FLAUBERT ~ SAND
THE CORRESPONDENCE

FLAUBERT ~ SAND

The Correspondence

Translated from the French by
Francis Steegmuller and Barbara Bray

WITH A FOREWORD BY FRANCIS STEEGMULLER

BASED ON THE EDITION BY ALPHONSE JACOBS
WITH ADDITIONAL NOTES BY FRANCIS STEEGMULLER

Alfred A. Knopf   New York   1993

THIS IS A BORZOI BOOK
PUBLISHED BY ALFRED A. KNOPF, INC.

Copyright © 1993 by HarperCollins Publishers

All rights reserved under International and Pan-American
Copyright Conventions. Published in the United States by
Alfred A. Knopf, Inc., New York. Distributed by
Random House, Inc., New York.

Originally published in France as *Correspondance Flaubert–Sand*
by Editions Flammarion, Paris, in 1981.
Copyright © 1981 by Editions Flammarion

This translation was published by Harvill, an imprint of HarperCollins
Publishers, by arrangement with William Collins Sons & Company Limited.

Library of Congress Cataloging-in-Publication Data
Flaubert, Gustave, 1821–1880.
[Correspondence. English. Selections]
Flaubert-Sand: the correspondence/translated from the French by
Francis Steegmuller and Barbara Bray; with a foreword by Francis
Steegmuller; edited by Alphonse Jacobs; with additional notes by
Francis Steegmuller.—1st American ed.
p.   cm.
"Originally published in France as Correspondance Flaubert-Sand
by Editions Flammarion, Paris, in 1981"—T.p. verso.
ISBN 0-679-41898-9
1. Flaubert, Gustave, 1821–1880—Correspondence. 2. Sand, George,
1804–1876—Correspondence. 3. Novelists, French—19th century—
Correspondence. I. Sand, George, 1804–1876. II. Steegmuller, Francis,
1906–. III. Bray, Barbara. IV. Jacobs, Alphonse. V. Title.
PQ2247.A2   1993
843´.8—dc20
[B]   92-16976
                                                            CIP

Manufactured in the United States of America

Published February 10, 1993
Second Printing, September 1993

CONTENTS

FOREWORD

At the time of his first acquaintance with George Sand, in the early 1860s, Gustave Flaubert already held a strong, controversial place in contemporary French literature. He had emerged from the publication, and "scandal", of *Madame Bovary*, in 1857–8, an important, innovative figure, esteemed by his literary peers. From the public point of view, he would long remain enigmatic, not only because of his relatively reclusive life in his family house at Croisset, near Rouen, but also from the uncompromising and divergent themes of his infrequent novels. (During his lifetime, Flaubert achieved, at most, intermittent success with a reading public that tended to find his fiction uncongenial and harsh.)

Since adolescence, Flaubert's private existence had been centred – despite the wish of his father, a respected doctor, that he enter the legal profession – on his love of literature and his literary labour, a dedication interrupted and nourished by travels to the Mediterranean and the Near East in 1849–50. In 1855, his liaison with the Parisian bluestocking Louise Colet had been pressed, through stages of incompatibility, to its forlorn conclusion. Thereafter, until his death in 1880, Flaubert's life and work would – with the grim interlude, in 1870–1, of the Franco-Prussian War and its fratricidal aftermath – revolve around his close relatives, in the region, and house, that had been home to him since childhood. This routine and its tribulations were interspersed with visits to Paris and meetings with fellow writers – George Sand among them – by whom Flaubert's genius was even then understood as a phenomenon to be fully defined in a later age. As will be seen from these letters, conviviality was, on occasion, welcome to Flaubert – although, like many another artist, he preferred it on his own terms.

In the years of her friendship with Flaubert – from 1863 to her death in 1876 – George Sand was at the height of her popularity as a prolific and beloved writer; and of her fame as an eminent personality in France. Born Amandine Aurore Lucile Dupin, in 1804, child of the romantic union between a proletarian girl and the illegitimate son of a noble house, product of the Romantic era and of an eccentric and affectionate upbringing, she had appeared on the literary scene in her twenties. Her early and turbulent marriage, her travels and legendary love affairs, her years with Frédéric Chopin, her liberalism and prominent friendships, and – above all – her independence of spirit had created the adventure and drama of her past. She was seventeen years older than Flaubert. When they met, she had long been established at Nohant, 175 miles south of Paris (near La Châtre), her country home since early youth –

where, with accustomed facility, she wrote novels, articles, and plays, and preserved the privacy of a life whose chief pleasures, aside from work, now lay in
family life with her son and grandchildren, in close and varied friendships, in
a delight in nature, and in a lively and benevolent curiosity towards the world.
Of this achieved serenity, George Sand would write to Flaubert, in her grief
over the events of 1870: "I'd sown my volcanoes with grass and flowers, and
they were getting on well." Yet the reader will discover, in the George Sand
of the present letters, no staid matron intent on quietude but a woman of keen
and vigorous mind, tender affections, and invincible humanity.

The close friendship of this disparate pair could not have been predicted.
Nevertheless, they were drawn to one another by common qualities: goodness,
candour, humour, and the passion of art. Vulnerability – and therefore trust –
was displayed on both sides, as they disclosed to one another their profound
needs. Their correspondence, so lively and, on occasion, so sombre, strikes a
note of mutual, affectionate scolding and encouragement. The great public
events of the Franco-Prussian War and the Commune drew from each of them
emphatic expressions of anguish, disagreement, and solidarity. The general
ease of their exchange may in part derive from its masculine-feminine
components, which were – because of differences of age, outlook, and situation
– complementary and, in respect to their work, without antagonism. Incapable
of envy or immodesty, George Sand paid unfeigned and unfailing tribute to
Flaubert's greater gift and to the slow suffering that, in contrast to her own
fluency, marked his creative life. When she challenged Flaubert's proclamations
– on human incorrigibility, or on his own indifference to worldly success – she
did so shrewdly and tactfully, and from the heart. Even when arguing passionately with his stated "creed" of authorial detachment, from which the signal of
human virtue was to be – as she felt – unrealistically excluded, she nonetheless
treated Flaubert's view as the vision of a master and disputed it within her
respect for his self-imposed task; recognizing, as more recent analysts have not
always done, that no doctrine or method can prevail in art unless as the adjunct
of genius.

If, in this fundamental matter of Flaubert's "creed", a recurring division of
opinion was never allowed to threaten the friendship, that often appears due
to George Sand's insight and forbearance: to her ready understanding of a
paradoxical nature exemplified in the rigorous artistic objectivity exercised by
a man of flaring private emotions. Her apprehension – that his stated creed
might ultimately detract from universality in his work – was shared by others
in Flaubert's lifetime, and remains, amid the modern acclaim for Flaubert's
mastery, a theme of literary discourse. Flaubert's artistic doctrine, eloquently
and nobly asserted in the present letters, has been challenged as a limitation,
and even as a form of surrender to the most bitter aspects of existence. (Thus
D. H. Lawrence, in certain of his own letters, deplores the "accurate-
impersonal school of Flaubert" as "an acceptance", adding, "I hate it.")

If at times, too, Flaubert's tirades against human nature could be consciously
provocative, George Sand responded without intemperance and with stalwart

invocation of beliefs verified in her past struggles: "My own conquest of despair was due to my will." At such times, as Stuart Hampshire wrote in 1982, George Sand, "surprisingly, seems to have the better of the argument, partly because her opinions appear to be at one with her character and not to be forced and too much cultivated and displayed, as Flaubert's sometimes were." That Flaubert returned repeatedly to these discussions with George Sand is itself indicative of a need and regard for her countering view. He could confide not only in her indulgence, but also in an integrity that enabled him to speak frankly of the central difficulties of his art: "Subjects impose themselves. Shall I ever find mine? Will there ever drop down on me from heaven an idea in perfect harmony with my temperament?" In 1872, Flaubert wrote to an old acquaintance: "Mme Sand is now, with Turgenev, my only literary friend."

George Sand's descents into obtuseness or mere sentimentality – as when she suggests to Flaubert that he console himself by marrying – are rare, and for that reason disconcerting. In publishing, in the wake of the war and the Commune, her refutation of Flaubert's despair in the form of a "Reply to a Friend", she seems precipitate. Similarly, the unforced sexual equality with which she customarily writes leaves us unprepared for her characterization of a particular topic in fiction as "too high for a mere woman to aim at". These lapses – as one feels them to be – are almost shocking to the reader, who has come, like Flaubert himself, to rely on her maturity and her sense of fitness.

It will be seen that George Sand withdrew from the anti-Jewish theme developed by Flaubert in reference to his quarrel with the publisher Michel Lévy; and that she sought – predictably, without success – to calm Flaubert's resentment. That she responded initially to Flaubert's introduction of this distasteful note seems uncharacteristic, and was perhaps regretted by Sand herself. For us, that particular exchange is shaded by the impending drama of the Dreyfus case, which neither of our protagonists lived to experience. Reading these letters, we will scarcely doubt where, in that affair, George Sand's sympathies would have lain.

From these letters we learn few details of the physical appearance of the protagonists. (It is, rather, the Goncourt brothers who have described the two writers in their latter years: George Sand's "mulatto-like" cast of features, her tiny hands inside lace cuffs, and her air of delicate shyness; Flaubert at Rouen, "wearing a broad-brimmed hat and short jacket, with his big behind in pleated trousers, and his kind, affectionate face".) After George Sand's funeral, Flaubert invoked her beautiful eyes when – "weeping", as he wrote to Turgenev – "I kissed her granddaughter Aurore (whose eyes, that day, were so like hers as to be a kind of resurrection.)" However, the two personalities are vibrantly, palpably present, bringing with them the daily circumstances of their lives, the atmosphere of their rooms and houses: we see George Sand among children, Flaubert by his cold river; we learn of their festivities *en famille* at Nohant; and of their talks at Croisset, by firelight, late into the night.

Flaubert's tribute to George Sand, "For me, you are like good bread," is succinct. In her he found authenticity, and a sustaining benevolence. In the

year of her death, Flaubert wrote to his *chère maître* with simple truth: "You
have never done me anything but good, and I love you tenderly."

Alphonse Jacobs' admirable annotated edition of the correspondence between
Flaubert and Sand,[1] from which the present translations have been made,
opens with a preface by M. Jacobs himself. After paying tribute to Flaubert
and Sand as noble souls, as artists and as correspondents, he assesses the
merits of earlier editions of their exchanged letters and the work of later scholars
who published additional letters in learned reviews. And he particularly salutes
the editors of the two modern, definitive master-texts from which he has derived
the present exchange of over four hundred letters: his friend and "guardian
angel", Georges Lubin, editor of the *Correspondance de George Sand* (24 vols.,
Classiques Garnier, 1964–90); and Jean Bruneau, editor of the *Correspondance
de Gustave Flaubert*, of which the first several volumes have appeared in Galli-
mard's Bibliothèque de la Pléiade.

"It has often been said that this is the finest correspondence of the past
century, perhaps the finest of all time." So M. Jacobs' preface begins. "Everyone has emphasized its historical importance, its great place in the literary,
philosophical, and political ideas of the nineteenth century. We are told that
all writers and students should be familiar with it as part of their education;
and that today's generations could profit from the moral lessons it provides.
Yet . . . Who is familiar with this correspondence? Who has really read it? How
strange that for the past half-century these letters between Flaubert and George
Sand – this 'masterpiece of sensibility', as René Dumesnil called it – should
have been accessible only to specialists!"

M. Jacobs does not presume, he says, to chronicle the stages of this great
friendship: "Such an account would be merely a résumé of the present volume."
Nor does he attempt to analyze its raison d'être: "Given Sand's character and
that of Flaubert, one would rather have expected reactions of scorn, of hatred.
It is impossible to imagine characters and temperaments more dissimilar, con-
ceptions of life more divergent, aesthetic and social ideas more opposed." The
most commonly invoked explanation of this "troubling mystery" are, M. Jacobs
continues, "on George Sand's part, her life-long compulsion to be the loving
mother, the nurse, the presence that protects and consoles; on Flaubert's, his
insatiable need for confidence, for affection, for someone to whom he could
pour out his heart."

M. Jacobs is sceptical concerning what he calls "a question whose importance has . . . been a trifle exaggerated" – the influence of each of these writers
on the other's work: "Although it is true that certain of Mme Sand's novels
written after 1865–6, *Monsieur Sylvestre, Le Dernier Amour, Césarine Dietrich*,

---

[1] *Gustave Flaubert - George Sand. Correspondance. Texte édité, préfacé et annoté par Alphonse
Jacobs.* (Flammarion, Paris, 1981.)

and a few others, give the impression of greater sobriety, of a less lofty idealism
– of being more 'realistic' than those written earlier, might this not be simply
because she is older? During the last decade of her life she had the habit of
inspecting the settings she chose for her novels: she travelled to Brittany for
Cadio, to Normandy for *Mademoiselle Merquem*, to the Ardennes for *Malgrétout*.
But she was not 'documenting herself' for her books: what she wanted was a
'general impression': 'All I need is to *see*,' she wrote to Flaubert, 'in order not
to falsify a bit of sunshine.' She will never adopt Flaubert's system, his style,
or his aesthetic and social ideology."

M. Jacobs writes similarly about Flaubert and his opinions, particularly those
concerning current events:

"In 1876, at the end of the correspondence, these remain exactly the same,
almost word for word, as those of ten years before. If he occasionally hesitates,
if he seems to contradict himself or to be somewhat confused, it is because
he realizes that his ideas, when pushed to their extreme, inevitably lead to
absurdity."

"The text of certain of the letters" – M. Jacobs' introduction continues –
"has often been taken as evidence that it was Sand's influence that led
to Flaubert's conception of the gentle, tender figure of Félicité in *Un Coeur
simple*. The idea is touching, but there are other elements to be considered.
Financial ruin, the sale of his farm at Deauville, the abandoning of his last
novel, *Bouvard and Pécuchet*, the threat of having to leave his beloved Croisset,
the uncertainty of his future – all these factors must have played their roles
in his choice of subject; and it was only after he had planned the work
and begun to write it that he realized what pleasure it would give his chère
maître.

"But – one might say – there is his letter to Maurice Sand of 28 August
1877: 'You speak of your beloved and illustrious mother. After yourself, I think
there can be no one who thinks of her more than I. . . . I began *Un Coeur
simple* exclusively for her, solely to please her. She died when I was in the
middle of my work. So it is with all our dreams. . . .' This formal declaration
that he had written his story to please Mme Sand – written it solely with her
in mind – is so strong that one is tempted to give it full credence. But one must
be wary – must remember, for example, that in a letter to his niece (of 16
October 1869), he had told her that he had written *L'Éducation sentimentale* 'to
please Sainte-Beuve'. Flaubert's literal sincerity, especially when he wishes to
impress or please a correspondent, is a complex problem: his exaggerating at
such moments can be quite naive. The Goncourts, always on the track of their
friends' human failings, several times mention Flaubert's 'claims to great feats
of performance and endurance'. The passage in question, obviously written to
convey to Maurice Sand the intensity of the affection he had borne his mother,
must not be taken literally: had Flaubert never known Mme Sand, this tale,
with its 'moral and human content' (Flaubert's words to Maurice), would have
been written as we read it today."

Such an assertion as that made here by M. Jacobs must, nevertheless, always retain an element of speculation. We cannot know for certain all the threads that are drawn together to fabricate a work of art. (We may recall, too, that during the composition of *Un Coeur simple*, Flaubert told George Sand – in his last letter to her – that, in this tale, "you will recognize your own direct influence." And that in another letter to Maurice Sand, four years later – and shortly before his own death – Flaubert wrote: "Your dear mother – how I think of her, and how I need her! Not a day when I don't tell myself 'If she were here, I'd ask her advice.'") It is clear, however, as M. Jacobs says, that the divergent personalities of the two friends were too firmly established – in their art as in their lives – to be radically altered by their exchange of ideas. The effects of the friendship may be felt, rather, in the stimulus and intimacy that pervade these letters, and in an expansiveness that was comforting and pleasurable – and, in literature, perhaps unique.

M. Jacobs' preface ends with thanks to the individuals and organizations of various nationalities that had helped him – "In the course of our work we have encountered only kindness, cordiality and friendship" – and with an emotional tribute to France:

"Who can they be, those contentious, blind individuals who claim that the French are not gracious, not easily given to friendship, loath to open their doors to strangers, jealously keeping their treasure to themselves? Our experience has been quite the opposite. Therefore, our thanks to France for all the joy and pleasure she has given us out of her marvellous culture – that treasure of which she is both creator and inheritor."

Alphonse Jacobs died at his home in Koudekerke, Holland, five years after the publication of his admirable volume. The following lines are drawn from an obituary of M. Jacobs by Jean Bruneau that appeared in *Le Monde* on Friday, 7 March 1986:

"Alphonse F.-J. Jacobs died, at the age of sixty-one, on 8 February 1986. He had known for some time that he was fatally ill, and wrote to a French friend [i.e. to Jean Bruneau] in July 1985: "I have been found to have an incurable cancer. I do not yet know how long I may have to live. And since by now I can barely move, my work on Flaubert is definitely at an end. Please do not pity me: I feel no pity for myself. I think that my life has had a certain usefulness. I have done one thing that I think will endure."

"That 'thing' is his volume of the Flaubert–Sand correspondence, published in 1981 by Flammarion. To that, Alphonse Jacobs devoted his entire life. His career as teacher and administrator in the Netherlands took him from his native province of Limbourg to the island of Walcheren, in Zealand.

"His edition of the Flaubert–Sand correspondence is admirable for the extent, as well as the quality and rigour, of his research. It is an honour for French literature that a foreigner, a great friend of our country, should have edited, and with such excellence, one of the most important and complex correspondences in modern French literature."

FRANCIS STEEGMULLER

Publisher's Note

In this edition Francis Steegmuller has translated the letters of Gustave Flaubert, as well as the linking passages and notes. Barbara Bray has translated the letters and diary extracts of George Sand.

GEORGE SAND
The Years 1804–65

1804   1 July: Birth, in Paris, of Amandine Aurore Lucile Dupin. She is the daughter of Maurice Dupin, an officer in Napoleon's *armée d'Italie*, and of Sophie Delaborde, a young woman of plebeian birth and little education, something of an adventuress. The couple had married secretly, 5 June, to legitimize their child.

1808   April–July. Aurore is taken by her mother to Madrid, where Dupin is serving with the French army. Mme Dupin gives birth to a son, who will die at Nohant on 8 September. A few days later, 16 September, Aurore's father dies, at thirty, the result of a fall from his horse.

1809–17   Aurore and her mother move to the château de Nohant, near La Châtre, in the Indre. This is the property of Aurore's maternal grandmother, Mme Dupin de Francueil, natural daughter of the celebrated eighteenth-century warrior the maréchal de Saxe. The family spends several months each year in Paris. From May 1812, Aurore's mother settles permanently in Paris, leaving the child with her grandmother at Nohant. Thenceforth the child sees her mother only during the latter's rare visits to Nohant. She studies grammar, Latin and science with a tutor, François Deschartres; her grandmother gives her music lessons. Much of the time she is free to roam the countryside, mingling with the peasants and playing with the village children. She makes her first communion at La Châtre, 23 March 1817.

1818–22   On 12 January 1818 Aurore continues her education with the English Augustinian nuns in Paris. There, the following year, she passes through a period of piety, and her grandmother finds it advisable to return her to Nohant. Early in March 1821, the old lady suffers an attack of apoplexy, and until her death on 26 December is devotedly cared for by Aurore, who inherits the property at Nohant. Almost immediately Mme Dupin takes her daughter with her to Paris. There Aurore, restless and unhappy, meets a young ex-army officer, Casimir Dudevant, the illegitimate son of a baron of the Empire, and they are married on 17 September 1822. The next month they take up residence at Nohant.

1823–9   The first years of their marriage are peaceful and even happy. Their son, Maurice, is born on 30 June 1823. But soon thereafter the young woman becomes bored, and seeks distraction in travel. During a trip to the

Pyrenees in July–August 1825 she meets Aurélien de Sèze: their relation remains platonic but causes stormy scenes between Aurore and her husband. Apparently less platonic are her relations with Stéphane Ajasson de Grandsagne, who is probably the father of Solange Dudevant, born 13 September 1828. In 1829 Aurore starts to write, but does not publish.

1830–3   On 30 July 1830 she meets a young student, Jules Sandeau, who soon becomes her lover. In November she happens to see a will, signed by her husband, that she considers outrageous. Seizing on this as a door to freedom, she succeeds in obtaining an agreement from Dudevant according to which he is to pay her an annual sum and allow her to spend half the year in Paris.

There, in the capital, she immediately meets a number of writers and begins to write for *Le Figaro* and *La Revue de Paris*. With Sandeau, using the pseudonym "J. Sand", she writes a novel, *Rose et Blanche*, which is published late in December 1831. The following year she writes, alone, two novels, *Indiana* and *Valentine*, both signed "G. Sand" and both very successful. On 11 December 1832 she signs an agreement to contribute regularly to *La Revue des Deux Mondes*. Her relations with Sandeau deteriorate and are broken off early in March 1833. At that time she is writing *Lélia*, which will be published on 18 July 1833.

1833–5   In June 1833 George Sand meets Alfred de Musset, who becomes her lover at the end of July, probably the 29th. In December they go together to Italy. Their stay in Venice, where they arrive on the 31st, is far from happy. Not only do they both fall ill, but there are dissensions, jealousy, violent scenes. At the end of February 1834 George Sand becomes the mistress of Pagello, the doctor whom she had summoned to tend the ailing Musset. On 29 March, Musset, only just recovered, leaves for Paris. George Sand remains in Venice, visiting its churches and palaces and enjoying some society. Short of money, she does considerable writing – several novels (*Jacques* among them), and several *Lettres d'un voyageur*. On 24 July she leaves Venice with Pagello, reaching Paris on 14 August. Late in October, following Pagello's departure, she resumes relations with Musset, but the liaison is as stormy as ever, and ends definitively on 6 March 1835.

1835–7   In April 1835 she begins a new affair, with the dominating Michel de Bourges, an active republican. He is said to have awakened her to physical passion. Following a violent scene with her husband on 19 October she brings an action for legal separation at the court in La Châtre. Michel de Bourges is her lawyer. She wins her case on 16 February 1836, and the following 29 July she and her husband sign the separation agreement. In September she goes to Switzerland for a rest, taking her children with her.

However, her life continues to be agitated. Several brief affairs; break with Michel de Bourges, July 1837; death of her mother, 19 August 1837; affairs with the social reformers Félicité-Robert de Lamennais and Pierre Leroux. Nevertheless she continues to write novels, the most important of which is *Mauprat*, published 7 August 1837. Her *Lettres d'un voyageur* appears in a volume, 18 February 1837; *Lettres à Marcie* is serialized in Lamennais' newspaper, *Le Monde*.

1838–47 The year 1838 marks a turning-point in George Sand's life. Her love affairs become less tumultuous, and she begins her involvement in humanitarian matters. In November 1836 she had met Frédéric Chopin, and now, in June 1838, she begins her liaison with him, destined to continue until 1847. On 18 October she sets out with her children for Majorca; Chopin joins them on the way, and they settle in the Certosa de Valldemosa. She writes *Spiridion* and the second *Lélia*, published respectively on 23 February and 28 September 1839. Leaving Majorca on 13 February, she arrives at Nohant on June 1st. Now she is to divide her time between Nohant and Paris, caring for Chopin, who is often ill, and writing novels that show the influence of Leroux: *Le Compagnon du tour de France* (1 December 1840), *Horace* (10 April and 28 May 1842), *Consuelo* (1842–3), *La Comtesse de Rudolstadt* (1843–4), *Jeanne* (21 December 1844), *Le Meunier d'Angibault* (5 July 1845) and others.

After breaking with *La Revue des Deux Mondes* (which is hostile to the socialist tendencies now present in her writing), she founds, with Leroux and Louis Viardot, *La Revue indépendante* (first number, 5 November 1841). She also participates in the founding of a local republican newspaper, *L'Éclaireur de l'Indre* (first number, 14 September 1844). Her love of nature and her increasing interest in provincial life lead her to write her first "rustic" novels: *La Mare au diable* (8 August 1846), *Le Péché de M. Antoine* (9 January 1847), *François le Champi* (not published in book form until 12 January 1850). During the year 1846 her relations with Chopin deteriorate, but as yet there is no rupture. He leaves Nohant on 11 November, never to return. Solange's marriage with the sculptor Auguste Clésinger, 19 May 1847, brings added strain. On 11 July painful scenes instigated by Solange and her husband force George Sand to ask them to leave the house. Relations with Chopin are brought to an end when he sides with Solange.

1848 When the Revolution breaks out, on 22 February 1848, George Sand goes to Paris, eager to participate in political affairs. She publishes several propaganda pamphlets, two *Lettres au peuple* (7 and 19 March), a *Lettre à la classe moyenne* (8 March), a *Lettre aux riches* (12 March), *L'Histoire de France écrite sous la dictée de Blaise Bonnin* (15 March). She founds a weekly, *La Cause du peuple* (only three numbers will appear), collaborates on the *Bulletin de la République*. After the demonstration of 15 May and the arrest of the leading radicals, she leaves Paris on 17 May and thereafter remains inactive. Deeply disappointed by the reaction in June, she

consoles herself by writing *La Petite Fadette*, which will be published as
a volume on 4 August 1849.

1849–55 During the years that follow, George Sand prudently avoids involvement
in political life and seldom leaves Nohant. After the coup d'état of 2
December 1851 she intercedes with Louis-Napoléon on behalf of his
exiled opponents. For financial reasons she begins to write for the
theatre. On 25 November 1849 a play drawn from *François le Champi*
begins a successful run at the Théâtre de l'Odéon. Between then and
1856, when she will temporarily renounce the theatre, ten of her plays
will be produced, among them *Claudie* (Porte-Saint-Martin, 11 January
1851), *Le Mariage de Victorine* (Gymnase, 26 November 1851), *Le Démon
du Foyer* (Gymnase, 1 September 1852), *Mauprat* (Odéon, 28 November
1853), *Flaminio* (Gymnase, 31 October 1854), *Maître Faville* (Odéon, 15
September 1855), *Françoise* (Gymnase, 3 April 1856). Beginning in
March 1851 she prepares a popular, illustrated edition of her novels (the
first volume is published by Hetzel on 3 April 1852), and begins to write
new ones: *Le Château des Désertes* (8 November 1851), *Mont-Revêche* (19
February 1852), *Les Maîtres sonneurs* (30 July 1853). But after April 1853
she devotes most of her time to writing her memoirs, *L'Histoire de ma
vie*. She had begun these in 1847, and now they are serialized in *La
Presse*, from 5 October 1854 to 17 August 1855. During these years her
life is simple, relatively calm. Chopin dies on 17 October 1849; Michel
de Bourges on 16 March 1853. But on 6 January 1850 there arrives at
Nohant a young friend of her son Maurice, the engraver Alexandre
Manceau, who becomes her secretary and soon her lover. This is a
peaceful liaison, which will end only with Manceau's death fifteen years
later. Relations with the Clésingers remain tense. Their daughter Jeanne,
born 10 May 1849, is often left in her grandmother's care – as in
childhood George Sand herself had been. Incessant quarrels between
Solange and her husband lead to their legal separation (16 December
1854). Jeanne's death, 13 January 1855, is a terrible blow to George
Sand: by way of distraction she leaves for Italy with Manceau and
Maurice on 28 February 1855, returning on 17 May.

1856–65 Thenceforth George Sand is to spend most of her time at Nohant,
writing, managing the household, devoting much time to botany and to
amateur theatricals in a theatre she had had constructed in the château.
Manceau buys her a small house in the nearby village of Gargilesse,
where she now and again retires for several days at a time. Her visits to
Paris are brief, always having to do with the theatre or other work. On
one of these occasions, at the Odéon, on 30 April 1857, she meets
Flaubert, whose first novel, *Madame Bovary*, has just been published.
Her novel *Daniella*, published at this time (30 May 1857) and reflecting
her impressions of Italy, causes a scandal because of its anticlericalism;
and *Elle et Lui* (14 May 1859), her version of the Musset story, also
arouses violent controversy. In late October 1860 she falls dangerously

ill with typhoid fever, and from mid-February to the end of May 1861 she is at Tamaris (near Toulon) with Maurice and Manceau, recuperating. On 17 May 1862 Maurice marries Lina, daughter of Mme Sand's friend the engraver Luigi Calamatta. Their first child, Marc-Antoine, born 14 July 1863, dies on 21 July of the following year. For the time being, George Sand is not at Nohant. Since 12 June 1864 she has been living with Manceau, who is ill with tuberculosis, in a small house at Palaiseau, not far from Paris: Manceau dies there on 21 August 1865.

During this decade Sand is prolific: pamphlets, prefaces, articles, and especially novels. In 1858 she resumes her connection with *La Revue des Deux Mondes*, which will publish almost all her works, among them *Les Beaux Messieurs de Bois-Doré* (published in a volume 20 March 1858), *L'Homme de neige* (28 May 1859), *Jean de la Roche* (3 March 1860), *Le Marquis de Villemer* (2 February 1861), *Valvèdre* (21 September 1861), *La Famille de Germandre* (9 November 1861), *Tamaris* (14 June 1862), *Mademoiselle La Quintinie* (4 July 1863). She also resumes work for the stage. On 18 March 1862 *Le Pavé*, originally written for the Nohant theatre, opens at the Gymnase. A few weeks later, 26 April 1862, *Les Beaux Messieurs de Bois-Doré* at the Ambigu-Comique. And – her greatest stage success – *Le Marquis de Villemer*, 29 February 1864 at the Odéon.

GUSTAVE FLAUBERT
The Years 1821–65

1821   12 December: Birth of Gustave Flaubert in the Hôtel-Dieu (Municipal Hospital) at Rouen in Normandy. He is the son of Achille-Cléophas Flaubert, chief surgeon at the Hôtel-Dieu, and of Caroline Fleuriot, daughter of a physician in Pont-l'Evêque. The couple already have one son, Achille, born in 1813, and in 1824 a daughter, Caroline, is born. Three other children, born between 1813 and 1824, died in infancy.

1829–35 The boy spends his earliest years in his parents' apartment in the hospital. At ten he is already interested in literature: *Don Quixote* is a special favourite. With his sister and his friends Alfred Le Poittevin and Ernest Chevalier he acts in plays on a stage set up in his father's billiard room. In 1832 he enters the Collège Royal in Rouen as a boarder. By now he is writing historical sketches and editing a handwritten "newspaper", *Art et Progrès*.

1836–9   The family spends summer vacations at Trouville, on the Channel coast. There, in 1836 or 1837, the adolescent Gustave conceives a hopeless passion for Elisa Schlésinger, wife of a music-publisher. Beginning in 1836 he writes stories, among them *Rage et Impuissance* (1836), *Rêve d'enfer* (1837), and *Passion et Vertu* (1837). In 1837 a small Rouen newspaper, *Le Colibri*, prints his first published work, *Une leçon d'histoire naturelle, genre commis*. In 1838 he writes, among other things, a play in five acts, *Loys XI*, and, more important, a novel, *Mémoires d'un fou*, which is later to serve as a preliminary sketch for *L'Éducation sentimentale*. In 1839 he writes a philosophical mystery-play, *Smarh*, which prefigures *La Tentation de Saint Antoine*. That October he begins his last year at the Collège, but is expelled because of his leadership in a student protest. He prepares for the *baccalauréat* – his final examination – at home.

1840–3   After passing his *baccalauréat* he spends several months travelling in the Pyrenees and Corsica. At a hotel in Marseilles he meets Eulalie Foucaud, recently arrived in France from South America, and with her has a few days' amorous adventure – his first consummated romance. (Earlier, he had visited Rouen brothels.) In November 1841 he registers at the Law School in Paris, preparing at home for his entrance examinations, and at the same time writing a small masterpiece, the short novel *Novembre* (completed 25 October 1842). He enters Law School that November, and on 28 December passes his first examination. In Paris he frequents an English family, the Colliers, whom he had met at Trouville: the two Collier daughters, Gertrude and Henriette, are in love with him. He also sees the Schlésingers, and the sculptor Pradier and the latter's wife Louise. In February 1843 he begins the first version of *L'Éducation sentimentale*, which he finishes two years later (7 January 1845). Also at this time, in March 1843, he becomes friendly with Maxime Du Camp. On August 21 he fails his second-year examination. Though very discouraged, he continues to attend classes.

1844–6 It is probably on Tuesday, 2 January 1844, while travelling at night to Pont-l'Evêque with his brother Achille, that he suffers his first nervous attack. Much to his relief, his father forbids him to continue his law studies. During the following summer his family moves into a house at Croisset, on the left bank of the Seine a few miles below Rouen. There Flaubert will spend most of his adult life. On 3 March 1845 his sister Caroline marries Emile Hamard, and the entire family accompanies the young couple on their wedding journey to Italy. At Genoa, in Palazzo Balbi, Flaubert sees the picture by Breughel that later inspires his *Tentation de Saint Antoine*. The year 1846 is a year of mourning. Dr Flaubert dies on 15 January; and Caroline, after giving birth to a daughter (baptized Caroline) on 21 February, succumbs to puerperal fever on 23 March. In May of this year Gustave becomes friendly with Louis Bouilhet, who will remain his confidant for more than twenty-five years.

1846–51 On 29 July 1846, at the Pradiers' in Paris, Flaubert meets the beautiful poet Louise Colet, wife of a professor at the Conservatory of Music and mother of a small daughter. This is the beginning of a stormy liaison that continues, with interruptions, until 1855. From 9 September 1846, the lovers meet periodically at the Hôtel du Grand Cerf at Mantes, half-way between Rouen and Paris. On 1 May 1847 Flaubert leaves with Maxime Du Camp for a three-months' walking tour in Touraine and Brittany. They narrate their experiences in a jointly-written account which they call *Par les champs et par les grèves*: Flaubert writes the even-numbered chapters, Du Camp the others, and they have two professional copies made of their manuscript. None of it, except for some pages by Flaubert on Carnac (in *L'Artiste*, 18 April 1858), is published during their lifetimes.

In Paris with Bouilhet and Du Camp, on 24 February 1848, Flaubert witnesses the outbreak of the Revolution. Back in Croisset, he begins (24 May 1848) the first version of *La Tentation de Saint Antoine*. But his nervous attacks persist, and doctors advise travel in a warm climate. He finishes the *Tentation* on 12 September 1849 and reads it to Du Camp and Bouilhet, who pronounce it a failure. Shortly thereafter, on 29 October, Flaubert and Du Camp leave for their "oriental journey". Arriving in Cairo on 28 November, they remain there until February 1850, when they set sail up the Nile, reaching the second cataract on 22 March. On 6 March, at Esneh, they had spent a night with the well-known *almeh* (courtesan) Kuchuk Hanem. After returning to Cairo on 26 June they set out for Palestine and Syria; they visit Rhodes in October, and on 13 November reach Constantinople, where they spend a month. On 16 December they are in Athens. They travel in Greece until 10 February 1851, when they sail from Patras to Brindisi. They visit Naples and its surroundings and reach Rome on 26 March. There Flaubert is joined by his mother, and Du Camp proceeds to Paris. After Florence, Venice, Cologne and Brussels, Flaubert and his mother return to Croisset in June. In the next month Flaubert resumes relations with Louise Colet, with whom he had broken in March 1848. (During his Eastern journey he had contracted a venereal disease, symptoms of which were to recur throughout his life.)

1851–5 On 19 September 1851 Flaubert begins to write *Madame Bovary* and, at the same time, to act as tutor to his niece Caroline. Relations with Louise Colet have become chiefly epistolary. Flaubert treats her with egotistical detachment: they see each other for a few days every two or three months, either at Mantes or in Paris. In June 1852 Flaubert's friendship with Du Camp has begun to cool: Du Camp, now editor of the *Revue de Paris*, is too insistent that Flaubert move to the capital and make a name for himself. In July 1853, a young Englishwoman, Juliet Herbert, comes to Croisset as Caroline's governess: in 1855 she and Flaubert begin a long, discreet liaison. There is little to record of these years: Flaubert is occupied at Croisset with the difficult and protracted composition of *Madame Bovary*. The progress of the work can be followed in his letters to Louise Colet and to Bouilhet, who is now living in Paris. In August, 1852, Part One is finished; at the end of that year, Chapters I to III of Part Two; all of 1853 is devoted to IV to VIII; 1854, IX to XIII. When he leaves for Paris in October 1855, he has reached Chapter VIII of Part Three. His relations with Louise Colet deteriorate. A widow since 1851, she seeks to marry Flaubert, and asks in vain to be introduced to his mother. She puts him to work revising her poems and her newspaper articles. By October 1854 the affair is all but over; Flaubert deals the coup de grâce with a harsh note written on 6 March 1855. In 1856 Louise takes her revenge with a short novel, *Une Histoire de soldat*, in which Flaubert, in the character of "Léonce", is disagreeably portrayed.

1856–7 When *Madame Bovary* is finished, in April 1856, Flaubert sends it to Du Camp, who asks for changes and cuts. The novel is serially published in the *Revue de Paris*, from 1 October to 15 December. Certain passages are omitted without Flaubert's permission. He insists on inserting a note of protest in the issue of 15 December. In December and January *L'Artiste* publishes a few fragments of *La Tentation de Saint Antoine*. But early in January the government begins legal action against the author of *Madame Bovary* and the editors of the *Revue*. The trial, opening on 29 January 1857 in Paris, ends on 7 February with acquittal; and at the end of April the novel is published by Michel Lévy. Despite its popular success, the critics, except for Sainte-Beuve and Baudelaire, are mostly hostile. Flaubert has now begun to participate in Parisian "literary life". He sees Feydeau, the Goncourts, Renan, Sainte-Beuve, and meets Victor Hugo, whom he has idolized from boyhood. He also frequents ladies of fashion – Mme Sabatier, Jeanne de Tourbey.

1857–62   In June 1856 Flaubert had begun to revise *La Tentation de Saint Antoine*; but when the new version is completed, fear of further prosecution makes him decide not to publish it. In May 1857 he begins to prepare a novel, tentatively called *Carthage* – the future *Salammbô*. From 16 April to 12 June he travels in Tunisia, studying the ruins of Carthage and the environs, with the result that he "demolishes" all he has previously written on this theme. As when he was writing *Madame Bovary*, he secludes himself at home – in Croisset, or, during the winter, in Paris, at 42, boulevard du Temple. He seldom goes out: on Sundays he is at home to his friends. Very occasionally he visits Bouilhet, now living in Mantes. The work progresses slowly: the first three chapters are completed in 1858; the next year he finishes IV to VII, and in 1860 VIII to XI. By the end of 1861 he has reached Chapter XIV, and on 15 February 1862, in Paris, he reaches the end. Negotiations with Lévy, begun in May, drag on for several months: only on 11 September, when he returns from a month in Vichy with his mother, does he sign the contract.

1862–5   When *Salammbô* is published, on 24 November 1862, the critics are at a loss, and generally hostile. Articles by Sainte-Beuve and Froehner irritate Flaubert, who writes ironic replies; but the review by George Sand, published in *La Presse* on 27 January 1863, marks the beginning of a magnificent friendship. The novel enjoys some popular success. In January 1863 Flaubert begins a long friendship with Princesse Mathilde Bonaparte and her brother, Prince Jérôme Napoléon Bonaparte, known as Prince Napoléon (cousins of the emperor, Napoleon III). Beginning in December 1862 he attends the Magny dinners, recently organized by Sainte-Beuve at the restaurant of that name. On 23 February 1863 he meets Turgenev – the beginning of a warm friendship between the two "giants". Following another stay in Vichy in June and July 1863 with his mother and his niece, he writes, with Bouilhet and Charles d'Osmoy, a *féerie*, *Le Château des cœurs*, which is finished on 26 October but never staged. The winter of 1863–4 is very social: dinners, balls, theatre, receptions. On 6 April 1864, at Flaubert's prompting, his niece Caroline reluctantly marries Ernest Commanville, a seemingly prosperous lumber merchant at Dieppe. After long hesitation, Flaubert finally decides on the subject of a new novel: this will be *L'Éducation sentimentale*. After his vacation he begins to write (1 September 1864). This time he does not avoid literary and social life as in the past. He stays for long periods in Paris, attending the Magny dinners and many receptions, including those given by Princesse Mathilde. From 12 to 16 November 1864 he is the guest of the Emperor and Empress at

Compiègne. In July 1865 he sees Juliet Herbert in London; and in Baden, where he visits Maxime Du Camp, he may have seen the Schlésingers, who have been living there since 1853. Nevertheless he works steadily at *L'Éducation sentimentale*, completing the first part in 1865.

SAND ~ FLAUBERT CHRONOLOGY
1866–76

1866   10 January Birth of Aurore, granddaughter of George Sand.

20 January *Monsieur Sylvestre*.

24 January – 22 May Flaubert in Paris.

12 February George Sand's first attendance at Magny dinners.

1 June Sand leaves for Nohant.

1 July – 15 August *Le Dernier Amour* published in *Revue des Deux Mondes*.

16 – 30 July Flaubert visits London and meets Juliet Herbert again.

1 – 19 August Flaubert visits Paris, Mantes, Ouville, Dieppe.

2 August to 5 September Sand in Paris and at Palaiseau.

9 August Première of *Les Don Juan de village* at the Vaudeville, Flaubert present.

15 August Flaubert appointed Chevalier de la Légion d'honneur.

28 – 30 August Sand at Croisset.

8 – 19 September Sand travels in Brittany and returns to Nohant.

24 October – 3 November Flaubert in Paris.

28 October Sand goes to Paris, staying there and at Palaiseau until 10 January 1867.

29 October Première of Bouilhet's *La Conjuration d'Amboise*; Flaubert and Sand present.

3 – 10 November Sand to Croisset.

9 November Sand's friend Charles Duveyrier dies.

1867   10 January Sand leaves for Nohant. Suffers from anaemia all winter.

19 February – 21 May Flaubert in Paris.

21 March – 2 April Sand in Paris and at Palaiseau.

23 March *Le Dernier Amour*.

2 May Bouilhet appointed Librarian at Rouen.

10 June Flaubert attends a ball at the Tuileries.

20 June – 14 July Sand in Paris and at Palaiseau.

10 July *Le Marquis de Villemer* revived at Odéon.

1 – 24 August Flaubert in Paris.

13 August Sand's close friend François Rollinat dies.

14 August *François le Champi* revived at Odéon.

1 September – 15 November *Cadio* published in *Revue des Deux Mondes*.

4 – 20 September Flaubert in Paris, Nogent and Dieppe.

16 September – 7 October Sand in Paris (after which she will seldom visit Palaiseau).

19 September *Les Beaux Messieurs de Bois-Doré* revived at Odéon.

17 – 19, 25 – 30 September Sand pays two visits to Normandy.

7 – 11 November Flaubert visits Paris to do research for *L'Éducation sentimentale.*

1868   15 January – 15 March *Mademoiselle Merquem* published in *Revue des Deux Mondes.*

29 January – 19 May Flaubert in Paris.

10 – 15 February Sand in Paris.

15 February – 12 March Sand visits the Midi: visits Juliette Adam at Bruyères, Charles Poncy at Toulon, then returns to Paris.

12 March Birth of Maurice Sand's daughter Gabrielle.

14 March Sand returns to Nohant.

25 April *Cadio*, the novel.

5 May – 2 June Sand in Paris.

24 – 26 May Sand at Croisset.

27 May Sand moves from rue des Feuillantines to 5, rue Gay-Lussac.

1 June – 15 August *Lettres d'un voyageur à propos de botanique* published in *Revue des Deux Mondes.*

4 – 20 July Juliette Adam and her husband at Nohant.

8 July – 13 August Flaubert visits Ouville, Dieppe, Paris, Fontainebleau and Saint-Gratien.

1 August *Mademoiselle Merquem.*

13 – 26 August Marguerite Thuillier and Mme Arnould-Plessy visit Sand at Nohant. Sand learns of the latter's conversion.

26 August – 13 October Sand in Paris and at Palaiseau (except 12–26 September).

3 October Première of *Cadio* at Porte-Saint-Martin. Flaubert attends.

22 November Turgenev visits Croisset.

15 December Sand's grandchildren baptized.

1869   25 January – 1 February Flaubert in Paris, researching *L'Éducation sentimentale.*

8 March Death of Luigi Calamatta.

27 March – 7 June Flaubert in Paris.

25 April – 9 June Sand in Paris.

29 April Sand sells her house at Palaiseau.

10 May Flaubert reads *L'Éducation sentimentale* to Sand.

16 May Flaubert finishes *L'Éducation sentimentale.*

30 May Flaubert signs lease for new apartment, 4, rue Murillo.

Mid-June Back at Croisset, Flaubert starts revising *La Tentation de Saint Antoine.*

15 June – 1 September *Pierre qui roule* published in *Revue des Deux Mondes.*

18 July Death of Bouilhet.

7 August Flaubert leaves for Paris (till 6 May 1870).

6 September – 23 October Sand in Paris.

11 September Première of *La Petite Fadette* at Opéra-Comique; Flaubert attends.

17 – 22 September and 28 September – 1 October Sand travels in Ardennes.

9 October Sand renews her contract with Michel Lévy.

13 October Sainte-Beuve dies.

17 November *L'Éducation sentimentale* published.

1 December *Lupo Liverani* published in *Revue des Deux Mondes*.

8–9 December Sand writes a review of *L'Éducation sentimentale*.

22 December Review published in *La Liberté*.

23–28 December Flaubert at Nohant.

1870   18 January – 5 March Sand in Paris.

1 February – 15 March *Malgrétout* published in *Revue des Deux Mondes*.

12 February Benefit at Odéon to raise funds for Bouilhet monument. Sand indisposed and does not attend.

25 February Première of *L'Autre* at Odéon. Flaubert does not attend, being in poor health.

1 March Flaubert's close friend Jules Duplan dies.

19 March Flaubert attends performance of *L'Autre*.

29 April Lévy offers to lend Flaubert 4,000 francs. Flaubert rejects offer.

6 May Flaubert returns to Croisset. Starts writing preface to Bouilhet's *Dernières Chansons* (completed 20 June).

20 June Jules de Goncourt dies; Flaubert attends his funeral, June 22.

26 June Sand's friend Armand Barbès dies.

19 July War declared on Prussia.

15 August – 1 October *Césarine Dietrich* published in *Revue des Deux Mondes*.

1 September French defeat at Sedan.

3 September *Malgrétout*.

4 September Republic proclaimed.

20 September – 12 November Sand visits Saint-Loup, Boussac and La Châtre.

27 October Metz capitulates.

5 December Germans occupy Rouen; Prussian troops billeted at Croisset, Flaubert moves to Rouen.

1871   28 January Armistice.

8 February Elections to the Assemblée nationale.

8 or 9 February Flaubert and his mother move in with his niece, just back from England, at Dieppe.

1 March Peace treaty ratified (it was signed on 26 February).

1 March – 1 April *Journal d'un voyageur pendant la guerre* published in *Revue des Deux Mondes*.

8 March Casimir Dudevant dies.

16 – 28 March Flaubert visits Princesse Mathilde in Brussels and Juliet Herbert in London.

18 March Start of insurrection in Paris.

1 April Flaubert returns to Croisset and resumes work on *Saint Antoine*.

4 (or 6) – 11 May Flaubert in Paris.

21–28 May "Week of bloodshed".

20 (or 21) July – 16 August Flaubert in Paris and at Saint-Gratien.

22 July German troops withdraw from Rouen.

22 August Sand begins to write for *Le Temps* with *Rêveries et Souvenirs*.

23 September *Césarine Dietrich*.

3 October *Le Temps* publishes *Réponse à un ami*.

9 – 18 October Flaubert in Paris attending to Bouilhet's affairs.

8 November Mme Schlésinger visits Croisset.

15 November Flaubert leaves for Paris (staying till 25 March 1872).

2 December Rouen municipal authorities reject plan for Bouilhet monument.

1872   6 January Première of Bouilhet's *Mademoiselle Aïssé* at Odéon.

20 January Bouilhet's *Dernières Chansons* published with preface by Flaubert.

26 January *Lettre au Conseil municipal* published in *Le Temps*.

February/March Maurice Sand ill.

7 March – 20 April *Nanon* published in *Le Temps*.

20 March Flaubert quarrels with Lévy.

25 March Flaubert returns to Croisset.

6 April Mme Flaubert dies.

April/June Sand and grandchildren ill.

1 May – 1 June *Francia* published in *Revue des Deux Mondes*.

28 May – 17 June Sand in Paris.

1 June *La Reine Coax* published in *Revue des Deux Mondes*.

12–22 June Flaubert in Paris.

29 June *Francia*.

1 July Flaubert completes *Saint Antoine*.

7 July – 14 August Flaubert at Luchon till 9 August, then Paris. Back in Croisset he starts reading for *Bouvard et Pécuchet*.

28 July – 23 August Sand at Cabourg.

7 – 22 September Flaubert in Paris for research on *Bouvard et Pécuchet*..

25 September – 3 October The Viardots at Nohant.

23 October Théophile Gautier dies.

About 25 November *Mademoiselle La Quintinie* banned by the censors.

28 December *Nanon* (released in November).

29 or 30 December Flaubert leaves for Paris, till 17 May 1873.

1873   January/February Flaubert ill in Paris. Reading for *Bouvard et Pécuchet*.

12 – 19 April Flaubert visits Nohant. Turgenev arrives on 16th. Reads *Saint Antoine*.

24 April – 10 May Sand in Paris.

3 May Probably last meeting between Flaubert and Sand, at dinner at Véfour.

17 May Flaubert returns to Croisset and starts rewriting Bouilhet's *Le Sexe faible.*

24 May *Impressions et Souvenirs.*

20 June Flaubert contracts with Charpentier for *Madame Bovary* and *Salammbô.*

9–12 July Michel Lévy at Nohant.

5 August – 4 September Flaubert visits Dieppe, Paris, Saint-Gratien. Excursion to Brie and Beauce countryside for *Bouvard et Pécuchet.*

5 – 25 August Sand travels in Auvergne.

7 September Flaubert starts sketching out *Le Candidat*, while reading for *Bouvard et Pécuchet.*

16 – 29 September The Viardots and Turgenev at Nohant (the latter from the 23rd).

2 – 5 October Turgenev at Croisset.

20–30 October Flaubert in Paris for *Le Sexe faible.*

29 October Ernest Feydeau dies.

Late October/Early November Sand ill with rheumatism and jaundice.

15 November *Contes d'une grand'mère* (first series).

22 November Flaubert finishes *Le Candidat.*

6 December Flaubert leaves for Paris, till 19 May 1874.

13 December Flaubert contracts with Charpentier for *La Tentation de Saint Antoine.*

1874   January/March At Nohant everyone ill by turns.

1 January – 15 March *Ma Soeur Jeanne* published in *Revue des Deux Mondes.*

11 March Première of *Le Candidat* at the Vaudeville; Sand does not attend. Flaubert withdraws the play after four performances.

28 March *Le Candidat* published.

31 March *La Tentation de Saint Antoine* published.

19 or 20 May Flaubert back at Croisset.

30 May – 10 June Sand in Paris.

June/August Back at Nohant, Sand frequently ill.

Early June *Ma Soeur Jeanne* published as a book.

18–23 June Flaubert and Laporte travel in Lower Normandy (for *Bouvard et Pécuchet*).

30 June – 31 July Flaubert at Kaltbad-Rigi, Switzerland, till 19 July; returns to Croisset via Geneva, Paris and Dieppe.

1 August Flaubert starts drafting *Bouvard et Pécuchet.*

25 August – 17 September Flaubert in Paris, for *Le Sexe faible.*

October/November Flaubert ill.

17 October Sand's close friend Charles Duvernet dies.

16 November Flaubert in Paris for rehearsals of *Le Sexe faible.* Withdraws the play a few days later. Stays in Paris till 9 May 1875.

1875   1 February – 1 May *Flamarande* published in *Revue des Deux Mondes*.
February/April Flaubert ill.

March Sand also ill.

April The Commanvilles' financial problems become acute.

9 May Flaubert returns to Croisset, setting aside *Bouvard et Pécuchet* for the moment.

14 July–1 November Several of the *Contes d'une grand'mère* published in *Le Temps* and *Revue des Deux Mondes*.

1 – 15 August *Marianne* published in *Revue des Deux Mondes*.

Throughout August Commanvilles threatened with bankruptcy.

14 August *Flamarande*.

18 August Sand's close friend Jules Boucoiran dies.

28 August *Les Deux Frères*.

13–14 September Flaubert sells his farm at Deauville.

16 September – 1 November Flaubert stays at Concarneau and starts his *La Légende de Saint Julien l'Hospitalier*.

1 October Commanville's business is put into liquidation.

1 November Flaubert settles into 240, rue du Faubourg Saint-Honoré, Paris.

1 December – 1 January *La Tour de Percemont* published in *Revue des Deux Mondes*.

1876   Late January *La Tour de Percemont–Marianne* published in volume form.

17 February Flaubert completes *Saint Julien* and begins *Un Coeur simple*.

7 March *Le Mariage de Victorine* revived at Comédie-Française. Flaubert attends.

18 March *La Coupe*.

10 – 11 April Flaubert visits Honfleur and Pont-l'Evêque for *Un Coeur simple*.

30 May Sand takes to her bed, suffering from an intestinal blockage, and leaving her novel *Albine* unfinished.

8 June Sand dies after great suffering.

10 June Sand buried in cemetery at Nohant, attended by Flaubert, Renan and Prince Napoléon.

8 May 1880 Flaubert dies at Croisset.

FLAUBERT ~ SAND
THE CORRESPONDENCE

CHAPTER I

Before 1866

"I have recently read *L'Uscoque*, by George Sand," the seventeen-year-old Gustave Flaubert – student and "Red Romantic" – wrote to his friend Ernest Chevalier on 11 October 1838. "Try to get hold of a copy and you'll find this Uscoque a man worthy of your esteem."

Flaubert's early enthusiasm for Sand was short-lived. By 1843, in the first version of *L'Éducation sentimentale*, he was proclaiming his scorn: "I do not address these remarks to the schoolboys and dressmakers who read George Sand ... but to persons of discrimination." His literary ideas had undergone a fundamental change: the credo of "impersonality in art" had become an obsession. *Conceal your feelings; don't put your self into your writings; don't try to prove anything; express no opinion*: these had become, and would remain, his maxims. On 16 November 1852, he expressed his principles in a turgid letter of advice to Louise Colet: "You will come into the fullness of your talent when you divest yourself of your sex, which must serve you as a means of objective comprehension, and not as an emotional outlet. In G. Sand, one smells the 'white flowers':[1] everything oozes, and ideas trickle between words as though between slack thighs." And in a letter to Louis Bouilhet of 30 May 1855: "Every day I read some G. Sand, and every day without fail I'm indignant for a quarter of an hour."[2]

George Sand, for her part, was long unaware of Flaubert's very existence. The publicity surrounding his prosecution as the author of *Madame Bovary* aroused her curiosity, and she had the novel read to her from 21 to 25 December 1856. "The book interests Mme Sand and is giving her great pleasure," her secretary and lover, Alexandre Manceau, noted in his diary. As for Flaubert, when his novel was published by Michel Lévy in April 1857, he did not fail – despite his earlier derision of Mme Sand's talents – to send the illustrious lady an inscribed copy: "*A Madame Sand, hommage d'un inconnu.*" A few days later, on 30 April, George Sand's diary records their first meeting – at the Théâtre de l'Odéon, during the opening performance of a play by Victor Séjour, *André Gérard*. They probably did no more than exchange greetings in an entr'acte: Flaubert's name is merely listed in the diary along with a number of others. Perhaps, at some time following that occasion, George Sand expressed to Flaubert her admiration for *Madame Bovary* and promised to write an article about the book. However that may be, on 29 September, in her weekly feuilleton for the *Courrier de Paris*, she contrived to include a few pages analyzing and defending it.

Mme Sand's sympathetic mention of the book must have pleased Flaubert, who had not been treated kindly by critics.[3] If he sent her a letter of thanks it has not survived. In any case, courtesy required that past differences be forgotten, and the way seemed clear for them to become friends. Some time passed before they found themselves in Paris simultaneously; and it was not until the spring of 1859, probably on 29 April, that their first significant meeting took place, in George Sand's apartment in rue Racine. Flaubert was won over immediately, even though he continued to have, at times, a poor opinion of Mme Sand's writings. "I gather you cherish la mère Sand," he wrote to Ernest Feydeau on 21 August 1859. "I find her personally a charming woman. As for her doctrines, as expressed in her writings – beware! A fortnight ago I re-read *Lélia*. Read it. I beg you, read that book again!"

There was no meeting, probably no letter, during the three years that followed; no mention in Mme Sand's diary or in the published correspondence.

Then, on 24 November 1862, *Salammbô* appeared, and Flaubert sent out the customary copies. On the 29th Manceau wrote in the diary: "Flobert [sic] sends Madame Sand his Carthaginian novel;" and on 26 December, when she had finished reading it, he tells us that "Madame Sand thinks well of this book."[4] The next day she began a laudatory article, which appeared in *La Presse* of 27 January.

Flaubert immediately thanked the reviewer, in a letter that has not been found. And in reply he received, sent on by Emile Aucante, Mme Sand's *homme d'affaires*, her letter of 28 January 1863. This appears to be the first letter written by George Sand to Flaubert.

---

[1] Leucorrhoea.

[2] He was referring to Sand's *Histoire de ma vie*, published in instalments in the newspaper *La Presse*, from 5 October 1854 to 17 August 1855.

[3] Although there is no formal proof that Flaubert was aware of Mme Sand's article, it is known that his friend Duplan combed the newspapers and magazines and sent him every printed mention of his book.

[4] This statement appears rather mild, if one compares it with Mme Sand's cries of admiration in her article and in her correspondence. For example, she wrote to her friend Juliette Lamber, the future Mme Adam: "You must read it: it is a superb book – one of those that mark an epoch." (J. Adam, *Mes Premières Armes littéraires et politiques*, Paris, 1904, p. 383.) A more moderate opinion appears in a letter from Sand to her son Maurice, 29 June 1865: "*Salammbô* – a very strong book, very fine, but really of interest only to artists and scholars. They may pick it to pieces, but they read it, whereas the public just says, 'It may be very good, but what do I care about people who lived so long ago?'"

1 SAND TO FLAUBERT

Nohant, 28 January [18]63

Mon cher frère,

Don't thank me for having done my duty. When the critics do theirs I'll keep quiet: I'd rather create than judge. But all I'd read about *Salammbô* before I read *Salammbô* itself was unfair or inadequate, and I'd have thought it either cowardly or lazy – they're much the same thing – to be silent. I don't mind adding your enemies to my own. A few more one way or the other . . .

I must apologize for my rather puerile criticism about *Le Défilé de la hache*.[1] I let it stand because a reservation only brought out the sincerity of my admiration.

We don't know each other very well. Do come and see me when you have time. It's not far, and I'm always here. But I'm an old woman[2] – don't wait till I'm in my second childhood.

Solve a puzzle for me. In September someone sent me an interesting pressed plant in an envelope with no name on the back. It now strikes me the address is in your handwriting. But how could that be? How could you have known that I take a keen interest in botany?

What I accept of your thanks is their friendliness. That I know I do deserve.

Tout à vous

G. Sand

---

[1] Chapter XIV of *Salammbô*. In her review, Sand had criticized it on the grounds of improbability.

[2] She was born on 1 July 1804.

2 FLAUBERT TO SAND

[Paris, 31 January 1863]

Chère Madame,

It's not that I'm grateful to you for having performed what you call a duty. I was touched by your goodness of heart; and your sympathy made me proud, that's all.

Your letter, which I have just received, adds to your article and goes beyond it, and I don't know what to tell you other than, quite frankly, that I love you for it.

M. Aucante has asked me to get you a copy of *L'Opinion nationale*.[1] You will receive it at the same time as this letter.

No, it wasn't I who sent you a flower in an envelope last September. But what is strange is that at that same time I was sent a leaf, in the same fashion.

As for your very cordial invitation, I answer neither yes nor no, like a true

Norman. Perhaps I'll surprise you some day this coming summer. Because I greatly long to see you and talk with you.

All my affection. I kiss both your hands, and am

All yours

Gve Flaubert

Boulevard du Temple 42; or Croisset, near Rouen

P. S. I should very much like to have a portrait of you to hang on the wall of my study in the country, where I often spend long months quite alone. Is the request indiscreet? If not, I send you my thanks in advance. Accept them along with the others, which I reiterate.

[1] The archaeologist William Froehner had published, in *La Revue contemporaine*, an article on *Salammbô*, in which he questioned the sincerity of Flaubert's research. Flaubert, in the *L'Opinion nationale* for 24 January 1863, published a "Réponse à M. Froehner", which refuted, with many references and quotations, all the critic's arguments. [For Flaubert's reply to Froehner see Francis Steegmuller, *The Letters of Gustave Flaubert*, II, 52–60.]

3 SAND TO FLAUBERT

Nohant, 10 February [18]63

There aren't many portraits of me, though all kinds are sold that weren't done from life. All I have here are unsatisfactory proofs. When I go to Paris I'll choose something presentable and send it to you. Thank you for the welcome you mean to extend to my face, which is insignificant in itself, as you well know. What is best is inside the head – understanding: and in the heart – esteem.

G. Sand

4 FLAUBERT TO SAND

[Paris, 12 February 1863]
Thursday morning

Thank you in advance, cher maître. Nothing about you is insignificant, whatever you may say. I'll be delighted to receive your gift, and shall be proud of it always.

I kiss both your hands, and am

all yours,

Gve Flaubert

If you come to Paris this summer, be good enough to let me know at Croisset. I'll come to meet you unless it should prove impossible – an improbability!

*

Despite that promising beginning, Flaubert did not immediately forget his reservations. "As for [Sand's] *Mademoiselle La Quintinie*," he wrote to his friend Mlle Leroyer de Chantepie, on 23 October 1863, "frankly, Art should not be made to serve as a pulpit for any doctrine: that is a debasement." He reproached Mme Sand also for complying too easily with the demands of publishers and theatre managers – a lack, as he considered it, of professional dignity.

During the remaining months of 1863, Flaubert and Sand did not correspond or meet. But, on 8 January 1864, Mme Sand arrived in Paris for rehearsals of her play, *Le Marquis de Villemer*. Flaubert, in the city for the winter as usual, visited her on 14 January and 1 February. A few weeks later the première of *Villemer* was a triumph unprecedented in the history of the Odéon. Flaubert was present, in Prince Napoléon's[1] box with Sand herself, and he "wept like a woman."

Sand returned to Nohant on 16 March. Before her departure she took leave of Flaubert in the following letter, to which no reply has been found.

[1] For identification of Prince Napoléon and his sister, Princesse Mathilde, see Flaubert Chronology, 1862–5.

5 SAND TO FLAUBERT

[Paris] 15 March [18]64

Cher Flaubert,

I don't know whether you gave me Monsieur Taine's excellent book[1] or only lent it. So I'm sending it back. I've only had time to read part of it here, and at Nohant I'm only going to have time to scribble for Buloz[2]. But when I come back a couple of months from now I shall ask you again for these excellent and noble volumes. I'm sorry not to have said goodbye to you. But as I shall be back soon, I hope you won't have forgotten me, and that you'll give me something of your own to read too. You were so kind and considerate to me at the first night of *Villemer* that I have come not only to admire your admirable talent but also to love you with all my heart.

George Sand

[1] The first volume of Hippolyte Taine's *Histoire de la littérature anglaise*, which Flaubert had read in January.
[2] Since 1858, almost all of Sand's books had been serialized in *La Revue des Deux Mondes*, of which François Buloz was editor. His name will appear frequently in the letters.

*

During the next year, no letters. But Sand noted in her diary, on 8 May 1865, that she had happened to meet Flaubert that day, in the Restaurant Magny.

CHAPTER II

1866

George Sand and Flaubert became better acquainted at the "Magny dinners". These Monday-evening gatherings of writers and artists, inaugurated by Sainte-Beuve, the artist Gavarni, and the brothers Edmond and Jules de Goncourt in November 1862, took place in a private dining room of the Restaurant Magny, in rue Mazet in the Latin Quarter. Often invited to join the group, Mme Sand first appeared among them on 12 February 1866: she was the only woman ever to be present as a member.[1]

They seem to have been a vociferous, self-approving lot, and that first evening Mme Sand did not feel at ease. She wrote to Maurice:

> Tonight I dined for the first time at Magny's with my *petits camarades* – the monthly dinner founded by Sainte-Beuve. Present were Gautier, Saint-Victor, Flaubert, Sainte-Beuve, Berthelot the famous chemist, Bouilhet, the Goncourts, etc. Taine and Renan were absent: there were only twelve of us. I was greeted with open arms – they have been inviting me for the past three years. I decided to go alone, preferring not to be escorted, and thus avoiding possible comment. They are all very witty and spirited, but there is a superabundance of paradox and self-esteem: only Berthelot and Flaubert didn't talk about themselves.

She also wrote about the occasion in her diary:

> Dinner chez Magny with my *petits camarades*. They couldn't have given me a warmer welcome. They were very brilliant, except for the great scholar Berthelot. Gautier constantly dazzling and paradoxical. Saint-Victor charming and distinguished. Flaubert, impassioned and more sympathetic to me than the others. Why? I'm still not sure. The Goncourts, too self-assured, especially the younger, who is very witty but too contentious with his elders. The best talker, and no less witty than the rest, is "l'oncle Beuve", as they call him. Everyone pays ten francs, the dinner is mediocre. There's a lot of smoking and loud talk, and you leave when you like. I was forgetting Louis Bouilhet, who looks like Flaubert and was modest.

Thenceforward, Sand attended the dinners regularly when she was in Paris. Flaubert, at that time plagued by boils, could not always come; but Sand's diary shows them there together on 12 March, 23 April, and 7 and 21 May.

[1] From the Goncourts' *Journal*, 12 February 1866:
"Mme Sand dines chez Magny. She sits beside me. With age, her fine, charming face is taking on a mulatto-like cast. She glances timidly around the table and murmurs to Flaubert: 'You're the only one here with whom I feel at ease.' She listens, says nothing. When someone recites a poem by Hugo tears come into her eyes at the most falsely sentimental passage. She has small hands, incredibly delicate, almost hidden in her lace cuffs."

For a clever re-creation of the Magny dinners, based on letters, journals, memoirs, etc. written by members of the group, see *Dinner at Magny's*, by Robert Baldick (London, Victor Gollancz, 1971). The talk was often very free, not to say rough: apparently the tone was somewhat moderated when George Sand was present. She patronized the restaurant independently, and was a friend of the proprietor, Magny, and his wife.

6 FLAUBERT TO SAND

[Paris, March–May 1866]
Sunday morning

Tomorrow, Monday, is Magny day, chère maître.[1] I'll be there, of course. Meanwhile, je vous embrasse.

Gve Flaubert

[1] From now on, in his salutations, Flaubert will use the feminine form of the adjective before the masculine noun – double homage to his friend.

*

Sand and Flaubert met on other occasions as well. On 19 February they dined chez Sainte-Beuve with Berthelot, the younger Dumas, and Sainte-Beuve's secretary, Jules Troubat: on the 23rd they were together at a dinner given by the actress Mme Arnould-Plessy ("Sylvanie" to her friends); on 10 March, Flaubert accompanied Sand to the Magny but could not stay: and on 2 May, Sainte-Beuve entertained Sand, Flaubert, Taine and Princesse Mathilde. Sand's diary records her pleasure on these occasions.

These were the months of the *farce de Goulard*, a series of burlesque letters to Flaubert from a character invented by Sand. The following is the only example known to survive.

7 SAND TO FLAUBERT

[Palaiseau, 9 May 1866]

Monsieur Flobaire,
You must be a reel lout to have taken my name and wrote a letter to a lady once kindly disposed to me and have no dout been received in my sted and

inherrited my cap, which I have recievd yours instead that you left there[.] This is very bad behavour on the part of the lady and you[.] She must be verry ill bread and laking in the feelings she ought to feel to understand the rude things you write and confuse our too stiles. If you are glad to have writen Fanie and Salkenpeau,[1] I am glad not to have red them. Nothing to get pufed up about there. I see from the papers they are vile works against Religion into which I have retired since the trobles I had because of that lady which mad me witdraw into myself and reppent of my ekceses with her, and so if I meat you with her which I hope not you will get a biff in the face. It will be Attonement for my sinns and Punishment for your wickednesses together. So now you no. Yrs ect.

Goulard

Palaisot, The Monastry

The bruthers say I've bin punnished for mixing with thearter women and awthers.

[1] Sand is satirizing literary critics who had long been boring Flaubert by linking *Madame Bovary* with Ernest Feydeau's novel *Fanny*. "Salkenpeau" is *Salammbô*.

*

The farce ended, the friendship prospered.

8 SAND TO FLAUBERT

Palaiseau, 14 May [1866]

This isn't a letter from Goulard. He's dead! The false Goulard[1] killed him off by being funnier and more real. Moreover the false Goulard is a rascal who stops at nothing!

My friend, this is to tell you I'd like to dedicate my forthcoming novel to you. But since, as Goulard would say, everyone has his own ideas about it, I want to know if you'll allow me just to put "To my friend Gustave Flaubert" at the top of my first page. I've got into the habit of placing my novels under the patronage of a name that is dear to me. I dedicated the last to Fromentin.

I'm waiting for it to be fine before I ask you to come and dine in Palaiseau with Goulard's *Sirenne*,[2] together with a few other Goulards of both your species and mine. Up till now it's been beastly cold and there's no point in coming to the country to catch a chill.

I've finished my novel.[3] What about you? A kiss on each of the two large diamonds that adorn your *trompette*.[4]

Jorje Sens

The elder Goulard is my little Lambert. I think that's enough literature from him.

[1] That is, Flaubert himself, who, as we know from letter 7, had outdone Sand in the

excellence of a Goulard letter he had composed and sent to "a lady" whom they both knew
– probably Mme Arnould-Plessy, who is also referred to in the present letter at (2).

² See Note 1.

³ *Le Dernier Amour.*

⁴ Apparently, Flaubert's eyes. *Trompette* (slang: *nose*) may mean here simply his face.

9 FLAUBERT TO SAND

[Paris, 15 May 1866]
Tuesday morning

Why – with pleasure, of course! With gratitude and affection, chère maître.

I must postpone my visit to Palaiseau until August, because I return to the country next Tuesday. My poor old mother keeps insisting that she needs me. So next Monday I'll say goodbye to you, or rather au revoir.

I read *Monsieur Sylvestre* without once putting it down, and have embellished it with some marginal notes (as is my habit).[1] If I have time on Monday I'll bring my copy with me and we'll talk about it before going on to Magny's.

You are right to love me: it's only a fair exchange.

Je vous serre les deux mains, vous baise sur les deux joues, et suis
votre

Gve Flaubert

[1] Flaubert's signed copy, along with other novels that Mme Sand sent him, is in the public library at Canteleu, near Croisset. He has marked a few passages, but there are no notes.

10 SAND TO FLAUBERT

Palaiseau, Wednesday 16 [May 1866]

Well, my dear fellow, as you're going away, and as I'm going to the Berry too for two or three months, do try to find time to come tomorrow, Thursday. You'll be dining with dear interesting Marguerite Thuillier, who is also off soon. So do come and see me and my Sylvestre's[1] hermitage. If you leave Paris by the Gare de Sceaux at 1 o'clock you can be at my place by 2, or if you leave at 5 you'll be here at 6, and you can go back in the evening with my "hams"[2] at 9 or 10.

Bring your copy of the book. Write in all the criticisms that occur to you. I'd like that very much. People ought to do this service for one another, as Balzac and I used to do.[3] It doesn't mean you change one another – on the contrary, it usually makes one cling more firmly to one's own point of view. But in so doing one supplements it, makes it clearer, develops it more fully, and that's why friendship is a good thing even in literature, where the first and foremost condition for having any sort of worth is to be oneself.

If you can't come I'll be extremely sorry, but in that case I'll count on you for Monday before dinner.

Sylvanie demands the death of all the Goulards. She's quite fierce about it. Nothing has been able to soften her stony heart. But they were charming rascals, weren't they! No, I haven't been clever enough to see why the idea does me credit: I agree it's *elegant*, but also rather *frivolous*, wouldn't you say? And the dénouement is risqué. I defy you to use it.

Au revoir, and thanks for your fraternal consent to the dedication.

G. Sand

[1] The village of Palaiseau, and George Sand's house there, are depicted in *Monsieur Sylvestre*. Marguerite Thuillier was an actress who had appeared in a number of Sand's plays.

[2] "*Cabots*": "ham actors" – Sand's breezy term for her stage friends.

[3] Sand to Balzac, in a letter written about 20 January 1840: "Come, dine with me tomorrow, and read me forty volumes if you can."

*

Flaubert did not go to Palaiseau; and Sand, disappointed, noted in her diary, the evening of the 17th, "Flaubert did not come." He was too busy with errands and with research for his novel. He could not even keep his promise to talk with her about *Monsieur Sylvestre* before dinner that following Monday. On 21 May they met at the Magny dinner to take leave of each other. Flaubert returned to Croisset the next day, and Sand to Nohant on 1 June.

On 1 July the *Revue des Deux Mondes* began the serialization of *Le Dernier Amour*.

11 FLAUBERT TO SAND

[Paris, 18 or 19 May 1866]

Chère maître,

Don't expect me to come to you on Monday. I must go to Versailles that day. But I'll see you at Magny's.

Mille bonnes tendresses from

Your

Gve Flaubert

12 FLAUBERT TO SAND

Croisset, near Rouen, 5 July [1866]

Chère maître,

I learn from some worthies here that the novel dedicated to me has begun to appear. I thank you again, very sincerely and deeply. I'll wait to read it until it's all in print. A book should be gobbled down whole, then re-read – when it is by you.

I expect to spend two or three days in Paris towards the end of this month. Shall we see each other?

For you I wish everything you might wish for yourself. Je vous aime et vous embrasse.

Your

Gve Flaubert

*

George Sand replied to that letter immediately, as we know from her "list of letters answered"; but her reply has not been found. A few weeks later she was in Paris for the opening of *Les Don Juan de village*, a play she had written in collaboration with her son Maurice. Flaubert, who had just spent a fortnight in London with his friend Juliet Herbert, his niece's former governess, arrived in Paris about 1 August.

13 SAND TO FLAUBERT

Nohant, 31 July [18]66

Mon brave cher camarade,

Are you going to be in Paris in the next few days, as you led me to hope? I leave here on the 2nd. What luck if I found you at next Monday's dinner! What's more, a play by my son and myself is being performed on the 10th. How could I do without you then? I shall be a prey to *emotion* this time, because of my dear collaborator. Try to be able to come, like a true friend! Hoping you will, I send all my love.

The late Goulard

G. Sand

14 FLAUBERT TO SAND

Paris, Boulevard du Temple, 42
Saturday morning
[4 August 1866]

Chère maître,

I doubt that I'll be at the next Magny, but I shall certainly be at the opening of your play.

Before that, I'm counting on paying you a little visit.

I send you a kiss, and remain

Your old Goulard, known as

Gve Flaubert

15 SAND TO FLAUBERT

[Paris] Saturday evening [4 August 1866]

Cher ami,

As I'm always out, I don't want you to come to the ends of the earth only to find the door shut. Come at 6 o'clock and have dinner with me and my children, whom I expect tomorrow. We always dine at Magny's at six o'clock sharp. You'll be giving us "appreciable pleasure", as the unfortunate Goulard would say — or, alas, would have said!

You're a very very kind brother to promise to come to the *Don Juan* do, and I send you twice as much love as before for it.

G. Sand

16 FLAUBERT TO SAND

[Paris, 5 August 1866]
Sunday morning 1 o'clock

Can you, mon chère maître, tell me positively the date of your opening? I have to know, to make my own little subsequent arrangements.

Forgive this bother.

Je vous baise les mains.

Gve Flaubert

17 SAND TO FLAUBERT

[Paris, 5 August 1866]
Sunday

It's next *Thursday*.

I wrote to you yesterday; our letters will have crossed.

A vous de coeur,

G. Sand

*

George Sand's diary tells us that they saw each other again on Monday, August 6; and, on Thursday the 9th, Flaubert attended the première of *Les Don Juan de village*. The play was poorly received. "The failure was complete, even though the critics weren't too harsh," Flaubert wrote to his friend Amélie Bosquet on 20 August. "Audiences puzzle me more and more: I completely fail to understand them. Why do they shout with enthusiasm at *Le Marquis de Villemer* and yawn with boredom at *Les Don Juan*? The two plays seem to me absolutely of the same calibre."

The following day he left Paris to resume his summer visits. He spent two days at Mantes with Bouilhet, went to see his mother, who was spending part of the summer with grandchildren and great-grandchildren at Ouville, and visited his niece Caroline at Dieppe.[1] He returned to Croisset on August 19, to resume work on *L'Éducation sentimentale*.

George Sand remained for a time in Paris, correcting the proofs of the printed edition of *Les Don Juan de village*. Then she too set off on holiday.

[1] Both towns are in the *pays de Caux* – "chalk country": that is, in Normandy north of the Seine, "*la haute Normandie*".

18 SAND TO FLAUBERT

Paris [22 August 1866]
Wednesday evening

Mon bon camarade et ami,

I'm going to see Alexandre[1] at Saint-Valery on Saturday evening. I'll spend Sunday and Monday there, and on Tuesday I'll return to Rouen and come and see you. Let me know how to get there. I'll spend the day with you if that suits you, go back to Rouen for the night if you haven't got room for me, and leave for Paris on Tuesday morning or evening. Do drop me a line straight away – by telegraph if you think an answer by post mightn't reach me before four o'clock on Saturday.

I think I'll be well enough, though I have an awful cold. If it gets too much worse I'll send you a wire. But I hope to be able to come; I feel better already.

Je vous embrasse

G. Sand

[1] The younger Alexandre Dumas. He had rented a seaside cottage at Saint-Valery-en-Caux, between Dieppe and Fécamp.

*

Flaubert replied immediately by telegraph. He had a room made ready at Croisset, and told the good news to his niece Caroline, so that she might come to see the famous novelist.

19 FLAUBERT TO SAND

Croisset near Rouen
Friday [24 August 1866]

Chère maître,

This is what you must do. As soon as you reach Saint-Valery, reserve your place in the old rattletrap that goes from Saint-Valery to Motteville. Otherwise you'll risk being delayed in leaving.

Leaving Saint-Valery at a quarter to 9 you'll reach Rouen at 1 o'clock. There you'll find me at the door of your compartment and you won't have to attend to anything. If you don't leave Saint-Valery in the morning, the only other departure is at four p.m.

You should have my telegram saying that your room awaits you. So you'll be staying with us.

Be good enough to wire me from Saint-Valery, giving me the exact time of your arrival.[1]

Je vous baise les deux mains et suis
Votre

Gve Flaubert

[1] To this letter Flaubert added some untranslatable comic references to a grotesque "poem" about a head-cold written to Lamartine by Casimir Delavigne, and quoted several lines of the verse itself. To the end of his letter Flaubert's mother, as hostess, appended a proper invitation to Mme Sand:

"I add my entreaties to those of my son, and I am counting, Madame, on having the honour of receiving you here. *Votre servante*, C[aroli]ne Flaubert."

20   SAND TO FLAUBERT

Saint-Valery, Monday 1 a.m.
[26–27 August 1866]

Cher ami,

I'll arrange to be in Rouen at 1 o'clock. I don't know the place, so leave me a little while to look around the town, or show it to me yourself if you have time.

Much love. Please tell your mother how touched and grateful I am to have her kind note.

G. Sand

*

George Sand greatly enjoyed her visit to Croisset.

FROM GEORGE SAND'S DIARY, 1866

Tuesday, 28 August

I arrived in Rouen at one o'clock. Found Flaubert waiting at the station with a carriage. He showed me around the town and the sights: the cathedral, the city hall, Saint-Maclou, Saint-Patrice: marvellous. An old graveyard and some ancient streets: very quaint. We got to Croisset at half-past three. Flaubert's mother is a charming old lady. A quiet place; the house comfortable, pretty and well arranged. Good servants; clean; plenty of water; every need thought-fully *provided for*. I'm in clover. In the evening Flaubert read me a superb *Tentation de Saint Antoine*.[1] We chatted in his study until two in the morning.

Wednesday, 29 August

At eleven o'clock we took the steam-boat to La Bouille, with Mme Flaubert, her niece, her friend Mme Vasse, and Mme Vasse's daughter, Mme de la Chaussée. Terrible weather: wind and rain. But I stayed on deck to watch the water and the river banks – all superb. We stopped at La Bouille for ten minutes, then came back with the bore, the tide, the *mascaret* or flood. We were back by one o'clock, lit a fire, dried ourselves and had some tea. I went out again with Flaubert to see around his place – garden, terraces, orchard, kitchen garden, farm, *citadel* – a strange little old house built of wood that he uses as a wine store, and Moses' Lane, a little footpath leading from Croisset to Canteleu. Everything charming and very poetic: the view looking down over the Seine, the orchard, on a height and very sheltered, the arid white land above. I dressed for dinner; a very good one. I played cards with the two old ladies, then talked with Flaubert and went to bed at two. Bed excellent; slept well. But I'm coughing again. My cold is sulking. Let it!

Thursday, 30 August

Left Croisset at noon with Flaubert and his niece, whom we dropped in Rouen. We had another look at the town and the harbour – huge and splendid. Fine baptistry in a Jesuit church.[2] Very thrilled with Flaubert.

[1] This was one of the early, unpublished versions of the *Tentation*. It would appear, in definitive form, in 1874.
[2] The church of St Romain.

*

Flaubert, too, was delighted. "[George Sand] was as always very natural, not at all a bluestocking," he wrote to Princesse Mathilde. And he added: "I think you are very severe about *Le Dernier Amour*. In my opinion there are some quite remarkable things in that book."

21 SAND TO FLAUBERT

Paris, Friday
[31 August 1866]

First of all, please give my love to your kind mother and charming niece. I'm really touched by the welcome I received in your cathedral close, where a roving creature like me might well be regarded as awkward and out of place. Instead I was treated like one of the family, and I could see that this graciousness came from the heart. Remember me to the other kind ladies too. I was really very happy staying with you.

And as to you yourself,[1] great man as you are, you are a good kind boy, and

I love you with all my heart. My head's full of Rouen, with its quaint houses and other sights. Seeing it with you makes it all doubly impressive. But your own house and garden and *citadel* – they're like a dream, and I feel as if I were still there.

Paris seemed quite small yesterday as we came in over the bridges. I feel like going away again. I haven't seen enough of you – of you and your setting. But I must rush after the children,[2] who are calling for me and showing their teeth.

Love and blessings to all,

G. Sand

Couture was here when I got back yesterday, and I told him from you that his photograph of me was the best there is. He was very pleased. I shall look out a very good print to send you.

I forgot to take a few leaves from the tulip tree, so you must send some in a letter – I need them for arcane purposes.

[1] Here George Sand hesitantly uses the familiar pronoun *tu*. She will alternate between *tu* and the more formal *vous* until early in 1867, when *vous* will be dropped. Flaubert, writing to Sand, always retained the seemly *vous*, out of respect for a woman who was also his senior.
[2] Maurice and his wife, Lina Sand Calamatta, married May 1862. Their daughter, Aurore, was born on 10 January 1866.

22 FLAUBERT TO SAND

[Croisset] Saturday, 11 o'clock
[1 September 1866]

How sweet, how nice it is, chère maître, your letter that came this morning. For me it is like a continuation of the final, farewell look you gave me the day before yesterday, from the train.

We have done nothing but talk about you since you left. Because everybody liked you so very much. So: there's no help for it – no holding out against the irresistible, involuntary charm that you diffuse.

You must come again, no? And for a longer stay.

You forgot a lace shawl, which would already be on its way to you by train were it not for the fear that you might not still be in Paris to receive it, and that it might lie forgotten by your porter. Let me know, and it will go off to you at once.

Thank you in advance for the portrait.

Je vous embrasse tendrement et suis
votre

Gve Flaubert

No need to tell you that everyone asks me to send you the most affectionate greetings imaginable.

23   SAND TO FLAUBERT
[Paris] Sunday evening
[2 September 1866]

You can send the lace shawl. My trusty porter will forward it to wherever I am. I don't yet know where that will be. If the children want to come with me to Brittany I'll go and pick them up. Otherwise I'll just go alone wherever chance leads me. The only thing I'm afraid of when I'm travelling is myself, and being distracted. But I'm taking myself in hand and shall eventually reform.

I'm touched by your good kind letter. Don't forget my tulip leaves.

The Odéon have asked if they can do *Nuit de Noël*, a fantasy we put on in the theatre at Nohant.[1] I shan't agree; it's too trivial. But if that's the kind of thing they want to do, why not try *your féerie*?[2] Would you like me to suggest it? It seems to me that would be the right theatre for such a piece. The Chilly and Duquesnel management[3] want plenty of *décor* and effects while remaining quite literary. We'll talk about it when I get back. Meanwhile there's still time for you to write – I'm not leaving for another three days.

G. Sand

Love to everyone.

I almost forgot! Lévy has promised to send you my complete works.[4] There's lots of it. Just stow it all away on some shelves in a corner, and dip into it when you feel like it.

[1] Madame Sand had had a stage built for Maurice in the billiard room at Nohant. There were frequent performances of improvised plays, pantomimes, marionette shows, etc. *La Nuit de Noël*, a dramatic dialogue adapted from one of Hoffmann's tales, had been played there in February 1863.

[2] A *féerie* was a spectacle with supernatural characters (fairies, wizards, etc.), requiring special effects. *Le Château des coeurs*, which Flaubert had written in collaboration with his friends Louis Bouilhet and Charles d'Osmoy, was an allegory, a contest between good impulses (fairies) and bad (gnomes) for possession of the human heart.

[3] Charles de Chilly and Félix Duquesnel, the managers of the Théâtre de l'Odéon, will be mentioned frequently in the letters.

[4] This would ultimately consist of 77 volumes.

*

On 5 and 6 September Flaubert made a brief visit to Paris to have *Le Château des coeurs* read to L. F. Dumaine, one of the directors of the Théâtre de la Gaîté.

24   FLAUBERT TO SAND
Croisset, Saturday [8 September 1866]

I had no luck during my short stay in Paris, chère maître. When I took your shawl and the tulip-tree leaves to your house on Wednesday, I intended, in case I didn't find you in, to return the following day. But the next day I had an appointment with M. Dumaine – who let us down twice that same day. In short, there was no reading. They were *afraid* to hear us. "Postponed." And I don't give a damn.

I'm impatient to see all your books in a row on a shelf. That's what I call a Present – a royal present, which touches me deeply.

And don't forget the portrait, so that I may have your loved and lovely face before my eyes always.

Where are you now? As to myself, I'll not appear in civilized surroundings until the end of October, for my friend Bouilhet's opening.[1]

I am quite alone. My mother is in the *pays de Caux* until the end of this week. We have spoken of you constantly since you left!

I wish you everything you may desire, chère maître. Je vous embrasse et suis Votre

Gve Flaubert

[1] *La Conjuration d'Amboise.*

25   FLAUBERT TO SAND

Croisset, Wednesday [12 September 1866]

Chère maître,

I have received the parcel of books. They are in a row in front of me. I thank you greatly for this present. You already had my love and admiration: I see that you wish to be adored as well!

Where are you? I am alone, my fire is burning, the incessant rain is falling in sheets, I'm hard at work, and thinking of you.

Je vous embrasse.

Gve Flaubert

*

When Flaubert had vainly tried to see Sand in Paris on 5 September she had been in Brittany with Maurice and his wife. She returned to Nohant the night of 19–20 September.

26   SAND TO FLAUBERT

Nohant, 21 September [18]66

I've been rushing about with my children for twelve days, and when we got home I found your two letters. This, together with the pleasure of finding Mlle Aurore well and in looks, makes my happiness complete.

And so you, my dear Benedictine, are all alone in your delightful monastery, working and never going out? That's what you get for having gone out too much before! What his lordship needs are quicksands, deserts, asphaltic lakes, dangers and fatigues![1] And yet he produces *Bovaries* in which the innermost details of life are examined and painted with the skill of a master. A strange body, fighting the battle both of the Sphinx and of the Chimera![2] You're a very special and mysterious being, and yet as meek as a lamb. Every so often I longed to ask you some questions, but I was held back by my great respect for you: my own disasters are the only ones I can handle – those a great mind must have gone through in order to be creative are too sacred to be touched roughly or lightly. Sainte-Beuve, although he's fond of you, says you're terribly dissolute. But perhaps he sees things through somewhat sullied eyes, like the learned botanist who says dropwort is a "dirty" yellow. This observation was so wrong I couldn't help writing in the margin, "No, it's you who've got dirty eyes." I assume that a man of intelligence may be exceedingly curious. I haven't been so myself – for want of courage I've chosen to leave my mind incomplete. That's my business: everyone's free to embark on either a great clipper or a little fishing boat. An artist is an explorer who oughtn't to shrink from anything: it doesn't matter whether he goes to the left or the right – his goal sanctifies all. It's up to him, after a bit of experience, to know the conditions that best suit the health of his soul. I believe your soul is in a state of grace because you enjoy working and being alone despite the rain. Do you know, while everywhere else was deluged we were having beautiful sunshine in Brittany, apart from a few showers? The wind was blowing great guns on the coast, but the heavy swell was beautiful. And as I was eager to botanize on the dunes, and Maurice and his wife are crazy about shells, we put up with it quite happily. All in all, Brittany's a great myth. We're fed up to the teeth with dolmens and menhirs, and came across local fêtes where the old people wore all the costumes that are supposed to have been abolished. Well, let me tell you it's ugly – all these ancients with their canvas breeches, long hair, and pockets up under their armpits, not to mention their dim expressions, half bigot and half drunk. The Celtic remains,[3] though undoubtedly interesting for an archaeologist, have no appeal for an artist. Their surroundings and layout are undistinguished, and even Carnac and Erdeven[4] are quite lacking in character. In a word, Brittany shan't have my bones – I'd a thousand times rather have your opulent Normandy, or, when I'm feeling histrionic, some region of real horror and despair. There's nothing to be had where the priest reigns supreme and Catholic vandalism has swept through, razing to the ground the monuments of the old world and sowing the squabbles of the future.

You speak of "us" in connection with the *féerie*. I don't know who collaborated with you in the writing of it, but I still think it ought to go to the *present Odéon*. If I knew what it was like I could do for you what one can never do for oneself, and get the management interested. Anything written by you is bound to be too original for crude old Dumaine to understand. So take care to have a copy by you, and next month I'll come from Paris to spend a day with you so that you can read it to me. Croisset is so close to Palaiseau! And I'm in a phase of peaceful activity when I'd love to watch your great river flow by, and daydream in your equally peaceful orchard on top of the cliff.

But here am I chattering while you're working. You must forgive this unusual excess in one who's been viewing stones and hasn't caught a glimpse of a pen for twelve days. You represent my first sojourn among the living after a period in which my poor "self" was completely buried. So life, and long life, to *you*! That's my prayer and my benediction. All my love.

G. Sand

[1] An allusion to *Salammbô*.

[2] An episode in *La Tentation de Saint Antoine*.

[3] For once Sand shows herself behind the times. The megaliths, formerly thought to be Celtic, were already known to date from the Stone and Bronze Ages.

[4] The menhirs.

27 FLAUBERT TO SAND

[Croisset,] Saturday night [22 September 1866]

I, "a mysterious being"! Chère maître, come now! On the contrary, I find myself revoltingly banal, and am often thoroughly bored by the bourgeois I have under my skin. Sainte-Beuve, between you and me, doesn't know me at all, whatever he may say.

I even swear to you (by your granddaughter's smile) that I know few men less "dissolute" than I. I have *dreamed* much, and *done* very little. What deceives superficial observers is the discrepancy between my feelings and my ideas. If you want my confession, I'll make you a full one.

A sense of the grotesque has kept me from slipping into a disorderly life. I maintain that cynicism is next to chastity. We'll have much to say to one another about this if you're willing, the next time we meet.

Here is the programme I suggest. This house will be cluttered and uncomfortable for a month, but towards the end of October or beginning of November (after the opening of Bouilhet's play), I hope nothing will prevent your coming back here with me, not for a day, as you say, but for at least a week. You will have your room, "with a table and everything needed for writing". Is it agreed? There will be just the three of us, counting my mother.

As for the *féerie*, thank you for your kind offer of help. I'll bellow it out to you when I see you (it was written in collaboration with Bouilhet). But I think it's a bit weak, and I'm torn between the wish to earn a few pennies, and shame at the thought of presenting something silly.

I think you're a little severe about Brittany. Not about the Bretons, who seem to me to be surly brutes, unlovable pigs. Apropos of Celtic archaeology, in 1858 I published a rather good little snippet on megalithic stones, in *L'Artiste*. But I don't have the issue here and don't even recall the month.[1]

I have read straight through the ten volumes of your *Histoire de ma vie* (I already knew about two thirds of it, but in fragments only). What struck me most is the convent life. I have many thoughts about it, which I'll remember to tell you.[2]

Such rain! Are you at Nohant for long?

What wish shall I make for you? *My* wish is to see you again. So: à bientôt. Je vous baise les deux mains, tendrement, et suis

votre

Gve Flaubert

My mother and I speak of you every day. She will be very happy to see you.

---

[1] Flaubert and his friend Maxime Du Camp had explored the megalithic remains in the Morbihan in May 1847. On their return they wrote the travel book which they called *Par les champs et par les grèves*, never published during their lifetimes. The chapter on Carnac alone was printed in the magazine *L'Artiste* for 18 April 1858.

[2] See Page 4, Note 2.

28 SAND TO FLAUBERT

Nohant, La Châtre, Indre.
28 September [18]66

It's all agreed, dear comrade and kind friend. I'll do my best to be in Paris for the opening of your friend's play, and afterwards I'll come and stay with you for a week – but only on condition that you don't turn out of your own room. I can't bear to be a nuisance, and I don't need all that to-do in order to sleep. I can sleep anywhere – in the cinders or under a kitchen settle, like a watchdog. Everything's spotless in your house, so it's comfortable anywhere. I'll stir up your mother, and you and I shall chat to our hearts' content. If the weather's fine I'll make you rush around. If it goes on raining we'll toast our shanks and tell one another our love problems. And the great river will run black or grey under the window, saying "Quick! Quick!" all the time and carrying away our thoughts and our days and nights without pausing for anything so trivial.

I've made up a package, marked "urgent", of a good print taken from Couture's drawing and signed by the engraver, my poor friend Manceau. It's the best I have, and this is the only place where I could find it. I also enclosed a photograph of a drawing by Marchal: it too used to be a good likeness, but one changes as the years go by. Age continually alters the faces of those who think or study, and so their portraits differ from one another and don't even resemble *them* for very long. I dream so much and live so little that I'm sometimes only three years old. But the next day I'm three hundred, if the dream has been sombre. Isn't it the same with you? Doesn't it occasionally seem to you as if you're starting out on life without even knowing what it is, while at other times you feel weighed down by thousands of centuries of which you have but a dim and painful memory? Where do we come from, and where are we going? Anything's possible because everything's unknown.

Please give my love to your kind and beautiful Maman. I so look forward to being with you both. Try to hunt out that "snippet" about the Celtic stones – I'd be very interested to read it. Had they opened up the *galgal* at Lockmariaker [sic][1] when you were there, or uncovered the dolmen near Plouharnel? The people who created these remains must have been able to write, as there are stones covered with hieroglyphics, and the elaborate neck-rings that have been found show they were also skilled at working in gold. The children, who like me are great admirers of yours, send their compliments, and I kiss you on the forehead, because Sainte-Beuve was lying.

G. Sand

Is it sunny there today? It's stifling here. The country is beautiful. When are *you* coming to see *me?*

[1] A Celtic funeral mound at Locmariaquer that Mme Sand had visited. A knowledgeable and graceful account of life in this region appeared in English in 1964: Eleanor Clark's *The Oysters of Locmariaquer.*

*

Flaubert received the two portraits before the letter telling him they had been sent. Thinking that Mme Sand was in Paris, he wrote to her there.

29 FLAUBERT TO SAND

Croisset, Saturday night [29 September 1866]

So now I have that beautiful, beloved, famous face! I'll have a large frame made for it, and hang it on my wall; and then, like M. de Talleyrand to Louis-Philippe, I can say, "This is the greatest honour ever paid my house."[1] But that's a poor joke, you and I being worth something more than those two fellows.

Of the two portraits, I prefer the drawing by Couture. Marchal saw only the "good woman" in you; but for me, old Romantic that I am, the other is the "portrait of the author" who so often set me dreaming in my youth.

You are back in Paris, aren't you? What are you up to there? The play goes forward?[2] As for your friend, he is at this moment being distracted by babes who fill the house – a great-nephew and a great-niece, who are as noisy as donkeys and active as monkeys. I work with such difficulty that I need a great deal of silence and concentration.

It is understood, you know, that you'll come here again toward the end of October. We'll be alone, with time to talk seriously and see something of each other.

Adieu chère maître – je vous embrasse bien tendrement et suis votre

Gve Flaubert

[1] Said to have been Talleyrand's final words to the monarch who visited him on his deathbed.

[2] *Cadio.* See note on the two *Cadio*'s, novel and play, on p. 33.

*

Flaubert had just posted that letter when Sand's of the 28th reached Croisset. He wrote again at once.

30 FLAUBERT TO SAND

Croisset, Saturday evening [29 September 1866]

Your sending me the two portraits made me think that you were in Paris, chère maître. And I wrote you a letter that is waiting for you in rue des Feuillantines.

I haven't found my article on the dolmens. But I have the entire manuscript of my trip to Brittany among my "unpublished works". We'll have plenty to talk about when you come here! *Courage!*

Unlike you, I never experience a sense of a life that is just beginning, the stupefaction of an existence freshly unfurling. It seems to me, on the contrary, that I have always existed! And I actually have memories that go back to the Pharaohs. I see myself at different moments of history, very clearly, in various guises and occupations. My present self is the consequence of all my vanished selves. I was boatman on the Nile, *leno* [procurer] in Rome at the time of the Punic wars, then Greek rhetorician in Suburra, where I was devoured by bedbugs. I died during the Crusades, from eating too many grapes on the beach in Syria. I was pirate and monk, mountebank and coachman – perhaps Emperor of the East, who knows?

Many things would be explained if we could know our *real* genealogy. For, since the elements that make a man are limited, surely the same combinations must repeat themselves? Thus "Heredity" is an accurate principle that has been incorrectly applied.[1] So it is with that word as with many others. Everybody takes hold of it from a different end, and nobody understands anybody else. The psychological sciences will remain where they are today – that is, at a dim and foolish stage – as long as there is no precise nomenclature, and as long as it is conventional and permissible to use the same expression to signify the most diverse ideas. When categories are confounded, farewell Morality!

Don't you think that *basically* we've lost the track since '89? Instead of continuing along the highroad which was broad and splendid, like a triumphal way, we've wandered off along little bypaths and are floundering in quagmires. Perhaps it would be wise to return to d'Holbach for a time? Before admiring Proudhon, shouldn't we know Turgot?[2]

But in that case, what would become of CHIC, that modern religion? Chic opinions: being *for* Catholicism (without believing a word of it);[3] being *for* slavery;[4] being *for* the House of Austria;[5] wearing mourning for Queen

Amélie;[6] admiring *Orpheus in the Underworld*;[7] taking part in Agricultural Fairs;[8] talking about sports;[9] cultivating a cold demeanour; being an Idiot even to the point of regretting the treaties of 1815:[10] such are the very latest.

Ah, you think that because I spend my life trying to write harmonious sentences, avoiding assonances, I don't have my own little judgments on the things of this world. Alas, I do; and I'll die mad from not having uttered them.

But I've chattered enough – I'd bore you if I went on.

Bouilhet's play will open early in November. So we'll see each other a month from now.

Give my thanks to your children for their nice message.

A big hug, chère maître, from

your

Gve Flaubert

[1] Flaubert can scarcely have seen Gregor Mendel's *Principles of Heredity*, published in German the previous year. It received little attention until 1900.

[2] Baron d'Holbach (1723–89) expounded an anti-religious, materialist philosophy; Turgot (1727–81) emphasized the utility of industry and commerce; Proudhon (1809–65) professed socialist ideas.

[3] Catholicism was one of the strengths of the Empire: for the bourgeois, religion was a means of stemming the increasing influence of international socialism.

[4] There had been considerable French support of the Southern side in the American Civil War.

[5] On 3 July, Prussia had defeated Austria at Sadowa, and the new threat of Prussian power was easing the old French hostility to Austria.

[6] Marie-Amélie, the widow of Louis-Philippe, had died in England on 24 March: fashionable royalists in France were wearing black.

[7] Flaubert considered Offenbach's popular operetta an offence against sacred literary and artistic traditions.

[8] Agricultural Fairs (*Comices Agricoles*), first instituted in 1785 and proliferating in the nineteenth century, were legendary for the banality of the opening speeches delivered by officials. (Cf. *Madame Bovary*, Part Two, Chapter 8.)

[9] The reference is probably to the new fashion of horse-racing, the Jockey Club, etc.

[10] The international treaties made by the Allies after the French defeat at Waterloo. Napoleon III had recently called them "detestable".

31 SAND TO FLAUBERT

[Nohant] Monday evening
[1 October 1866]

Cher ami,

Your letter didn't miss me – it was sent on to me from Paris. They're too important to me to be allowed to get lost. You don't say anything about floods. So I suppose the Seine has been behaving itself in your part of the world, and the tulip tree hasn't been paddling in the river. I was afraid you might be in trouble, and wondered whether your embankment was high enough to keep you safe. We don't have to worry about anything of that kind here. Our streams are very badly behaved, but we're a long way away from them.

You're lucky to have such clear recollections of other lives. A good deal of imagination and learning – that's what your "memory" is! But even if one doesn't recall anything distinctly, one does have a very vivid sense of existing through eternity. I had a very amusing brother[1] who often referred to the times "when I was a dog . . ." He thought he'd only become a man quite recently. *I* think *I* was once a plant or a stone. I'm not always sure I completely exist at all, and at other times I feel such an accumulation of weariness it's as if I'd existed too long. I simply don't know. I couldn't, like you, say I actually "possess" the past. Does that mean you believe that since we are reborn into various new lives we don't die? If you dare tell the bluffers that, you're a brave man, and I approve. I have the same sort of courage myself. It makes people take me for a fool, but that doesn't bother me because I'm a fool in so many other ways!

I'd love to have your written impressions of Brittany. I didn't see enough of it to speak of. But I did try to get a general impression, and that has come in useful in writing one or two scenes I needed. I'll read you *my* play too, though it's still a shapeless mess as yet. Why hasn't your journey been published? You're too coy: you don't consider everything you do is worthy to be seen. That's wrong. Anything a master does is instructive, and he shouldn't be afraid to show his drafts or sketches. They're still far above the heads of his readers, who are presented with so much that's at their own level the poor wretches never rise above vulgarity. We ought to love dolts more than we love ourselves – aren't they the real unfortunates of this world? Aren't people devoid of taste and ideals bound to be bored – to enjoy nothing and be good for nothing? We ought to put up with being run down and mocked and misjudged – it's inevitable. But we ought not to abandon the fools, and should always throw them good bread to eat whether or not they prefer sh—— When they've had their fill of rubbish they'll eat the bread, but if there isn't any bread to be had they'll go on eating sh—— *in secula seculorum.*

I've heard you say: I write just for ten or a dozen people. In the course of conversation people say lots of things merely on the spur of the moment. But you weren't the only one to say that. It was the general opinion of the group that Monday,[2] or rather its theme that day. I protested inwardly. The twelve readers for whom an author might write, the dozen people capable of appreciating his work, would have to be either equal to or better than himself. But *you* have never needed to read the other eleven in order to be yourself. One writes for everyone, for all those who need to be initiated. If one's not understood, one resigns oneself to it and tries again. That's the whole secret of our unremitting labours and our love of art. What is art without the hearts and minds into which we pour it? A sun that radiates no light and gives life to nothing. If you think it over, don't you agree with me? And if you do agree, you'll never be weary or discouraged. Even if the present is barren and unrewarding, even if the public ceases to value or react to us, if we do our best to serve it we can still look to the future, which keeps up our courage and soothes any hurt to our pride. A hundred times over in life the good we do seems useless, and may indeed serve no immediate purpose, but nevertheless it maintains the tradition of meaning and doing well, without which everything would perish.

Have we been floundering since '89? Didn't we have to flounder in order to arrive at '48, in which we're floundering still, though we do so in order to arrive at what has got to be in the future? Tell me what you think, and I'll re-read Turgot to please you. But I don't promise to go as far as Holbach, even if "there are some good things about him, the beast!"[3]

Let me know when Bouilhet's play comes up. I'll be here, slogging away, but ready to come running, and loving you with all my heart. Now I'm no longer a woman I'd become a man if God were just. I'd have a man's physical strength and I'd say to you, Let's take a trip to Carthage or somewhere. But there, what really lies ahead is second childhood, which has neither sex nor energy, and it's in some other place, some quite other place, that one is regenerated. But *where?* I shall find out before you do, and if I can I'll come back and tell you in a dream.

[unsigned]

---

[1] Hippolyte Chatiron, son of George Sand's father and of a maidservant at Nohant.

[2] In the French, George Sand's phrase reads simply: "c'était l'opinion du *lundi*." Literal translation could lead to confusion: because on Monday (*lundi*) mornings, Sainte-Beuve's weekly newspaper articles, his "Causeries du Lundi", appeared, and were commonly referred to simply as his "*lundis*". On Monday evenings, there was the weekly dinner at Magny's – the dinner to which Mme Sand here refers to simply as the "*lundi*".

[3] A quip attributed to the comic actor Grassot. (See Letter 46, Paragraph 4; and Letter 63, Note 3.)

---

32 SAND TO FLAUBERT

Nohant, 19 October [1866]

Cher ami,

They write from the Odéon that Bouilhet's play is on the 27th. I have to be in Paris on the 26th anyhow on business, and shall dine at Magny's that day, and the next, and the next. So you'll know where to find me, if, as I expect, you're coming up for the first performance.

Yours ever, and with all my heart,

G. Sand

33   FLAUBERT TO SAND

[Croisset] Sunday morning
[21 October 1866]

Chère maître,

La Conjuration d'Amboise is announced, or will be announced, for next Saturday, but in fact it will open only on Monday the 29th. We're counting on you, of course.

I shall be at 42 boulevard du Temple from Wednesday evening.

So – à bientôt. Love from

your

                   Gve Flaubert

We'll both come back here at the end of the week after next – that is, about November 2nd or 3rd. Then you and I will have some long, quiet, serious talks.

34   SAND TO FLAUBERT

Nohant, 23 [October 1866]

Cher ami,

As the play's not until the 29th I'll give my children a couple of extra days and leave here on the 28th. You haven't said whether you'd like to dine with me and your friend, just the three of us, on the 29th at Magny's – early, at whatever time suits him. Let me find a note with your answer at 97 rue des Feuillantines on the 28th.

We'll go to your place afterwards, on the day of your choice. My great talk with you will consist in listening, and in loving you with all my might. I'll bring you what I'm working on at the moment. It will put me in heart, as we say in our part of the world, to read you my "foetus".[1] If only I could bring you the Nohant sunshine! It's splendid.

Love and blessings,

                   G. Sand

[1] *Cadio.*

35   FLAUBERT TO SAND

[Paris] Saturday morning
[27 October 1866]

Chère maître,

One doesn't dine on the evening of a première, when one is extremely nervous oneself and has to take care of another nervous type. So thanks and regrets from the two of us. Nevertheless I hope to see you during an entr'acte, in your box (ticket enclosed).

We'll dine and talk peacefully at Croisset on Thursday or Friday.

Meanwhile a thousand affectionate greetings from

your

Gve Flaubert

*

Sand arrived in Paris on the 28th and was present at the very successful opening of Bouilhet's play the following evening. She and Flaubert saw each other, and two days later he wrote her a reminder about Croisset.

36 FLAUBERT TO SAND

[Paris] Boulevard du Temple, 42
[1 November 1866]
Thursday noon

Chère maître,

My mother definitely expects us next *Saturday*. Therefore, since the express leaves at one o'clock sharp, I'll be on the platform at half-past twelve. So: that's settled. No need to answer.

A thousand affectionate greetings from

your

Gve Flaubert

*

The visit to Croisset was very pleasant. There were expeditions in the neighbourhood, long talks, and readings into the small hours. As usual, Sand recorded events and impressions in her diary.

FROM GEORGE SAND'S DIARY, 1866

Saturday, 3 November

Left Paris at one with Flaubert. Very fast train. Delightful weather, charming country, good talk. We were met at Rouen station by Mme Flaubert and her other son, the doctor. At Croisset, walk round the garden, talk, dinner, more talk and reading aloud until half-past one. Good bed, deep sleep.

Sunday, 4 November

Beautiful weather. Walked through the garden to the orchard. Worked. I'm very comfortable in my little room; it's very warm. At dinner, the niece and her husband and old Madame Crépet, Valentine's Crépet aunt. She leaves tomorrow. Games of patience. Then Gustave read me the *féerie*.[1] It's full of good and attractive things, only too long, too rich, too dense. We went on talking. By half-past two I felt hungry. We went down to the kitchen for some cold chicken. Popped out into the yard to get water from the pump. It was as mild as spring. We ate, went upstairs again, smoked, had more talk. Separated at four in the morning.

Monday, 5 November

Still beautiful weather. After breakfast we went for a walk. I made Gustave come with me; very heroic of him.[2] He got dressed and took me to Canteleu; it's only a short distance away, up the coast. What a lovely landscape, what a pleasant, broad, magnificent view! I brought home some ossified sea-anemones; there were masses of them! We were back by three. I worked. After dinner, more talk with Gustave. I read *Cadio*[3] to him. We talked some more and supped off a bunch of grapes and a slice of bread and jam.

Tuesday, 6 November

It rained. At one o'clock we set out for Rouen on the steam-boat, with Maman. Gustave took me to the little Natural History Museum. We were received by M. Pouchet: deaf as a post and ill, though he did his utmost to be charming. Impossible to exchange a word with him. But from time to time he explained something, and that was interesting. The apteryx; the longipod; the nest with a circumference of eighty metres and the eggs abandoned in the dungheap; the young born with feathers; a superb collection of shells. M. Pouchet's collection: his live bird-eating spider; his crocodile. We called at the Pottery Museum: garden, statues, fragments, Corneille's door.[4] We came back and went to dinner with Mme Caroline Commanville. Then to the Schmidt menagerie.[5] Superb animals as tame as dogs. Foetuses; bearded lady; a puppet-show (Fair of Saint-Romain).[6] We got back to Croisset at half-past twelve at night, with Maman, who's very game and had walked a long way. We went on talking till two.

Wednesday, 7 November

Dull weather but not cold. Walked round the garden. Worked at *Mont-Revêche*.[7] Reasonable day. In the evening Flaubert read me the beginning of his novel.[8] It's good, good. He read from ten o'clock till two. We talked till four.

Thursday, 8 November

Same dull weather. Walked round the garden. Worked. Had dinner. Talked. Flaubert read from his novel. Talked.

Friday, 9 November

Felt ill this morning. Missed lunch. Fine weather. Glimpse of the sun. I worked. I packed.

Saturday, 10 November

Left Croisset, almost well again, at half-past twelve. Flaubert and his mother took me to the station. The train left at a quarter to two.

[1] *Le Château des coeurs.*

[2] Flaubert detested physical exercise.

[3] This is the first mention of *Cadio* by name. There would be two *Cadio*'s: the novel, on which Sand was now working, and which would be serialized in the *Revue des Deux Mondes*, 1 September–15 November 1867; and the play, produced 3 October 1868.

[4] Pierre Corneille was born in Rouen, 1606.

[5] *La Chronique de Rouen* for 1 and 15 November mentions the presence of this menagerie in the annual fair, the Foire Saint-Romain. It included thirteen lions, a Bengal tiger, leopards, hyenas, black bears, white bears, an elephant, snakes and crocodiles.

[6] It was perhaps on this occasion that Flaubert showed Sand the puppet-show of the temptations of Saint Anthony, a feature of the fair since Flaubert's youth.

[7] See Letter 67, Note 2.

[8] *L'Éducation sentimentale.*

*

"My illustrious friend, Mme Sand, left on Saturday afternoon," Flaubert wrote to Mme Roger des Genettes on the 12th. "There was never a better woman, more good-natured and less of a bluestocking. She worked all day, and at night we chattered like magpies until three in the morning. Though she's a bit too benevolent and benign, she has insights that evince very keen good sense, provided she doesn't get on to her socialist hobby-horse. Very reserved concerning herself, she talks freely about the men of '48[1] and frankly stresses their goodwill rather than their intelligence. I showed her the sights of Rouen. My mother finds her delightful."

[1] Mme Sand would continue to supply Flaubert with memories of 1848 for what are some of the best scenes in *L'Éducation sentimentale.*

37 SAND TO FLAUBERT

Paris, Saturday evening
[10 November 1866]

There was sad news waiting for me in Paris. While we were talking about him yesterday evening – and I believe we did so the day before yesterday too – my friend Charles Duveyrier was dying. He had the tenderest of hearts and the most innocent of minds. And he's to be buried tomorrow! He was a year older than me. My generation is disappearing, bit by bit. Shall I outlive it? I don't very much want to, especially at times of bereavement or separation. But as God wills, so long as he lets me go on loving in this life and the next. I still feel a great affection for people after they die. But the love one has for the living is different. I give you the part of my heart that he used to have, which together with what you already possess makes up a very large share. Sending you this gift is a kind of consolation. From the literary point of view he wasn't in the highest class, but he was loved for his goodness and spontaneity. He'd have had an attractive enough talent if he'd spent less time on business and philosophy, and he leaves behind a charming play called *Michel Perrin*.

I was alone for half of the journey, thinking of you, your Maman and Croisset, and looking at the Seine, which thanks to you has become a friendly "divinity". After that I had the company of one man and a couple of women, whose loud and affected stupidity reminded me of the music that accompanied the puppet show the other day. E.g.: "When I looked at the sun it seemed to leave two spots on my eyes." Husband: "That's what they call sun spots." And so on for an hour without stopping.

I shall do all the "family" errands, for I'm one of the family now, am I not? I shall go to bed exhausted, I've been crying like anything all the evening, but that only makes me salute you all the more fondly, dear friend. Love me even more than before because I'm sad.

G. Sand

Do you happen to have a friend among the lawyers in Rouen? If so, do write him a note asking him to remember the name Amédée Despruneaux.[1] He has a civil law case coming up in Rouen any day now, and I'd like you to let it be known that he is the most decent of men. You can answer for him as you would for me. If the thing is possible, you'd be doing me a personal favour. You must let me do as much for your friends in return.

[1] Amédée Despruneaux, whom Sand had known in La Châtre (his birthplace), was a builder. He was involved in a dispute concerning his recent purchase of land at Yport, on the Normandy coast.

38 SAND TO FLAUBERT

[Paris] Sunday
[11 November 1866]

I think you'll be really pleased to know that what my porter calls the *Conjuration d'Ambroise* looks like being a financial success. This evening there was as long a queue as for *Villemer*, and Magny's, which is another barometer, is set fair.

So be glad. If it keeps up, Bouilhet's launched.

G. S.

39 SAND TO FLAUBERT

Paris, Sunday
[11 November 1866]

I send you herewith my friend Despruneaux in person. If you know a judge or two, or if your brother could give him a note backing him up, do arrange it, and I'll kiss you three times on each eye.

G. Sand

A five-minute interview is all the inconvenience I ask.

40 FLAUBERT TO SAND

[Croisset] Monday night
[12–13 November 1866]

You are sad, pauvre amie et chère maître. It was you I thought of on learning of Duveyrier's death. You loved him, and I feel for you. It's another loss. How many of the dead we have in our hearts! Each of us carries his necropolis within him.

I've been all at odds since you left: I feel I haven't seen you for ten years. My mother and I speak only of you; everyone here loves you. What constellation were you born under, to be endowed with so many qualities, so diverse and so rare? I don't know what to call the feeling I have for you: it's a very particular kind of affection, such as I have never felt for anyone until now. We got along well together, didn't we? It was nice.

It was so very good, in fact, that I don't want to let others enjoy it. If you make use of Croisset in one of your books, disguise it, so that it won't be recognized. That would oblige me. The memory of your presence here is for the two of us, for me. Such is my selfishness.

I missed you particularly last night at ten o'clock. A fire broke out at my woodseller's. The sky was pink and the Seine the colour of red-currant syrup. I worked at the pumps for three hours and came home as tired as the Turk with the giraffe.[1]

What did Chilly and Duquesnel say about your play? When will it be put on? What are you going to do now? Your scenes from the Revolution, probably? etc. etc.

A Rouen newspaper (*Le Nouvelliste*) reported your visit to Rouen, with the result that on Saturday, after leaving you, I ran into several bourgeois who were indignant with me because I hadn't exhibited you. The best thing was said to me by an ex-magistrate. "Ah! If only we'd known she was here ... We'd have ..." – pause for five minutes while he hunted for the phrase – "we'd have ... *given her a smile!*" That would have been little enough, no?

Speaking of magistrates, you must send me more detailed information about the Despruneaux case. What is it about? When does it come up? Is it an appeal, or a first hearing? I'll do what I can, you may be sure.

It would be difficult for me to love you "more", but I embrace you fondly. Your letter of this morning, so melancholy, went deep. We parted at a moment when many things were just rising to our lips? All doors between us are not yet open. You inspire great respect in me, and I dare not ask you questions.

Adieu. I kiss your kind and lovely face, and am
Your

G. Flaubert

[1] An allusion to an old vaudeville skit about the first live giraffe brought to France, in 1827.

41   SAND TO FLAUBERT

Night of Tuesday-Wednesday
[Paris, 13–14 November 1866]

I haven't given a reading of my play yet. I still have some re-working to do, and there's no hurry. Bouilhet's piece is doing remarkably well, and I'm told my young friend Cadol's play may be coming on next.[1] And I wouldn't shoulder the boy aside for the world. This puts me off for quite a while, but I don't mind that and it won't do me any harm. What an awful sentence – a good thing I'm not writing for Buloz. I saw your friend yesterday in the foyer at the Odéon. I shook hands with him. He looked happy. And then I talked to Duquesnel about the *féerie*. He's very anxious to find out more about it. You only need to let him know when you're ready and you'll be received with open arms.

Mario Proth will give me precise information about the changes in the paper tomorrow or the day after.[2] I'm going out tomorrow, and will buy the shoes for your dear mother. Next week I go to Palaiseau and will look out my book on pottery.[3] Do remind me if I forget anything.

I've been ill for a couple of days but am better now. Your letter does my heart good. I'll answer all your questions quite frankly, as you've answered mine. We're lucky, aren't we, to be able to tell one another our whole life stories? It's much less difficult than the bourgeois think, and the mysteries one can reveal to a friend are always the opposite of what outsiders imagine.

I was very happy, the week I spent with you. No worries, a comfortable nest, beautiful landscape, affectionate hearts, and your fine, frank and somehow fatherly face. Age has nothing to do with it; there's a protectiveness, an infinite kindness about you; you brought tears to my eyes one evening when you called your mother "my girl". I didn't want to come away, but I was getting in the way of your work. And then, and then – one of the maladies of my old age is that I can't keep still. I'm afraid of getting too attached or of outstaying my welcome. The elderly ought to be very discreet. But from a distance I can tell you how fond I am of you without any danger of overdoing it. You are one of the *rare* people who remain sensitive and sincere, who go on loving art uncorrupted by ambition and unintoxicated by success. You'll always be twenty-five years old in terms of all kinds of ideas which the senile youth of today dismiss as out-of-date. I'm quite ready to believe that theirs is just a pose, but it's a stupid one. And if it's due to mere impotence it's even worse. They may be men of letters, but they're not men.

Good luck to the novel. It's very fine, but it's also funny. There's a whole aspect of you that doesn't reveal or betray itself in what you do, something you yourself probably don't know about. But it'll emerge later, I'm sure.

Fondest love to you, to your Maman, and to your charming niece. Oh, I almost forgot – I saw Couture this evening, and he said that as a favour he'd do you a portrait in pencil, like the one he did for me, for whatever fee you decide. You see how good I am at doing errands; find me some more.

[unsigned]

---

[1] *Les Ambitions de M. Fauvelle*, a play in 5 acts, which would run at the Odéon from 28 February to 31 March 1867.
[2] Proth, a journalist, would supply information Flaubert needed concerning political events in 1848, for *L'Éducation sentimentale*.
[3] Not a book, but an article: "Les Maioliques florentines et Giovanni Freppa", which had originally appeared in *La Presse*, 5 July 1855 and had been reprinted in Sand's *Souvenirs et Impressions littéraires* (1862). This, too, was information for *L'Éducation sentimentale*.

42 FLAUBERT TO SAND

[Croisset] Wednesday night
[14–15 November 1866]

Chère maître,

Your friend Despruneaux seems a nice fellow. But he's not very practical. His case comes up tomorrow morning at 10 o'clock, and he didn't call on me until just now, at 4 in the afternoon! There are about a dozen names on the list of the magistrates concerned with the case – how can I make the necessary moves in so short a time? If he loses because he has no one to come forward on his behalf, he'll have only himself to blame.

The only lawyer we know intimately is at a wedding today and can't be reached. Nevertheless my niece will call on him tomorrow morning before the court convenes and see whether he can mention your friend to his colleagues.

If the verdict won't be pronounced until a week from now, we'll have time to look around. My brother goes to bed at nine o'clock and spends the entire morning at the hospital, so tomorrow he'll be unable to do anything. But I am counting on my niece. I have a friend who is very close to the judge, but – once again – there's no time.

It was so kind of you – more than kind, it was goodness itself – to write me about Bouilhet's success. Nothing is lost on me. I am well aware of the subtleties. Greatness of heart shows itself in just such delicacy.

Adieu. I love and kiss your hands, your cheeks, your eyes.

Gve Flaubert

43   SAND TO FLAUBERT

[Paris, 16 November 1866]

Thank you, dearest friend, for all the trouble I've given you over my Despruneaux from the Berry. They're old local friends, a whole delightful family of worthy folk, fathers, sons, wives, nephews, all part of the Nohant circle. He must have been overcome at seeing you – he was so pleased about it, self-interest quite apart. And I, who am not at all "practical" either, forgot to tell you the case won't be decided for another fortnight, so anything you could do between now and then would be very useful. If he wins his case over the buildings at Yport he means to go and live there, and I shall be able to carry out an old plan of going to stay with him every year. He has a charming wife, and they've all been fond of me for ages. So you're in danger of having me keep dropping by to knock at your door, give you a kiss on the brow, wish you good luck with your slogging, and then dash off.

I'm still waiting for our information about the paper. Apparently it's difficult to be quite definite about '48. I've insisted on the utmost accuracy.

For the past couple of days I've been trailing my "Cascaret"[1] around with me – the young engineer I told you about. He's grown very handsome, the ladies ogle him, and he could easily become a slave and giraffe trader[2] if he wanted to. But he's *in love*, and engaged, and has to wait and work for four years to be in a position to marry, and he's made a *vow*. You'd tell him he's foolish, but I treat him to my old troubadour's morality. Morality apart, I don't think young people nowadays have the energy to cope with science and debauchery, tarts and fiancées, all at the same time. Witness the fact that youthful bohemians don't manage to produce anything any more.

Goodnight, friend; work and sleep well. Go for a walk sometimes, for the love of God, and of me. Tell those judges of yours who promised me a smile to smile on my friend from Berry.

[unsigned]

¹ *cascaret* — a puny individual. This was a twenty-two-year-old friend, Francis Laur, later a Deputy.

² An obscure allusion to the subject of Letter 40, Note 1.

44 SAND TO FLAUBERT

[Paris, l6 November 1866]
Friday

Don't bother with any more efforts. Quite unexpectedly Despruneaux has won his appeal outright. Whether you were instrumental or not, he's very grateful, and asks me to thank you with all his good and honest heart.

Bouilhet is going from strength to strength. I've just seen the directors; they're delighted.

Love and kisses. Think sometimes about your old troubadour,

G. Sand

45 FLAUBERT TO SAND

[Croisset, 17 November 1866]
Saturday morning

Well, Despruneaux won his case right off – the verdict was announced then and there, immediately following the speeches on both sides. He gave me the news this morning.

I expect that your name helped him somewhat? My niece Caroline had set to work that morning and charmed one of the lawyers, who must then have spoken to his colleagues (as he promised). So – it's over. You'll be a Norman, chère maître, and we'll see you every summer.

Don't go to too much trouble getting information about the newspapers. They won't loom large in my book, and I'm in no hurry. But when you have nothing else to do, jot down on a scrap of paper what you remember about '48. Then you can expand it when we talk. I'm not asking for a treatise, needless to say – just a few of your own recollections.

Do you know an actress at the Odéon who played Macduff¹ in *Macbeth* – Duguéret? She would like to have the part of Nathalie in *Mont-Revêche*. She will be recommended to you by Girardin,² Dumas, and me. I saw her in *Faustine*,³ where she showed considerable style. So: you're warned. Be prepared. My opinion is that she's intelligent and would be an asset.

If your young engineer has made a vow, and if that vow comes easily to him, he is right to keep it: otherwise, it's pure foolishness, between you and me. Where is liberty to exist, if not in passion? Catholicism, whose only idea has been to prevent philandering – that is, to repress Nature – has made us set too high a value on chastity. We give such things a grotesque importance! One must no longer be spiritually-minded or materialist, but a "naturalist". Isis seems to me superior both to the Virgin and to Venus. No! "In my day" we made no such vows. We made love! And boldly! But it was all part of a broad eclecticism. And if we kept away from the "Ladies", as I did, absolutely, for two years (from 21 to 23), *it was out of pride*, as a challenge to oneself, a show of strength. After which, we would give ourselves over to excesses of the opposite kind. We were Romantics, in short – Red Romantics, utterly ridiculous, but in full efflorescence. The little good left in me comes from those days!

Adieu, ma chère maître. I love you, and embrace you tenderly.

Gve Flaubert

Do you know, you're spoiling me with all the sweet things you say to me in your letters.

¹ The text says "Macduff". "Lady Macduff", probably?
² Emile de Girardin (1806–81), liberal journalist and writer on politics and economics. In 1836 he had founded *La Presse* (in which George Sand's *Histoire de ma vie* was serialized), and now, in 1866, he had bought another newspaper, *La Liberté*.
³ Bouilhet's play, staged in 1864.

46   SAND TO FLAUBERT

Palaiseau, 22 November [18]66

I feel it will bring me good luck to say goodnight to my dear comrade before I start work.

Here am I *all alone* in my cottage. The gardener and his family live in the lodge, and we're the last house at the lower end of the village, completely surrounded by country – a lovely oasis. Meadows, woods, apple trees just as in Normandy; no big river with its steam hooters and infernal clanking, just a brook flowing silently under the willows; and such silence . . . Oh, I feel as if I were in the middle of a virgin forest: no voice but that of the little spring forever amassing diamonds in the light of the moon. The flies drowsing in the corners of the room wake up in the heat from the fire. They went there to die, but when they get near the lamp they go wild with joy, they buzz and dart about and laugh – they even have vague thoughts of love, but it's time to die, and bang! down they crash right in the midst of the dance. It's all over – farewell to the ball!

I feel sad here, though. The absolute solitude that has always been holiday and recreation to me is shared now by one of the dead,¹ who ended here like a light going out but is still present. I don't suppose he's unhappy where he is now, but the image he's left around me, which is now no more than a gleam, seems to grieve at not being able to speak to me any more. Never mind! Sadness isn't bad for us; it stops us from drying up.

And you, my friend, what are you doing at this hour? Slogging away too, no doubt, and on your own too, for Maman is no doubt in Rouen.² It must be beautiful at night there too. Do your thoughts sometimes turn to the "old troubadour on an inn clock, who sings of perfect love and always will"?[3] Yes, of course they do! Your lordship's not in favour of chastity – well, that's your business. For my part, I say "there are some good things about it, the beast"![4]

Whereupon I embrace you with all my heart, and shall now, if I can, put words in the mouths of some people who love one another in the old way.

[unsigned]

You don't have to write to me if you don't feel like it. There's no real friendship without *absolute* freedom.

I'll be in Paris next week, then in Palaiseau again, and then in Nohant.

I saw Bouilhet at the *lundi*. I'm quite smitten with him. But some day one of us is going to snuff it at Magny's. I'm very strong, but even I broke out in a cold sweat and nearly passed out.[5]

[1] Alexandre Manceau had died at Palaiseau, of tuberculosis, on 21 August the previous year. Mme Sand had bought the house there in 1864, to be with him. She would soon sell it and return to Nohant.

[2] For the winter months Mme Flaubert had taken an apartment in Rouen, 7, quai du Havre, close to the one occupied by her granddaughter Caroline.

[3] Had Sand and Flaubert perhaps recently seen, in some inn, a clock of the Romantic period with the figure of a troubadour painted on its case? Or does the passage refer to something they had read together? From mid-November the word "troubadour" frequently appears in the correspondence.

[4] See Letter 31, Note 3.

[5] From Sand's diary, 19 November 1866: "Monday dinner. . . . It was so hot that I felt faint; but I soon recovered."

47 FLAUBERT TO SAND

Croisset, Tuesday, 5 o'clock
[27 November 1866]

You're lonely and sad down there: it's the same with me, here. Where do they come from, these waves of black depression that engulf one from time to time? It's like a rising tide. You feel you're drowning, you have to flee. At such moments I lie flat on my back. I do nothing – and the flood recedes.

My novel is going very badly at the moment. On top of that, I've heard of the deaths of Louis de Cormenin (a friend for twenty-five years), and of Gavarni.[1] And then there's all the rest. But this will pass.

You don't know what it is to spend an entire day with one's head in one's hands, taxing one's poor brain in search of a word. With you, the flow of ideas is broad, continuous, like a river. With me it's a tiny trickle. I can achieve a cascade only by the most arduous effort. I know them well, the Pangs of Style! In short, I spend my life racking both my brain and my heart: such is the true essence of your friend.

You ask him if he sometimes thinks of "his old troubadour on the clock". I should say he does! And misses her, too. They were very sweet, our nighttime chats. There were moments when I had to restrain myself from giving you little kisses, as though you were a big child! Your ears must have burned last night. I dined at my brother's with all the family. We spoke only of you, and everyone sang your praises. Except me, of course: I disparaged you to the utmost, beloved chère maître.

Apropos of your last letter (and by a natural train of ideas), I reread old Montaigne's essay called "Some Lines of Virgil". What he says about chastity is precisely what I believe.[2] It's the Effort that's virtuous – not the Abstinence in itself. Otherwise one would have to curse the flesh, like Catholics. And God knows where that leads! So, at the risk of always harping on the same string, and of being a Prud'homme,[3] I say again that your young man is wrong. If he's celibate at twenty, he'll be a disgusting old rake at fifty. Everything has its price! Large natures (and those are the good ones) are above all prodigal, and don't keep such strict account of how they expend themselves. We must laugh and weep, love, work, enjoy and suffer – *vibrate* as much as possible, to the entire extent of our being. That's what it is, I believe, to be truly human.

Goodbye. Try to be calm. You'll soon be seeing your granddaughter, and that will do you good. And think of your old friend, who sends you all his affection.

Gve Flaubert

[1] Louis de Cormenin had been one of the editors of *La Revue de Paris* during its serialization of *Madame Bovary*. Gavarni, the caricaturist, was one of the first *convives* at the Magny dinners.

[2] "I protect myself from temperance as I once did from *volupté*. It diminishes me, even makes me a bore. I desire to be master of myself in all respects. Wisdom has its own excesses, and has no less need of moderation than does folly."

[3] A character in a play by the popular dramatist Henri Monnier (1805–77). The name came to typify the self-satisfied bourgeois.

48   SAND TO FLAUBERT

To G. Flaubert
For some reason or other this letter got left in my blotter.[1]
G. S.

Palaiseau, 29 November [1866]
Paris, the following week

We should be neither spiritualists nor materialists, you say, but naturalists. It's a large question.

My Cascaret, as I call the young engineer, will resolve it as he thinks best. He's not a fool, and he'll go through a lot of ideas and deductions, not to mention emotions, before he fulfils your prediction. I'm careful not to catechize him too much, as he can outmatch me on a number of points and is not overburdened with Catholic spirituality.

But the matter itself is very serious, and hovers over the art of us more or less penduliferous or penduloid troubadours. Let us treat it quite impersonally, for what's good for one individual may very well be just the opposite for another. Let us ask ourselves, setting aside our own propensities and experiences, whether a human being can aim at and attain all the limits of his physical possibilities without harming his intellect. Yes, it might be so in an ideal, rational society. But in the one we live in and with which we're obliged to make do, doesn't the pursuit of pleasure go together with excess, and can anyone except the wisest of sages keep the two things separate? And if one *is* a sage, it's goodbye to the impulse that engenders true joys.

The problem for us artists is to decide whether abstinence helps us, or keys us up so much that it degenerates into weakness. You'll say there's a time for everything, and enough strength to meet any expenditure of it. So in fact you do make a distinction and set yourself limits – one can't avoid it. You believe nature itself imposes limits and saves us from excess. But no – nature is no wiser than we are, who are part of it. We kill ourself by overindulging in work as well as by overindulging in pleasure, and the greater our own natures the more likely we are to break through barriers and push back the frontiers of our powers.

I don't have any theories, myself. All my life I've asked questions and heard them answered one way or the other, but I've never come across a single completely successful and irrefutable conclusion. I expect light to be shed by a new state of my mind and organs in another life, for anyone who thinks in this one becomes all too aware of the limits of pros and cons. It was Monsieur Plato, I believe, who sought for and thought he'd found the link. But he hadn't, any more than we have. And yet there must be such a link, because the universe goes on existing without the pros and cons on which it is based destroying one another. What would it be called, as regards material nature? Equilibrium, no doubt. And as regards thinking nature? Moderation, a certain chastity, abstention from excess, anything you like – but it would still manifest itself as equilibrium. Am I right or wrong, *mon maître*?

Think about it, for what the characters in our novels do or don't do depends on that very thing. Will they or will they not win the object of their ardent desires? For by the very fact of existing they aspire to some goal, whether it be love or glory, wealth or pleasure. If we writers have a philosopher inside us, our characters follow what we consider a straight path; if we haven't, they proceed at random, unduly influenced by the events we put in their way. If we endow them with our own ideas, they often shock those of other people. If we don't, but merely subject them to fate, they don't always seem logical or natural. Should we put little or much of ourselves into them, or only that which society puts into each of us?

For my part I follow my old bent and put myself in my people's shoes. I'm criticized for it, but it doesn't matter. I'm not sure you yourself, by either method or instinct, don't do the same. But what you do suits you, and that's why I ask if we differ on the question of inner struggles, and whether man-as-he-exists-in-the-novel should or shouldn't experience them.

You always surprise me when you say you work with difficulty. Is this just coyness? The difficulty isn't at all apparent! What I find hard is selecting, from the thousands of different dramatic permutations and combinations, with the infinity of alternatives they involve, a definite and striking situation that won't seem arbitrary or forced. As for style, I don't set as high a value on it as you do.

The wind plays on my old harp at its own sweet will. It has its ups and downs, its strong notes and its feeble ones – that's really all one to me so long as the emotion comes. But I can't find anything in myself – it's "someone else" who sings as he pleases, badly or well, and if I try to think about it I only frighten myself and tell myself I'm nothing, nothing at all.

But we're saved by a great wisdom. We're able to say to ourselves, "Ah well, even if we're absolutely nothing but instruments, it's still a very pleasant state to be in, and a quite incomparable sensation, to feel oneself vibrating." So let the wind stray through your strings a bit. I think you go to more trouble than is necessary, and ought to give that "someone else" a chance more often. You'd get on just the same, and be less tired. The instrument might sound fainter now and then, but the inspiration would gather strength as it swept along. Then afterwards you could do what I ought to do but don't – go back and tone up the whole picture, eliminating anything that might seem overdone in the light of day.

Vale et me ama,

G. Sand

[1] This sentence, written in black ink (whereas the letter itself – never sent – is written in blue) seems to have been added by Sand several years later: perhaps she discovered the letter while arranging papers. After writing it she must have considered it unsuitable, and put it aside.

The next day, she wrote quite differently:

49   SAND TO FLAUBERT

Palaiseau, 30 November [1866]

There's a great deal to be said about all this, my friend. My Cascaret – as I call the fiancé in question – is keeping himself for his fiancée. She's told him: "Let's wait until you've solved certain problems concerning work" – so he works. She's told him: "Let's save our purity for one another" – so he's saving himself up. He's not overburdened with Catholic spirituality, but he entertains a very high ideal about love, and why should one advise him to get rid of it when he's invested his conscience and virtue in preserving it?

Nature itself, which rules over us, imposes a certain equilibrium on our instincts, and soon sets a limit to our appetites. The greatest of men are not the most robust. We don't receive an education that develops us fully in all directions. We're hemmed in on all sides, and send out roots and branches as and where we can. Thus great artists are often invalids; some of them have actually been impotent. Some, all too potent, have exhausted themselves prematurely. On the whole I think the joys and sorrows of those of us who work with our brains are too intense. A peasant, who has to cope day and night with his land and his wife, isn't very energetic physically, and has a mind quite lacking in power. You talk about developing in all directions? How is that possible in all directions at once, and without any respite? Those who boast of doing so must be joking, or if they really are jacks of all trades they must be masters of none. If they regard love as a little treat and art as a little job, all well and good; but if pleasure is something intense, verging on the infinite, and art something ardent, verging on exaltation, they don't switch from one to the other as easily as between sleeping and waking. Personally I don't believe in these Don Juans who are also Byrons. Don Juan didn't write poems, and Byron is said to have been a very poor lover. But he must sometimes have experienced complete ecstasy through the heart, the mind, and the senses – one does experience such things, if rarely. It happened to him often enough to make him one of the great love poets. So it is with the instruments that produce our own vibrations. The continual wind of petty appetites would break them. Try some time to write a novel with a (genuine) artist for a hero, and you'll see what a delicate and restrained, though strong, current of sap and strength will flow through him; how carefully, curiously yet calmly he observes things in general; and how rare and weighty are the occasions when he's really carried away by the things he examines. You'll see, too, how careful he is of himself, knowing that if he abandons himself he destroys himself, and how a fundamental modesty keeps him from scattering and frittering away the treasures of his soul. An artist is such a fine subject I've never really dared attempt it. I didn't feel worthy to touch so beautiful and complicated an image – it's too high for a mere woman to aim at. But it might well tempt you some day, and would certainly repay the effort. Where's the model? I don't know. I've never really known any artist who didn't have some spot on his sun, some aspect that gave him a touch of the grocer. It may be you haven't any such spot; you should paint your own portrait. I *have* got a flaw. I like classification: I have a touch of the teacher. I like sewing and wiping babies' bottoms: I have a touch of the servant. I'm absent-minded and have a touch of the fool. And lastly, I wouldn't like perfection. I have a sense of what it is, and yet I couldn't demonstrate it. Perhaps it might be allowed to have some flaws; but which? We'll go into that one day. But it has nothing to do with your present subject, and I mustn't distract you. So be less cruel to yourself and forge ahead, and when inspiration has done its work, then you can go back and tone up the picture as a whole, eliminating any detail that stands out too much. Isn't this possible? I think it is. What you do seems so easy and prolific, a perpetual brimming over. I simply can't understand your anguish.

Goodnight, dear brother. Fond love to all your family. I'm back in my solitude at Palaiseau. I love it. I return to Paris on Monday.

Much love. Work well.

G. Sand

*

Early in December, in Paris, Sand and Bouilhet together composed another
farcical letter to Flaubert.

50 SAND (AND BOUILHET) TO FLAUBERT

[Paris, 4 December 1866]

Monsieur,

The faim yr distingished talents have erned you in literatture I oncet knew
myself inso far as in me laid I mad my daybew in 1804 under the hospisses of
the selebrated Mde Saqui[1] and won gt succsess leaving memories world wid
in the anals of the acrabatic art and titerope coriography I was much apreeciated
by the genrals and other oficers of the empire and more sort after even in
advancd age than the wives of som Minister and Prefects I cd name Having
red yr distinguished works e.g. Mde Bovary I blieve I could serv you as a
moddle when she carsts of her fettrs and goes where her hart call I am wel
preservd for my age and shd you fel any repugnce for an artiste cum down in
the world I wd make doo with ideel sentiments on yr part. You may therfor
count on my heart not being abl to dispose of my person being maried to a
hedless felow who ran thru my Waxwks of famus peeple: kings emperers ansient
and moden and famus crimes, which if i had had yr permision i wd hav included
you. I then had a plaice in the Railway under the station loking after the WWCC
but a jellous Rivall done me out of that. And so if you wd write the story of my
Unfortunat Existance you alon wd be equel to it and find out things you alon
are worthy to apreciate. I shall pressent myself at yr residenc in rouen whch I
got the adress from monsieur Bouilhet who knows me wel having bin keen on
me in his yewth. He will tel you Im still agrable in phisic and loyl to all who
have know me wether civill or millitry

Hopping this finds you wel ever your affectnate

Victoire Potelet
allas Marengo Lirondelle
ex-Mde Dodin

rue Lanion
47, belleville

[1] A celebrated acrobat and tight-rope dancer (1786–1866).

51 FLAUBERT TO SAND

[Croisset, 5–6 December 1866]
Wednesday night

Oh, what a splendid letter from Marengo l'Hirondelle! Truly, I think it a masterpiece. Every word has a touch of genius. I laughed aloud several times as I read. Thank you greatly, chère maître – you are everything that's nice.[1]

You don't tell me what you are doing. How far along are you with the play?

I'm not a bit surprised that you fail to understand my spells of literary anguish. I don't understand them myself. They exist, however, and are violent. At such times I no longer know how to go about writing, and after infinite fumbling I succeed in expressing a hundredth part of my ideas. Nothing spontaneous about your friend! Far from it! These last two days, for example, I've been casting and recasting a paragraph, and still haven't solved it. At times I want to weep. I must seem pitiable to you. How much more so to myself!

As for our subject of discussion (apropos of your young man), what you write me in your last letter is so much my way of viewing things that I've not only put it into practice, but preached it. Ask Théo![2] Let's be clear, however. Artists (who are priests) risk nothing by being chaste. On the contrary! But bourgeois – what's to be gained by their being so? *Some* people have to remain within the human race. Happy indeed are those who never stir beyond it!

My view – contrary to your own – is that nothing good can be done with the character of the "ideal Artist". Anything of the kind would be monstrous. Art isn't intended to depict exceptional beings.[3] I feel an unconquerable aversion to putting anything of my heart on paper. I even think that a novelist *hasn't the right to express his opinion* on anything whatsoever. Has God ever expressed his opinion? That is why there are so many things that stick in my throat – things I long to spit out, and which I choke down instead. Indeed, what would be the use of uttering them? Any Tom, Dick, or Harry is more interesting than Monsieur G. Flaubert, because they are more *general* and consequently more typical.

There are days, nevertheless, when I feel I'm worse than moronic. I now have a bowl of goldfish. And they entertain me, they keep me company while I eat my dinner. Imagine taking an interest in anything so inane!

Adieu – it's late and I have a headache. I kiss you fondly. And am your

Gve Flaubert

[1] Among Flaubert's notes concerning material he expected to use in his last (unfinished) novel, *Bouvard et Pécuchet*, is the following: "Letters characteristic of various classes of society in divers situations: Letter from Marengo l'Hirondelle, G. Sand." The reader will recall that *l'Hirondelle – The Swallow –* is the name of the stage-coach that carries Emma Bovary back and forth between Yonville and Rouen.

[2] Théophile Gautier.

[3] So says the depictor of Salammbô, Saint Anthony, and Hérodias!

52 SAND TO FLAUBERT

[Paris, 7 December 1866]

   Not put any of one's heart into what one writes? I don't, I simply do not understand. For my part I don't see how one can put anything else. Can one separate one's mind from one's heart? – are they two different things? Can limits be set to what one feels, can one's being be split in two? Not to give the whole of oneself in one's work seems as impossible to me as weeping with something other than one's eyes or thinking with something other than one's brain. What did you mean? Answer when you have the time.

[unsigned]

53 SAND TO FLAUBERT

Paris, 8 December [18]66

   You ask what I'm doing? Your old troubadour is pleased this evening. He spent the night rewriting a second act that wouldn't come right and now has, so much so that my two directors are delighted[1], and I have high hopes of pulling off the end – I'm not satisfied with it yet, but I must manage it. In short, I haven't got anything very interesting to tell you about myself. When you have the patience of an ox and a wrist used to breaking stones as best it can, you don't have any events or emotions to relate. My poor Manceau used to call me the "roadmender", and there's nothing less poetic than that.
   And you, my dear and excellent friend, you're suffering the pains and anguish of parturition, are you? That's fine, that's young – not everyone is so lucky! When my daughter-in-law gives birth to her little darlings I enter into the effort so completely, holding her in my arms, that it affects me too, and by the time the child arrives I'm in a worse state than she is – sometimes quite seriously ill. And I feel as if your present suffering were affecting me too and giving me a headache. But alas, I can't help with the birth, and I almost wish we still lived in the days when people thought they could hasten delivery by lighting candles in front of a statue or a picture.
   I see that rascally Bouilhet has given me away. He promised to copy out the Marengo letter in odd handwriting to see if you'd be taken in. I get sent genuine letters just as extraordinary as that. How good and kind he is, your great friend! They adore him at the Odéon, and this evening I was told the play is doing better and better. I went to hear it again two or three days ago, and found it even more delightful than I did the first time.
   Come now, cheer up, and when you stop for a rest remember that we love you.

G. Sand

Love to your Maman and brother and niece.

[1] She notes in her diary: "For two hours I read the first two acts of *Mont-Revêche* to Chilly and Duquesnel. They're finally satisfied."

54 FLAUBERT TO SAND

[Croisset, 15–16 December 1866]
Saturday night

All to the good that they're pleased at the Odéon, chère maître. I look forward to a re-*Villemer*, and of course I'll be at the opening. It's in April, isn't it? No matter – I'll be there whether I'm in town anyway, or come up from here.

Oh – while I think of it, give me the address of your good shoemaker. My mother has worn out her shoes and wants to order new ones.

Mlle Bosquet (the author of *La Normandie merveilleuse*) has published a novel called *Une femme bien élevée*. It definitely has its merits. I have presumed to ask her to send you a copy.[1] If you could have it reviewed by Mario Proth, or by one of your friends, you'd be doing a kindness.

Now let's talk about ourselves. I have seen citizen Bouilhet, who has been enjoying a veritable triumph on his native heath. The locals who previously wouldn't give him the time of day have been cheering themselves hoarse since learning of the plaudits in Paris. He'll be back here next Saturday for a banquet being given in his honour. At least 80 at table, etc.!

As for Marengo l'Hirondelle, Bouilhet kept your secret so well that he read the letter in question aloud with an air of astonishment, taking me in completely. Poor Marengo! She's a character – shouldn't you make use of her somewhere? What would her memoirs be like, I wonder, written in the same style?

Mine (my style) continues to cause me no little trouble. Still, I hope that in a month I'll have got through the emptiest stretch. For the moment, however, I'm lost in a desert. Anyway, what the hell – one can only trust in God.

How happy I'd be to give up this sort of thing and never return to it for the rest of my days! Depicting the modern bourgeoisie – and the *French* bourgoisie at that – stinks in my nostrils remarkably. Mightn't it be time now to enjoy myself a little, and deal with subjects I like?

I expressed myself badly when I told you "one shouldn't write with one's heart." What I meant was: don't put your own personality on stage. I believe great art is scientific and impersonal. What you have to do is transport yourself, by an intellectual effort, into your Characters – not attract them to yourself. So much for the method – which amounts to this: strive to have a great deal of talent – and genius as well, if you can. What vanity all Poetics, all works of criticism! The complacency of the gentlemen who produce such things is flabbergasting. Oh! Nothing daunts those numbskulls!

Have you noticed how, sometimes, certain ideas seem to be in general circulation? For example, I have just read my friend Du Camp's new novel, *Les Forces perdues*. In many ways it resembles the one I'm writing. It's a book – his,

I mean – that is very naive and gives an accurate idea of the men of our generation – veritable fossils in the eyes of young people today. The Reaction of 1848 gouged an abyss between France as she had been and the France we have now.[2]

N.B. Have you found me a title? It's not easy, I'm sure.

And where are you now? In Paris or Nohant?

Bouilhet told me that at one of the recent Magny's you weren't at all well, "made of oak" though you claim to be. No, no – you are not made of oak, dear great heart, my beloved old troubadour.

Might this be a good time to bring *Almanzor*[3] back to the stage? I can just see him with his turban, his guitar, his apricot tunic, up on a pinnacle haranguing the stockbrokers. The speech could be splendid.

So – goodnight. . . . Tender kisses on both cheeks. . . .

                              Gve Flaubert

---

[1] Here, in the margin, Flaubert inserted the exclamation "*Quel style!*" He had written *de* twice in the same sentence, introducing two infinitives in succession. He seldom failed to underline, in self-accusation, any careless repetitions of *de* and *que*.

[2] Flaubert writes "*entre les deux France*".

[3] *Almansor* is a tragedy by Heinrich Heine. Pursued by Saracens and Christians, the young Moor Almansor and his Christian fiancée kill themselves, leaping from the rock on which they had taken refuge. But it is not clear why Flaubert should mention *Almansor*, nor what he means by saying that it should be "brought back to the stage." It had never been performed in Paris. Does he mean (in a free association with "troubadour") that George Sand might take it as a subject for a play?

55   SAND TO FLAUBERT

                            [Paris, 17 December 1866]
                                        Monday

One morning about a week ago someone called at my house to ask for the shoemaker's address. But my maid didn't want to wake me and I didn't read the letter until noon. As the bearer had said he was from the hotel du Helder,[1] in the street of that name, I answered at once saying Simonin lived at 15 rue Richelieu. I addressed my note to your mother, thinking it must have been she who'd written to me. I see she never received the message, and I can't understand it; but it wasn't my fault.

Your old troubadour is still beastly unwell today, but that won't stop him from going to Magny's this evening. He couldn't kick the bucket in better company – though he'd prefer to do it by a ditch, in spring.

Apart from that all's well and I leave for Nohant on Saturday. I'm doing my best to launch the book on entomology that Maurice is bringing out;[2] it's very good. I'm doing for him what I've never done for myself – writing to the editors of journals. I'll recommend Mlle Bosquet to everyone I can. But her work aims at a different public from mine, and I'm not so well received by literary people as by scholars.

I quite agree that Marengo l'Hirondelle should be "done," and the apricot troubadour too. They belong among the Cadios[3] of the Revolution, who started or tried to make something of themselves, it hardly mattered what. I'm one of the last of them, and those of you who are our heirs are caught between the illusions of my day and the raw disillusions of the present. It's quite natural that you and Du Camp should have a number of ideas and observations in common. It's of no consequence. There can't be any real resemblance.

Oh no, I haven't found you a title! It's too serious a matter, and I'd need to know all about the work. Anyhow, all I'm fit for today is to write my own epitaph! *Et in Arcadia ego*,[4] of course.

I love you, dear friend and brother, and bless you with all my heart.

G. Sand

[1] Where Mme Flaubert stayed when in Paris.

[2] His book on butterflies: *Le Monde des papillons*.

[3] The peasant-born Cadio, in Sand's novel and play, becomes a fanatical republican.

[4] An anonymous Latin saying, depicted, as carved in stone, by various artists, notably by Poussin in a painting in the Louvre. The words have been variously interpreted: "I too once lived in Arcadia" – (a memory of past joys: probably the sense in which Sand used it); or: "I (death) am present even in Arcadia." For interesting reflections on the meaning of the phrase, see John Hall, *Dictionary of Subjects and Symbols in Art* (London, 1974); and two articles by Erwin Panofsky: *Et in Arcadia ego, Philosophy and History*, Essays presented to Ernst Cassirer (Oxford, 1936, p. 223ff.); and *"Et in Arcadia Ego" et le Tombeau Parlant*, Gazette des Beaux-Arts, 1938, 305–6.

*

Mme Sand found herself too ill to travel to Nohant for Christmas – she was suffering from anaemia – but Flaubert did not know of her change of plan, and wrote to her in the country.

56 FLAUBERT TO SAND

Croisset, Thursday
[27 December 1866]

So – are you better, chère maître, since being at Nohant? What *is* your illness, first of all? Seeing your little Aurore must have done you good?

What should I wish you for 1867? First of all, everything; and then everything else, including 200 performances of *Mont-Revêche*.

I have absolutely nothing to tell you, as you well know, except that I miss seeing you. That's all.

How long will you be staying down there? That is, when do you return to Paris? I expect to be in the city toward the middle of February.

Not having you near me, I'm reading you. Or rather re-reading. I've taken up *Consuelo*, which I devoured when it ran in the *Revue indépendante*.[1] Once again I'm *charmed* by it. What talent! Mon Dieu, what talent! I keep saying that to myself over and over again "in the silence of my sanctum".[2] Just now I've been weeping, really, as I read about Porpora kissing Consuelo on the forehead. I can only compare you to some great American river: Vastness and Calm.

I haven't yet read *Les Odeurs* by the great man called Veuillot.[3] If it contains no attack on you it's incomplete. And yet intelligent people admire it! Oh! Saint Polycarp![4]

Adieu – I feel so stupid that I'm afraid of boring you to death. So I'll stop. Give me your news and think of me sometimes.

I kiss you tenderly and am
your old

Gve Flaubert

Mme Maurice must have received the cheeses quite some time ago?

Ah! I was forgetting a commission: old Pouchet asked me to say *that* he was so unnerved by your presence *that* he forgot to tell you *that* he admires not only your works immeasurably, but also those of your son, etc. (When he wants to be diverted he opens *Masques et Visages*.)[5] And once again he mentioned his beard, which he hadn't trimmed that day. Oh!

[1] In 1842–3, when Flaubert was in his early twenties.

[2] "*Dans le silence du cabinet*": Flaubert enjoyed the pomposity of this cliché.

[3] *Les Odeurs de Paris* (Paris, 1866), by Louis Veuillot, the Catholic propagandist. Veuillot had attacked Sand in earlier books.

[4] Flaubert had taken St Polycarp, bishop of Smyrna (69–155), as his patron, after discovering, and acquiring, an engraving in which the saint is shown raising his arms to heaven and crying "My God! My God! In what a century hast Thou decreed I should be born!"

[5] The proper title of the book is *Masques et Bouffons, comédie italienne*. Text and drawings by Maurice Sand, engravings by Manceau, preface by George Sand (Paris, 1860). Flaubert, or Pouchet, probably confused the title with that of Gavarni's *Masques et Visages*.

CHAPTER III

1867

Concerned at having no reply to his letter of 27 December (1866), Flaubert wrote again:

57 FLAUBERT TO SAND

Croisset [6 January 1867]
Sunday

Well, chère maître? What does this mean? Has a letter from you gone astray? I've had no news of you for a long time. I miss you, and worry about you – *voilà*. When you last wrote to me, you were sick. Are you, still? I don't know whether you're at Nohant, at Palaiseau, or in Paris.

A kiss while awaiting a few lines in your dear hand.

Votre vieux

Gve Flaubert

58 SAND TO FLAUBERT

Paris, 9 January [1867] p.m.

Cher camarade,

Your old troubadour has been tempted to kick the bucket. He's still in Paris, though he was supposed to leave on 25 January[1] and his trunk was packed. Your first letter languished day after day at Nohant. But now here is your troubadour, quite fit enough for travel, and setting out tomorrow morning with his son Alexandre,[2] who is good enough to escort him.

It's stupid to be laid up, to lose all notion of oneself for three days, and then to get up as weak as if you'd been doing something onerous and useful. However, it was nothing, really, but a temporary inability to digest anything. Due to cold, or weakness, or work – I don't know. I've almost stopped thinking about it. Sainte-Beuve is a greater anxiety, as you must have learned from your correspondents. He's better too, but he'll be seriously weakened and at risk. I'm very sad and anxious about him.[3]

I haven't done any work for more than a fortnight. So I haven't made any progress, and as I don't know if I'm going to be fit right away I've given the

Odéon *campo*.⁴ They'll take me when I'm ready. I'm thinking of going to the
South of France when I've seen the children. The plants that grow on the coast
keep running through my head. I've completely lost interest in anything else
but my own little ideal of peaceful work, country life, and disinterested and
affectionate friendship. I don't think I have very long to live, even though I'm
better and feeling quite well. I see a sign of this in the great calm, "ever more
calm",⁵ that's beginning to reign in my once agitated soul. My brain proceeds
only from synthesis to analysis now; before, it used to do the opposite. What
presents itself to me now when I wake in the morning is the world as a whole.
I find it quite hard to find the "I" that once interested me, and which I've
started to address as "you", in the plural. The world's very charming, very
interesting and strange, but rather backward and still pretty inaccessible. I hope
to move on into an oasis that's easier to get to and accessible to everyone. It
takes so much money and equipment to travel in this world! And the time you
spend acquiring the necessary paraphernalia is lost to study and contemplation.
I think I'm due for something less complicated and civilized, something more
naturally luxurious and easily good than this fevered phase of existence. Will
you come to the world of my dreams if I manage to find the way there? But
who knows if I shall?

So how is the novel coming along? Your courage hasn't failed? Your solitude
isn't getting you down? I imagine it isn't quite absolute, and that there's a lovely
lady friend somewhere who comes and goes or lives thereabouts. But there's
something of the anchorite about the life you lead, and I envy your situation. I
myself am too much alone when I'm at Palaiseau with one of the dead, and not
alone enough when I'm at Nohant, with children I love too much to be able to
keep myself to myself. As for Paris, one doesn't know *what* one is there; one
forgets oneself entirely for a thousand things no better than oneself.

All my love, dear friend. Remember me to your mother and the rest of your
dear family, and write to me in Nohant – it will do me good.

The cheeses? I can't remember. I seem to recall someone saying something
about them, but I've forgotten what. I'll let you know from there.

[unsigned]

¹ Lapsus for 25 December.
² Sand's friendship with the younger Dumas dated from 1851, when, travelling in eastern
Europe, he had been able to obtain, and return to her, letters she had sent to Chopin. In
their correspondence they addressed each other as "*cher fils*" and "*chère maman*".
³ Sainte-Beuve was suffering from retention of urine.
⁴ The correct spelling is *campos*: *donner campos* – take a vacation.
⁵ "*toujours plus calme*": this phrase is found in several of Sand's letters, always as a
quotation. In one place she calls it a translation of a phrase by Goethe. Jean Bruneau suggests
that that phrase might be the celebrated "*Über allen Gipfeln ist Ruh*" – adding: "but I am
suspicious."

59 FLAUBERT TO SAND

Croisset, Saturday night
[12–13 January 1867]

No, chère maître, you are not near your end. So much the worse for you, perhaps? But you will live to be old, very old – like the giants, since you belong to that race. Only, you *must* rest. It astonishes me that you haven't died twenty times, you've thought so much, written so much, suffered so much. Why don't you go to the Mediterranean for a bit, as you'd like to? Blue skies relax and restore one. There are places – such as the Bay of Naples – that are Gardens of Youth.[1] Perhaps they can be depressing at times? That I don't know.

Life isn't easy! What a complicated business, and so expensive! I know something about that: one needs money for *everything*! To such a point that with a modest income and an unremunerative profession one must resign oneself to living on little.[2] And that's what I do. I've got used to it, but on days when work goes badly or not at all it's no fun. Yes – I'd be glad to follow you into another world. And, speaking of money, that's what will make ours uninhabitable in the near future. It will be impossible even for the very rich to live without giving all their attention to their "holdings". Everyone will have to spend several hours a day fiddling with his capital. Charming!

As for me, I continue to fiddle with my novel. And I'll be off to Paris when I reach the end of my chapter, about the middle of next month. It proceeds at its usual slow pace. Every day I chip away at my coconut, like a convict breaking stones. I'm one myself. Not a convict. A nut.

And whatever you may suppose, no "lovely lady" comes to see me. Lovely ladies have greatly occupied my mind – but consumed little of my time. To speak of me as an anchorite is perhaps a more apt comparison than you think. Whole weeks go by without my exchanging a word with a soul. And at the end of the week it's impossible for me to recall a single day, or any fact whatever. I see my mother and my niece on Sundays, and that's all. My only company is a tribe of rats that make an infernal racket in the garret overhead: I hear them whenever the river stops roaring and there's a drop of the wind. The nights are black as ink, and I'm enclosed in a silence like that of the desert. One's sensibility becomes vastly exalted in such an atmosphere. My heart beats wildly for no reason at all – understandable, in an old hysteric like me. For I maintain that there are male hysterics as well as female, and that I am one of them. When I was writing *Salammbô* I consulted "the best authors" about this, and recognized all my own symptoms – choking, pain in the back of the head.[3] Our charming occupation is to blame for that: we torment ourselves body and soul. But what if the torment is the only thing that's valid, here below . . . ?

I told you, didn't I, about re-reading *Consuelo* and *La Comtesse de Rudolstadt*? It took me four days. We'll have a long talk about them whenever you like. Why am I "*amoureuse*" with Liverani?[4] Because I belong to both sexes, perhaps.

Oh yes – you promised to find me an article on pottery, at Nohant. If you come across it, do send it on.

Make a bow for me to your daughter-in-law. A handshake to your son. Kiss
Mlle Aurore on all four cheeks. And take good care of yourself, partly for love
of your old

Gve Flaubt

¹ For Flaubert in Naples, see Steegmuller, *The Letters of Gustave Flaubert*, I, 138.
² Flaubert had no private fortune, and his books brought him little financial reward. His
principal income was an allowance from his mother.
³ For Flaubert on his hysterical symptoms, see his letters to Hippolyte Taine in *The
Letters of Gustave Flaubert*, II, 96–9.
⁴ A male character in *La Comtesse de Rudolstadt*. The reference is to Flaubert's use of
the feminine form of the adjective *amoureux* (in love).

60 SAND TO FLAUBERT

Nohant, 15 January [1867]

So here I am back home, fairly flourishing except for a few hours in the
evening. Still, it will pass: as my old priest¹ used to say, "Either the ill or he
who endures it can't last." I got your letter this morning, cher ami de mon
coeur. Why do I love you more than I do most others – more even than some
old and well-tried comrades? I try to find the answer, for at the moment I'm
like one "seeking his fortune at sunset".² Yes – intellectual fortune: light! The
thing is that when one's old, in the sunset of one's life – the best time of all
for richness of colour and light – one acquires a new approach to everything,
and especially to affection. During the phase of power and personality you test
a friend, as you might test the ground, for reciprocity. You're strong and firm
yourself, and you want that which is to support or guide you to be strong and
firm as well. But when you feel your own "self" getting less intense, you love
people and things for what they are in themselves, what they represent in the
eyes of your soul, and not at all for what they will contribute to your own
destiny. It's like a picture or a statue that you covet and would like to possess
when you dream of having a fine place of your own to put it in. But when
you've rolled your stone through Bohemia³ and not gathered any moss, you
end up still poor, sentimental and a troubadour, knowing full well it will always
be the same and you'll die without hearth or home. Then, when you think of
the statue and the picture, you know that if you did own them you wouldn't
know what to do with them or how to house them suitably. And you're
glad to know they're in some out-of-the-way temple unprofaned by cold
analysis, and you love them all the more. You think to yourself: I'll go back
to their places of origin and I'll see again, and go on loving for ever, what
it was that made me love and understand them in the beginning. They won't
have been modified by contact with my own personality; I shan't merely be
loving myself when I profess to love them. And that is how an ideal that you
no longer try to fix and appropriate fixes itself in *you* because it remains itself.
That's the whole secret of the beautiful, the good, and the "one truth";⁴ of

love, friendship, art, devotion and faith. Think about it and you'll see.

I'd find the kind of solitude you live in delightful when the weather was fine. But in winter it strikes me as stoical, and I have to remind myself that you have no moral need of regular locomotion. I've been reflecting that you expend energy in other ways while you're shut away as you are. Now that's all very fine, but it mustn't go on for ever. If the novel is going to take longer you must interrupt it or intersperse it with periods of recreation. That's the truth, my friend. Give a thought to the life of the body, which gets cross and rebels if it's put on too short commons. When I was ill in Paris I saw a very crazy but very clever doctor who had some sound things to say on the subject.[5] He told me I had an alarming tendency to "spiritualize" things, and when I said, thinking precisely of you, that it was possible to abstract oneself from everything but work, and yet increase rather than lessen one's energy thereby, he answered that it was as dangerous to accumulate power as to lose it. And I wish I could reproduce for you a lot more excellent things he said in this connection. But you know them already; it's just that you disregard them. The work you apply such rough words to is really a passion – and a *grande passion*, at that! So I'll say to you what you say to me: for the love of us all, and in particular for the love of your old troubadour, take it easy.

Consuelo, La Comtesse de Rudolstadt – what are they? Did I write them? I don't remember a word of them![6] And you're reading that stuff? Does it really amuse you? I'll read it again then one of these days, and if you like me I'll like myself.

What does it mean to be a hysteric? Perhaps I was one too, perhaps I'm one still, but I couldn't say, not having gone into it but only heard about it. Isn't it a discontent, an anguish, caused by desire for something or other that's unattainable? In that case all of us who have any imagination suffer from that strange malady; why should it be attributed to only one sex?

What's more, those who are learned in anatomy say there *is only one sex*. Men and women are so much alike it's hard to understand all the subtle distinctions and theories on the subject that have coloured our various human societies. I myself have observed the childhood and subsequent development of my son and daughter. My son was the image of me, and so more a woman than my daughter; she was a failed man.

All my love. Maurice and Lina, who smacked their lips over the cheeses, send their kind regards, and Mlle Aurore shouts "Wait, wait, wait!" That's all she can say, and she says it laughing like anything. When she laughs at all, that is, because she's really very serious and attentive, as clever as a monkey with her hands, and more amused with the games she invents for herself than with any suggested by other people. I think *she*'ll have a phiz all of her own.

If I don't get better here I shall go to Cannes, where some friends press me to join them. But I mustn't breathe a word of that yet to my children. It isn't easy to move when I'm with them. Passion and jealousy are involved. And all my life has been like that – I've never been at my own disposal! So complain if you dare, you who belong to yourself!

[unsigned]

¹ The old curé of Saint-Chartier, the abbé Pierre de Montpeyroux, much spoken of in *L'Histoire de ma vie*.

² A reference to a song quoted by Maurice Sand in *Le Monde des Papillons*.

³ i.e. "When you've lived *la vie de Bohème*..."

⁴ An allusion to Victor Cousin's *Du Vrai, du Bien et du Beau*(1858).

⁵ From Sand's diary, 22 December 1866: "Dr Favre came to see me at 7 o'clock. He examined me again. He gave me good advice, and talked until midnight. He is very intelligent, very learned, very interesting, very witty, but I'm afraid he may be a bit cracked. He believes he's the only sane person of this century: *diable*! And he says all this in the most moderate language. Very dangerous."

⁶ Despite the obvious exaggeration of these words, it seems to be true that George Sand, a prolific writer, cared so little about what she had written that she sometimes forgot she had written it. One day, when a friend quoted a passage that he much admired in one of her novels, she said: "Really not bad. Who wrote it?"

61 FLAUBERT TO SAND

[Croisset, 23–24 January 1867]
Wednesday night

I have followed your advice, chère maître. I have taken some exercise! Am I a splendid fellow, or not? On Sunday night at eleven o'clock, the moonlight on the river and the snow was such that I was seized by the itch of locomotion. And I walked for two and a half hours – working myself into a state and pretending that I was travelling in Russia or Norway. When the tide came in and cracked the ice floes on the Seine and the frozen surface of the stream – no joking: it was superb. I thought of you and wished you were there.¹

I dislike eating alone. I have to associate someone or the idea of someone with the things that give me pleasure. But that someone is rare. I, too, ask myself why I love you. Is it because you're a great man, or a "charming human being"? I have no idea. What is certain is that for you I have a *particular* feeling, one I cannot define.

By the way, do you believe (you who are a Master in psychology) that one can love two people in the same way? And that one ever has two identical feelings? I think not, since one's *self* keeps changing at every moment of existence.

You write beautifully about "disinterested affection". What you say is true. But so is the opposite, is it not? We always make God in our own image. At the heart of all our loves and all our admirations don't we discover – ourselves, or something resembling ourselves?

But what does that matter, if "ourselves" are good?

My *me* bores me to death at the moment. What a heavy burden that fellow is, at times! He writes too slowly! And he isn't striking the slightest pose when he complains about his work. What a chore! And what an idea, to have picked such a subject! You should give me a recipe for working faster. And you complain of seeking your Fortune!

As you know, you've never told me what your illness is. What is it? Is it serious? Are you going to spend the winter in the Midi? Don't stay there too long, eh? I shouldn't like it if we weren't to see each other soon. I'll be in Paris a month from now – and you?

I've had a little note from Sainte-Beuve that reassures me about his health but is lugubrious nonetheless. He seems disconsolate at no longer being able to haunt the Cyprian groves! He is right, after all, or at least right according to his lights, which is the same thing. Perhaps I'll be like him when I'm his age? I think not, however. Not having had the same youth, I'll have a different old age. That reminds me that I once thought of writing a book about Sainte-Périne.[2] Champfleury treated that subject idiotically. For I see nothing comic there (neither in the subject nor in Champfleury). I would have made it dreadful, pitiful. I believe the heart does not grow old. In some people it even expands with age. I was more dry, more harsh, twenty years ago than I am today. I've been feminized and softened by wear and tear – which harden other people. That makes me indignant. I feel I'm becoming *vache*.[3] I get emotional over nothing. Everything troubles me, agitates me. To me, everything is like the north wind to the reed.[4]

Something you said came back to my mind and is making me reread *La Jolie Fille de Perth*.[5] It's charming, whatever people may say. That chap had imagination – no question.

So: adieu. Think of me. I send you my best love.

Your

Gve Flaubert

[1] The river Seine is tidal for forty miles or so above its mouth in the English Channel – that is, beyond Rouen, of which Croisset is a down-river suburb.

[2] That is, a book about old age set in L'Institution de Sainte-Périne. This was an endowed residence for elderly persons, particularly retired civil servants or their widows, who could afford to pay modest sums for board. Founded in the very early 1800s, under the patronage of the Empress Joséphine, it was originally in Chaillot, then transferred in 1862 to buildings in Auteuil. Most of these have been demolished and replaced by modern hospital facilities. Champfleury published his novel, *Les Amoureux de Sainte-Périne*, in 1859.

[3] See Letters 64 and 65.

[4] An allusion to La Fontaine's fable *The Oak and the Reed*. The oak says to the reed: "To you everything is north wind; to me all seems zephyr."

[5] Sir Walter Scott's *The Fair Maid of Perth*. Flaubert owned a thirty-two-volume set of Scott's novels in French translation. His adjective for the book is *coquet*: the translation "charming" might be improved were one sure of his meaning. *La Jolie Fille de Perth* was literally "in the air" in 1867: Georges Bizet's four-act opera of that name, its libretto taken from the novel, would have its first performance at the Théâtre Lyrique in Paris on December 26.

62 SAND TO FLAUBERT

[Nohant, 27 January 1867]

Pooh! To hell with it! Tralala! Ouch, ouch! I'm not ill now, or at least only half as ill as before. The local air is curing me – either that, or patience, or "the other", the person who wants to go on working and creating. What is the illness I'm suffering from? Nothing. Everything's in good condition, but there's something called anaemia, an effect without discernible cause, a collapse that has been threatening for some years and manifested itself openly in Palaiseau, after I got back from Croisset. Weight loss too rapid to be natural; slow, weak pulse; lazy or uncertain digestion; together with a feeling of breathlessness and vague fits of apathy. Sometimes for several days this poor stomach couldn't keep even a glass of water down, and it lowered me so much I didn't really think I'd get over it. But everything's improving now, and since yesterday I've even been able to work.

And you, dear friend – you go walking in the snow at night. Rather farfetched for someone who ventures out so rarely; it could easily make you ill too. It was the sun I prescribed for you, not the moon: we're not owls, for heaven's sake. We've just had three spring days. But I bet you haven't been up to my dear orchard that's so pretty and that I'm so fond of. You ought to climb up through it at noon every fine day, if only in memory of me. The work would flow more freely afterwards and more than make up for lost time.

Have you got money worries, then? I haven't known what they are since I stopped having any possessions. I live off my day's work, like the proletariat; when I stop being able to do a day's work I'll be tipped for the next world and shan't need anything any more. But *you* must go on living. And how are you to live from your pen if you're always letting yourself be cheated and fleeced? I'm not the person to teach you how to look after yourself. But haven't you some friend capable of acting for you? Alas, yes! the world is going to the devil in that respect. I was talking about you the other day to a very dear friend of mine, and pointing out how an artist, now such a rarity, may be driven to curse the necessity of thinking about the material side of life. I enclose the last page of his letter. As you'll see, you have an unsuspected friend in that quarter. I expect the signature will surprise you.[1]

No, I shan't go to Cannes, although I've been strongly tempted. Yesterday I received a little box of cut flowers picked five or six days ago, which went first to Paris and Palaiseau by mistake. Yet they still look and smell delightfully fresh and pretty. Oh, how I'd love to go away, to leave at once for sunny climes! But I have neither the money nor the time. My illness has hampered me and set me back. So let's stay, then! Aren't I comfortable where I am? And if I can't get to Paris next month, won't you come and see me here? Yes, it does take eight hours to get here! But you can't not see this old nest of mine. And you owe me a week's stay, or else I shall think I love a monster of ingratitude who doesn't love me back.

Poor Sainte-Beuve! He's worse off than we are, since he never had great sorrows and no longer has material worries. So there he is lamenting the things that should be missed the least, the most unimportant things in life, understood as he used to understand it! And he takes a very lofty tone for one who was once a Jansenist. His heart has grown cold in this respect. Perhaps his mind has grown greater. But mind alone can't help us to live or teach us to die. Barbès, who for so long has been expecting to be carried off by a syncope, is gentle and smiling. It doesn't seem to him, or to his friends, that death will separate him from us. The sort of person who really does disappear is the one who *thinks* he will, and who doesn't hold out a hand to others, beckoning them to accompany him or rejoin him.

So goodnight, cher ami de mon coeur. They're just giving the signal for the show to begin. Maurice is entertaining us this evening with the marionettes. It's very amusing, and the theatre's so pretty! A real actors' delight. Why aren't you here? It's silly not to live next door to those one loves.

[unsigned]

¹ This was Armand Barbès (1809–70), the republican revolutionary, who had been condemned to death in 1839, charged with murdering a lieutenant in the National Guard. He had not committed the crime, but was the leader of an insurrectionary group one member of which had fired the fatal shot. His sentence was commuted to life imprisonment the day before his scheduled execution, when Victor Hugo sent a plea in verse to Louis-Philippe. (Hugo had possibly been inspired by the example of La Fontaine, who in 1662 or 1663 had written an "Ode to the King" on behalf of the imprisoned Fouquet.) After four years at Mont-Saint-Michel (at that time used as a prison), Barbès was transferred to the milder climate of Nîmes because of ill health caused in part by maltreatment. Released in 1848 and playing a role in the revolutionary government, he was again imprisoned after the June Days, and in 1854 was again released, almost against his will, by Napoleon III. At the time of this letter he was living in self-imposed exile in Holland. George Sand had been one of his political comrades. The passage of a letter from Barbès which Sand encloses contains praise of *Madame Bovary*.

63 FLAUBERT TO SAND

[Croisset, 6 February 1867]
Wednesday

I received your son's volume yesterday.¹ I'll begin it when I have finished some reading that is probably less amusing. Meanwhile, please thank him for me, chère maître.

First, let's talk about you. Anaemia! I'm not surprised! You *must* take a tonic of iron, and walk and sleep – and go to the Midi, whatever it costs! Yes! Otherwise, made of oak though you may be, you'll crack. As for money, it can be found; as for time, just take it. You'll do nothing that I advise, naturally. Well, you're wrong. And it grieves me.

No, I do not have what are called money worries. My income is very limited, but secure. Only, since it's your friend's habit to anticipate said funds, he's occasionally a little short, and grumbles about it "in the silence of his sanctum".

But not elsewhere. Barring the unexpected, I'll be able to keep myself in food and firewood to the end of my days. My heirs are, or will be, rich. (I'm the poor man of the family.) But enough of that.

As for earning money by my pen, it's something I've never envisaged, recognizing that I'm fundamentally incapable of it. Therefore one leads a modest country life on what one has. Not a supremely amusing existence. But there are so many other people, more deserving than I, who haven't a sou, that it would be wrong to complain. Besides, railing against Providence is such a common way of going on that one should refrain, if only for good form.

One more word about lucre, which will be a secret between us. As soon as I'm in Paris, that is from the 20th to the 23rd of this month, I'll be able easily, with no strain whatever, to lend you a thousand francs[2] in case you need it to go to Cannes. I propose this to you bluntly, as I would to Bouilhet or any other intimate. No fuss about it, please. Among conventional folk this would be thought improper, I know, but between troubadours much can be dispensed with.

You are very kind, with your invitation to Nohant. I *will* come. Because I long to see your house. It bothers me not to know it, when I think of you. But I must postpone that pleasure until next summer. Just now I should stay in Paris for a while. Three months is not overlong for all I want to do there.

I return herewith the page by the excellent Barbès. Of his *true* biography I know very little. All I know about him is that he is honest and heroic. Shake hands with him for me, to thank him for his words of appreciation. Between you and me, is he as intelligent as he is good? I need some men of that camp who will speak frankly with me. Because I'm about to study the revolution of '48.

You promised to look out for me, in your library at Nohant, 1st an article of yours on faience, 2nd a novel by Father X, a Jesuit, about the Virgin Mary.

But such severity toward old [Sainte-] Beuve, who is neither Jesuit nor Virgin! You say he laments "the things that should be missed the least in life, understood as he used to understand it". Why so? Doesn't everything depend on the *intensity* one puts into the thing? I find you fundamentally tainted (in this matter) with Catholicism, O chère maître. Men will always consider sexual pleasure the most important thing in their lives. Woman, for all of us, is the Archway to the Infinite. This isn't noble, but such is the very core of the Male. There's an immense amount of joking about all this. Thank God there is – for the sake of Literature, and for individual Happiness, as well. No matter! Glory be to Venus!

[. . .][3]

Ah! I missed you greatly just now. The high tides are superb. The wind is moaning, the river is white and overflows its banks. It seems to bring sea breezes, and one feels the better for it.

Adieu. I embrace you the way I love you – very tenderly.

Gve Flaubert

[1] *Le Coq aux cheveux d'or, récit des temps fabuleux* (Paris, 1867).

[2] After much persuasion, the publisher Lévy had recently given Flaubert an advance of 5,000 francs on the total fee of 10,000 francs he was to receive for *L'Éducation sentimentale*.

[3] Omitted here are a few lines, inadvertently absurd, of a high-flown drinking song – "*Des voluptés essayons le délire*" etc. – by the abbé Delille. Flaubert includes them for Sand's amusement, suggesting that they should be recited by the comic actor Grassot.

64 SAND TO FLAUBERT

Nohant, 8 February [18]67

No, I'm not a Catholic, but I do draw the line at monstrosities. I say an ugly old man who buys little girls isn't making love, and that all this has nothing to do with Aphrodite or archways or infinity or male or female. There's something unnatural about it, for it isn't desire that throws the girl into the ugly old man's arms, and where there's no freedom and reciprocity there's sacrilege against Nature. So what *he* laments is not something that should be missed, unless he believes his little tarts miss *him* – and I ask you, are they likely to miss anything but their ill-gotten gains? That has been the gangrene of this great and admirable thinker, so lucid and wise in all other respects. We forgive the people we love anything when it's a matter of defending them against their enemies. But what we say between our two selves is completely private, and I can tell you this defect has quite spoiled my old friend in my eyes.

We really must love one another in earnest, dear comrade, for we both thought of the same thing at the same time. You, who are as penniless as I am, offer me a thousand francs to go to Cannes; and when *you* wrote that *you* were bothered about money, *I* opened the letter *I'd* written you to offer you half of what I possess, which always amounts to 2,000. That's my reserve. And then I didn't dare. Why not? It was very silly, and you were better than I and actually did it. So my best love for your kind offer, though I don't accept it. I would have done so, you may be sure, if I'd had no other option. But what I say is that if anyone ought to give me a loan it's Master Buloz, who's bought châteaux and estates with my novels. He wouldn't refuse me, I know. He's even offered. So I'll get it from him if necessary. But I'm not in a fit state to travel. My health has worsened again in the last few days. I was so exhausted I slept for 36 hours at a stretch. I'm up and about again now, but weak. I don't mind admitting it to you – I haven't the energy to *want* to live. I don't really feel like it. To leave a place where I'm comfortable, go out of my way in search of more exertions, get dog-tired just to go on living a dog's life – all that seems rather silly to me, when it would be so pleasant just to go off like this, still loving, still loved, at war with no one, not displeased with oneself, and dreaming of such marvels in other worlds that one's imagination must still be fairly lively.

But I don't know why I'm talking to you about such reputedly sad things. I'm so much in the habit of facing them calmly, I forget that to people in the prime of life they may seem distressing. Let's change the subject and trust to spring – perhaps its breezes will kindle in me a desire to get back to work. I'll be as ready to obey an inner voice that tells me to walk as one that tells me to sit.

It wasn't I who promised you a novel about the Virgin Mary – at least I don't think so. As for my article on pottery, I can't find it. So do look and see if it hasn't been printed at the end of a volume of my collected works, to fill up some odd pages. It was called *Giovanni Freppa ou les majoliques*.

Just a minute ... What luck! As I was writing I suddenly remembered a place I hadn't looked in. I rushed there at once, and found the article! I did even better, and enclose three studies on the subject which will make you as expert as I am. Passeri's is delightful.[1]

Barbès certainly is intelligent! But his mind is like a sugar-loaf – too sweet and lofty. An Indian skull full of mild, almost imperceptible instincts; all in favour of metaphysical thought merging into instinct and passion that governs all. Hence a character which can only be compared with that of Garibaldi. So saintly and perfect he's almost incredible. Of immense worth, but a worth without immediate relevance in France. He's a hero of another age or another country, born into the wrong environment.

And so goodnight. Lord, what a *veau* I am! I won't deprive you of the title of *vache* which you apply to yourself in your off moments.[2] Anyhow, let me know when you'll be in Paris. I shall probably have to spend a few days there myself for some reason or other. We shall throw our arms round one another, and then you're coming to Nohant this summer. It's all arranged; you *must*!

My love to your Maman and lovely niece.

Do let me know when the 3 booklets reach you. I shouldn't like them to get lost.

[unsigned]

---

[1] *L'Histoire des peintures sur majoliques faites à Pesaro et dans les lieux circonvoisins* (1853).
[2] See Letter 65.

65   FLAUBERT TO SAND

[Croisset, 12 February 1867]
Tuesday

I've just received your three booklets, along with your letter, chère maître. Thank you for all this.

I shall be in Paris toward the end of next week. If you come, when will it be?

Take care of yourself for all our sakes!

Adieu. I send you a kiss.

[unsigned]

I'm in the middle of *Le Coq*. It's very strange! In other words, just what I like.

Certainly: I use the word *vache* in my own way. I have even invented the verb *vacher: Je vache, tu vaches*. But the best is the imperative: *"Vachons!"*[1]

[unsigned]

[1] In this, and in Letters 61 and 64, Flaubert and Sand play on the various derogatory popular uses of the words *vache* (cow) and *veau* (calf), all conveying ideas of stupidity, slowness, weakness, feeble-mindedness. In *vache* there is also a possibility of nastiness or aggression, and it may be this that Flaubert wants to evoke with his invented verb: *je vache, tu vaches, vachons* – "I am beastly, you are beastly, let's be beastly!"

*

Flaubert went to Paris on the 19th, chiefly to study the events of the Revolution of 1848. He worried about not hearing from George Sand.

66 FLAUBERT TO SAND

[Paris] Saturday 2 [March 1867]

Chère maître,

What's become of you? I hear you're still ill – is it true?

Shall you be attending Dumas' opening?[1] Le père Sainte-Beuve was splendid at the last Magny. There was an American there, who I think is a friend of yours.[2]

You know that my poor Bouilhet has lost his mother. I went to see him at Mantes and found him shattered.

I have so many things to say about *Le Coq aux cheveux d'or*, by your son (who is quite a Coq himself), that I prefer to tell them to you. Otherwise I'd have to write *"une lettre de grand Homme"*, and that would be too silly.

Such cold! It cuts right through you.

I long to see you: here's a kiss for you.

Votre vieux,

Gve Flaubert

I hear the most contradictory things about your play.[3] Also, that *Villemer* will be revived during the Exhibition.[4]

I'm continuing to write a little, but am chiefly engrossed in the Revolution of '48.

[1] *Les Idées de madame Aubray* was to open at the Théâtre du Gymnase on 16 March 1867.
[2] Henry Harrisse (1829[?]–1910), born in Paris of American parents, wrote (in French) many historical works on the discovery and exploration of portions of North America.
[3] *Mont-Revêche*.
[4] *Le Marquis de Villemer* was to return to the stage from 10 July to 13 August 1867, during the Exposition Universelle.

67 SAND TO FLAUBERT

Nohant, 4 March [1867]

Cher bon ami,

The friend of your heart, the old troubadour, is as well as ten thousand men who are all well, and as happy as a lark because the sun's shining again and the work's progressing. He'll probably be in Paris soon for his son Dumas' play. Let's try to be there together.

Maurice is very proud to be labelled a cock by an eagle. At the moment he's at a party, with veal and sour wine, in honour of his firemen.[1]

The American in question is charming. He has, literarily speaking, a passion for you, and writes that he loves you even more after having met you. It doesn't surprise me.

Poor Bouilhet. Please pass on to him the enclosed note. I share his grief; I know what it's like.

Are you enjoying yourself in Paris? Are you as sedentary there as you are in Croisset? If so I shan't see much of you unless I actually come to visit you. Let me know the times when you won't admit the fair sex but when you don't mind receiving troubadours in their sixties.

Cadio is revised and rewritten up to where I finished reading it to you. It's not so awful now. I'm not doing *Mont-Revêche* – I'll tell you all about it. It's a long story.[2]

Je t'aime et je t'embrasse de tout mon coeur
Your old

George Sand

Have you received the pottery booklets? I haven't heard from you about them. They were sent to Croisset the day after your last letter.

[1] Maurice was head of the local fire department.
[2] In October, 1864, after the success of *Le Marquis de Villemer*, the Odéon had asked George Sand to dramatize her novel *Mont-Revêche* (1852). After several attempts to do so, she abandoned the task, which was then undertaken by the younger Alexandre Dumas.

68 FLAUBERT TO SAND

[Paris, 5 March 1867]
Tuesday, 4 o'clock

I'm relieved and delighted to know you're well, but you mustn't exhaust yourself with work, or imagine you're made of oak!

I thought I'd told you that the booklets on faience had arrived:[1] a thousand pardons, chère maître.

But of course I'm counting on your visiting me in my private quarters! As for embarrassing situations involving the Fair Sex, you'll encounter none, you may be sure, nor will anyone else. My little stories concerning the heart and the senses are kept out of the front of the shop. But since my part of town is far from yours, and you might not find me in, choose a day and an hour as soon as you arrive in Paris. Then we'll make another appointment, for dinner, just the two of us, and we'll huddle together over our table.

I've sent your affectionate note on to Bouilhet.

As I write this I'm revolted by the crowds outside my window, celebrating Mardi Gras. So much for the saying that "True wit is found in the streets"!!![2]

Adieu — à bientôt. It's strange how I long to see you! A big hug.

Votre vieux

Gve Flaubert

[1] He had, on 12 February.
[2] ["*L'esprit court les rues.*"]

69   SAND TO FLAUBERT

[Nohant] 14 March [1867]

Your old troubadour has been laid up again. His old guitar keeps threatening to break. Then he sleeps for forty-eight hours and is better — but weak, and he can't be in Paris on the 16th as he intended. Maurice has just left on his own. I'll join him in five or six days' time.

Little Aurore consoles me for this set-back. She warbles away like a bird, and the birds themselves are already warbling as if it were the middle of spring. The Sylvie anemones that I found in the woods and transplanted into the garden, and that had difficulty acclimatizing themselves there, are at last sending up thousands of white and pink stars amid the blue periwinkles. It's hot and damp. One can't break one's guitar in weather like this.

A bientôt cher bon ami.

G. Sand

70   SAND TO FLAUBERT

[Paris] Friday [22 March 1867]

Your old troubadour is here and not too peaky. He'll be dining at Magny's on Monday. We'll settle on a day for us to have dinner together, with Maurice. The troubadour is to be found at home at five o'clock, but not until Monday. He's dashing about!

He is yours with love.

[unsigned]

71 FLAUBERT TO SAND

[Paris, 23 March 1867]
Saturday, 11 o'clock

Ah! At last! So we'll be seeing each other!

I'll not go to the Magny next Monday, because I have a disgusting grippe.
But what's to prevent our dining at my place next Wednesday or Thursday?
Whom would you like as a "fourth"? Or shall we not have a fourth? If le père
Beuve could come, would that be nice?

A bientôt, chère maître. Je vous embrasse tendrement.

Gve Flaubert

72 SAND TO FLAUBERT

[Paris, 23 March 1867]
Saturday evening

Wednesday, then, if you wish, mon cher vieux. With anyone you like. Certainly, cher Beuve if possible, and no one if you prefer.

Love from us both.

G. S. Maurice[1]

[1] Mme Sand signed for both.

*

Sainte-Beuve was too ill to come. Mme Sand wrote in her diary: "We dined
with Flaubert – he's so nice." She returned to Nohant on April 2nd.

73 SAND TO FLAUBERT

Nohant, 11 April [18]67

Here I am back in my nest and almost recovered from a bad attack of fever
that struck me down in Paris just before I left. Your old troubadour's health
really has been all over the place these last six months. March and April make
him stupid. Never mind, he's coming round again, and once again sees the
trees and plants coming into flower. It's always the same, and that's why it's
beautiful and good. Maurice was very touched by your friendliness; he's not
demonstrative, but you delighted and won him over completely. He and his
wife – who's not at all an ordinary woman – insist that you visit us this year. I
am instructed to tell you so very seriously – *persistently* if necessary.

Are you over that nasty grippe? Maurice meant to call and ask how you were,
but when he saw me so flattened with fever his one thought was to wrap me
up and carry me off like a parcel. I slept all the way from Paris to Nohant, and
was bucked up by Aurore's kisses – she has learned to give great big smackers,
laughing uproariously. She thinks that's very funny.

And how about the novel? Is it progressing as well in Paris as it does in Croisset? It seems to me you lead the same hermit-like existence wherever you are. When you have time to think of friends, remember your old comrade and send him a couple of lines to say you're well and haven't forgotten him.

Goulard

74 FLAUBERT TO SAND

[Paris, 13 April 1867]
Saturday

Chère maître,

You really should seek the sun somewhere. It doesn't make sense to be unwell all the time, so do get away and rest. Resignation is the worst of the virtues.

I need plenty of those, to put up with all the stupidities I keep hearing! You have no idea of the pass things have come to. France, which has had occasional attacks of St Vitus' dance (as under Charles VI),[1] now seems to me to be stricken with paralysis of the brain. Fear is making everybody idiotic: fear of Prussia,[2] fear of strikes,[3] fear concerning the Exhibition,[4] which "isn't going well," fear about everything. You have to go back to 1849 to find such a degree of cretinism. At the last Magny dinner the conversation was on such a servants'-hall level that I swore to myself never to set foot there again. Nothing was talked about except M. de Bismarck and Luxembourg! I'm still fed to the teeth with it. All in all, I'm becoming "difficult". Instead of getting blunted, my sensibility grows ever more acute; I'm pained by all kinds of trivialities. Forgive me this weakness, you who are so Strong and so tolerant!

The novel isn't progressing at all. I'm deep in the newspapers of '48. I've had to look into things in various places – Sèvres, Creil, etc. – and I still haven't finished.

Old Sainte-Beuve is preparing a speech on Free Thought that he'll read in the Senate – concerning the law on the Press. He's been very stalwart, you know.[5]

Tell your son Maurice that I'm very fond of him. First because he's your son, and second because he's himself. I think he's good, witty, well-read, natural – in a word, charming. "And talented!" – (as people add).

Of course I'll come to Nohant. But when do you return to Paris?

Much love from your

Gve Flaubert

[1] Flaubert refers here to outbursts of religious excitement, frequent in the Middle Ages, which caused people to dance until they fell to the ground, their limbs twitching. On such occasions, prayers were said to St Vitus and St John. These phenomena sometimes became epidemic, notably in 1375 and in 1418 during the reign of Charles VI.

[2] After the battle of Sadowa (1866), which left victorious Prussia predominant in central Europe, France wanted to avenge itself by annexing the Grand Duchy of Luxembourg. This

small state was allied to Germany by a customs union and occupied by a Prussian garrison. Bismarck had let Napoleon III know that he would not oppose France's move if it were done quickly and in secrecy. But at the last moment the secret was leaked, and France had to abandon the project. Then the French Emperor sought to obtain, at least, the withdrawal of the Prussian garrison. Bismarck refused; France began to arm; there were rumours of war. Finally, at a conference in London (7–11 May 1867), an agreement was arrived at, declaring the Grand Duchy neutral, under European guarantee; and the fortress was evacuated and dismantled. In a footnote, Alphonse Jacobs attributes this information to Lavisse, *Histoire de France*, VII.

³ Strikes in industry and commerce had threatened to wreck the Exposition Universelle, set to open on 1 April 1867.

⁴ The Exhibition opened on time in the Champ de Mars, despite complaints of high prices, rumours of postponement, and the threat of more strikes.

⁵ At the urging of Princesse Mathilde Bonaparte and her brother, the Emperor had appointed Sainte-Beuve a Senator, with a salary of 30,000 francs a year. His maiden speech, on 29 March 1867, was on the subject of freedom of thought. He was now preparing a second speech, on freedom of the press. (Flaubert's "Free Thought" is a moment of absent-mindedness.)

75 FLAUBERT TO SAND

[Paris, 6 May 1867]
Monday evening

I'm worried at having no news of you, chère maître. What is happening with you? When shall I see you again?

My visit to Nohant must be postponed, and this is why. A few days ago my mother had a slight stroke. It has passed off completely, but might recur. She misses me, and I'll be returning to Croisset sooner than planned. If she is well, say by August, and if I'm not anxious about her, I don't have to tell you that I'll hasten towards your penates.

As for news: Sainte-Beuve seems to me seriously ill. And Bouilhet has just been appointed librarian at Rouen.

Today is Magny day, but I shan't go, as the best of them won't be there.

Since the war-rumours have subsided, people seem to me to be less idiotic. I'm getting over the desperation I felt about the public cowardice.

I have been twice to the Exhibition: it's overwhelming. There are some splendid things, very curious indeed. But man isn't made to absorb the infinite! One would have to be familiar with all the Sciences and all the Arts, to find interest in everything on view in the Champ de Mars. Still, someone who had three whole months to spare and went every day and took notes could save himself no end of reading and travel. One feels very distant from Paris there, in a new and ugly world, an enormous world that is perhaps the world of the future. The first time I lunched there I kept thinking about America, and felt I should be talking like a black.

And so, in a fortnight I'll go back to Croisset, after having been here three months. As usual, I'll have accomplished a fifteenth part of what I intended to do.

A thousand friendly greetings to Maurice. To you a tender kiss.

Your old

Gve Flaubert

I'm told that Girardin serves at Mass in his wife's chapel. It's he who tinkles the bell. Nice picture, what?[1]

---

[1] Jacobs says: "We have been unable to verify this piece of gossip." Girardin's wife was the poet and novelist Delphine Gay. Flaubert was always on the lookout for religiosity among "liberals".

76 SAND TO FLAUBERT

Nohant, 9 May [18]67

Cher ami de mon coeur,

I'm well, I'm working, I'm finishing *Cadio*. It's hot, I'm alive, I'm calm – and yet sad, I scarcely know why. In the even, tranquil and pleasant life I lead here I find myself in an element that, while it strengthens me physically, debilitates me mentally, and I gets fits of spleen that are none the less fits of spleen for being made of honey and roses. I feel as though I'm forgotten by all the people I've loved, and that it's only fair, because I live selfishly and do nothing for them. I *have* been very devoted in my time, and made sacrifices which crushed me and tried me beyond my strength, and which I often cursed. And it may be that, not being called on for that sort of thing any more, I'm just bored with being comfortable. If the human race were doing either very well or very badly one could link on to some general concern and live for an idea, whether wisdom or mere illusion. But you, who fulminate so strongly against the faint-hearted, can see the state people's minds are in. You say the panic's fading – but it will only recur! What sort of society is it that's paralyzed in the midst of its own expansion because there may be a storm on the way? Never before have people been so demoralized by the thought of danger. Have we fallen so low we won't eat anything unless we're assured it won't give us indigestion? Yes, it's stupid and shameful. Is it the result of excessive wellbeing? Is civilization itself going to drive us into this craven, morbid egotism? My optimism has taken a hard knock lately.

I was so looking forward to having you here – the thought of it put new heart in me. I felt I was cooking up my own cure. And now here you are worried about your dear old mother, and of course I can't say anything. Still, if before you leave Paris I can finish *Cadio*, which I must buckle down to if I'm to pay for my shoes and my tobacco, Maurice and I will come in and say hello to you. Otherwise I'll hope to see you in the middle of the summer. The children too, who are quite cast down by the postponement, would like to look forward to your visit. Our hearts are all the more set on it because it would mean your dear Maman was well again.

We're deep in natural history once more. Maurice aims to be an expert on *micros*.[1] His learning rubs off on me. It'll do me a lot of good, won't it, to burden my brain with the names and shapes of two or three thousand almost invisible species? But, you see, this kind of research is like an *octopus* that envelops you in its tentacles and opens up some kind of infinity. You ask if men are meant to "drink in the infinite." Yes, they certainly are! It's their destiny, because it's their dream and their passion. *Imagining* is fascinating too, but how tired one is afterwards! How empty and intellectually exhausted you feel when you've been scribbling away for weeks and months about the two-legged animal who's the only permissible subject for a novel! I can see Maurice is quite refreshed and rejuvenated when he gets back to his insects and stones, and if I want to escape from my woe I do so by burying myself in the sort of research that grocers call useless. Anyway, it's better than saying Mass and "tinkling" adoration of the Almighty. Is what you say about G. true? Is it possible? I can't believe it. Do you think the earth is exhaling laughing-gas or some other vapour that attacks the brain and causes peculiar behaviour – like the irritating fluid that made people commit cruelties in the first Revolution? We've fallen out of Dante's inferno into Scarron's.[2]

What do you, with your excellent head and heart, think in the midst of these bacchanalia? They make you angry. Which is as it should be – I'd rather that than have you laugh at them. But what about when you calm down and think about it all?

But we have to find some way of accepting the honour, duty and burden of living, don't we? I myself fall back on the idea of an everlasting journey through more amusing worlds. But you'd need to travel fast and keep changing your surroundings. This present life, which we're so afraid of losing, is always too long for those who get the hang of it early. Everything keeps repeating itself over and over.

There's only one pleasure, I assure you – to learn something you didn't know before. And one happiness: to love all that's exceptional. And so I love you and send my affectionate greetings.

Your old troubadour

G. Sand

I'm worried about Sainte-Beuve. How greatly he'd be missed! I'm pleased if Bouilhet is pleased. Is it a real job, and a good one?

[1] Maurice would publish his *Catalogue raisonné des Lépidoptères du Berry et de l'Auvergne* in 1879.
[2] The reference is to Book VI of Paul Scarron's *Enéide travestie* (1652), in which Aeneas goes to the underworld. In the view of Jean Bruneau this parody of Virgil is "one of the masterpieces of the Burlesque genre".

77   FLAUBERT TO SAND

[Paris, 17 May 1867]
Friday morning

I return to my mother next Monday, chère maître, and between now and then I have little hope of seeing you. But when you're next in Paris what is there to prevent your continuing on to Croisset, where everyone adores you, including me?

Sainte-Beuve has finally consented to see a specialist and have some serious treatment. Already he feels better – his morale has improved.

Bouilhet's post brings him four thousand francs a year and lodging. Now he need no longer think of "earning his living"[1] – true luxury.

The war talk has stopped – *all* talk has stopped. Only the Exhibition "occupies everyone's attention," and the cab drivers are exasperating all the bourgeois. They (the bourgeois) made a spectacle of themselves during the tailors' strike: you'd have thought "Society" was about to collapse.

Axiom: hatred of the Bourgeois is the beginning of virtue. As for me, I include in the word "bourgeois" the bourgeois in overalls as well as the bourgeois in frock coat. It's we, we alone – that is, the educated[2] – who are the People, or, to put it better, the tradition of Humanity.

Yes, I am given to useless rages, and I love you the more for loving me on that account. Stupidity and injustice make me roar. And I *thunder*, in private, against a lot of things that don't concern me.

How sad not to be living together, chère maître! I admired you before I knew you. And from the day I first saw your beautiful, sweet face I loved you. So! A big kiss.

Your old

G. F.

I'm having the booklets on faïence returned to the rue des Feuillantines. A hearty handshake to Maurice. A kiss on Mademoiselle Aurore's four cheeks.

[1] That is, by doing odd jobs of writing, tutoring, etc., as in the past.
[2] "*les lettrés*".

78   SAND TO FLAUBERT

Nohant, 30 May [18]67

So you're back home, vieux de mon coeur, and Maurice and I must come and say hello to you there. If you're still hard at work we'll only stay a minute. It's so close to Paris there's no need to make an occasion of it.

I, for my part, have finished *Cadio* – phew, what a relief! I've only got to lick it into shape a bit. It's crazy, to have been carrying this great thing around in one's noddle so long. But I was interrupted so often by real illness it was hard to get down to work. However, now the fine weather's here I'm as fit as a fiddle, and am going to take a refreshing dip into botany. Maurice is steeping *him*self in entomology. He and a friend who's in the same case walk for miles over vast moors in search of some little creature you can only see through a magnifying glass. That's genuine happiness! Being well and truly cracked.

My woes faded away as I worked on *Cadio*. Now I'm only fifteen years old, and consider all is for the best in the best of all possible worlds. Who knows how long it will last? Such moods are resurgences of innocence, with youth's inexperience replaced by age's oblivion of evil.

How is dear Maman? Happy to have you with her again, I'm sure. And the novel? Dash it, it must be getting on! Are you walking sometimes and being more sensible?

We had some people here the other day, not too stupid, who talked enthusiastically about *Madame Bovary* but didn't like *Salammbô* so much. Lina flew into a flaming rage and wouldn't let the poor wretches express the slightest criticism. Maurice had to calm her down, and then, speaking as an artist and a scholar, he gave such an excellent appraisal of the book that the renegades surrendered. *I'd* have liked to write what he said. He doesn't often speak, and when he does he often acquits himself badly. But this time he was remarkably good.

I shan't say goodbye, then – only au revoir, because I'll be seeing you as soon as I can manage it. I do love you very much, you know, mon cher vieux. How perfect it would be to spend a long year living close to such a good and great heart. But then one would no longer want to die, and when you really are "vieux", like me, you must be ready for anything.

Maurice joins me in sending much love. Aurore is the sweetest and most waggish creature imaginable. When her father gives her a drink he says "*Dominus vobiscum*," and she drinks and answers "*Amen*". And here she is, walking already. How wonderful it is, the way a child develops! And it's never been done. It would be valuable from every point of view to follow the process day by day. It's one of those things we all see without really seeing them. Farewell again. Think of your old troubadour, who never stops thinking of you.

G. Sand

79 FLAUBERT TO SAND

[Croisset] 12 [June 1867]
Wednesday night

Chère maître,

First, a question: when will you come to Croisset with my friend Maurice? I'm not the only one who longs to see you: my mother feels the same. In a week or so she intends to go to Dieppe and Ouville to be with her two granddaughters. Then, at the end of June, I'll take her to Paris to see the Exhibition. She'd be desolated to miss your visit, and will arrange her plans to suit yours. So, don't stand on ceremony. Come when you wish (except in August). The sooner, and the longer the stay, the better.

Early this week I spent 36 hours in Paris in order to attend the ball at the Tuileries.[1] No joking whatever: it was splendid. Indeed, the whole trend in Paris now is toward the colossal. Everything is becoming crazy and out of proportion. Perhaps we're returning to the ancient East. I keep expecting idols to come out of the ground. There's the threat of a Babylon. And why not? The *individual* has been so negated by Democracy that he'll eventually be wiped out altogether, as under the great theocratic despotisms.

I deeply disliked the Czar of Russia. I thought he was a boor. Just like the noble Floquet, who at no risk to himself shouts "Long live Poland," we have the chic people who sign the visitors' book at the Elysée.[2] What an era!

As for my novel, it goes *piano*. As I advance, new difficulties arise. It's like dragging a heavy cartload of stones. And you complain of something that takes you six months! I still have two years to go, at least. How the devil do you handle transitions of ideas? That's what's delaying me.

Moreover, this book requires tedious research. On Monday, for example, I visited, one after the other, the Jockey Club, the Café Anglais, and an attorney.

Oh, by the way, I forgot to tell you that our friend Chilly read *Le Château des coeurs*.[3] I gather he can't understand a word of it. So the bear has returned to his pit.

Do you like old Hugo's preface to the *Paris-Guide?*[4] Not much, no? To me, Hugo's philosophy always seems vague.

A week ago I was enraptured by an encampment of gypsies who had stopped in Rouen.[5] This is the third time I've seen them, each time with new pleasure. The wonderful thing is that they were arousing the *Hatred* of the Bourgeois, even though they were harmless as lambs. The crowd looked its great disapproval when I gave them a few sous. I heard some delightful remarks à la Prud'homme.[6] This kind of hatred stems from something very deep and complex. It's to be found in all "champions of law and order". It's the hatred felt for the Bedouin, the Heretic, the philosopher, the hermit, the Poet. And there is fear in this hatred. I'm infuriated by it, being always on the side of minorities. It's true that many things infuriate me. The day I stop being indignant I'll fall flat on my face, like a puppet whose prop has been removed.

For example, the stake that held me upright last winter was my indignation against our great national historian M. Thiers, who has been elevated to the status of demigod; and the Trochu pamphlet, and the eternal Changarnier surfacing again.[7] Thank God, the delirium of the Exhibition has delivered us temporarily from those buffoons.

Adieu, chère maître. Let me give you a hug as great and strong as my love for you. Do come! I long to see your illustrious and beloved face.

Gve Flaub.

---

[1] Flaubert had written to Caroline a few days earlier: "Their Majesties wishing to take a look at me, as one of the most splendid curiosities of France, I am invited to spend the evening with them next Monday." After the ball he wrote to Princesse Mathilde: "The Tuileries ball stays in my memory as something from a fairy tale, a dream. The only thing

lacking was an opportunity to have a closer view of you and speak with you. Don't I sound like Madame Bovary, dazzled by her first ball?" To his friend Jules Duplan he wrote: "I did some very good observing. . . . I immediately stored everything I saw, everything I felt, in a corner of my memory, to make use of it at the proper time."

2 The Palais de l'Elysée was being used during the Exhibition to house distinguished guests, the Czar among them. Following the Russian repression of the Polish uprising of 1863, French sympathy for Poland was seized upon by those in opposition to the imperial regime at home. During the Czar's visit to the Sainte-Chapelle on June 4 someone shouted "Vive la Pologne, Monsieur!" Charles Floquet, a leading republican, was generally credited with the "outrage", but denied it, putting the responsibility on Gambetta.

3 It was Sand who had suggested that *Le Château des coeurs* be shown to Chilly at the Odéon.

4 *Paris-Guide* (2 vols.) was published to coincide with the opening of the Exposition Universelle. Many prominent French writers and specialists contributed articles on aspects of the city. In the preface, Hugo proclaimed an "ideal future", in which Paris would be the centre of an utopian Europe.

5 The newspaper *Le Nouvelliste de Rouen* reported on May 30 that "Forty-three individuals of the Zingaro type, come from Hindustan, fleeing the invasion of the Mongols," had arrived in the city two days before and set up their tents in the Cours la Reine. On June 8 the same newspaper announced that they had left on the sixth for Le Havre, where they would take ship for America.

6 Adolphe Thiers, for Flaubert as archetypal a bourgeois as "Joseph Prud'homme" (the character invented by the writer Henri Monnier), had been officially dubbed "national historian" by Napoleon III. He was nevertheless in the opposition, and, on 4 March 1867, had made a speech, lamenting France's loss of prestige because of misgovernment, which brought him much acclaim.

7 General Louis-Jules Trochu had recently published a pamphlet attacking the government for its plans to reorganize the French army. An article on the same subject had appeared in *La Revue des Deux Mondes* for April 15, written by the ex-General Nicolas-Anne-Théodule Changarnier, who had been arrested during the coup d'état of 1851, expelled from France, and given amnesty in 1859. He had until now been living obscurely in the provinces.

80   SAND TO FLAUBERT

Nohant, 14 June [18]67

Cher ami de mon coeur,

I and my son and his wife leave on the 20th of this month to spend a couple of weeks in Paris – perhaps longer if the revival of *Villemer* keeps me. So your good kind mother – *I* don't want to miss *her* either – has plenty of time to go and see her granddaughters. I'll wait for you to let me know in Paris when she's back, or if I pay you a real visit you'll tell me when would suit you best. My immediate intention was just to come and spend an hour with you, and Lina was tempted to come too. I'd have shown her Rouen, then we'd have dropped in to say hello to you and come back to Paris the same evening – the dear girl is always on tenterhooks when she's away from Aurore, and she doesn't often take a day off because of that anxiety. I do understand. Aurore is a sweet treasure and we're all engrossed in her. So if it can be arranged we'll just hurry out and shake hands with you. If that's not possible I'll come later on my own, whenever you feel like it. And if you go to the South of France I'll put it off until all can be accomplished without in any way upsetting your plans, or your mother's. I myself am very free. So don't worry – arrange your own summer and don't be concerned on my account. I have umpteen plans but am not particularly wedded to any of them. What I like is for something to descend on me unexpectedly and carry me off. Travelling is like a novel: it's what happens that counts. But going from Paris to Rouen isn't travelling, and I can always come out at a moment's notice when I'm in town. I feel rather guilty at the thought of taking up whole days when you might be working, though I myself never tire of lounging about. You can leave me for hours under a tree or in front of a log fire, and be sure I'll find something to interest me. I'm very good at living *outside myself*! I haven't always been like that. I was young myself once, and subject to fits of indignation. But that's all over! Ever since I started poking my nose into real Nature I've found in it and its revolutions an order, a consistency, a placidity lacking in man, but which man can to a certain extent assimilate so long as he's not too directly embroiled in the difficulties of his own existence. Of course, when those difficulties present themselves again he has to deal with them as best he can, but if he's drunk of the cup of eternal truth he's no longer too passionately engaged for or against the evanescent and relative variety.

But why am I telling you all this? Merely because it comes to me as I write, for when I really think about it I see that your state of extreme excitability is probably more appropriate, or at any rate more productive and human than my *senile* tranquillity. I wouldn't want to make you resemble me even if by some magic process I could. I wouldn't be interested in myself if I had the honour of meeting me. I'd say one troubadour was quite enough to cope with, and send the other to Chaillot.[1]

Speaking of Bohemians, did you know there were maritime gypsies? I once saw some big boats moored in the shelter of some remote rocks near Tamaris[2] which were inhabited by a very small and very swarthy population of inshore fisherfolk who lived off their catch and what little of it they could sell. They spoke a language of their own that the local people couldn't understand. Their only homes were these boats, which, whenever there was a storm, were blown out of their rocky coves and up on to the sand. They intermarried among themselves and were harmless but dour, and either too shy or too uncouth to answer when spoken to. I forget what they're called. I was told, but it's slipped my mind. I could ask and find out. Naturally the locals loathed them and said they were utterly godless. If so they must be better than we are.

I ventured all alone into their midst. "Good-day, gentlemen." The only answer was a brief nod. I looked at their camp; no one took any notice. It was as if they didn't see me. I asked if my curiosity bothered them. A shrug of the shoulders, as if to say "It's all the same to us." I spoke to a young boy who was very skilfully mending a net, and showed him a gold 5-franc piece. He looked away. I showed him a silver coin. This he did condescend to look at. "Do you want it?" He bent over his work. I put it down beside him. He didn't move. I walked away. He watched me go. When he thought I wasn't watching any more he picked up the coin and went and spoke to some others. I don't know what happened then. I imagine the money went into a common fund. I started botanizing a little way off, where they could see me, to find out whether they'd come and ask me for more or thank me for what I'd given already. No one made the slightest move. I wandered back in their direction, as if by chance. The same silence, the same indifference. An hour later, on the cliffs, I asked the coastguard who these people were who spoke neither French nor Italian nor the local dialect. It was then he told me the name that I've forgotten. According to him they were Moors who'd stayed on the coast since the days of the great invasions of Provence, and maybe he was right. He said he'd looked down from his observation post and seen me mixing with them, and that I shouldn't have done it because they were capable of anything. But when I asked him what harm they did he admitted they didn't do any. They lived off their fishing and even more off flotsam and jetsam, which they got to before anyone else. But they were the object of great contempt. Why? Always the same old story: anyone who behaves differently from everyone else is bound to be doing wrong. If you ever go to that part of the world you might meet some of these people at Point Le Brusq. But they're birds of passage, and it's been some years since they put in an appearance.

I haven't so much as glimpsed the *Paris-Guide*. I should have been sent a copy, as I gave them something without asking any fee. I expect that's why they've forgotten me.

To conclude, I'll be in Paris from 20 June to 5 July. So please write to me there – the address is still 97 Feuillantines. I may stay on longer, but I don't know.

Je t'embrasse tendrement, mon grand vieux. Walk a little, I beg you. I'm not worried about the novel, but I am worried lest you concentrate on your nervous system at the expense of your muscular one. I'm very well, apart from the occasional thunderbolt, when I collapse on to my bed for forty-eight hours and don't want anyone to speak to me. But it doesn't happen often, and so long as I don't weaken and let them call the doctor I'm perfectly well again when I get up. Maurice sends his love. The entomology has started up again this year and he's finding some wonderful things. Give your mother my love and take good care of her. Je vous aime de tout mon coeur.

G. Sand

---

[1] Chaillot, now a quarter of Paris, was at that time a suburb; but as used here the name refers to one of its buildings, an asylum for the insane. Sand is using a popular expression that means merely "The devil take him!"

[2] A village near Toulon.

*

George Sand arrived in Paris on 20 June and attended the opening of the revival of *Le Marquis de Villemer* at the Odéon on 10 July. From her diary: "First night of the revival of *Villemer*. 178th performance. Very well done. Full house. Receipts, after deduction of expenses, 2,080 francs."

81   SAND TO FLAUBERT

[Paris, late June or early July 1867]

Ami,
I'll come whenever you say: I've finished.
Je t'embrasse et je t'aime.

G. Sand

*

But Flaubert was deep in *L'Éducation sentimentale*, the house at Croisset was being repaired, there were guests.
Sand left Paris on July 14th.

82   FLAUBERT TO SAND

[Croisset, 18 July 1867]
Thursday

You must be in Paris, chère maître? Will you still be there a fortnight from now? I'll be bringing my mother to show her the Exhibition.
Is *Villemer* making money? Give me your news. I miss you, and long to kiss you.
Wasn't le père Sainte-Beuve splendid![1]
I'm going to have to be away all of August. But from the beginning of September until mid-February I'll stay right here, in order to push on with the interminable novel that's giving me more and more trouble. We must arrange to meet this autumn: it's too stupid not to see each other a little when we love each other so much.
So – till soon. Mille tendresses
from your old

Gve Flaubert

[1] On 25 June 1867 Sainte-Beuve had delivered a second speech in the Senate, this one against a proposal to ban the works of Voltaire, Rousseau, Michelet, Renan, Sand, etc. from public libraries.

83   SAND TO FLAUBERT

Nohant, 24 July [1867]

Cher bon ami,

I spent three weeks in Paris with the children, hoping you'd either come or send word for me to go and see you. But you were "submerged", and I respect those moods when one has to work; I know all about them myself!

So here I am back in old Nohant, while Maurice is in Nérac negotiating a settlement to end a lawsuit that does him out of his inheritance. His charming father is stealing about 300,000 francs from his children to please his cook.[1] Fortunately, while his lordship was leading this edifying life I was working and not touching my capital. I haven't got anything myself, but I shall leave my heirs enough to live on.

Little Aurore is pretty as a picture and full of charming antics. My daughter Lina remains my real daughter. The other one[2] is well and beautiful, and that's all I ask of her. I'm working again,[3] but not feeling up to much. I'm paying the price for the energy and activity of Paris. But no matter – I hold no grudge against life.

Je t'aime de tout mon coeur. Whenever I'm "gloomy"[4] I see your kind face and feel the goodness radiating from the power of your being. You are a kind of magic amid my peaceful, pure autumnal friendships, devoid of egotism and thus devoid also of disappointment. Think of me sometimes, work well, and send for me if ever you have a spell of idleness. Otherwise, never mind. If you felt like coming here it would be a red-letter day for all of us.

I've seen Sainte-Beuve. I'm pleased with him and proud of him.

Bonsoir ami de mon coeur. Je t'embrasse ainsi que ta bonne mère.

G. Sand

They write that *Villemer* is doing well.

---

[1] Since their separation in 1836, Casimir Dudevant had been living in his château de Guillery, near Nérac, with Jeanny Dalias, whom he had engaged as governess in 1844 and by whom he had a daughter. To forestall the danger of a legacy to this illegitimate daughter, Maurice and Solange had brought a lawsuit against their father that had gone on for several years. The verdict, finally delivered on 20 April 1866, declared Maurice and Solange to be the owners of the buildings at Guillery, whereas their father would keep the land and the income from the part awarded to the children. However, the two parties agreed that the property should be sold, and this was done on 23 July 1867. From the results of the sale, Casimir kept 149,000 francs, Maurice and Solange the rest – 130,000 francs. (From L. Vincent, *G. Sand et le Berry*, Vol. I, p. 623 ff).

[2] Solange, who was on bad terms with her mother.

[3] She was writing *Mademoiselle Merquem*, which would be published in *La Revue des Deux Mondes*, 15 January - 15 March 1868, and in book form a few months later.

[4] In English in the original.

84   FLAUBERT TO SAND

[Croisset, 27 July 1867]
Saturday

That word must be struck out, chère maître: I was not so "submerged" in work as not to want to see you. I have already made enough sacrifices to literature, without adding this one. What happened was that the front of my house was being repainted, and stank to high heaven,[1] so that I spent a fortnight in my mother's flat in Rouen and then a week in the little pavilion at the edge of the garden.[2] That was why we didn't invite a certain dear friend to visit us. But what's to prevent our seeing each other some time from September on? I shall be away all of August: my address for letters will be Boulevard du Temple, 42.

And your work? What is happening with *Cadio*?

I feel as old as a pyramid and as tired as a donkey. My mother doesn't add to my merriment. She grows feebler, more bitter, more sad – and that saddens me also. It's to distract her a little that I'm taking her to the Exhibition.

Nonobstant I continue to plough my furrow, and I hope by the end of the year to have finished my second part. The whole thing won't be done for at least another two years! And then farewell forever to the Bourgeois! Nothing is more exhausting than delving into human stupidity.

Speaking of stupidity, it seems that the world of officialdom is furious with old Sainte-Beuve. Camille Doucet's distress verges on the sublime.[3] For the sake of future liberty, we really ought to bless the religious hypocrisy of the worldly, which so revolts us. The later the question is settled, the better the settlement will be. *They* can only weaken, and *we* can only grow stronger.

Bouilhet and I have written the scenario of a farcical comedy,[4] which it would be fun to stage in your little theatre at Nohant. It's true that the play itself remains to be written! No small task.

Adieu, chère grand et bon maître. Many affectionate kisses from

Gve Flaubert

Greetings to my friend Maurice.

As for coming to Nohant, I reply as we do in Normandy: "I'm not saying no." I'd let you know two or three days in advance.

---

[1] "*schlinguait comme un homme.*"

[2] Although the house at Croisset was demolished soon after Flaubert's death, the pavilion still stands, a rather sad relic in what is now an industrial suburb. It houses a small Flaubert Museum.

[3] Doucet was director of the Administration des Théâtres. The world of officialdom had been angered by Sainte-Beuve's speech.

[4] The "scenario", never developed, seems to have been the few autograph pages, entitled *La Queue de la Poire de la Boule de Monseigneur*, which were sold at auction in Paris in 1933 and printed in facsimile, also in Paris, in 1958. (See p. 106, Note 2, for mention of this work in G. Sand's diary.)

85   SAND TO FLAUBERT

Nohant, 6 August [18]67

When I see the trouble my vieux goes to to write a novel I'm depressed at my own facility and tell myself my work is only botched stuff. I've finished *Cadio*, and it's been in Buloz's clutches for a long while. I'm on something else now, but can't see my way very clearly – what's one to do without sun or warmth? Now is the time I ought to be in Paris, visiting the Exhibition again at leisure and helping you take your mother around. But I must work – that's all I have to live on now. And then there are the children! Aurore really is a wonder. A sight for sore eyes. Perhaps I shan't be seeing her for much longer. I don't think I'm destined to make very old bones: one must love before it's too late!

Yes, you're right, and that's what consoles me. This fit of hypocrisy is storing up a devastating reply, and it won't lose anything by the delay. On the contrary. You'll live to see it, because you're a vieux who's still quite young. You're the same age as my son. You'll laugh together as you watch that heap of rubbish come tumbling down.

You mustn't be a Norman – you must come and stay for a few days. You'll make a lot of people happy, and as for me, it will restore blood to my veins and joy to my heart.

Go on loving your old troubadour and tell him about Paris. Just a few words when you have time. Sketch out something for Nohant with four or five characters and we'll put it on.

Best love and pressing invitations.

G. Sand

*

From 1 or 2 August Flaubert was in Paris. But an intestinal upset spoiled his stay, and he returned to Croisset.

86   SAND TO FLAUBERT

[Nohant] 18 August [18]67

Where are you, mon cher vieux? If by chance you were to be in Paris early in September, do try to arrange for us to meet. I'm to spend three days there and then return here. But I don't really hope to see you in town. You're bound to be in some pleasant region far away from Paris and its dust. I don't even know if my letter will reach you. Never mind – if you can let me hear from you, please do.

I'm in despair. I've suddenly, and without even knowing he was ill, lost my poor dear old friend Rollinat,[1] an angel of goodness, courage and devotion. It's a crushing blow. If you were here you'd help me bear it, but my poor children are just as dismayed as I am. We adored him – the whole region adored him.

Please keep well yourself, and think sometimes of absent friends. We all send much love. The baby is very well and very sweet.

G. Sand

---

[1] François Rollinat, deputy from the département of the Indre to the Assemblée Constituante of 1848, which had proclaimed France a republic and elected Louis-Napoléon president. He and Sand had been friends for thirty-five years.

87 FLAUBERT TO SAND

[Paris] 19 [August 1867]
Monday night

Chère maître,

I didn't answer your letter because I intended to do so "in person". That is, I wanted to come and surprise you at Nohant. But I'd reckoned without the rather bad stomach pains that have been tormenting me for the last twelve days, and a train journey of several hours would be very inconvenient indeed. Now I shall return to Croisset and fresh air, and look after myself.

Why will you be staying in Paris for so short a time? Won't you be able to come as far as Croisset, with your dear son?

I know who Rollinat was. And I am sorry for you, pauvre chère maître. As friends we love disappear, we must cling all the harder to those who remain. That is why I hope to see you at Croisset.

I'm stupefied by the heat – and by my colic (forgive the candour). Still, I have the strength to embrace you and beg you to bestow, as coming from me, four good kisses on Mlle Aurore's four cheeks. Mille tendresses from your old troubadour.

Gve Flaubert

88 SAND TO FLAUBERT

[Nohant, 21 or 22 August 1867]

Bless you, mon cher vieux, for kindly thinking of coming, but you were right not to travel when you were ill. Oh Lord, all I think about is illness and misfortune. Do take good care of yourself, mon vieux camarade. I'll come and see you if I can buck myself up, for since this last blow I've been weak and depressed and dogged by a kind of fever. I'll drop you a line from Paris. If you can't come, send me a telegram. No need for explanations, of course: I know from experience the sort of things that can crop up, and I never doubt the hearts of my friends.

What I'd like now, if you have a moment to write, is your advice as to where to go for a few days to see the Normandy coast without stumbling on places patronized by "society". In order to get on with my novel I need to see a part of the region that hasn't already been dealt with by everyone else, and where there are real local people in their own surroundings: peasants, fishermen, a genuine village among the rocks.[1] If you were in the mood we could go together. Otherwise, don't worry about me. I go about all over the place and never worry about anything. You told me the people who live on the coast are the best there are in those parts – the salt of the earth, some of them. I'd like to see their faces, their clothes, their houses, and the landscapes they live in. That's enough for my purposes; I only need them as props. I don't really mean to describe things; I just need to *see* them, so as not to get the lighting wrong.

How is your mother? Have you been able to take her around and amuse her a little? My love to her and to you.

G. Sand

Maurice sends his love. He's not coming to Paris with me as he's been let in for jury service from 2 September until ... we don't know when. What a chore. Aurore is very flirtatious with her arms, which she holds out to be kissed; her hands are wonderful and incredibly nimble for her age.

So I'll be seeing you soon, if I can hoist myself out of my present state. The worst is not being able to sleep. One makes inordinate efforts during the day so as not to depress other people. But at night one relapses back into oneself.

[1] *Mademoiselle Merquem* is "set" in Normandy.

89 FLAUBERT TO SAND

Croisset, 25 [August 1867]
Sunday

Two places "society" doesn't go to are Arromanches and Grandcamp (both of them villages near Caen); into the bargain, there are very few bathers at Langrune. But an amusing place, with a "special quality", is Cayeux, about fifteen miles beyond Tréport (Seine-Inférieure). The sand dunes are higher than the roofs of the houses; and the boats – like those of the Greeks on the Trojan beach – are drawn up on the shingle. But to see the coast of Normandy properly, chère maître, you must wait for *la saison normande* – autumn, October. The most beautiful cliffs are near Dieppe and Etretat. As for dwellings along the coast – the houses of sailors and fishermen – I'm well acquainted with Honfleur, Trouville and Villerville.[1]

So, if you're not in a hurry with the novel, I advise you to wait until October. You'll come here, and we'll think about making a tour together. It would be even better in mid-winter – not better for me, because I long to see you at once, but for the thing itself.

I'm still exhausted by colic.

My mother asks me to send you a kiss: so here is one from her and one from me. Greetings to your family, and to you all my love.

Gve Flaubert

[1] In his youth Flaubert had spent his holidays in this region.

On 4 September, Flaubert returned to Paris for two days. Then, on holiday, he visited members of his father's family in Champagne and spent a few days with his niece in Dieppe. Returning to Croisset on 20 September, he found the following letter from George Sand:

90 SAND TO FLAUBERT

Nohant, 12 September [18]67

Cher vieux,

I'm worried at not having heard from you since that indisposition of yours. Are you better?

Yes, we'll both go and see the shingle and the cliffs next month, if you feel like it. The novel's galloping ahead, but I can sprinkle the local colour on afterwards.

Meanwhile I'm still here, up to the chin in the river every day and quite getting my strength back in the shady, cold, beloved stream where I've spent so many hours of my life reviving after over-lengthy sessions with the inkpot.

I'm finally going to Paris on the 16th, and on the 17th at 1 o'clock I leave for Rouen and Jumièges, where my friend Mme Lebarbier de Tinan will be waiting for me at the house of M. Lepel-Cointet, landowner. I'll stay there on the 18th and return to Paris on the 19th. Can I be so close to you without coming to say hello? I'll be dying to do so, but I'm so absolutely obliged to spend the evening of the 19th in Paris I don't know if I shall have time.[1] Do let me know. A note from you could reach me in Paris on the 16th at 97, rue des Feuillantines. I shan't be alone: a charming young femme de lettres, Juliette Lamber, will be travelling with me. If you wanted to be really sweet you'd make your way to Jumièges yourself on the 19th, and we could come back together so that I'd be back in Paris at 6 in the evening at the latest. But if you're still at all unwell, or "submerged" in ink, forget I ever suggested it and we'll put off our meeting until next month. As for that *winter* trip to the Normandy strand, it sends cold shivers down my spine – I was planning to go to Golf-Juan then!

It's the death of my poor Rollinat that has made me ill. My body's better now, but the soul . . . ! I need a week with you to recharge myself with the force of affection: cold and purely physical courage is no more help to me than a plaster on a wooden leg.

Love, and to your mother. And from Maurice. What awful French! Let's forget it as soon as possible. Nothing but a bore.

Ton troubadour

G. Sand

[1] On Thursday evening, 19 September, she will attend the opening of the revival of "her" play, *Les Beaux Messieurs de Bois-Doré*. It is in five acts, drawn by Paul Meurice from her novel of the same name. It had first been staged at the Théâtre Ambigu-Comique, 26 April 1862. That night Sand wrote in her diary: "The play seemed charming to me, and very well acted. It was much appreciated: people wept."

91 FLAUBERT TO SAND

[Croisset, 20 September 1867]
Friday, 3 o'clock

Chère maître,

I feel abashed, mortified, cheated! I've just arrived from Dieppe and find your letter from La Châtre. You have already left Jumièges – and so we shan't meet!

Your telegram reached me at Dieppe only yesterday afternoon, and I posted you a note immediately.[1]

So, when shall we see each other in October? From the 1st to the 15th I'll have some visitors from Champagne, who would be in our way. But after the 15th I'll be completely free. A thousand tender greetings from your old

Gve Flaubert

I'm well again. The sea air set me up.

[1] No trace of either document has been found.

92 FLAUBERT TO SAND

[Croisset, 24–25 September 1867]
Tuesday night

Chère maître,

What's this? No news? But you'll answer me now, because I seek your help.

In my notes I find the following: "*National* of 1841. Maltreatment of Barbès. Kicked in the chest; dragged by beard and hair and transferred to an *in-pace*.[1] Consultation with a group of lawyers against these abominations, signed: E. Arago, Favre, Berryer." Find out from Barbès whether that is accurate, will you? I'll be much obliged.[2]

On your way back from Jumièges you must have passed through Canteleu? *So* close to Croisset! But I forgive you because of *Les Beaux Messieurs de Bois-Doré*! Are you happy about it? Is it going well?

I don't yet know when my Nogentais will be leaving. But as soon as they've gone, that's to say about three weeks from now, my mother and I (I especially, I need scarcely say) are counting on you. Those aren't mere words. You *must* come. It's too stupid to go so long without meeting.

I'm afraid I mis-read your street number in my last letter. You received it even so, didn't you?

Till soon, then. Mille tendresses. Je vous embrasse.

Gve Flaubert

[1] Literally "in peace": solitary confinement for life. A synonym is *oubliette*: a place where one is *oublié* – forgotten.

[2] See Letters 62 and 63.

93   SAND TO FLAUBERT

Paris, Tuesday, 1 October [1867]

Cher ami,

You shall have your information. I asked Peyrat yesterday evening and am writing to Barbès today. He'll reply to you direct.

Where do you think I've come from? Normandy! A delightful chance carried me off six days ago. I was fascinated by Jumièges. This time I saw Etretat, Yport – the prettiest of all the villages – Fécamp, Saint-Valery, which I knew already, and Dieppe, which dazzled me, together with places like the château d'Arques and the ruined city of Limes nearby. What a region! So I passed quite close to Croisset again, twice, and sent you lots of kisses, and am always ready to go back with you to the seaside and to chat with you at your place whenever you're free. If I'd been on my own I'd have bought an old guitar and come and sung a serenade under your mother's window. But I couldn't bring a whole *smala*[1] down on you.

I'm going back to Nohant et je t'embrasse de tout mon coeur.

G. Sand

I believe the *Bois-Doré* is doing well, but I don't know. I have a way of being in Paris while being by the English Channel which rather prevents me from keeping in touch. But I *have* picked gentians among the tall grasses in the huge oppidum at Limes, with a view over the sea – pretty marvellous, that. I've covered the ground like an old horse, and I return full of beans.

[1] From the Arabic. The tents of a powerful chief – his mobile home: hence, "household", "large family", "tribe". Sand had been travelling with several friends.

94   FLAUBERT TO SAND

[Croisset, 8 October 1867]
Tuesday evening

Chère maître,

I enclose a few lines of thanks for Barbès, who has written me a charming, fascinating letter.[1] Since I am far from having a "patriotic" past, and since I was bellowing out sentences "in the silence of my sanctum" while he was risking his life in the streets in the cause of liberty, I didn't think it appropriate for me to tell him how very highly I think of him: I'd have seemed like a sycophant. What first gave me a high opinion of this man is the account (written by himself)[2] of the days when he was awaiting execution. He read Lord Byron and smoked his pipe. Rather decent! Besides, he loved liberty, *without spouting empty phrases*: like a figure in Plutarch. Furthermore he seems to me to have remained on the high, right road, whereas the rest (almost all of us) have strayed from it, alas.[3]

Now perhaps we are very gradually returning to it, and by the right track – by way of an issue on which all else depends: the religious question. Whatever may soon be happening in Italy,[4] and whatever the result may later be for France, we are witnessing the last hour, the last gasp, of "government by Grace". Justice is rising over the horizon. All is well.[5]

Re-reading my notes on '48, I am astonished by the enormous role played by *messieurs les ecclésiastiques*! and I'm no longer surprised by the outcome.

But: amidst all that, when are you and I going to see each other for God's sake?

What an idea, to come back to Normandy and pass by Rouen without letting me know! Such behaviour must be expiated.

My Champenois are still here. But they'll be gone in a week; and even if they aren't. . . .

The fact is, I'm *dying* to see you. A hug from your old.

                                                            Gve Flaubert

[1] After hearing from Sand, Barbès had written directly to Flaubert on 2 October, giving a vivid account of maltreatment during his imprisonment. For Barbès' letter and Flaubert's reply of the 8th sent via Sand, and for Flaubert's use of Barbès' details in *L'Éducation sentimentale*, see *The Letters of Gustave Flaubert*, II, 108–11.

[2] *Deux jours de condamnation à mort* (Paris, 1848).

[3] This reproach to "almost all of us" often recurs in Flaubert's correspondence. He refers to the literary men, the scholars, the intellectuals – the "mandarins", as he often calls them – who followed, or were supposed to follow, Voltaire's "high road", the road of free thought. He contrasts them with the bourgeois, the professional politicians, the neo-Catholics, and the revolutionaries influenced by Christian ideals.

[4] In 1864 Napoleon III had made a pact with Victor Emmanuel binding the Kingdom of Italy not to attack Papal territory, while France promised to withdraw her troops gradually from Rome. Accordingly, the last French troops had left by the end of 1866. But during the summer of 1867 Garibaldi had threatened Rome: arrested by order of the Italian government he had been imprisoned; but shortly thereafter he escaped and was soon again at the gates of Rome.

[5] The concepts of "government by Grace" and "government by Justice" are to be found in Michelet's optimistic introduction to his *Histoire de la Révolution*.

95   SAND TO FLAUBERT

                                                Nohant, 12 October [1867]

I sent your letter on to Barbès; it's good and worthy, like yourself. I know it will make the excellent fellow happy.

But I feel like jumping out of the window, because the children won't hear of my going away again so soon. Yes, it's very stupid to have seen your roof 4 times without going in. But I'm sometimes so scrupulous it amounts to dread. I did think of asking you to Rouen for twenty minutes while I was there. But you're not like me, who've got itchy feet and am always ready to leave at a moment's notice. You live in your dressing-gown, the great enemy of freedom and activity. To make you dress and go out, perhaps in the middle of an engrossing chapter, merely to meet someone who isn't any good at impromptu speech and whom happiness only makes more stupid! – I just didn't feel I could do it.

I've also got to finish something that's been dragging on, and before the last going-over I'll probably make another trip to Normandy. I'd like to sail up the Seine to Honfleur; that'll be next month if the cold doesn't make me ill. And this time I shall try to carry you off in passing. At the very least I shall see you, and then I'll go to Provence.

Oh, if only I could carry you off to there! And if only you could, if only you would, come and see me here in the second half of October, when you're going to be free! You did promise, and it would make the children so happy! But you don't love us enough for that, you blackguard! You imagine you've got lots of better friends. But there you're quite wrong; it's always the best who are neglected and ignored.

Come on now, make an effort! You leave Paris at a quarter past 9 in the morning, arrive at Châteauroux at 4, find my carriage waiting, and are here by 6 for dinner. It's not that bad a journey, and here we lead an easy, rough and ready, self-sufficient life, without dressing up, without ceremony, with plenty of affection. Say yes.

Je t'embrasse. I too find it dreadful that it's *a year* since I saw you.

Ton vieux troubadour

96 SAND TO FLAUBERT

Nohant, 27 October [1867]

I've just been summarizing in a few pages my impressions, as a landscape painter, of what I saw in Normandy. That's of no consequence, but I was able to quote three lines from *Salammbô* that seem to me to depict the countryside better than all my own phrases. The passage in question has always struck me as a masterly piece of work. As I was leafing through the pages to find it I naturally re-read most of the book, which I'm convinced is one of the finest of all books ever.

I'm well and working well and hard, so as to be able to live "off my income" this winter in the South of France. But what will the delights of Cannes be to me, and where shall I find the heart to plunge into them? It makes me so glum to think of us fighting for the Pope![1]

I've tried in vain this month to go and see "my Normandy" – i.e. mon gros cher ami de coeur – again. The children threatened to slay me if I left them so soon. And now we've got company coming. You're the only one who talks about not coming. And it would be so nice! But next month I'll stop at nothing to be with you wherever you are, and meanwhile I love you very very much.

And how are you? And the work? And your mother's health? And yours? I'm worried at not hearing from you.

G. Sand

¹ Because in his opinion the Italian government was not doing enough to prevent Garibaldi from entering Rome, Napoleon III, after two warnings, sent several regiments, which reached Rome on 30 October. This exasperated King Victor Emmanuel, and he ordered his troops to enter Roman territory: however, wishing to avoid war with France, he withdrew a few days later. On 3 November, French and pontifical troops defeated the Garibaldians at Mentana.

97   FLAUBERT TO SAND

[Croisset] Wednesday 30
[October 1867]

Chère maître,

I was as shamed as I was touched, last night, on receiving your "very kind epistle". I'm a wretch not to have answered your previous one. What can have happened? – because in such matters I'm usually not unreliable.

Work goes not too badly. I hope to finish my second part in February. But if the whole thing is to be done in two years, this old fellow mustn't budge from his chair during that time. That is why I don't come to Nohant. One week of vacation would mean for me three months of day-dreaming. I'd do nothing but think about you, and yours, and the Berry, and everything I'd seen. My wretched mind would be navigating in distant waters. I have so little energy! I'm such a hopeless case!

I'll not conceal from you the pleasure your little mention of *Salammbô* gave me. That book needs to be pruned of certain inversions; there are too many "then"s, "but"s and "and"s. The writer's labour is too apparent.¹

As for the one I'm writing, I'm afraid the idea itself may be defective: and for that there's no remedy. Will such vague characters interest anybody? Grand effects are achieved only by simple things and clear-cut passions. But I see simplicity nowhere in the modern world.

A sad world! How deplorable and lamentably grotesque, what is happening in Italy! All these orders, counter-orders, and countering of counter-orders! The earth is certainly a very inferior planet.²

You haven't told me whether you were satisfied with the revivals at the Odéon. When will you go to the Midi? And where abouts, in the Midi?

Beginning a week from today, I'll be in Paris for three days – 7 to 10 November. I have to wander about a bit in Auteuil, to find some suitable little corners there.³ What would be nice would be for us to return to Croisset together. You well know that I hold your two last visits to Normandy against you.

Till soon, no? No if's or but's. I kiss you the way I love you, chère maître – by which I mean very tenderly.

Gve Flaubert

Bonjour chère Dame, merci de vous souvenir encore d'une vieille bourgeoise comme moi.

Votre bien dévouée
Cne Flaubert
J'aurai bien du plaisir à vous voir, et j'espère que vous viendrez bientôt.[4]

[Omitted from the translation of this letter are, again, a few lines of bathetic French verse that Flaubert had found and that he thought might amuse Maurice].

[1] Flaubert made many small alterations in later editions of *Salammbô*. Scholars have noted 128 eliminations of conjunctions and adverbs for the Charpentier edition of 1874, and 187 more for the Lemerre edition of 1879.
[2] Flaubert is quoting a remark by Littré. (See Letter 410.)
[3] Chiefly to find a proper address for Mme Arnoux' suburban house, in *L'Éducation sentimentale*.
[4] In French these lines written by Flaubert's mother have a charming flavour – a tone of dignified respect, and at the same time diffident affection, for someone recognized as a special being. Something like:
"Bonjour, dear lady: Thank you for still remembering a simple old person like me. . . . I should greatly enjoy seeing you again, and hope that you will come soon."

98   FLAUBERT TO SAND

Croisset, 3 December [1867]
Tuesday

I do not think this is nice. No news for what will soon be two months!!! Why? I begin to be worried.

That is all I have to tell you, chère maître, except that I give you a big hug. Le vieux

Gve Flaubert

99   SAND TO FLAUBERT

Nohant, 5 December [18]67

I agree, your vieux troubadour is horrible. He worked like a horse to earn the wherewithal to go away this winter to Golf-Juan, and now it's time to leave he wants to stay. He doesn't like the thought of leaving his children and little Aurore; but he *is* suffering from the cold, he *is* afraid of anaemia, and he thinks it's his duty to seek a place that's not made impracticable by snow, and skies beneath which one can breathe without the sensation of needles sticking into one's lungs. So that's the situation.

He has been thinking of you, probably more than you of him, for his work comes to him stupidly and easily, and when his hand tires of writing his thoughts wander about far away from him and his task. But you really work, and concentrate, and you couldn't have heard my mind going tap-tap more than once at the door of your study to say "It's me!" Or else you just thought to yourself, "It's a sprite – let him go to the devil!"

Aren't you coming to Paris? I'll be there from the 15th to the 20th. I'm just staying in town for a few days, and then off to Cannes. Will you be there? Please heaven you will!

All in all I'm fairly well. I'm furious with you for not coming to Nohant, but I don't say so because I'm no good at complaining. I've covered lots of paper with squiggles. My children are still excellent and good to me in every sense of the word. Aurore is an angel.

We *have* fumed over politics, but are trying to be patient and not to think about it any more.[1]

We think of you often, and love you. Especially your old troubadour, who sends you all her love and asks to be remembered to your good mother.

G. Sand

[1] French feelings about Italy were running high. Republicans were vociferously opposing French intervention, whereas a leading conservative was cheered in the Chamber of Deputies for shouting: "Never will Italy enter Rome! Never!"

100 FLAUBERT TO SAND

[Croisset, 18–19 December 1867]
Wednesday night

Chère maître, chère amie du Bon Dieu,

"*Parlons un peu de Dozenval!*"[1] Let's do some roaring against M. Thiers![2]

Is it possible to find a more triumphant imbecile, a more abject ass, a more turd-like[3] bourgeois? No! Nothing can give an idea of the vomiting inspired in me by this old diplomatic idiot, rounding out his stupidity like a melon ripening on a dung heap – the dung heap of the bourgeoisie! Is it possible to treat philosophy, religion, peoples, liberty, the past and the future, history, natural history – everything and all the rest – with more naive, inept crudity? To me he seems as eternal as mediocrity itself! I'm flattened by the very thought of him.

But what is really splendid is our glorious National Guard, whom he threw into the clink in 1848, now beginning to cheer him again! What infinite madness! It only goes to show that Temperament is everything. Prostitutes, like France, have a weakness for old humbugs.

I shall try, in the third part of my novel (when I reach the reaction that followed the June Days) to slip in a panegyric of said gentleman, apropos of his book on Property, and I hope he'll be pleased with me.

What is the best form in which to express one's opinion, occasionally, about affairs of this world without risking being taken later for a fool? It's a difficult problem. It seems to me that the best way is simply to depict the things that exasperate you. Dissection is a form of revenge.

Well, he's not the one I blame, nor the rest of them – but *us*. If we had followed the high road of Mr de Voltaire instead of taking little neo-Catholic byways, if we had thought a little more about Justice instead of preaching so much about Fraternity, if we had concerned ourselves with educating the upper classes and left the Agricultural Fairs until later – if, in short, we had put the Head before the Stomach, we probably wouldn't be where we are now.[4]

This week I read Buchez' preface to his *Histoire parlementaire*.[5] It was Parlement and other places like it that disseminated much of the nonsense that weighs on us today.

And then it's unkind to say that I'm not thinking of my old troubadour. What else would I be thinking of? My book, perhaps? But that comes less readily and gives less pleasure.

Until when do you stay in Cannes? I'm jealous of Mme Lamber. After Cannes won't you return to Paris? I'll be there towards the end of January.

If I'm to finish my book by the spring of 1869, I mustn't take a single week of vacation. That's why I don't come to Nohant. It's the old story of the Amazons:[6] the better to draw the bow, they flattened their breasts. But is that such a good method, after all?

Adieu, chère maître. Write to me, won't you? I send you great affection.

Gve Flaubert

It's three o'clock. Now I'm going to down a cup of chocolate, thinking of our suppers of last year. Can't we repeat them? My mother often speaks to me of Mme Sand, whom she "likes very much."

[1] These words, put between quotation marks by Flaubert, have not been identified.

[2] Thiers, using historical, philosophical and religious arguments, had come out against the unification of Italy and that of Germany, both of which he considered dangerous for France.

[3] *Etroniforme* – term coined by Flaubert.

[4] Flaubert, probably influenced by Renan, would always be convinced that the education of the upper classes should precede that of "the people".

[5] *Histoire parlementaire de la Révolution française, ou Journal des Assemblées nationales depuis 1789*, a massive collection of documents published by Philippe Buchez in collaboration with Roux-Laverne (40 vols., 1833–38).

[6] The word "Amazon" (from the Greek) connotes "without breasts". Legend has it that a race of warrior women in Scythia amputated the right breast of their daughters at an early age in order to make their right arm stronger and more adept at drawing the bow.

101   SAND TO FLAUBERT

Nohant, 21 December [1867]

At last! At last someone agrees with me about that boor of a politician. It could only be you, ami de mon coeur. "Turd-like" is a sublime expression to describe this kind of "merdoid" vegetable. I have friends who are quite good fellows yet who kowtow to any sign of opposition, whatever it's like and wherever it comes from, and who regard this empty-headed charlatan as a god. But they've had their tails between their legs since that speech with all the stops out. They're beginning to think he goes a bit too far, and maybe it's a good thing that in support of parliamentary supremacy the rascal has emptied out his huckster's packful of dead cats and cabbage stumps in front of everybody. It'll open some people's eyes. Yes, you ought to dissect this balloon of a soul and cobweb of a talent! Unfortunately by the time your book comes out he may have snuffed it and no longer be dangerous – such men leave nothing behind them. On the other hand perhaps he'll be in power; anything is possible. In that case it'll teach him a lesson.

I don't go along with you about the need to flatten the breast in order to draw the bow. I personally act in accordance with a completely opposite belief, which I think valid for many if not most other people. I've just set out my views on the subject in a novel that I've sent to the *Revue*[1] and that's due to appear after About's.[2] I think an artist ought to live as much as possible in accordance with his own nature. Let those who like fighting have war; those who like women, love; let old stagers like me who like nature and travel and flowers have rocks, great landscapes, children, a family, everything that militates against moral anaemia. I think art calls for a palette brimming over with both soft and strong colours, to be used according to the subject of the picture, and that an artist is an instrument on which everything ought to play before he starts playing on others. But perhaps all this doesn't apply to a mind like yours, which has acquired much and merely needs to digest. I insist on one point only, which is that one's physical being is a necessary adjunct to one's moral being, and I worry lest some day a deterioration in your health might force you to suspend your work and let it grow cool.

Anyhow, you're coming to Paris early in January and we shall see each other, for I'm not going to town until after the New Year. My children have made me promise to spend New Year's Day with them, and I couldn't refuse despite a great need for locomotion. They're so sweet! Maurice is always cheerful and inexhaustibly inventive. He's turned his puppet theatre into a marvel of sets and effects and various "*trucs*" or capers, and the plays they put on in those delightful surroundings are incredibly imaginative. The most recent is called *1870*. It shows Isidore, together with Antonelli,[3] leading the Calabrian brigands in an attempt to regain his throne and restore the Papacy. Everything else is to match. At the end the Widow Ugénie marries the Grand Turk,[4] the only sovereign left standing. Admittedly he's a former "*démoc*", and it's agreed he's only the great ladykiller in disguise.[5] The plays last until 2 in the morning and everyone's wild at the end. Supper goes on till 5 a.m. There are two perform- ances a week, and the rest of the time they do "*trucs*", in which the play continues with the same characters having the most incredible adventures. The audience consists of 8 or 10 young men, my three great-nephews and the sons of some old friends of mine. They get so excited they shriek. Aurore isn't allowed in; she's not old enough yet for such entertainments. I laugh until I'm exhausted, and I'm sure you'd enjoy yourself hugely too – the improvisations are done with such splendid freedom and verve, and the characters Maurice has carved look just as if they're alive and leading a farcical existence at once real and impossible. As in a dream.

That's how I've been passing the time in the fortnight since I stopped working. Maurice provides me with this kind of recreation when my intervals of rest coincide with his own, and he brings as much passion and enthusiasm to it as he does to science. He really is of a happy disposition, and one's never bored in his company. His wife is charming – very round at the moment, but carrying her little tummy[6] proudly, always on the go, taking care of everything, lying down on the sofa twenty times a day, getting up again to run to her daughter, her cook or her husband, who keeps asking for things for his theatre, coming back to lie down again, calling out that she's got a pain, roaring with laughter at a fly, sewing baby clothes, reading newspapers that make her cross and novels that make her cry, and weeping again whenever the puppet theatre gets a bit emotional, for it does deal in feelings too. In short, she's a personality and a character; sings beautifully, is both irascible and affectionate, and cooks delicious treats to "surprise" us. Every day of this resting-period of ours is a little fête organized by her.

Young Aurore looks as if she's going to be very gentle and thoughtful: she's wonderfully quick to understand what's said to her, and *is accessible to reason* at 2 years old. It's quite extraordinary: I've never seen such a thing before. It would even be rather worrying if one didn't sense a great tranquillity in the workings of that little brain.

But how I do run on when I'm talking to you! Does it amuse you? I hope so, and that a chatty letter makes up to you for one of our suppers, which I miss too, and which would be so nice *here* if you didn't have a leaden posterior that won't let you be enticed into *life for life's sake*. Oh, how strange and nonsensical work and logic and reason all seem when one's on holiday! You wonder if you'll ever be able to go back to the old grind.

Je vous embrasse tendrement, mon cher vieux, and Maurice thinks your letter's so fine he's going to put words and phrases from it straight into the mouth of his chief philosopher.[7] He won't forget turd-like, which he finds delightful; turdiform, turdifer. . . . He tells me I'm to kiss you for it.

Ton vieux troubadour qui t'aime.

Mme J. Lamber is really charming; you'd like her very much.[8] What's more, it's 18 degrees above zero down there, and here we have to walk through the snow. It's very disagreeable, so we seldom go out, and even my dog[9] won't go and pee. He's not the least splendid member of our society. If anyone calls him Badinguet[10] he lies down looking desperately ashamed and sulks for the rest of the evening.

¹ *Mademoiselle Merquem* would be published in *La Revue des Deux Mondes* from 15 January to 15 March 1868.

² Edmond About's *Les Mariages de province*.

³ Isidore was one of Napoleon's nicknames. French republicans deplored the strong influence exerted by Cardinal Antonelli on Pope Pius IX.

⁴ Abd-ul-Aziz, sultan of Turkey from 1861 to 1876. The early years of his reign had been marked by liberal reforms: hence Sand's "former '*démoc*'".

⁵ "Coq-en-bois", one of the most amusing of the Nohant marionettes.

⁶ Her daughter Gabrielle would be born on 12 March 1868.

⁷ Probably "Balandard", the "chief" marionette, who always opened the performance by announcing the programme.

⁸ Flaubert would later meet Juliette Lamber (Mme Adam) and would promise her *Bouvard et Pécuchet* for her magazine, *La Nouvelle Revue*.

⁹ The beloved Fadet.

¹⁰ Another of Napoleon III's nicknames.

CHAPTER IV

1868

[Croisset] 1 January [1868]

Trite as it may seem to wish someone a happy New Year, that's in fact what I wish you, chère maître. Mathieu Lansberg's prediction[1] – "Today, as always on this day, there will be much kissing of the Judas kind" – does not touch our case. Quite simply, I embrace you with great affection.

It's unkind of you to depress me with tales of the good times at Nohant, since I can't be part of them. It takes me so long to achieve so little, that I haven't a moment to lose (or gain) if I'm to finish my tome by the summer of 1869.

I didn't say that we must suppress the heart's affections. Only curb them, alas!

As for my way of life, which violates all rules of health, it doesn't date from yesterday. I'm long accustomed to it. Still, I am suffering from a clear case of exhaustion, and it's time for me to finish my Part Two, after which I'll go to Paris. That will be towards the end of this month. You don't tell me when you'll be back from Cannes. Let's hope we'll not be as foolish in 1868 as we were in 1867, and that we'll see each other.

Lord, this cold![2]

My best to Maurice. And to you, chère maître, mille tendresses from

Gve Flaubert

P.S. My fury against Monsieur Thiers has not abated. Far from it! It's becoming an *ideal*, and it's growing.

[1] The allusion is to an almanac, which had first appeared in 1636, entitled *Almanach de Liège*, and was attributed to Matthieu de Liège, a canon of Liège cathedral. It predicted events, gave medical advice, etc. It continued to be published in Flaubert's day, its title changed to "Almanach Liègeois." [Jean Bruneau]

[2] Most of France was suffering from a particularly cold winter. At Rouen and Paris the Seine was frozen over and could be crossed by carriages.

103   SAND TO FLAUBERT

Nohant, 12 January [1868]

No, it's not stupid to exchange kisses on New Year's Day. On the contrary, it's good and kind. I thank you for thinking of it, and kiss you on your beautiful big eyes. Maurice sends love too.

I'm cooped up here by the snow and the cold, and my journey is postponed.[1] We're enjoying ourselves *hugely* at home so as to forget that we're prisoners, and I'm extending my holiday quite crazily. Not a stroke of work from morn till night. How good it will be when you can say the same! But what a beautiful winter, eh? Isn't it lovely, the moonlight on the snow-covered trees? Do you look out at the night as you work?

If you go to Paris at the end of the month I might still be able to meet you there.

But from near or far, cher vieux, I think of you and love you with all my old heart, which knows nothing of the mounting up of the years.

G. Sand

Affectionate greetings, as ever, to your mother. I suppose she's in Rouen during this cold weather.

[1] Alphonse Jacobs, in a note, says that there was another reason for the postponement: George Sand's daughter, Solange Clésinger, had arrived at Cannes, accompanied by "a foreign prince", and Sand had no wish to see them.

*

We know from George Sand's diary that she and Flaubert saw each other in Paris in February, when they dined chez Magny with Maxime Du Camp and Prince Napoléon; but any letters that may have been written between 12 January and 15 March are missing. Sand had been making her postponed visit to the south of France.

104   FLAUBERT TO SAND

[Paris] bd du Temple 42
Sunday evening 15 [March 1868]

Well? A nice thing, I must say! No news for over a month! If it weren't for Harrisse I wouldn't even know where to write to you, chère maître.

He told me that you'd soon be returning to Paris, and would then go on to Nohant. And after that? Paris again, no? And then to Croisset.

Please: a little note, eh? A line in the dear handwriting that I. . . . etc.

Je vous aime et vous embrasse tendrement.

Your old troubadour

Gve Flaubert

On March 17th, in a letter that has not been found, Sand wrote to Flaubert of the birth, at Nogent, of another granddaughter.

105 FLAUBERT TO SAND

[Paris, 19 March 1868]

A thousand respects to Mlle Gabrielle, compliments to her maman, and two great fond kisses to her grand'mère!

So: news from you at last, chère maître – and good news, which makes it doubly pleasant.

I shan't leave Paris before May 20th. But in mid-April I'll be away for forty-eight hours in Champagne, for the wedding of a cousin who wants me as her witness. Then I hope to return to my rural abode with Mme Sand, and my mother hopes the same. What do you say? Because otherwise, what with all these comings and goings, we never manage to meet, damn it!

As for my moving about, it's not the wish to do so that's lacking. But I'd be *lost* were I to budge before the end of my novel. Your friend here is made of wax: everything leaves a mark on him – a mark that goes deep and endures. On my return from a visit to you I'd be thinking only of you, your family, your house, your part of the world, the faces of the people I'd met, etc. To concentrate costs me enormous effort. The slightest thing distracts me. That, my dear, good, adored maître, is why I don't allow myself to visit you, to sit down and dream aloud with you. But by the summer (or autumn) of 1869 I'll be let loose into the fresh air, and you'll see me behaving like a veritable travelling salesman. I'll be impossible, I warn you. As for news, everything is quiet again since the charming demise of the Kervéguen incident. What a farce! And so stupid.[1]

Sainte-Beuve is preparing a speech on the Press Law. His health is decidedly better. On Tuesday I dined with Renan. He was marvellously witty and eloquent. More of an *artist* than I have ever known him to be. Have you read his new book?[2] The preface is much spoken of.

I worry about poor Théo.[3] To me he seems far from robust.

It was good of you to answer me so promptly. And I love you with all my heart. Your old troubadour.

Gve Flaubert

When will I be able to read *Cadio?* When will it appear as a book?

[1] On 10 December 1867, the vicomte de Kervéguen, deputy from the Var, had declared to the Legislature – on the basis of a report in a Belgian newspaper – that Bismarck had given fifty thousand thalers to several of the chief French newspapers. A *jury d'honneur* had declared the report unfounded, but the accusation had been repeated in the Legislature by Granier de Cassagnac on 19 February 1868.

[2] *Questions contemporaines.* It opens with an article written in 1859, predicting a liberal hereditary monarchy.

[3] Théophile Gautier.

Sand's list of "Letters answered" records two to Flaubert, 23 March and 1
April, both now lost.

106 FLAUBERT TO SAND

[Paris] Saturday [4 April 1868]

Mon chère maître,

Information, please. What is the address of the terrible Couture? And about
how much would a man like this charge a bourgeoise like my niece (the niece
you know) for a portrait such as the one he did of you?[1]

In your last letter, among other nice things, you praise me for not being
"lofty". One cannot be lofty with someone who stands high. Thus *you* cannot
judge whether I am lofty or not.

Though I do think of myself as a kindly sort of fellow, I'm not always an
agreeable gentleman, as may be demonstrated by something that happened last
Thursday. After lunching with a lady whom I called an imbecile, I visited
another lady whom I called an idiot. Such is my old French gallantry. The first
had been boring me to death with her talk about spirituality and her pretensions
to "the ideal". The second had made me indignant by calling Renan a scoundrel
(she admitted she hadn't read his books). There are things that put me out of
patience. And when someone belittles a friend to my face, my savage blood[2]
boils over: I see red. Nothing could be more foolish: it achieves nothing, and
leaves me feeling wretched.

That vice, by the way – the failure to defend one's friends against other
people – seems to be taking on gigantic proportions, don't you agree?

During Easter week I go to Champagne to be a witness at a cousin's wedding.
That will occupy three days. Then I'll return here and wait for you.

What about your fever?

And Miss [sic] Gabrielle?

Friendly greetings to all. But to you my affection.

Gve Flaubert

[1] See Letter 29.
[2] According to family legend, one of Mme Flaubert's ancestors had returned from
Canada with an Indian wife.

*

Sand's reply, written on April 11th, has disappeared, but we know from one of
Flaubert's letters to his niece that it confirmed reports he had received from
others about improper behaviour by the painter Thomas Couture. It also contained Sand's promise to visit Croisset in the near future.

107   FLAUBERT TO SAND

[Paris] Monday 13 [April 1868]

Mon chère maître,

I'll be back in my rural abode by May 20 or 24. So you have time to do your packing. Besides, you mustn't travel in such abominably cold weather as this. Your friend has a frightful grippe – which won't keep him from setting out for Champagne tomorrow to act the sheik[1] as Witness. What a rôle!

Last night the Prince[2] and I had a long talk about you. I was touched by his great respect and affection for you.

Have you read the preface to *La Dame aux camélias?* Do you know the abominable story about Mme Feydeau?[3] etc. etc. Ah, I long to see you, to relieve myself of a lot of things that aren't fit to put on paper.

You must spend at least a week with your old troubadour – not two days!

My mother is sitting here beside me and adds her entreaties to mine. . . . *Ex imo. . . .*[4]

Gve Flaubert

Write to me in Paris. I'll be there at the end of this week. How is Mme Plessy? Greetings to all.

[1] Ever since his trip to Egypt Flaubert had enjoyed using the term "sheik" to convey "self-important old bourgeois".

[2] Prince Napoléon (Jérôme).

[3] The yellow press had printed a false report in March, 1868, that the wife of the playwright Ernest Feydeau, Flaubert's friend, had stolen lace from a shop, "on an impulse due to her pregnancy", and that her lover had returned the stolen goods. The shoplifting had in fact been done by Feydeau's sister, abetted by her daughter.

[4] *Ex imo corde* ("from the bottom of my heart"). Victor Hugo had used the expression in one of his letters to Flaubert from Jersey in 1853. [J. B.]

*

Sand had apparently told Flaubert, either in her missing letter of April 11th or subsequently, that she would arrive in Paris on May 5th, to remain about a month.

108   FLAUBERT TO SAND

[Paris, 5 May 1868?]
Tuesday, 3 o'clock

Chère maître,

I'm just going to pass by, on the off chance. I wonder if I'll find you in.

If you aren't busy this evening, let me know by messenger chez Mme Commanville, rue de Luxembourg 35. I'll be there until 9 o'clock, and would join you wherever you like.

I'm busy tomorrow evening and the next. But on Friday and Saturday I'm completely free.

If by chance you're in my part of town tomorrow, I'll be here until 6 o'clock. But I'll be out all day Thursday.

Je vous embrasse.

Gve

*

The date of the above letter is uncertain. In any case, Flaubert and Sand did see each other on the evening of the 5th, and during the next few weeks would exchange many short notes.

109 FLAUBERT TO SAND

[Paris, 9 May 1868]
Saturday morning

Chère maître,

Be ready to leave for Croisset at the beginning of next week – that is, towards the 18th or 20th. Does that suit you?

I shan't be calling on you, because 1° I'm afraid of not finding you in, and 2° because I have a lot of little things to do just now.

Mille tendresses from the old troubadour. . . .

Gve Flaubert

110 SAND TO FLAUBERT

Paris, 10 May [1868]

Yes, ami de mon coeur, though I myself haven't any real troubles, poor little Mme Lambert *is* in danger.[1] I saw M. Depaul today. We have to be prepared for anything! If the crisis is over or delayed, for there's some question of *inducing* the event, I'll be very glad to spend a couple of days with my vieux troubadour que j'aime tendrement.

G. Sand

[1] Esther Lambert, wife of the painter Eugène Lambert, was facing a possibly dangerous confinement.

111 SAND TO FLAUBERT

[Paris, 11 May 1868]
Monday evening

If you were at home on Wednesday evening I'd come and have an hour's chat alone with you after dining in your part of town. I rather despair of getting to Croisset. It's tomorrow they decide the fate of my poor friend.

A word in reply will suffice, and whatever you do don't alter any of your plans. Whether I see you or not, I know the two old troubadours are fond of one another!

G. Sand

112 FLAUBERT TO SAND

[Paris, 12 May 1868]
Tuesday, 9 o'clock

No, chère maître, don't come tomorrow evening, because I'll be dining chez la Princesse and it will be impossible for me to be home before 11 o'clock.

I'm planning to pay you a little visit some morning this week, before noon, and we'll make our arrangements then.

I grieve for your grief and am tormented by your worry.

Et je vous embrasse comme je vous aime, c'est-à-dire tendrement.

Le vieux

Gve Flaubert

113 FLAUBERT TO SAND

[Paris, 13 May 1868]
Wednesday, 3 o'clock

Chère maître,

Would you like to dine with me at Magny's *next Friday*? I have errands to do in your neighbourhood from 4 o'clock to 6.

If this suits you, no need to reply.

Mille tendresses du vieux

Gve Flaubert

114 SAND TO FLAUBERT

[Paris, 17 May 1868]
Sunday

I have a brief respite because they've decided not to induce the birth. So I hope to come and spend a couple of days at dear Croisset; so don't you go and leave before Thursday. I've invited the Prince to dine at Magny's, and I've told him I'll get you to come too, by force if necessary. Tell me you will, as quick as you can.

Je t'embrasse et je t'aime.

G. Sand

115 FLAUBERT TO SAND

[Paris, Monday 18 May 1868]

Chère maître,

Not only shall I not be dining with you on Wednesday – I shan't be seeing you before you come to Croisset. When will that be?

Because I'm leaving Paris immediately, so full of rage that I'm afraid I'll burst. It is now 2 in the afternoon. And since this morning I have tried *two hotels* without being able to sleep. I haven't closed an eye since Friday night. My poor noddle is splitting.[1]

Forgive me – we'll see each other soon.

Mille tendresses.

Gve Flaubert

[1] In a serio-comic letter to the Goncourts written a few days later Flaubert lists the noises that had kept him awake. [*The Letters of Gustave Flaubert*, II, 114–15.]

116 SAND TO FLAUBERT

[Paris, 19 May 1868]

I shan't come to Croisset with you: you need sleep, and we talk too much. But Sunday or Monday if you're still agreeable; though I forbid you to put yourself out. I know my Rouen, and that the pine trees by the railway lead straight to your place without any difficulty.

I'll probably come in the evening. Give my love to your dear mother. I'm looking forward to seeing her again.

G. Sand

If the days I propose don't suit, drop me a note and I'll suggest others.

I'd be grateful if you'd address the enclosed letter and have it posted.

117 FLAUBERT TO SAND

Croisset, Wednesday 20
[May 1868]

Sunday or Monday, chère maître – whenever you wish. We await you, your room is ready.

Coming on Sunday you'd give us 24 hours more. So you must come on Sunday, no?

The letter to Renan is being mailed along with this.

Send me a word to tell me the time and day of your arrival.

Mille tendresses du vieux qui vous aime.

Gve Flaubert

118 SAND TO FLAUBERT

Paris, Thursday 21 May 1868

I see the trains are very slow during the day, so I'll make a great effort and leave at eight o'clock on Sunday so that I can lunch with you. But if that gets me there too late don't wait for me. I lunch off a couple of eggs, fried or as an omelette, and a cup of coffee. I dine off a bit of chicken or veal and a few vegetables.

Since I gave up forcing myself to eat "real meat" my digestion has been all right again. I drink cider with gusto – and champagne! At Nohant I live on the local wine and bread, and since I've stopped trying to "feed myself up", no more anaemia! So much for what the doctors say!

In short, I need as little looking after as the cat; perhaps less. Be sure to tell that to your little Maman. So at last I'm going to be able to feast my eyes on you for two whole days! Do you realize that in Paris you're inaccessible? Pauvre vieux, have you been sleeping like a dormouse now you're back in your own hole? I wish I could give you some of my own capacity to snooze: not even artillery can disturb it.

But for the last fortnight I've been having awful dreams about my poor Esther, and now at last, yesterday, Depaul, Tarnier, Guéneaux and Nélaton[1] have told us she'll give birth all on her own to a child that has every chance of being perfect! I breathe again, I'm reborn myself, and I'm going to give you such a hug you'll be shocked. Till Sunday, then, and don't go to any trouble.

G. Sand

---

[1] Mme Sand had seen to it that her friend was examined by these well-known doctors.

119 FLAUBERT TO SAND

[Croisset, 22 May 1868]
Friday morning

Right! We'll lunch together on Sunday.

But do arrange in advance to stay more than two days, since nothing calls you away.

So now you're relieved of worry – good news.

A hug from me, chère maître. Till Sunday, then.

Tout à vous,

Gve Flaubert

*

Sand accordingly arrived in Rouen the morning of the 24th. As before, she went on excursions with Flaubert to places of interest in the region, and at night he read to her from *L'Éducation sentimentale*.

FROM GEORGE SAND'S DIARY, 1868

Sunday, 24 May

. . . I travelled with a soldier, who woke me up by tapping me on the shoulder and offering me some barley sugar. We parted good friends. Flaubert was waiting for me at the station and made me go and pee so that I wouldn't become like Sainte-Beuve. It was raining in Rouen, as usual. I found Maman less deaf, but alas! unable to walk. I had lunch, and chatted as we strolled in the arbour, sheltered from the rain. I slept for an hour and a half in an armchair; Flaubert on a divan. We chatted some more. Dined with the niece, her husband and Mme Frankline.[1] Then Gustave read me a religious farce.[2] I went to bed at midnight.

Monday, 25 May

Croisset. Wonderful weather. We had lunch and drove to Saint-Georges[3] along a charming sunken lane running through the woods. Masses of flowers everywhere: splendid geranium purpureum; polygalas; a figwort. Saint-Georges is a fine old romanesque abbey with a well-preserved chapter. On to Duclair,[4] where we rested the horses, and back via Canteleu: I sat up by the coachman to get a better view of the lovely countryside. Beautiful drive down. Dined with the same people as yesterday, and M. Commanville, who has a *flat* forehead. Mme Frankline sang, *badly*. We went upstairs at nine o'clock. Flaubert read me three hundred excellent pages, which I think delightful. I went to bed at two. Coughed a lot. The tulip tree is covered with flowers.

Tuesday, 26 May

Left Croisset at noon with Gustave. Town library; called on flabbergasted Bouilhet. Left at half-past one. Dozed till Paris [. . .] Dined with Maxime Du Camp; he is very nice; a worthy fellow [. . .]

[1] A friend of Caroline Commanville.
[2] Probably *La Queue de la Poire de la Boule de Monseigneur*. (See Letter 84.)
[3] A church and the remains of a thirteenth-century abbey, at Saint-Martin-de-Boscherville.
[4] A town on the Seine twenty kilometres west of Rouen.

*

As before, Flaubert was both touched and impressed by George Sand's presence at Croisset. On July 5th he would write to Mlle Leroyer de Chantepie: "Last month we had a few days' visit from our friend Mme Sand. Such character! Such strength! And at the same time there is no one whose company is more soothing. Her serenity is contagious."

120   SAND TO FLAUBERT

[Paris, 26 May 1868]
rue Gay-Lussac 5
Tuesday evening

Dozed on the journey. Dined with your worthy and charming friend Du Camp. We talked of you, nothing but you and your Maman, and said a hundred times that we loved you both. Now I'm going to get some sleep, to be ready to move house tomorrow. I've got a charming place on the Luxembourg Garden.[1]

Love to the two of you, mother and son, from a heart that belongs to you both.

G. Sand

[1] This apartment would be Sand's Parisian pied-à-terre until 1875, her last year in the city.

121   FLAUBERT TO SAND

[Croisset,] Thursday [28 May 1868]

I'm thinking of you, missing you, longing to see you again – *voilà!* I'll be hanged if I have anything new to tell you, chère maître: no, absolutely nothing.

My mother asks me to tell you once again that she loves you dearly. And don't I!

Mille tendresses du vieux

Gve Flaubert

Yesterday evening I began *Cadio*.

You *must* arrange to come here for a fortnight next autumn.

122   SAND TO FLAUBERT

[Paris, 28 May 1868]
Thursday evening

My little friend had her baby this morning after a crisis lasting two hours – a boy who appeared to be dead, but whom they "teased" to such effect that this evening he's very much alive and very sweet. The mother is doing well. What a relief! But what a scene! It really was a sight to see. I'm very weary but very happy, and I tell you about it because you love me.

G. Sand

I leave on Tuesday for Nohant.

123   SAND TO FLAUBERT

Paris, Friday evening
[29 May 1868]

Halcyons skim on the water, and are common everywhere. It's a pretty name, and quite well known.[1]

Je t'embrasse.

Ton troubadour

October – yes, I'll try!

---

[1] While Sand was at Croisset Flaubert had probably asked her about halcyons in connection with the Fontainebleau scenes in *L'Éducation sentimentale*. (See the following letter.)

124   FLAUBERT TO SAND

[Croisset, 5 June 1868]
Friday evening

I have received your two notes, chère maître. In one you give me the news of Mme Lambert's delivery, and I rejoice for you. Do you remember that I expressed some doubts about the diagnosis? *A priori*, without knowing any particulars – I'm so familiar with the *boutique*.[1]

In the other, you send me the word *alcyons* [halcyons] to replace *libellules* [dragonflies]. Georges Pouchet has suggested *gerre des lacs* (genus *gerris*). Well, neither of them suits me, because neither evokes a picture for the ignorant reader. So, there would have to be a description of said beasties. But that would hold things up! It would fill the entire landscape! I'll say "long-legged insects", or "long insects", and that will be succinct and clear.[2]

Few books have gripped me more than *Cadio*, and I entirely share Maxime's admiration. I'd have spoken of it sooner if my mother and my niece hadn't made off with my copy. They finally gave it back this evening. It's here on my table, and I'm turning the pages as I write.

First of all, it seems to me that "it must have been just like that!" One sees it all; one is there, and thrilled to be so. There must have been many people like Saint-Gueltas, like the comte de Sauvières, like Rebec! And even like Henri, though fewer. As for the character of Cadio, who is more fictional than the rest, what I like especially is his ferocious anger. That is his particular quality. Humanity changed into fury, the guillotine become mystical, existence no longer anything more than a bloody dream – that is what must have gone on in such minds as his. One of your scenes, I think, is Shakespearian – that of the delegate to the Convention with his two secretaries: it's incredibly strong. One wants to shout. And another, which struck me on first reading: the scene in which Saint-Gueltas and Henri have, each of them, a pistol in their pocket. And many others! Your page 161 is splendid. (I have just opened the book there at random.)

In the play, wouldn't you have to strengthen the part of Saint-Gueltas' legal wife? It shouldn't be difficult to adapt the book – just some condensing and cutting. If it's allowed to be staged I'm sure the success will be tremendous. But the censor?

You've gone and written a masterpiece! – and it is *very entertaining*. My mother claims that it reminds her of stories she heard as a child. Speaking of the Vendée, did you know that her paternal grandfather was head of the Vendéan army after M. de Lescure? His name was M. Fleuriot d'Argentan. It isn't something I boast about. Especially since it's problematical: my mother's father, a raving royalist,[3] never spoke of his political background.

In a few days my mother will be going to Dieppe, to stay with her granddaughter. I'll be alone a good part of the summer, and intend to keep my nose to the grindstone.[4]

But my everlasting novel gets me down at times. Manipulating such lightweight characters is a heavy task. Why take pains over such a paltry crew?

I wanted to write you at greater length about *Cadio*. But it's late, and my eyes are smarting. So, quite simply, I thank you, ma chère maître.

I love you and kiss you.

Gve Flaubert

Greetings to Maurice.

[1] Literally "shop", as in "shop talk" – here, the medical profession. Flaubert's older brother had succeeded their father as chief surgeon in the Rouen hospital.
[2] Flaubert seems in the end to have banished all these troublesome creatures from his description of the forest of Fontainebleau in *L'Éducation sentimentale*.
[3] Jacobs says that this is a lapsus for "republican".
[4] Here again Flaubert inserts a bit of faux-naïf popular verse. Of uncertain authorship, it lauds the virtues of toil.

125 SAND TO FLAUBERT

Nohant, 21 June [18]68

Here I am, bothering you again over M. Du Camp's address, which you've never given me – though you did forward a letter to him for me – and which I forgot to ask him for when we dined together in Paris. I've just read his book, *Les Forces perdues*. I promised to tell him what I thought of it, and I'm keeping my word. Will you write the address on the note and give it to the postman? Thanks.

So there you are, in this hot sun, all alone in your charming villa! Why am I not the . . . river, cradling you in its "gentle murmur" and bringing coolness into your lair! I'd talk to you very unobtrusively between the pages of your novel, and I'd silence the strange clanking that you hate but that I like.[1] I like anything that typifies a place: the rumble of carriages and the noise of workmen in Paris, the sounds made by thousands of birds in the country, and those made by ships on rivers. I also like deep and absolute silence. In short, I like everything around me, wherever I am. It's a new form of "aural idiom". Admittedly I choose my surroundings, and avoid the Senate and other places of ill repute.[2]

All goes well here, mon troubadour. The children are lovely and we all adore them. It's hot, and I adore that. All I have to tell you is the same old thing, and I love you as the best of friends and comrades. Nothing new about that, is there! I still have a very vivid and favourable impression of what you read me. It struck me as so fine it's impossible for it not to be good. As for me, I'm not doing a stroke; just loafing about. It will pass. What won't pass is my friendship for you.

G. Sand

Love from all here, as ever.

[1] The sound made by the chains with which the Seine tug-boats towed large sailing-vessels past Flaubert's house, either toward Rouen or to the open sea.

[2] The Senate was "a place of ill repute" because its members were appointed by the Emperor.

126 FLAUBERT TO SAND

Croisset, Sunday, 5 July [1868]

Yes – with me, too, it's "the same old thing", chère maître. I love you, truly, and greatly. And I'm conceited enough to believe that you don't doubt it. You *must* come here again in the autumn, and stay, so that we may have a long time together. Besides, you *swore* you would.

Now your friend is coming up for a breath of air. The day after tomorrow I'm going off to visit my two nieces until the end of the week. Then to Fontainebleau (for my book) and to Paris. I won't be back here until early August. So from the 12th on, write to me at Boulevard du Temple, 42.

I've been slaving away madly for the past six weeks. The patriots won't forgive me this book, nor the reactionaries either![1] Too bad: I write things as I feel them – that is, as I believe them to exist. Is this foolish of me? But it seems to me our unhappy situation is attributable exclusively to people of our own kind?[2] Everything about the Christianity that I find in the [socialist] revolutionaries appals me!

Here, for example, are two little notes now lying on my table:

"This system [Louis Blanc's own] is not a system of disorder. For it has its source in the Gospels. And from this divine source *there cannot flow* hatred, warfare, total conflict of interests. For the doctrine formulated from the Gospels is a doctrine of peace, union, and love." (L. Blanc)

"I even make bold to assert that with the disappearance of respect for Sunday, the last spark of poetic fire has been extinguished in the souls of our rhymesters. As the saying has it: 'Without religion, no poetry.'" (Proudhon)

Talking of the latter, I beg you, chère maître, to read, at the end of his book on Sunday observance, a love story entitled, I think, *Marie et Maxime*. One must know this to have an idea of the Style of our Thinkers. It should be set beside the excursion to Brittany in *Çà et là*, by the great Veuillot. This doesn't prevent some of our friends from admiring these two gentlemen. Whereas they deride Voltaire.

In my old age I intend to write criticism: it will be a relief to me because I often choke with suppressed opinions. No one understands better than I Boileau's outbursts against bad taste: "The stupidities I hear uttered at the Academy are hastening my end." There was a man for you!

Whenever I hear the clanking of the steamboats I think of you: I remind myself that you like the sound, and it irritates me less. What moonlight on the river last night!

I have been completely alone for a week. My mother is visiting Caroline. She is better physically, and her spirits have improved as well.

Friendly greetings to all your family. And to you much love.

Gve Flaubert

[1] The pages of *L'Éducation sentimentale* are full of scorn for the "reactionaries" of 1848 – the bourgeois. A typical passage: "Most of the men present [at a reception given by Mme Dambreuse] had served under at least four governments, and they would have sold France and the entire human race to guarantee their fortunes, to avoid trouble, or out of mere baseness." As for the "patriots", Dussardier is one of the few sympathetic characters in the novel, but Sénécal, a fanatical republican and socialist, turns police spy and kills a friend during Louis-Napoléon's coup d'état.

[2] See Letter 94, Note 3.

*

During July and August Flaubert visited relatives in Normandy and spent a week as the guest of Princesse Mathilde at her château de Saint-Gratien (today an apartment house) on the lac d'Enghien.

127 SAND TO FLAUBERT

Nohant, 31 July [1868]

I write to you at Croisset anyhow. I doubt if you're still in Paris in this Toledo heat. Unless the shades of Fontainebleau have made you linger there. Isn't the forest pretty? But it's especially elegant in winter, without its leaves but with all those bright mosses. Did you see the sands at Arbonne?[1] A little Sahara that must be very nice just now. We're very happy here. A bathe every day in a stream that's still cool and shady; 4 hours' work in the daytime, and at night relaxation and mummery. We've had a *Roman comique*[2] here on tour, a group from the Odéon company that included several old friends. We invited them and their whole troupe to supper at La Châtre two nights running after the performance: singing and laughter and iced champagne till 3 o'clock in the morning, to the great scandal of the bourgeois, who nevertheless grovelled to be invited. One of the people there was a very funny Norman comic, a real Norman who sang authentic peasant songs in the authentic language. Did you know some of them have a wit and waggishness that's truly Gallic? There's an unknown mine there, full of "genre" masterpieces. It made me even fonder of Normandy than I was already. Perhaps you know the actor concerned. His name's Fréville. He's the one who always plays the oafish manservant and gets his behind kicked. He's horrible, impossible – but outside the theatre he's a charming fellow, amusing enough for ten! There's fate for you!

We've had some delightful guests[3] here and been having a high old time, but without prejudice to the *Lettres d'un voyageur* in the *Revue* and botanical excursions to out-of-the-way and very surprising places. Best of all are the little girls. Gabrielle is a fat lamb who sleeps and laughs all day. Aurore is slimmer, with bright eyes soft as velvet; at thirty months she's talking as well as other children do at five years, and is adorable in every way. We try to keep her from developing too fast.

You worry me when you say your book's going to blame the patriots for all that went wrong. Is that really true? And don't forget they're the losers! It's bad enough to be responsible for your own defeat, without having all your blunders thrown in your teeth. Be merciful. After all, there've been a lot of great souls among them! Christianity has been a dead loss, but I have to admit it's always had appeal. It can capture people emotionally if they see only the attractive side. You have to remember the evil it's done if you want to get rid of it. But it doesn't surprise me that someone as magnanimous as L. Blanc should dream of seeing it purified and restored to its ideal form. I've entertained the same illusion myself, but as soon as you actually venture into the past you realize it can't be resuscitated; I'm quite sure that by now L. Blanc himself is smiling at his dream. One has to think about that too! To remind oneself that everybody with any intelligence has come a long way since he was twenty, and it would be ungenerous to reproach such people for things they probably regret themselves. As for Proudhon, I never thought he was sincere. People say he was an "inspired" orator. Personally I can't understand him. He's an example of perpetual and incomprehensible paradox. He makes me think of the sophists old Socrates used to make fun of.

But I rely on *you* to illustrate *magnanimity*. With one word more, or one less, it's possible to flick without wounding when the hand holding the whip is both gentle and strong. And you're so good you're incapable of being cruel.

Shall I come to Croisset this autumn? I begin to fear I shan't, and that *Cadio* will be in rehearsal then. But I'll try to escape from Paris, even if it's only for a day.

My children send their greetings. Lord, there's been a fine old set-to about *Salammbô*! Someone you don't know ventured not to like it. Maurice called him a bourgeois, and fiery little Lina improved the shining hour by saying her husband had chosen the wrong word – he should have called him an idiot.

There. I'm in rude health. Je t'aime, et je t'embrasse.

Ton vieux troubadour

G. Sand

[1] A sandy stretch in the forest of Fontainebleau.

[2] Sand is referring allusively to *Le Roman comique*, by Paul Scarron, published in two parts, 1651 and 1657, a novel recounting the adventures of a troupe of travelling players.

[3] The guests were the statesman Edmond Adam, his wife Juliette Lamber, and their daughter.

128 FLAUBERT TO SAND

Dieppe, Monday [10 August 1868]

Yes, chère maître, I was indeed in Paris during the heat: it was truly "Tro Pical" (to adopt the pronunciation of M. Amat, governor of the palace of Versailles), and I sweated profusely. I was twice at Fontainebleau. And the second time, following your advice, I saw the sands at Arbonne. They're so beautiful they made my head swim.

I went to Saint-Gratien[1] as well. Now here I am at Dieppe, and on Wednesday I'll be at Croisset. From there I shan't budge for a long time – I must forge ahead with the novel.

Yesterday I saw Dumas. We talked about you, needless to say. And since I'll be seeing him again tomorrow we'll talk about you again.

I expressed myself badly if I told you that my book will "blame the patriots for all that went wrong." I don't claim the right to blame anyone. I don't even believe that the novelist should express his opinion on matters of this world. He can communicate it, but I don't like him to state it. (This is part of my poetics.)

So I limit myself to describing things as they appear to me, expressing what seems to me the Truth. Hang the consequences. Rich or poor, winners or losers – I take none of that into account.

I want to have neither love nor hate, pity nor anger. As for sympathy, that's different. One can never have enough of it. The Reactionaries, by the way, will be treated even less gently than the others. For they seem to me more criminal.

Isn't it time to inject Justice into Art? Then wouldn't objectivity of portrayal attain the majesty of the Law and the precision of Science?

So: since I have absolute confidence in the greatness of your spirit, I will read my third part to you when it's done, and if there's something in my work that seems cruel to you I'll remove it. But I'm convinced in advance that you'll make no objection. As for allusion to individuals, there's no trace of that whatever.

Prince Napoléon, whom I saw Thursday at his sister's, asked me for news of you and sang the praises of Maurice.[2] Princesse Mathilde told me she thinks you "charming" – which makes me like her somewhat more.

What's this? The rehearsals of *Cadio* will prevent you from coming to see your old chum this fall? Not possible! Not possible!

I know Fréville: a fine man, highly cultivated.

Je vous baise sur les deux joues tendrement.

Gve Flaubert

[1] The château de Saint-Gratien, outside Paris, was the country house of Princesse Mathilde Bonaparte.

[2] Prince Napoléon and Maurice Sand had long been friends. Maurice had been the prince's guest aboard the latter's yacht in 1861, on a voyage to Canada and the United States.

129 FLAUBERT TO SAND

[Croisset, 2–3 September (?) 1868][1]
Wednesday night

Chère maître,

I shall be in Paris the last day, or the next to the last, of this month. No two ways about it: we *must* see each other and have a good talk.

So, Sylvanie and Thuillier have become perfect Catholics! O Saint Polycarp! Le Père Hyacinthe seems to me to be a decidedly dangerous man.[2]

This is what my mother said to me yesterday: "Tell Mme Sand that I think of her very often, that I want to see her again, and that I love her as though I were her equal."

My eyes are starting out of my head. Time for a nap.

So much love from your old troubadour,

Gve Flaubert

[1] This letter, approximately dated, would appear to be Flaubert's reply to two lost letters from Sand written in late August.

[2] In the lost letters Sand may have lamented Sylvanie Arnould-Plessy's conversion. In any case, she will do so in Letter 133. Flaubert seems to have been mistaken in thinking that Marguerite Thuillier, too, had been "converted". (For this, again, see Letter 133.) (However, after appearing in *Cadio*, Thuillier abruptly quit the stage, retired to the country, and refused to see or correspond with her friends.) Charles Loyson (1827–1912), known as Le Père Hyacinthe, was a "liberal" Catholic priest and writer.

130 FLAUBERT TO SAND

Croisset, Wednesday night
9 September [1868]

Is this the way to behave, chère maître! Almost two months without writing to your old troubadour?

Are you in Paris? At Nohant? Or somewhere else?

I'm told that *Cadio* is in rehearsal at the Porte-Saint-Martin? So you have broken with Chilly? I hear also that Thuillier will make her return to the stage in your play? (But I thought she was dying.) And when will the play open? Are you happy about it? etc. etc.

I am living absolutely like an oyster. My novel is the rock I'm attached to, and I know nothing of what is happening in the world.

I don't even read (or rather I didn't) *La Lanterne*. I find Rochefort a great bore, be it said between ourselves.[1] It takes courage to venture to suggest that he may not be the greatest writer of the century. "O Velches, Velches!" as M. de Voltaire would sigh (or roar).[2] But – apropos of Rochefort again – haven't they[3] been IDIOTIC! What a wretched lot!

If you're too busy, ask nice Maurice to write and tell me how you are.

And Sainte-Beuve? Do you see him? As for me, I'm working furiously. I have just done a *description* of the forest of Fontainebleau that made me want to hang myself from one of its trees.[4] I had interrupted myself for three weeks, and had great trouble getting back into my stride. I'm like a camel – you can't stop him when he's on the go, nor make him start when he's resting. I still have a year's work ahead. After that, I'll abandon the bourgeois for good. Too difficult and too ugly. It's time for me to do something Beautiful, something I'll enjoy.

What I would greatly enjoy, at this moment, would be to kiss you. When will that be?

Until then, so much love from your

Gve Flaubert

My mother is very well and sends you a thousand affectionate greetings.

[1] A new law concerning the press (9 March 1868) had given the opposition permission to found a newspaper without specific authorization. Henri Rochefort, former editor of *Le Figaro*, began in May 1868 to publish *La Lanterne*, a largely humorous political weekly. It enjoyed a great success, the first issue selling 120,000 copies; but was suppressed by the government early in August. Rochefort, sentenced to three years in prison, took refuge in Belgium.

[2] "Velche" is the usual French spelling of "Welsch", a scornful German term for anything foreign, especially French. Voltaire made use of it in his *Discours aux Welches* (1764) to indicate the ignorant, the tasteless, and those insensitive to beauty.

[3] The government of Napoleon III.

[4] For this description (four printed pages in the novel) Flaubert wrote various drafts that filled seventy-two pages in all.

131 SAND TO FLAUBERT

Paris, 10 September 1868

There really is a combined attack on the correspondence front, cher ami. On all sides I'm being reproached, quite unfairly, for not answering. I wrote to you from Nohant about a fortnight ago to say I was going to Paris for the rehearsals of *Cadio*. And now I'm going back to Nohant, tomorrow at dawn, to see my own Aurore.[1] In the last week I've written four scenes for the play, and I've no more work to do for the rest of the rehearsals, which my friend and colleague Paul Meurice is kindly taking charge of. For all his efforts, the preliminary sorting is as always a frightful mess. You need to see the difficulties involved in putting on a play in order to credit them; and if you haven't got enough humour and inner cheerfulness to study human nature in the real people about to embody your fiction, it can make you tear your hair out. But I don't tear my hair out any more; I laugh. I'm too familiar with it all to let it bother me, and I'll tell you some good stories when we meet.

As I'm an optimist I look on the bright side of things and of people, but the truth is that in this world everything is both good and bad.

Poor Thuillier isn't in brilliant health, but she hopes to be able to bear the burden of work one more time. She needs to earn her living; she's horribly poor. I told you in the letter that got lost that Sylvanie[2] had spent a few days at Nohant. She's more beautiful than ever, and quite revived after a terrible illness.

Would you believe it? I haven't seen Sainte-Beuve – I've only just had time to sleep a little and snatch a bite since I've been here. That's how it is: I haven't heard anyone say a word about anything except the theatre and the actors. I sometimes longed to drop everything and surprise you with a visit, but I was under arrest every single day.

I'm coming back here at the end of the month, and when *Cadio* is on I shall beg you to come and spend twenty-four hours in town for my sake. Will you? Yes, you're too kind a troubadour to refuse.

Je t'embrasse de tout mon coeur, ainsi que ta chère maman. I'm very glad she's well.

G. Sand

---

[1] A play on the juxtaposition of sunrise and her granddaughter's name Aurore, which was also her own.

[2] Mme Arnould-Plessy.

132 FLAUBERT TO SAND

Croisset, Sunday
[13 September 1868]

Agreed, chère maître: I'll come for the opening of *Cadio*. You hardly needed to ask me!

Just let me know five or six days ahead.

It will be in the middle of October, won't it? About a month from now?

You seem not too satisfied with things?

Oh! How good it would be to have a book giving a *true* picture of theatre people![1]

So – until soon.

Mille tendresses from your old

                                        Gve Flaubert

¹ Flaubert did not know that Sand had already begun a novel about actors. She will
mention it for the first time in Letter 133. It was originally called *La Chambre bleue*, then
Bellamare; its final title would be *Pierre qui roule*.

133   SAND TO FLAUBERT

                              Nohant, 18 September [1868]

I think it will be on the 8th or 10th of October. The director's announcing
it for September 26th, but everyone regards that as impossible. Nothing is
ready, but they'll inform me and I'll inform you. I've come here for the respite
accorded me by my very conscientious and devoted colleague. I've started work
again on a novel about the *theatre* – I'd left a draft of Part I on my desk – and
every day I pitch myself into an icy brook that shakes me up and makes me
sleep like a top. How comfortable one is here, with the two little girls laughing
and chattering like birds from morn till night, and how foolish one is to go
writing and putting on *fictions* when reality is so easy and good! But you get
into the habit of looking at it all as a kind of military duty, and go out into the
firing line without thinking about whether you're going to get killed or wounded.
Do you think that bothers me? No, I assure you it doesn't. But it doesn't amuse
me either. I just go straight ahead, stupid as an ox and patient as a Berry
peasant. There's nothing interesting in my life except other people. Seeing you
soon in Paris will delight me more than my own affairs will exasperate me.
Your novel interests me more than all of mine. Impersonality, my special idiom,
is making great progress. If I weren't so well I'd think it was an illness. If my
old heart didn't grow more loving every day I'd think it was selfishness. In
. short, that's how it is, I don't know why. I've had some sorrow lately; I told you
about it in the letter you never received.¹ It was on August 31st; it's written in
my book. Someone you know and of whom I'm very fond, "Célimène",² has
turned religious – ecstatically, mystically and Molinistically and I don't know
how else, the fool! I emerged from my shell, I stormed, I said some very harsh
things, I ridiculed her – but it's no good, it's all one to her. As far as she's
concerned, Father Hyacinthe has taken the place of all friendship and esteem.
Can you credit it? A very noble spirit, a genuine intelligence, a worthy character!
And she does this! Thuillier is religious too, but it hasn't changed her; she
doesn't like priests and doesn't believe in the devil – she's a heretic without
realizing it. Maurice and Lina are furious with the other one. They simply
don't love her any more. It grieves me very much to stop loving her.

But we love you, and send you affectionate greetings. Thank you for coming
to *Cadio*.

                                        G. Sand

¹ Flaubert had received it, and refers to the matter in his letter of 2–3 September.

² At the Comédie-Française, Mme Arnould-Plessy played the role of Célimène in *Le Misanthrope*. But it was purely from discretion that Mme Sand used the name here and in the lost letter: i.e. without reference to the unpleasant character of Molière's lady. "Molinistically" refers here to the Spanish Miguel de Molinos (c.1640–97), who revived Quietism and was favoured in Louis XIV's court by Madame de Maintenon.

134 FLAUBERT TO SAND

[Croisset, 19 September 1868]
Saturday evening

You are surprised, chère maître? Not I! *I told you, but you wouldn't believe me.*
I feel for you. For it's sad to see people you love change. The substitution of one spirit for another, in a body that remains unaltered, is heartbreaking to witness. One feels *betrayed*. I have experienced that, and more than once.

Still, what is your conception of women, then, oh you who are of the Third Sex? Are they not, as Proudhon says, "the desolation of the Just"? Since when have they been able to dispense with chimeras? After love, Piety; that's the way it goes. Sylvanie has no more men; she takes up with God. That's all it amounts to.¹

Rare are those who have no need of the Supernatural. Philosophy will always be the portion of aristocrats. Fatten the human herd, bed them with straw up to their bellies, even gild their stable – to no avail: they will remain brutish, whatever anyone may say. The only progress to be hoped for is that the brutes may be made a little less vicious. But as for elevating the ideas of the masses, giving them a conception of God that is broader and therefore less Human, I am very dubious, very dubious.

I am just now reading a most respectable little book (by a friend of mine, a judge) about the Revolution in the department of the Eure.² It is full of documents written by bourgeois of the period, ordinary small-town citizens. Well, I assure you there are few of that calibre nowadays. They were well-read, admirable people, full of good sense, ideas, and generosity. Neo-Catholicism on the one hand and Socialism on the other have made France stupid. Everything is either the Immaculate Conception or workers' lunches.

I told you that I don't flatter the Democrats in my book. But I assure you the Conservatives aren't spared, either. I'm now writing three pages on the abominations committed by the National Guard in June '48,³ which will make me highly popular with the bourgeois. I'm doing my best to rub their noses in their own turpitude.

You give me no details about *Cadio*. Who are the actors? etc. I'm wary of your novel about the theatre. You are too fond of those people. Have you known many of them who love their art? So many actors are merely bourgeois gone astray!

So we'll see each other three weeks from now, at the latest. I'm very happy about that, and send you a kiss.

Gve Flaubert

What about the Censor? For your sake I hope he'll commit some howlers; indeed it would grieve me were he false to his traditional role.[4]

Did you see this in a newspaper: "Victor Hugo and Rochefort, the greatest writers of our day"? If Badinguet doesn't feel himself avenged by that, he's certainly hard to please.[5]

[1] Mme Sylvanie Arnould-Plessy (1819–1897) had had her first success at the Comédie-Française at the age of fifteen. A liaison with Prince Napoléon had ended in 1858. She would retire from the stage in 1876.

[2] *Notice pour servir à l'histoire de la Révolution dans le département de l'Eure*, by L. Boivin-Champeaux (1864).

[3] The reference is particularly to the fate of captured revolutionaries confined in the basement of the Tuileries palace. "Le père Roque", a member of the National Guard, fires point-blank at a young prisoner who asks for bread. (*L'Éducation sentimentale*, Part III, end of Chapter 1.)

[4] In addition to speaking here as veteran of the censuring and prosecution of *Madame Bovary*, Flaubert shows himself the former law student in his use of a legalistic phrase: "*si elle manquait à ses us.*" ("Elle" is *la Censure*, the censorship office.)

[5] That is, the humiliation and anger that Flaubert thinks Hugo must feel at being linked as an equal with the scribbler Rochefort must be sweet revenge for Napoleon III, against whom Hugo had written the scathing *Napoléon le Petit*.

135 FLAUBERT TO SAND

Croisset, Saturday evening
[26 September 1868]

When, chère maître? Do you know?

As soon as there's a definite date, tell me. I need to know because of some little personal arrangements I must make.

So much love from your old

Gve Flaubert

136 SAND TO FLAUBERT

[Paris, 29 September 1868]

Cher ami,

It'll be next Saturday, 3 October. I'm in the theatre from six every evening till two in the morning. There's talk of putting mattresses backstage for the actors when they're not actually required. I myself, like you, am used to late hours and don't get at all tired, though I'd get very bored if it weren't for the fact that one can always think of something else. While one play is being rehearsed I quite often compose another; and there's something rather exciting about a huge dark auditorium full of mysterious characters in strange costumes talking to one another in whispers. It's just like a dream – or a conspiracy of lunatics escaped from Bicêtre.[1]

I've no idea what the performance will be like. If one hadn't seen the prodigies of cooperation and effort that can be put into these things at the last minute one would say it was hopeless, with only five or six out of a cast of thirty-five or forty who really know how to speak their lines. We spend hours making characters in white or blue smocks run in and out; eventually they're supposed to represent soldiers or peasants, but meanwhile their manoeuvres are utterly incomprehensible. Again, just like a dream. You have to be crazy to attempt this sort of thing. And then there's the frenzy of the actors: they drag themselves into place, pale and weary and yawning, and then suddenly come to life and fire off their speeches as if inspired. Again like a bunch of madmen.

The censors haven't bothered us as far as the text is concerned, but tomorrow they're to see the costumes, and perhaps they'll take fright at *them*.

I haven't bothered my dear ones, but left them in peace at Nohant. If *Cadio* is a success it will provide a little dowry for Aurore; that's all I ask. If the play fails I'll have to try again, that's all.

I shall be seeing you, so it will be a happy day whatever happens. Come and see me the day before, if you arrive in town then; or else on the day itself. Come and have dinner with me either day; I'm in from one till five.

Merci; je t'embrasse et je t'aime.

G. Sand

[1] The huge hospital at Bicêtre, outside Paris, included an asylum for the insane. Sand's succinct phrase is: "*une conspiration d'évadés de Bicêtre*".

FROM GEORGE SAND'S DIARY, 1868

1 October

Today saw Flaubert, come from Rouen especially to see *Cadio*.

2 October

Dinner with Thuillier, Plauchut,[1] Flaubert. . . . Flaubert stays with me until 11 o'clock.

[1] Edmond Plauchut (1824–1909), world traveller and devoted admirer of Mme Sand, was one of the habitués of Nohant. He is buried in the family cemetery there.

*

Cadio opened on 3 October and enjoyed a certain *succès d'estime*.

137 SAND TO FLAUBERT

Paris, 6 October [18]68

Cher bon ami,

Once again I'd be very grateful if you would do what you can to help my friend Despruneaux in a just cause that has already been decided in his favour.[1]

A toi.

G. Sand

[1] Apparently on an explanatory document Sand had given him or sent him, Flaubert had scribbled: "Work on the Judge at Le Havre. Recommend Despruneaux against Helie."

138 SAND TO FLAUBERT

Nohant, 15 October [1868]

Here I am at home, where after being reunited with my children and grand-children I slept for thirty-six hours at a stretch. I must have been tired without realizing it. I'm now coming out of my animal-like hibernation, and you are the first person I want to write to. I didn't thank you properly for coming to Paris on my account when you usually travel so little. And I didn't see enough of you, either; when I found out you'd had supper with Plauchut I was cross with myself for staying to look after my seedy Thuillier, for whom I could do nothing and who wasn't particularly grateful. Actors are spoiled children; even the best of them are great egoists. You say I'm too fond of them. I feel for them what I feel for the woods and the fields, for everything and everybody that I know a little and never stop studying. It's amid all these that I make my life, and as I love my life I love everything that sustains and stimulates it. I realize people are nasty to me sometimes, but I don't feel it any more. I know bushes have thorns, but that doesn't ever stop me thrusting my hands into them and finding flowers. If they're not all beautiful, at least they're all fascinating. The day you took me to the abbey at Saint-Georges I found some *scrofularia borealis*, a plant that's very rare in France. I was delighted; yet there was plenty of *merde* where I picked it. *Such is life!*[1]

If you don't take life like that you can't take it at all, and then how are you to bear it? I myself find it amusing and interesting, and the fact that I accept everything makes me all the more delighted and enthusiastic when I come across the good and the beautiful. If I hadn't had a great knowledge of the human race I couldn't have immediately sympathized with you and understood and loved you. I may be very indulgent with people, too easy-going perhaps – I've had so much practice. But admiration is another matter, and I don't think your old troubadour's capacity for *that* has been worn out yet.

I found my children good and affectionate as always, and the little girls, as ever, pretty and sweet. I was still dreaming this morning as I woke up, and found myself saying, "There's always a part for a *jeune premier* in the play of life." Very odd. The *jeune premier* in my life is Aurore. The fact is, it's impossible not to idolize the child. She's so perfectly intelligent and sweet-natured it's like a dream.

You too are a dream without realizing it. Plauchut has met you only once and he adores you. That's proves he's not stupid. When he left Paris he asked me to remember him to you.

I left *Cadio* selling lots of seats one day and not so many the next. The cabal against the new management died down the second day. The notices have been half favourable and half hostile. The fine weather doesn't help. Neither does Roger's awful acting.[2] So we don't know yet if we shall make money. For my part, if it comes I'm glad without going into ecstasies, and if it doesn't I'm sorry without being the slightest bit upset.[3] Money wasn't my object, so it shouldn't be my concern. And it's not a true sign of success – a lot of things that are worthless or downright bad make money. I'm already writing another play so as not to lose the knack.[4] I've also got a novel going, about the mummers. I studied them closely this time, though I didn't learn anything new. I already knew what makes them tick. It's quite simple and natural.

Je vous embrasse tendrement ainsi que ta petite Maman. Show me a sign of life. Is the novel making progress?

G. Sand

[1] In English in the original.

[2] Raphaël Félix, the new manager of the Théâtre de la Porte-Saint-Martin, had not been having an easy time with the actors. Now he had engaged, to play the principal role in *Cadio*, the tenor Gustave Roger – an excellent singer but a poor actor, with the handicap of an artificial arm.

[3] On October 28th Flaubert would write to Henry Harrisse: "I'm afraid that *Cadio* may not play more than thirty or forty nights. But you know our friend. Her stoicism in such matters confounds the imagination."

[4] *L'Autre.*

139 FLAUBERT TO SAND

[Croisset, 17 October 1868]
Saturday evening

Chère maître,

Your letter of yesterday *inspires* me. That's the only word that suits the case; and what you say about the indulgence one should have for egoists is so beautiful that I was close to tears.

I would like to answer you at length. But I can't think any more. Since returning here I have never slept more than five hours a night, and now that my chapter is done I'm dying for a long slumber.

Yes, I was cross about Thuillier too! And delighted with your friend Plauchut: I took to him immediately.

I kiss your two hands, your two cheeks, and all four of Mlle Aurore's.

Gve Flaubert

What with everything that's been going on, when shall we see each other? Keep me informed about *Cadio*. What a shame about that Roger!

140   FLAUBERT TO SAND

[Croisset, 31 October 1868]
Saturday evening

I feel guilty at not having answered your last letter at greater length, ma chère maître. In it you spoke of people being "nasty" to you. Do you think I was unaware of it? I'll even admit to you (between ourselves) that I was wounded, on that occasion, even more on the score of good taste than through my affection for you. I found a number of your close friends insufficiently zealous. "*Mon Dieu! Mon Dieu! comme les hommes de lettres sont bêtes!*" (from the correspondence of Napoleon I).[1] It's nice, isn't it? And doesn't it seem to you that he's being excessively denigrated these days, said gentleman?

The infinite stupidity of the masses makes me indulgent toward "individuality", however odious a form it may assume. I have just swallowed the first ten volumes of Buchez and Roux.[2] What I have come away with is, above all, an immense disgust with *les François*. Nom de Dieu! How inept we have always been in this lovely country of ours! Not a liberal idea that hasn't been unpopular, not a decent thing that hasn't raised a scandal, not a great man who hasn't been pelted with rotten apples, or knifed. "The history of the human mind is the history of stupidity," as M. de Voltaire says.

And I am more and more convinced of this truth: we are putrid with Catholicism. The doctrine of Grace has entered so deeply into us that the sense of Justice has evaporated. What frightened me in the story of '48 was its natural origins in the Revolution, which never freed itself from the Middle Ages, whatever anyone may say. In Marat I have found whole fragments of Proudhon, and I'll wager they go back as far as the preachers of the Ligue.[3]

What was the measure proposed by the most advanced thinkers, after Varennes? Dictatorship – and military dictatorship, at that. They closed the churches, but they built temples, etc. I assure you that the Revolution is consuming my intellect. It's like an abyss drawing me in.

Nevertheless I'm ploughing ahead in my novel like a team of oxen. I hope that by the New Year I'll have no more than a hundred pages to go. That is, another good six months of work. I'll move to Paris as late as possible. My winter will be spent in complete solitude – a fine way to make one's life flow swiftly by.

Maurice has written me an ultra-nice letter. But why does he let himself be bullied by Buloz?[4] We are all too restrained in our dealings with such gentlemen.

When will you come and pay me a visit? I'll perhaps go to Paris for three or four days towards the end of December.

What are you up to? etc. etc.

All my affection.

Gve Flaubert

[1] "My God, aren't men of letters idiots!" Letters to Cambacérès and Fouché, 24 January 1806.

[2] See Letter 100, Note 5.

[3] The militant Sainte-Ligue of sixteenth-century France, which waged war against the Protestants.

[4] François Buloz, editor of *La Revue des Deux Mondes*, had asked Maurice to make changes in his novel *Miss Mary* before its serialization in the magazine. Both Maurice and his mother (who always "corrected" his manuscripts) had objected.

141 SAND TO FLAUBERT

[Nohant] 20 November [18]68

You ask me when we shall meet. Around December 15th we're christening our two little girls here – christening them Protestants. It's Maurice's idea. He was married by a Protestant minister and doesn't want his daughters to suffer from Catholic influence or persecution. Our friend Napoléon[1] is Aurore's godfather, and I'm the godmother. My nephew is godfather to the other girl. We're keeping it all in the family. You must come. Maurice wants you to, and he'll be very upset if you don't. You can bring your novel and read it to me when we have a break; it will do you good to read it to a good listener. It gives one a chance to tighten things up and get a clearer view of what one's written, as I know from my own experience. Say yes to your vieux troubadour and he'll be mightily pleased with you.

Six kisses if you say yes.

G. Sand

[1] Prince Napoléon.

142 FLAUBERT TO SAND

[Croisset, 24 November 1868]
Tuesday

Chère maître,

You can't imagine the anguish you cause me. Despite my longing to come, I say "No." However, I'm torn by the longing to say "Yes." It makes me appear to give myself airs – as if I were "Not to be disturbed"; and that's absurd. But I know myself: were I to come to Nohant I'd spend the ensuing month day-dreaming about the visit. My poor brain would be filled with real pictures instead of the fictive ones I'm at such pains to invent; and my house of cards would crumble to dust.

Three weeks ago, after idiotically accepting a dinner invitation in the country near here, I lost four days [sic]. What would it be like, after leaving Nohant? But you won't understand that, strong creature that you are!

I'll come to you when I'm "in a more tranquil state of mind". Please give Maurice not my apologies but my sad regrets.

My mother returns to Rouen next Thursday. And I shall probably stay here until the end of February. By that time, I hope, I'll have reached my last chapter – which will take another three months. I must finish the book in June if it's to appear in October.

And you? What are you up to?

Your old troubadour embraces you as he loves you – that is, with all his strength.

Gve Flaubert

143 FLAUBERT TO SAND

[Croisset, 19–20 December 1868]
Saturday night

I have the impression you're a bit annoyed with your troubadour? (a thousand pardons if I'm mistaken), and that you think him a swine (forgive the word) not to have attended the baptism of his friend Maurice's two Adorables?

The dear maître must write to me to tell me if I'm wrong, and to give me her news.

Herewith mine: I'm working excessively hard, and rejoicing in the prospect of The End, which is now in sight. In order to reach it the more swiftly, I have resolved to stay here all winter, probably until the end of March. Even if all goes as well as possible, I won't finish the entire thing before the end of May.

I know nothing of events, and my only reading is a little about the French Revolution after meals, to aid digestion. I have lost my good old habit of reading some Latin every day, with the result that I no longer know a single word of that language. I'll take it up again seriously when delivered of my odious bourgeois – to whom I have no intention of ever returning!

My only distraction is to have dinner every Sunday in Rouen with my mother. I leave here at six and return at ten. Such is my existence.

Did I tell you that I had a visit from Turgenev?[1] How you would love him!

Sainte-Beuve is holding his own. I'll see him next week, as I shall be in Paris for two days, seeking some necessary information. Information about what? About the National Guard!!

What say you to the following? The *Figaro*, not knowing how to fill its columns, took it into its head to say that my novel tells the story of Chancellor Pasquier.[2] Great apprehension on the part of the family of same, who wrote to another branch of said family, living in Rouen, who consulted a lawyer, who called on my brother for the purpose of. . . . In short, I was foolish enough not to "take advantage of the situation".[3] A fine bit of idiocy, don't you think?

I kiss you as I love you, from the bottom of my heart and with all my strength.

Gve Flaubert

[1] Turgenev came to Croisset on 22 November. [For the friendship of the two writers see *Flaubert and Turgenev. The Complete Correspondence*. Edited and translated by Barbara Beaumont (1985). Also, *The Letters of Gustave Flaubert*, II, passim.]

[2] The duc de Pasquier (1767–1862) was a statesman in various regimes. *Le Figaro*, 11 December 1868, reported: "New information concerning the novel being written by M. Gustave Flaubert: This book portrays one of the longest lives, one of the most striking characters, of our day, the duc de Pasquier. The book begins, we hear, with a scene showing the young member of Parlement strolling with [the celebrated actress] Mlle Clairon about the ruins of the Bastille, in order to see with his own eyes the notice '*Ici l'on danse*'; and ends with a fantastic scene in the Cour des Pairs."

[3] That is, the episode, had it been developed in the press, would have been good "publicity" for his novel. [J. B.]

144   SAND TO FLAUBERT

Nohant, 21 December [18]68

I certainly am rather peeved with you, not because I'm demanding or selfish but on the contrary, because we were so happy and merry and you wouldn't come and enjoy yourself too. If it was only in order to go and have a better time somewhere else you'd be forgiven in advance, but it's just to coop yourself up and make yourself miserable, and all for work that you hate and that, seeing you want and have to do it, you ought to be able to do at leisure and without sacrificing everything else. You say it's how you're made. There's no answer to that, but other people are allowed to grieve at having a dear friend who's a fettered prisoner far away and beyond rescue. Perhaps you're just being rather coy, to make us feel sorry for you and love you even more. I haven't buried *my*self in literature, and I had a very lively and amusing time during the celebrations, but all the while I was thinking of you and talking about you to our friend from the Palais-Royal,[1] who would have been happy to see you and who greatly likes and admires you.

Turgenev was more fortunate than we, as he managed to tear you away from your inkpot. I've only the slightest acquaintance with him, but I know him by heart.[2] What talent, and how original and strong! I think foreigners are much better than we are. They don't play-act, whereas we either swank or wallow. The French no longer have any social or intellectual standards.

You're an exception – you create an exceptional life for yourself. I'm another, because of the bohemianism and insouciance I was born with. But I can't polish and pore – I love life too much ever to be a *littérateur*, I'm more amused by the condiments than by the dinner. I have had attacks of the malady, but it didn't last. An existence where you forget about your self is so pleasant, a life in which you're not acting a part is such an agreeable play to watch and listen to! When I *have* to get involved personally I draw on courage and resolution, but I don't enjoy myself. But you, you fanatical troubadour, I suspect you get more enjoyment from your work than from anything else in the world. Whatever you say, it's quite possible that *art* is your only passion, and that your seclusion, over which I fret like the fool that I am, is your form of ecstasy. If that's the truth of the matter, so much the better, but do console me by admitting it.

I leave you now, to dress the puppets: because of the bad weather we've taken up fun and games again, and I suppose this will continue for a good part of the winter. So much for the idiot you love and call Maître. A fine sort of maître, who would rather play than work!

Despise me thoroughly, but always go on loving me. Lina tells me to tell you you're a mean thing, and Maurice is furious too, but we love you in spite of ourselves and *on t'embrasse* just the same. Friend Plauchut asks to be remembered to you. He adores you too.

A toi, ungrateful creature.

G. Sand

I'd seen and laughed at the howler in the *Figaro*. The thing seems to have swelled to grotesque proportions. The press has saddled me with a grandson instead of my two little girls, and a Catholic baptism instead of a Protestant one. It doesn't matter. People have to tell a few lies to amuse themselves.

[1] Prince Napoléon.
[2] Sand had met Turgenev in 1845 in the house of their common friend Pauline Viardot, but had not seen him since. They would later become close friends.

CHAPTER V

1869

The two friends began the New Year by writing to each other.

145 FLAUBERT TO SAND

[Croisset, 1 January 1869]
New Year's Eve, 1 a.m.

Why shouldn't I begin the year 1869 with the wish that for you and yours it may be "good, and happy, and followed by many more"? Rather rococo, but I like it.

So let's chat. I am not "working myself to death", for I've never been better. In Paris I was told that I was "fresh-faced as a girl", and people ignorant of my biography attributed that healthy look to the country air. So much for ready-made ideas. Everyone looks after his health in his own way. I, when I'm not hungry, can eat only dry bread. And the most indigestible foods, such as unripe cider-apples, and bacon, are my cures for stomach ache. And so on. A man who has no common sense mustn't live according to common-sense rules.

As to my mania for work, I'll compare it to a rash. I keep scratching myself and yelling as I scratch. It's pleasure and torture combined. And nothing that I write is what I want to write. For one doesn't choose one's subjects: they impose themselves. Shall I ever find mine? Will there ever drop down on me from heaven an idea in perfect harmony with my temperament? Shall I be able to write a book into which I put my entire self? It seems to me, in my moments of vanity, that I'm beginning to glimpse something that might be a novel. But I still have three or four to write before that one (which is as yet very vague); and at the rate I'm going it will be all I can do to write those three or four. I'm like M. Prud'homme, who thought the most beautiful church of all would have the spire of Strasbourg, the colonnade of St Peter's, the portico of the Pantheon, etc. I have contradictory ideals. Hence confusion, stoppage, impotence!

As to the cloistered life to which I condemn myself being a "form of ecstasy" – no! But what to do! To get drunk on ink is better than to get drunk on brandy. The Muse, crabbed though she may be, is the source of less grief than Woman! I cannot accommodate the two. There has to be a choice. Mine was made long ago. There remains the question of the senses. Mine have always been my servants. Even in the days of my greenest youth I did with them exactly as I pleased. I am now almost fifty, and their ardour is the least of my worries.

This regime is not very amusing, I agree. There are moments of emptiness, of hideous boredom. But these decrease as one grows older. To be truthful, *living* strikes me as a business I wasn't cut out for! And yet! . . .

I was in Paris for three days, which I spent doing research and errands for my book. I was so exhausted last Friday that I went to bed at 7 o'clock. Such are my wild orgies in the capital.

I found the Goncourts in a state of frenzied [sic] admiration for a book called *Histoire de ma vie* by G. Sand – which goes to show that they are stronger in good taste than in erudition.[1] They even wanted to write you to express their admiration. On the other hand I found our friend Harrisse stupid. He compares Feydeau to Chateaubriand, greatly admires *Le Lépreux de la Cité d'Aoste*,[2] considers *Don Quixote* tedious, etc. How rare a true feeling for literature is! A knowledge of languages, archaeology, history, etc. – all that should help. But not at all! So-called enlightened people are becoming more and more inept about art. They don't even know what it *is*. Glosses are more important for them than the text. They value crutches more highly than legs.

Old Sainte-Beuve seemed to me quite restored to his usual good cheer. He is permanently infirm, not ill.

I didn't have time to call on the Prince, who has – or had – tertian fever. "I permitted myself to be told" (as Brantôme[3] puts it) that he overdid things a bit on the island of Cythera.[4] What a strange man! Not because of that, but because of all the rest!

I shan't budge from here before Easter. I expect to have finished by the end of May. You'll see me at Nohant this summer, though bombs should fall.

And your work? What are you doing now, chère maître?

When shall we see each other? Will you be coming to Paris in the spring? Je vous embrasse.

Gve Flaubert

[1] Flaubert means that because the last volume of *Histoire de ma vie* had been published in 1855, the Goncourts should have read the work long since.

[2] A novel by Xavier de Maistre (1811).

[3] The chronicler Pierre de Bourdeilles, seigneur de Brantôme (c.1540–1614), "permitted himself to be told" – and to include in his various biographical works – many scandalous anecdotes that were *perhaps* true.

[4] It was on the Ionian island of Cythera that Aphrodite – Venus – landed as she emerged from the sea. The suggestion is that the Prince's fever was venereal.

146 SAND TO FLAUBERT

[Nohant] 1 January [18]69

It's 1 o'clock in the morning. I've just kissed my children goodnight. I'm tired after having spent last night dressing a large doll for Aurore, but I don't want to doss down without kissing you too, mon grand ami et mon gros enfant chéri. May '69 be kind to you and see the end of your novel. May you keep well and always be *you!* I can't think of anything better to wish, et je t'aime.

G. Sand

I don't know the Goncourts' address. Would you mind posting them the enclosed answer?

147 FLAUBERT TO SAND

[Croisset, 14 January 1869]
Thursday evening

I have nothing, absolutely nothing, to tell you, except that I miss a certain person called Georges [sic] Sand, and that I long for news of said individual.

You know, chère maître, it's very nice about the two of us – writing to each other simultaneously on New Year's Eve. There is clearly some strong bond between us.

I see no one, I know nothing about anything, I live like a stuffed bear. Last week, however, I was in Rouen – in the *Salon de la Préfecture*, no less! – to sign the Prefect's daughter's marriage contract. My fellow citizens are a weird-looking lot, and I enjoyed it all immensely.

Why is it that we don't appreciate the Comic when we're young?

I sent your letter on to the Goncourts immediately, needless to say.

I assure you (once again) that they're very nice. And there are so many Pignoufs![1] He's a product of the XIXth century, is Pignouf! Now we even have Pignouflard (his son), and la Pignouflarde (his daughter-in-law).

Do you know the details of the Sainte-Beuve story? I know absolutely nothing. Is he definitely turning against the Empire? Giving in, I mean, to that of his[2] anger? Forgive me!

I embrace you as I love you – with all my strength.

Gve Flaubert

[1] *pignouf:* colloquial: "boor".
[2] "That" – "the empire", in the sense of "dominating force". Flaubert apologizes for the pun. (See Letter 149, Note 2.)

148 SAND TO FLAUBERT

Nohant, 17 January [18]69

A certain person called G. Sand is well, enjoying the marvellous Berry winter, picking flowers, communicating interesting botanical anomalies, making dresses and coats for her daughter-in-law and costumes for puppets, cutting out stage sets, dressing dolls and reading music – but above all spending hours with little Aurore. She's an amazing child. There's no one in the world so inwardly calm and happy as this old retired troubadour, who sings a little serenade to the moon every now and then without bothering much if it's sung well or ill so long as it expresses what he has in mind; and who, the rest of the time, is deliciously idle. He hasn't always been as comfortable as this. He was foolish enough, once, to be young, but as he didn't do any harm, or have any "unwholesome passions", or seek just to satisfy his vanity, he's lucky enough now to be peaceful and easily amused. And this insipid creature takes great pleasure in loving you with all his heart, and not letting a single day go by without thinking of the other old troubadour, confined to the solitary splendour of the rabid artist, scorning the pleasures of this world, and sworn enemy of the magnifying glass and its delights.[1] I don't think there can be two workers in the world more different from one another than we are. But as we're so fond of each other it doesn't matter. If we think of one another at the same moment it must be because we need our opposite number. We complete ourselves by identifying every so often with what is not ourselves.

I believe I told you I'd written a play when I got back from Paris. They like it,[2] but I don't want it to be put on in the spring, and the end of their season is full unless the play they're rehearsing now is a failure. As I'm not one to *wish* misfortune on my colleagues, I'm in no hurry, and my manuscript is in abeyance. I've got plenty of time. I go on with my little annual novel[3] when I have an hour or two to spare. I don't mind not being able to think about it. It matures in the interval. And I always have a pleasant few minutes, before I fall asleep, to go on with it in my head.

I know nothing, absolutely nothing, about the Sainte-Beuve incident. I get a dozen or so newspapers, but it's so rarely I as much as undo the wrappers that if it weren't for Lina, who occasionally tells me the main gist of what's going on, I wouldn't even know if Isidore is still of this world. Sainte-Beuve is very irascible, and so completely sceptical when it comes to ideas, that I wouldn't be surprised at anything he did, one way or the other. He hasn't always been like that, or not to such a degree; he was once more religious and more republican than I was. And he was thin, pale and gentle. How people change! His talent, knowledge, and intelligence have increased enormously. But I liked him better before, as a person. Never mind, there's still a lot of good in him. He loves and respects literature, and he'll be the last of the critics. The others are either artists or idiots. There won't be any more critics in the real sense of the word. Perhaps there's no more need for them. What do you think?

You seem to make a study of *pignoufs*. Personally I avoid them – I know them too well. I like the Berry peasant, who's never, never a boor even when he doesn't amount to much. The word *pignouf* has a special meaning, and was invented exclusively for the bourgeoisie, don't you think? Out of a hundred bourgeois provincial ladies, ninety are confirmed *pignouflardes*, even when they have pretty little ways that would seem to indicate refined instincts. But one is surprised to find these sham ladies are all crude conceit inside. Where will you find a real woman today? She's become a kind of a freak.

Bonsoir, mon troubadour. Je t'aime et je t'embrasse bien fort. So does Maurice.

G. Sand

[1] The allusion is to Sand's love of botanizing, not shared by Flaubert.

[2] That morning, Sand had received a letter from Duquesnel, one of the directors of the Odéon, agreeing to stage *L'Autre*.

[3] This time the "*petit roman de tous les ans*" is *Pierre qui roule*, her novel about actors.

149 FLAUBERT TO SAND

Croisset, 2 February [1869]
Tuesday

Ma chère maître,

Your old troubadour is the very picture of exhaustion. I spent a week in Paris verifying boring details (7 to 9 hours of cabs a day, a fine way to get rich with Literature! Ah well . . .) I have just read over my outline. The amount I still have to write overwhelms me, or rather it makes me almost vomit from discouragement. It's always like this when I get back to work. It's then that I'm bored, bored, bored. But this time it's worse than ever. That's why I so dread any interruption of the grind. I had no choice, however. I had myself carted to undertakers' establishments, to Père-Lachaise, to the valley of Montmorency, past shops selling religious paraphernalia, etc.[1]

In short, I still have four or five months' work ahead of me. What a sigh of relief I'll send up when it's done! And what a long while it will be before I tackle the bourgeois again! It's time I enjoyed myself!

I have seen both Sainte-Beuve and the Princess. And I know everything about their quarrel: it seems to me irreparable. Sainte-Beuve was angry with Dalloz,[2] and went over to *Le Temps*. The Princess begged him not to. He wouldn't listen. That's the whole story. My opinion, if you care to have it, is this: the first fault was committed by the Princess, who was intemperate: but the second and more serious offender is Sainte-Beuve, who acted ungallantly. When you have so accommodating a friend, and when this friend has provided you with an income of 30,000 livres a year, you owe her some consideration. It seems to me that in Sainte-Beuve's place I'd have said: "If you disapprove, let's say no more about it." He was bad-mannered and lacking in magnanimity. What disgusted me a little, just between ourselves, was the way he sang the praises of the Emperor. Yes: to me! Praise of Badinguet! And we were alone, too.

The Princess took things too seriously from the start. I wrote to her, siding with Sainte-Beuve, whereas he, I'm sure, found me unresponsive. That was why, to justify himself in my eyes, he protested his love for Isidore, which I found rather humiliating. For it amounted to taking me for an utter imbecile.

I think he's preparing himself for a funeral like Béranger's, and that he's jealous of old Hugo's ability to speak the language of the people. Why write for newspapers when you can write books and aren't starving to death?

He's far from being a sage; he's not like you! Your Strength charms and amazes me. I mean the Strength of your entire person, not only your brain.

You spoke of criticism in your last letter, saying it will soon disappear. I think, on the contrary, that it's only just beginning. The trend is the opposite of what it used to be, that's all. (In the days of La Harpe, critics were grammarians; in the days of Sainte-Beuve and Taine they're historians.) When will they be *artists*, only artists, but *real* artists? Where have you ever seen a piece of criticism that is concerned, intensely concerned, with the work in itself? The setting in which it was produced and the circumstances that occasioned it are very closely analyzed. But the *inner* poetics that brought it into being? Its composition? Its style? The author's point of view? *Never.*

Such criticism as that would require great imagination and great goodwill. I mean an ever-ready faculty of enthusiasm. And then *taste* – a quality rare even among the best, so very rare that it is no longer even mentioned.

What infuriates me daily is to see a masterpiece and a disgrace put on the same level. They put down the mighty, and exalt those of low degree.[3] Nothing could be more stupid or immoral.

Speaking of stupidity, "I permitted myself to be told" (as le sieur de Brantôme puts it) that Plessy is becoming boring and unsociable. Her friends avoid her.

In Père-Lachaise I was overcome by a deep and painful disgust for mankind. You cannot imagine the fetishism of the tombs. Your true Parisian is more idolatrous than a black. I felt like dropping down into one of the graves.

And people with "advanced ideas" can find nothing better to do than rehabilitate Robespierre! Look at Hamel's book! If there were to be another Republic they'd start blessing Liberty Trees again as a powerful contribution to politics.[4]

Give your two granddaughters my love. Je vous baise sur les deux joues, tendrement.

Your old

Gve Flaubert

When are we going to meet? I expect to be in Paris from Easter to the end of May. This summer I'll come and see you at Nohant. I promise myself.

[1] Continuing to document himself for *L'Éducation sentimentale.*

[2] Sainte-Beuve had broken with the semi-official *Moniteur universel* and its editor Paul Dalloz over the insistence that he delete an unfavourable reference to Mgr Le Courtier, bishop of Montpellier, from one of his weekly articles. He had gone over to *Le Temps*, the mouthpiece of the liberal opposition, despite Princesse Mathilde's request that he not do so. In her displeasure the princess revealed the spirit of her benefactions to Sainte-Beuve in saying that his acceptance of a senatorship (for which she had recommended him) had made him "a vassal of the Empire". (André Billy, *Sainte-Beuve, Sa vie et son temps*, Paris, 1952.)

[3] A reference to *Luke*, i, 52.

[4] Since the recent restoration of permission to hold public meetings, there had been a number in which orators invoked the spirit of 1789, exalting Robespierre, etc.

Ernest Hamel's *Histoire de Robespierre* had appeared in three volumes between 1865 and 1867.

In the 1790s it had been a patriotic fashion to plant trees, called *arbres de la Liberté*, "in honour of the Revolution".

150 SAND TO FLAUBERT

Nohant, 11 February [18]69

While you've been trotting about for your novel I've been doing my best not to get on with mine. I let myself indulge in *indefensible* fantasies. I get caught up in a book I read, which sets me off scribbling something that will merely lie on my desk, bringing in absolutely nothing.[1] It amused, or rather compelled, me – for it's no good my struggling against such whims. They just irrupt and take me over ... I'm not as strong as you think, you see.

As for our friend [Sainte-Beuve], he's ungrateful, whereas our other friend [Princesse Mathilde] is too exacting. As you say, they're both in the wrong; and neither is at fault. It's the social mechanism that's to blame. The kind of gratitude, or rather obedience, that she insists on belongs to a tradition which the present age still exploits (and there's the rub) but no longer accepts as a duty. The attitudes of a person who receives a favour have changed; those of a person who bestows a favour ought, correspondingly, to change. A benefactress should remember that she can't buy another's moral liberty – and as for *him*, he should have realized he'd seem to be under an obligation. The simplest solution would have been not to want an income of 30,000 livres. It's so easy to do without it! We must just let them get on with it. They won't catch us at that game – we've got more sense.

You say some very good things about criticism. But it would take artists to practise it as you prescribe, and artists are too busy with their own work to delve into that of others.

Heavens, what lovely weather! I hope you at least enjoy it through your window? I wager the tulip tree is in bud. Here the peach and apricot trees are flowering. Everyone says they'll get spoiled. That doesn't stop them from being pretty and unconcerned.

We've had our family carnival. Niece, great-nephews and so on. We all wore fancy dress. No difficulty about that here – you've only got to go up to the wardrobe room and come down again as Cassandra or Scapin, Mezzetino, Figaro or Basilio. All the costumes are accurate and very handsome. The best of the lot was Lolo as young Louis XIII in crimson and white satin trimmed with silver braid. I spent three days making that extremely stylish costume, and it looked so pretty and droll on a little girl of three that we were all quite taken aback. Then we played charades, had supper, and larked about till dawn. We still have plenty of energy, you see, even if we are stuck in the back of beyond. So I put off business and going to Paris as long as I can. If you were there I wouldn't be so reluctant. But you're only going to town at the end of March and I can't hang back as long as that. Still, you do promise to come here this summer, and we're absolutely counting on it, even if I have to come and drag you by the hair. Much love in return for that welcome hope.

G. Sand

[1] Sand had been reading a French translation of *El Condenado por Desconfidado*, by Tirso de Molina, which preached the Catholic dogma of Grace. It inspired her to write a short novel, *Lupo Liverani*, published in *La Revue des Deux Mondes* beginning 1 December 1869.

151   SAND TO FLAUBERT

Nohant, 21 February [1869]

I'm all alone at Nohant, as you are at Croisset. Maurice and Lina have gone to Milan to see Calamatta,[1] who's dangerously ill. If they're unfortunate enough to lose him they'll have to go on to Rome to settle his affairs, thus adding bother to bereavement. It's always the way. The sudden separation was very sad: Lina wept both at having to leave her daughters and at not being already with her father. They left me in charge of the children. I'm with them nearly all the time, and the only chance I get to work is when they're asleep, but I'm lucky to have that to take my mind off things. I have news every day from Milan; a telegram takes only a couple of hours to get here. The patient's condition has improved – but as my son and daughter-in-law have only got as far as Turin today, I know about this and they don't. What an effect telegrams have had on things, and how full of fact and free of uncertainty life will be when such procedures have been still more simplified.

Aurore, who usually sits on her father's or mother's lap basking in adoration, and cries every day when I'm not there, hasn't once asked where her parents are. She plays and laughs, then stops and stares out of her beautiful wide eyes and says "Papa?" – or sometimes "Maman?" I distract her, she forgets, and then it happens again. Children are very mysterious! They think without understanding. One sad word would be enough to bring out the sorrow she feels unconsciously. She looks me straight in the eye to see if I'm sad or worried. If I laugh, she laughs. I think children's sensitivity should be allowed to slumber as long as possible, and that Aurore would never cry for me if no one ever mentioned me. What do you think, after bringing up such an intelligent and charming niece?[2] Is it a good thing to make children affectionate and sensitive when they're still very young? I used to think so, but I was disturbed when I found Maurice too impressionable and Solange too touchy and self-willed. I'd like little children to be exposed only to the good, gentle side of life until reason can help them either accept or challenge the bad aspect. What do you think?

Lots of love. Tell me when you're going to be in Paris. As the children may be away for a month, my trip has to be postponed, and I might perhaps be in town at the same time as you.

Ton vieux solitaire

G. Sand

To my surprise I find an excellent definition in the fatalistic Pascal! "Nature advances in fits and starts, *itus et reditus*. She progresses, then regresses, then advances further, then takes two steps back, then thrusts forward further than ever."[3]

What eloquence, eh? How flexible, expressive and concise language becomes, handled by that magnificent talent!

[1] Luigi Calamatta (1801–69), an Italian-born engraver, whose only daughter, Lina, married Maurice Sand in 1862. Parisian by preference, he is the author of several portraits of George Sand.

[2] Flaubert's sister Caroline had died in 1846, leaving an infant daughter, also named Caroline. Flaubert educated his niece, giving her regular lessons which were supplemented by instruction in languages, etc., by tutors. After a youthful attachment had been discouraged by her uncle and great-aunt, Caroline married Ernest Commanville in 1864.

[3] *Pensée* No. 355 in the edition edited by Léon Brunschvicg. Sand had copied it, and it hung over her work table.

152 FLAUBERT TO SAND

[Croisset, 23–24 February 1869]
Tuesday night

You ask me what I think, chère maître? About whether sensitivity in children should be fostered or repressed? It seems to me one shouldn't have preconceived ideas in this matter. It depends on whether they tend to have too much or too little. You can't alter basic character. There are affectionate natures and cold natures – there's no remedy for that. And then the same sight, the same lesson, can produce opposite effects. I ought to have been hardened by being brought up in a hospital and playing as a small child in a dissecting room. And yet no one is more easily moved than I by the sight of physical suffering. It's true that I'm the son of a man who was extremely humane, and sensitive in the good sense of the word. The sight of a dog in pain brought tears to his eyes. Yet this didn't impair his efficiency as a surgeon. He even invented some operations that were quite dreadful.

"Expose children only to the good, gentle side of life until reason can help them either accept or challenge the bad aspect," you say. I don't agree. For then something terrible is bound to take place in their hearts, an infinite disillusionment: and besides, how can reason develop if it doesn't apply itself (or isn't applied daily) to distinguishing right from wrong? Life is perforce an incessant education. Everything has to be learned, from Talking to Dying.

You say some very true things about the inner life of children. Anyone who could see clearly into their little brains would discover the roots of human genius, the origin of the Gods, the sap that determines subsequent actions, etc. A black speaking to his idol and a child to its doll seem to me very close.

The child and the barbarian (the primitive) do not distinguish reality from fantasy. I remember very clearly that when I was five or six I wanted to "send my heart" to a little girl I was in love with. (I mean my *physical* heart.) I pictured it lying on a bed of straw in a basket – the sort of hamper they put oysters in.

But no one has gone as far as you in these analyses. Your *Histoire de ma vie* has pages on the subject that are extraordinarily profound. What I say must be true, because minds quite different from yours have found the work amazing – witness the Goncourts.

Have you read *Madame Gervaisais?*[1] You should.

Your poor daughter-in-law must be very distressed. And Maurice, in consequence? And you too? I'm sorry for all of you. I met M. Calamatta twice: once at Mme Colet's, and the second time at your house, rue Racine, the first time I called on you. Tell me how he gets on.

Winter is approaching its end. I have seldom passed a better, despite an abominable grippe that's kept me coughing and streaming for three weeks. In about ten days I hope to begin my next-to-last chapter. When it's well under way (half done), I'll be off to Paris – toward Easter, not before. Because I miss you madly – or rather, very intelligently.

Our good Turgenev should be in Paris by the end of March. It would be nice if the three of us could dine together.

I have been thinking more about Sainte-Beuve. To be sure, one can "do without 30,000 livres a year." But there's something simpler yet: if you do have them, not to go spouting every week in those rags called newspapers. Why doesn't he write books? – he's rich enough, and talented.

I'm just re-reading *Don Quixote*. What a giant of a book! Can anything be more splendid?

Soon it will be four o'clock. Time to climb between the sheets.

Adieu. I kiss you on both cheeks – you're like fresh bread – and Mlle Aurore too, with all the affection of your troubadour.

Gve Flaubert

---

[1] By the Goncourt brothers, recently published.

153 SAND TO FLAUBERT

Nohant, 7 March [1869]

Still all on my own with my granddaughters. My nephews and friends come most days, but I miss Maurice and Lina. Poor Calamatta is at death's door.

Why don't you give me the Goncourts' address? You never have. Am I never to know it? My letter to them is still waiting to be sent.

Je t'aime et je t'embrasse; je t'aime beaucoup, beaucoup, et je t'embrasse bien fort.

G. Sand

154 FLAUBERT TO SAND

[Croisset] Monday 8 [March 1869]

The Goncourts live at Boulevard de Montmorency 53, Auteuil, Paris.

Let me remind you, by way of excuse, chère maître du bon Dieu, that you never asked me for their address! You sent me a letter for them this past winter, and I forwarded it. *Voilà!*

I am sad because you are. Keep me informed of everything.

How I long to see you! How stupid it is to spend one's life far from those one loves!

Je vous embrasse bien tendrement.

Gve Flaubert

I have nothing whatever to tell you, except that I'm working like the very devil and that it all comes harder and harder.

155 SAND TO FLAUBERT

[Nohant] 12 March [1869]

Poor Calamatta died on the 9th. The children are returning. My Lina must be very upset. The only news I've had is by telegram. It only takes an hour and a half from Milan to here. But it doesn't go into detail, and I worry.

Je t'embrasse tendrement.

G. Sand

Thank you for the address.

156 FLAUBERT TO SAND

[Croisset, 13 March 1869]
Saturday evening

How sorry I am for your poor daughter-in-law, Maurice, and you! Give me their news when they return.

The journey back will have been a distraction, and seeing the children again will do them good. Like a gift.

There's a frightful lot of dying this winter! Rossini, Berryer, Lamartine, Mérimée. . . . Not to mention the rest.[1]

Anyone would think I'd nothing more interesting to tell you! I'll stop. But I greatly long to embrace you, ma très chère maître!

Votre vieux troubadour

Gve Flaubert

[1] Rossini had died on 13 November, 1868; Berryer on 29 November; Lamartine on 28 February, 1869. Mérimée died later, on 3 September, 1870, after a long illness.

With his penultimate chapter completed at last, Flaubert set out for Paris on 27 March, the day before Easter.

157 FLAUBERT TO SAND

[Paris] bd. du Temple 42
Wednesday [31 March 1869]

I miss you and worry about you, chère maître. How are you all? When shall I see you? etc. etc.!

I arrived here on Saturday evening. All my errands are done. And this afternoon I resume work.

Sainte-Beuve looks very ill to me. I fear he's not long for this world.

The day before yesterday, and yesterday, I dined with Turgenev. That man paints such powerful pictures, even in conversation, that he *showed* me G. Sand, leaning over a balcony of Mme Viardot's château at Rosay. Below the turret was a moat; in the moat, a boat. And Turgenev was sitting in that boat, looking up at you. The setting sun was falling on your black hair.

Du Camp and Prince Napoléon asked after you.

Je vous embrasse très fort.

Gve Flaubert

I'm in the midst of paying bills. It makes me irritable, "naturally!" Next time, we'll have a better chat.

158 SAND TO FLAUBERT

Nohant, 2 April [18]69

Cher ami de mon coeur,

All is peaceful and quiet again. The children came back to me very tired. Aurore's been a little unwell. Lina's mother came to see her and settle their affairs. She's an excellent, honest woman, very artistic and amiable. I've had a bad cold too, but everything's getting back to normal, and our charming little girls are a consolation to their dear mother. If the weather wasn't so dreadful and I hadn't got such a cold. I'd come straight to Paris, for I do want to see you there. How long are you staying? Let me know right away.

I'd very much like to renew my acquaintance with Turgenev: I knew him a little, before I'd read any of his work, and I've read it since with the utmost admiration. It seems to me you're very fond of him, so I am too, and I want you to bring him to see us when your novel's finished. Maurice also knows him, and has a very high opinion of him – my son always loves what's unusual.

I'm working away like a slave at my novel on the mummers, trying to make it amusing and instructive about the "art". It's a new form for me, and takes my fancy. But it may not be a success. The current fashion is for marchionesses and midinettes – but what does it matter? You really ought to find me a title that would suggest a modern *Roman comique.*

The children send their love; ton vieux troubadour embrasse son vieux troubadour.

G. Sand

Let me know soon how long you mean to stay in Paris.

You say you're paying bills and getting irritated. If you need any of the ready, I've got a bit on hand at the moment. You know you offered me a loan once, and I'd have taken it had it been needed.

Give Maxime Du Camp my best wishes and thank him for not forgetting me.

159 FLAUBERT TO SAND

[Paris, 3 April 1869]
Saturday morning

Chère maître,

I don't expect to leave Paris before June 10 or 12, when my novel will be finished and a fair copy made.

Thank you for the pecuniary offer! At present I'm not in need.

Since your novel is about actors, why not call it *Les gens du théâtre* [*Theatre People*]? You know the subject inside out. The only thing that bothers me is that you might be too easy on them. Because you know as well as I – those rascals care nothing for art.

Talking of titles: you promised to find one for my novel. Here is what I've decided on, in desperation:

L'Éducation sentimentale[1]

– histoire d'un jeune homme.

I don't say it's good, but so far it's the one that best conveys what I've had in mind. This difficulty in finding a good title makes me wonder whether the *idea* of the work (or rather the concept behind it) isn't clear.

I'd very much like to read you the end.

Now I'll dress and go to meet my mother, who will be staying here, with my niece, until the end of the month.

Cure your cold and join us.

Friendly greetings to all. Et à vous, chère bon maître, toutes mes tendresses.

Gve Flaubert

---

[1] The title, whether in French, or in English translation as *The Sentimental Education*, has long been a source of dissatisfaction. (See Letter 411, Note 1.)

160 FLAUBERT TO SAND

[Paris, 16 April 1869]
Friday morning

I'm worried about you, chère maître. Because despite your usual punctiliousness you haven't answered my last letter. You should have been in Paris long ago, should you not?

Tell Maurice to write if you're ill.

Je vous embrasse très fort.

Gve Flaubert

161 SAND TO FLAUBERT

[Nohant] 17 April [1869]

I'm quite well. I'm finishing (today, I hope) my modern *Roman comique*, which will be called I don't know what. I'm rather tired, because I've been doing lots of other things as well,[1] but I'm going to have a rest in Paris in the next week or so, and say hello to you, and talk to you about yourself, and your work, and forget my own, thank God! and as always love you, bien fort et bien tendrement.

G. Sand

Best wishes from Maurice and his wife.

[1] In addition to finishing *Pierre qui roule*, she was re-writing *Mauprat*, a play adapted from the novel of the same name. In an early form it had enjoyed a run at the Odéon in 1853. The new version was not performed until 1877, after Sand's death.

162 FLAUBERT TO SAND

[Paris, about 19 April 1869]

Chère maître,

I'm busy every evening next week. *Nonobstant*, as soon as you arrive do send me a telegram and I'll come running. So we'll see each other again at last!

I have been worried recently about my mother, who is here in Paris with her granddaughter. (At the moment she's better, thank God.) This has obliged me to go out every day, and is holding up the last part of my novel, which is proving hard to finish. I'll be at it for another month.

How I long to see you!

All good wishes to your family. And to you all my love.

Gve Flaubert

*

Sand finally arrived in Paris on 25 April. But arrangements for her play, *L'Autre*, took up all her time.

163 SAND TO FLAUBERT

[Paris] Monday [26 April 1869]

I got here yesterday evening and am rushing about like a mad thing. But every day at six I'm sure to be found at Magny's, so the first day you're free do come and have dinner with your vieux troubadour qui t'aime et t'embrasse.

But let me know in advance, so that if something unforeseen crops up I shan't be unlucky enough to miss you.

[unsigned]

*

The following evening, 27 April, George Sand went to the Théâtre du Vaudeville to see a double bill of short plays by Meilhac and Labiche. "Flaubert, whom Martine[1] calls M. Flambart, joined me there," she wrote to Maurice that night, "and during one of the acts we sat in the smoking room in the moonlight."

[1] "Martine", whose last name has not been recorded, was an usher, apparently at the Vaudeville, and a helpful friend to Mme Sand.

164 FLAUBERT TO SAND

[Paris] bd. du Temple 42
Thursday 2 o'clock [29 April 1869]

Chère maître,

Since you have no engagement for Saturday night, and especially since you (or rather our) friend Plauchut will be out with his nephew, would you come and dine *en tête à tête* with your old troubadour? I'd spout a few pages.

I'm entirely free tomorrow and the day after, from dawn to dark.

The first part of next week (until Friday) I shan't be free. So, come on Saturday. Tell me what you'd like to eat. My mameluke doesn't cook too badly.

I'll take you home afterwards, or else your maid can pick you up in a cab after she's through at the Vaudeville.

Tomorrow I hope to finish my last chapter?? Then I'll have only the epilogue: 12 pages.

So: till Saturday?

Je vous embrasse.

Gve Flaubert

P.S. Come *very early*, so we'll really have time to see one another.

165 SAND TO FLAUBERT

[Paris, 29 April 1869]
Thursday evening

I've just got back from Palaiseau to find your letter. I can't be sure of being free on Saturday – I have to read through my play with Chilly, as I told you, to settle a few details. But I'm seeing him tomorrow evening and will try to get him to give me another day. So I'll write to you tomorrow evening, Friday, and if he sets me free I'll come to your place at about 3 on Saturday so that we can get some reading in before and after dinner. For which I have a bit of fish, a wing of chicken, an ice, and a cup of coffee – never anything else. If I stick to that, no digestive problems. If Chilly won't let me off, we'll postpone till next week, after Friday.

I sold Palaiseau today, to a master cobbler who has a *leather* patch over his right eye and calls garden sumacs "schumakres".

So by Saturday morning you'll have a line from your vieux camarade.

G. Sand

166 SAND TO FLAUBERT

[Paris, 30 April 1869]
Friday evening

Can't possibly get out today. Isn't it idiotic, being a slave to one's work like this? I'll write before Friday so that we *do* manage to meet one day.

Je t'embrasse, mon vieux troubadour aimé.

G. Sand

167 SAND TO FLAUBERT

[Paris] Monday [3 May 1869]

I'm being more and more invaded. All my days are taken up, up to and including Sunday. Tell me right away if you'll have me on Monday, today week, or if it's to be another day let's fix it, because I'm being attacked on all sides.

Your troubadour, who doesn't want *this* to go on much longer!

G. Sand

168 FLAUBERT TO SAND

[Paris, 4 May 1869]
Tuesday, 11 o'clock

Certainly, chère maître. Agreed! Next Monday – I'll expect you. For dinner! Come in the afternoon, at whatever time you like.

I don't think I'll be going out on Friday or Saturday. So if you should happen to be in my part of town, climb my four flights, s.v.p.

In any case, until Monday.

Mille tendresses.

Gve Flaubert

How difficult life is in Paris!

169 SAND TO FLAUBERT

[Paris, 4 May 1869]
Tuesday evening

Till Monday then, and if I have an hour free I'll come and say hello to my troubadour before. But don't put yourself out – I know all too well one isn't one's own master in this place. In any case, till Monday between 3 and 4, and sweep your flue[1] so as to read me part of the book before dinner.

G. Sand

[1] Sand writes this in slang, "*ramone ton galoubet*": "*ramoner* is to sweep (a chimney), *galoubet*, a small flute.

*

On Monday May 10, the much-awaited reading of *L'Éducation sentimentale* took place, from three o'clock to eleven, with an hour's interruption for dinner. George Sand enjoyed it greatly. "Prime example of beautiful painting," was the way she put it in her diary.

A few days later, on May 12, Flaubert and Sand saw each other again at a dinner given by Princesse Mathilde. Among others present were the Goncourts, Gautier and Taine. "They demolish everybody except Hugo and *us*," Sand laments in her diary. "The princess defends Feuillet. I observe the battle. I hear them demolish Alexandre [Dumas, the younger] as thoroughly as they do Sardou. So: go ahead – be rivals! To defend anyone would have been useless: I wouldn't even have been heard." And the next day, in a letter to her son: "Only literature was discussed, and as usual nobody agreed with anybody."

That evening Flaubert must have complained to Sand about the contract for *Salammbô*, which bound him to give his future "modern" novel to the publisher Michel Lévy for 10,000 francs: and apparently Sand promised to speak to Lévy about improving the terms.

170 FLAUBERT TO SAND

[Paris, 13 May 1869]
Thursday night

Herewith my contract with the child of Israel. (One might cry, as one reads it, *"Dieu des Juifs, tu l'emportes!")*[1] Look at it and act accordingly, chère maître.
I still count on having *everything* finished by the middle of next week.
Tell me your evening plans after Thursday.
We have a lot of things that we must go over together, don't you think?
Je vous embrasse tendrement.

Gve Flaubert

My mameluke asks me to remind you about theatre tickets.

[1] From Racine's *Athalie*, V, 6. "God of the Jews, thou prevailest!"

*

On May 16th, "at 4 minutes to 5 in the morning", as he wrote in a letter to his friend Jules Duplan, Flaubert finished *L'Éducation sentimentale*. The next day he called on Mme Sand to tell her the news, probably reminding her of her promise to speak to Lévy.

171 SAND TO FLAUBERT

[Paris, 18 May 1869]
Tuesday evening

I saw Lévy today. First I sounded him out; I could see he didn't want to give up his contract at any price. Then I sang the praises of the book and told him he'd got it very cheap. But, he said, if the book runs to two volumes that will be 20,000 francs – that's agreed. Am I right in thinking there *will* be two volumes? But I kept on at him, and he said, if the book's a success I shan't make a fuss about another two or three thousand francs. I said you wouldn't ask him for anything – that wasn't your way; but that *I* would insist for you, without your knowing. And when he left he told me not to worry, if the book's a success I don't say I won't see the author gets something out of it. But will he keep his word? That's all I've been able to do for the moment, but I'll return to the charge as and when. Leave it to me. I'm sending you back your contract.
What day next week will you come and dine with me at Magny's? I'm a bit tired. It would be very kind if you'd come and read to me at my place – we'd be alone and one evening would be enough for what's left. Tell me what day suits you, and come at half-past 6 if you don't mind – my digestion's beginning to suffer a little from these Parisian habits.
Ton troubadour qui t'aime.

G. Sand

The rest of this week will conclude the Palaiseau business. But I'm free on Sunday if you like. Let me know if half-past 6 on Sunday at Magny's suits you.

172   SAND TO FLAUBERT

(in reply to a lost letter from Flaubert)   [Paris, 20 May 1869]
                                                             [Thursday morning]

Yes, Monday, mon cher bon ami, I count on you et je t'embrasse.
                                                             G. Sand

I'm just off to Palaiseau *and it's 10 in the morning!*

173   SAND TO FLAUBERT

                                                             [Paris, 20 May 1869]
                                                             Thursday evening

I count on you for Monday, then, at half-past 6, but as I'm going to Palaiseau I may be a few minutes late or early. The first to get to Magny's waits for the other. I'm so looking forward to hearing what comes next. Don't forget the manuscript.

                                                             Ton troubadour

                                                             *

Sand did not go to Palaiseau on the 24th.

Instead, she called on Sainte-Beuve, who continued ill. There she saw Flaubert, and they dined together that evening at Magny's. "Before dinner he read me the end of his novel, which is excellent," she wrote in her diary. "Later I read him my play, which moves him to tears.[1] Martine and I drive Flaubert home along the boulevards: they are full, but marvellously quiet – no singing or shouting. Beautiful moonlight."[2]

They made another appointment for dinner at Magny's the following Friday, with Prince Napoléon.

---

[1] *L'Autre*, which she had finished on May 14. On the 25th she wrote in her diary: "I work all day on Flaubert's suggestions."

[2] Elections for the legislature had been held that day, with large Liberal gains. Sand wrote to Maurice and Lina: "... I went on foot to call on Sainte-Beuve. I saw the Prince at my house on my return, then Flaubert, and the three of us made an appointment to dine at Magny's on Friday.... I dined with Flaubert, who read me the end of his novel and will come to see us this summer without fail. I read him my play, which is much improved and made him cry his eyes out. We went out at 11 o'clock to see Paris in its peaceful triumph."

174 FLAUBERT TO SAND

[Paris, 26–27 May 1869]
Wednesday night

Chère maître,
So it's agreed that we dine next Friday chez Magny instead of chez moi?
I have just replied to the Prince, saying I'll be there.
Mille tendresses.

Gve Flaubert

175 SAND TO FLAUBERT

[Paris, 29 May 1869]
Saturday

This morning I had to sign the contract with the Odéon. I had no choice in
the matter. I'm to read my play[1] in October and it will be put on in November
– not the time of year I like, but they can't guarantee the time I wanted. They
swear they never make a contract for a play which isn't absolutely ready;[2] that
Bouilhet's[3] isn't finished; that when it *is* finished it still won't be *au point*; that
getting to be *au point* is often the largest and most difficult part of the author's
work, because it sometimes calls for lengthy revisions. In short, whether they're
telling the truth or not, they're treating Bouilhet as they treated me about *my*
play. It was to have been staged last February, but they postponed it and didn't
let me put it into final shape straight away, as I could and would have done.
They preferred to put on *Guttemberg*,[4] which was ready but wasn't a success.
This way of doing things can be very disappointing for authors and directors
alike. But the opposite procedure, the one La Rounat used to follow, ran the
risk of leaving the theatre without a play to put on. At least, that's *their* explanation. Keep this letter to yourself, but explain to Bouilhet that I had to yield
to *force majeure*.
   See you soon, I hope? Je t'embrasse. It was the Prince who stole your
overcoat.[5] I sent it on to you this morning.

[unsigned]

----

[1] *L'Autre* was to have its première at the Odéon on 25 February 1870.
[2] "*au point*".
[3] *Mademoiselle Aïssé*, a verse drama championed by Flaubert after the author's death.
[4] Verse drama in five acts, by Édouard Fournier.
[5] Prince Napoléon had walked away with Flaubert's coat following the dinner at Magny's
the previous evening.

176 FLAUBERT TO SAND

[Paris, 4 June 1869]
Friday, 11 o'clock

Chère maître,

I'm counting on coming to see you Sunday morning. Between 11 and noon. Is that too early?

For the past week I've been "engaged in the most frenzied activity". My novel is copied, and I have found an apartment.[1] But I'm exhausted.

I'm definitely leaving on Monday. Shall I be leaving alone? Try to make it not so.

Je vous embrasse.

Gve Flaubert

[1] At 4, rue Murillo, overlooking the Parc Monceau.

*

Sand did not accompany Flaubert to Croisset: they exchanged farewells that Sunday morning. Flaubert immediately took up *La Tentation de Saint Antoine* again,[1] while awaiting a visit from Louis Bouilhet, who was to help him with a final revision of *L'Éducation sentimentale*. Sand, at Nohant, set about correcting the proofs of *Pierre qui roule* for serial publication in *La Revue des Deux Mondes*.

With *L'Éducation sentimentale* finished, Flaubert allowed himself to write longer letters, often more spirited than in the past.

[1] The reader may recall that in 1856 Flaubert had written a new version of the first (1848-9) *Tentation de Saint Antoine*, and put it aside. It was this version that he had read to George Sand at Croisset in 1866. Now in 1869 he began yet another version. He would work sporadically on this third – and final – version of the *Tentation* until its publication in 1874.

177 FLAUBERT TO SAND

[Croisset] Thursday 24 [June 1869]

Well, chère maître, how are you? Is your stomach better? Did you find your family well? etc. etc.?

Aren't you planning to come to Paris at the beginning, or in the middle, of July? And will you push on a bit then, as far as Croisset?

I shan't have great distractions to offer you. My poor dear mother is aging rapidly: she grows deafer and weaker every day. At the moment she has the Vasse ladies with her, from Saint-Ouen (you know them, and they ask me to send you ... etc.), and thanks to their company she's a little less depressed. But when we're alone, just the two of us, I assure you, it's lamentable.

But let's talk about something else.

Is it true that you and Renan have quarrelled?[1] I heard it from the Prince, the day before I left Paris.

My prediction has proved correct. By running for office my friend Renan has merely made himself ridiculous.[2] It's his own fault: when a man of style lowers himself to action he falls from grace and must be punished. Besides: is there such a thing as true Politics, at present? The citizens who are hot for or against the Empire or the Republic seem to me as useful as those who used to argue about efficacious and efficient grace.[3] Now, thank God, Politics is as dead as Theology! It lasted for three hundred years: quite long enough!

Do you remember I foretold the religious conversion of that nice Mme Plessy? Well, now I predict another. *When* it will be I don't know. But it will happen. This time it will be Alexandre Dumas, *fils*. I was struck by the mystical expression on his face the last time I saw him. Everything persuades me that I'm not wrong about this. Note the increasing tendency toward Catholicism in all his works, and especially in his most recent prefaces.[4] Keep these remarks to yourself, of course. But don't be surprised if some day you see him go to Mass.

For my part, I'm at present lost among the Fathers of the Church. (As for my novel, *L'Éducation sentimentale*, I no longer think about it, thank God. It has been copied. Other hands have passed over it. So it's no longer mine. It no longer exists. That's that!) I have taken up my old infatuation – St Anthony. I have re-read my notes, made a new outline, and am devouring Lenain de Tillemont's *Mémoires ecclésiastiques*. I'm hoping to find a logical development (and thus a dramatic interest) in the saint's various hallucinations. I like this extravagant milieu, and am plunging into it. *Voilà*.

I'm worried about my poor Bouilhet. He's in such a nervous state that he's been advised to spend a while in the south of France. He's suffering from invincible hypochondria. How strange: he used to be such a cheerful fellow.

My niece is greatly enjoying herself in Norway.[5] I shan't leave my mother until she comes back, about the middle of August. Then I'll come to see you. And move into my new apartment in Paris.

God! The life led by those old Desert Fathers! – how fascinating, and how weird! They were probably all Buddhists. This is a problem well worth time and thought, and solving it would be much more useful than choosing between Jouvencel and Renan. "Oh, ye of little faith!" *Vive St Polycarpe!*

Kiss your granddaughters for me. Je vous baise sur les deux joues.

Your old friend, still "hindignant"!

Gve Flaubert

Fanjat, back in the news these last few days, is the individual who on 25 February '48 [sic] called for the death of Louis Philippe "without trial". Thus is the cause of Progress served.[6]

---

[1] No evidence of such a quarrel exists.

² Renan had campaigned as deputy for the department of Seine-et-Marne, but was defeated by Hippolyte-Félicité-Paul Jouvencel, the radical candidate.

³ In a footnote, M. Jacobs points out that the proper theological terms here are *la grâce efficace* (in English "efficacious") and *la grâce suffisante* ("sufficient"). Commenting on this ecclesiastical dispute, he adds: "The Thomists (Dominicans) maintain that grace always has an effect, whereas according to the Molinists (Jesuits) man's will is free to resist grace." But Professor Giles Constable has suggested that Flaubert's "mistake" may have been wilful – a satirical jibe at ecclesiastical jargon.

⁴ Flaubert had perhaps read Dumas' preface to his *Théâtre complet* (1868–9), in which a moralizing tendency is evident.

⁵ Mme Commanville and her husband, a lumber dealer, were on a business trip to Norway and Sweden.

⁶ There had recently been rumours in the press that the deputy Jouvencel had been killed in a duel by Fanjat (or Fangeat), a republican ultra-radical who had been living as an exile in Belgium since the coup d'état. Actually there had been no duel, but Fanjat had accused Jouvencel in a newspaper of having committed "certain acts of a nature to put his honour into question". Jouvencel had appealed to a *jury d'honneur*, which had declared him blameless.

*

Sand's reply, sent on June 30th (as we know from her records), seems not to have survived. A pity, as one infers from Flaubert's next letter.

178   FLAUBERT TO SAND

[Croisset, 5 July 1869]
Monday

What a sweet and charming letter, maître adoré! Certainly there is no one like you, my word of honour: if I wasn't convinced of that before, I am now. A gale of stupidity and folly is sweeping over the world these days. Rare are those who stand firm and strong.

My poor mother continues to drive me crazy. When she's not worrying about her granddaughter and has finished tormenting herself over her health, she's fretting about the housekeeping. And then it starts all over again. The Vasse ladies are taking her to Vernon with them tomorrow, and I hope the change of air will do her good. I'll stay alone with the Church Fathers and a number of other things. Your troubadour has his nose to the grindstone. The joy of no longer having to depict bourgeois and make them talk puts me into high spirits despite it all.

My poor Bouilhet is now at Vichy. From there he'll go on to Mont-Dore. His last letter wasn't bad, and I hope he may be cured. But the last time I saw him (ten days ago) I was very upset. No one knows what's really wrong with him. He's very short of breath, and lives in an almost continual state of terror.

I believe absolutely, like you, that one can cure oneself if one wants to. But will isn't given to everyone. There's a certain sensuousness in pain that causes people to give way to it.

My religious studies have inspired me with such disgust for theology and Christians that I'm reading Cicero's philosophical works with delight. What a difference between that society and its successor! I have just re-read Renan's *Jesus*: a charming book rather than a splendid one. What a strange mind! The feminine element and the episcopal are too dominant. His *Saint Paul*[1] is dedicated to his wife, as his *Jesus* was to his sister. It seems to me that someone whose intellect was devoted above all to Truth and Justice wouldn't have flaunted a pair of skirts in this way on his opening pages?

If he took care to remain on good terms with all parties for the purpose of his election, he was only acting according to his nature, which is all nuances, mists, compromises. That's why his wanting to become involved in the business of this world struck me as grotesque. Action, which is a debasement for men of his stamp, calls for a single-mindedness of which he is incapable.

That is what I meant when I wrote that the time of Politics is past. In the eighteenth century, Diplomacy was the great thing. "*Le secret des cabinets*" really existed in those days. Entire nations were still allowing themselves to be manipulated, or divided, or merged. That order of things seems to me to have ended in 1815. Since then, we've done little but argue about the exterior Form we should give to that fantastic and odious entity called the State. Experience proves (it seems to me) that no Form contains the Good in itself. The terms Orléanism, Republic, and Empire are now meaningless, because the most contradictory ideas can co-exist in all those compartments. All the flags have been so sullied with blood and shit that it's time to do away with them. Down with words! No more symbols or fetishes! The great moral of the present regime will lie in demonstrating that universal suffrage is as stupid as divine right, even if somewhat less odious.

The "question" is therefore misconceived. It is no longer a matter of dreaming of the best form of government, since one is as good as another, but of ensuring that Science[2] prevails. That is the most pressing matter. The rest will follow of itself. Purely intellectual men have rendered greater service to the human race than all the St Vincent de Pauls in the world! And politics will continue to be nonsense as long as it's not a department of science. A country's government should be a branch of its *Institut*, and the most minor branch at that.[3]

But before concerning ourselves with "social security"[4] and even with agriculture, we send a Robert-Houdin to all the villages of France to work miracles![5]

Isidore's greatest crime is the squalor in which he leaves our beautiful country. *Dixi*.

I admire Maurice's activities and his healthy way of life.[6] But I'm incapable of emulating him. Nature, far from invigorating, exhausts me. When I lie in the grass it seems to me that I'm already below ground, and that lettuces are beginning to sprout from my stomach. Your troubadour is a congenitally unhealthy man. I only like the country when I'm travelling, because then the independence of my self obliterates my awareness of my nothingness.

My respects to your ram, Monsieur Gustave. Whose idea was it? It gave me a good laugh.[7]

Aimez-moi toujours.

Toutes mes tendresses.

Gve Flaubert

I wish you good work, good health, and good humour. Many kisses to your granddaughters.

[1] Renan's *Saint Paul* had just been published. About his *Vie de Jésus* (1863), Flaubert had written to his friend Mlle Leroyer de Chantepie (23 October 1863): "I am less enthusiastic than the public about it. I like such matters to be treated more scientifically. But because it's gracefully written, women and superficial readers will enjoy it. That's a great deal, and I consider it a great victory for philosophy to compel the public to think about such matters."

[2] i.e. objective thought.

[3] Here Flaubert's ideas reflect those put forward by Renan, especially in his article "La Monarchie constitutionelle en France", which would appear in *La Revue des Deux Mondes* for 1 November 1869. The two writers had doubtless discussed these matters during their various meetings.

[4] "*Caisses de secours*". Flaubert is probably alluding to the "*Caisses d'assurance en cas d'accident et de décès*" (National accident and life insurance), instituted on 11 July 1868.

[5] In 1857 the French government had sent the celebrated conjuror Robert-Houdin (Houdini) to North Africa in an attempt to destroy the nefarious influence of the marabouts on the native population. His feats, announced as "miracles", were a great success.

[6] Early in June 1869, Maurice and Lina had begun to practise scientific farming and stock-breeding at Nohant.

[7] The ram ("a wonder", according to George Sand's diary) had been bought on June 17th and named at once after Flaubert.

*

About July 10th, Bouilhet, his condition now hopeless, returned to Rouen. Flaubert went to see him every other day. "I found him improving," he was to write to Maxime Du Camp on the 23rd. "His appetite was excellent, as were his spirits. . . . I left for Paris hoping he might live a long time." But Bouilhet had died on the 18th; and Flaubert, returning in haste to Rouen, found himself in charge of his friend's funeral. "For me, this is an irreparable loss," he wrote to Frédéric Fovard, his Paris notary. "What I buried two days ago was my literary conscience, my judgment, my compass – not to mention the rest." At the funeral he broke down and had to be escorted home. There he found a parcel from Mme Sand, containing several portraits of herself, and a letter that is lost.

179 FLAUBERT TO SAND

[Croisset, 20 July 1869]
Tuesday, 5 o'clock

I have just *buried* my poor Bouilhet. And back here at Croisset I find your portraits. It's as though you sent them to me as a consolation: thank you, chère maître.

Now I'll let myself go for a bit. Then I'll feel better – at least I hope so. But it's hard. An old friend – a friend of 37 years – gone!

And I was in charge of the ceremony. Grotesque, horrible details, etc.

I can say no more. I embrace you.

Gve Flaubert

*

George Sand's reply, written on July 22 and no doubt eloquent with sympathy, has disappeared. If Flaubert sent a letter in return, that too has vanished.

His friend's death left him with much to do: among other things, he supervised the publication of Bouilhet's posthumous verse (Flaubert wrote a preface for the volume), and the production of Bouilhet's most recently written drama, *Mademoiselle Aïssé*, which had been accepted by the Odéon, "subject to correction".[1]

[1] Mlle Aïssé was a Circassian, born in the late 1690s and sold in the Constantinople slave market, when she was a mere child, to the French ambassador, the comte de Ferrol. Ferrol brought her to Paris and supervised her education: her beauty, wit and exotic story made her a favourite in the salons of the Regency. Bouilhet's play is based on episodes in her life and in that of her lover, the chevalier d'Aydie.

180 SAND TO FLAUBERT

Nohant, 6 August [1869]

Well, cher bon ami, here we are in August, and you promised you'd come. We haven't forgotten, we count on it, dream about it, and talk of it every day. You were supposed to go on a trip to the seaside first, if I'm not mistaken. You must be feeling the need to throw off your grief. The effort doesn't drive it away, but does force it to live beside us without weighing us down too much. I've been thinking about you a lot lately. I'd have hurried to see you if I hadn't thought you'd have older friends around you, friends with more right to be there than I. I wrote to you at the same time as you were writing to me: our letters must have crossed. Come and see us, mon vieux chéri. I shan't go to Paris this month – I don't want to miss you. My children will be so pleased to spoil you and try to distract you. We all love you, and I love you *passionately*, as you know.

[unsigned]

181 FLAUBERT TO SAND

[Croisset] Friday 6 August [1869]

Chère maître,

I leave tomorrow for Paris, so write to me at bd. du Temple 42.

My poor Bouilhet's death (which has convulsed my entire life) makes it necessary to change my vacation plans.

When shall I come to Nohant? Not before the winter, probably. I'm going to be overburdened with things to do. I have to 1st move; 2nd attend to the printing of my novel; and 3rd supervise the production of *Aïssé*. And much more besides.

And you? Give me your news. When things are a bit calmer I'll write at greater length.

Je vous embrasse bien tendrement.

Your old

Gve Flaubert

182 SAND TO FLAUBERT

Nohant, 14 August [18]69

We're very upset at your change of plan, cher ami, but given all your troubles and cares we don't like to complain. We can only want you to do what will distract you most and give you least pain. I do hope to be seeing you in Paris as you're going to stay in town for a while and I always have things to do there. But we see so little of one another in Paris, and are worn out with so many tedious obligations! In short, it really grieves me not to be able to look forward to having you in our own home, where we'd have vied with one another to love you, and you'd have felt as if you were in *your* own home – sad when you wanted to be sad, busy when you felt inclined. But I resign myself, so long as you're better off elsewhere for the moment and will make it up to us as soon as you can.

Have you at least settled matters with Lévy? Is he paying you for two volumes? I want you to have enough to be independent and free to dispose of your own time.

Here it's a haven of intellectual repose amidst the boisterous activity of Maurice and his brave little wife, who's set herself to like whatever he likes and help him fervently in everything he undertakes. I look like the personification of idleness, surrounded by all this positive effort. I do some botany and bathe in a little cold stream. I'm teaching my manservant to read, I'm correcting proofs,[1] and I'm well. What a life! And nothing bores or troubles me in a world where it seems to me, *as far as I'm concerned*, that all is for the best. But I'm afraid of becoming even more boring, myself, than I used to be. People like me aren't popular. They're too harmless. But *you* must still love me a little, for from the sorrow I feel at not seeing you I can tell how terribly grieved I'd be if you were deliberately not writing.

Et je t'embrasse tendrement, cher vieux.

G. Sand

---

[1] The final proofs of *Pierre qui roule*, which was appearing in *La Revue des Deux Mondes* between 15 June and 1 September, 1869.

183 FLAUBERT TO SAND

[Croisset] Sunday morning, 15 August 1869]
Isidore's birthday[1]

Chère bon maître adoré,

For some days I've been wanting to write you a long letter telling you everything I've been feeling this past month. It's strange. I've been passing through all kinds of curious states of mind. But I haven't the time or peace of mind to collect my thoughts properly.

As to Nohant, I'll come this winter, when *Aïssé* and my novel are off my hands.

Lévy has given me 6 thousand fr. (first payment); we haven't discussed the rest. There will be two octavo volumes. Don't worry about your troubadour. He will always retain "his independence and freedom", because he'll do as he's always done. He's let everything go rather than submit to any kind of obligation.

And then, with age one's needs are fewer. I no longer pine because I don't live in castles in Spain.

What would do me good, now, would be to plunge furiously into *Saint Antoine*. But I have no time even to read. And as for travel – a couple of Sundays at Dieppe with Caroline!

Hear ye this: Originally, your play was to have opened after *Aïssé*. Then it was agreed that it should go on *before*. Now Chilly and Duquesnel want it to go on after. Solely to "take advantage of the occasion" – my poor Bouilhet's death. They'll give you some kind of compensation. Well, I – who am in sole charge of *Aïssé* exactly as though I were its author – I won't have it. I simply won't – please understand this – have you disadvantaged in any way.

You think I'm as meek as a lamb. Don't you believe it! Act precisely as though *Aïssé* didn't exist. And no "delicacy", please, or I'd be vexed. Between ordinary friends there's need for consideration and niceties. But that sort of thing would be out of place between you and me. We owe each other nothing but love. *Dixi*.

I believe the managers of the Odéon are going to miss Bouilhet in every way. I'll be less easy-going at rehearsals.

Weren't you to come to Paris for *La Petite Fadette*,[2] in September? I'd like to read you *Aïssé*, so that we could talk of it a little. Some of the actors who have been suggested are to my mind impossible. It's so difficult to deal with illiterates!

Friendly greetings to your family, cher [sic] maître, and to you all my affection.

Gve Flaubert

[1] August 15, the feast of the Assumption, is also the feast-day of St Néopolus, martyred at Alexandria in the fourth century. In France he came to be considered the patron saint of men named Napoléon. Beginning in 1852, the day was celebrated as a national holiday. In 1869, the centenary of the birth of Napoleon I, there were special festivities.

[2] *La Petite Fadette*, an *opéra comique* by Michel Carré based on George Sand's novel of the same name, was to open on 11 September 1869.

184 SAND TO FLAUBERT

Nohant, 17 August [1869]

As, cher vieux troubadour chéri, you want me to settle things without sacrificing my own interests, I've decided to stick to the letter of agreement I have with the Odéon. According to that I'm supposed to read the play on October 10th, and it's to be performed around the 15th or 20th of November. They were the ones who insisted on this, though I wanted them to do *Aïssé* then. They swore *Aïssé* wasn't finished and that they wanted my play. They signed. I signed. And now I've arranged all my plans and business for the whole year to fit in with that, and it would be extremely inconvenient to have to change everything. What's more, if you allow one promise to be broken in the theatre, you can never be sure of anything with them again, and they won't regard any agreement as binding. So please tell them I don't want to change the dates. The later in the year *Aïssé* is put on, the more interest and success it will meet with. Death is not a suitable subject for exploitation, and if my play fails our friend's will be all the more likely to triumph.

You say you won't be so easy-going as poor Louis. You'll soon see one has to be easy-going, or else one hampers the work and thereby harms the play's chances. Actors are fragile instruments; if you play them too hard they break. You have to keep telling them they're good; they only react to praise; criticism shatters them. If you want to consult me about who would be the best for each part, I think I know almost all the Odéon people and their abilities pretty well. And – which is always useful to know – their effect on the Odéon audience. I've seen so much of them, from both sides of the footlights! I'm sorry you can't come and read me the play. But I'll try to come to Paris for the purpose, if you need me before I'm due to arrive anyway.

I can't write any more. I've got a bad hand. A cut and a graze. As I can't scribble, I botanize. But I can still put my arms round you and give you a hug.

[unsigned]

185   FLAUBERT TO SAND

[Paris, 31 August or 1 September 1869]

Chère maître,

About a fortnight ago I told Chilly of your intentions, which are mine as well, but I've had no reply. Have you?

Your old troubadour is demoralized – the result of correcting his proofs. How can some people be thrilled by seeing their works in print? I find it nauseating.

My move to rue Murillo is another headache. What I need is either to see some Blue or to work like mad.

Je vous embrasse.

Gve Flaubert

When do you come to Paris? And *La Petite Fadette*? Tell me your plans.

186   SAND TO FLAUBERT

[Nohant, 2–4 September 1869]
Thursday

I don't know anything about Chilly either, nor about *La Petite Fadette*. I set out for a trip to Normandy in a few days' time, and shall be passing through Paris. If you feel like jaunting around with me – oh no, you don't jaunt around, do you? – but we'll see one another in passing. I've earned a little holiday. I've been working like a horse.[1] I need to see some blue too, but the blue of the sea is good enough for me, whereas you feel we should have the blue of the artistic and literary firmament overhead. Pooh, there's no such thing! All is prose, flat prose, in the surroundings men have concocted for themselves. It's only by getting away from it all for a bit that one can return to the normal being inside oneself.

I resume after a couple of days when my hand hurt too much for me to write. I'm not going to Normandy after all: my friends the Lamberts, whom I was going to see in Yport, are coming back to Paris, and I have to go to town for my own affairs too. So I'll probably see you there next week, when I'll give my own lad a good hug. If only I could substitute Aurore's ruddy face for my own. She's not what people call pretty, but she's adorable, and so quick it amazes us all. Her chatter's as amusing as the talk of a grown-up person – if by any chance that *is* amusing.

So I'm going to have to start thinking of my own affairs again! I can't bear the thought – it's the only thing that disturbs my serenity. But you'll console me by chatting to me a little when you have the time.

A bientôt, and good luck with the nauseating proof-reading. I always scamp it, but I don't set myself up as an example.

The children send their love, et ton troubadour t'aime.

G. Sand

Saturday evening

I've just heard from the Odéon. They're busy on the production of my play, and don't mention anything else.

[1] She has been re-copying *L'Autre.*

187 FLAUBERT TO SAND

[Paris, 5 September 1869]
Sunday morning

So we'll see each other! At last!

Send me a line as soon as you arrive.

Chilly is going to put your play into rehearsal immediately. I saw him yesterday. It's definite.

Your troubadour is still not very frisky. Il vous embrasse tendrement.

Gve Flaubert

I'll be at bd. du Temple for another fortnight.

188 SAND TO FLAUBERT

[Paris, 6 September 1869]
Monday evening

They wrote yesterday saying they needed me at the Opéra-Comique. So here I am in the rue Gay-Lussac. When are we going to meet? Just let me know. All my days are still free.

Je t'embrasse.   G. Sand

*

From George Sand's Diary, 7 September:

"Rehearsal of *La Petite Fadette*; very nice [...] Flaubert comes in at the end. I go with him to see his apartment on the *jardin* Monceau [sic]. Splendid view."

189 SAND TO FLAUBERT

[Paris, 8 September 1869]
Wednesday morning

I'm sending you back the muffler you left in the cab.[1] It *is* tomorrow, Thursday, that we're dining together? I've written to fat Marchal telling him to come to Magny's too.

Ton troubadour

G. Sand

[1] Sand uses the slang, *sapin:* in effect, "the rattle trap".

On the 9th, Mme Sand, Flaubert and the painter Charles-François Marchal dined together at Magny's; and later, in Sand's apartment, were joined by Plauchut. "They are my three best *camarades*," Sand wrote in her diary.

Two days later, *La Petite Fadette* opened at the Opéra-Comique. Sand was in the manager's box with Flaubert and other friends, and from the theatre Plauchut took them all home to celebrate.

190 FLAUBERT TO SAND

[Paris, 12 September 1869]
Sunday morning

We – rather I – forgot Mme Espinasse[1] again. Stick that name on your mirror, so that the matter can be attended to when you return.

What a good time we had last night!

A bientôt. Et mille tendresses de votre vieux troubadour.

Gve Flaubert

[1] Mme Espinasse was Princesse Mathilde's "*dame pour accompagner*" – her lady-in-waiting. The "matter" has not been identified.

*

Shortly thereafter, Sand paid two brief visits to the Ardennes, the setting for her new novel, *Malgrétout*.

191 SAND TO FLAUBERT

Paris, Tuesday [5 October 1869]

Where are you, mon cher troubadour? I'm writing to you at the boulevard du Temple still, but perhaps you've taken possession of your delightful apartment. And I don't know the *address*, even though I've seen the house, the place it's in, and the view. I myself have been to the Ardennes twice, and in eight or ten days from now, if neither Lina nor Maurice has come to Paris, as they'd like to do, I'll go back to Nohant. So you and I must get in touch and see one another.

I'm more or less *sfogata*[1] now of my need to jaunt, and charmed with what I've seen. Tell me what day – except tomorrow, Wednesday – you can spare to dine with me at Magny's or somewhere else, with or without Plauchut – with anybody you like so long as I can see you and give you my love.

Ton vieux camarade qui t'aime

G. Sand

[1] Italian: "freed".

Flaubert and Sand met for dinner at Magny's on 7 October, together with Plauchut and Sand's daughter Solange. They discussed the situation at the Odéon, which they both found disquieting; and a few days later Sand reported to Flaubert on a meeting she had had there with the director, Chilly.

192 SAND TO FLAUBERT

[Paris, 11 October 1869]
Monday evening

I saw Chilly this evening: he's scared lest you take *Haïssé* [sic] away from him. He asked me to plead his cause, and I do think it's a good one. I had an agreement with him which I'd have broken if you'd wanted me to, and which I'll break still if you like. Self-interest is nothing beside friendship. If my play had been done next month, you'd have had all spring for *Aïssé* (I don't think it's really got an H). But *Le Bâtard*[1] is a success, and one can't just push it out and take its place. *It* will push *us* back until December, though. I won't mention the Latour-Saint-Ybars piece[2] – they say it won't last a week. Anyhow, it's certain mine will be put on in late December or early January. Of course, I mightn't last any longer than the Saint-Ybars play – luck is something one can't predict – and in that case they'd hurry *Aïssé* on, and it would open in February. But suppose I do have a success, and last through January, February, March. That's a good long time. You'd come on in April and have April, May, and June, which is a good long time too. The Odéon doesn't *have* to close before the summer. When they have a success on their hands they don't act as stupidly as La Rounat,[3] who closed *Villemer* when it was bringing in 3,000 francs because he felt like going to the country. Besides, Parisian habits have changed since then. People don't leave Paris, nowadays, till the middle of the summer, and don't come back till mid-winter. *Villemer* was on in March, and could have gone on until July. But what does it matter if a run *is* interrupted before the 100th performance? It will do all the better when it starts up again; after La Rounat's blunder *Villemer* lasted for over 100 more performances. It's not in the managers' interests to drop a success, and Chilly's no fool. And he's a man of his word: if he promises you a good, prompt revival he'll give you one. So don't take the play to the Français. You can't imagine what a bear garden it is,[4] and Bouilhet's name isn't revered there as it is at the Odéon.[5] And you wouldn't want to lose Berton![6] – he's the only actor who's really congenial and serious. I know you have an appointment with Chilly on Wednesday – will you call in on me beforehand?

You weren't well the other day. Are you better, cher ami de mon coeur?

Ton vieux camarade

[1] By Alfred Touroude.
[2] *L'Affranchi de Pompée*, by Latour-Saint-Ybars, the pen-name of Isidore Latour (1807–91).

³ Léon La Rounat (1823–86), theatre director and dramatic critic.

⁴ Sand professed great scorn for the Théâtre-Français. "It's extraordinary what a chill that theatre casts over me," she wrote in her diary for 5 June 1869, "and how false, pretentious and stupid I find the audiences, the plays and the actors."

⁵ Several of Bouilhet's plays had been successful at the Odéon: *Madame de Montarcy* in 1856 (78 performances), *Hélène Peyron* in 1858 (80), and *La Conjuration d'Amboise* in 1866 (105).

⁶ The celebrated actor Charles-Francisque Montan-Berton (1820–74).

*

A few minutes after Flaubert reached Sand's apartment on the morning of 13 October, as she had suggested, her daughter Solange entered with the news that Sainte-Beuve was dying. Flaubert hurried to Sainte-Beuve's house, arriving a few minutes after the end.

This death, though long expected, again greatly moved Flaubert. "Another one gone," he wrote that day to Maxime Du Camp. "The little band is shrinking. The rare survivors on the raft of the *Méduse*¹ are disappearing! Who is there to talk about literature with now? Sainte-Beuve loved it, and though he wasn't precisely a friend, his death affects me deeply."

Later that day George Sand went to the Odéon to discuss theatrical matters, and reported to Flaubert by letter.

¹ The raft mentioned by Flaubert, famed for carrying survivors of the ship *Méduse*, wrecked off the west coast of Africa in 1816, had been immortalized by Théodore Géricault's painting of the event, exhibited in the Salon of 1819 and now in the Louvre. The administration of the Salon had refused to reproduce Géricault's title *Le Radeau de la "Méduse"* – *The Raft of the "Medusa"*; it was listed in the catalogue simply as *Scène de Naufrage* – *Scene of Shipwreck*. This was because the loss of the ship had become a political matter, involving charges against the ship's commander, and against the government responsible for his appointment. But the subject of the painting immediately became known, and Géricault's title prevailed.

Julian Barnes has written admirably of the wreck itself, and about the painting, in the chapter "Shipwreck" in his *A History of the World in 10½ Chapters, a Novel* (London and New York, 1989).

See also Léon Rosenthal, *Géricault*, quoted in *Géricault, Raconté par lui-même et par ses amis* (Pierre Cailler Editeur, Vésenaz-Genève, 1947), p. 222.

193   SAND TO FLAUBERT

[Paris, 13 October 1869]
Wednesday evening

They're not burying our poor friend until the day after tomorrow. They'll let me know where we have to go and when, and I'll inform you by telegram.

I've seen the directors twice today. This morning it was agreed with Duquesnel that an approach should be made to Latour-Saint-Ybars. I was to give up my own turn in favour of *Aïssé*, and my play wouldn't come on until

March. This evening I went back. Chilly wouldn't agree to that arrangement, and Duquesnel had thought better of it and now considered it pointless and even harmful. I cited my agreement and my rights. But – there's the theatre for you! – M. Saint-Ybars' agreement takes precedence over mine. They'd expected *Le Bâtard* to run for a fortnight, but it's going to run for another six weeks. So Latour-Saint-Ybars comes before us, and I can't give my turn up to *Aïssé* without having to wait until next year which I'll do if you want me to but it would make things very difficult, as I'm in debt to the *Revue* [*des Deux Mondes*] and need to fill my purse.

So are the directors a couple of rascals? No, but they're clumsy – they're always afraid of being short of plays, and take on too many, on the assumption that most of them won't run. When they do have a success and the authors they've made promises to get cross, then there has to be a lot of begging and praying. I've no liking for quarrels or for backstage and newspaper scandals; and neither have you. And what would be the result? Meagre compensation and much ado about nothing. One just has to be doggedly patient. Which is what I am, and I repeat: if the delay really upsets you I'm ready to sacrifice myself.

Whereupon je t'embrasse et je t'aime.

G. Sand

194 FLAUBERT TO SAND

[Paris, 14 October 1869]

Chère maître,

No! No sacrifices! It's quite all right! If I didn't consider Bouilhet's affairs absolutely as my own, I'd have accepted your suggestion at once. But 1° it *is* my business, and 2° the dead mustn't injure the living.

The fate of the *féerie*, of the volume of poems, and other works depends on how *Aïssé* is received. No matter, though: let's hope for the best. But I do hold it against these gentlemen, and I don't mind saying so, that they told us nothing about the Latour-Saint-Ybars play.[1] Latour had been scheduled a long time ago. Why did we know nothing about it?

In short, let Chilly write me the letter we agreed about on Wednesday. And let that be the end of it.[2]

It seems to me that you can open on 15 December, if *L'Affranchi* begins about 20 November? Two and a half months [sic] make about 50 performances: if you run longer than that, *Aïssé* won't come on till next year.

I'm very much afraid Berton will be exhausted when March comes round.

So, it's agreed! Since there's no cancelling Latour-Saint-Ybars, you'll be played after him. And then *Aïssé*, if I think fit.

We'll see each other on Saturday, at poor Sainte-Beuve's funeral. How the little band is shrinking! One by one the rare survivors on the raft of the *Méduse* are disappearing!

Mille tendresses de votre

Gve Flaubert

¹ *L'Affranchi de Pompée*. [The reader, sharing Flaubert's and Sand's difficulties with theatrical scheduling, will recall Sand's wry comment on the subject in the previous letter.]

² Chilly's letter to Flaubert, 14 October 1869: "If, because of the success of Mme Sand's play, which is to precede *Mademoiselle Aïssé*, it should prove impossible to stage Bouilhet's play between next February 25 and March 10, you will have the right to insist that it be held over to the next theatrical season, and staged between October 20 and November 20, 1870."

*

On October 15th Flaubert and Sand were among the many who paid their last respects to Sainte-Beuve before his body was taken from his house to the Cimetière Montparnasse. On that occasion they had no chance to speak. As Sand left, she was moved to find herself greeted with spontaneous homage by the mourners, who drew back silently to let her pass. Later that day, Lina arrived in Paris for a brief visit; and on the 21st Sand asked Flaubert to join them before they returned to Nohant. With her invitation, she sent a gift for his new flat.

195 SAND TO FLAUBERT

[Paris, 21 October 1869]
Thursday morning

Lina and I leave on Saturday morning and will be running about all the time till then. If you cared to come and dine with us on Friday at Magny's at 6, at least we could say goodbye. You'd be free by 9. We'll be going to bed early so as to leave betimes the next day. So what do you say?

Je t'aime de tout mon coeur.

[unsigned]

196 FLAUBERT TO SAND

[Paris, 21 October 1869]

Chère maître,

First of all, thank you for the cushion! But it's so gorgeous I shan't dare touch it. Only the empress of China is worthy to rest her head on it! And the empress of China doesn't come to my humble retreat! Isn't it sad?

I didn't need that, chère maître adoré, to think of you many times a day.

I accept the invitation for tomorrow. But since you'll be out doing things all day, would you mind if we dined somewhere other than at Magny's? – where I'm always seedy and cantankerous, it seems to me? Besides, the memory of . . .¹

¹ Sainte-Beuve? The rest of the letter is lost, but it will be evident from Sand's reply that Flaubert proposed the restaurant Paul Brébant, boulevard Poissonnière.

197 SAND TO FLAUBERT

[Paris, 22 October 1869]

Impossible, cher vieux chéri. Brébant is too far – I've got so little time. And I've already asked Marchal and Berton to come to Magny's to say goodbye. If you can be there I'll be very pleased, but if it will make you ill, don't come – I know you love me and I shan't feel at all ill-used.

G. Sand

*

Flaubert did not dine at Magny's that night; but the following afternoon he called at the rue Gay-Lussac to make his farewells. The next day George Sand left for Nohant, where she busied herself with *Malgrétout* while waiting to be summoned to rehearsals of *L'Autre*. Flaubert remained in Paris, revising the *féerie* and "hatching mighty intrigues," as he wrote to Caroline, to get it produced.

198 SAND TO FLAUBERT

Nohant, 15 November [1869]

What are you up to, mon vieux troubadour chéri? Slogging away till the last minute at your proofs? Your book's been announced for "tomorrow" for two days now. I'm awaiting it eagerly – you're not going to forget me, are you? You're in for both praises and slatings – but you're prepared for that. You're too genuinely superior not to be envied, but you don't give a damn, do you? Nor do I, on your behalf. You're strong enough to be stimulated by what shatters others. And the fur certainly will fly. Your subject will be very apt in these days of Régimbards.[1] The genuine progressives and true democrats will approve, the idiots will be furious, and you'll say "Let 'em all come!"[2]

I'm correcting proofs too – those of *Pierre qui roule*[3] – and I'm halfway through a new novel which won't cause much of a stir.[4] That's all I ask for the moment. I write alternately a novel that *I* like, and one that the *Revue* doesn't dislike too much but that I don't like at all. That's how it is – I'm not sure if I'm right or wrong. Perhaps the ones I like best are the worst. But I've stopped worrying about myself – if I ever did, much. Life has always swept me out of myself, and will do to the end. My heart is always engaged at the expense of my head. At present it's the children who eat up all my intellect – Aurore is a pet, I'm lost in admiration at her personality. Will this last?

You're going to spend the winter in Paris, and I don't know when I'll be there. The *Bâtard*'s success goes on. But I don't fret – you promised to come as soon as you're free, at Christmas at the latest, to celebrate festive season with us. I think of nothing else, and if you break your promise we shall all be in despair.

So saying, je t'embrasse à plein coeur comme je t'aime.

G. Sand

¹ Régimbard is the chronic recusant, or recalcitrant, in *L'Éducation sentimentale*.
² Fr. *"vogue la galère!"*
³ For its publication as a volume the following May.
⁴ Sand is greatly mistaken here: as we shall see, the new novel, *Malgrétout*, caused a scandal.

199 FLAUBERT TO SAND

[Paris, 16 November 1869]
Tuesday noon

Chère maître,

I begin by declaring that *I'm a pig*. I should have written to you. But I've had 1° my proofs, 2° the *féerie*, which I have been reworking steadily for a fortnight, 3° errands to do concerning my niece's apartment (she is at present in Poland), 4° my mother's arrival – she will stay with my niece but for the moment is in a hotel, and 5° a matter that doesn't concern me and that I'll recount to you *dans le silence du cabinet*.

My book appears tomorrow, I think. The day after, at latest. You'll have the first copy, needless to say.

Will the political situation work against me? I'm afraid so. Unless it helps me. The wind has turned. Rochefort's stock is very low, for the moment.¹

Since *Le Chevalier de Maison-Rouge*² is a total flop, perhaps Félix will want our great show?³ We have smoothed all the rough edges, modernized the whole, and removed the comedy, as we agreed. *Voilà.*

I don't see why I shouldn't come to Nohant toward Christmas?

Until then, friendly greetings to your family: and to you, chère maître, mille tendresses.

Your old

Gve Flaubert

¹ The various anti-Imperial parties were in conflict, making the parliamentary situation confused. Rochefort (see Letter 130), returned from exile, was to win a seat as deputy, despite Flaubert's remark.
² By the elder Dumas and Maquet; revived 9 November 1869.
³ The *féerie*, *Le Château des coeurs*.

*

As Sand had predicted, *L'Éducation sentimentale*, published on November 17th, was greeted coldly by most critics.

200 SAND TO FLAUBERT

[Nohant] Tuesday, 30 November [1869]

Cher ami de mon coeur,

I made a point of re-reading your book, and my daughter-in-law has read it too, as have some of my young men, all sincere and sensitive readers and not at all stupid. And we all agree it's a fine book, as forceful as the best of Balzac's novels and more real – that's to say, more faithful to the truth throughout. It takes great art, exquisite form, and rigour such as yours to be able to dispense with the ornaments of fancy. And yet, to the picture you depict, you add poetry with a lavish hand, whether your characters understand it or not. Rosanette doesn't know what kind of grass she's walking on at Fontainebleau, yet she's poetic all the same. All that is masterly, and your place is assured for ever. So take things as easy as possible, so that you may live long and produce much.

I've seen a couple of short articles that didn't seem too hostile to your success, but I don't really know what goes on – politics seems to be swallowing up everything else. Let me know what happens. If anyone should fail to do you justice I'd lose my temper and say what I think.

I don't know exactly when, but some time in the coming month I'll probably come and see you – and pick you up if I can tear you away from Paris. My children are still counting on it, and we all send you our praise and our love.

A toi, ton vieux troubadour

G. Sand

201 FLAUBERT TO SAND

[Paris, 3 December 1869]

Chère bon maître,

Your old troubadour is being greatly berated in the press. Look at last Monday's *Constitutionnel* and this morning's *Gaulois* – they don't mince their words. They call me a cretin and a scoundrel. Barbey d'Aurevilly's piece in the *Constitutionnel* is typical, and the one by our friend Sarcey, though less violent, is no more complimentary than the rest.[1] These gentlemen protest in the name of morality and the ideal! I have also been flayed in the *Figaro* and in *Paris*, by Cesena and Duranty.

I don't care in the least, but it does surprise me that there should be so much hatred and dishonesty.

The *Tribune*, the *Pays* and the *Opinion nationale*, on the other hand, praise me to the skies.[2]

As for my friends – people who received copies adorned with my signature – they are afraid of compromising themselves, and speak to me about everything except the book. Instances of courage are rare. Nevertheless, the book is selling very well despite the political situation, and Lévy seems satisfied.

I know that the Rouen bourgeois are furious with me because of old Roque and the cellar of the Tuileries.[3] Their opinion is that "the publication of such books should be forbidden" (I quote verbatim), that I favour the Reds, that I am guilty of fanning revolutionary passions, etc. etc!

In short, I have gathered very few laurels so far, and have been wounded by no rose petals.[4]

I told you, didn't I, that I'm re-working the *féerie?* I am now writing a horse-racing scene,[5] and have removed everything I considered conventional. Raphaël Félix doesn't seem in any hurry to read it. *Problème!*

In a fortnight I'll be finished, and ready to set off in your direction.

Comme j'ai envie de vous embrasser!

Mille tendresses de votre vieux

Gve Flaubert

All the papers adduce as proof of my iniquity the episode of la Turque[6] – which they garble, of course; and Sarcey compares me to the marquis de Sade, whom he admits he hasn't read!

None of this destroys my composure. But I keep asking myself: what's the point of publishing?

[1] Barbey d'Aurevilly reproached Flaubert especially for his "lack of originality" and for his "endless descriptions". Sarcey concluded his indictment by exclaiming, "What a wretched abuse of talent!"

[2] Articles by Emile Zola, Paul de Léoni and Jules Levallois.

[3] See Letter 134, Note 3.

[4] An allusion to one of the Roman "histories" of Claudius Aelianus (d. A.D. 140), in which the Sybarite Smindyrides complains of spending a sleepless night because one of the rose petals strewn on his bed was folded in two.

[5] The final, published text of *Le Château des coeurs* contains no such episode.

[6] The much discussed last scene in the book, when Moreau and Deslauriers recall the fiasco of their adolescent approach to a brothel as having been "the best moment of their lives".

202 FLAUBERT TO SAND

4 rue Murillo, parc Monceau, Tuesday, 4 o'clock.

[Paris, 7 December 1869]

Chère maître,

The way they're all jumping on your old troubadour is incredible. People to whom I've sent a copy of my novel are afraid to talk to me about it,[1] either for fear of compromising themselves or out of pity for me. The most indulgent are of the opinion that what I've written is merely a series of scenes, and that composition and pattern are completely lacking. Saint-Victor, who extols the books of Arsène Houssaye, won't write about mine, finding it too bad. *Voilà.* Théo is away,[2] and no one (absolutely no one) is coming to my defence.

Therefore (you can guess what's coming), if you would care to take on that role you'd oblige me. If it embarrasses you, do nothing. No mere indulgence between us.

Another thing: yesterday Raphaël and Michel Lévy heard me read the *féerie*. Applause, enthusiasm. I felt that they were about to give me a contract on the spot. Raphaël understood the play so well that he made two or three excellent suggestions. I found him a charming fellow, by the way. He asked me to give him until Saturday for a definite answer.

But just now, a letter (very polite) from said Raphaël, in which he tells me that the *féerie* would involve him in expenses he cannot afford. Another blow! We must look elsewhere.

Nothing new at the Odéon.

Sarcey has published a second article against me. Barbey d'Aurevilly claims that I pollute a stream by washing myself in it[3] (Sic). All this upsets me not the slightest. But God! How stupid people are!

When are you coming to Paris?

Je vous embrasse.

Gve Flaubert

[1] Of the hundred and fifty or so people to whom he had sent copies of *L'Éducation sentimentale*, Flaubert wrote to Jules Duplan on December 9, thirty at most had replied.

[2] Théophile Gautier was in Egypt, sent by the *Journal officiel* to cover the festivities celebrating the opening of the Suez Canal.

[3] In his second article (*Le Gaulois*, 4 December) Sarcey reproached Flaubert especially for his impassivity and superabundance of descriptions, and he ended: "*Oh, quel ennui! quel ennui!*" Barbey d'Aurevilly had written in his article in the *Constitutionnel*: "Flaubert has neither grace nor melancholy: his robustness is like that of Courbet's painting 'Women Bathing' – women washing themselves in a brook, polluting it."

*

Sand began her article the next day. Her diary for 8 December 1869: "Letter from Flaubert, and article immediately [. . .] I go upstairs early to finish my article."

203 SAND TO FLAUBERT

[Nohant, 9–10 December 1869]
Thursday, 2 a.m.

Mon camarade, the thing is done. The article will go off tomorrow. I'm sending it to . . . whom? The answer, please, by telegram. I feel like sending it to Girardin, but perhaps you've a better idea – I'm not very well up in the importance and prestige of the various papers. Send me a wire with a name and the address (I've got Girardin's).

I'm not altogether pleased with what I've written. I've had a kind of sprain and a temperature the last couple of days. But I don't want to lose any time.

Je t'embrasse.

G. Sand

204 FLAUBERT TO SAND

[Paris, 10 December 1869]
Friday, 10 p.m.

Chère maître, bon comme du bon pain,

I have just sent you a telegram saying "To Girardin". *La Liberté* will print your article immediately.

What do you say about my friend Saint-Victor, who refused to write one, because he found the book "bad". You don't have so squeamish a conscience!

I continue to be dragged through the mud. *La Gironde* calls me Prud'homme. That's something new.

How can I thank you? I long to say all kinds of affectionate things. I have so many in my heart that none comes to my fingertips. What a kind woman you are, and what a *brave homme*! Not to mention the rest.

Je vous embrasse.

Your old troubadour,

Gve Flaubert

Take care of the sprain, and the temperature, and give me news of both.

205 SAND TO FLAUBERT

[Nohant, 10–11 December 1869]
Fri. to Saturday night

I've spent today and this evening rewriting my article. I'm feeling better, and it's a bit clearer. I'll expect to have your telegram tomorrow. If you don't veto it I'll send the article to Ulbach – his paper starts up on the 15th of this month[1] and I had a letter from him this morning begging me for some sort of contribution. I imagine a lot of people will read this first number, so it should be good publicity. Lévy ought to be more knowledgeable than we are about what's best to do: consult him.

You sound surprised by all the ill-will. You're being too naive. You don't realize how original your book is, and how many people it's bound to offend because of the force of the writing. And there are you fondly imagining you're producing things that will pass unnoticed!

I've laid stress on the book's construction. That's what people understand the least, yet it's the novel's strongest point. I've tried to show the unsophisticated reader how to read it: that's the kind of reader who makes a book a success. The clever ones can't bear anyone else to *have* a success. I haven't bothered with the people who are actuated by malice: it would be doing them too much honour.

[unsigned]

PS from Lina:
My mother got your telegram and is sending her manuscript to Girardin.

Lina

4 in the afternoon.

[1] *La Cloche.* The first number appeared on 19 December.

206 SAND TO FLAUBERT

[Nohant] 14 December [1869]

My article doesn't seem to have come out yet, but I have seen others that are spiteful and unfair. People always give their friends shorter shrift than their enemies. And when one frog starts to croak all the others join in. Once the bounds of respect have been broken, vandals vie with one another to deface the statue. It's always the way. You are reaping the disadvantages of a style that hasn't yet been hallowed by repetition, and people outdo one another in their stupid refusal to understand. The notion of *absolute impersonality* is debatable, and I don't accept it *absolutely*, but it amazes me that Saint-Victor, who has advocated it so much and castigated my plays for *not* being impersonal, deserts you instead of defending you!

Don't bother about all that – just press on. Don't adopt any system; follow your inspiration.

The weather's set fair, here at least, and we're getting ready for a family Christmas round the fire. I told Plauchut to try to abduct you, and we're waiting for him to arrive. If you can't come with him, at least come to spend Christmas with us and escape New Year's Day in Paris. It's so tedious! Lina says I'm to tell you you'll be allowed to wear your dressing gown and slippers all the time. There aren't any ladies or strangers present. In short, we'd be very happy to see you, and you've been promising for a long time.

Je t'embrasse, and am angrier than you are about these attacks – but not put out, and if I had you here we'd buck one another up to such effect that you'd start out on a new novel right away.

Je t'embrasse.

Ton vieux troubadour

G. Sand

207 FLAUBERT TO SAND

[Paris, 17 December 1869]
Friday evening

Chère maître,
I hope that at this time a week from now I'll be arriving chez vous. I think that Plauchut, whom I saw yesterday, should be reaching Nohant at the same time as my letter?

Your article hasn't yet appeared in *La Liberté*. I asked someone to enquire from Girardin what that means: no answer. Politics, I think, is the only reason for this delay. Unless my poor book is the victim of a "Holbachian conspiracy".[1]

I assure you the hostility to your old troubadour is *personal*. That is evident in the articles. Fortunately I'm not sensitive!

This morning I finished correcting the *féerie* – it has taken up all my time for the last six weeks. Raphaël having declined it, it goes into a drawer, and I return to good old Saint Anthony.

This week, only three demolition jobs. (That's very few.) Read the one in the *Revue des Deux Mondes*.[2] A friend, Mlle Bosquet, to whom I've been of real service a number of times, has written me two very cutting letters. The second was accompanied by an article in *La Voix des femmes*, in which she tears me to pieces.[3] I prefer Saint-Victor's behaviour: he at least abstains.

All this doesn't pain me in the slightest, but it does greatly surprise me.

A bientôt et tout à vous.

Gve Flaubert

My intention is to leave next Friday by the 9 o'clock train.

[1] Flaubert alludes to the conspiracy which Jean-Jacques Rousseau claims, in his *Confessions*, had been formed against him by baron d'Holbach and others.

[2] In the issue of December 15, by Saint-René-Taillandier, who reproaches Flaubert for the "silliness" of his chief character, for imitating the style of Michelet, for lack of form, and so on.

[3] For Mlle Amélie Bosquet see above, Letter 54. The article in question appeared on December 11 in *Le Droit des femmes* (not *La Voix des femmes*, which had been a feminist newspaper of 1848); and a second appeared on December 18. Perhaps Mlle Bosquet thought herself portrayed in Flaubert's antipathetic character la Vatnaz.

208 SAND TO FLAUBERT

[Nohant] 17 December [1869]

Plauchut writes telling us you *promise* to come on the 24th. But come on the evening of the 23rd, so that you'll be rested in time to celebrate Christmas Eve with us on the 24th-25th. Otherwise you'll arrive from Paris tired and sleepy, and our pranks won't amuse you. I warn you, you're coming among children, but then you love children because you're so kind and affectionate. Plauchut will have told you to bring your dressing gown and slippers, because we don't want to force you to dress. But I hope you'll bring a manuscript of some kind too. The *féerie* re-done, or *Saint Antoine* done. I do hope you *are* working. Criticism is merely a challenge and a stimulus. Poor René-Taillandier is as priggish as the *Revue* he writes for. How mealy-mouthed can they get in that monument? I'm rather peeved with Girardin. I know I don't have any literary influence and am not cultivated enough for these fine gentlemen, but the good old public reads me just the same and pays some attention to what I say.

If you don't come we'll be shattered and you'll be an ungrateful monster. Would you like me to send a carriage to meet you at Châteauroux on the 23rd at 4 o'clock? I'm afraid you might be uncomfortable in the old rattletrap of a coach that makes the regular run, and it would be so easy to spare you two and a half hours' queasiness!

We send you our love and hopes. I'm working like an ox to finish my novel, so as not to have to waste a minute thinking about it while you're here.

[unsigned]

209 SAND TO FLAUBERT

[Nohant, 19 December 1869]
Sunday

So the women are poking their noses in too? Come and forget this persecution a hundred thousand leagues away from Paris and things literary; or rather come and rejoice at it all, for such savage attacks are the inevitable consecration of great merit. Don't forget that those who haven't experienced this sort of thing are only good for the Academy.

Our letters crossed. I asked you, and now ask you again, not to come on Christmas Eve itself – come the day before, to be ready for the celebrations on the 24th. This is the programme for Christmas Eve: we dine at 6 sharp, and then have the Christmas tree and the puppets for the children so that they can go to bed at 9. After that we confabulate, and have supper at midnight. But the coach doesn't get here till half-past 6 at the earliest, which would mean we couldn't dine till 7, and then the little ones would be kept up too late to enjoy themselves properly. That means you really ought to leave on the 23rd at 9 in the morning, so that you and I can see one another comfortably, so that everyone can get together at leisure, and so that we're not distracted, by demanding and over-excited infants, from the joy of your arrival.

You must stay with us a long, long time: we'll have some more larks on New Year's Eve and Twelfth Night. Ours is a foolish, happy household, and now is a time of recreation after toil. This evening I finish my own task for the year.[1] Seeing you, cher vieux ami bien aimé, would be my reward. Don't deprive me of it.

G. Sand

Plauchut has gone hunting with the prince today and may not come till Tuesday. I'm writing to tell him to wait and come with you on Thursday so that you won't find the journey so tedious.

I've just written a letter of complaint to Girardin.

[1] The novel *Malgrétout*.

210 FLAUBERT TO SAND

[Paris, 20 December 1869]
Monday 10 a.m.

Agreed, chère maître! I'll leave for Nohant on Thursday by the 9 a.m. train. And I'll bring the *féerie*, so that I can bellow it on your stage. I'm going now to see our friend Plauchut and ask whether we can set out together.

As for remaining a long time in your good company, that will be impossible. I must be back in Paris on Tuesday evening.

Je vous embrasse bien fort.

Your old troubadour.

Gve Flaubert

*

On December 22, the day before Flaubert's arrival at Nohant, *La Liberté* printed George Sand's article on *L'Éducation sentimentale*, a welcome Christmas gift for Flaubert.

FROM GEORGE SAND'S DIARY, 1869

Thursday, 23 December

[...] Flaubert and Plauchut arrived at half-past five. We met, dined, talked, played Arab tunes on the serpent.[1] Flaubert told some stories. We separated at one o'clock.

Friday, 24 December

Snow and rain all day. We were merry. I went down to breakfast with the others at eleven. The little girls were delighted with Flaubert's presents. Lolo carried her doll about with her all day. She played in my room while Flaubert and Plauchut were there, and they were very struck with her. She was wearing her best frock; so was Titite. All the young men came and stayed to dinner. Afterwards the puppets and the tombola in a fairy-tale décor. Flaubert enjoyed himself like a schoolboy. Christmas tree on the stage. Presents all round. Lolo enjoyed herself, was charming, and went to bed like a good girl. Lina enthusiastic and delighted. We saw Christmas Day in in splendid style. I went to bed at three o'clock.

Saturday, 25 December

We lunched at noon. Everyone stayed on except Planet. From three to six Flaubert read us his great *féerie*,² which is very delightful but not likely to succeed. Everyone enjoyed it very much and discussed it at length. As we were dining late, Lolo had dinner with her sister. I scarcely saw her today. We were very merry this evening. Flaubert made us split our sides with *L'Enfant prodigue*.³

Sunday, 26 December

Fine but very cold. We went out into the garden – even Flaubert, who wanted to see the farm. We went all over the place. Introduced him to Gustave the ram. Then some quiet conversation in the drawing room. The little girls were sweet. René and Edme left. At three o'clock Maurice decided to put on an impromptu show with Edme;⁴ it was delightful. Act I extremely good, Act II too long but still very funny. Flaubert was in stitches. He liked the puppets. Edme was excellent and very witty. I went up to bed at two.

Monday, 27 December

Snowed all day. Fadet⁵ wouldn't set foot outside. Lunched at noon. Lolo performed all her dances. Flaubert dressed up as a woman and danced the chachucha⁶ with Plauchut. It was grotesque; everyone went wild. A visit from M. and Mme. Duvernet calmed us down. The doctor came. Edme and Antoine left. We spent the evening quietly, talking. Flaubert said his goodbyes.

¹ The "serpent horn", a now obsolete musical instrument usually made of wood, consisting of a serpentine tube about eight feet long – "the natural bass of the ancient cornet family". (Grove's *Dictionary of Music and Musicians*, 1935.)
² *Le Château des coeurs*.
³ Unidentified. Perhaps one of Flaubert's "turns" as a mime.
⁴ But hadn't Edme left?
⁵ The family dog.
⁶ Sic for *cachucha*, a Spanish dance.

211 FLAUBERT TO SAND

[Paris] 30 December [1869]
Thursday morning

I had a good journey back, chère maître. The worst was the stretch from the Jardin des Plantes to the rue de Clichy. The Paris streets were abominable, and in my cab I was frozen.

All the way, I thought only of Nohant. I cannot tell you how touched I was by your welcome. What splendid, lovely people you all are! Maurice seems to me to be the happiest of men. And I cannot help envying him. *Voilà!*

Give Mlle Lolo a little kiss from me: I miss her extremely. My compliments to Coq-en-Bois[1] and to all the dear "lewd" [!] young friends[2] with whom I so enjoyed celebrating. And since this is the moment for New Year's wishes, let me wish you all a *continuation of the same*: because I cannot see that you lack for anything.

All the very best you can think of to Mme Maurice; and to you, chère maître, mille tendresses de votre

vieux troubadour

Gve Flaubert

[1] One of the characters in the marionette shows at Nohant.

[2] "*chers lubriques*". This seems to have been the term used by "Balandard", the (puppet) master of ceremonies, in greeting the guests at the show. One senses the charming fun at Nohant, with young friends from the neighbourhood joining in.

212   SAND TO FLAUBERT

[Nohant] 31 December [18]69

We were hoping to have a line from you this morning. The sudden cold is so severe, I was anxious about your journey. We know you got to Châteauroux all right, but did you get a compartment to yourself on the train, and weren't you uncomfortable on the way? Do set our minds at rest. We were so happy to have you, and would be very upset if you had to suffer for your winter escapade.

All's well here, and everyone adores everyone else. It's the end of the year. We send you your share of the seasonal kisses.

G. Sand

CHAPTER VI

1870

[Paris, 3 January 1870]
Monday morning

Chère maître,

I wrote last Thursday to tell you that I had a very good return journey. That letter was probably delayed, what with New Year and the weather. I didn't have a separate compartment. But I was alone in my carriage as far as Orléans.

I haven't told you properly how charming I found the hospitality at Nohant. Those were the best moments of 1869, a year that wasn't at all kind to me.

I hear that you've withdrawn your play from the Odéon. And that *L'Affranchi* is announced there for January 10th. I'll go to see Duquesnel on Wednesday, to find out what's going on and what they want. The date of my departure for Croisset will be determined by the opening of *L'Affranchi* and your coming to "honour our humble abode."

Thank God, there's an end to Troppmann.[1] And we have a government![2] What bliss!

I've begun to read for *Saint Antoine* again, and the *féerie* has been put aside. *Voilà!*

Kiss Lolo for me, and give my love to everyone: don't forget anybody, even Fadet!

Tout à vous, chère maître.

Gve Flaubert

[1] The newspapers had been featuring the trial and sentencing of the nineteen-year-old Jean-Baptiste Troppmann, who the previous September, in the working-class suburb of Pantin, had murdered a mechanic named Kinck, his wife and five children.

[2] Napoleon III had been forced to agree to the formation of the first parliamentary ministry of the Second Empire. It was inaugurated on January 2, 1870, with Emile Ollivier as premier.

214   FLAUBERT TO SAND

[Paris, 6 January 1870]
Thursday morning

Chère maître,

I saw Chilly and Duquesnel yesterday. They told me *L'Affranchi* will definitely open on the 17th (a week from next Monday), and that your play will be
put on as soon as it's ready – that is, toward the middle of February at the
latest. They seemed to me to be expecting less and less of *L'Affranchi*.

So I'm going to see you. About twelve days from now?

Mille tendresses de votre vieux troubadour qui vous embrasse.

Gve Flaubert

215   SAND TO FLAUBERT

Nohant, 9 January [18]70

I've had so many proofs to correct[1] I'm quite dazed. But I needed occupation
to console me for your going, troubadour de mon coeur, and for the departure
of my idiot of a Plauchemar;[2] not to mention that of Edme, my favourite
great-nephew, the one who helped Maurice with the puppets. He's passed his
examination for the registration department and is to be sent away to Pithiviers,
unless we can pull some strings and arrange for him to do his probationary
period in La Châtre. Do you know M. Roy, supreme head of the Crown Lands
Office? I was wondering if by any chance the Princess knew him, and would
be willing to have someone put in a word for young Simonnet? I'd be so grateful
for this favour – it would be a blessing for the whole family, and save expense
for his mother, who is poor. It seems it's quite easy to arrange, and there's no
rule against it. But one needs backing, and a word from the Princess or a line
from M. Roy would transform our tears to rejoicings. I'm very fond of the lad.
He's so affectionate and kind! He was a delicate child, always ailing, always
having to be nursed on our laps, yet always gentle and sweet. He's very
intelligent, and works hard in La Châtre, where his chief adores him and
doesn't want him to go. So please do what you can, if indeed you can do
anything at all.

They're still slating your book. That doesn't prevent it from being a fine
and good novel. Justice will be done later; justice always *is* done. It seems the
book didn't come at the right time; or rather it came *too* aptly. It showed too
plainly the mental confusion that prevails nowadays. It touched an open wound.
People recognized themselves in it too clearly.

Everyone here adores you, and they are all too unspoiled to shy away from
the truth; we talk about you every day. Yesterday Lina told me she greatly
admired everything you write, but preferred *Salammbô* to your modern rep-
resentations.

And if you'd been sitting here in a corner, this is what you'd have heard her, and me, and others say:

He is bigger and greater than ordinary beings. His mind, like himself, is of more than common dimensions. There is at least as much of Hugo in him as of Balzac, but he has the taste and discernment Hugo lacks, and he is an artist whereas Balzac is not. – Does that mean he's greater than either of them? – *Chi lo sa?* He hasn't said all he has to say yet. The vastness of his brain bewilders him. He doesn't know whether he's going to be a poet or a realist, and is hampered by the fact that he's both. – He has to choose among all his visions. He sees everything and wants to grasp everything at once. – He's not on the same scale as a public that wants only to nibble at things and chokes on anything large. But the public will come round to him once it has understood. – It will come round very soon, if he condescends to want to be understood. – For that to happen, perhaps he'll need to make some concessions to the public's intellectual sloth. – One would need to think hard before daring to offer that advice.

That, in a nutshell, is what was said. It can be of some use to know what honest folk and young men think. The youngest say they found *L'Éducation sentimentale* depressing. Not that they recognized themselves in it; they haven't lived yet. But they do have illusions, and they say: Why does this man, who's so kind, so amiable, so cheerful, so unaffected, so congenial, want to put us off living? What they say is illogical, but as it's instinctive perhaps one should take it into account.

Aurore talks about you and clasps your doll to her heart all the time. Gabrielle calls Punch her little boy, and won't eat her dinner unless he sits opposite her. We still idolize the little brats.

After your letter of the day before yesterday I got one yesterday from Berton, who doesn't think *L'Affranchi* is coming on until the 18th or so. Wait for me, since you may have to delay your departure slightly. The weather's too bad for travelling to Croisset. And though it's always an effort for me to leave my beloved nest to exercise my wretched trade, it's less of one when I can hope to see you in Paris.

Love from myself and on behalf of all the brood.

G. Sand

[1] Of *Malgrétout*, for *La Revue des Deux Mondes*.
[2] Sand's pun-nickname for her friend Edmond Plauchut. (Plauchut-Plauchemar-*cauchemar* – "nightmare".)

*

Sand was well aware of how keenly Flaubert must be feeling the hostility of many reviewers, and wrote to cheer him even before receiving a reply to her previous letter.

216   SAND TO FLAUBERT

Nohant, 11 January [1870]

Plauchut writes this morning to say your novel is a great success in Paris, I'm so glad to be proved right.

Je t'embrasse.

G. S.

217   FLAUBERT TO SAND

[Paris, 12 January 1870]
Wednesday afternoon

Chère maître,

Your business was attended to yesterday at 1 o'clock. Before my eyes the Princess made a note to see to the matter immediately. She seemed very happy to be able to do you a service.

No one speaks of anything but the death of Noir![1] The general feeling is Fear, pure and simple!

What wretched behaviour everywhere! There's so much stupidity around, it makes people violent. But I'm less indignant than plain disgusted. What do you think of gentlemen who come to negotiate armed with pistols and swordsticks? Or, on the other hand, of a Prince who maintains his private arsenal and doesn't hesitate to make use of it? Delightful!

What a splendid letter you wrote me two days ago! But you are blinded by your friendship, chère bon maître! I don't belong to the family of those you speak of. I know myself. I know what I lack – and the lack is immense.

In losing my poor Bouilhet I lost my midwife, the person who saw into my thinking more clearly than I do. His death has left me with a void that I'm more aware of every day.

But what's the use of making concessions? Why force oneself? No: I'm determined from now on to write for my own pleasure, without any restraint. Let things fall out as they may. I shall soon be fifty. It's time to enjoy oneself – that is, to let oneself go.

I shan't leave Paris before you arrive. So I can hope to see you in about ten days, can't I?

My greetings to all "*les chers lubriques*", many kisses to my two little lady friends, etc. etc.

And to you, all tender thoughts from the old troubadour.

Gve Flaubert

[1] Prince Pierre-Napoléon Bonaparte, a cousin of the Emperor, had engaged in a news-paper polemic with Paschal Grousset, one of Rochefort's collaborators. On January 10, 1870 Grousset sent his seconds to the Prince, and one of them, Victor Noir, was said to have slapped the Prince's face. The Prince drew his revolver and killed the young man. The news infuriated the republicans. On January 12, at Neuilly, more than 100,000 people attended Noir's funeral.

218 SAND TO FLAUBERT

[Nohant,] 15 January [18]70

L'Affranchi is on Tuesday. I'm hurrying to finish my corrections and I leave on Tuesday morning. Come and dine with me at Magny's at 6. Can you? If not, should I keep a seat for you in my box? Drop a line to my place during the day. You won't have to sit through the whole performance if it bores you.

Je t'aime et je t'embrasse for myself and the brood. Thank you for Edme.

G. Sand

219 FLAUBERT TO SAND

[Paris, 17 January 1870]
Monday 3 o'clock

Chère maître,

I can't dine with you tomorrow, Tuesday, and I'm engaged also Wednesday, Thursday and Friday. But keep Saturday for dinner at my place with our friend Plauchut.

You'll see me at the Odéon in the evening[1] in your box or in the lobby. Would it be possible for me to bring Turgenev?

I must return to Croisset. But I'm postponing my departure until Monday.

Mille tendresses de votre vieux

Gve Flaubert

[1] Apparently – as we may gather from what follows – Wednesday evening, 19 January.

*

Sand, somewhat ailing, arrived in Paris on Tuesday, 18 January, and Flaubert called on her that evening.

L'Affranchi de Pompée, the cause of such tribulation the previous October, opened the next night at the Odéon. Despite his promise, Flaubert did not attend.

220 SAND TO FLAUBERT

[Paris, 19 January 1870]
Wednesday evening

Cher ami de mon coeur,

I didn't see you at the theatre. The play was both clapped and booed, more clapped than booed. Berton very fine, Sarah[1] very pretty, but the characters uninteresting, and too many minor parts that weren't good. I don't think it will be a success.[2]

I'm better. But not well enough to go to your place on Saturday and come back such a long way in this cold. I saw Théo this evening and told him to come and dine with us both on Saturday at Magny's. So say yes, *I'm* inviting *you*, and we'll have a quiet room to ourselves. We can smoke at my place afterwards.

Plauchut wasn't able to come to see you. He was invited to the Prince's.

A line if it's no. Don't bother if it's yes. So I want you *not* to write to me. I saw Turgenev and told him how much I admire him. He was bewildered as a child.[3] We said horrid things about you.

[1] Sarah Bernhardt.

[2] She was right. *L'Affranchi* would run for only a week.

[3] From Sand's diary, 19 January: "Cross with Martine – she forgets everything. Finally I get dressed, in time for Turgenev's arrival at 4. He's charming: age, and white hair and beard, make him more handsome. He speaks better French, and tells me about Troppmann's execution (he witnessed it). He was quite astonished and disconcerted when I told him he's a great artist and a great poet."

221 FLAUBERT TO SAND

[Paris, 19 January 1870]
Wednesday, 6 o'clock

Chère maître,

I'll come to see you tomorrow, Thursday, between 3 and 4, after I've been to the Bibliothèque Impériale.

D'ici là, je vous baise sur les deux joues.

Gve Flaubert

*

Flaubert was now beginning research in libraries for the new *Saint Antoine*, and preparing a benefit to be held at the Odéon on February 12 to raise funds for a bust of Bouilhet. (It would be placed outside the library in Rouen, where Bouilhet had been director.) Sand was attending rehearsals of her new play, *L'Autre*, also at the Odéon.

They saw each other, as agreed, on 20 January; and again, on the 22nd, chez Magny. From Sand's diary: "22 January. I go on foot to Magny's. Théo sends a telegram: he is ill. . . . I dine with Flaubert. We return on foot. Milder weather. We chat chez moi for an hour, then walk to the Odéon and see two acts of *L'Affranchi*." Flaubert went to Croisset from the 24th to the 28th, then saw Sand again on 1 February.

222 SAND TO FLAUBERT

[Paris, 5 February 1870]

I never see you. You drop in at the Odéon, they tell me you're there, I rush to the spot and find you're gone. So tell me when you'll come and let me give you a cutlet.

Your exhausted old troubadour qui t'aime.[1]

[unsigned]

[1] This note is written on the last page of a letter from Edme Simonnet, thanking Flaubert for his successful help in the matter mentioned in Letters 215 and 217. Dated February 4, it had been sent first to Mme Sand.

223 FLAUBERT TO SAND

[Paris, 12–13 February 1870]
Saturday night, 2 a.m.[1]

Chère maître,

I've just learned at the Odéon that you're ill and that your doctor has forbidden you to talk or to see anyone. I'd like to think the report exaggerated. Is it simply a bad grippe?

Give me some news, or ask someone to tell me about you.

Tonight's performance went very well. I'm exhausted, and at last am going to sit by my fire, with Saint Epiphanius.[2]

Your old troubadour,

Gve Flaubert

[1] This had been the evening of the benefit at the Odéon. Sand, ill with bronchitis and unable to attend, had sent Plauchut to take her place. The programme consisted of several one-act plays by several authors, the recitation of some of Bouilhet's unpublished verse, and the last act of his *Conjuration d'Amboise.*

[2] For *La Tentation de Saint Antoine.* Saint Epiphanius (310–403) was the author of several works against Arianism and the doctrines of Origen.

224 FLAUBERT TO SAND

[Paris, 15 February 1870]
Tuesday afternoon

Chère maître,

I wrote to you on Saturday night, asking for news. Why have I had no answer? This worries me.

I'm still very tired. My grippe is a thing of the past, but I have a boil in the middle of my face that disfigures me completely.

I'm sitting by the fire, dozing and thinking of you.

Gve Flaubert

225   SAND TO FLAUBERT

[Paris, 15 February 1870]
Tuesday evening

Mon troubadour,

We're a couple of old crocks. I've had a serious attack of bronchitis and am
only just up. I'm better, but still confined to my room. I hope to start work at
the Odéon again in a couple of days.

Get better, and don't go out unless there's a genuine thaw.

My play opens on the 22nd. I do hope I'll see you then. Meanwhile je
t'embrasse et je t'aime

G. Sand

226   FLAUBERT TO SAND

[Paris, 17 February 1870]
Thursday, 3 o'clock

Of course! Certainly I'll be at the opening of *L'Autre*. Even if I have to
appear with the bandage that's at present disfiguring my mug. It's hideous!

But I'm taking it easy, and studying the Gnostics.

The 22nd is a bad day, because it's a Tuesday.[1] But the opening will
probably be put off to Wednesday or Thursday. As soon as the date is fixed,
let me know.

Be careful in this cold weather.

Je vous embrasse comme je vous aime, chère maître, c'est-à-dire très fort.

Gve Flaubert

[1] Flaubert does not mean this factually – that Tuesday is a bad day for an opening. He
was superstitious about Tuesdays. He would write to Caroline, for example, on 4 December
1877: "Your letter is sad. I'm not surprised, since I got it on a Tuesday, an unlucky day for
me." There are many such examples in his correspondence.

Flaubert's dislike of Tuesdays probably stems from the onset of his nervous attacks, the
first of which seems to have occurred on Tuesday, 2 January 1844. [J.B., F.S.]

227   SAND TO FLAUBERT

[Paris, 20 February 1870]
Sunday evening

I went out today for the first time. I'm better, but not well. I'm worried at
not having news of the *féerie* reading.[1] Were you pleased with it? Did they
understand?

L'Autre opens on Thursday, or Friday at the latest. Would your nephew and
niece mind having seats in the dress or upper circle? It's impossible to get a

box. If that's all right, let me know and I'll send you the tickets out of my allocation, which as usual won't be very brilliant.

Ton vieux troubadour.

[unsigned]

¹ Flaubert had offered it to the management of the Théâtre de la Gaîté.

228 FLAUBERT TO SAND

[Paris, 21 February 1870]

Chère maître,

My head's spinning – too much is happening.

Jules Duplan, a very intimate friend (my closest after Bouilhet), a wonderful old confidant and utterly devoted, is at death's door or very near it.¹

I have a fine outbreak of eczema on my face.

My servant has rheumatism of the joints and is in bed in my dining room.

The *féerie* has been refused again, though pronounced "very good". I'm sending your letter on to my niece. As for me, I don't know whether I'll be able to get to your opening. Physically I'm worn out and worn down, and my morale is even lower.

Be good enough to thank Duquesnel for me. I'll write him, or go to see him, as soon as I can.

Je vous embrasse.

Tout à vous

Gve Flaubert

I'll send you an answer tomorrow about the seats.

¹ Flaubert and Jules Duplan had been friends since 1851. It was Duplan who collected Flaubert's press notices for him, and he had often helped with research for the novels, especially for *L'Éducation sentimentale*.

229 FLAUBERT TO SAND

[Paris, 22 February 1870]
Tuesday, 3 o'clock

Either gallery or balcony, it doesn't matter, chère maître.

N. B. If the performance isn't till Friday, send no tickets, as my niece won't be in Paris. She asks me to give you her best thanks.

Je vous embrasse.

Gve Flaubert

My poor friend is worse and worse. I'm going back to him now. Your old troubadour's nerves are in a sorry state!

230   SAND TO FLAUBERT

[Paris, 22 February 1870]

It *is* on Friday. So I've still got the two seats I was going to send your niece.

If you have a moment's respite and come to the Odéon that evening, you'll find me in the directors' box, by the front of the stalls.

What you tell me makes me very sad. You're in for more gloom and sadness and grief, pauvre cher ami! Let's hope you may still save your patient. But you're ill yourself, and I'm so anxious about you. I was quite shattered when I got your note this evening, and can't turn my mind to anything else.

Drop me a line when you can, to let me know how things are.

G. Sand

231   FLAUBERT TO SAND

[Paris, 24 February 1870]
Thursday morning

Chère bon maître,

It will be impossible for me to be at your opening tomorrow. Won't Plauchut please come on Saturday morning and tell me how it went?

I'm going to have to put my servant into hospital – because if I were to continue like this I'm the one who'd soon have to go there. I can no longer climb stairs, but I'll be all right as soon as I'm alone and quiet.

My poor Duplan is still extremely ill. But last night things were a bit hopeful. Life is decidedly "a grim joke", as M. de Voltaire used to say.

And you? The grippe is entirely gone? How I long to see you!

Good luck for tomorrow.

Je vous embrasse très fort.

Gve Flaubert

*

The opening of *L'Autre*, on February 25th, was a triumph. "*Quelle soirée, mes enfants!*" Mme Sand wrote to Maurice and Lina. "What a success! What a good house! Everybody all attention, not coughing, scarcely breathing, appreciating everything – spontaneous applause from all parts of the theatre. The claque had little to do, and could give their hands a rest!"

Despite what he had written her two days before, Flaubert called on Mme Sand the next morning to congratulate her, arriving before she was awake. They made an appointment for the following Thursday; but on Wednesday, March 1, Jules Duplan died.

232 FLAUBERT TO SAND

[Paris, 1 March 1870]

Chère maître,

It's over. My poor Duplan died today at noon. He will be buried the day after tomorrow. So don't count on me for Thursday.

Let me know how you are. I'll write to you as soon as I feel a bit better.

Je vous embrasse.

Gve Flaubert

Oh! your poor troubadour is far from cheerful!

233 SAND TO FLAUBERT

[Paris, 2 March 1870]
Wednesday evening

Pauvre cher ami,

I grieve for your sorrows. They come too thick and fast, and I go away on Saturday morning, leaving you amid all these woes! Would you like to come with me to Nohant for a change of air, if only for two or three days? I've reserved a separate compartment, so we'll be alone, and my carriage will be waiting at Châteauroux. You could be sad in comfort at our house. We've had a bereavement in the family, too.[1] Sometimes a change of quarters, with new faces and habits, is a help physically. One's trouble isn't forgotten, but one forces one's body to bear it.

Je t'embrasse de toute mon âme. A word and I'll be expecting you.

[unsigned]

[1] Mme Chatiron, George Sand's sister-in-law, had died on 20 February.

234 FLAUBERT TO SAND

[Paris, 3 March 1870]
Thursday, 6 p.m.

No! chère bon maître, what I need now is not the country, but work. My grippe has come back, but as soon as it's over I'll rush to the library of the Institut, where I'll be busy every day for at least six weeks.

This morning, when I was almost overcome with grief,[1] I was invaded by a flood of bitter, grotesque thoughts. And there was no one to talk to, no one who *feels*, as you do.

Since Sunday I've been very worried about my brother, who has pleurisy. But today I hear he's better.

Later this week I'll ask at the Odéon for two seats for *L'Autre*.

For whom is your family in mourning?

When you're rested, let me have your news.

Give Aurore a big hug from me.

Mille tendresses from your poor old troubadour, not very merry at the moment!

Gve Flaubert

---

[1] At the funeral of Jules Duplan.

235 SAND TO FLAUBERT

[Nohant] 11 March [18]70

How are you, mon pauvre enfant? I'm glad to be here, surrounded by my family darlings. I'm sorry too, to have left you sad and ill and beset by vexations. Do let me have at least a line to say how you're getting on, and be sure we're all deeply concerned about your troubles and sufferings.

G. Sand

236 FLAUBERT TO SAND

[Paris, 15 March 1870]
Tuesday evening

Chère maître,

I'm still very weak, exhausted in mind even more than in body. And I'm turning cantankerous and misanthropic: everything and everybody annoys and irritates me. I feel old age taking over! I no longer see anyone I can talk with!

For ten days I deliberately wallowed in black depression. I closed my door and saw no one. Then I got back to work, reading crabbed things like Plotinus's *Enneades*. I go to the Bibliothèque Impériale or the Bibliothèque de l'Institut every day, dine at home alone, go to bed at 11, and sleep till 9. *Voilà.*

I haven't yet seen *L'Autre*. I'll give myself that pleasure at the end of this week or the beginning of next.

My face is getting back to normal. I'm taking cod liver oil as a tonic.

And you? When are we going to see each other? At the beginning of April, no?

My brother had a severe case of pneumonia, but has recovered.

Amitiés à tous les vôtres, et à vous, chère bon maître, mille tendresses.

Gve Flaubert

237 SAND TO FLAUBERT

Nohant, 17 March [1870]

None of that, now! Old age *isn't* creeping up on you. Anyhow, old age doesn't imply cantankerousness and misanthropy. On the contrary, a good person only becomes better, and as you're better than most people to start with, you're bound to become positively exquisite. What's more you're only boasting when you propose to be angry with everyone and everything. You couldn't do it. You're defenceless against sorrow, like all who are tenderhearted. Strong people are those who can't love. So you'll never be strong, and a good thing too. It's not right to live alone, either. When strength comes back one must live, and not just hoard it up for oneself.

What I hope is that spring will bring you to life again. Today the rain is relenting, tomorrow the sun will revive us. We're all getting over something. The girls have had bad colds. Maurice a chill and aches and pains. I've had the shivers and anaemia again. But I'm very, very patient, and as far as I can I prevent the others from being *im*patient. That's the secret: fretting at trouble only doubles it. When shall we be wise as the Ancients understood the word? In other words, patient. Come, cher troubadour, you must be patient – just a little effort to start with and then you get into the habit. If we don't shape ourselves, how can we hope to be gradually shaping others?

Anyway, in the midst of all this don't forget that we love you, and that when you hurt yourself you hurt us.

I shall come and see you and brace you up as soon as I've got my legs and my willpower back. They're overdue, but I know I shan't wait for them in vain.

Love from all my invalids. Punch has lost nothing but his stick so far, and he's still got his smile and his gilt. Lolo's doll has been in the wars, but her dresses have been handed down to others. I'm not up to much myself, mais je t'embrasse et je t'aime.

G. Sand

238 FLAUBERT TO SAND

[Paris] 17 March [1870]
Thursday

Chère maître,

Last evening I received a telegram from Mme Cornu[1] that read as follows: "Please come. Important." So I called on her today. And this is the story:

The Empress claims that you have made very unfavourable allusions to her in the last number of the *Revue [des Deux Mondes]*.

"How could she! With everybody attacking me now! I wouldn't have believed it! And I wanted to have her elected to the Academy! What have I done to her? Etc." In short, she is very unhappy, and the Emperor as well. He wasn't indignant, but "prostrated" (sic).[2]

Mme Cornu vainly insisted that she was mistaken, that you had meant no allusion to her whatever, and tried to explain how novels are written.

"Well then, have her write to the newspapers that she had no intention of offending me."

"That she won't do, I'm sure."

"Then you write to her, and ask her to tell you so."

"I wouldn't presume to take such a step."

"But I want to know the truth! Do you know someone who . . ."

At that point Mme Cornu named me.

"Oh, don't say that I spoke to you about this."

Such is the dialogue that Mme Cornu reported to me. She'd like you to write me a letter saying that the Empress was not your model. I am to send your letter to Mme Cornu, who will pass it on to the Empress. That's all.

I find the whole thing idiotic. Those people are certainly thin-skinned! You and I have to put up with a good deal more than that!

Now, chère maître du bon Dieu, you must do exactly as you please.

The Empress has always been very pleasant with me, and I wouldn't mind doing her a kindness. I have read the passage in question, and find nothing offensive in it. But women's brains are so peculiar!

I am very tired of my own (my brain, I mean), or rather it's at a decidedly low ebb for the moment. Try as I may, I don't get ahead with my work. Things aren't going well at all. Everything irritates and wounds me; and sometimes after controlling myself in the presence of others I'm seized by fits of weeping during which I think my end has come. In short, I'm experiencing something quite new: the onset of old age. The shadows are closing in on me, as old Hugo would say.

Mme Cornu spoke to me enthusiastically about a letter you wrote her concerning a method of teaching. I'm going to see *L'Autre* with my niece next Saturday.

I'm waiting with redoubled impatience for your return to Paris. Because as soon as you leave it again I'll return to Croisset. Paris is beginning to get a little too much on my nerves.

Did I tell you that I'm taking cod liver oil, like a baby? Pathetic, isn't it?

Je vous embrasse bien fort.

Your crusty old troubadour,

Gve Flaubert

[1] Mme Sébastien Cornu (born Hortense Lacroix) was namesake and goddaughter of the Emperor's mother, Queen Hortense, and was what the French call his *soeur de lait* (foster-sister): that is, they had shared the same wet-nurse. She had grown up with him, and was now a confidante of the Empress.

[2] Alphonse Jacobs' notes to this and the following passage read in substance as follows:

"In fact, George Sand had no reason to complain of the Empress Eugénie. Several times in the past the latter had helped her give aid to the poor. In 1861, when the French Academy refused to award Sand the Gobert prize [for French historical writing], the Empress had suggested that Sand be elected to the Academy (a suggestion that Sand herself declined). As for Napoleon III, Sand had on several occasions appealed successfully to him on behalf of imprisoned or exiled dissidents."

[However, the reader will decide whether the beautiful, Spanish-born Eugénie, known for her ambition when she was Mlle de Montijo, had reason to think herself alluded to in the following passage, spoken by a Spanish beauty, "Mlle d'Ortosa", in the second instalment of Sand's novel, *Malgrétout*, in the *Revue des Deux Mondes* for 15 March 1870:

"I know about all the eminent men, all the powerful women, of the past and the present. I have taken the exact measure of them all, and I fear none of them. The day will come when I will be as useful to a sovereign as I can be today to a woman who asks me for advice on how to dress. I give the impression of attaching great importance to trivialities; no one suspects the serious preoccupations that engross me; this will become known later, when I am queen, czarina, grand duchess. . . ."]

239 SAND TO FLAUBERT

Nohant, 19 March [1870]

I know you're very devoted to her, mon ami. I know that *She* is very kind to people one recommends to her as needing help. That's all I know about her private life. I've never heard any revelations or read any documents about her – not a single word or fact to enable me to describe her. So I swear the character I depict is purely imaginary; and, at all events, anyone who claimed to recognize her in some kind of satire would be no well-wisher, and indeed no friend.

I myself don't write satire. I don't know what it is. Nor do I paint portraits. It isn't my job. I invent things. The public don't know what invention and imagination are, and look for models everywhere. They deceive themselves, and they demean art.

That is my sincere reply. I've only just got time to put it in the post.

G. Sand

240 FLAUBERT TO SAND

[Paris, 20 March 1870]

I have just sent on your letter (for which I thank you), to Mme Cornu, enclosing it in an epistle by your troubadour in which I permit myself to say what I think, in no uncertain terms. The two documents will be submitted to the gaze of the lady, and will give her a little lesson in aesthetics.[1]

Last night I saw *L'Autre*, and was in tears more than once. It did me good. How tender and stirring it is! What a charming thing! And how it makes one love its author! I missed you greatly: I wanted to give you little kisses, as if to a child. It raised my sunken spirits: thank you! I think I'll be better now.

There was a large audience, and Berton and his son had two curtain-calls. Take care of yourself: don't work too hard.

Kiss Lolo and the others for me.

Mille tendresses de votre vieux troubadour.

Gve Flaubert

¹ "I was very sure that Mme Sand had no intention of painting a portrait," he wrote in
his letter to Mme Cornu, "first because of her high-mindedness, her taste, and her respect
for Art, and second because of her character, her sense of decorum and fairness."

241 SAND TO FLAUBERT

Nohant, 3 April [1870]

Your old troubadour has been going through anxious times. Maurice has
been seriously, dangerously ill. Fortunately Favre, my own doctor and the only
one I have faith in, got here in time. After that, Lolo had some bad attacks of
fever. More alarms! But our saviour departed this morning, leaving us with
minds almost at rest, and our invalids took their first stroll round the garden.
But they still want watching and looking after, and I shan't leave them for
another two or three weeks. So if you're waiting for me in Paris and the sun
calls you elsewhere, don't bother about me. I'll try to come out to Croisset
from Paris for an hour or two one day.

But at least tell me how you are, what you're doing, and if you're up and
about. My invalids and my well ones all send you their love, et je t'embrasse
comme je t'aime, which is a lot.

G. Sand

My friend Favre is very drawn to you and would like to meet you. He's not
looking for patients: he only treats his friends, and would be offended if they
tried to pay him. He's interested in you as a person, and I've promised I'll
introduce him to you if you agree. And he's something else as well as a doctor –
I don't quite know . . . a researcher. Into what? Everything. He's tremendously
amusing, original and interesting. Let me know if you'll see him. If not I'll see
he forgets about it. I'd be grateful for an answer.

242 FLAUBERT TO SAND

[Paris, 4 April 1870]
Monday morning, 11 o'clock

I *felt* that something bad had happened to you, and had just written to ask
you for news when your letter was brought to me. I retrieved mine from the
porter downstairs, and here is a second.

Pauvre chère maître! How worried you must have been! And Mme Maurice,
too! You don't tell me what Maurice's illness was.

In a few days, before the end of the week, write and tell me that all's right
again. I think that the abominable winter we've had is to blame: one hears of

nothing but illness and funerals! My poor servant is still in the maison Dubois,[1] and I'm distressed when I go to see him. It's two months now that he's been bed-ridden, in great pain.

I picture you beside Lolo's cradle, watching over her. That can't have been much fun. Give her a kiss from me as a reward for getting well.

As for me, things are better. I've been reading enormously, I've been over-working, and now I'm pretty much back on my feet. Except that the black gloom in my heart is a little blacker. I hope it may soon become less notable. I spend my days in the Institute library: the Arsenal library lends me books that I read at night; and then I begin all over again the next day. At the beginning of May I'll return to Croisset. But I'll see you before that. The sun will put things right again.

The lovely lady in question has sent me very proper apologies concerning you, assuring me that she had "never intended any insult to genius."

Certainly, I'll be glad to make the acquaintance of M. Favre: I'm sure to love any friend of yours.

Mille tendresses, chère bon maître. Je vous embrasse très fort.

Gve Flaubert

[1] The Paris hospital, popularly so-called from the name of its principal surgeon.

243 FLAUBERT TO SAND

[Paris, 14 April 1870]
Thursday

M. Favre sent me news of you on Saturday. So now I know that all's well and that your worries are over, chère bon maître.

But how are you yourself?

The fortnight's almost gone, and there's no sign of your coming. I'll be leaving Paris on May 8 or 9.

I had yet another attack of the grippe, and a sort of haemorrhage in my left eye. Spirits still not very high. I keep reading my abominable tomes, but it's time for me to stop – I'm beginning to be disgusted with my subject.

Are you reading Taine's splendid book?[1] I devoured the first volume with infinite enjoyment. In fifty years, perhaps, his will be the philosophy taught in schools.

And what about the preface to *Les Idées de Madame Aubray*![2] I tell you once again: *he'll* end up in the bosom of the church.

How I long to see you and chat with you.

A thousand kisses to Lolo – and ask her to kiss her grandmother for me.

I haven't yet spoken to Lévy, being incorrigibly diffident in such matters.

Gve Flaubert

[1] *De l'intelligence*, published in two volumes at the beginning of April.
[2] By Dumas *fils*. In the preface to the 1870 edition of the play, the author invokes a

sermon preached at the Tuileries in 1867 by Mgr Bauer, in which the latter says that "God has made the mother the source of the child's faith." Dumas claims that those words gave him the idea for his play. See Letter 177.

244 SAND TO FLAUBERT

Nohant, 16 April [18]70

What shall I say to Lévy so that he makes the first move? Remind me of the present state of affairs – my memory isn't reliable. You sold him one volume for 10,000; there are two, and he told me himself that that would bring it up to 20,000. How much has he paid you so far? And what was said on either side at that point? When I have your answer I'll act.

We're making excellent progress here: the little girls are better and Maurice convalescent, though I'm tired from sitting up with him, which I still do because he needs to wet his whistle during the night and I'm the only one in the house who's able to do without sleep. But I'm not ill, and manage to dabble with some work. As soon as I can leave him I'll go to Paris. If you're still there it'll be all the better for me, but I don't like to ask you to prolong your servitude – I can see you're always ill when you're in town, and you work too hard. Croisset will cure you if you'll only take things easy.

Je t'embrasse tendrement pour moi et toute la famille qui t'adore.

G. Sand

245 FLAUBERT TO SAND

[Paris, 19 April 1870]
Tuesday morning

Chère maître,

It's not my stay in Paris that's exhausting me, but the series of afflictions that have befallen me during the past eight months. I'm not working excessively. Because without work, what would become of me? But I'm finding it very hard to be reasonable. I'm afflicted by a black melancholy that recurs persistently, several times a day, in connection with everything and with nothing. Then it passes, only to recommence! Perhaps I've gone too long without writing – without a nervous outlet.

As soon as I'm in Croisset I'll begin the article about my poor Bouilhet[1] – a painful, dispiriting task that I'm eager to put behind me so that I can return to *Saint Antoine*. That's such an extravaganza that I hope it may take me out of myself.

And you? Maurice isn't completely well, I see, since you spend your nights at his bedside.

I have seen your doctor, M. Favre, who seemed to me very strange – a bit mad, between you and me. He probably thinks well of me, because I let him talk the whole time. There are great flashes in his conversation, things that dazzle one for a moment. Then all is darkness.

As for Lévy, here's the story. He gave me 16 thousand francs. Calculating by the number of pages, he owed me, strictly speaking, only fourteen. At the time of the last payment I expressed my surprise at his not giving me 20 thousand. Whereupon he replied: "Don't worry. We'll see later. You'll be pleased. But wait a bit."

I *dare not* remind him of his promise, and yet God knows that I'd welcome those 4 thousand francs. Because my prolonged stay in Paris this year has been disastrous for my small means, and I have debts besides. If Lévy isn't quite polite with me, if he forces me to beg, if he doesn't hand over said cash in full, I'll be rude and violent with him. That's certain. I know myself. Especially since your troubadour is very unsociable and none too accommodating at the moment. Monsieur is *upset*. I know how ridiculous I am, even if I don't find it funny. And Lévy has the right to resist a bit, because after all my novel hasn't done as well as we'd hoped. (I keep wondering why, but such is the case.) On the other hand, I've made money enough for him to fork out a bit. And I deserve some small consolation.

Such is the situation, chère maître. So, you can write to said Michel that I expect the immediate fulfilment of his promise (of which I'll not remind him). If he refuses, I'll not say a word, but I'll hold it against him. If he's ready to open his money-bags, I'll rush to his office.

I intend to leave here about May 8th. Until then, I have things to do.

Kiss all the household for me, and all "*les chers lubriques*". I miss Lolo – I often think of her.

To you, a big hug and greetings from the heart.

Gve Flaubert

---

[1] This is to be the preface to *Dernières Chansons*. Preface completed 20 June (date on the manuscript). Flaubert later rewrites it and it is published only in January 1872.

*

Whereupon Sand wrote to Lévy, and reported to Flaubert as follows:

246   SAND TO FLAUBERT

Nohant, 26 [April 1870]
3 o'clock in the morning

Lévy writes to say he's very fond of you and will do anything he can to prove it. I wrote to him as from myself, and he'll be coming to see you. Don't leave without seeing him – he'll be round very shortly.

Je t'embrasse. All well here but I can't leave yet.

G. Sand

247 FLAUBERT TO SAND

[Paris, 29 April 1870]
Friday, 9 p.m.

Chère maître,

Michel Lévy has just been here. He arrived at 6 o'clock, and after speaking of this and that:

"Mme Sand wrote me that you're short of money."

"That's true. I always am."

"Well. . . ." Whereupon he launched into a rigmarole to convince me that his business brought him no money, that he'd even had to borrow for his new quarters near the Opéra, and that with *L'Éducation sentimentale* he hasn't yet covered expenses. In short, do you know what he suggested? That he *lend* me, without interest, 3 or 4 thousand francs, *on condition* that my next novel go to him on the same terms, namely 8 thousand francs per volume.[1] I'll be hanged if he didn't repeat thirty times: "I'm doing this to oblige you, my word of honour!"

Thus his great generosity, his great affection for me, consists in lending me money on my next book – he setting the price in advance. I behaved splendidly, I assure you. He must think me a perfect idiot. Because: I gave no sign of surprise. I said I'd "think about it." But all my thinking is done. I have no lack of friends – beginning with you – who'd lend me money "without interest". But, thank God, I haven't reached that point yet. I can never see the point of borrowing money (except for some emergency), because sooner or later one has to return it. And then you're back where you started from.

Psychological problem: why have I felt so light-hearted since Michel Lévy's visit? My poor Bouilhet often said to me: "There isn't a man more moral than you, or one who loves immorality more: a vile deed positively delights you." There's some truth in that. Is it due to my pride? Or a certain perverseness?

Anyway, enough's enough. Such things don't upset me. I can only say, with Athalie: "*Dieu des Juifs, tu l'emportes*,"[2] and think no more about it. In fact, I ask you not to speak of it again with Lévy when you write to him or see him. He'll have my preface to Bouilhet's volume of poems. From then on, I intend to be perfectly free. *N I ni, c'est fini!*

And you, chère maître: so we shan't be seeing each other in Paris? I go back to Croisset next Thursday. And I'll not budge from there until October.

Note: I saw Dr Favre again, yesterday, chez Dumas. Strange fellow! I'd need a dictionary to understand him.

You don't tell me how Maurice is?

Greetings to everyone, and to you all affection.

Gve Flaubert

Have you read Taine's 2 volumes?

I knew Spinoza's *Ethics*, but not the *Tractatus theologico-politicus*, which bowls me over. It's dizzying! I'm in transports of admiration! *Nom de Dieu!* What a man! What a brain! Such learning, and keenness of mind! Definitely better than M. Caro.[3]

You have no idea of the stupidity into which the Plebiscite is plunging the Parisians.[4] It's enough to make one die of disgust. At which point I bid you goodnight.

Give Lolo a good kiss from me. When shall we see each other? Can't I count on a little visit to Croisset? Not little: a *good* visit. I have to talk with you at length about *two* projects.[5]

[1] In letters exchanged with George Sand on this subject, Lévy speaks of an advance of four to five thousand francs, and a suggested price of ten thousand francs for the next volume.

[2] See Letter 170, Note 1.

[3] The philosopher and moralist Elme-Marie Caro (1826–87).

[4] There was to be a plebiscite on May 8 to vote on a new, liberal constitution.

[5] Probably those for the completion of an unfinished play by Bouilhet, *Le Sexe faible*, and for the revision of Flaubert's *Saint Antoine*.

248 SAND TO FLAUBERT

Nohant, 1 May, in the evening [1870]

What can you expect? Once a Jew, always a Jew. He could have been worse. He bought one volume from you and the agreement wasn't clear. He *might* have given you only 10,000 and said that covered the rest of the manuscript. He wasn't really expecting two volumes: he was surprised when I mentioned it to him, and blurted out "But that makes 20,000 francs!" Then later he must have thought it over, and gone into it, and seen you were rather at his mercy. He may even have consulted a lawyer. Anyhow, the fact is that although I spoke to him several times I could never make him say it should be 20,000 again. He kept prevaricating and saying, Just let him wait and we'll come to some arrangement – and I admit I expected a positive gesture, though I did have moments of apprehension. So he's paid you 16,000 francs and would like to get out of disgorging the rest. I still hope to get him to do so *myself*. But I'll need to see him, and to persist, but carefully. Don't you do anything. Your job is to think, and the thing to do if you're troubled by debts is accept my money – I don't need it. The first part of the *L'Autre* run has brought in 10,000 francs or so that I was going to invest, but my instructions mayn't have been carried out yet. Even if they had, bonds can be sold again from one day to the next, so just take it as I'd take it from you, and pay me back when you can. I don't need my few penn'orth of savings except for illness or infirmity. As long as I can work I can easily make ends meet now. This has been the case for only the past three years, which shows how unprofitable our calling is unless one's . . . a thousand things that you and I can never be. We must just make up our minds to it. But don't stop me from pursuing the negotiations with Lévy. My patience gradually wears him down, and you may be sure I shan't compromise you. Even if he won't shell out the 4,000 francs, he must at least commit himself to paying 10,000 per volume for the next book. And if he won't do that, then it'll be time enough for you to leave him. But in these days of plebiscite and confusion, which look likely to continue, don't forget that Lévy is the most, if not the only, reliable publisher there is. I was offered a better agreement by someone else, but I took fright and compromised rather than leave him.[1]

I was hoping to go to Paris in a few days' time, but Maurice has an inflammation of the eye. His illness keeps erupting all over the place, for he's only just got rid of a little abscess in the mouth, a consequence of his throat trouble. I don't want to leave him yet. He's getting on very well really, but he still needs some looking after. So I'll come and see you in Croisset when the weather's fine. And you'll let me roam the woods a bit during the day, and at night you'll tell me about all your projects.

I haven't read Taine, or anything else whatever since my people have been ill. I need to wallow in some delightful out-and-out trash. Lolo sends her love. Punch still smiles affably by Gabrielle's bed. Both girls are altogether better and altogether sweet. I spend every day closeted with the elder one, and I never tire: she gets me to make up stories that last for ever, for the children don't want them to end and I always have to think of a sequel the next day. A weird mode of composition, I assure you, and one that breaks every known literary rule.

Je t'embrasse, and so does everyone else here.

Favre, who corresponds with Lina about the convalescents, writes some charming things about you. He's extremely witty and inventive, and expresses himself more succinctly on paper. When he's speaking he gets carried away, though I myself bring him down to earth and make him explain himself, except when it's a question of fancy. I'm not ashamed to tell him I don't understand. What's certain is that when it comes to medicine he's both marvellous and realistic. He turned Maurice's illness round completely, with wonderful steadiness and vision. If it hadn't been for him . . . things were going very badly, and there were times when I was desperate. And so I'm very, very weary! But it will pass.

Everything passes, mon gros enfant, except friendship when it's made up of affection and devotion.

G. Sand

[1] The publisher Dentu had offered her a higher royalty, but she had decided not to accept. "Lévy is so solid and so punctual," she wrote to Maurice on 9 October 1869, "and the political situation so threatening."

249 FLAUBERT TO SAND

[Paris, 4 May 1870]
Wednesday

Chère bon maître,

I owe you thanks for many things. 1° Thank you for your offer. But I'm not in need of money. Because I find that my nephew has been holding three

thousand francs for me that I knew nothing about. That's the way I am! 2°
Thank you for what you have done and 3° for what you are going to do.

For my part, I'll leave Lévy quite alone – not even answer him. I find such
matters intolerable, so atrociously unpleasant that I could scream. I prefer to
live less well and not concern myself about money.

But I consider myself perfectly free from now on, as regards Michel. Against
whom I hold no grudge, let me say.

Yesterday I was at the Odéon. Chilly told me that *L'Autre* was picking up
again and that he hoped to keep it on until the end of this month.[1]

I'm sorry to hear Maurice isn't well. Keep me informed about him. I'll be
at Croisset Friday evening – and shall await you there.

Mille tendresses de votre vieux troubadour.

Gve Flaubert

[1] In Sand's diary for May 2nd: "I had a note saying that *L'Autre* will close tonight." In
fact it would run through May 19th.

250 SAND TO FLAUBERT

Nohant, 20 May [18]70

I haven't heard from my old troubadour for a long time. You must be at
Croisset. If it's as hot there as it is here you must be very uncomfortable. We're
having temperatures of 34 degrees in the shade; 24 at night. Maurice has had
another bad attack of sore throat, but this time there were no membranes and
it wasn't dangerous. The swelling was so bad, though, that for three days he
could scarcely swallow a little wine and water. He couldn't take broth. But this
insane heat has cured him – it suits all of us here, and Lina set off this morning
hale and hearty for Paris. Maurice gardens all day. The children are merry,
and grow prettier before our very eyes. I don't do a stroke – I've got my hands
full looking after and sitting up still with my boy, and the little girls keep me
busy too now their Maman's away. But I do get some work done – planning
and daydreaming. It will come in useful when I can scribble again.

I'm still active, as Dr Favre would say. I'm not old yet. Or rather this is
normal old age, carrying with it the "peace due to virtue" that people make
fun of and that I myself mention in jest; but its stupid, over-emphatic name
denotes a pleasant and harmless state, even though it *is* inevitable and therefore
without merit. One has to try to make it serve art when one believes in that,
and serve family and friends when one's devoted to them. I don't like to say
how primitive and naive I am about all this. It's fashionable for people to mock
it. Let them – I don't intend to change.

So there you have my spring *examen de conscience*, and now for the whole of
the summer I'm going to think only of things that don't concern me. And what
about you? Your health, to begin with? And is the sadness and discontent that
Paris brought you a thing of the past? No more outward sorrows? You've been

sorely tried too! Losing two wonderful friends one after the other. There are times in life when fate is cruel to us. You're too young to fall back on the thought of recovering those you love in a better world, or an improved version of this one. At your age you ought (and even at my age I still try) to hold on all the more closely to what remains. You wrote and said so to me when I lost Rollinat,[1] my double in this life, the true friend whose pure affection was never, even when we were young, flawed by any sense of the difference between the sexes. He was my Bouilhet, and even something more, because the emotional intimacy I felt for him was accompanied by a kind of religious respect for a model of moral courage who'd come through every kind of ordeal with sublime gentleness. Everything that's good in me I owe to him. And I try to preserve it for love of him. For do not our loved ones, when they are dead, leave a legacy behind them? And any despair that might make us give up would be ingratitude to them, and treachery. Tell me you're calm and have mellowed down, and that you're working well and not too hard. I must say I'm a little anxious at not having had a letter for so long. But I didn't want to ask you for one until I could tell you Maurice was really better. He sends his love and the children haven't forgotten you. Moi je t'aime.

G. Sand

I've written off my own bat to Lévy. I should have a reply soon, and will let you know what it says.

[1] See Letters 86 and 87.

251 FLAUBERT TO SAND

[Croisset, 21–22 May, 1870]
Saturday night

No, chère maître, I'm not ill, but I've been busy with my move from Paris and settling in again at Croisset. Furthermore, my mother was not at all well: now she is herself again. And then I've had to sort out the papers left behind by my poor Bouilhet, and have begun my piece about him. This week I've written almost six pages – quite an accomplishment for me; the task is a painful one for all kinds of reasons. The difficulty is to know what not to say. I'll relieve my feelings a little by spouting two or three dogmatic opinions on the art of writing. It's an opportunity to express what I think: an agreeable occupation, which I have always denied myself.

You write to me very beautifully and with great goodness, seeking to restore my courage. I have none, but proceed as though I had, which perhaps amounts to the same thing.

I no longer feel the *need* to write, because I wrote especially for one sole being who is no more. That is the truth. And yet I will continue to write. But the taste for it is gone, the enthusiasm has vanished. There are so few people who love what I love, who are concerned with the things that are my chief care. Do you know, in all the vastness of Paris, a single house where the talk is about Literature? And when it is alluded to incidentally, it is always in connection with its minor, external aspects – the question of success, morality, utility, relevance, etc. I feel I'm becoming a fossil, a being unconnected with the life around me.

I should like nothing better than to find comfort in some new attachment. But how? Almost all my old friends are married, set in their ways, thinking all year round of their little concerns, with shooting during the holidays and whist after dinner. I don't know a single one who is capable of spending an afternoon with me reading a poet. They have their worldly involvements: I have none. Note that I am in the same position as regards company as when I was 18 years old. My niece, whom I love as though she were my daughter, does not live with me, and my poor old mother is growing so old that any conversation with her (except about her health) is impossible. All that scarcely makes for a madcap existence.

As for the Ladies, there are none available hereabouts, and even if there were! . . . I have never been able to accommodate Venus with Apollo. For me it has always been the one or the other—being, as I am, a creature of excess, given over entirely to whatever I'm engaged in.

I keep repeating to myself Goethe's words: "Forward! Beyond the tombs!" and I hope to grow accustomed to this new emptiness around me. But no more than that.

The more I know you, the more I admire you. How strong you are!

But you are too good to have written once again to the child of Israel. Let him keep his gold! The rascal has no idea what a fine specimen he is. Perhaps he considers himself very generous in proposing to lend me money without interest, but on condition that I bind myself with a new contract. I bear him no grudge whatever, for he hasn't hurt me – he hasn't touched any sensitive spot.

Except for a little Spinoza and Plutarch, I have read nothing since my return, being fully occupied with my present task. This will take me to the end of July. I'm eager to be rid of it, so that I can plunge back into the extravagances of good old Saint Antoine, though I'm afraid of not being able to crank myself up to the proper pitch.

A lovely story, isn't it, about Mlle d'Hauterive?[1] This suicide of two lovers to escape from a poverty-stricken existence should inspire Prud'homme with some splendid moral sentiments. I understand it very well. It's not American, what they did, but how Latin, how antique! They weren't *strong*, but perhaps they were very fine?

When shall we see each other?

Friendly greetings to Maurice: he must take care of himself and cure his windpipe once and for all. Four big kisses to your little girls, handclasps to the "*chers lubriques*" and to you.

Your old troubadour –

Gve Flaubert

252   FLAUBERT TO SAND

[Croisset] 26 June [1870]
Sunday

You've been forgetting your old troubadour, who has just buried another friend.[1] Of the seven of us who were at the Magny dinners when they began, we are now only three! I'm crammed with coffins, like an old cemetery. I've had enough of that, frankly.

And in the midst of it all, I go on working! Yesterday I finished, for better or worse, the introduction to the Bouilhet poems. Now I'm going to see whether there may be some way of fixing up a play of his, in prose. After which I'll get back to *Saint Antoine*.

And you, chère maître? What is happening with you – all of you?

My niece is in the Pyrenees, and I'm living alone with my mother, who grows deafer every day: my existence is anything but jolly, I assure you. What I need is to go and sleep for six months on a hot beach, somewhere. But for that I have neither time nor money. So one simply has to keep writing – and re-writing – working as hard as possible.

I'll go to Paris at the beginning of August. Then I'll spend all October there for the rehearsals of *Aïssé*. My vacation will just be a week or so at Dieppe towards the end of August. Such are my plans.

Jules de Goncourt's funeral was awful. Théo wept buckets.

But when shall we see each other?

Je vous embrasse très fort.

Gve Flaubert

[1] Jules de Goncourt had died on June 20th, destroyed by syphilis.

253   SAND TO FLAUBERT

Nohant, 27 June [18]70

Another sorrow for you, mon pauvre vieux. I've had an affliction too – I've just lost Barbès,[1] one of my religions, one of those beings who reconcile one to humanity. So you are mourning poor Jules and pitying unhappy Edmond. Perhaps you're in Paris trying to comfort him. I've just written to him, and have been thinking of your own affections receiving yet another blow. What a time this is! Everyone and everything is dying, including the earth, consumed by the sun and the wind.[2] I don't know where I get the heart to go on living amid all these ruins. Let us go on loving each other to the end.

You write so seldom – I'm quite worried about you.

G. Sand

[1] See Letter 62, Note 1.
[2] Exceptional heat and drought were ruining crops in many parts of France.

254 SAND TO FLAUBERT

Nohant, 29 June [1870]

Our letters always cross, and I'm now superstitiously convinced that if I write to you in the evening I shall hear from you the next morning. We might say to one another:

"To me as I slept you appeared, looking sad."[1]

What worries me about the death of poor Jules is the brother who survives. The dead are all right – they're resting, perhaps, before coming back to life; in any case they're back in the melting pot, to emerge with whatever was good about them intact, plus something else. Barbès did nothing but suffer all his life. Now he's fast asleep, and soon he'll wake. But we poor survivors can't see our dead any more. Just before he died, Duveyrier,[2] who seemed to have recovered, said to me, "Which of us two will go first?" We were just the same age. He regretted that those who went first couldn't let those who remained know whether they were happy and remembered their friends. I said, "Who knows?" Then we promised that whichever of us died first would appear to the other and at least try to speak to him. He hasn't come, though. I've waited for him, but he hasn't spoken. Yet he was one of the most affectionate of men, and completely dependable. So he must have been unable to keep his promise; or it isn't allowed; or else I've failed to hear or understand.

As I said, it's poor Edmond I'm worried about. Now that shared life of theirs is over, I can't see how he can bear the bond being broken, unless he too believes we don't really die.

I wish I could come and see you. It seems you have some cool at Croisset, since you speak of wanting to sleep on a hot beach. Come here – you won't find a beach, but you will find a temperature of 36 degrees in the shade and a river as cold as ice, which is not to be sniffed at. I go and splash about in it every day after work – for I have to work. Buloz has advanced me so much money. So here I am "plying my trade," as Aurore says, and unable to budge till the autumn. I wasted too much time getting over my sick-bed exertions. Young Buloz[3] came recently to chase me up. So I've got my nose to the grindstone.[4]

You must come and spend a few days with us if you're going to be in Paris in August. You *did* get a laugh here. We'll do our best to amuse you and stir you up a bit. You'll find the little girls grown taller and prettier. The tiny one is starting to talk. Aurore prattles and argues. She calls Plauchut "old bachelor". Speaking of whom, the excellent fellow asks me to give you his best wishes, and all the family send their love.

Moi, je t'embrasse tendrement and beg you to be well.

G. Sand

[1] La Fontaine, *Fables*, "The Two Friends".

[2] See Letter 37.

[3] Charles, the elder son of the editor of *La Revue des Deux Mondes*. He had turned up without notice at Nohant on 17 June.

[4] She was writing *Césarine Dietrich*, a novel that would appear in *La Revue des Deux Mondes* from 15 August to 1 October, 1870. The manuscript is dated "Nohant, 15 July 1870."

255 FLAUBERT TO SAND

[Croisset] 2 July [1870]
Saturday evening

Chère bon maître,

The death of Barbès has greatly saddened me, for your sake. We both have our bereavements. What a procession of deaths during the past year! It leaves me dazed, as though I'd been hit over the head. What distresses me (for we always refer everything back to ourselves) is the terrible solitude I live in. I no longer have anyone – no one at all – to talk with.

"Qui s'occupe aujourd'hui de faconde et de style?"[1]

Apart from you and Turgenev, I don't know a single mortal with whom I can share the things closest to my heart; and you both live far away.

I continue working, however. I have sworn to myself to take up my *Saint Antoine* tomorrow or the next day. But to begin a long and exacting work one must feel a certain liveliness that I lack. Still, I hope the exoticism of this work will take hold of me. Oh, how I'd love to be able to stop thinking about my poor *me*, about my miserable carcass! Actually, my carcass is in very good shape. I sleep tremendously. "I have a strong constitution," as the bourgeois say.

Bouilhet's affairs will take me to Paris in August. Then I'll spend five or six days with my niece at Dieppe. All that bothers and upsets me no end. I detest short trips. Because it's just as hard for me to resume work as it is to interrupt it. And then I'll have to spend all October in Paris for the rehearsals of *Aïssé*. After which I'll return here, to remain all winter. Such are my plans, at least.

My mother is well! My niece is at Luchon with her husband. Lately I've been reading some deadly theological works, interspersing them with a little Plutarch and Spinoza. That's all I have to tell you.

Poor Edmond de Goncourt is in Champagne with his relatives. He has promised to come here at the end of the month. I don't think the hope of being reunited with his brother in a better world is much consolation for having lost him in this. One hears a lot of nonsense about immortality. The question is, does the *self* survive? To say that it does seems to me a mere reflection of our presumptuousness and pride, a protest by our weakness against the eternal order! Death has perhaps no more secrets to reveal to us than life.

What an accursed year! I feel as though I were lost in the desert. Nonetheless I assure you, chère maître, that I'm keeping a stout heart. And making prodigious efforts to be stoical. But the poor brain is weak at times. I need only one thing (and it's not had for the asking): to feel some sort of enthusiasm.

Your last letter but one was very sad. You too, you heroic being: you too feel weary! What's to become of us?

Je vous embrasse comme je vous aime: c'est-à-dire bien fort.

Gve Flaubert

I've just read the *Conversations of Goethe and Eckermann*. There was a man, that Goethe! But he had everything: everything was in his favour!

[1] "Who cares today about fluency and style?" A line from Bouilhet's *Melaenis*.

*

But the *Malgrétout* business still wasn't forgotten. In an article in *La Liberté*, 25 June 1870, a critic signing himself "Panoptès" once again stated that, in the character of Mlle d'Ortosa, George Sand had portrayed the Empress. Mme Sand sent a letter of protest to Girardin, editor of *La Liberté*, and kept Flaubert informed about it.

256 SAND TO FLAUBERT

[Nohant] 3 July [18]70

They're harping on Mlle d'Ortosa again, and someone in *La Liberté* has said I was deliberately aiming at someone. I was neither aiming at nor describing any real or living subject. Aiming at people isn't my style, and I couldn't have been painting a portrait from the life because there isn't anyone who could have posed for me. It seems to me the habit of interpreting everything in this way degrades the writing profession and confirms the public as a whole in its mania for trying to identify fictional characters. I've already told you this; no need to add that I don't know "Panoptès", I don't even know his real name; nor, again, do I have to tell you I didn't authorize him to interpret me or fathom out my "intentions".

We've had some rain, but not enough. Our trees and grass are still dying. But we're all well and nous t'aimons.

G. Sand

*

Flaubert accordingly sent on George Sand's letter to Mme Cornu once again.

But political events soon threw the lives of the two writers into confusion. The expanding power of Prussia under Bismarck had been alarming France, particularly since the Prussian victory over Austria at Sadowa in 1866. Greatly increased tensions in 1870 brought the two countries to the brink; and in July, in a deceitfully insolent message known to history as "the Ems telegram", Bismarck tricked France into becoming the "Aggressor". On Bastille Day, July 14, inflamed Paris mobs chanted "On to Berlin!" That night, the singer Marie Sasse, explicitly authorized by the Emperor and draped in the tricolour, sang *La Marseillaise* at the Opéra to wild applause from the audience. On July 19, France, though hopelessly unprepared, declared war.

257 FLAUBERT TO SAND

Croisset [22 July 1870]
Friday evening

What has become of you, chère maître – of you and yours?

As for myself, I am nauseated, and heartbroken, by the stupidity of my compatriots. The incorrigible barbarism of mankind fills me with blackest gloom. This enthusiasm [for war], unmotivated by any idea, makes me long to die, that I might witness it no longer.

The worthy Frenchman wants to fight 1° because he is jealous of Prussia; 2° because man's natural condition is savagery; 3° because in war there is an inherent mystical element that enraptures the masses.

Have we reverted to wars between races? I fear so. The frightful butchery now being prepared lacks even a pretext. It's just a craving to fight for fighting's sake.

I lament the destruction of bridges, the blowing-up of tunnels, the waste of so much human work, such fundamental *negation*.

Conferences about peace are anathema for the moment.[1] Civilization seems to me a far-off thing. Hobbes was right: *Homo homini lupus.*[2]

Here the bourgeois is at the end of his patience. He considers that Prussia was too insolent, and wants to "avenge himself." Did you see that a gentleman in the Chamber [of Deputies] has proposed the sacking of the [Grand] Duchy of Baden?[3] Ah, why can't I go and live with the Bedouins!

I have begun *Saint Antoine*. And it might go well if I could stop thinking about the war.

And you?

My mother is at Dieppe with Caroline. I am alone at Croisset, for a long stay. We're having quite a nice little hot spell. But I splash in the Seine like a porpoise.

Et je vous embrasse très fort, chère bon maître.

Gve Flaubert

[1] Flaubert probably refers to the "Congress for Peace and Liberty", held in Lausanne in September, 1869, with Victor Hugo as honorary president. The announced goal of the congress was "To determine the bases of a federal organization of Europe."

[2] "Man is wolf to man." Originally what seems to be a proverb, in Plautus, *Asinaria*: "*Lupus est homo homini, cum qualis sit non novit.*" Flaubert had read Hobbes' *Leviathan*, in which it is quoted.

[3] It was the comte de Kératry, deputy from Finisterre and later prefect of police, who made the proposal, to punish the Grand Duchy of Baden for not having signed a proposed international agreement about the use of explosive bullets.

258 SAND TO FLAUBERT

Nohant, 26 July [1870]

I consider the war infamous and the authorization of the *Marseillaise* a sacrilege. Men are vainglorious and ferocious beasts. We're now in the "two steps back" phase. How long will it be till we move forward again?[1]

We're having temperatures of 40 and 45 degrees *in the shade*. People are starting forest fires – another stupid barbarity. Wolves come and stroll round our courtyard and we hunt them at night, Maurice with a revolver and I with a lantern. The trees are losing their leaves; their lives too, perhaps. We'll soon be short of drinking water. There are practically no crops to harvest, but fortunately we do have the war! Agriculture is dying, famine threatens, want only bides its time to break out into a *Jacquerie*.[2] But we're going to beat the Prussians! *Malbrough s'en va-t-en guerre!*[3]

You were right to say one can't work without a certain amount of elation. But where is one to find it in these unhappy times? Fortunately we haven't anyone ill here. When I see Maurice and Lina active and Aurore and Gabrielle playing, I daren't complain for fear of losing everything.

Je t'aime, mon cher vieux, nous t'aimons tous.

Ton troubadour

G. Sand

[1] See Letter 151.

[2] A fourteenth-century revolution of French peasants, which gave its name to subsequent rural uprisings. (Originally, from "Jacques Bonhomme", a name derisively given to peasants by the nobility.)

[3] A famous song from the eighteenth century, inspired by the military exploits of the first Duke of Marlborough during the War of the Spanish Succession.

259 FLAUBERT TO SAND

Croisset [3 August 1870]
Wednesday

What, chère maître? You too! Demoralized, sad? What's to become of weak souls, then?

As for me, my heart is oppressed in a way that astonishes me. And I wallow in a bottomless melancholy, despite my work, despite our friend Saint Antoine, who ought to distract me. Is it the result of my series of griefs? But the war has much to do with it. I feel we're entering into black darkness.

Behold "natural man"! What price theories now? Extol Progress, enlightenment, the good sense of the Masses, and the sweet nature of the French people! I assure you that anyone who ventured to preach Peace here would get himself murdered.

Whatever happens, it will be a long time before we move forward again.

Perhaps there's to be a recurrence of racial wars? Within a century we'll see millions of men kill each other at one go? All the East against all Europe, the old world against the new? Why not? Perhaps great enterprises like the Suez Canal are some kind of sketch, or preparation for monstrous conflicts we can only guess at?

But maybe Prussia is going to get a good drubbing, as part of the schemes of Providence for restoring Europe's balance of power?[1] That country [Prussia] was tending to become hypertrophied, like France under Louis XIV and Napoleon. The other organs are unfavourably affected. Hence universal disorder. Might tremendous bloodletting be salutary?

Ah, literate folk that we are! Mankind is all too far from our ideal! And our huge mistake, our fatal mistake is to imagine that it is no different from us, and to expect to treat it accordingly.

The general reverence for the fetish of universal suffrage revolts me more than the infallibility of the Pope, who has misfired nicely, by the way, poor old chap.[2] Do you think that if France, instead of being governed, in effect, by the mob, were to be ruled by the "Mandarins", we'd be where we are now? If instead of wanting to enlighten the lower classes we'd busied ourselves educating the upper, we wouldn't have M. de Kératry proposing the sack of the duchy of Baden – a measure the public finds quite right and proper.

Have you been watching Prud'homme these days? He's marvellous! He admires Musset's *Rhin*[3] and asks whether Musset has written anything else. So Musset becomes our national poet, ousting Béranger! What a huge farce it all is! But one that's far from funny.

Poverty begins to be very evident. Everybody is hard up, starting with me! But perhaps we were too accustomed to comfort and tranquillity. Perhaps we were sinking into materialism. We must return to the great tradition: cling no longer to Life, to Happiness, to money, to anything; but be what our grandfathers were – bright, untethered beings.

In former times men passed their entire lives in a state of starvation. Now that same prospect is on the horizon. What you tell me about poor Nohant is terrible. The countryside here has suffered less than yours.

The day after tomorrow I leave for Dieppe, where my mother is staying with her granddaughter. She is aging and failing dreadfully. In that respect, too, the future doesn't look very bright for me.

On Monday I'll be in Paris, so write to me at 4 rue Murillo, where I'll be staying for about a week. I must find out what's going to happen to *Aïssé*. And to Bouilhet's volume of verse. For this I have to see the excellent M. Lévy once more.

And us? When shall we see each other again?

Amitiés à tout le monde et à vous mes tendresses.

Gve Flaubert

[1] This reflection was perhaps inspired by the French capture of Saarbrücken on August 1 – an insignificant battle, embarked upon by the Emperor to satisfy an impatient public.

[2] The doctrine of papal infallibility had been promulgated on July 18. It would soon be followed by the loss of the papal states to the kingdom of Italy. Flaubert seems to make the common mistake of thinking that the infallibility claimed by the doctrine was total: actually, it is "restricted" to matters of dogma and morality.

[3] *Le Rhin Allemand* (*The German Rhine*, 1840), a short patriotic poem by Alfred de Musset, was a rejoinder to a provocative German poem of the same name, written in the same year by Nikolaus Becker (1809–45). Musset's words had been set to music and were enjoying new popularity at this moment. Lamartine had also answered Becker, in a poem called *La Marseillaise de la paix* (1841).

260 SAND TO FLAUBERT

Nohant [7 August 1870]
Sunday evening

Are you in Paris, in the midst of this turmoil? What a lesson it all is for countries that want to have absolute masters! France and Prussia cutting one another's throats over matters neither of them understands! So here we are, plunged into great disasters, and it will all end in oceans of tears, even if we win. Round here you see nothing but poor peasants weeping over their children going off to fight. The *mobile*[1] takes away any that were left to us, and the way they treat them, for a start! What chaos and confusion – in an army that soaked up everything and ought to have been able to take on anything![2] Will this horrible experience teach people at last that war must be abolished or civilization will perish?

The position here this evening is that we know we've been defeated.[3] Tomorrow, perhaps, we'll know we've been victorious. And in either case, what good or advantage will come of it?

It has rained at last – a terrible storm that battered everything to pieces. But the peasants go on ploughing and putting their fields to rights, toiling away whether they're happy or sad. People say they're stupid. Not so. A peasant is a child in prosperity and a man in adversity – more of a man than us, with all our self-pity. He says nothing, and while others are killing he sows, for ever repairing on the one hand what is being destroyed on the other. We're going to try to be like him, and look for a spring 50 or 100 metres underground. The engineer is here, and Maurice is teaching him soil geology. We're exploring the bowels of the earth in the hope of forgetting what's going on on the surface.

But it's impossible to distract oneself from the present consternation!

Write and tell me where you are. I'm sending this to the rue Murillo on the day you said you'd be arriving. Nous t'aimons et nous t'embrassons tous.

G. Sand

¹ The *garde nationale mobile*: an auxiliary army (1868–71), made up of young men who didn't do ordinary military service.

² When the crisis came, the French army was found to be badly undermanned and ill-equipped. Even maps were not available.

³ The government had just announced two French defeats, at Froeschwiller and Forbach.

261   SAND TO FLAUBERT

[Nohant] 15 August, evening [1870]

I wrote to you in Paris on the 8th, as indicated. Aren't you there?¹ Probably not. It's hardly the moment, in the midst of all this confusion, to be publishing Bouilhet, a poet.

I must admit *my* heart fails me: there's still a woman inside the old troubadour, and this human butchery reduces me to tatters. I tremble too for all my children and friends who may get cut to pieces. And yet in the middle of it all my soul revives and even has flashes of faith. We need these harsh lessons in order to realize our own foolishness, and we must make good use of them. Perhaps this is our last relapse into the errors of the past. Some clear principles that are evident to all should emerge from this turmoil. Everything has a use in the material order of the universe. And that applies to the moral order too. Out of evil comes good. I tell you, we're going through Pascal's phase of "two steps backward" just so as to advance "further than ever"! That's all the mathematics I understand.

I've finished a novel in all this uproar,² working as fast as I could so as not to collapse before I'd done. I'm as weary as if I'd been fighting with our poor soldiers.

Je t'embrasse. Tell me where you are and what you're thinking.

Nous t'aimons tous.

G. Sand

A fine St Napoleon's Day, eh?³

¹ As military defeats multiplied and the government fell, Flaubert had left the tense city for Croisset.

² She had finished *Césarine Dietrich* on 11 August.

³ See Letter 183, Note 1.

262 FLAUBERT TO SAND

Croisset [17 August 1870]
Wednesday

I arrived in Paris on Monday and left on Wednesday. Now I know what the Parisian is really like! And in my heart I apologize to the most ferocious politicians of 1793. I understand them now. For I've seen such stupidity! Such cowardice! Such ignorance! Such presumption! My compatriots made me want to vomit. They're to be lumped together with Isidore, absolutely.

Perhaps this country *deserves* to be punished, and I fear it will be.

It's impossible for me to read anything whatever; let alone to write. I spend my time like everybody else, waiting for news. Ah! If it weren't for my mother I'd certainly have joined up by now.

Not knowing how to keep busy, I've volunteered as a nurse at the Hôtel-Dieu in Rouen, where my services may be of use, as my brother has no more students.[1] My inaction is stifling me: I feel I'm about to burst.

If the Germans besiege Paris, I'll go and fight. My rifle is ready. But until then I'll remain at Croisset because I must. I'll tell you why.

The vile things I witnessed in the capital are enough to add years to a man's life.

And we're only in the first act, because soon we'll be moving into "*la Sociale*".[2] Which will be followed by a vigorous and lengthy reaction!

This is what we've been brought to by Universal Suffrage, the new God I consider as stupid as the old. No matter. Do you think it will be abashed, good old Universal Suffrage? Not at all! After Isidore we'll have Pignouf I.[3]

What makes me wretched about this war is that the Prussians are right! Their turn now! Then Russia's! Ah! how I wish I were dead, not to have to think about all this!

At Nohant you must be less bothered than we are by the question of money. In a few days all the workers in the Seine-Inférieure will be begging. My nephew Commanville is showing a good deal of spirit, keeping his workmen busy despite everything.[4] My brother has abandoned his patients and is devoting himself to public affairs.[5] Rouen is arming and maintaining its entire *garde mobile* at its own expense. That idea hasn't yet occurred to any other municipality.

Poor literature! Utterly forsaken, chère maître. *Saint Antoine* is only at page 14! Impossible to press on with it.

Where is Maurice?

Give me your news often, and kiss your dear little girls for me.

Tout à vous,

Gve Flaubert

[1] They had probably been called up.

[2] Current slang for "Socialist Republic".

[3] That is, "After Napoleon the Third, Lout the First." The "lout" would be Thiers.

Sand may have replied directly to this tirade of Flaubert's against universal suffrage.

(Letters from her to him dated, according to her diary, August 22 and September 7, are lost.) In any case, she answered it publicly, with no mention of Flaubert, in a few sentences contained in her "*Letter to a friend*" in *Le Temps* for 5 September 1870:

"France, always in the forefront of the action, has a weapon the Teutons will not snatch from her, a supreme weapon in battles of will: universal suffrage. Recently I have heard it much execrated, even by serious-minded men, this formidable missile we have so often turned on ourselves. But so it is with all weapons one doesn't know how to use. This one is the universal salvation of the future. This is the machine gun that must peacefully resolve all the questions that have been set aside in days of tumult and terror – let us not forget it! The day it begins to function properly, the errors of the powers-that-be will become impossible."

It must be remembered that "universal suffrage" meant universal *male* suffrage. Even with George Sand, there was no question of "Votes for Women".

[4] Since the end of July the blockade of the Normandy coast had closed factories, causing unemployment and poverty. But Commanville had obtained a government order for his lumber mill.

[5] On August 10, Dr Achille Flaubert had been elected to the Rouen Municipal Council.

*

September 1 brought the annihilating Prussian victory at Sedan in the Ardennes: over eighty thousand French troops, and the Emperor himself, surrendered to the enemy and became prisoners of war. French killed and wounded numbered about nine thousand. On September 4 the Third Republic was proclaimed in Paris, its "Government of National Defence" resolving to continue the fight. On September 5, George Sand wrote in her diary: "Maurice wakes me, telling me that the republic has been proclaimed in Paris without a shot being fired! A tremendous event, unique in human history! . . . May God protect France! Once again she has become worthy of His regard."

263 FLAUBERT TO SAND

[Croisset, 10 September 1870]
Saturday

Chère maître,

Here we are, "in the depths of the abyss": even a shameful peace may not be accepted.[1] The Prussians want to destroy Paris – such is their dream. Our only rational hope is in *chemistry*. Who knows? Perhaps methods of defence have been found, new ones?[2]

I don't believe that the siege of Paris is imminent. But to force its surrender they will 1° intimidate it by bringing up their big guns, and 2° ravage the nearby provinces.

At Rouen, we're expecting the visit of those gentlemen. As I've been lieutenant of my company[3] since Sunday, I drill my men and go into Rouen to take lessons in military art.

The deplorable thing is that opinion is divided: some are for a fight to the death and others for peace at any price.

I am dying of grief.

What a house this is! Fourteen people, all moaning and groaning and driving me crazy.[4]

I curse women: they are the cause of all our woes.[5]

I expect Paris to suffer the fate of Warsaw.[6]

And you distress me with your enthusiasm for the Republic. At this moment, when we're being defeated by Positivism at its purest, how can you still believe in Phantoms? Whatever happens, those now in Power will be sacrificed. And the Republic will suffer the same fate. Please note that I defend it, the poor Republic. But I have no faith in it.

Yesterday I saw Dumas in Dieppe, where I went especially to talk with him, to quash an idiotic piece of slander about the Princess, who has been accused of stealing 51 million *in gold*. In fact she left France with clean hands. But the same cannot be said of her brother, who since the beginning of the war has cut down and sold the trees at the Château de Meudon for his profit. Splendid, isn't it? Badinguet is (has become?) an imbecile, an idiot. He keeps repeating, "No arms! No supplies!" The Prince Imperial is dying. These last details were given me (indirectly) by Mme Trochu.[7]

That's all I have to tell you now. I have many other things in my head, but can't collect them – I feel I'm drowning in sorrow – in cascades, rivers, oceans of it. It is impossible to suffer more than this: at times I'm afraid I'm going mad. When I look at my mother's face, the sight of it drains me of all energy. And I dare not tell you what I sometimes wish for.

This is where our crazy refusal to recognize the truth has led us, our passion for humbug and for all things meretricious. We'll become another Poland, another Spain. Then it will be Prussia's turn – she'll be devoured by Russia.

As for me, I consider myself *finished*. My brain will never recover. One cannot write when one has lost one's self-esteem. I ask but one thing – to die, so as to be at peace.

Adieu, chère maître. And above all, don't try to comfort me!

I embrace you with as much tenderness as is left in me. I feel my heart is withered and dry. I'm becoming stupid and nasty.

A vous encore,

G.

---

[1] Jules Favre, Minister of Foreign Affairs in the "Government of National Defence", had published, on September 6, a "manifesto to the Powers", declaring that France would not surrender "a single stone of her fortresses, not an inch of her territory".

[2] Flaubert is probably thinking of the "Scientific Committee for Defence", instituted on September 2. It was presided over by his associate at the Magny dinners, the chemist Marcelin Berthelot, and concerned itself chiefly with the manufacture of nitro-glycerine and dynamite.

[3] The Croisset company of the National Guard.

[4] The Bonenfant family, fearing the arrival of the Prussians at Nogent-sur-Seine, had been at Croisset since the end of August.

[5] Perhaps a reference to the Empress, who had fled to England on September 7. She was blamed for having encouraged her husband to listen to pro-war advisers, or, more popularly, was hated as the wife of the man who had brought the country to defeat. Crowds were calling for her head when she left Paris. Readers of earlier letters will recall numerous misogynistic pronouncements by Flaubert; and most of the Nogent refugees (the Bonenfant family) were women. But the remark seems particularly offensive in a letter to George Sand,

unless Flaubert had made George Sand, "le vieux troubadour", an honorary male. Of course Aurore Dupin, Baronne Dudevant, had already done this to herself.

⁶ The scene of savage Russian repression following the Polish insurrection of 1863.

⁷ Princesse Mathilde had left Paris on September 4 and taken shelter with Alexandre Dumas the younger at Puys, near Dieppe. Her baggage had already been put aboard a steamer for England when a rumour arose that it included the crown jewels and pictures from the Louvre. The captain ordered it opened, to convince the crowd of onlookers that it contained only personal effects; and the princess was allowed to depart. The story about Prince Napoleon's trees may also belong to the realm of wartime rumour. Similarly, the Emperor had not lost his mind, nor was the Prince Imperial (the fourteen-year-old son of the Emperor and Empress) dying; after serving in the army he too had gone to England. He was killed in Zululand in 1879, a volunteer in a British army expedition. Mme Trochu was the wife of General Louis-Jules-Trochu, recently appointed military governor of Paris.

*

By September 19, German armies had encircled Paris; but the new government, refusing Bismarck's terms for an armistice, voted to continue the war.

264 FLAUBERT TO SAND

[Croisset, 28 September 1870]
Wednesday

I have stopped being sad. Yesterday I took up my *Saint Antoine*. What can we do? We must resign ourselves – accustom ourselves to man's natural condition: that is, to evil.

In Pericles' time, the Greeks devoted themselves to Art without knowing where the next day's bread might come from. Let us be Greeks! I confess, however, chère maître, that I feel more like a savage. *Lettré* though I am, the blood of my forefathers, the Natchez or the Hurons,¹ seethes through my veins, and I have a grim, stupid, animal *desire to fight*. Explain that if you can! The idea of signing a peace now infuriates me, and I'd rather see Paris burned, like Moscow, than occupied by the Prussians. But we haven't reached that point yet, and I think the tide is turning.

Do you know the story about Mme Pourtalès? Nice, isn't it? France is paying dear for her immorality.²

I have read several letters from soldiers. They are exemplary: a country in which such things are written can't be swallowed up. France is a resourceful jade, and will rise again.

Whatever happens, another world is in the making. But I feel too old to adjust myself to new ways.

My nephew Commanville is making a thousand biscuit-boxes a day for the army, not to mention huts. As you see, we're not idle in these parts. Paris is overflowing with troops and provisions. In those respects, all is secure.

How I miss you! How I long to see you!

Je vous embrasse tous.

Your old troubadour,

Gve Fl

Here we're resolved to march on Paris should Hegel's fellow-countrymen besiege it. Try to put some guts into your neighbours in Berry. "Help, *chers lubriques*! Help us prevent the enemy from eating and drinking in a country that isn't theirs!"[3]

The war will (I trust) deal a heavy blow to the "Authorities". Will the individual, rejected and trampled on by the modern world, come into his own again? Let's hope so.

[1] See Letter 106, Note 2.

[2] Nothing is known about this "story".

[3] In one of her lost letters from Nohant (in the old province of Berry), Mme Sand had apparently written of lethargy or fatalism among her rural neighbours. Once again, "*chers lubriques*" seems to have been an affectionate or jollying phrase used by the Nohant puppets in addressing their youthful audience. The quoted exhortation might be an allusion to one of the plays.

265 FLAUBERT TO SAND

[Croisset] Tuesday 11 October [1870]

Chère maître,

Are you still alive? Where are you – you, Maurice and the others? I don't know how it is I'm not dead, I've been suffering so atrociously for the past 6 weeks!

My mother and her cousins from Nogent have taken refuge in Rouen. My niece is in London. My brother is busy with municipal affairs, and I am here alone, chafing with helplessness and grief. I assure you I've tried to be of use: impossible!

What wretchedness here! Today I've had 271 poor people at the gate. We gave them all something. What will it be like this winter? The Prussians are now 12 leagues from Rouen,[1] and we have no orders, no one in command, no discipline, nothing, nothing! We're still being told stories about the army of the Loire. But where is it? Do you know anything about it? What is happening in central France?[2]

Paris is well on its way to starvation, and no one is coming to its aid!

The stupidities of the Republic are outstripping those of the Empire. Is some abominable intrigue going on in secret? Why such inaction?

I'm so sad! I *feel* that the Latin world is in its death-throes. Everything that we stood for is dying.

My entertainment consists of the patrolling and drilling of the National Guard!

Adieu, chère bon maître. I haven't the heart to write more. Send me your news: it will be an act of charity.

Je vous embrasse.

Gve Fl

[1] Actually, the Germans were at Gisors and Gournay, more than fifty kilometres from Rouen, awaiting the capitulation of Metz, which surrendered on October 27. They did not venture further, so as not to expose their lines of retreat; but their short forays from Gisors and Gournay were enough to cause alarm in Rouen.

[2] With parts of various regiments put together here and there, two armies had been formed – the army of the Vosges and that of the Loire. The army of the Vosges had been driven back by German regiments enabled to do so by the fall of Strasbourg (27 September). The army of the Loire was crushed at Artenay on October 10 by the Bavarians, who entered Orléans the next day.

266 SAND TO FLAUBERT

[La Châtre, 14 October 1870][1]

We're alive, and at La Châtre. Nohant is being ravaged by a terrible compound smallpox epidemic, so we had to take the children to stay with some friends who live in the Creuse, where we spent three weeks trying in vain to find a place fit for a family to live in for a few months. We were offered hospitality in the south of France, but didn't want to leave our own area, where we might be able to make ourselves useful at any moment, though we haven't much idea how to set about it. So we're back here with the friends who live nearest our own deserted home,[2] and are waiting to see what happens.

There'd be no point in listing all the dangers and uncertainties involved in setting up a republic in the provinces. Why delude ourselves? – we're staking our all, and Orleanism[3] may be the result. But we're so far advanced into the unforeseen it would be childish to attempt prediction. The thing is to escape impending disaster. We mustn't say, or believe, that it's impossible. We mustn't despair of France: she's expiating her own folly, but she'll be reborn no matter what. Perhaps we ourselves will be carried off. What difference does it make whether we're killed by a bullet or by pneumonia? We die just the same. Let's die without cursing our own species!

Nous t'aimons toujours et tous, nous t'embrassons.

G. Sand

[1] Probable date.

[2] The family of Charles Duvernet. La Châtre is five kilometres from Nohant.

[3] That is, the return of the Orléans family to the throne. The Orléanist pretender was the comte de Paris, grandson of Louis Philippe.

*

By November 11, Mme Sand was once again at Nohant. There she learned that one of two balloons that the Republican government had sent out from Paris early in October for Tours, carrying delegates to encourage resistance in the provinces, was named the "George Sand". The other, which had carried Gambetta, was the "Armand Barbès".

The Germans had now encircled Paris, beginning the famous siege: no foodstuffs could enter, and there was occasional bombardment. To escape that fate, Rouen declared itself an open city and awaited the arrival of the Germans. Some sort of postal service continued to function: from Croisset Flaubert wrote in anguish to Caroline in England, to Princesse Mathilde, now in Brussels, and to George Sand, who on November 25 had written him a letter that has disappeared.

267 FLAUBERT TO SAND

[Croisset] 27 [November 1870]
Sunday evening

I'm still alive, chère maître, but only just, I'm feeling so sad. I didn't write earlier, because I was waiting to hear from you. I didn't know where you were.

For six weeks we've been expecting *messieurs les Prussiens* to arrive, from one day to the next. We keep listening, thinking we hear gunfire in the distance. They now surround the Seine Inférieure, with a radius of 15 to 20 leagues. In fact they're even closer, since they've occupied – and completely devastated – the Vexin. What horrors! It makes one blush to be a man.

If we have a victory on the Loire, their coming will be delayed. But will we have that victory? When I feel hope I try to suppress it. And yet deep within me, despite everything, I can't help hoping a little, just a little.

I don't think there can be a sadder man than I am in the whole of France. (Everything depends on how sensitive a person happens to be.) I am dying of grief. That is the truth. And any attempt to console me irritates me. What breaks my heart is 1° human ferocity; 2° the conviction that we're about to enter an era of stupidity. We'll be utilitarian, militaristic, American, and Catholic. Very Catholic! You'll see! This war with Prussia concludes and destroys the French Revolution.

"But what if we're victorious?" you'll ask. That hypothesis goes against all historical precedent. Where have you ever seen the south defeat the north, or Catholics prevail over Protestants?[1] The Latin race is in its death throes. France is going to follow Spain and Italy. *Pignouflisme*, the Age of the Boor, is upon us.

What a collapse! What a fall! What wretchedness! What abominations! Is it possible to believe in progress and civilization in the face of all that's happening now? What good is science, since this nation of scientists is committing abominations worthy of the Huns? And worse, because the Prussians are systematic, cold-blooded and deliberate, without the excuse of passion or hunger.[2]

Why do they execrate us so? Don't you feel crushed by the hatred of 40 million men? The thought of such an immense, hellish abyss makes my senses reel.

There's no lack of ready-made slogans. "France will rise again!" "Do not despair!" "It's a salutary punishment! We were really so immoral!" Etc. Oh, eternal nonsense! No! One does not recover from such a blow.

I feel stricken to the core. If I were twenty years younger, I mightn't be thinking like this; if I were twenty years older, I'd resign myself.

Poor Paris! I call it heroic. But if we see it again it will no longer be our Paris. All the friends I had there are dead or scattered. I no longer have a centre. Literature seems to me a vain and useless thing. Shall I ever be capable of writing again?

I find it impossible to devote attention to anything. I spend my days in gloomy, devouring idleness. My niece Caroline is in London. My mother grows older by the hour. Every Monday we go to Rouen and stay there till Thursday, to escape from the solitude of the country. Then we come back again!

Oh! if only I could flee to a country where there aren't any uniforms and one doesn't hear the sound of drums! Where there's no talk of massacres, where one doesn't have to be a *citizen*. But the earth is no longer habitable for us poor Mandarins!

Adieu, chère maître. Think of me, and write. I feel I'd be stronger if you were nearby. Embrassez pour moi tous les vôtres, et à vous cent mille tendresses de votre

vieux troubadour

Gve

[1] It was in the works of Renan that Flaubert found this idea of the superiority of Protestants to Catholics.

[2] The Germans were ruthless in punishing any sign of resistance in occupied territory – burning villages, shooting inhabitants found with arms, and deporting local officials to Germany.

*

Sand replied to that letter of lamentation – in her diary she speaks of doing so – but her letter was lost in the chaos of the occupation. There would be no further letters between her and Flaubert until the following February.

Flaubert continued to write to his niece in England: his letters to her tell of the arrival of the Prussians in Rouen and Croisset in early December. In both places Flaubert and his mother were forced to lodge officers and men, and Flaubert was obliged to do their errands. "At present we are in Rouen," he wrote to Caroline on December 18, "with two soldiers quartered on us. At Croisset there are seven, plus three officers and six horses. . . . I am writing to you in your old bedroom, and can hear the snores of the two soldiers sleeping in your dressing room. I toss and plunge in my sorrow like a boat foundering at sea. I never thought my heart could hold so much suffering and still remain alive."[1]

[1] For a selection of Flaubert's letters written during the occupation, see *The Letters of Gustave Flaubert, 1857–1880*.

CHAPTER VII

1871

The war was rapidly nearing its end. On 8 December the seat of government, in danger at Tours, had been transferred to Bordeaux. Of the two armies of the Loire, one was annihilated at Le Mans (12 January); and the other, defeated at Héricourt (15–17 January), sought internment in Switzerland. The army of the North was put to flight at Saint-Quentin (19 January). Paris, exhausted by cold and famine, was subjected to bombardment that began on 5 January: continued resistance was clearly impossible.

On 18 January 1871, as though to emphasize the shift of power resulting from the French defeats, the king of Prussia was proclaimed emperor of Germany in the palace of Versailles. At last, on the 28th, hostilities were ended by an armistice: discussion of peace terms began.

George Sand, in the relative quiet of Nohant, recorded her impressions in her diary as usual. The armies hastily organized by Gambetta inspired her with little confidence. Her dream was a true republic, legitimized by elections: the "Bordeaux dictatorship" horrified her. She greeted the armistice with relief. "I breathe again! My children and I weep and embrace each other," she wrote to Henry Harrisse on 29 January. "Enough of politics! Enough of the ferocious heroism coming out of Bordeaux, that seeks to reduce us to despair and conceals incompetence under a fanatical, hollow, gutless lyricism."

When correspondence became possible again she at once sent an anguished note to Flaubert.

268 SAND TO FLAUBERT

Nohant, 4 February [18]71

Aren't you receiving my letters? Do send me just a word, I beg, saying "I'm well." We're so anxious!

Everyone's all right in Paris.

Nous t'embrassons.

G. Sand

*

Flaubert and his mother were now in Dieppe with Caroline, who had recently returned from England.

269 FLAUBERT TO SAND

Neuville near Dieppe
Wednesday 15 February [1871]

Chère maître,
Your letter of the 4th has just come. I have had no other. Will this reach
you? I wonder.
I'm still alive. But only just. However, I have no personal misfortunes to
complain of.
Mille tendresses pour vous et les vôtres.
The old troubadour

[unsigned]

I'll write to you as soon as possible, and let's hope we may soon meet again
in Paris. But, – poor Paris! . . . . .

270 SAND TO FLAUBERT

Nohant, 22 February [1871]

I got yours of the 15th this morning, and what a painful thorn it removes
from my heart! One goes crazy with anxiety these days if a letter isn't answered.
Let's hope we can soon have a chat and tell one another all about what's
happened during our "separation".
I too have been fortunate in not losing any of my friends, young or old.
That's the only good thing to be said. I shan't shed any tears over the republic:
it's been the worst ever – unsuccessful in Paris and inept in the provinces. But
even if I'd liked it I wouldn't mind anything so long as this hateful war comes
to an end!
Nous t'aimons et nous t'embrassons tendrement.
I shan't be in any hurry to come to Paris. It'll still be pestilential for some
time to come.
A toi.

[unsigned]

*

Elections to the National Assembly were held on 8 February. The great question, as represented by opposing candidates, was: Peace or war? The Peace
party won by a large majority. When the Assembly met at Bordeaux on 12
February, Thiers was named "*chef du pouvoir exécutif de la République française*":
it was he who would negotiate peace terms with Bismarck.
The treaty, signed on 26 February, was ratified at Bordeaux on 1 March.
Alsace and part of Lorraine were ceded to Germany; France agreed to pay an
indemnity of five billion francs; the Prussians were to make a triumphal entry
into Paris. "It's all over: we've drunk shame to the dregs," Flaubert wrote to
Princesse Mathilde on March 4th.

271 FLAUBERT TO SAND

Dieppe, 11 March [1871]

Chère maître,

When shall we see each other again? Paris doesn't sound very gay. Ah! What kind of a world are we going to inhabit? Paganism, Christianism, Boorism:[1] such are the three great evolutions of mankind. It's depressing to find oneself at the beginning of the third.

I won't recount everything I've suffered since September. How have I stayed alive? That's what surprises me! No one has been more *desperate* than I. Why? I have had bad times in my life, I have suffered great losses, I have often wept, endured much anguish. Well, all those griefs put together are nothing – nothing at all – compared with these. And I don't become reconciled to it. I find no consolation. I have no hope.

I didn't consider myself a believer in progress, or a humanitarian. No matter! I did have illusions! But what barbarism! What retrogression! I have a grudge against my contemporaries for making me feel like a brute of the twelfth century. I am choking on gall. These officers who smash your mirrors with white-gloved hands, who know Sanskrit and fling themselves on your champagne, who steal your watch and then send you their visiting-card, this war for money – these civilized savages horrify me more than Cannibals. And everybody is going to emulate them and turn military. Russia now has 4 million troops. All Europe will be in uniform. If we take our revenge, it will be ferocious. And you can be sure we'll be thinking of nothing but avenging ourselves on Germany. The government, whatever it may be, will only be able to maintain itself by harping on that passion. Mass murder is going to be the object of all our efforts – France's ideal!

I cherish the dream of going to live in some peaceful country in the sun.

And we must expect new hypocrisies: declamations about virtue, diatribes about corruption – and austerity in dress, etc. Priggishness triumphant.

At this moment I have *forty* Prussians at Croisset. As soon as my poor house (which is now a horror to me) is emptied and cleaned, I'll go back to Paris, insalubrious or no – I don't give a damn.

Amitiés aux vôtres, et tout à vous.

Your old troubadour

Gve

not very merry!

[1] *Muflisme.*

*

The Germans levied taxes on each occupied city, increasing them at the least sign of resistance. In addition, heavy "reparations" were part of the peace terms. In 1914, at the outbreak of the First World War, France would still be paying "reparations" to Germany for the war of 1870–1.

As future letters will show, Flaubert retained a hatred of Germany for the rest of his life.

272   SAND TO FLAUBERT

Nohant, 17 March [1871]
(Yesterday I got your letter of the 11th)

We've all suffered in spirit more than ever before in our lives, and shall never cease to feel the wound. It's clear that the instinct for savagery tends to prevail, but I fear a worse one – the instinct for selfishness and cowardice, the base corruption of the false patriots and ultra-republicans who cry out for revenge but make sure to keep out of the way, while providing a good excuse for the bourgeois who want a "strong" reaction. But I'm afraid we mayn't even be vindictive: we'll be so revolted by this craven bravado we'll just live from day to day, as we did under the Restoration, putting up with everything so long as our slumbers aren't disturbed. An awakening will come, though I shan't be here to see it, and you'll be old! You talk about going to live in some peaceful country in the sun. Where? What country is going to be peaceful in the struggle between barbarism and civilization which will spread all over the world? And isn't the sun itself a myth? Either it refuses to come out or it scorches you to a cinder. And so it is with everything on this unfortunate planet. But let's go on loving it just the same, and get used to suffering on it.

I wrote down my thoughts and impressions every day during the crisis, and the *Revue des Deux Mondes* is publishing them in the form of a journal.[1] If you read it you'll see that life was entirely disrupted everywhere, even in places the war never reached. You'll also see that although I'm very gullible by nature I didn't swallow the tripe handed out by the political parties. But I don't know if you agree with me that complete and unalloyed freedom would save us from such disasters and set us back on the road to progress. Abuses of liberty don't worry me in themselves – it's just that those they do frighten tend to resort to abuses of power. M. Thiers seems to understand this at the moment; but will he be able to stick to the principle that has made him the arbiter of this great question?[2]

Whatever happens, let us go on loving one another, and don't leave me ignorant of anything that concerns you. My heart is heavy and permanently anxious, and a sign from you always lightens it a little. I worry lest your awful guests should have ruined Croisset, for they continue to make themselves loathsome and disgusting everywhere in spite of the peace. If I had five billion francs I'd spend it all to get them thrown out! And I wouldn't ask for it back.

Why don't you come and stay with us, where it's quiet? It always has been, physically. One tries to start working again. One accepts things – what else is there to do? And we love you here – life here still consists of loving one another. We still have our Lamberts,[3] and mean to keep them as long as possible. All our children are back from the war safe and sound. You could live in peace, and work too – for one must work, whether one feels like it or no! It's going to be a delightful spring. And Paris will have time to quieten down while you're here. You're looking for a peaceful spot. Well, it's ready to hand, together with hearts devoted to you!

Je t'embrasse mille fois on behalf of myself and all my brood. Our little girls are marvellous, and the Lamberts' little boy is charming.

G. S.

¹ *Journal d'un voyageur pendant la guerre* was printed in the issues of 1 and 15 March and 1 April. Sand had written her diary entries for publication.

² See Sand on Thiers in Letter 101. It was thought probable that he would have the comte de Paris, eldest son of Louis-Philippe, called to the throne.

³ For the Lamberts, see Letter 110.

*

Flaubert was unable to read this letter until a fortnight later, having set out with Dumas *fils* on 16 March to spend a few days with Princesse Mathilde in Brussels. From there he went to London, where he visited Juliet Herbert, and returned to Dieppe on the 28th.

Meanwhile, Paris was in tumult. On 18 March, in the working-class districts of Montmartre and Belleville, rebellious mobs that included women and children prevented regular army troops from seizing cannon belonging to the Garde Nationale – the long-established, legally organized and equipped citizens' army, which the central government had recently been threatening to abolish. That afternoon, Thiers ordered all government officials and employees, and all regular army troops, to leave Paris for Versailles, which was declared the new national capital. The central committee of the Garde Nationale assumed control of Paris, and the city was declared an independent, self-governing unit, or commune. The lines were drawn. A provisional revolutionary popular government, calling itself La Commune de Paris, was hastily organized, with headquarters in the city hall, the Hôtel de Ville. Now began the second siege of Paris, the besiegers this time being the "Versaillais", the troops of the French national government.

273 FLAUBERT TO SAND

Neuville near Dieppe
Friday, 31 March [1871]
In reply to yours of 17 March.

Chère maître,

Tomorrow, at last, I shall resign myself to returning to Croisset. It will be hard, but I must do it. I'll try to take up my poor *Saint Antoine* again, and forget France.

My mother will stay here with her granddaughter until it becomes clear where one can go without fear of the Prussians or of riots.

A fortnight ago, I set out from here with Dumas for Brussels, thinking to return direct to Paris. But "the new Athens" seems to me to surpass Dahomey in ferocity and imbecility.[1]

Have we reached the end of the swindle? Are we done with hollow metaphysics and clichés? All the evil stems from our colossal ignorance. What ought to be pondered is simply believed. Instead of observing, people assert.

The French Revolution must cease to be mere dogma, and become an object of scientific inquiry, like all else that's human. If people had known more, they wouldn't have believed that a mystical formula is capable of creating armies, or that the word "Republic" suffices to defeat a million well-disciplined men. They would have left Badinguet on the throne *expressly* to make peace, even if they sent him to the galleys afterwards.[2] If they had known more, they would have realized the truth about the volunteers of '92, and the retreat of [the duke of] Brunswick, bribed by Danton and Westermann.[3] But no! always the same story! Always nonsense! And now we have the Paris Commune, a throw-back to sheer mediaevalism.[4] They're frank enough about it! The business about controlling rents is particularly splendid. Now government meddles in Natural Law and interferes in contracts between individuals.[5] The Commune asserts that we don't owe what we do owe, and that one service is not to be paid for by another. It's monstrous ineptitude and injustice.

Many conservatives who wanted to preserve the Republic out of love for law and order are going to miss Badinguet and in their hearts call back the Prussians. The people in the Hôtel de Ville have *deflected our hatred*. That's why I resent them. It seems to me that we have never sunk lower.

We're being tossed back and forth between the Society of St Vincent de Paul and the International.[6] But the latter is committing too many idiocies to last long. If it should defeat the Versaillais and overthrow the government, the Prussians will enter Paris and "order will prevail" – as it did in Warsaw.[7] If, on the contrary, it is beaten, the reaction will be fierce and all liberty strangled.

What can one say of socialists who imitate the methods of Badinguet and Wilhelm: requisitioning, banning of newspapers, executions without trial, etc.? Ah! What a vile beast the crowd is! And how humiliating to be a man!

Je vous embrasse bien fort.

Your old troubadour

Gve

[1] Flaubert refers to the cruelty of the insurgents – executions without trial, firing on hostile demonstrators, etc. There were atrocities on both sides. Dahomey, during the slave trade, was famous for the ferocity of its warriors, both men and women.

[2] Maxime Du Camp says in his *Souvenirs Littéraires* that he had suggested this in a letter to Flaubert.

[3] In 1792, the army of the First French Republic repulsed the German invaders in the Battle of Valmy, arousing great popular enthusiasm in France. Considerable surprise was expressed, however, that the German commander, the Duke of Brunswick, should immediately withdraw his troops instead of continuing the campaign; and there were rumours that he had accepted French bribes.

Flaubert is saying that, just as in 1792 – when victory was won not, as patriotic tradition would have it, by the "spirit of the Republic", but by corrupting the enemy – so in 1870 and 1871 the mystical idea of "proclaiming the Republic" would not win the war. [J. B.]

⁴ In a manifesto, the Communards had evoked the "heroism of the mediaeval artisans" – a reference to the communal movement of the tenth century, which had aimed to free cities and guilds from central and feudal authority.

⁵ On 29 March, the Council of the Commune had cancelled rent increases imposed after October 1870.

⁶ That is, between Catholic reaction and Communism.

⁷ See Letter 263, Note 6.

*

If George Sand did not reply to that letter, it may well have been because she was depressed and outraged by the horrors of the Commune. She saw her hopes, and all her humanitarian dreams, crumbling. "It is a great sorrow for me," she wrote to Jules Boucoiran, "– for me, who love the proletariat in the classical sense and have dreamed only of its future."

Flaubert, back in Croisset after April 1st, began to be impatient.

274 FLAUBERT TO SAND

[Croisset] 24 [April 1871]
Monday evening

Chère maître,

Why no letters? Perhaps you didn't get mine, sent from Dieppe? Are you ill? Are you still alive? What does this mean? I do hope that neither you nor any of your family are in Paris. "Capital of the arts, seat of civilization, centre of fine manners and urbanity"!

Do you know the worst thing about all this? It's that one becomes accustomed to it. Yes! We're "getting used" to it. We're getting used to doing without Paris, to not caring about it – almost to imagining it no longer exists.

As for me, I am not like the bourgeois. My feeling is this: that after the invasion, there can be no further disaster. The Prussian war has affected me like a natural disaster, one of those cataclysms that occur every six thousand years; whereas the insurgents in Paris strike me as something very clear, quite obvious and almost simple.

What a throw-back! What savages! How like they are to the supporters of the Ligue, and to the Maillotins![1] Poor France! She'll never free herself of the Middle Ages! Still dragging herself along on the Gothic idea of the *commune* – which is nothing but the Roman *municipium*!

I'm afraid that the destruction of the column in the Place Vendôme may sow the seed of a Third Empire![2]

Ah! I can hardly bear it, I swear.

And the nice little reaction we'll have after all this? All the worthy ecclesiastics will bob up again, large as life!

I've got back to *Saint Antoine* and am working hammer and tongs.
So: write to me!
Je vous embrasse très fort.

                                        Gve Flau.

---

[1] For the Ligue, see Letter 140, Note 3. "Maillotins" was the name given to the Parisians who armed themselves with mallets (*maillets*) and revolted against the government of the uncles of Charles VI (1381).

[2] For the Communards, the Vendôme column was the symbol of Bonapartism and militarism. As early as September 1870, the painter Gustave Courbet had asked the provisional government to demolish it, but it was not until 12 April 1871 that the Council of the Commune did so. Courbet was to pay dearly for his activities during the Commune. See Letter 288, Note 6. The column was re-erected in 1874.

275   SAND TO FLAUBERT

                                        Nohant, 28 April [1871]

No, I certainly haven't forgotten you, but I'm sad, very sad – that's to say, I try to deaden my sorrow, I contemplate the spring, I keep myself busy, I talk as if nothing had happened. But since these horrible events I haven't been able to stay alone for a moment without lapsing into bitter despair. I make great efforts, I try not to be depressed, I don't *want* to renounce the past and dread the future! But the fact is, my will and my reason are fighting against a deep and insurmountable impression as to the present. That is why I didn't want to write to you until I felt better. Not because I'm ashamed of these attacks of despondency, but because, knowing you were so sad, I didn't want to increase your sorrow by adding the weight of my own.

In my view, the vile experiment that Paris is attempting or undergoing in no way disproves the laws of eternal progress that govern both men and things, and if I have acquired any intellectual principles, good or bad, this business neither undermines nor alters them. A long time ago I accepted the necessity for patience in the same way as one accepts the weather, the long winter, old age, and failure in all its forms. But I think that people who take a stand on things – if they are sincere – need to be able to change their slogans, or perhaps even to realize the emptiness of all *a priori* formulae.

That's not what makes me sad. When a tree dies you just have to plant two others. My grief comes from a sheer failing of the heart that I can't overcome. I can't sleep for thinking of the suffering or even the ignominy of others. I pity those who do evil; while acknowledging that they're not in the least interesting, I'm distressed by their state of mind. We pity a little bird fallen from its nest; how can we fail to pity whole masses of consciences fallen into the mud? The situation was less painful during the Prussian siege. We loved a Paris that was suffering against its will. We pity it all the more now because we can no longer love it. Those who have never loved now indulge in implacable hate. What should we say to them? Perhaps we shouldn't answer at all. The contempt of the whole of France is perhaps the inevitable punishment for the signal cravenness with which the Parisians have knuckled under to the revolt and its outlaws. It's a natural sequel to acceptance of the outlaws of the Empire. Different traitors, the same cowardice.

But I didn't mean to talk to you about that – you "bellow" about it quite enough already! We ought to try to think about other things. If we think about *that* too much we lose all sensation in our limbs, and let them be lopped off too stoically.

You don't tell me how you found your delightful nest in Croisset. The Prussians occupied it; did they knock it about, dirty it, steal from it? Your books, your bibelots – were they all still there? Did they respect your name? And your study? If you can get yourself to work there again, your mind will be at peace once more. I'm waiting for mine to get better; I know I have to forward my own cure by means of some kind of faith, and though that faith has received many knocks, I've made it my duty to do so.

Tell me whether the tulip tree suffered from the frost this winter, and whether the peonies are doing well. I often make the journey there in my mind, and see your garden and its surroundings again. How far away it all seems; how much has happened since! I sometimes feel I must be a hundred years old.

My little girls, and they alone, give me some sense of time again. They're growing up, they're funny and affectionate, and it's through them and the two beings who gave them to me that I feel I'm still of this world. Through you too, cher ami, whose heart I still feel to be vital and kind. How I wish I could see you! But there's no means of getting about at present.

Nous t'embrassons tous et nous t'aimons.

G. Sand

*

Flaubert knew his *chère maître* well enough to recognize the fundamental cause of her sadness and disenchantment. "Mme Sand has written me a desperate letter," he wrote to Princesse Mathilde on May 3rd. "She sees that her old ideal was hollow, and her republican faith seems completely extinguished! That's a disaster that won't befall me." And in his reply to his friend he expressed his political conviction more energetically than ever – of course without converting her.

276 FLAUBERT TO SAND

Croisset, 30 April [1871]

Chère maître,

Let me answer your questions at once insofar as they concern me personally. No, the Prussians did not loot my house. They made off with a few trifles – a dressing case, a cartoon, some pipes; but on the whole they did no damage.

My study they respected. I had buried a large box full of letters, and hidden my voluminous notes for *Saint Antoine*. All that, I found intact.

The worst effect of the invasion *for me* is that it has aged my poor mother by ten years. What a change! She can no longer walk alone, and her frailty is heart-rending. How sad it is to watch the slow deterioration of people you love!

And the death of Mme Viardot, which I learned of this morning! I've just written to Turgenev. He must be shattered.[1]

To stop thinking about public miseries and my own, I have plunged furiously back into *Saint Antoine*, and if I can continue at this pace without interruption it will be finished next winter. I really long to read you the 60 pages that are done. When railway journeys become possible again, come and see me. Your old troubadour has been waiting a long time. Your letter this morning touched me. What a fine fellow you are, and what a great heart you have!

I'm different from all the people I hear lamenting the [civil] war in Paris. I find it more tolerable than the invasion, because after the invasion any further despair is impossible – another proof of the depths to which we have sunk. "Ah, thank God the Prussians are there!" is the universal cry of the bourgeois.[2] I put Messieurs the workers into the same bag, and I'd like to throw the whole lot of them into the river!

That's where they're headed anyway – and then things will subside. We'll become a big, dreary, industrial country – a kind of Belgium. The disappearance of Paris (as the seat of government) will make France dull and stagnant. She will have no heart, no centre – and, I think, no mind?

As for the Commune, which is in its death throes, it's the latest manifestation of the Middle Ages. Will it be the last? Let's hope so!

I hate democracy (at least as it is understood in France), because it is based on "the morality of the Gospels", which is immorality itself, whatever anyone may say: that is, the exaltation of Mercy at the expense of Justice, the negation of Right – the very opposite of social order.

The Commune is rehabilitating assassins,[3] just as Jesus forgave thieves; and they are looting the houses of the rich[4] because they have learned to curse Lazarus – who was not a *bad* rich man, but simply a rich man.[5] The slogan "The republic is above all argument"[6] is on a par with the dogma that "The Pope is infallible." Always slogans! Always gods!

The God-before-last – universal suffrage – has just played a terrible joke on his faithful by electing "the assassins of Versailles".[7] What are we to believe in, then? Nothing. That is the beginning of Wisdom. It is time to rid ourselves of "Principles" and to espouse Science, objective inquiry. The only rational thing (I keep coming back to it) is a government of Mandarins,[8] provided the Mandarins know something – in fact, a great many things. The *people* never come of age, and they will always be the bottom rung of the social scale because they represent number, mass, the limitless. It is of little importance that many peasants should be able to read and no longer listen to their priests; but it is infinitely important that many men like Renan or Littré be able to live *and be listened to*. Our only salvation now lies in a *legitimate aristocracy*, by which I mean a majority composed of something more than mere numbers.

If we had been more enlightened, if in Paris there had been more people familiar with history, we wouldn't have had to suffer Gambetta or Prussia or the Commune. "What did the Catholics do to avert a great danger? They crossed themselves, putting their trust in God and the saints. We, who are 'advanced', cry *'Vive la République!'* and evoke the memory of '92."[9] And remember: we never doubted we should win. The Prussians no longer existed. We embraced each other in our joy. We had to restrain ourselves from rushing to the passes of the Argonne,[10] where there are no passes. No matter: such was tradition. I have a friend in Rouen who suggested that we forge pikes – *pikes*, to use against rifles!

Ah! How much more practical it would have been to keep Badinguet, so that he could be gaoled once peace was signed! Austria didn't stage a revolution after Sadowa, nor Italy after Novara, nor Russia after Sebastopol![11] But the good Frenchman rushes to tear down his house as soon as the chimney catches fire.

Enfin: I must share a ghastly thought with you: I fear that the destruction of the Vendôme column may sow the seed of a 3rd Empire? Who knows whether in twenty years or forty years a son of Plon-Plon may not be our master?[12]

For the moment, Paris is completely epileptic. It's the result of congestion of the brain caused by the siege. Besides, during the past few years France was living in an abnormal mental state. The success of the *Lanterne*, and Troppmann,[13] were very clear symptoms.

This madness springs from excessive stupidity; and the stupidity from a superfluity of nonsense. Our lying had turned us into idiots. We had lost all notion of good and evil, of the beautiful and the ugly. Remember what criticism has been like these last few years. Could it tell the difference between the Sublime and the Ridiculous? What lack of respect! What ignorance! What a muddle! *"Bouilli ou rôti même chose!"*[14] And, at the same time, such servility toward the "opinion of the day" – *le plat à la mode*.

Everything was fakery: fake realism, fake army, fake credit, and even fake whores. They were called *"Marquises"*, just as *grandes dames* called each other "cochonnettes".[15] Girls who continued in the tradition of Sophie Arnould, like my friend Lagier, were looked on with horror.[16] You never witnessed Saint-Victor's display of respect for la Païva.[17] And this falsity (which is perhaps a legacy of Romanticism – the predominance of passion over form, of inspiration over precept) played a particularly strong role when it came to making judgments. An actress was praised not for being a good actress, but for being a good mother. Art had to be moral, philosophy had to be clear, vice decent, and knowledge "accessible to everyone".

But this letter is too long. When I start cursing my compatriots I don't know when to stop.

Je vous embrasse bien fort.

Votre vieux

Gve Flaubert

[1] A false report. Turgenev's great friend, the singer Pauline Viardot (sister of the celebrated Marie Malibran), lived until 1910.

[2] The following lament from an unidentified French village was printed in the newspaper *Le Drapeau tricolore*, 2 May 1871:

"I assure you that the Germans were fine men, and have been greatly slandered. When we learned that they were being withdrawn we were all very sad. No more Prussians meant no more police, no more order or security. You should have seen how we all tried to prevent their leaving – everyone: the mayor, the Municipal Council, the entire population."

[3] Probably an allusion to the assassination, more or less officially approved by the Commune, of Generals Lecomte and Thomas.

[4] On April 18 the Commune had issued orders that the houses of those who had left the city (especially rich bourgeois) should be entered and any arms found in them seized.

[5] Flaubert has mis-remembered his *Luke* xvi, 19–31. Lazarus was the poor man.

[6] During the elections the Revolutionary Republican party declared: "The Republic must never be questioned. . . . The Republic is above all principles, even that of universal suffrage."

[7] After the first encounters with the Communards, on April 2, the Versaillais had shot several prisoners: thenceforth the Commune called the members of the Assembly and the Versailles government "assassins".

[8] See Letter 178, Note 3, and Letter 284, Note 1.

[9] Apparently a quotation, unidentified. Here and there in this letter, as in the present paragraph, Flaubert grows almost incoherent with indignation.

[10] It was at the entrance of the "*défilés de l'Argonne*" that General Dumouriez won the Battle of Valmy in 1792.

[11] For the Austrian defeat at Sadowa, see Letter 30, Note 5. At Novara, in 1849, the defeat of the king of Sardinia by the Austrians resulted in his abdication. The taking of Sebastopol by the French and English armies in 1855 ended the Crimean war.

[12] Plon-Plon was the nickname of Prince Jérôme Napoléon Bonaparte. Flaubert does not mention the Prince Imperial (son of Napoleon III), thinking perhaps that Jérôme Napoléon, considered a liberal, had a greater chance of being elected.

[13] For *La Lanterne*, see Letter 130, Note 1; for Troppmann, Letter 213, Note 1.

[14] Molière, *Le Malade Imaginaire*, Act II, scene 6. The correct text is: "*Rôti, bouilli, même chose*" – "Roast or boiled, it's all the same." "*Le plat à la mode*" – "the going thing".

[15] These bits of gossip, uncharacteristic of Flaubert, perhaps came to him from Maxime Du Camp. Some of them can be found in the latter's memoirs, *Souvenirs d'un demi-siècle* (1883).

[16] Sophie Arnould (1744–1802), and Suzanne Lagier, Flaubert's contemporary and friend, were both singers – talented, charming, beautiful and promiscuous.

[17] A beautiful Polish adventuress, Thérèse Lachmann, who preferred to be known by the name of one of her several husbands, the Portuguese marquez de Païva. In the 1860s, Flaubert had attended some of the literary and artistic receptions given in her mansion on the Champs-Elysées after her marriage to a wealthy German, Graf Henckel von Donnesmarck. The pair acted as agents for Bismarck, left France during the Franco-Prussian War, returned, and were later deported. For Saint-Victor, see Letter 204. Flaubert had not forgiven him.

*

The end of the Commune was in sight. All attempts at conciliation had failed: now it was war, and without mercy. On May 2 the executive committee was replaced by a five-member Committee of Public Safety, invested with dictatorial powers.

But it was too late. The forts at Ivry, Clamart and Vanves fell to the Versaillais. And on May 21 there began "*la semaine sanglante*" – "The Week of Blood". Unperceived by the insurgents, government troops entered the city by the undefended Porte de Saint-Cloud. Street warfare began, with barricades. Setting "strategic fires" to impede the enemy, the Communards put the torch to houses and public buildings. On both sides, thousands of people were shot without trial. On May 28 the last, sporadic street-fighting died out in the Faubourg du Temple, and the tricolour flew over all Paris.

As soon as communications were re-opened, Flaubert hastened to Paris, probably on June 4, to resume research for *Saint Antoine*. He went to Versailles, to speak with his friends Bardoux and d'Osmoy, both of whom had been elected deputies in February, about "Bouilhet's affairs". But the air of Paris, polluted by the stench of corpses, and the uncertainties of railway travel obliged him to return to Croisset on the 11th.

George Sand, meanwhile, remained at Nohant, depressed and distraught by the tragedy. "It's a long time since I've had news of Mme Sand," Flaubert wrote anxiously to Princesse Mathilde. "Does she resent my 'disillusioning' letters, I wonder? But no: that would be to underrate her." The day of his return to Croisset he unbosomed himself in a letter filled with indignation.

277   FLAUBERT TO SAND

Croisset [11] June [1871][1]
Sunday evening

Chère maître,

Never did I have a greater desire or greater need to see you than now! I've just come from Paris, and don't know whom to talk to! I'm stifling – I'm so distressed, or rather distraught. The smell of the corpses revolted me less than the miasmas of egotism exhaled from every mouth. The sight of the ruins is as nothing compared with Paris's immense stupidity. With very rare exceptions, it seemed to me that *everybody* was absolutely crazy. Half the population wants to strangle the other half, and vice versa. You can see it in the eyes of people in the streets. And the Prussians no longer exist! People excuse them, *admire* them!!! "Sensible" people want to be naturalized as Germans. I assure you, it's enough to make one despair of the human race.

I was in Versailles on Thursday. The excesses of the Right are frightening. The vote on the Orléans[2] is a concession made to appease the Right and gain time to prepare action against it.

Did you know that Troubat[3] had written articles urging the murder of the hostages? Even so, he was not arrested. He admitted to me that he had been "imprudent": charming word.

From the general madness I except Renan, who on the contrary seemed to me very philosophical. Our friend Soulié charged me with a thousand affectionate messages for you. Princesse Mathilde asked for news of you several times.

She is losing her wits. She wants to return to Saint-Gratien "despite every-thing". I've collected a mass of horrible and unheard-of details, all of which I spare you.

My short stay in Paris has upset me extremely, and I'm going to have a hard time getting back to work.

What do you think of my friend Maury, who kept the tricolour flying over the Archives throughout the Commune? I think few men would be capable of such pluck.[4]

The imperialists are the scum of the earth. I am sure of that. And I have proof – fantastic.

When history disentangles the story of the burning of Paris, many elements will unquestionably be found to have played their parts: 1° Prussia, and 2° the men around Badinguet. There is still no written evidence against the Empire. And Haussmann is boldly[5] entering himself as a candidate at the Paris elections.

Have you read the outline of a novel by Isidore that was among the docu-ments found in the Tuileries last September? What a scenario![6]

Adieu, and let me hear from you. My poor Maman seems a bit stronger these last few days.

Your old troubadour,

Gve Flaubert

I wrote you a long letter about a month ago.

[1] The original reads "10 June", but that was a Saturday.

[2] The abrogation of the 1848 law exiling members of the French royal houses.

[3] Jules Troubat, formerly Sainte-Beuve's secretary, had been secretary to Félix Pyat, publisher of pro-communist newspapers; but no article by him of the kind mentioned by Flaubert has been found.

[4] Other public buildings in Paris flew the red flag of the Commune. In a letter to his friend Mme Roger des Genettes, Flaubert added, in another tribute to Maury: ". . . which didn't keep him from continuing to write his little articles on the Etruscans. So there are still a few philosophers left. I'm not one of them."

[5] Because he had been so closely associated with the Imperial regime. He was defeated.

[6] The present whereabouts of this outline are not known. It was entitled *L'Odyssée de M. Benoît*, and is said to have been "probably political, intended to demonstrate the benefits of the imperial regime".

278 SAND TO FLAUBERT

[Nohant, 14 June 1871]

You want and need to see me, and you don't come! That's not nice – because I too, and all of us, are longing to see *you*. We were so cheerful when we parted eighteen months ago, and so many dreadful things have kept us apart! Having survived them, we deserve the consolation of seeing one another again. But I can't stir – I haven't a sou, and I have to work like a black.[1] Moreover, I haven't seen a single Prussian, and I'd like to keep my eyes unsullied. What times we're living through, my friend! It's all too much, for hope is being swept away with all the rest.

What will be the reaction to the infamous Commune? Isidore, or Henri V,[2] or will anarchy bring the incendiarists[3] back to power? I, who used to have such patience with my own species, and who for so long saw everything through rose-coloured spectacles, now see only darkness. I used to judge others by myself. I'd made great progress in schooling my own character: I'd sown my volcanoes with grass and flowers, and they were getting on well. And I imagined that everyone could enlighten and correct and control themselves – that the years which had passed over me and my fellow-creatures were bound to show the effects of reason and experience. And now I awake from a dream to find a whole generation divided between idiocy and delirium tremens. Anything is possible now!

But it's wrong to despair. I shall make a great effort, and perhaps I'll manage to recover patience and equanimity. But at present I can't. I'm as upset as you are, and I daren't talk or think or write for fear of opening up everyone's gaping wounds.

I did get your letter, but was waiting until I had the heart to answer it. I don't want to do anything but good to the people I love – especially you, who feel everything so deeply. I'm no good for anything at the moment. I'm consumed with anger and dying of disgust.

Je t'aime – that's all I know. My children send the same message. Give my love to your bonne petite mère.

G. Sand

[1] Sand was working with her son Maurice on a novel, which was published as *Mademoiselle de Cérignan* in *Le Temps* from 27 June to 2 August 1872. She soon began an article on *La Lettre de Junius*, by Dumas *fils*; but the article was refused by *La Revue des Deux Mondes*. And at the end of the month she refurbished a little *"proverbe"* she found among her notes, *Un Bienfait n'est jamais perdu*, which the *Revue* printed on 15 February 1872.

[2] Following a reconciliation between the legitimists and the Orléanists, it was thought that the comte de Chambord would soon be on the throne as Henri V. But his public declaration that he would abolish the tricolour in favour of the ancient, pre-Revolution national flag – a white banner bearing the fleur-de-lys – spelled the end of his chances.

[3] Sand refers to the so-called *pétroleuses*, "women who, during the Commune, were said to have poured kerosene on certain buildings to quicken the fires" *(Grand Larousse Encyclopédique)*. Their existence is questioned by many historians, but in the hysteria of reprisal a number of women were executed on the charge.

*

Throughout this period of disorder and uncertainty George Sand was indeed undergoing a *crise de conscience*. Her letters to the Adams, to Harrisse, to Prince Napoléon and to Plauchut all make this clear. She often seemed unaware of the extent to which some of her own ideas had changed since 1848. [In the chaos of 1870–1, however, she adhered to her humanistic principles, abandoning political formulas that had proved inadequate to such events.] Her severity toward the Commune astonished and distressed her friends; and she, in turn, reproached them for having allowed the mob to overturn the government. "Don't attempt to justify me," she wrote to Plauchut on June 16, "when I'm accused of not being 'sufficiently republican': on the contrary, tell them I'm not republican *in their way*. They have ruined and will continue to ruin the republic, exactly as the priests have ruined Christianity. They are proud, narrow, doctrinaire, and never have the slightest doubt about what they can and cannot do." It is hardly surprising that during these anguished weeks she felt no eagerness to write to Flaubert, who, according to mood, might express himself as an arch-conservative.

After his return to Paris, Flaubert worked as best he could at *Saint Antoine*. But he was in constant need of documentation, and went to Paris again on July 20 or 21. There, in the *Paris-Journal* for the 21st, he read that George Sand was seriously ill. He wrote immediately to Nohant (this letter is lost), and Sand quickly sent him reassurance.

279 SAND TO FLAUBERT

Nohant, 23 July [1871]

No, I'm not ill, mon chéri vieux troubadour, despite the sorrow that is France's daily bread. I have an iron constitution and an unusual, even peculiar old age – my energies increase at a time when they ought to be diminishing. On the day I decided to put youth behind me I immediately felt twenty years younger. You'll say the bark of the tree still has to bear the ravages of time. I don't mind that – the core is sound and the sap goes on doing its work, as in the old apple trees in my garden; the more gnarled they grow the more fruit they bear. Thank you for being worried about the illness the papers bestowed on me. Maurice thanks you too and sends his love. He still intersperses his scientific, literary and agricultural researches with excellent puppet performances. He thinks of you every time, and says he wishes you were here to see the progress he continues to make.

How do you see the present situation? It's something that you've got rid of the Prussians from Rouen,[1] and it looks as if the bourgeois republic is here to stay. I've no doubt it will be a stupid one, as you predicted. But after the grocers' inevitable period in power, life must expand and start up again in general. The vile excesses of the Commune have shown us dangers that weren't sufficiently foreseen, and which call for a new kind of politics all round, consisting of looking after one's own affairs and forcing the charming proletariat created by the Empire to realize what's possible and what isn't. You can't educate people to be decent and disinterested overnight. The vote is a kind of instant education – and they went and elected men like Raoul Rigault.[2] But now they've learned from experience. If they go on like that they'll die of starvation. That's the only thing they can be taught quickly.

Are you working? Is *Saint Antoine* making progress? Tell me what you're doing in Paris, what you see and what you think. I haven't the heart to go there. So come and see me before you go back to Croisset. I do miss seeing you. It's a kind of death.

G. Sand

¹ The German troops had just left Rouen, on 22 July.
² Raoul Rigault, named Prefect of Police by the Central Committee of the Commune, had been responsible for numerous arrests and for the murder of several hostages. He was shot by the Versaillais on 24 May 1871.

280 FLAUBERT TO SAND

[Paris] 25 July [1871]

So: yet another of those charming benefits we derive from the Press! I suspected as much. Still, those wretches at the *Figaro* gave me a nasty scare. It's indestructible, that sheet. The Empire has been overturned, France conquered, and Paris gone up in flames, but Magnard, La Fargue and Villemessant flourish more than ever.¹ That stupidity should be eternal I well understand: but that those same louts should continue blithely on their way whatever happens – that I do find amazing.

However, Paris seems a little less panicky than in June. At least on the surface. People are beginning to hate Prussia in a way that is *natural*: that is, they're returning to French tradition. One hears fewer remarks in praise of those *civilisateurs*. As for the Commune, everybody expects it to be reborn "later on", and the "forces of law and order" are doing absolutely nothing to prevent its return. To new diseases they apply old remedies that never cured (or prevented) any ill. (The restoration of the *cautionnement²* seems to me a gigantic piece of ineptitude.) One of my friends has made a good speech against it. He's the godson of your friend Michel de Bourges – Bardoux, mayor of Clermont-Ferrand.

I believe as you do that the bourgeois Republic may last. Perhaps its very lack of edification is a guarantee of solidity? For the first time, we are living under a government that has no principles. Perhaps the age of Positivism in politics is about to begin?

The immense disgust my contemporaries inspire in me is driving me back to the past, and I'm working full force on my good Saint Antoine. I have come to Paris solely for him: in Rouen it's impossible to find the books I need just now. I'm lost amid the religions of Persia. I'm trying to form a clear idea of the god Hom – no easy task. I spent all June studying Buddhism, a subject on which I'd already made a good many notes. But I wanted to have as complete a picture of it as possible, and I've been able to put together a little Buddha that I think very nice. How I long to read you the book – mine, I mean. I shan't be coming to Nohant, because I no longer dare go very far from my mother.

Her company is both distressing and irritating: she is a dear but painful burden, which my niece Caroline helps me to bear. In a fortnight I'll be back at Croisset.

From August 15 to 20 I expect le bon Turgenev here.[3] It would be very nice if you would come here after that, chère maître. I say "after that" because, since the Prussians were here, we've had only one suitable bedroom. Come! Be kind and make the effort! In September!

Have you had any news from the Odéon? I can extract no reply whatever from the great De Chilly. I called at his office several times, and have written him three letters: not a word. Those fellows have a lordly way about them that's so charming! I don't know whether he's still manager, or whether the Berton-Laurent-Bernard group is now in charge.[4] Berton wrote to me, asking me to recommend him (and them) to d'Osmoy, the Deputy who is president of the Commission dramatique. But since then I've heard nothing about anything.

P. S. You had no telegram from me because it was too late to send one that evening, and the next morning the report of your illness had been corrected.

I forgot to tell you that Princesse Mathilde asked me several times for your news. I saw her on Friday, and she wanted to know all about you.

Adieu, chère maître. Je vous embrasse très fort.

Your old troubadour,

Gve Flaubert

---

[1] Villemessant, who had founded *Le Figaro* in 1854, was still its director: Magnard and La Fargue were his principal editors. Flaubert's scorn for the press in general is well known: he particularly detested *Le Figaro*.

[2] A sum of money a newspaper was obliged to deposit with the government as a "*caution*" – to be forfeited should the paper displease.

[3] Flaubert greatly looked forward to this visit; but Turgenev disappointed him, apparently preferring to prolong his shooting trip to Scotland.

[4] The management of the Odéon seemed for a time to be in a state of flux, but "the great De Chilly" remained.

*

In Paris Flaubert did little except research for his book. He spent a day at Versailles – he wanted to see the Conseil de guerre at work – and a week-end with Princesse Mathilde at Saint-Gratien. On 16 August he was back at Croisset, beginning a new chapter.

George Sand, still unwilling to leave Nohant, forced herself to return to work. Her contract with the *Revue des Deux Mondes* had ended, and she agreed to write a fortnightly article for the newspaper *Le Temps*. For a time she had the idea of founding a new magazine with Dumas *fils*, one that "would attract a younger, livelier set of readers than the old *Revue des Deux Mondes* – people more attuned to modern ideas." But Dumas vigorously declined the proposal, and nothing came of it.

After six weeks of silence, she and Flaubert wrote to each other on the same day.

281 SAND TO FLAUBERT

Nohant, 6 September 18[71]

Where are you, mon cher vieux troubadour? I haven't written to you – I've been so completely, profoundly distressed. It will pass, I hope, but I'm ill with the illness of my country and my species. I can't isolate myself in my own reason and "irreproachability". All important ties seem to be loosened, almost broken. It looks to me as if we're all heading into the unknown. Have you got more spirit than I have? If so, give me some!

I'm sending you likenesses of our little girls. They remember you and say we must send you their portraits. Alas, they are girls, and we're bringing them up lovingly, as carefully as if they were rare plants. But will they meet any men who will protect them and carry on our work? It looks to me as if in twenty years' time there'll be nothing left but hypocrites and louts!

Let me hear from you. Tell me about your poor Maman, and your family, and Croisset. Continue to love us as we love you.

G. Sand

282 FLAUBERT TO SAND

6 September [1871]
Wednesday evening

So, chère maître, it seems you've forgotten your troubadour? I suppose you must be overwhelmed with work? It's so long since I've seen your dear great handwriting! So long since we've spoken together! How sad that we live so far apart! I need you so badly!

I no longer dare leave my poor mother. When I must be away Caroline takes my place. Otherwise, I'd come to Nohant. Will you be there indefinitely? Must we wait until midwinter to be together?

I'd love to read *Saint Antoine* to you – the first half is done – and then just relax and "bellow" in your company.

Someone who knows I love you, and who admires you, brought me a copy of *Le Gaulois*, with extracts from an article by you, on the workers, that had appeared in *Le Temps*. How *right* it is! How accurate, and well put![1] Sad! Sad! Poor France! And I've been accused of being a sceptic! What do you think of Mlle Papavoine, a *pétroleuse*, who was "attacked" by no fewer than 18 citizens on one day in the middle of one of the barricades?[2] That puts to shame the closing scene of *L'Éducation sentimentale*, where they merely present flowers. How stupid people are! how stupid![3]

But what goes beyond everything at the moment is the Conservative Party, which isn't even going to vote,[4] and keeps shivering in its shoes! You can't imagine the terror of the Parisians. "In ten years, Monsieur, the Commune will be in power everywhere:" such is the opinion – or rather the wail – one hears on all sides.[5]

I don't believe in an imminent cataclysm, because nothing expected ever happens. Perhaps the International will triumph eventually, but not in the way it hopes to, not in the way everybody fears. Ah! How sick I am of the ignoble worker, the inept bourgeois, the stupid peasant and the odious ecclesiastic!

That is why I bury myself as best I can in antiquity. At the moment I have all the gods talking before they give up the ghost. Perhaps the sub-title of my book will be "The Height of Insanity". And typography grows ever fainter in my mind. Why publish? Why worry about art, now? I "make literature" for myself, these days, the way a bourgeois makes napkin rings in his attic.[6] You'll tell me that it would be better to be useful. But how? How can one make oneself heard?

Turgenev writes to tell me that in October he'll be coming to Paris for the entire winter. So there will be someone to talk to! Because at present I haven't a soul with whom to discuss anything.

Today I made arrangements about poor Bouilhet's grave. With the result that tonight I feel more gloomy than ever. Speaking of friends, we have some still alive who are pretty strange!

Princesse Mathilde is always asking for news of you.

Things at the Odéon seem very confused. If state support is withdrawn, Duquesnel and Chilly keep the theatre anyway! But what actors will they have? And the Berton-Laurent group: what capital will *it* have? And what theatre? In short, what am I to do with *Aïssé*?

Adieu, chère bon maître. Je vous embrasse très fort.

Your old

Gve Flaubert

Little kisses to the little girls. Best greetings to the others.

---

[1] The article had appeared in *Le Temps* of 5 September and portions in *Le Gaulois* of the 6th. In it, Sand expressed her disgust for the corruption and demoralization resulting from industrial development. It was later reprinted in the volume *Impressions et Souvenirs*. Flaubert wrote to Princesse Mathilde: "Have you read an article by Mme Sand (published in *Le Temps*) on the workers? She is gradually coming to see the most difficult thing of all: the truth. For the first time she calls the rabble by its real name."

[2] On September 4 and 5, five "*pétroleuses*", among them Eulalie Papavoine, had appeared before the Conseil de Guerre at Versailles. According to the *Figaro* of the 6th, "A person appearing in open court gave details of an accusation she had brought against *la fille* Papavoine – an accusation of which yesterday's report spoke in guarded terms. '*Cette fille*,' she said, 'had eighteen lovers in a single day.' The accusation seemed not to have a deep effect on *la fille* Papavoine, who merely smiled and shrugged – apparently flattered rather than vexed by the charge."

[3] In the last page of the novel, Frédéric and Deslauriers recall how they had paid their first visit to a brothel, but had fled, after offering a bouquet of flowers to the ladies. Flaubert is contrasting the innocence of that scene (which had been branded "immoral" by some of the novel's critics), with the squalor of recent public news.

[4] Probably an allusion to the fact that sections of the Assembly had shown themselves reluctant to tackle the proposal of a tax on income.

[5] This was in fact a widespread fear at the time. In late August several newspapers,

among them *Le Gaulois* and *La Liberté*, had predicted that the Commune would soon be established in Lyons and other large cities. *Le National* and *Le Temps* had branded the articles as vicious, designed to stir up trouble.

⁶ Flaubert was obviously thinking of *Madame Bovary*, II, ch.1.

283 SAND TO FLAUBERT

Nohant, 8 September [1871]

Our letters crossed as usual. Today you should receive the portraits of my little girls, not pretty at this point of their development, but blessed with such lovely eyes they can never be ugly.

As you can see, I'm as disgusted and angry as you, but unfortunately unable to hate either the human race or our poor dear country. I *am* weighed down, though, with the feeling that there's nothing I can do to revive its heart and mind. One just goes on working anyway, if only, as you say, to make napkin-rings. And for my part, while trying to serve the public, I think about it as little as possible. *Le Temps* has done me the favour of making me turn out my wastepaper basket, in which I find prophecies inspired by all our various views. These little delvings into the past ought to be cheering. But no. The lessons of experience are always learned too late.

I don't think the Odéon will be able to put on a literary play like *Aïssé* properly without a subsidy, and it would be unwise to put its fate in the balance in advance of possible upheavals. Better to wait and see. As for the Berton group, I have no news of them; they're roaming around the provinces, but Chilly won't take them back – he's furious with them. The Odéon has let Reynard go – a first-rate artist whom Montigny[1] has had the sense to take on. There's really no one left at the Odéon as far as I know. Why don't you consider the Théâtre-Français?

Where is Princesse Mathilde? In Enghien or Paris? Or in England? I enclose a note for you to forward to her next time you have occasion to write.

I can't come to see you, cher vieux, though I've earned a brief spell of such a delightful holiday. But I can't leave *home*[2] for all sorts of reasons which it would take too long to explain, and which are as imperative as they're uninteresting.[3] I don't even know if I'll be going to Paris this winter. I'm getting so old! It seems to me I'm bound to be a nuisance to other people, and that I'm only really tolerable in my own home. So since you do intend to go to town this winter, you absolutely must come to see me here, and bring Turgenev. Warn him he's going to be abducted.

Je t'embrasse comme je t'aime, and so do all my folk here.

G. Sand

¹ Manager of the Théâtre du Gymnase.
² In English in the original.
³ Agitated and depressed by the war and the Commune – she was feverish and sleeping badly – Sand obviously wanted to stay as quietly as possible where she was.

284 FLAUBERT TO SAND

Croisset, 8 September [1871]

Ah! how sweet they are! What darlings! What good little faces, so serious and charming! My mother was greatly touched, and so was I. That is what I call a "delicate attention", chère maître, and I thank you greatly for it. I envy Maurice! His existence isn't arid, like mine.

Our two letters crossed again. That proves, doesn't it, that we're affected by the same things, at the same time, and to the same degree.

Why are you so sad? Mankind is displaying nothing new. Its irremediable wretchedness has embittered me ever since my youth. So I am not disillusioned now. I believe that the crowd, the mass, the herd, will always be detestable. Nothing is important save a small group of minds, ever the same, which hand on the torch. As long as no deference is paid to the Mandarins, as long as the Academy of Sciences doesn't take the place of the Pope, all Politics, and Society down to its very roots, will be nothing but an assortment of disgusting humbugs.[1] We are floundering in the afterbirth of the Revolution, which was a miscarriage, a failure, a gross blunder, whatever people may say. And the reason is that it had its origin in the spirit of the Middle Ages and Christianity, an antisocial religion. The idea of equality (which is all that modern democracy is) is an essentially Christian idea and opposed to that of justice. Observe how *Mercy* predominates now.[2] Sentiment is everything, the law nothing. There is no longer even any public indignation against murderers. And the people who set fire to Paris get let off more lightly than the slanderer of M. Favre.[3]

If France is to rise again, she must pass from Inspiration to Science, she must abandon all metaphysics in favour of objective inquiry – that is, the examination of reality.

Posterity will consider us very stupid, I'm sure. The words "Republic" and "Monarchy" will make them laugh, just as we laugh at "Realism" and "Nominalism". For I defy anyone to show me one essential difference between those two terms. A modern republic and a constitutional monarchy are identical. No matter: there's great squabbling over it anyway – shouting, fighting!

As for the worthy "People" – "free and compulsory" education will be the end of them.[4] When everybody is able to read the *Petit Journal* and the *Figaro*, they won't read anything else, since those are the only things read by the bourgeois, the rich gentleman. The press is a school for stultification, because it absolves people from thinking. Say that! It will be courageous of you, and if you prevail you'll have performed a noble service.

The first remedy would be to abolish universal suffrage, that insult to human intelligence. As it is constituted at present, one element prevails to the detriment of all the rest: *Number* dominates over mind, education, race, and money itself – and even *that* is preferable to Number.[5]

But perhaps a Catholic society (which always needs a beneficent God, a Saviour)[6] isn't capable of self-preservation. The conservative party hasn't even the instinct of the Brute Beast, (for the brute beast at least knows how to fight for its lair and its food.)[7] It will be devoured by the Internationals, those Jesuits of the future. But the Jesuits of the past, who had neither Country nor Justice, did not prevail. And the International, too, will founder, because its principles, like theirs, are false: no ideas, nothing but greed!

Ah, chère bon maître, if you could only hate! That is what you lack: Hate. Despite your great sphinx eyes, you have seen the world through a golden haze. That comes from the sun in your heart. But so many shadows have loomed that you no longer see things for what they are. Come, now! Shout! Thunder! Take your great lyre and pluck the brazen string. The Monsters will flee. Sprinkle us with the blood of the wounded Themis.[8]

Why do you feel that "important ties have been broken"? What is broken? *Your* ties are indissoluble, for your affinity can only be for things that are Eternal.

Our ignorance of history makes us slander our own time. People have always been like this. A few years of quiet fooled us, that's all. I too used to believe in the progressive "civilizing" of the human race. We must expunge that mistake and think no better of ourselves than people did in the age of Pericles or Shakespeare, dreadful periods in which great things were accomplished.

Tell me you're in better spirits. And think sometimes of your old troubadour, who loves you.

Gve Flaubert

[1] Here, in his ideas about "Mandarins", Flaubert comes close to Socrates' words in Plato's *Republic*, Book V: "Until philosophers are kings, or the kings and princes of this world have the spirit and power of philosophy, and wisdom and political greatness meet in one, and those commoner natures who pursue either to the exclusion of the other are compelled to stand aside, cities will never have rest from their evils, – no, nor the human race, as I believe – and then only will this our State have a possibility of life and behold the light of day." (Translation by Benjamin Jowett.)

[2] This idea, long dear to Flaubert (see Letter 94, Note 5), was probably suggested to him by the Commission des Grâces (Committee on Pardons), created by the Assembly on June 15th. It had begun to function concurrently with the first death sentences passed on Communards, September 2nd.

[3] Jules Favre, Minister of Foreign Affairs, had recently been the successful plaintiff in a libel suit. Even though Favre admitted to being guilty of peculation, his accuser was sentenced to a year in prison and a fine of a thousand francs.

[4] Since the revolution of 1848, free and compulsory elementary schooling had held an important place in the republican programme; but attempts made in that direction before and during the Second Empire had come to nothing. In 1871 the question of schooling had again become active thanks to the proposal, by Jules Simon, of a law on the subject. This, which would make schooling compulsory but not necessarily free, was not debated, because the majority of the Assembly was in favour of maintaining clerical influence in the schools. On August 8th, deputy Lacretelle returned to the charge, demanding that primary education be made free and compulsory throughout France from 1 November 1871.

[5] Here Flaubert reproduces the opinion expressed by Renan in his article, "*La Monarchie constitutionnelle en France.*" Renan wanted, "along with the simple numerical representation of citizens, representation also of various interests, functions, specialities and skills". (*La Réforme intellectuelle et morale*, p. 294.)

[6] Flaubert is perhaps being ironic here. The word "Saviour", with a capital "S", inevi-

tably invokes Jesus Christ, but Flaubert may also be referring to a recently published pamphlet, by H. de Noyers, entitled *Le Sauveur de la France* – a biography, with portraits, of Thiers.

[7] Probably an allusion to the attitude of the conservative majority, which, though always resisting measures proposed by Thiers, gave in when he threatened to resign.

[8] In Greek mythology, the deity representing divine justice.

285 SAND TO FLAUBERT

Nohant, 16 September [18]71

Cher vieux,

I answered your last the day before yesterday, but my letter became so long I sent it to *Le Temps* to be used as my next fortnightly article: I promised to let them have two a month.[1] This letter "to a friend" doesn't refer to you even by an initial: I don't want to argue with you in public. In it I give you my reasons for still suffering, still wishing. I'll send it to you, and it will be like continuing our conversation. You'll see that my grief is a part of myself, and that it's beyond my powers to believe that progress is only a dream. Without that hope, no one can do anything. "Mandarins" aren't in need of knowledge, but there's no point in going on educating the few if it's not in the hope that they'll influence the many. Philosophers don't come into it, and the great minds you're attached to by your soul's need – Shakespeare, Molière, Voltaire and the rest – don't have to assert their existence. Just let me suffer – it's better than, as Shakespeare says, "calmly contemplating injustice."[2] When I've drained my cup of bitterness to the dregs I'll recover. I'm a woman, I have feelings of affection, pity and anger. I'll never be a sage or a scholar.

I had a nice note from Princesse Mathilde. She's settled in Paris again, has she? Has she got enough to live on from M. Demidoff, her late and I believe unworthy husband?[3] Anyhow, it's kind and courageous of her to come back among her friends, despite the risk of fresh upheavals.

I'm glad the little faces gave you pleasure. You're so kind I was sure they would. Je t'embrasse très fort. You may be a mandarin, but I don't find you at all inscrutable, et je t'aime à plein coeur.

G. Sand

I'm working like a galley slave.[4]

[1] This was her second in the series. The first had been an article on the workers (5 September), which had inspired Flaubert's letter to her of the 8th.

[2] Sand's words appear to paraphrase a French translation (by Guizot and A. Pichot, 1821) of a passage from *Julius Caesar*, II, i: "such suffering souls that welcome wrongs".

[3] Princesse Mathilde had married Count Demidoff in 1840, but his behaviour had been so scandalous that in 1846 she had petitioned Czar Nicholas I for an annulment. Demidoff was ordered to pay her 200,000 francs a year. He died in April, 1870.

[4] Her contract with *Le Temps* for an article every two weeks was proving more burdensome than she had expected. She was also writing her yearly novel – this time *Nanon*, which would appear early in 1872.

The "Reply to a Friend" appeared in *Le Temps* for October 3,[1] and brought Sand many letters of commendation. "I'm certainly enjoying a rejuvenated success in *Le Temps*," she wrote, in some astonishment, in her diary for the 6th. She must have sent the promised copy to Flaubert, who replied by return of post.

[1] Reprinted in the volume *Impressions et Souvenirs* (1873), and, in translation, in *The Letters of Gustave Flaubert, 1857–1880*, Appendix II.

286 FLAUBERT TO SAND

[Croisset, 7 October 1871]
Saturday

Chère maître,

I received your article yesterday, and would answer it at length were I not preparing to leave for Paris. I'm going to try to wind up the business of *Aïssé*.

The middle section of your piece made me "shed a tear" – without converting me, of course! I was moved, that was all, but not persuaded.[1]

I comb your article for a certain word and find it nowhere: "Justice". Our entire affliction comes from forgetting utterly that first premise of morality, which to my mind embraces all morality.

Mercy, humanitarianism, sentiment, the ideal, have played us sufficiently false to make us try *Integrity* and *Science*. If France doesn't soon enter a period of self-appraisal, I think she will be irrevocably lost. Free compulsory education will do nothing but swell the number of imbeciles. Renan has said that superbly, in the preface to his *Questions contemporaines*.[2] What we need most of all is a *natural aristocracy* – that is, a legitimate one. Nothing can be done without a ruling element; and universal suffrage as it now exists is more stupid than divine right. You'll see some extraordinary things if it's retained. Mass, numbers, are invariably idiotic. I hold few convictions, but I do hold that one, and strongly. Nevertheless the masses must be respected, however inept they are, because they contain seeds of incalculable fertility. Give them liberty, but not power.

I believe no more than you do in class distinctions.[3] Castes belong to archaeology. But I do believe that the Poor hate the Rich, and that the Rich fear the Poor. It will be ever thus. It is as futile to preach love to the one as to the other. The most urgent thing is to educate the Rich, who after all are the stronger. Enlighten the bourgeois first! For he knows nothing, absolutely nothing. The entire dream of democracy is to raise the proletariat to the level of bourgeois stupidity. That dream is partly realized! They read the same newspapers and share the same passions.

The three levels of education have shown within the past year what they can accomplish. 1° higher education made Prussia the victor; 2° secondary, bourgeois education produced the men of the 4th of September;[4] 3° primary education gave us the Commune. Its Minister of Public Education was the great Vallès,[5] who boasted that he despised Homer.

Suppose that three years from now all Frenchmen know how to read. Do you think we'll be the better off for it? Imagine, on the other hand, that in each community there was *one* bourgeois, one only, who had read Bastiat,[6] and that that bourgeois was respected: things would change!

I learn today that most Parisians are sorry to have lost Badinguet. A plebiscite would declare for him, I'm sure. That's universal suffrage for you!

However, unlike you, I'm not discouraged, and I like the present government, because it has no principle, no metaphysics, no humbug.

I'm expressing myself very badly. You deserve a different answer, but I'm in a great hurry – ce qui m'empêche pas de vous embrasser très fortement.

Your old troubadour,

Gve Flaubert

Not such a troubadour as all that, however! Your "friend", as dimly glimpsed through your article, is a rather disagreeable fellow and a first-rate *HHégoiste*!

[1] Flaubert refers to the following high-flown passage in Sand's article: "Until my heart stops beating it will be open to pity: it will always take the part of the weak; it will refute calumny. If today the populace is being trodden under foot, I will offer my hand; if it becomes the oppressor, the executioner, I will tell it that it is cowardly and hateful."

[2] For *Questions contemporaines*, see Letter 105, Note 2. Renan says, in his preface, "Do your best to create upper classes inspired by a liberal spirit: otherwise you build on sand." Comparing teaching in Germany and France, he says: "The strength of public education in Germany comes from the quality of education among the upper echelons in that country. The education of the masses is a by-product of the advanced culture of certain classes."

[3] Flaubert refers to the following passage in Sand's article: "'The people' are you and I ... There are not two races: distinction between classes now consists only of inequalities that are merely relative and usually illusory."

[4] Date of the proclamation of the Third Republic, in 1870.

[5] The tirade by the journalist Jules Vallès (1832–85) against "old Homer" first appeared in *L'Evénement*, 17 February 1866, under the title "L'Académie". Vallès says, in part, "I'm tired of old Homer. . . . You're considered a miserable wretch if you don't cross yourself and tip your hat to this immortal *Patachon* . . . The only part I like about Homer's epic is what he says about cooking: the great oxen and fat sheep roasted over huge logs." And Vallès ends his diatribe with words that according to M. Jacobs have become famous: "*Et toi, vieil Homère aux Quinze-Vingts!*" ("And you, old Homer, off with you to the hospital for the blind!") After the end of the Commune, Vallès took refuge in Holland. Later, following the amnesty, he revived his radical Paris newspaper, *Le Cri du peuple*.

"*Patachon*": originally "driver of a public coach"; later, commonly, "one given to 'wine, women and songs'".

[6] Frédéric Bastiat (1801–50), economist and politician. In his writings, especially in *Les Harmonies économiques*, he championed free trade and opposed socialism.

287 SAND TO FLAUBERT

Nohant, 10 October [1871]

I'm answering your postscript. If I'd been replying to Flaubert himself [in the article] I wouldn't have replied at all, as I'm well aware your heart doesn't always agree with your mind. We're all constantly bound to fall into such inconsistency. In my article I was answering part of a letter from a friend whom no one knows or can recognize, as I address myself to an element in your argument which doesn't represent you completely.

You *are* a troubadour in spite of all, and if I were indeed writing to you in public I'd address you as you really are. But our real discussions must remain between ourselves, like lovers' caresses, only more delightful, since friendship has its own mysteries, untroubled by the storms of personality.

Your letter, even written in haste, is full of admirably expressed truths that I do not challenge. But we need to find the link, the reconciliation, between your truths of reason and my truths of feeling. Unfortunately France doesn't agree with either of us. It's on the side of blindness, ignorance and stupidity. Oh, I don't deny it – that's precisely what upsets me.

Is this really the moment for putting on *Aïssé*? You tell me it's distinguished and sensitive, like everything our dear Bouilhet did; and people say theatre audiences are more insensitive now than they've ever been. It would be a good idea for you to go and see two or three other plays, to find out the literary level of the Parisians at present. The provinces' contribution will have shrunk. People who aren't very wealthy have lost so much they can't afford to come to Paris often. If, as when I was young, Paris provided an élite audience of intelligent and influential people, a good play wouldn't run for 100 performances, but a bad one wouldn't run for 300. But such a public scarcely exists now, and its influence is swamped. So who is likely to fill the theatres? Paris shopkeepers unguided by any decent criticism? But anyway, you're probably not in a position to decide all by yourself what happens to *Aïssé*. I expect there's an heir waiting impatiently in the wings.[1]

I've had a letter saying Chilly is seriously ill and Pierre Berton has been taken on again.

You must be very busy, so I don't want to write at too much length. Je t'embrasse tendrement. My children love you and ask to be remembered to you.

G. Sand

[1] Louis Bouilhet's heir was Philippe, his son by his mistress, Léonie Leparfait. Bouilhet had legally adopted him.

*

That letter reached Flaubert in Paris, where he arrived on October 9th to arrange for the staging of Bouilhet's *Aïssé* and the publication of *Dernières Chansons*. Because of the precarious situation at the Odéon, he "intrigued and lied shamelessly" (as he wrote to Caroline) to get the play accepted by the Théâtre-Français; but in the end he did not succeed. He spent two days at Saint-Gratien with Princesse Mathilde, and returned to Croisset on the 18th.

288   FLAUBERT TO SAND

[Paris, 12 October 1871]
Thursday evening

Never, never, chère bon maître, have you given such proof of your incredible innocence! Do you really, seriously, think that you could have offended me!! The first page of your letter sounds almost like a series of apologies! Really, it made me laugh![1] You, of all people, can always say anything to me – anything: for me, a blow from you will always be a caress.

You endow others with your own qualities, and assume *a priori* that they're full of fine feelings. This is an allusion to one of your recent letters, in which you called Princesse Mathilde's return to Saint-Gratien "kind and courageous". I too consider it a "very good thing" – that is, good for me, because I like her and find her company agreeable. But I think she should have remained in exile for a time. That would have been more courageous and shown greater pride. I wrote and told her as much. And then, seeing that she was dying to return to France, I kept my peace, and even did what I could for her: it was a close friend of mine who took the necessary measures. She returned because she is a spoiled child who can't control her passions. That's the entire psychology of the thing. And I made a great concession (of which she was totally unaware) in going to see her at Saint-Gratien, among the Prussians! There were two sentries at the gate. Though I have no imperial blood in my veins, I turned red as I passed those sentry-boxes. I deliberately did without my house while the Prussians were there. I think she might have done the same. Keep this to yourself, of course, and let's say no more about it.

So – back to what we were saying: I repeat: *Justice* is what counts. See how it is flouted on all sides. Hasn't modern Criticism abandoned art for history? The intrinsic value of a book is nothing, according to the Sainte-Beuve–Taine school. Everything is taken into account except talent. And that leads, in the lesser press, to over-emphasis on personality, biography and diatribes. The result is disrespect on the part of the public.

In the theatre, the same thing. Nobody worries about the play – but about the idea that's being preached. Our friend Dumas dreams of the notoriety of a Lacordaire. Or rather of a Ravignan.[2] All he thinks of is that a woman should never show her ankles. You can see how far we have advanced when you think that morality for a woman consists entirely in avoiding adultery, and for men in abstaining from theft.

In short, the first wrong is committed by Literature, which cares nothing for Aesthetics, the prime justice. The Romantics will have a lot to answer for, what with their immoral sentimentality and their neo-Christianity, worse than the old. Remember a piece by old Hugo, in *La Légende des Siècles*, in which a sultan is saved because he takes pity on – a pig.[3] Always the story of the Good Thief, Blessed because he repented.[4] It is good to repent, but to do no evil is better. The preachers of rehabilitation have brought us to the point of seeing no difference between a rascal and an honest man. I once burst out, in front of witnesses, against Sainte-Beuve, begging him to show as much indulgence to Balzac as he did to Jules Lecomte.[5] He replied by calling me a blockhead. That's what comes of being "broad-minded".

We have so lost all sense of proportion that the Counseil de Guerre (at Versailles) gave harsher treatment to Pipe-en-Bois than to M. Courbet.[6] Maroteau is condemned to death like Rossel![7] Madness! But I have little interest in such gentlemen. In my opinion the entire Commune should have been sent to the galleys, and the bloodthirsty fools chained by the neck like common criminals and made to clean up the ruins of Paris. But that would have been an offence against "humanity". We have a soft spot for mad dogs, but not for the people they bite.

That will not change as long as universal suffrage remains what it is. Every man (in my view), no matter how insignificant, has the right to *one* voice, his own. But he is not the equal of his neighbour, who may be worth a hundred times as much. In an industrial enterprise, a company, every shareholder votes according to his holdings. So it should be in the government of a nation. I am certainly worth twenty other Croisset voters! Money, intelligence, even breeding – in short, all qualities – should count. Whereas up to now I see only one: number. Ah! chère maître, you who have so much authority – *you* should sound the alarm. So many people read your articles in *Le Temps*, which are having such a success. And who knows? You might do France a great service.

Aïssé is taking up an enormous amount of my time. Or rather it's giving me enormous trouble. I haven't seen Chilly, who has piles (fascinating detail), and thus I have to deal with Duquesnel. They are definitely withdrawing old Berton, and they suggest his son. He is very nice – despite his hunch back – but not at all the type envisaged by the author. Might the Français really want to take on *Aïssé*? I'm very perplexed. And I'm going to have to decide. As for waiting for a literary wind to blow, since it won't blow during my lifetime it's better to take the risk, right away.

I find these theatre matters very distracting. And I was working so well! This past month I was "almost out of my mind with excitement".

I ran into the inevitable Harrisse, the man who knows everybody and all about everything – theatre, novels, finance, politics, etc. What a race they are, the "educated classes"!

I saw Plessy – charming, and still beautiful. She asked me to give you "mille amitiés". As for me, I send you mille tendresses.

Votre vieux

Gve Flaubert

[1] "Would you believe it, la mère Sand was afraid she might have offended me in her article, and almost sent me apologies?" Flaubert wrote the same day to his niece. "Such naiveté seems to me at once very silly and very delicate." These words, and their tone, suggest that Flaubert was in fact irritated by Mme Sand's article.

[2] Xavier de Ravignan, Jesuit and preacher (1795–1858), successor to Père Lacordaire at Notre-Dame, where for ten years he delivered celebrated *conférences* (lectures not open to the general public).

[3] The poem *Sultan Mourad*.

[4] The allusion is to the thief crucified with Jesus. "And he said unto Jesus, Lord, remember me when thou comest into thy kingdom. And Jesus said unto him, Verily I say unto thee, Today shalt thou be with me in paradise." (Luke xxiii, 42–3.)

[5] Literary critic and journalist with the newspaper *L'Indépendance belge*. Author of a book full of scandal and indiscretions, *Lettres sur les écrivains français* (1837). He died in 1864.

[6] Georges Cavalier, nicknamed "Pipe-en-Bois", sometime leader of the *contre-claque* (paid to hiss at actors or the author) in various Paris theatres, had become an official of the Commune, and was sentenced to deportation. Gustave Courbet was heavily fined for his rôle in the destruction of the Vendôme column. He fled to Switzerland, where he died in 1877. (Neither Flaubert, nor Jacobs in writing this note, mentions Courbet's genius.)

[7] The journalist Gustave Maroteau had written violent articles during the Commune. Captured, rifle in hand, on a barricade, he was condemned to death, but would be reprieved and deported. Louis Rossel had escaped from Metz during the surrender and joined the Paris insurrection, trying unsuccessfully to organize the popular army. He was condemned to death, and executed on 28 November 1871.

289 SAND TO FLAUBERT

Nohant, 25 October [1871]

Your letters fall on me like a good shower of rain, making all the seeds in the ground start to sprout. And making me want to answer your arguments, because they're weighty and call for a reply. I don't say my answers are weighty too, but they're sincere, and spring from my roots like the plants aforementioned. And so I've just written an article on the subject you raise, addressing it this time "to a female friend" who writes to me along the same lines as you, only needless to say not so well, and rather from the point of view of an intellectual aristocracy to which she can scarcely claim to belong.[1]

"My roots" – one can't change them, and I'm surprised you should ask mine to produce tulips when all they can give you is potatoes. From the earliest days of my intellectual awakening, when I began to educate myself at my grandmother's bedside (she was paralyzed) (or, when I could leave her with Deschartres, roaming the countryside), I asked myself the most basic questions about society. At 17 I was no more advanced than a child of 6, if that, thanks to Deschartres (my father's tutor), who was made up of contradictions from head to foot – much information and no common sense. Thanks also to the convent they'd shoved me into – heaven knows why, as they didn't believe in anything. Another factor was my being immersed in a completely pro-Restoration atmosphere, in which my grandmother, though a philosopher, was dying and could no longer resist the monarchist trend. So I read Chateaubriand

and Rousseau; I went from the New Testament to the *Contrat social*; I read the history of the Revolution as written by bigots and the history of France as written by sceptics. And one fine day I added it all together like a light from two lamps, and found myself with "principles".² Don't laugh – they were childish, innocent principles that have stayed with me through everything – through *Lélia* and the romantic period; through love and doubt, enthusiasms and disillusions. To love, to sacrifice oneself, never to withdraw unless the sacrifice comes to harm the people it's meant to benefit, and then to sacrifice oneself again in the hope of serving a true cause – love. I'm not talking now of personal passion, but of love of the human race; of an extension of self-love that abhors concentration on the self alone. I've never been able to separate the ideal of justice that you speak of from love: for if a natural society is to survive, its first law must be mutual service, as with the ants and the bees. In animals we call this collaboration of all to achieve the same end, instinct. The name doesn't matter. But in man, instinct is love, and whoever omits love omits truth and justice.

I lived through the revolutions and had a close view of the major participants.³ I saw into the depths of their souls, or rather into their depths pure and simple: no principles, and therefore no genuine intelligence or strength or perseverance. Nothing but means, and to one personal end. Only one of them, Barbès, had principles – they weren't all good, but he counted himself as nothing in comparison with loyalty to them. Among artists and writers I didn't find anything of substance. You're the only one with whom I've ever been able to exchange anything but professional ideas. I don't know if you were at Magny's one day when I told them they were all "gentlemen". They said one shouldn't write for the ignorant, and shouted me down because the ignorant were the only people I did want to write for, since they are the ones that need it. The masters are provided for; they're rich and self-satisfied. The fools have nothing, and I pity them. Love and pity go together. There you have the not very elaborate mechanics of my philosophy.

I have a passion for good, and no partisan sentimentalism whatever. I loathe with all my heart anyone who claims to have the same principles as mine but whose acts contradict his words. I don't feel sorry for convicted arsonists or murderers. I do feel deeply sorry for a class condemned to a life that's harsh, degraded, without hope or help, and reduced to producing such monsters. I pity humanity and wish it to be good because I don't want to set myself apart from it; because it *is* me; because the harm it inflicts on itself wounds me; because its shame makes me blush; because its crimes turn my stomach; and because I can't conceive of a paradise, either in heaven or on earth, for myself alone. You, who are all goodness yourself, must understand what I'm saying.

Are you still in Paris? We've been having such fine weather I've been tempted to come and see you. But I don't like spending money, however little, when there's so much poverty about. I'm tight-fisted because I know I'm extravagant when I forget; and I always do forget. And I've so much to do! . . . I know nothing and learn nothing – I'm always having to re-learn things. But I do need to be with you again for a while. It's as if a part of me were missing.

My Aurore takes up a lot of time.[4] She understand things so fast it's all one can do to keep up with her. She adores to know but hates to learn. She's lazy, as her father used to be, but he's made up for it so well I don't let it bother me. She says she's going to write you a letter soon. She hasn't forgotten you, you see. Titite's Punch has literally lost his head through being kissed and cuddled so much. But his owner loves him just as much without a head; what an example of fidelity through thick and thin! His stomach has become a container for keeping toys in.

Maurice is deep in archaeological studies, Lina delightful as ever, and all's well in general, except that the maids aren't clean. What a long way people who don't comb their hair still have to go!

Je t'embrasse. Let me know how you're getting on with *Aïssé*, the Odéon, and all the rest of your bothers. Je t'aime – that's how all my dissertations end.

G. Sand

[1] Juliette Lamber (Mme Adam).
[2] Sand recounts this evolution in her *Histoire de ma vie*, Part 3.
[3] She is referring to her part in the Revolution of 1848.
[4] Mme Sand herself was teaching her granddaughter to read and write.

290 FLAUBERT TO SAND

[Croisset,] 14 November [1871]

Ouf! I have just finished my Gods! That is, the mythological part of my *Saint Antoine*, which I've been on since the beginning of June. How I long to read it to you, chère maître du bon Dieu!

Why did you resist your good impulse? Why didn't you come this autumn? You mustn't be so long without seeing Paris. I'll be there myself the day after tomorrow. And I don't expect to have much fun there all winter, what with *Aïssé*, the printing of a volume of [Bouilhet's] verse (I'd like to show you my preface), and I don't know what else. A lot of not very amusing things.

I haven't received the second article you spoke of.

Your old troubadour is worn out. For the last three months I've slept at most 5 hours a night. I've been working frantically, and as a result I think I've brought my book to a high point of insanity. The thought of the stupidities it will evoke from the bourgeois buoys me up. Or rather, I don't need to be buoyed up, I'm feeling so at home in the company of my characters.

Le bon bourgeois grows ever more stupid! He won't even vote! Brute beasts are better than he when it comes to self-preservation. Poor France! Poor *us*!

Do you know what I'm reading at the moment, to distract myself? Bichat and Cabanis,[1] both of whom afford me vast amusement. They knew how to write books in those days. Ah! How far removed such men are from our doctors of today!

We are suffering from one single thing: *Stupidity*. But that one thing is formidable and universal.

When people talk about the mindlessness of the *plebs* they are saying something that is unfair and partial. I forced myself to read the election addresses of *all* the candidates for the General Council of the Seine-Inférieure.[2] There were a good sixty of them, all emanating, like so many farts, from the fine flower of the bourgeoisie, rich, well-placed, etc. Well, I defy anyone to be more benighted and daft, even in darkest Africa.[3] Conclusion: we have to educate the educated classes. Begin with the head: that's where the body's sickest. The rest will follow.

You're not like me! You're full of forbearance. There are days when I can hardly breathe for sheer anger. I long to drown my contemporaries in the latrines. Or at least to bring torrents of abuse and cataracts of invective down on their noddles. Why? That's what I wonder.

What kind of archaeology is Maurice engaged in?[4] Kiss your little girls for me.

Votre vieux

Gve Flaubert

[1] Celebrated physiologists. Xavier Bichat (1771–1802) is best known as the author of an *Anatomie générale* (1801) and *Recherches physiologiques sur la vie et la mort* (1800). Pierre Cabanis (1757–1808) published, among other works, *Rapports du physique et du moral* (1802).

[2] Elections for the Conseils généraux had taken place on 8 October 1871.

[3] Flaubert's words are: "*Je défie qu'on soit plus ignoblement âne en cafrerie.*" "*La cafrerie*" is "the land of the Kaffirs".

[4] A fair question. Nothing is known about Maurice as "archaeologist". His mother might conceivably have used the word in reference to his investigations into historical characters, customs and costumes, for his marionette theatre.

*

George Sand's "second article" – another "Reply to a Female Friend" – appeared that same day, November 14th. In it she criticizes Flaubert's ideas about justice:

"A friend of mine, a very great intellect, as I said before and as I think still, criticizes me for not caring enough about the principle of justice. Justice is my friend's ideal, and a very good ideal it is too. I flatter myself it's mine as well, but we can't agree about its application. My friend tells me justice requires that power be in the most capable hands; who could deny it? But my friend believes in using legal means to ensure that intelligence reigns, whereas I say it's not for the law to impose such means. If the State is to judge the value of individuals we'll be living in an out-and-out theocracy . . .

"I wouldn't have the Academy of Sciences, any more than Louis XIV, say '*L'Etat, c'est moi.*' The tyranny of the intelligence may not justify the tyranny of stupidity, but it makes it inevitable; every abuse secretes its opposite."

*

Flaubert must have read this article in Paris, where he arrived the evening of 15 November. He made no comment to Sand on its contents.

291 SAND TO FLAUBERT

Nohant, [24] November [1871]

I hear from Plauchut that you don't want to be abducted and carried off to our Christmas celebrations. You say you've too much to do. So much the worse for us, who would have been so happy to see you.

You were at Charles-Edmond's play,[1] which was a success, you're well, you've got lots to do, you still hate the stupid bourgeois, and in the midst of all that have you finished *Saint Antoine* and shall we soon be reading it?

I'm going to ask you to do me a very easy favour: I've been trying to help a respectable and interesting person,[2] to whom the Prussians left nothing but an old garden seat by way of furniture. I sent her 300 francs, she needed 600, so I appealed to other people's charity. Everyone sent the necessary except Princesse Mathilde, whom I'd asked for 100 francs and who replied on the 19th of this month asking "How shall I send it?" I replied the same day telling her just to send it through the post. But it hasn't come. I don't want to make a fuss, but I'm afraid the money might have got stolen or lost, and I'd be grateful if you could clear the matter up as soon as possible.

Whereupon je t'embrasse, et Lolo

t'embrasse aussi

Aurore[3]

et toute la famille, qui t'aime.

G. Sand

[1] The opening of *La Baronne*, by Charles-Edmond and Edouard Foussier, on 23 November.

[2] This was Mlle Pauline de Flaugergues, a writer who had been the *amie* of Henri de Latouche – poet, novelist and journalist, who in turn had been a considerable presence in Sand's early life. Mlle de Flaugergues' house at Aulnay (inherited from Latouche) had been wrecked by the Prussians.

[3] In the child's own hand.

292 FLAUBERT TO SAND

[Paris] 1 December [1871]

Friday evening

Chère maître,

I'm filled with remorse: on re-reading your letter I realize I haven't yet done what you asked about Princesse Mathilde. But for several days I didn't know her whereabouts. She was to have moved into her Paris house, and to have let me know. At last, today, I learn that she is remaining at Saint-Gratien, where I shall probably go next Sunday evening. Whatever happens, your errand will be done by next week.

You must forgive me. During the past two weeks I've barely had ten minutes to myself. I've had to have the revival of *Ruy Blas* postponed (it was scheduled to go on before *Aïssé*, and I had a hard time bringing about the change).[1] Rehearsals are at last scheduled to begin next Monday. Today I went and read the play to the actors. And tomorrow we collate the various parts. I think it will go well. I'm having Bouilhet's volume of verse printed, and have re-written my preface. In short, I'm exhausted. And sad! Deathly sad! When I have to act, I charge ahead. But at heart I feel a deep disgust with it all. And that's the truth.

So far I've seen none of our friends except Turgenev, whom I find more charming than ever.

Give Aurore a big kiss for her nice message, and tell her to pass it on to you.

Votre vieux

Gve Flaubert

---

[1] Flaubert wrote about this imbroglio to Philippe Leparfait on 13 December. "Yes, they have a contract to revive *Ruy Blas* on 25 January. After much tortuous talk, here's what Chilly and I worked out a fortnight ago: he'll go ahead with *Aïssé*, and then, on January 20, Père Hugo will be put off, with talk about sets, for a fortnight; then I'll go, myself, and in some way persuade him to postpone it for another fortnight or a month."

In the end, Victor Hugo's *Ruy Blas* was revived on 19 February 1872.

293 FLAUBERT TO SAND

[Paris, 5 December 1871]

Tuesday morning

On hearing from you the Princess immediately sent you 100 fr. in a letter sealed with five seals and with the amount of the enclosure written on the envelope.

But (an important point, which only came to light when we talked about it on Sunday) she forgot to have the letter properly stamped. So the 100 fr. have probably been stolen?

Je vous embrasse.

Votre vieux

Gve Flaubert

294 SAND TO FLAUBERT

Nohant, 7 December [1871]

The money *has* been stolen. I haven't received it, but it can't be claimed back because that would mean the sender might be prosecuted. Still, please thank the Princess on my behalf and on behalf of poor Mlle de Flaugergues, who as it happens has been awarded an extra 200 francs by the ministry. She now has a pension of 800 francs.

So now you're in the middle of rehearsals. I pity you, and yet I imagine that when one's acting on behalf of a friend one puts more energy and confidence into it, and thus more patience. Patience is the key to everything, and it's learned by experience.

Je t'aime et je t'embrasse – and how I'd have loved to have you here for Christmas! But you can't come – so much the worse for us. But we'll drink a toast to you, and you'll be the subject of several "speaches" [sic].

G. Sand

*

The month of December 1871 strained Flaubert's energy to the utmost. In the space of a few days he re-wrote the preface to Bouilhet's *Dernières Chansons*, which he had composed before the events of *l'année terrible* and which he now found "cold, awkward, inept". The printing of this posthumous collection also involved further difficulties with printer, publisher and engraver.

With the thermometer below 17 degrees (Fahrenheit) and with few cabs available, he trudged through the snow to the rehearsals of *Aïssé* at the Odéon, the most tedious chore of all. "What a world!" he wrote to Mme Regnier, referring to the theatre. "I'm not surprised it killed Bouilhet." He had to hire the actors, study costumes at the Cabinet des Estampes, supervise the sets, the production, the extras – everything. "Ah, if Bouilhet had ever taken the trouble with his plays that I'm taking with this one!"

To his fatigue was added a great disappointment. On December 2nd the Municipal Council of Rouen rejected the committee's proposal for a Bouilhet memorial in the form of a fountain. In a rage, Flaubert began to write an open letter for publication in *Le Nouvelliste de Rouen*, in which he would fling his anger and contempt in the faces of the bourgeois, "conservatives who conserve nothing".

CHAPTER VIII

1872

Beset by troubles, Flaubert sent no New Year's greetings for 1872, but Sand did not forget him.

295 SAND TO FLAUBERT

Nohant, 4 January [18]72

I write to give you New Year's greetings and to tell you I love my vieux troubadour now and always. But I don't want you to answer this – you're in the midst of the last-minute rush at the theatre, and haven't the time or the peace and quiet to write. Here we called out to you on the stroke of midnight on Christmas Eve: we shouted your name three times. Did you hear us a little?

We're all well. Our little girls are growing fast; we speak of you often. My children send their love too. May our affection bring you luck!

G. Sand

*

That note reached Flaubert on January 6th, the day of the opening of *Aïssé*. The play was poorly received. "It limped along, the audience displaying respect for a deceased author's hexameters," Edmond de Goncourt wrote in his *Journal*. A few weeks later, when his "Bouilhet business" had been largely attended to, Flaubert could resume his correspondence with George Sand.

296 FLAUBERT TO SAND

[Paris] 21 [January 1872]
Sunday afternoon

At last I have a moment's peace and can write to you! But I have so many things to spill out that I don't know how to begin.

(1)[1] Your note of January 4th reached me the very morning of the première of *Aïssé*, and brought tears to my eyes, chère maître bien aimé. There's no one like you for doing such thoughtful things.

The opening night was splendid. And then – nothing: the next day, an all but empty house. The press was for the most part stupid and vile. I was accused of wanting to draw attention to myself by *inserting* an inflammatory speech! I'm supposed to be a Red![2] [sic] You see what we've come to!

The management of the Odéon did *nothing* for the play! Quite the contrary! On the day of the opening, it was I who brought to the theatre, in my own hands, the properties needed for the first act! And, at the third performance, it was I who drilled the extras.

Throughout the rehearsals, they filled the newspapers with announcements of the revival of *Ruy Blas*, etc. etc. They made me kill off *La Baronne*, just as *Ruy Blas* will kill off *Aïssé*. In short, Bouilhet's heir will get very little money. All that can be said is that we came honourably out of the affair.

I have had *Dernières Chansons* printed. You'll be getting a copy at the same time as *Aïssé*, and a printed letter from me to the Rouen Municipal Council. That little elucubration was considered so violent by the *Nouvelliste de Rouen* that they didn't dare print it. But it will appear next Wednesday in *Le Temps*. Then at Rouen, as a pamphlet.[3]

What a stupid life I've been leading for the past two and a half months! It's a wonder I didn't collapse! I've never had more than five hours' sleep at a time! So many errands! So many letters! And such fits of anger – suppressed, alas! Finally, these past three days I've been sleeping round the clock, and feel groggy as a result.

I went with Dumas to the opening of *Le Roi Carotte*.[4] Impossible to imagine anything so putrid! It's more stupid and empty than the worst of Clairville's *féeries*. The audience agreed with me completely. Only a rascal could be guilty of such trash.

The worthy Offenbach has had another fiasco at the Opéra-Comique with his *Fantasio*.[5] Are people beginning to be fed up with such fakery? That would certainly be a step in the right direction!

Turgenev has been in Paris since the beginning of December. Every week we make an appointment to read *Saint Antoine* and dine together, but something always comes up to prevent it and we don't see each other. I am more than ever harassed by existence, and disgusted with everything. That doesn't keep me from feeling in better physical form than ever. Explain that if you can!

I've had news of you from Charles-Edmond. What's this about your not coming here in April? When are we to see each other? Oh, how badly I've *needed* you during all this time, chère maître! How I've missed you! You're the only person I could have talked to about so many things!

Je vous embrasse bien fort, en vous envoyant toutes mes tendresses.

Gve

---

[1] Flaubert inserted the (1) at the beginning of this paragraph apparently with the intention, subsequently forgotten, of numbering the "many things" he had to say.

[2] Flaubert refers to remarks by pro-royalist reviewers, blaming him for not "correcting", or accusing him of expanding, some of Bouilhet's anti-royalist details. Close to the end of Act III, the chevalier d'Aydie, driven desperate by (false) accounts of the infidelity of his beloved Aïssé with the Regent, predicts to the latter, before a group of courtiers, that the outraged populace will one day burn the Palais Royal (in which the scene is taking place).

The fact that the Communards set fire to the Palais Royal in May 1871, whereas Bouilhet had died in 1869, gave weight to the accusation that Flaubert had invented, or emphasized, the scene, to give the production topicality. Goncourt reports that d'Aydie's lines were cheered.

³ *Dernières Chansons* and *Mademoiselle Aïssé* had both been published the day before. The *Letter to the Municipal Council* was published in *Le Temps* not on Wednesday the 24th, but on Friday the 26th.

⁴ *Le Roi Carotte*, by Victorien Sardou, with music by Jacques Offenbach, had opened at the Théâtre de la Gaîeté on 15 January. Despite Flaubert's opinion, it had considerable success.

⁵ *Fantasio*, opera by Jacques Offenbach after a play by Musset, had opened on the 18th.

297 FLAUBERT TO SAND

[Paris, 23 January 1872]
Tuesday evening

You'll very soon be receiving *Dernières Chansons, Aïssé*, and my *Letter to the Municipal Council of Rouen*, which is to appear tomorrow[1] in *Le Temps*, before coming out as a pamphlet.

I forgot to warn you of the following, chère maître: I have made use of your name. I have "compromised" you by listing you as one of the illustrious contributors towards the Bouilhet monument. I thought your name would "look well" in the context; and, style being sacred, please don't give me the lie!

Today I resumed my metaphysical reading for *Saint Antoine*. Next Saturday I'm to read 130 pages of it – all that's completed – to Turgenev. Why won't you be there!

Votre vieux

Gve Flaubert

¹ In fact, on the 26th.

298 SAND TO FLAUBERT

[Nohant] 25 January [18]72

You did quite right to put me down for a contribution; I *want* to give something. Name whatever sum you like, and let me know the figure so that I can have it sent to you.

I read your preface (in *Le Temps*)[1] and found the end very fine and touching. But I see your poor friend was incurably irascible, like you, and I do wish that, at your age, you yourself were less angry, less preoccupied with other people's stupidity. In my view it's a waste of time, like complaining about flies or the rain. If you tell the public they're stupid they just become offended and more stupid still; if you offend or anger someone intelligent he rises above it, but if people are stupid to begin with they end up yet more foolish.

But still, chronic indignation may be an organic necessity for you. It would kill *me*! I have an enormous need for calm if I'm to think and reflect. At the moment I'm risking your anathema by doing something "useful". I'm trying to give a child an enlightened introduction to the life of the mind. I believe early education affects all the rest of a person's studies, and that official pedagogy always complicates everything unnecessarily. In a nutshell, I'm working at a primer. Don't eat me alive![2]

There's only one thing I regret about having to miss Paris, and that's not being able to make a third when you read Turgenev your *Saint Antoine*. Apart from that, Paris has no appeal for me. There are people there I'm fond of, and whom I don't want to upset by having to disagree with their ideas. One's bound to get tired of the spirit of faction or sect that won't let anyone be a Frenchman, a man, or himself any more. People haven't a country – they only belong to a Church; they do what they disapprove of so as not to disobey party orders. I can't quarrel with those I love; nor can I lie. I prefer to say nothing. Everyone would think me cold or stupid. Better to stay at home.

You don't say anything about your mother – is she in Paris, at her grand-daughter's? I trust your silence means they're both well. Here everything's getting through the winter splendidly. The children are in great form and give us nothing but happiness. After the dire winter of '70-'71 we oughtn't to complain about anything.

Is a peaceful life possible, you'll say, when the human race is so absurd? I manage by telling myself that perhaps I'm just as absurd as the rest of mankind, and that it's time I thought of mending my ways.

Je t'embrasse on behalf of myself and all my family.

G. Sand

[1] An extract from Flaubert's preface to *Dernières Chansons* had appeared in *Le Temps* for 23 January. He had written to Charles-Edmond, the *directeur littéraire* of that newspaper, shortly before:

". . . . I will give you . . . the conclusion of my preface. Paragraph IV is the only personal passage, and, in my opinion, the best, or the least bad. It contains an exposition of Bouilhet's aesthetic opinions, with a tirade by

Votre

Gve Flaubert."

[2] George Sand was preparing three articles for *Le Temps*, entitled "*Les Idées d'un maître d'école*" ("*Thoughts of a Schoolmaster*").

299 SAND TO FLAUBERT

[Nohant, 26 January 1872]
Friday

I wrote this on top of a notebook by mistake.[1]

I didn't know about all that business in Rouen, but now I realize why you were so angry.[2] But you're *too* angry – that's to say, too kind, and too kind to them. With someone harsh and vindictive those boors would be less spiteful and less bold. But you and Bouilhet have always treated them unceremoniously, and now they're getting their own back on both the living and the dead. Oh yes, that's the explanation; no doubt about it.

Yesterday I was exhorting you to cool disdain, but I see it's the wrong moment for that. But you're not malicious – strong men aren't cruel. If they'd had a bloodthirsty mob at their heels, those worthy gentlemen of Rouen wouldn't have dared do what they're doing now!

The *Chansons* have come, and tomorrow I'll read the whole of your preface.

Je t'embrasse.

[unsigned]

[1] Sand added this to explain the slightly crumpled edges of the letter.
[2] She had just read, in *Le Temps*, Flaubert's scathing *Letter to the Municipal Council of Rouen*.

300 FLAUBERT TO SAND

[Paris, 28 January 1872]
Sunday evening

No, chère maître! It's not true. Bouilhet never offended the Rouen bourgeoisie. No one was kinder to them – I might even say craven, to tell the truth. As for me, I've always kept my distance from them. That's the full extent of my crime.

I found, just today, by chance, in Nadar's *Mémoires du Géant*, a paragraph about me and the Rouennais which is utterly exact. Since you own the book, see p. 100 or so.[1]

Had I remained silent, I'd have been accused of being a coward. I protested quite spontaneously: that is, violently. And I did the right thing. The result has been this: people in Rouen are afraid of me, and I'm considered "*un homme sérieux*" because I quoted figures [sic]!

I don't believe one should ever be the first to attack. But when you strike back you should try to kill your enemy outright. That's my system. Candour is an ingredient of Loyalty: and why should Loyalty be less whole-hearted in blame than in praise?

We are perishing from indulgence, from clemency, from *Cowardice*; and (I repeat my eternal refrain) from lack of *Justice*!

Besides, I insulted no one. I kept to generalities. As for M. Decorde, what I say is perfectly fair in war.[2] But enough about those imbeciles.

I spent the best part of yesterday with Turgenev, reading him the 115 pages I have written of *Saint Antoine*. What a good listener! And what a critic! He dazzled me with the profundity and precision of his judgment. Ah! If all those who take it on themselves to judge books could have heard him, what a lesson! Nothing escapes him. And after listening to a hundred-line poem he could still remember a weak epithet. For *Saint Antoine*, he gave me two or three excellent bits of advice concerning details.

The day before yesterday, I resumed my reading, and when I have mailed out all the copies of my *Letter* I'll get back to my usual routine.

Charles-Edmond told me that the novel of yours that he's to publish in *Le Temps* is a marvel. Entirely possible![3]

My mother is well. But her character is becoming *intolerable*. My poor niece is at the end of her tether.

Kiss everybody for me – and to you, chère bon maître, trop bon, *ex imo*.

Gve Flaubert

You must consider me idiotic if you think I'm going to scold you about your primer. I'm too much of a philosopher not to realize that such a thing can be a very serious work.

Method is the most precious part of criticism, for without it there can be no creation.

[1] Here is the passage alluded to by Flaubert:

"Be banal if you want to live. . . . I still remember a nice young man, something of a dandy, in Rouen, whom I congratulated on the very great, very deserved, and at that time recent success of his fellow-citizen, the author of *Madame Bovary*. 'You find it a good book?' that young Rouennais of good family replied, with a tone of superiority utterly crushing towards Flaubert. 'Not I! The author is a kind of eccentric – something we don't at all care for in Rouen. He was always trying to attract attention to himself. He didn't want to belong to the National Guard. And then, suddenly, *without saying a word*, he left for Africa! We don't like that sort, in Rouen.'" (Nadar: *Mémoires du Géant*, Paris, Dentu, 1864.)

[2] Decorde, a lawyer, member of the Rouen Municipal Council and himself an occasional poet, had composed a preparatory report describing Bouilhet as "an often clever pupil of Musset", with a talent that "is not totally exempt from criticism." In his *Letter*, Flaubert, quoting many passages, demonstrates Decorde's own very mediocre talent.

[3] *Nanon* would be serialized in *Le Temps*, 7 March to 20 April 1872.

301   SAND TO FLAUBERT

Nohant, 28 January [18]72

Your preface is splendid, the book is divine! Dear me, I've written a line of verse without realizing it! God forgive me!

Yes, you're right. Your friend was certainly not second-rate, and anyway ratings aren't something to be handed out by society in general, especially at a time when criticism destroys everything and promotes nothing. Your whole heart is in your simple and sober account of his life. I can see now why he died so young: he lived too much in the mind. I beg *you* not to be so completely absorbed in literature and learning. Travel, move about, have mistresses – or wives, just as you like; and during such phases, don't work. One shouldn't burn the candle at both ends; the thing is to light each end turn and turn about.

Even at my age I still plunge into the waters of idleness sometimes: I don't despise the most childish and silly amusements – I emerge from my bouts of foolishness more lucid than before.

Bouilhet's premature death is a great loss to art. Ten years from now there won't be a single poet left. Your preface is beautiful and good. Some pages are exemplary, and certainly the bourgeois won't see anything out of the way in *them*. Oh, if we didn't have a little inner shrine or pagoda where we can take refuge without having to account to anyone, where we can contemplate and dream about beauty and truth, we'd have to say, What's the point of it all?

Je t'embrasse bien fort.

Ton vieux troubadour.

[unsigned]

*

The "divine book" is, of course, *Dernières Chansons*. As for *Mademoiselle d'Aïssé*, Sand doubtless preferred to say nothing about it to Flaubert: her diary for 5 February records her dislike of the work. "I read *Aïssé*, which I found *very bad*, and I wasn't prejudiced against it, quite the contrary."

302   FLAUBERT TO SAND

[Paris, 15 February 1872]

Chère bon maître,

Can you do an article for *Le Temps* about *Dernières Chansons*? I'd be very much obliged.

So much for that!

I was sick all last week – my throat was in a ghastly state. But I slept a lot, and now I'm myself again. I've resumed my reading for *Saint Antoine*.

Je vous embrasse comme je vous aime, c'est-à-dire très fort.

Gve Flaubert

It seems to me that *Dernières Chansons* could be the occasion for a splendid article – a funeral oration on poetry. Poetry will not perish, but it will be in eclipse for a long time! And the darkness is just beginning.

See if you're in the mood, and drop me a line.

303   SAND TO FLAUBERT

Nohant, 17 February [18]72

Mon troubadour,

I'm thinking over what you asked, and I'll do it. But this week I have to rest. I overdid it larking about with my great-nephews and great-nieces at Mardi Gras.

Je t'embrasse on behalf of myself and all my brood.

G. Sand

[Paris, 26 February 1872]
Monday evening

How long it is since I last wrote to you, chère maître! I have so many things to tell you that I don't know where to begin! How stupid it is for people who love each other to live so far apart!

Have you bidden Paris an eternal farewell? Am I never to see you here again? Will you come to Croisset this summer, to listen to *Saint Antoine*?

As for me, I can't come to Nohant because my time—considering the flatness of my purse – has to be carefully portioned out, and I still have a good month's reading and research to do in Paris. After which I'll relieve my poor niece of the company of her grandmother, who has become unsociable, intolerable. What a decline! And how sad it is, the indifference that creeps into our hearts! (We're looking for a lady companion – not easy to find.) So, towards Easter I'll be back at Croisset, to resume my copying. I'm beginning to feel a desire to write.

These evenings I'm reading Kant's *Critique of Pure Reason*, translated by Barni, and going over my Spinoza. During the day I enjoy leafing through mediaeval *belluaires*[1] looking, in those authorities, for the most baroque animals. I'm in the midst of fantastic monsters. Soon, when I'll have about finished with these volumes, I'll go to the Natural History Museum and brood over real monsters. And then my research for good old Saint Antoine will be concluded.

In your letter before the last you seemed worried about my health. You needn't be. I have never been so convinced of having a strong constitution. The life I've led this winter has been enough to kill three rhinoceroses. Yet I've come through it in splendid form. The sheath *has* to be sturdy, the blade being so very keen. But there's always a feeling of sadness. Activity of any kind fills me with a disgust for existence. I took your advice and had a little "distraction". But I didn't much enjoy it. No question that only one thing really interests me: literature, the sacrosanct.

My preface to *Dernières Chansons* has inspired Mme Colet with a Pindaric rage. She has sent me an anonymous letter, in verse, depicting me as a charlatan banging the big drum over my friend's grave, a dullard always up to scurvy tricks to please the critics, and always "fawning on Caesar."[2] A sad lesson in the passions, as Prud'homme would say.

Speaking of Caesar, I have no belief in his imminent return,[3] whatever the talk may be. Pessimist though I am, we haven't reached that point. Still, if one were to consult the god called Universal Suffrage, who knows? . . . Ah! We've sunk very low, very low.

I saw *Ruy Blas*, wretchedly acted except by Sarah. Mélingue is a sleepwalking sewer worker, and the rest are just as bad.[4] *Le père* Hugo having complained in a friendly way that I hadn't called on him, I felt I had to do so. And I found him . . . charming! I say it again: *charming*. Not at all the great man: no pontificating whatever. This discovery greatly surprised me, and did me a lot of good. Because I have a gift for veneration. And I love to love what I admire. This is a personal allusion to you, chère bon maître.

I have met Mme Viardot, and find her personality quite strange. Turgenev took me to see her. I understand his liking for her, and hers for him.

What are you up to? What are you writing? When will your article appear in *Le Temps?*

To your granddaughters, a hug from me. And to you mes meilleures, mes plus hautes tendresses.

Votre

Gve Flaubert

[1] It is puzzling that Flaubert did not write *bestiaires* — "bestiaries" – the usual term for the mediaeval stories about fanciful animals that he was reading. *Belluaire*, derived from the Latin *bellua*, "ferocious beast", signifies, according to Littré, the gladiator who fought the animals.

[2] Louise Colet, Flaubert's mistress in earlier years, made a show of republican sympathies, and here uses the name "Caesar" in scornful reference to the ex-emperor Napoleon III, author of a two-volume *Histoire de Jules César*. "Fawning" is her term of contempt for Flaubert's occasional attendance at court functions during the 1860s.

[3] Taking advantage of a period of political confusion, the partisans of the Empire were trying to revive their cause, founding newspapers, organizing meetings, and calling for a plebiscite.

[4] See Letter 292, Note 1. The young Sarah Bernhardt played the role of the queen, Etienne Mélingue that of Don César. Despite Flaubert's opinion, this revival of *Ruy Blas* enjoyed a long run.

305   SAND TO FLAUBERT

[Nohant, 28–29 February 1872]
Wednesday to Thursday
3 a.m.

Mon cher vieux, I've been having such a sad time these last twelve days! Maurice has been very ill. Those terrible sore throats again, that don't seem at all serious to begin with but develop into abscesses with a tendency to quinsy. He hasn't been in danger, only in danger of danger all the time, with awful pain, loss of voice, inability to swallow, and all the discomforts attached to bad throats. You've just had one yourself, so you know all about them. With him it always tends to deteriorate, and the same tissues have been attacked so often they've lost their powers of resistance. Although he has little or no fever and rarely keeps to his bed, his morale does suffer very much, as it's bound to do when someone who's always active in body and mind finds both of these flagging. But we've taken such good care of him that I think he's over it now, though I was worried again this morning and sent for Dr Favre, our saviour *in ordinary*.[1]

During the day, to distract him, I told him about your research into monsters. He sent for his sketch books to see if he had anything that might be of use to you, but found only pure fantasies of his own invention. I found them so original and amusing, though, that I encouraged him to send them anyway. They won't be of any use, but they might give you a good laugh in your moments of leisure.

I hope we shall get back to normal now without any relapses. He's the life and soul of the household, and when he's laid low the rest of us – mother, wife and daughters – are all as good as dead. Aurore said she wished she could be ill instead of her father. All five of us love one another passionately, and what you call "sacrosanct literature" is only secondary in my life. I've always loved someone more than literature, and my family more than that someone.

Why is your poor little mother so irritable and hopeless in the middle phase of an old age that was still so youthful and gracious when I met her? Is it the sudden deafness? Or did she lack patience and philosophy before her health started to fail? I share your sufferings about all this, because I understand what they must be like.

Mme Colet's old age is even worse, because it has degenerated into malice. I used to think her hatred was all directed against myself, which struck me as rather crazy, as I've never said or done anything against her, even after the chamber-pot of a book into which she excreted her causeless fury.[2] And what has she got against you, now passion has passed into legend? *Strange, strange!*[3] And why in connection with Bouilhet? Did she hate the poor poet too?[4] She's mad.

As you may imagine, I haven't been able to write a word for the last twelve days. I hope to be able to get back to work properly as soon as I've finished my novel, which has had to be left dangling at the last few pages. Publication's just due to start, and the writing's still not finished. I sit up night after night until dawn, but my mind's not tranquil enough to think of anything but my patient.

Goodnight, cher bon ami de mon coeur. For goodness' sake don't *you* work too hard or sit up too late, because you, also, are subject to bad throats. It's a painful and treacherous thing to have. Nous t'aimons et nous t'aimons tous. Aurore is sweet, with a strange ability to learn anything at all quite effortlessly.

What sort of woman have you in mind as companion for your mother? I may know of someone who'd do. Should she be good at reading and conversation? I suppose the deafness makes that unnecessary. Is it only a question of physical care and constant attendance? What are the requirements, and how much do you wish to pay for them?

Tell me how and why it was you hadn't been to see old Hugo once since *Ruy Blas*. Do Gautier and Saint-Victor, his old friends, neglect him too? Have people quarrelled with him over politics?[5]

[unsigned]

---

[1] [See Concise Oxford Dictionary: "*in ordinary*: applied to 'physician', etc., meaning by permanent appointment, not temporary or extraordinary".] The adjective *ordinaire* was added here by Sand, and underlined, perhaps after the rest of the letter was written – no doubt to distinguish this permanent "saviour" from Thiers, to whom we have seen the term applied in Letter 284, Note 6.

² In the early 1840s, Louise Colet had sought George Sand's friendship; but the latter, recognizing their incompatibility, had politely but firmly held aloof. Following Sand's attempt, in her much-discussed novel *Elle et Lui* (1859), to explain her relations with Alfred de Musset, Colet had published a novel of her own, *Lui*, in which Musset is a hero and Sand his tormentor.

³ In English in the original.

⁴ Louise Colet had blamed Louis Bouilhet – not without justification – for encouraging Flaubert to break with her. In *Une Histoire de soldat* (1856), a novel in which she writes about herself and Flaubert, Bouilhet is depicted as the false friend responsible for the rupture.

⁵ As he grew older, Victor Hugo had become increasingly radical in his political views. Several of his friends had broken with him over his defence of the Commune and the Communards.

306 FLAUBERT TO SAND

[Paris, 3 March 1872]
Sunday evening

Chère maître,

The fantastic drawings arrived, and I've been enjoying them. Perhaps there's a deep symbol hidden in what Maurice has done, but I haven't discovered it. Food for thought! There are two very pretty monsters: (1) a foetus in the form of a balloon with four feet; (2) a skull with a tapeworm coming out of one side.[1]

Can Maurice really be as ill as you say, when he's able to enjoy himself like this? Nevertheless I well understand that those persistent sore throats should worry you. Are they perhaps caused by bad habits? I lay the blame on cigarettes. Why doesn't he smoke long wooden pipes? – they're the least irritating.

We haven't yet found a lady companion. It seems to be difficult. We'd need a very gentle person who'd be able to read aloud. She'd also be asked to do a little housekeeping. But her chief occupation would be to converse. My poor mother can't be alone for a moment now! The lady would not have to attend to any major physical details: my mother would keep her maid. The wages would be 800 francs to begin with, then a thousand if things worked out. What we need above all is someone pleasant and absolutely honest. Religious principles not required! The rest is left to your perspicacity, chère maître. That's all I can tell you.

I'm worried about Théo. He seems to be aging in a strange way. He must be very ill – a heart ailment, probably? Yet another preparing to leave me! . . .

No! Literature is not what *I* love best in the world, either. I expressed myself badly (in my last letter). I was speaking of distractions, and nothing more. I'm not so far gone as to prefer words to human beings. The longer I live, the more my sensitivity exasperates me. But the outer man is solid, and the machine continues to function. Besides, after the Prussian war nothing can trouble me unduly.

At the moment I'm impatiently awaiting the outcome of the Janvier case. I'm well acquainted with the mother of this rascal. The poor woman idolizes her son: for the past eight months she's been staying with him in his prison: I pity her profoundly. I believe ex-prefect Janvier is innocent of what he's charged with, but he's so criminal in other respects that I don't know what to think.[2] If he's acquitted it will be a triumph for the execrable Bonapartists. If he's sentenced I'll grieve for his mother. That's how all's the best in this best of all possible worlds. Oh, Serenity of the great Goethe, no one admires thee more than I, for no one possesses thee less!

And the *Critique of Pure Reason*, by a gentleman named Kant, translated by Barni, is heavier reading than Marcelin's *La Vie Parisienne*.[3] No matter! Eventually I'll get to understand it!

I've almost finished sketching the last part of *Saint Antoine*. I'm eager to begin to write. It's too long since I've written anything! I'm famished for *style*!

And for you still more, chère bon maître. Send me, quickly, news of Maurice. And tell me whether you think the lady you know might suit us.

Et là-dessus, je vous embrasse tous à pleins bras.

Votre vieux troubadour

Gve Flaubert

perpetually excited, perpetually "Hindignant", like Saint Polycarp.

---

[1] Flaubert seems not to have made use of these drawings for his book, but he preserved them among his notes. They are reproduced in the Conard edition of *La Tentation de Saint Antoine*, p. 678.

[2] Eugène Janvier de la Motte, prefect of the Eure from 1855 to 1868, was known for his dissipation. He was arrested in June 1871, accused of falsifying public documents, misuse of funds, and extortion. His trial took place from 26 February to 3 March, 1872. Thanks to influential witnesses for the defence, among them Pouyer-Quertier, the Minister of Finance, he was acquitted. Flaubert knew Janvier fairly well, and was close to his mother, Mme Parrot, and his sister, Mme Lepic. In one of his Notebooks, under "Projects", there is the following anecdote: "A midwife in Evreux, who had brought up her daughter very properly, was given a six-year prison sentence for abortion. J[anvier], speaking to the woman's husband, offered to release her if her daughter would come to the prefecture. She went, and was all but raped. Her mother was not released: her sentence was reduced from six years to five." (M. J. Durry, *Flaubert et ses projets inédits* [Librairie Nizet, 1950, pp. 291 ff.]).

[3] *La Vie Parisienne*, an illustrated weekly chronicling literature and society, was founded in 1862 by the graphic artist Emile Planat, known as Marcelin.

---

307 FLAUBERT TO SAND

Paris, 11 March 1872
Monday

Chère maître,

Is Maurice worse? Your silence worries me, especially since you usually answer immediately when you're asked for a favour.

Where is the lady companion you spoke of? I'll be bringing my mother back to Croisset in a fortnight, and would like to have found someone for her by then. Not an easy matter.

Mille tendresses de votre vieux

Gve Flaubert

V. Hugo sends you every kind of greeting. He spoke of you in the highest terms. He's a shrewd old codger who knows what's what.

308   SAND TO FLAUBERT

[Nohant, 13] March [18]72

No, cher ami, Maurice is nearly better, but I've been tired, overwhelmed with the urgent job of finishing my novel and correcting a mass of proofs for its earlier stages. Not to mention unanswered letters and business – I haven't had a minute to breathe! That's why I've not managed to write the Bouilhet piece yet, and as *Nanon* has just started coming out in five weekly instalments in *Le Temps*, I don't see how I can bring the article out in the immediate future. The people at the *Revue des Deux Mondes* don't want me to engage in criticism. Anyone who isn't now or hasn't in the past been part of their set has no talent, and they won't allow me to say any different. True, there's a new review that would welcome me with open arms, and it's produced by very decent people. But it has more readers abroad than in France, and you might consider that the article wouldn't attract enough notice if they published it. It's called *La Revue universelle*, and the editor is Amédée Marteau. Talk to Ch.-Edmond about all this. Ask him if he could find a little space for me in the main body of *Le Temps*, despite the fact that *Nanon* is appearing there in instalments.

As for the matter of the lady companion, of course I've been doing something about it. But the person I had particularly in mind wouldn't do as she couldn't read aloud, and I'm not sure enough about the others to put them forward. I'd supposed your poor Maman was too deaf to converse or have someone read to her, and assumed she only needed someone kind and agreeable to look after her and keep her company. So there you are, mon cher vieux – I'm not to blame.

Je t'embrasse de tout mon coeur. For the moment my heart's the only organ that still functions. My mind is completely stupefied.

G. Sand

309   FLAUBERT TO SAND

[Paris, 14 March 1872]
Thursday morning

It was Charles-Edmond himself who told me to ask you for an article on *Dernières Chansons*, and no one but you will do it for *Le Temps*. Schérer offered, but I declined. So, first rest, take your time, and whenever you wish you can be sure that your article will be published.

The said Charles-Edmond is now in Antibes, staying with Dennery, "to complete a long and urgent piece of work". The scoundrel! I wonder what he's up to?

I'll be back in Croisset in a fortnight at the latest. We haven't succeeded in finding a lady companion for my poor Maman.

I'm delighted Maurice is better. Greetings to him from me, and to all the others as well, et tout à vous, chère bon maître.

Votre vieux

Gve Flaubert

Try to get hold of *Tartarin de Tarascon*, by Alph. Daudet.[1] It will make you laugh. It's very nice – there's a real comic vein in it.

[1] *Les Aventures prodigieuses de Tartarin de Tarascon* had been published on 29 February 1872.

*

For Flaubert, the winter spent in Paris had been full of disappointments. And an incident that occurred shortly before he left was particularly galling: on 20 March, a trivial quarrel concerning Bouilhet's *Dernières Chansons* put an end to his relations with his publisher. "I kept going very well this winter, until my quarrel with Lévy," he wrote to his niece on the 28th, "but since then I've been tired to the very marrow of my bones."

He returned to Croisset on Monday, 25 March, with his mother, whose steady decline was an increasing anxiety.

310 FLAUBERT TO SAND

Croisset, [31 March 1872]
Easter Sunday

Here I am, chère maître – back at home, and not very merry. My mother is a great worry. She is failing day by day, almost hour by hour. She wanted to return here even though the painters haven't finished their work, and we are very uncomfortable. At the end of next week she'll have a lady companion, and I'll be relieved of some of the stupid housekeeping tasks.

Ten days ago I had a violent quarrel with the great Michel Lévy, who is certainly a fine, a very fine, piece of goods! He flatly denied having made me a certain promise. I felt as though he had slapped me in the face, and turned first pale, then fiery red. And then your troubadour . . . was magnificent! Never before had the Maison Lévy experienced such a drubbing.

It was about *Dernières Chansons*. Do you know how much that book and *Aïssé* have earned for Bouilhet's poor little Philippe, who sacrificed 30 thousand francs to save Bouilhet's manuscripts from being burned?[1] At the final reckoning he'll have to *pay* about 400 francs! I'll spare you the details, but that's the situation. Such always are the rewards of virtue. But then if it *were* properly rewarded, it wouldn't be virtue!

No matter! That last episode with Lévy has taken it out of me like an excessive blood-letting. It's humiliating to realize one has failed. And when one has given, for nothing, all one's heart, one's thought, one's nerves, one's muscles and one's time, one simply collapses. My poor Bouilhet did well to die: the times are not kind.

As for me, I'm determined not to "make the presses groan" for many a long year, solely in order to have no "business" – to avoid all contact with printers, publishers and newspapers, and above all not to have to talk about money.

My inadequacy in such matters is assuming frightening proportions. Why does the mere sight of an "account" send me into a rage? It borders on madness. I'm quite serious. You must realize that I failed at everything this past winter. *Aïssé* made no money. *Dernières Chansons* has come close to involving me in a lawsuit with Lévy. The business of the Bouilhet fountain isn't yet resolved. I'm weary, bone-weary, of everything.

Let's hope I won't botch *Saint Antoine* as well. I'll get back to it in a week, after finishing with Kant and Hegel. These two great men make me feel all the more stupid. And when I leave their company I fall hungrily on my old, thrice-great Spinoza. What a genius! What a work, the *Ethics*!

I've been reading a little astronomy, also for *Saint Antoine*. But I don't feel in good form. How could I, with this constant worry about my poor Maman?

I have made the acquaintance of your old friend Mme Viardot, whom I find very pleasant.

Adieu, chère bon maître. Mille amitiés aux vôtres, et à vous toutes mes tendresses.

Votre

Gve Flaubert

[1] The details of Philippe Leparfait's "sacrifice" are not known. Perhaps it involved Bouilhet's next-of-kin, the bigoted sisters mentioned by Flaubert in a letter to Maxime Du Camp of 23 July 1869. (See *The Letters of Gustave Flaubert*, II, 131.)

311 FLAUBERT TO SAND

[Croisset, 6–7 April 1872]
Saturday night, 1 a.m.

Chère bon maître,
My mother *has just died*!
Je vous embrasse

Gve Flaubert

*

"Letter from my poor friend Flaubert," George Sand wrote in her diary, on the 8th. "One line: his mother is dead." She replied immediately, and wrote again a few days later.

312 SAND TO FLAUBERT

Nohant, 9 April [1872]

I am with you all the time, day and night, mon pauvre cher ami. I imagine all the distressing things going on around you. I wish I could be with you. The frustration of being stuck here makes it all worse for me. I hope for a word saying you're finding the necessary courage. The end of that worthy and beloved life has been painful and protracted: as soon as she became infirm she declined, and none of you could distract or comfort her any more. Alas, your continual anguish and worry have ended in the way everything in this world ends, with struggle terminating only in sorrow! What a grievous way to earn repose! And I know you will miss even your anxiety. I've experienced myself the kind of consternation that follows the fight against death. All I can do, mon pauvre enfant, is offer a motherly heart which, though it cannot make up for any loss, suffers closely and keenly with your own in all your misfortunes.

G. Sand

313 SAND TO FLAUBERT

Nohant, 14 April 1872

My daughter-in-law has gone to spend a few days near our friends in Nîmes,[1] to keep Gabrielle away from Aurore, who's suffering from a bad bout of whooping cough. Lina herself has been ailing for some time and needs to recuperate. I myself am quite well again, though the child's indisposition and the business of the lightning departure did rather upset me. I had to see to it that Aurore accepted things without fretting too, and I haven't had a moment to write to you again. I also wonder whether you wouldn't prefer to be left to yourself in these early days. But I ease my longing to be near you at this sad time by telling you, and telling you again, mon pauvre cher ami, how very much I love you.

Perhaps, too, your family took you off to Rouen or Dieppe, so that you didn't have to go back straight away to that sadly empty house. I don't know what your plans are, should you have changed your mind about concentrating entirely on work. If you feel at all like travelling and lack the wherewithal, I've just earned a few sous which are at your disposal. Don't stand on ceremony with me, any more than I would with you, cher enfant. *Le Temps* will be paying me for my novel in five or six days, and you'd only have to drop me a line and I'd see the money got to you in Paris.

A line when you can. Je t'embrasse ainsi que Maurice, bien tendrement.

[unsigned]

¹ The family of Jules Boucoiran, Maurice's former tutor. Since 1835 Boucoiran had been editor of the regional newspaper, *Le Courrier du Gard*, at Nîmes. See Letter 318 for the explanation of this rather confused passage.

*

Stricken by his loss, uncertain of the future, Flaubert replied to Sand's two letters.

314 FLAUBERT TO SAND

[Croisset,]16[April 1872]
Tuesday

Chère bon maître,

I should have answered your first letter at once. It was so kind and affection-ate! But I was too shattered. I lacked the physical strength. Today I'm at last beginning to hear the birds singing and see the fresh green of the leaves. I've stopped resenting the sunshine! That's a good sign. If only I could feel like working again, I'd be saved.

Your second letter (that of yesterday) moved me to tears. How good you are! What a wonderful being! I have no need of money at the moment, thank you. But, should I feel the need, it is certainly to you I would turn.

My mother has left Croisset to Caroline, with the condition that I retain my quarters here. So until things are finally settled I'll stay on. Before deciding about the future, I must know what I'll have to live on. After that we'll see. Shall I have the fortitude to live absolutely alone here, in solitude? I doubt it. I'm growing old. Caro cannot live here now. She already has two places of her own. And the Croisset house is expensive to maintain.

I think I'll give up my apartment in Paris – there's no longer any reason for me to be there. All my friends are dead. And the last of them, poor Théo, isn't long for this world, I fear. It's hard to make a new start at fifty!

I've realized for a fortnight now that my poor dear mother was the being I loved most. I feel as though part of my entrails had been torn out.

I need to see you so badly! So badly! As soon as things are cleared up I'll come and visit you. If you go to Paris, let me know, and I'll come running.

Mme Viardot, Turgenev and I have a plan – to visit you at Nohant in July. Will this little dream come true?

Je vous embrasse bien fort.

Votre vieux troubadour

Gve Flaubert

Much love to Maurice, whom I envy more than ever, because he has you. And kisses to Mlle Aurore, despite (or because of) her whooping cough.

315   SAND TO FLAUBERT

Nohant, 28 April [1872]

I've got my poor Aurore whooping terribly in my arms day and night. I've also got some forced labour to finish, and I *am* finishing it in spite of all.[1] If I haven't done the Bouilhet article yet, you may be sure it's because it's been impossible. I'll do it at the same time as the piece on *L'Année terrible*.[2]

I'll go to Paris from May 20th to 25th at the latest. Perhaps sooner, if Maurice takes Aurore to join Lina and the younger one in Nîmes before that. I'll write, and either you'll come to see me in Paris or I'll come to see you. I'm longing to see you and . . . not comfort you, but tell you how truly your troubles are my own. Until then, just send a word to let me know if things are sorting themselves out and you yourself are recovering.

Ton vieux

G. Sand

[1] Sand was trying to write a play adapted from her novel *Nanon*, in the hope of having it produced at the Odéon during her next visit to Paris.

[2] Sand's remarks on *Dernières Chansons* would appear in *Le Temps* for 31 July. They would be included in an article in which she discusses, as well, Victor Hugo's *L'Année terrible*, translations from Aeschylus by Lecomte de Lisle, and a musical evening given by Pauline Viardot.

316   FLAUBERT TO SAND

[Croisset, 29 April 1872]
Monday evening

What good news, chère maître! In a month, even less than a month, I'll see you – at last. Arrange things so that you won't be too busy in Paris: we'll want time to talk. What might be nice would be for you to return here with me, to spend a few days. It would be more peaceful than in town. "My poor old lady" was very fond of you. It would be sweet to see you here, in her house, now, while her presence still lingers.

I'm working again. Because existence is tolerable only if one forgets one's wretched self.

It will be a long time before I know how much I'll have to live on. Because everything left to us is in the form of real estate, and we'll have to sell everything in order to share it out.

In any event, I'll keep my rooms here. Croisset will be my refuge. And perhaps my only home. Paris no longer holds much attraction for me. Before long I'll have no friends left there. Except for Ed. de Goncourt and Turgenev, all my colleagues make me shudder, with their grocer's-shop mentality or their grotesque pretensions. The human race amuses me less and less (and that includes the eternal feminine).

Do you know that Théo is *very* ill? He is dying of boredom and general misery. No one speaks his language any more. That's what we are – a few surviving fossils, lost in an altered world.

Did I tell you about the impudence of the great M. Lévy, who denied, to my face, having given me his word about a certain matter? I never had many illusions about that Jew. No matter! The indignation he aroused still weighs on me, even though heavier burdens have since fallen to my lot. Why do I even think of him? It proves that my brain is empty indeed.

Kiss Mlle Aurore for me despite her whooping cough, and tell her to pass the kiss on to you. A vous, chère maître, mes meilleures, mes plus hautes tendresses.

Gve

317 FLAUBERT TO SAND

Croisset, 15 May [1872]
Wednesday

Chère maître,

It will be impossible for me, because of business – these everlasting money matters! – to be in Paris before June 3rd or 4th. Can you postpone your trip? But if you were to stay in Paris a little longer than a fortnight we could still meet there.

We *must* see each other before autumn – either I must come to Nohant or you here. In August I hope *Saint Antoine* will be finished. I long to read it to you. I'm re-working it. But my heart's not in it: I'm finding it deathly boring.

Je vous embrasse très fort.

Votre vieux

Gve Fl

318 SAND TO FLAUBERT

Nohant, 18 May [1872]

Cher ami de mon coeur,

Your contretemps doesn't complicate things; on the contrary. I've got the grippe and the prostration that goes with it. So I shan't be able to go to Paris for another week, and shall still be there in early June.

My little girls are both back home again. I took good care of the elder one and cured her; she's strong. The other is very tired, and the journey didn't stop her from catching whooping cough. I've been working hard despite looking after my darling, but as soon as my task was finished, as soon as I saw all my dear ones together again and up and about, I collapsed. It's nothing serious, but I haven't the energy to write.

Je t'embrasse. I look forward to seeing you soon.

G. Sand

*

While Flaubert was working over the last pages of *Saint Antoine*, Sand was finally able to leave for Paris on May 28th, taking with her the two new plays, *Nanon* and *Mademoiselle La Quintinie*. It was her first sight of the city since the events of 1870–1. It made the same impression on her as it had on Flaubert the year before: "The city is dreadful, and the stupefied population even more so," she wrote in her diary.

The day after her arrival she read *Nanon* at the Odéon, but the political allusions frightened the management. Fortunately, there was enthusiasm about *Mademoiselle La Quintinie*.

She wrote to Flaubert on one of the dates he had mentioned in his latest letter.

319 SAND TO FLAUBERT

Paris, rue Gay-Lussac 5
Monday [3 June 1872]

I'm in Paris, and submerged in the awfulness of personal affairs all this week. But will you come next week? I'd like to come and see you in Croisset, but I don't know if I can. I've caught whooping cough from my Aurore, and it hits you hard at my age. But I'm better, though not quite up to rushing about.

Write me a note so that I can set aside the times you can spare me. Je t'embrasse comme je t'aime, à plein coeur.

G. Sand

320 FLAUBERT TO SAND

[Croisset] 4 [June 1872]
Tuesday

"How much time can I spare you?" Chère maître! But *all* my time! Now, then, and ever.

I was planning to leave for Paris at the end of next week, on the 14th or 15th. Will you still be there? If not, I'll leave earlier.

But I'd much prefer that you came here. We'd be more peaceful – no calls to make, no unwelcome visitors. Now more than ever I'd like to have you here, in my poor Croisset, sleeping near me in my mother's room.

We must have enough to tell one another to go on for 24 hours without stopping. Then I'd read you *Saint Antoine*: I've only got fifteen pages to go before it's finished.

However, don't come if you haven't shaken off your cough: I'd be afraid that the damp might be bad for you.

You speak of "the awfulness of personal affairs". I know what you mean! I'm just emerging from the same sort of thing. And I'm still exhausted by it! The repugnance I feel for everything to do with money has become a kind of mania. I'm really serious.

And, while we're on the subject, if you have business with M. Lévy, beware! Did I tell you that he was abominable with me? If there wasn't one other publisher on earth I'd stay out of print rather than go back to him.

The mayor of Vendôme has invited me to "honour with my presence" the inauguration of the Ronsard statue, which will take place the 23rd of this month. I shall go, and would even like to "deliver a speech", a protest against modern Panmuflisme.[1] It would be a good opportunity. But I haven't the spirit or verve to do the thing properly and produce "something noteworthy".

A bientôt, chère maître.

Votre vieux troubadour

Gve Flaubert

qui vous embrasse.

[1] A term coined by Flaubert from the noun *mufle*, meaning rotter, or cad: "universal caddishness".

321 SAND TO FLAUBERT

[Paris, 7 June 1872]
Friday

Cher ami,

Your old troubadour has such a bad cough that a bit more would be too much. On the other hand, they can't do without me at home, so I can't stay beyond next week, i.e. the 15th or 16th. If you could come next Thursday, the 13th, I'd keep the 13th, the 14th and even the 15th free to be with you, at my place during the day and at dinner in the evening. In short, we could talk and read as if we were in the country. Everyone would think I'd already left.

Let me have a word right away. Je t'embrasse comme je t'aime.

G. Sand

*

On 12 June Flaubert left for Paris, and that same evening he called for Mme Sand and dined with her at Magny's.[1] They saw each other again two days later at a musical evening at Mme Viardot's.

Between those two meetings, Flaubert wrote the following note, occasioned by the sudden death of Chilly, the manager of the Odéon, on 12 June.

[1] The next day he wrote to Caroline: "Yesterday I spent the evening with Mme Sand, whom I found quite unchanged. She asked very kindly about you and all our affairs." The reader might be reminded that it was now more than two years since Flaubert and Sand had last met.

322 FLAUBERT TO SAND

[Paris] 13 June [1872]

Chère maître,

Have you promised to support Duquesnel? If not, let me beg you to use all your influence to support my friend Raymond Deslandes, as though the candidate were

your old troubadour.

Give me a definite answer, so that we know what you mean to do.[1]

[1] Sand voted for Duquesnel.

*

They saw no more of each other during their stay in Paris: on the 15th Flaubert went to spend three days at Saint-Gratien with Princesse Mathilde, and on Monday the 17th Sand returned to Nohant.

On 21 June, "in an acute attack of misanthropy", Flaubert suddenly cancelled his trip to Vendôme. "I felt too depressed to stand the crowd," he wrote to Princesse Mathilde on 1 July. "I'd have had to travel with Saint-Victor, and I deeply dislike that gentleman. . . . He has always been worse than ill-mannered with me, and I couldn't have avoided 'having words' with him, which would have been ridiculous and absolutely pointless."[1] Back at Croisset, he finished the last chapter of *Saint Antoine*, and then made preparations for a stay in the Pyrenees, where his niece was to go for her health.

[1] Flaubert never forgot that Saint-Victor, to whom he had sent one of the rare copies of a specially printed edition of *L'Éducation sentimentale*, had not only refused to review it but never acknowledged its receipt. He also resented Saint-Victor's having sneered at *Aïssé* in *Le Moniteur*.

323 FLAUBERT TO SAND

Croisset, 1 July [1872]
Monday

Chère maître,

We didn't see each other in the right way at all, in Paris. I had a hundred things still to tell you. And you were hindered by your nephew's being there. I would have liked to know in what respect Troubat was (or is) a "scoundrel",[1] because I had wanted him to do some business for me – to get me clear of the Maison Lévy. That child of Israel continues to make my flesh creep. In connection with my account, he cheated Claye the printer out of two months' interest, etc. It's enough to make one vomit. I'm so disgusted by it all that I never want to publish anything again, much though I need the money. But since what I earn with my pen is laughable anyway, there's no great merit in abstaining.

I have finished *Saint Antoine*! Thank God! I'm going to work over a play by

Bouilhet[2] – it's full of possibilities. Then I'll begin a modern novel, a counterpoint to *Saint Antoine* – I intend it to be comic.[3] A little job that will take me two or three years at least!

While I was at Saint-Gratien I saw Mme de Voisins, who seemed to regard you with a mixture of respect and resentment. She has since sent me her *Contes algériens*.[4] She's a strange little woman, with a lot to her, I'm sure. I well remember Sainte-Beuve telling me anecdotes about her that were . . . spicy.

Next Friday, I take my niece to Luchon. I'll stay there five or six weeks, then go to the seaside for a while.

Will you be coming to Paris again soon, as you wrote to the Princess?

Not all the actors at the Odéon want Duquesnel as manager. They gave in to his pressure – out of cowardice, as usual. But since he's a real rascal he'll probably be appointed, and as his associate he'll have M. Blum, author of *Vlan dans l'oeil*, but worth 500 thousand francs and a protégé of Hugo's.[5]

Tendresses à tous les vôtres. Je vous embrasse.

Votre

Gve

I'll write you from Luchon to give you my address.

[1] Troubat had refused to return to G. Sand the letters she had written to Sainte-Beuve. In speaking of Troubat in her letter of 19 July (See Letter 326), Sand will not mention this, but Flaubert will already be *au courant*. Cf. his letter to Princesse Mathilde of 16 July: "I learned from Harrisse that my friend Troubat tried to behave with Mme Sand as he at first behaved with you – i.e. tried to keep her letters. What a wretched fellow!"

[2] *Le Sexe faible.*

[3] *Bouvard et Pécuchet.*

[4] Anne Devoisin, who called herself Mme de Voisins and used the pen-name Pierre Coeur. She lived for a number of years in Algeria, and in 1870 published the volume of stories mentioned by Flaubert. In 1866, when she had begun to write for the newspaper *La France*, she was a protégée of George Sand.

[5] Among the 75 or so plays, sketches and revues written by Ernest Blum, there is no *Vlan dans l'oeil*. Flaubert is probably thinking of *Pan! dans l'oeil*, revue in five acts by Jules Dornay and Gaston Marot (1867).

324[1] SAND TO FLAUBERT

[Nohant, 5 July 1872]

I want to write to you today, when I'm 68.[2] In perfect health in spite of the whooping cough, which lets me sleep since I've started plunging it every day into a furious little stream as cold as ice. It foams along among stones and flowers and tall weeds, beneath delicious shade – an ideal bathtub.

We've had some terrible storms. A thunderbolt fell into our garden, and our little Indre rivulet has become a Pyrenean torrent. It's rather nice. What a marvellous summer! The grass is seven feet high, the cornfields are sheets of flowers. The peasants say it's too much, but I just let them talk; it's so beautiful!

I walk down to the river and am boiling hot when I go into the icy water. The doctor thinks it's crazy, but I don't mind him either. I get better, while his patients follow their treatments and croak. I'm like the grass in the fields: all I need is water and sun.

Are you on your way to the Pyrenees? How I envy you – I love them so! I've made some wild excursions there,[3] but I don't know Luchon. Is it beautiful too? You won't visit those parts without going to see the Cirque de Gavarnie, will you, and the path that leads there? And Cauterets, and the lake at Gaube? And the route de Saint-Sauveur? Oh, how lovely it is to travel and see mountains and flowers and precipices! Does it all bore you? Do you remember, as you go along, that there are such things as publishers, theatre managers, readers and audiences? *I* forget everything, as I do when Pauline Viardot sings.

The other day, about nine miles from here, we found a wilderness, an absolute wilderness, a huge stretch of woods with not a cottage to be seen, not a human being nor a sheep nor a chicken, only flowers and butterflies and birds the whole day long.

But where can my letter reach you? I'll keep it until you send me your address.

[unsigned]

[1] Although Sand apparently thought she had mailed this letter, Maurice found it among her papers, never even folded, after her death.

[2] For many years George Sand had been mistaken about the date of her birth (1 July 1804). She had always celebrated it on 5 July, and after discovering the true date she preferred not to change the family custom.

[3] It was in the Pyrenees, in July or August, 1825, that Sand (at that time still Aurore Dudevant) met her first love, Aurélien de Sèze. In 1837 she visited the region again, with her daughter Solange.

325 FLAUBERT TO GEORGE SAND

> Bagnères-de-Luchon (Haute Garonne).
> Maison Binos
> 12 July [1872]

I've been here since Sunday night, chère maître, and no more cheerful than at Croisset – even a little less so, being idle. The house we are living in is so noisy that it's impossible to work. Besides, the sight of the bourgeois around us is unbearable! I'm no longer fit for travel. The slightest disturbance upsets me. Your old troubadour is old indeed, very much so! Dr Lambrou, the medical man here, thinks my weak nerves are due to too much tobacco! To be amenable, I'll smoke less, but I greatly doubt that my good behaviour will cure me.

I have just read Dickens's *Pickwick*.[1] Do you know it? Parts of it are superb, but it's so badly put together! All the English writers are like that, except W. Scott. They have no idea of construction! We Latins can't abide that!

Le sieur Duquesnel is definitely appointed, it seems? Everybody in any way connected with the Odéon, beginning with you, chère maître, will regret having backed him. Having nothing more to do with that place, thank God, I don't care one way or the other.

My last adventure with Lévy has completely disgusted me with publishing. *Saint Antoine* is finished, but it will slumber in a drawer until better days, if they ever come.

I'm about to begin a book that will require vast reading, and don't want to ruin myself buying books: do you know a bookseller in Paris who could let me hire all the books I would list for him?

What are you up to now? We saw each other too little the last time, and not in the right way.

This is a stupid letter. But they're making such a noise overhead that mine (my head) can't function.

Dazed though I am, je vous embrasse ainsi que les vôtres.

Your old dotard who loves you.

Gve Flaubert

[1] Among the numerous French translations of *The Posthumous Papers of the Pickwick Club*, the most successful seems to have been that by P. Grolier (Paris, Hachette, 2 vols., 1859): there were seventeen reprintings before 1900.

326 SAND TO FLAUBERT

Nohant, 19 July [18]72

Cher vieux troubadour,

We're going away as well, but we don't know where to yet. It's all one to me. I wanted to take my brood to Switzerland, but they prefer to go in the opposite direction, towards the sea. So be it – as long as we're travelling and get some bathing I'm wild with joy. Our two old troubadourships certainly are as unlike each other as possible. What bores you amuses me. I like movement and noise, and even annoyances so long as they're part and parcel of travelling. I'm much more sensitive to anything that disturbs the sedentary peace of home than I am to the normal, necessary upsets involved in locomotion. I'm exactly like my granddaughters, who are drunk with excitement beforehand without knowing why. But it's strange how children, while loving change, want to take their familiar surroundings, their favourite toys, with them into the outside world. Aurore packs for her dolls, while Gabrielle, who prefers animals, wants to take her rabbits, her puppy, and a piglet she makes a pet of until the time comes for her to eat it. *Such is life.*[1]

I think your trip will do you good despite your grumpiness. It will force you to rest your brain, and if you have to smoke less, what does it matter? Health above everything. I hope your niece makes you stir about a bit. She's to all intents and purposes your child, so she must have some authority over you unless the world's been turned upside-down.

I can't help you about a bookseller to hire books from. I consult Mario

Proth[2] about that sort of thing, but I don't know where he is at the moment. When you're next in Paris, get in touch with him and mention my name. He's a most obliging and devoted fellow, and lives at 2 rue Visconti. I think Charles-Edmond might be able to help you too. And Troubat.

Talking of whom, perhaps I did wrong to warn you against him. It's probably just that he's got something badly wrong with his brain. But still, it's a bit far-fetched to ask someone who works for the Maison Lévy to look after your interests there! I got a friend of mine a job there, and he promised to look into my accounts. But I had to give it up, because I was putting him in a position where he had to choose between letting me have the wool pulled over my eyes and losing his job, which he simply couldn't afford to do. And Troubat needs *his* job no less desperately. Besides, though I know Lévy drives a hard bargain, I really don't believe he's dishonest once he's signed his name to something. You're surprised because words aren't regarded as bonds. You're very naive. In business it's only documents that count. You and I are a couple of Don Quixotes, mon vieux troubadour, and we must resign ourselves to being got the better of by inn-keepers. That's life, and anyone who doesn't want to be deceived must go and live in the desert. One isn't really living at all if one avoids all the evil in this vale of tears. We have to take the rough with the smooth.

As for your *Saint Antoine*, with your permission I'll try to find you a publisher or a magazine the next time I'm in Paris. But we must talk about it and you must read it to me. Why not come and stay with us in September? I'll be there until the winter.

You ask what I'm doing now. Since I was in Paris I've written an article on Mademoiselle de Flaugergues which is to appear in *L'Opinion nationale*, together with a piece by herself;[3] and an article for *Le Temps* on Victor Hugo, Bouilhet, Leconte de Lisle and Pauline Viardot.[4] I do hope you'll be pleased with what I've said about your friend. I've done a second fantastic tale for the *Revue des Deux Mondes*, a story I wrote for the children;[5] and I've written about a hundred letters, mostly to repair the stupidities or alleviate the sufferings of fools of my acquaintance. Sloth is the plague of the present day, and one spends one's life working for people who won't work themselves. But I'm not complaining – I'm in excellent health! I plunge my 68 years and my whooping cough into the Indre and its chilly waterfall every day. When I'm no longer useful or agreeable to other people, I'd like to depart peacefully without a sigh, or at least with no more than a sigh over the poor human race: it doesn't amount to much, but I'm a part of it, and perhaps I don't amount to much either.

Je t'aime et je t'embrasse. My family, including Plauchut, do the same. He's coming with us on our travels. When we're settled for a few days somewhere I'll send you the address so that I can hear from you.

G. Sand

---

[1] In English in the original.

[2] Mario Proth (1832–91), journalist, founder of the *Revue internationale* (1859), was a con-

stant opponent of the Empire. After the revolution of 1870, he was a member of the cabinet and one of the editors of the *Journal officiel*.

³ For Mlle Flaugergues see Letter 291, Note 2. Her piece, entitled *Mes campagnes*, was published in *L'Opinion nationale*, 15–21 December 1872, with a *Notice préliminaire* by George Sand. The *Notice* was reprinted in Sand's *Dernières Pages*, pp. 221–47.

⁴ See Letter 315, Note 2, and Letter 355, Note 7.

⁵ For some time, Sand had been in the habit of composing fantastic tales for the entertainment and instruction of her granddaughters. One of the first, *La Reine Coax*, had appeared in *La Revue des Deux Mondes* for 1 June 1872; the second, *Le Nuage rose*, followed on 1 August. Finally, fourteen tales were published in two volumes under the title *Contes d'une grand-mère* (1873 and 1876).

*

The stay at Luchon, where he had arrived on 7 July, did not bring Flaubert the rest he had hoped for. Harassed by noise that prevented his working, he left the Maison Binos for the Maison Bonnette. There he could busy himself with his revision of *Le Sexe faible*, which he hoped would be put on at the Vaudeville and "earn a little money for Bouilhet's heir." Leaving Luchon on 9 August, he spent a few days in Paris, documenting himself for his new novel; and returned to Croisset on Wednesday 14th.

George Sand's vacation was very different. Leaving Nohant on 25 July, she reached Cabourg on the 28th, via Paris and Trouville. She spent several happy weeks there with her family, sea bathing, enjoying herself, making excursions, and having pleasant company. They returned by way of Normandy, Maine, and a part of Berry that was largely unfamiliar to Sand, and were back at Nohant on 23 August. There she found a letter from Flaubert, written the previous day.

327   FLAUBERT TO SAND

Croisset, [22 August 1872]
Thursday

Chère maître,

In the letter I had from you at Luchon a month ago, you told me that you were packing your bags, and that was all. No news since then. "I heard tell," as good old Brantôme used to say, that you were in Cabourg? When do you leave there? Where will you go then – to Paris or Nohant? A problem.

As for me, I shan't be at Croisset from the 1st to the 20th or 25th of September. I have to vagabond a bit, on "business". I'll be passing through Paris, so write to me at 4 rue Murillo.

I'd love to see you. First of all simply to see you, and then to read you *Saint Antoine*, and then to talk with you about another, more important book, etc. etc., and to have long chats about a thousand things, just the two of us.

Until then, je vous embrasse à deux bras et sur les deux joues.

Votre vieux troubadour

Gve Flaubert

328 SAND TO FLAUBERT

Nohant, 31 August [18]72

Mon vieux troubadour,

Here we are, home again after a month indeed spent in Cabourg, where we alighted more by luck than judgment. We all, Plauchut included, had some lovely sea bathing, and often talked about you with Mme Pasca,[1] who had the next table and the next bedroom to ours. We all came home in splendid health, and are very glad to be in our old Nohant again, though we'd been glad enough to leave it for a while for a change of air.

I've got back to ordinary working, and go on taking my dips in the river, but no one else will come with me – it's too cold. Who would think, to look at me, and considering my peaceful old age, that I still dote on excess?

But my ruling passion is really my Aurore. My life hangs upon hers. She was so sweet while we were travelling – so cheerful, so grateful for everything that was done to amuse her, taking such an intelligent interest in all she saw, that she's a constant source of true, congenial company. I'm not very "literary", am I? Despise me if you like, but go on loving me.

I don't know if I'll find you in Paris when I go there for my play. I haven't yet settled with the Odéon about the date of the production. I'm waiting for Duquesnel to arrange the final reading. And then I'm expecting Pauline Viardot here around September 20th, and Turgenev as well, I hope. Couldn't you come too? It would be so nice, and make everything complete.

Clinging to this hope, je t'aime et t'embrasse de toute mon âme, and my children join me in loving you and asking you to come.

G. Sand

[1] A well-known actress, a friend of Flaubert.

329 FLAUBERT TO SAND

[Paris] rue Murillo 4
Sunday, 15 September [1872]

No, chère maître, I shan't come to Nohant now, since I've already tramped around a good deal this summer. For what will soon be three months I've scarcely lived in my own house. I *must* get back there.

How I long to see *you* there for a while, to talk about many things one can't say in letters! First of all I'd like to read you *Saint Antoine*, and then talk to you about another book that I'm about to begin, and which will take me five years at least!

When does your play go into rehearsal at the Odéon? When do you come to Paris? It seems to me you might reserve me two or three days, in the midst of your theatre business?

I'm afraid you may have trouble with the amiable Duquesnel. Just now he's suing Sarah Bernhardt.[1] A fine beginning! The company will be seeing more of the same: I *know* him!

One of these days, since we're talking theatre, I'm going to read Carvalho[2] *Le Sexe faible*, a prose comedy by Bouilhet that I've touched up a little. But I have no hope. In any case, never have I been more indifferent about publicity. The success of *L'Homme-Femme*[3] (and its satellites) has been the last straw: my demoralization is now complete. And today, as I was passing the Vaudeville, I saw on the posters: "*Ragabas* [sic], 224th performance!"[4]

All this reinforces my . . . Religion. You'll understand what I mean.

Your troubadour is now studying medical theory – most amusing. After that, I'll go on to make other preparations.[5]

Our nice Turgenev will soon be on his way to you. I miss him, and wish I could be there with you all.

Embrassez pour moi tous les vôtres, chère maître, and arrange things so that we can see each other for a good long while, alone and in peace.

Tout à vous, encore.

Gve Flaubert

[1] Sarah Bernhardt had broken her contract with the Odéon in the midst of the run of *Ruy Blas*, and signed an agreement with the Théâtre-Français. Duquesnel had sued her, and she was ordered to pay the Odéon a fine of 5,000 francs.

[2] Léon Carvaille, known as "Carvalho" (1825–97), was manager of the Théâtre du Vaudeville.

[3] The quarrel about *L'Homme-Femme* was the "great literary event" of the year. Inspired by several recent *crimes passionnels*, Henry d'Ideville had published in *Le Soir* for 15 May 1872 an article entitled "L'Homme qui tue et l'homme qui pardonne", in which he protested against the French law authorizing a husband to kill his wife if she is discovered in the act of committing adultery. A. Dumas *fils* replied to this article in a volume of 177 pages, *L'Homme-Femme*, published on 16 July and enormously successful: 37 reprintings in 1872 alone. Whereas d'Ideville had advised pardoning the adulterous wife, Dumas demanded that she be punished: his cry of "Kill her!" created a sensation. Flaubert was irritated by this quarrel, as may be seen in his scornful allusions to it in his correspondence: "It's enough to put you off adultery altogether," he wrote to Mme Roger des Genettes on 19 August. His allusion to "satellites" refers to the numerous books inspired by *L'Homme-Femme*, notably E. de Girardin's *L'Homme et la Femme, l'homme suzerain, la femme vassale*, published on 3 August and also extremely successful. Flaubert was doubtless unaware that G. Sand herself had participated in the quarrel: her most recent article for *Le Temps*, in the issue of 4 September, was entitled "*L'Homme et la femme*" (reprinted in *Impressions et Souvenirs*, p. 258).

[4] *Rabagas* (not *Ragabas*), comedy in five acts by Victorien Sardou, had opened at the Vaudeville on 1 February 1872.

[5] All for *Bouvard et Pécuchet*. Flaubert would later say that he had read at least 1,500 volumes for this novel.

*

Flaubert had returned to Paris on 7 September to document himself for *Bouvard et Pécuchet* and to have *Saint Antoine* copied. "The copyists were out of their minds with bewilderment and exhaustion," he wrote on the 14th, with obvious satisfaction, to his niece. "They told me it was too much for them, and made them positively ill."

It was during this stay in Paris that he was visited by the publisher Georges Charpentier, who offered to buy from Lévy the rights to all his books. As usual, Flaubert included Bouilhet's interests along with his own, and asked that there be an edition of his friend's complete works. For the time being the matter remained open.

Back at Croisset on the 22nd, he resumed his reading, sometimes for eight or ten hours a day. His only companion was the young greyhound Julio (named after Juliet Herbert), a recent gift from his new friend Edmond Laporte.

George Sand, meanwhile, was at Nohant, writing articles for *Le Temps* while prolonging, in a way, the vacation spent at Cabourg. "All through September we had fifteen or twenty house guests, with dancing, marionettes, and especially music," she wrote to Mme Adam on 16 October. "Especially music" indeed: Mme Viardot had arrived, with her daughters, on September 25th. Turgenev soon joined them. Following her guests' departure on 3 October Mme Sand set to work to revise her play, *Mademoiselle La Quintinie*.

Throughout this period, there were no letters between Croisset and Nohant. It was George Sand who finally broke the silence, when she read in the newspapers of the death of Théophile Gautier on 23 October.

330 SAND TO FLAUBERT

Nohant, 26 October [18]72

Cher ami,

Another sorrow for you, no less grievous for being foreseen. Poor Théo – I pity him very much, not because he's dead but because he wasn't really alive for the last twenty years. If he *had* agreed to live, to exist, to act, to forget his intellectual side for a while in order to preserve his physical person,[1] he might still be alive now and for some time to come, developing the talents he treated too much as a barren and unprofitable treasure. It's said he suffered a great deal from deprivation. I can understand that, during the siege. But afterwards? Why and how?

I'm worried at not hearing from you for so long. Are you in Croisset? You'll have had to go to Paris for your poor friend's funeral. All these painful partings! But I don't like to see you becoming so unsociable and discontented with life in general. It strikes me you have too strong a tendency to regard happiness as possible, so that the absence of happiness, which is our chronic state, surprises and angers you. You avoid your friends, you bury yourself in work, and time spent on loving or on letting yourself be loved you regard as wasted. Why didn't you come to see us with Mme Viardot and Turgenev? You like and admire them, you know all of us here adore you, and yet you run away and stay alone.

Well now, why don't you get married? Being alone is horrible, deadly, and it's cruel to those who love you, too. All your letters are so sad – they make my heart bleed. Isn't there some woman you love, or whom you'd like to love you? Have her to live with you. Or isn't there some young sprig somewhere of whom you might suppose yourself the father? Bring him up, make him your slave, forget yourself in him.

How shall I put it? – living for oneself is a bad thing. The keenest intellectual pleasure comes from being able to return to the self after being absent from it for a spell. But living all the time inside the self, that most tyrannical, demanding and capricious of companions – no, one shouldn't do it.

Please, please, listen to me! You're keeping an exuberant nature shut up in jail! You're trying to turn a kind and tender heart into a jaundiced misanthropist – though you'll never quite manage it. In short, I'm worried about you and am perhaps saying stupid things. But we live in cruel times and we shouldn't just accept and anathematize them. We should overcome and pity them. So. Je t'aime; do write.

I shan't be in Paris until I go for the production of *Mademoiselle La Quintinie* a month from now. Where will you be then?

[unsigned]

¹ Gautier's unhygienic habits were legendary.

*

"Why don't you get married?" It is not surprising that the "hermit of Croisset" was somewhat irritated by such counsel, well intended though it was. "Today I received, from Mme Sand, a letter about Théo that is very kind and contains much advice concerning myself," he wrote to Princesse Mathilde. "I'll confess to you, just between ourselves, that her perpetual pious optimism – her peculiar brand of logic, if you will – sometimes sets my teeth on edge. I'm going to answer her with some invective against democracy that will relieve my feelings." But Mme Sand was soon forgiven, and Flaubert's "invective against democracy" took the form of a magnificent eulogy of Gautier.

In their exchange about matrimony, the two troubadours were not at their best. George Sand, with her suggestion that Flaubert embrace domesticity, descended into obtuseness and sentimentality. Flaubert, while justly provoked, proposed, in turn, to "punish" her – as it were – with an attack on her principles. We may also feel that Flaubert could have refrained from condemning democracy – and George Sand's espousal of it – to Princesse Mathilde, who would have interpreted his view as being, in this regard, consonant with her own.

On each side, however, affection was undisturbed. George Sand was too magnanimous to take serious offence at Flaubert's tirades. As for Flaubert, we may recall – in this quite different context – his assertion to Louis Bouilhet, in the far-off days of 1855: that, after reading George Sand, he was "indignant for a quarter of an hour".

331 FLAUBERT TO SAND

[Croisset, 28–29 October 1872]
Monday night

Chère maître,

You guessed aright that there had been a redoubling of my grief, and your letter is sweet and kind. Thank you. And I embrace you even more warmly than usual.

Expected though it was, poor Théo's death leaves me heart-broken. With him, the last of my *intimate* friends is gone. The list is closed. Whom shall I see now when I go to Paris? Who is there to talk with about what interests me? I know thinkers (or at least people who are called such), but an *artist* – where is there one?

If you want my opinion, he died of disgust with the "putrefaction of the modern world". That was his expression, and he repeated it to me several times last winter. "I'm dying of the Commune," etc. September 4th inaugurated an order of things in which people like him have no place. You can't expect apples from orange trees. Makers of luxuries aren't needed in a society dominated by the *plebs*. How I miss him! He and Bouilhet have left a great void in my life, and nothing can replace them. Besides, he was so good, and, whatever they say, so *simple*! He will be recognized later (if anyone ever again cares about literature) as a great poet. Meanwhile he is an absolutely unknown writer. But then, so is Pierre Corneille.

He had two hatreds. In his youth, hatred of Philistines. That gave him his talent. In his maturity, hatred of the rabble. That killed him. He died of suppressed rage, of fury at being unable to speak his mind. He was *stifled* by Girardin, by Turgan, Fould, Dalloz.[1] And by the present Republic. I tell you this because I have seen some abominable things, and because I was perhaps the only man in whom he confided fully. He lacked the quality that is most important in life — for oneself as well as for others: *character*. His failure to be elected to the Academy[2] was a real source of grief to him. What weakness! What lack of self-esteem! To seek an honour, no matter what, seems to me an act of incomprehensible self-abasement!

That I missed his funeral was due to Catulle Mendès,[3] who sent me a telegram too late. There was a great crowd. A lot of idiots and rascals came to show off, as usual, and today being Monday, the day for theatre news in the papers, there will certainly be articles. He will make "good copy".

To sum up, I don't pity him. *I envy him.* For, frankly, life is not much fun.

No, I do not think of happiness as being possible — but tranquillity, yes. That's why I keep away from what irritates me. I am unsociable; therefore I flee Society, and find myself the better for doing so. A trip to Paris is a great undertaking for me, these days. As soon as I stir the water, the dregs rise up and becloud everything. The slightest discussion with anyone at all exasperates me, because I find everybody idiotic. My sense of justice is continually outraged. All talk is about politics — and *such* talk! Where is there the least sign of an idea? What is there to hold on to? What cause is there to be passionate about?

Still, I don't consider myself a monster of egoism. My *me* is so dispersed in my books that I spend whole days unaware of it. I have bad moments, it's true. But I pull myself together by reminding myself that at least nobody is bothering me — and soon I'm back on my feet. All in all, it seems to me that I'm following my natural path. Doesn't that mean I'm doing the right thing?

As for living with a woman, marrying, as you advise, it's a prospect I find fantastic. Why? *I have no idea.* But that's how it is. Perhaps you can explain. The feminine existence has never fitted in with mine. And then I'm not rich enough. And then, and then . . . Besides, I'm too old. And also too decent to inflict my person on another in perpetuity. Deep down, there's something of the priest in me that no one suspects. We'll go into all this much better in conversation than in a letter.

I'll see you in Paris in December. But in Paris one is constantly disturbed by "the Others". I wish you 300 performances of *Mademoiselle La Quintinie*. However, you'll have a lot of trouble with the Odéon. It's an odious place. I suffered horribly there last winter. Every time I've ventured into the world of action I've come a cropper. So – enough is enough! "Conceal your life," says Epictetus. My entire ambition now is to avoid trouble. And by doing that I'm certain to avoid causing any to others, which is saying much.

I'm working like a madman, reading about medicine, metaphysics, politics, everything. For I'm undertaking a work of enormous scope. It will be very long in the doing – a prospect I like.

For the past month I've been expecting Turgenev from one week to the next. But gout keeps preventing him from coming. Adieu, chère bon maître. Continue to love me.

Your old

Gve

[1] The poet Théophile Gautier had earned his living by journalism: Girardin, Dalloz and Turgan were editors of newspapers for which he wrote art and theatre criticism. Achille Fould, Finance Minister under Napoleon III, responsible for literary pensions, had always passed over Gautier: only a year before his death, when he had become old and decrepit, was the poet awarded three thousand francs a year by the new ministry. Gautier had also been helped by Princesse Mathilde, who had appointed him her "librarian", at six thousand francs a year.

[2] Gautier had made three unsuccessful attempts to be elected to the French Academy: in 1867, 1868, and 1869.

[3] The poet Catulle Mendès was Gautier's son-in-law, the husband of his second daughter, Judith.

*

There was no reply for a time, and Flaubert doubtless realized that Sand must have been displeased by his recent letters, so *disillusioned*. He wrote to Turgenev on 13 November: "The excellent Mme Sand is probably annoyed by my bad humour. I no longer have news from her."

But Mme Sand was very busy – with her pieces for *Le Temps*, and difficulties with the end of *Mademoiselle La Quintinie*. But on learning that the opening of that play had been postponed, she immediately interrupted her work to resume the dialogue.

332   SAND TO FLAUBERT

Nohant, 22 November [18]72

I don't think I'll be in Paris before February. My play has been put off because they're having difficulty finding an actor to play the lead.[1] I'm glad, for I didn't at all like the idea of leaving Nohant and my delightful walks and other occupations. This mild autumn is so good for old folks! A couple of hours from here we have some absolutely deserted forest that's as dry as a bone the morning after it rains, and where there are still flowers for me and insects for Maurice. The little girls scamper about like rabbits through heather taller than they are. Lord, how good life is when all you love is alive and active. You are the only "black speck"[2] in my emotional life, because you're sad and won't look at the sun any more. As for people I don't care about, I care just as little about any harm or folly they may inflict either on me or on themselves. They'll pass over like the rain. What is eternal is the sense of beauty in a good heart. And you've got both, dash it! – you've no right not to be happy! Perhaps it would have been better if the "feminine feeling" you say you've snapped your fingers at *had* found a place in your life. I know things "feminine" are noxious but perhaps to be happy one needs to have been unhappy first. I've been unhappy, and I know all about it. But then I'm so good at forgetting! Anyhow, happy or sad, I love you and keep on hoping to see you, even though you never mention coming yourself and are quick to reject any opportunity that offers. But we all love you just the same. We're not literary enough for you here, I know, but we love, and that gives life a purpose.

Is *Saint Antoine* finished, then, that you speak of a work of enormous scope? But if it's *Saint Antoine* himself who's going to spread his wings over the whole universe, I'm sure he can – it's a vast subject.

Je t'embrasse – should I still say "my old troubadour" when you're determined to turn into an old monk? Well, I'm still a troubadour – there's no getting away from it.

G. Sand

I'm sending you two novels[3] for your collection of my works. You don't *have* to read them just now if you're deep in serious matters.

[1] Francis Berton, the first choice, had to be replaced because of mental instability.
[2] In 1867, at a moment of early threats from Prussia, Napoleon III had said, in a speech, that "a few black specks threaten our horizon." The understatement had become an ironic cliché.
[3] *Francia* and *Nanon*.

333 FLAUBERT TO SAND

[Croisset, 25 November 1872]
[Monday night, 11 o'clock]

[. . .]¹

This is for your dear *Maman*.

At five o'clock today the postman brought me your two volumes. I'm going to begin *Nanon* at once – I'm very curious about it.

And don't worry any more about your troubadour, who quite frankly has been acting like a silly brute. But I hope to get over it. I've had a number of sombre periods in the past, and always come out of them. Everything wears itself out, the spleen along with the rest.

I expressed myself badly. I didn't say that I scorned "feminine feeling", but that women, physically speaking, had never been part of my usual way of life – which is quite a different matter. I have *loved* more than anyone – a presumptuous statement, which means "like anybody else, and perhaps even more than just anybody". I have experienced all kinds of affection: "storms of the heart" have rained down on me. And then chance, the force of circumstances, has gradually intensified my solitude, until now I am alone, utterly alone.

On my income I could not support a wife, and even to live in Paris for half the year is beyond my means. So I cannot change my way of life.

How I envy your son! How pleasant his life is, so well-ordered and wholesome! Did I really not tell you that *Saint Antoine* has been finished since June? What I am meditating at the moment is a more considerable work, with an element of what I hope will be comedy. It would take too long to explain it to you in writing. We'll talk about it when we're together.

Adieu, chère bon maître adorable. A vous avec mes meilleures tendresses. votre vieux

Gve Flaubert

perpetually *H*indignant like Saint Polycarp

Do you know, in the history of the entire universe, including that of the Botocudos,² anything more stupid than the gentlemen of the Right in the National Assembly? They don't like to hear the simple, empty word "Republic", and they consider Thiers "too progressive"!³ What profundity! What confusion! What fantasy!

---

¹ The text seems to be that of the second part of a letter written by Flaubert to Maurice Sand, thanking him for his recently published novel, *L'Augusta*. (See the first paragraph of Letter 335.) The present editor has not found the autograph: the date and the hour have been taken from the Conard edition of Flaubert's works.

² A tribe of once-cannibal Brazilian Indians.

³ On 13 November, in a presidential message to the Assembly, Thiers had come out openly for the Republic, provoking indignation from the Right.

334 FLAUBERT TO SAND

[Croisset, 26 November 1872]
Tuesday night, 11 o'clock

Chère maître,

A night and a day – all spent with you! I finished *Nanon* at 4 this morning and *Francia* at 3 this afternoon. It's all still dancing around in my head. I'm going to try to collect my thoughts so that I can talk to you about these two fine books. They have "done me good." So, thank you, chère bon maître. Yes, it has been like a great breath of fresh air; and, after being moved to tears, I feel revived.

In *Nanon*, I was first of all charmed by the style, by the thousand simple, strong things that are present in the texture of the work and that constitute it, such as this: "Comme la somme me parut énorme, la bête me sembla belle," etc.[1] And then I stopped paying attention to such things: I was caught up, like the most ordinary reader. (However, I don't believe that the ordinary reader is capable of admiring you as much as I.) Then, with *Le Mouton* [*The Sheep*], the utter enchantment began. What a marvel, the first hundred pages! The life of the monks, the first relations between Emilien and Nanon, the fright caused by the brigands. And the incarceration of Père Fructueux, who might easily have been a hackneyed character but isn't so at all. Page 113 – what a page! And how difficult it must have been not to overdo it!

"A partir de ce jour-là *je sentis du bonheur dans tout* et comme une joie d'être au monde"! . . .[2]

I love your lawyer Cortejoux, with his surge of anger, and then the way he welcomes Nanon. But what seems to me quite simply *sublime* is Dumont's drunkenness when it comes to freeing Emilien. I know nothing more pathetic, more *grand*. It's heart-rending: two or three times I found myself saying aloud – "*Nom de Dieu, comme c'est beau!*"

La Roche aux Fades is an exquisite idyll. One longs to share the life of those three fine people.

The interest flags a little, I think, when Nanon decides to grow rich? Doesn't she become too strong-minded, too intelligent?

Nor do I care for the episode of the robbers. But Emilien's reappearance with his arm amputated affected me again, and I shed a tear over the last page, at the portrait of the Marquise de Franqueville in her old age.

Let me mention one or two doubts. Emilien seems to me rather too strong on political philosophy. At that time, were there really people with such lofty views? Same objection to the Prior, whom I find charming, however, especially in the middle of the book. How well it's all put together and presented – so captivating and charming! What a great person you are! Such power!

So: great kisses on both cheeks – the kind that a nurse gives a baby – and on to *Francia*!

A different style, but no less good. First of all, I admire your Dodore. This is the first time anyone has painted a true picture of a Paris street urchin. He's not goody-goody, not too nasty, not too stagey. The dialogue with his sister when he consents to her being "kept" is a real tour de force. Your madame de Thièvre, fussing with her shawl on her fat shoulders: straight out of the Restoration!

And the uncle who wants to steal his nephew's grisette! And Antoine, the fine big tinsmith, so polite in the theatre! The Russian is a simple soul, a "natural", not easy to portray.

When I saw Francia plunge her dagger into his heart I frowned, fearing this was going to be a classic case of revenge, untrue to that excellent girl's delightful character. But not at all! I was mistaken. This unconscious murder completes your heroine.

What strikes me in this book is that it is very lively and utterly *right*. One feels one is living in the period.

I thank you from the bottom of my heart for this double reading pleasure. It has relaxed me. So: everything isn't dead! There is still some Beauty and Goodness in the world! You edify me, and fill me with admiration! *Voilà!*[3]

Two books like these seem to me more important events than Rochefort's civil marriage,[4] for example. But here I am, beginning to bellow again about the times I live in – a very silly way to go on. I prefer to think of *you*, et vous dire que je vous chéris et vous embrasse.

Votre vieux

Gve Flaubert

[1] "As the sum seemed enormous to me, the animal seemed handsome."

[2] "From that day on, I found happiness everywhere – a kind of joy at being in the world."

[3] One sometimes suspects that Flaubert's admiring letters to Sand about her work are entirely dictated by friendship. This time, however, we can be sure of his sincerity: on 30 November he wrote to Princesse Mathilde: "Last week Madame Sand sent me two of her books, *Nanon* and *Francia*, which I have read with pleasure." One understands that Flaubert should have enjoyed them. *Francia* may be somewhat weak, but *Nanon* is a very good novel.

[The foregoing is one of M. Jacobs' rare expressions of opinion concerning George Sand's work. F.S.]

[4] Henri Rochefort (former editor of *La Lanterne* – cf. Letter 130, Note 1) had been condemned to deportation to New Caledonia because of the articles he had published during the Commune; but his poor state of health had so far impeded the execution of the sentence. From his internment in the citadel of Saint-Martin-de-Ré, he was taken on 4 November 1872 to Versailles, where on the 6th he was married to Mlle Renaud, the mother of his several children. It was a marriage *in extremis*: the bride died a few days later. Rochefort was returned to his prison immediately after the ceremony.

335   SAND TO FLAUBERT

Nohant, 27 November [18]72

Your letter to Maurice makes him very happy and proud. There's no one else who could give him so much pleasure, or whose encouragement means more to him. I thank you for his letter too, for I value it just as he does.

What, you've finished *Saint Antoine*? Well, we'll have to see about a publisher, for I presume you're not doing anything about it? But you can't just leave it lying about. You don't want anything to do with Lévy, but there are others. Just say the word and I'll go ahead, just as if I were acting for myself.

You promise me you'll get better in due course. But meanwhile you won't do anything to shake your ideas up. Come and read me *Saint Antoine* and we'll talk about getting it published. What effort is required for a man to come here from Croisset? If you don't want to come when we're in the midst of celebrations and merrymaking, come while the weather's mild and I'm alone.

Toute la famille t'embrasse.

Ton vieux troubadour

G. Sand

*

That letter had scarcely gone off when Flaubert's of the 26th arrived at Nohant. Sand wrote in her diary: "A good letter from Flaubert, who has read *Nanon* and *Francia* and likes them both."

336   SAND TO FLAUBERT

Nohant, 29 November [18]72

You spoil me. The novels had been wrapped up and addressed to you for a week and I didn't dare send them. I was afraid I might interrupt your train of thought and annoy you. And you dropped everything to read first Maurice and then me. We'd feel guilty if we weren't egoists, and delighted to have a reader worth ten thousand others. It's a great boon, because Maurice and I labour away in the wilderness with only one another to tell us if what we do succeeds or fails, just exchanging our own criticism and bereft of any contact with recognized judges. Michel never lets us know for a year or two whether anything has *sold*. As for Buloz, whenever we have dealings with him he always says it's bad or nothing special. Charles-Edmond is the only one who encourages us by actually asking for copy. So we write without an audience in mind – not necessarily a bad thing, but carried too far in our case. So encouragement from you puts new heart into us – not that we ever lose heart, but it often gets rather sad. Whereas you make it brilliant and gay and robust.

I was right, then, not to throw *Nanon* on the fire, as I was ready to do before Charles-Edmond came and told me it was very good and he wanted it for his paper.

So I send you my thanks, and return your kisses, especially for *Francia*, which Buloz published only reluctantly and for want of anything better.[1] I'm not usually spoiled, you see. But I never let that kind of thing vex me, and I don't talk about it. That's how things are, and it's only natural. When literature is treated as a kind of merchandise, the vendor is interested only in the customer, and if the customer belittles the goods the vendor tells the author his product isn't popular. The republic of letters is nothing but a fair at which books are sold. Our only virtue is not to make concessions to publishers, so let us hang on to that and live in peace, even with curmudgeonly publishers. It's not they who're to blame. They'd have taste if the public did.

So now I've unburdened myself, and we can concentrate our talk on what to do about *Saint Antoine*, bearing in mind that the publishers are bound to be stupid. Lévy isn't, but you've quarrelled with him. Will you come here? Or wait till I go to Paris? But when will that be? I don't know. I'm rather afraid of bronchitis in the winter, and travel only when it's absolutely necessary for reasons of state.

I don't think they're going to do *Mademoiselle La Quintinie*. The censors have pronounced it a "masterpiece of the highest and soundest morality", but said they couldn't "take the responsibility" of authorizing its production. So it "has to go higher up" – that is, to the minister, who'll send it to General Ladmirault.[2] It's enough to make a cat laugh. But I won't agree to all that – I'd rather everyone just did nothing *jusqu'à nouvel ordre*. And if the "new order" is a clerical monarchy, things will be even worse. As far as I personally am concerned, it's all one to me if I'm suppressed – but what about the future of our generation?

[unsigned]

[1] Before appearing as a volume, *Francia* had been printed in *La Revue des Deux Mondes*, 1 May – 1 June 1872.

[2] The words quoted are taken more or less literally from a letter of 26 November from Charles-Edmond to Sand. The Minister in question was Jules Simon, Minister of Fine Arts and Religion. General Ladmirault, as military governor of Paris (the city was still officially in a state of siege), had the final say about all questions of "public order".

337 FLAUBERT TO SAND

[Croisset, 4 December 1872]
Wednesday 3

Chère maître,

Let me quote a sentence from your last letter. It's about Lévy, who never says anything to you about your books, and about Buloz, who suavely disparages them: "The publishers would have taste if the public did." Or if the public obliged them to have it – which is asking the impossible. But we can at least require that the publisher be polite, and that he not lie boldly to our faces in order to exploit us the more. Publishers have "literary ideas", don't you know, and so do theatre managers. Both claim to be connoisseurs. And a fine result they produce, with their combination of aesthetics and commerce!

Why does Lévy, who has made, and continues to make, every day, a lot of money out of you and old Dumas (I use the two of you as examples) disparage you both as much as he can? Your latest book is *always* "inferior to the one before". I'll be hanged if that's not his way. Lévy has academic tastes: he prefers writers like Ponsard and Octave Feuillet. I've earned more money for him than Cuvillier-Fleury, haven't I? Well, make that same comparison between you and me, and you'll see what's coming to you. You're not unaware that he has refused my work:[1] he didn't want to sell more than 1,200 copies of *Dernières Chansons*. And the 800 that remain are in my niece's attic in the rue de Clichy! I'm being very intolerant about this, I know. But I confess that his behaviour simply enraged me. It seems to me that my writing might be treated with greater respect by a man for whom I've made a little money. But publishers deal only with infants, and take advantage of them. That's what it amounts to.

Since I never want to speak to said Michel again, my nephew Commanville is going to conclude my business with him. I'm going to pay him for the printing of *Dernières Chansons* – about 1,500 francs – and then I'll be through with him.

Why publish, in these abominable times? To earn money? What a joke! As though the money were an adequate reward for one's work! As if it could be! It may be, when Speculation is abolished. Until then, no! And besides, how can one weigh the Labour? Or assess the Effort? Then there remains the commercial value of the book. To determine that, it would be necessary to abolish all the middlemen standing between Producer and Purchaser. And even so, this question is essentially insoluble. Because I write (speaking as a self-respecting author) not for the reader of today, but for all readers as long as language exists. Therefore: my merchandise cannot be consumed at once, because it was not created exclusively for my contemporaries. Thus my usefulness remains imponderable, and consequently cannot be paid for.

So: why publish? To be understood, applauded? But you yourself, the great George Sand, confess that your life is one of solitude.

Is there, now, I don't say admiration or understanding, but any sign of the slightest *attention* being paid to works of art? Where is there a critic who actually reads the book he judges?

Ten years from now perhaps no one will know how to make a pair of shoes, so frightfully stupid is everyone becoming! All this is to tell you that until better times (in whose advent I have no faith) I shall keep *Saint Antoine* in a cupboard. If I do allow it to be published, I'd prefer that it came out at the same time as another book that is completely different. I am working on one now that may possibly constitute its counterpart. Conclusion: the best thing to do is to keep calm.

Why doesn't Duquesnel go and see General Ladmirault, Jules Simon, Thiers himself? It seems to me it's up to him to take such a step. What a wonderful thing is censorship! It will always exist – of that we can be sure: it always has existed. Didn't our friend the younger Dumas make an amusing paradox, lauding its benefits, in his preface to *La Dame aux camélias*?[2]

And you wish I weren't depressed! I suspect that we'll soon be seeing more abominable things, thanks to the obdurate ineptitude of the Right. Even our worldly Normans here, the most conservative people in the world, are leaning towards the Left – very markedly!

If the bourgeoisie were to be consulted now, they'd make old Thiers king of France. And were Thiers out of the running, they'd throw themselves into the arms of Gambetta. I'm afraid they may soon do so in any case.

I console myself by reflecting that next Thursday I'll be 51.

If you're not coming to Paris in February, I'll come to see you in January before returning to the Parc Monceau. I've made myself that promise.[3]

The princess has written to ask me whether you're at Nohant. She wants to write to you.

I have just read *Nanon* to my niece, and she's enchanted by it. What strikes her is its *youthfulness*. That seems to me a sound observation. It's a marvellous book. And so is *Francia*: though simpler, it's perhaps even more successful, more completely realized as a work of literature.

This week I've been reading *L'Illustre docteur Mathéus*, by Erckmann-Chatrian.[4] What vulgarity! Those two fellows have revoltingly plebeian souls.

Adieu, chère bon maître.

Votre vieux Troubadour vous embrasse.

[unsigned]

I keep thinking of Théo. I can't get over this loss.

[1] "*refusé ma copie*". This is not entirely clear. Flaubert was proud of his preface to *Dernières Chansons* – the only preface he ever wrote. Apparently the phrase reflects his indignation that Lévy, by restricting the size and sale of the edition (his reason for doing so is not stated), thus belittled the preface as well, and ruined any possibility of its becoming properly known.

[2] Dumas, in the preface to the 1868 edition of *La Dame aux camélias*, writes ironically of his troubles with the censor: it would be wrong, he says, to abolish that office, because in the long run it quite often brings fame and success to the work it has tried to ban or mutilate.

[3] A few days earlier, on 30 November 1872, Flaubert had written again to Princesse Mathilde: "[Mme Sand] is doing all she can to raise my morale, and keeps inviting me to visit her. But for the moment I'm too dull and too depressed to accept. It would be cruel to inflict my company on people I love."

[4] A novel first published in 1859. Erckmann-Chatrian was the pen name of the "two fellows" who were its authors: Emile Erckmann (1822–99) and Alexandre Chatrian (1826–90), who collaborated on many works.

338 SAND TO FLAUBERT

Nohant, 8 December [18]72

Well, if you're in the ideal state of having a future book in mind, if you're working on something you can do confidently and with conviction, there'll be no more anger and sadness. Let's look at the facts logically. I myself have arrived at a very satisfactory and philosophical state of serenity, and I wasn't exaggerating at all when I said that no injury or indifference coming from others can really affect me any more. Not only can they not prevent me from being happy outside literature, but they can't stop me enjoying being a writer and getting great pleasure from my work. Were you pleased with my two novels? That's enough reward for me. I think they're good too, and the silence that has come to fill my life (I must admit I asked for it) echoes with a kindly voice. To have that voice speaking to me is enough. My ambition has never flown as high as yours. You want to write for all time; I think *I* shall be completely forgotten, perhaps severely denigrated, in fifty years' time. That's the natural fate of things that are not of the highest order, and I have never thought my work was of the highest order. What I've tried to do is rather to act upon my contemporaries, even if I influence only a few, and make them share my idea of goodness and poetry. Up to a point I've attained this goal; at least I've done and continue to do my best to reach it; and my reward is to draw always a little nearer.

So much for me. For you, as I can clearly see, the goal is much greater and success more distant. That only means you ought to be even calmer and more contented than I am, so as to be more in harmony with yourself than you are. Your temporary rages are good. They're the result of a generous temperament, and as they're neither malicious nor vindictive I like them! But your sadness, your weeks and weeks of spleen, I don't understand, and I don't like them at all. I've always thought, and think still, that they stem from too much isolation, too great a detachment from the ordinary bonds of life.

You dispose of powerful arguments to answer me, so powerful that you're bound to win the day. But look inside yourself and answer me, if only to assuage the anxiety I often feel on your account: I don't want you to burn yourself away. You're fifty years old; almost the same age as my son. He's in the prime of life, at his peak, and you can be, too, if you don't overheat the oven of ideas. Why do you often say you wish you were dead? Don't you believe in your work? Do you let yourself be influenced by passing circumstance? Perhaps. We are not gods, and something inside us, some weakness or whim, occasionally clouds our theodicy.[1] But victory grows easier every day when one is sure of loving logic and truth. Sometimes it even anticipates occasions of anger, resentment and discouragement, and conquers them in advance.

All that's easy enough, it seems to me, when it's a matter of governing ourselves. The causes of really great sorrow lie elsewhere, in the spectacle of the history unfolding all around us. The eternal struggle of barbarism against civilization is a subject of much grief to those who have cast off the element of barbarity and are in advance of their time. But even in that great pain and in its secret angers there is a great stimulus, which gives us new heart by inspiring us with the need to act. If it weren't for that I confess I would just give up.

I've had plenty of compliments in my life, in the days when people were still concerned about literature. But I was always nervous of them when they came from people I didn't know; they made me too uncertain of myself. As for money, I've earned enough to make me rich. If I'm *not* rich it's because I haven't wanted to be – what Lévy makes for me is enough (he's better than you give him credit for). What I'd like is to devote myself entirely to botany; that would be heaven on earth for me. But I mustn't. It wouldn't do anyone any good but myself, and if sorrow is good for anything it's to defend us from egoism. So – we oughtn't to curse or despise life. We oughtn't to wear it out deliberately. You are in love with justice – start by being just to yourself. You owe it to yourself to preserve and develop what you are.

Listen, I'm terribly fond of you; I think of you every day and in connection with everything; I think about you even when I'm working. I've managed to acquire certain mental benefits which you deserve more than I do and of which you must make longer use. Remember too that my spirit is often close to yours, and that it wishes you long life and an inspiration that will bring you many true delights.

You've promised to come, and that is cause for joy and celebration in my family and in my heart.

Ton vieux troubadour

You must tell me all about Michel's misbehaviour. If he has done you any wrong I'll try to see he puts it right.

¹ This complex word, coined by Leibnitz, indicates a branch of philosophy concerned with the existence of good and evil in the divine context.

339   FLAUBERT TO SAND

[Croisset,]12 December [1872]

Chère bon maître,

Don't worry about Lévy, and let's speak no more of him. He doesn't deserve to occupy our thoughts for a minute. He wounded me deeply in a sensitive spot: the memory of my poor Bouilhet. That is irreparable. I am not a Christian, and cannot achieve the hypocrisy of forgiveness. All I can do is to have no further dealings with him. That's the entire situation. I hope never to see him again. Amen.

And don't take the dramas of my "ire" too seriously. Don't go thinking I'm counting on Posterity to avenge the "indifference" of my contemporaries. I meant only this: when you don't address yourself to the Crowd, it's only right that the Crowd shouldn't reward you. That's Economics. Now I maintain that a work of art (worthy of the name and conscientiously executed) cannot be evaluated, has no commercial worth, and cannot be adequately compensated. Conclusion: if the artist has no money of his own, he *has* to starve. A charming situation.

And people talk about the independence of literature! They say that the Writer, because he no longer receives a pension from some grandee, is much freer, much nobler. His entire nobility in today's society consists in being the equal of a grocer. Great progress! As for me, you say "Look at the facts logically:" but there's the difficulty.

I am not at all *sure* of writing good things, or that the book I'm at present thinking about will turn out well. That doesn't stop me from undertaking it. I think the idea is original – no more than that. And since I hope to spit out into it the bile that's choking me – in other words, utter a few truths – I hope in this way to purge myself and thereafter be more Olympian. A quality I lack completely at present. Ah! How I wish I could admire myself!

Today I enter my 52nd year, et je tiens à vous embrasser aujourd'hui. I do so with the greatest affection, because I know you truly love me.

Votre vieux troubadour

Gve Flaubert

Another bereavement. Last Monday I was chief mourner at the funeral of Père Pouchet.[1] I had to console his son Georges, who was sobbing his heart out. The father led a very worthy life: I wept for him too. Nothing but funerals! It's enough to turn one into an undertaker!

[1] The reader will recall the elder Pouchet's emotion on meeting Mme Sand. See Letter 56.

*

On 29 or 30 December 1872 Flaubert returned to Paris for his usual winter stay.

CHAPTER IX

1873

[Paris] 4, rue Murillo
[3 January 1873]
Friday evening

Chère bon maître,

To you and yours I send all imaginable good wishes for the New Year. But what, indeed, *is* imaginable? It seems to me you have everything!

Here I am, back in Paris, far from cheerful. But I did well to leave Croisset: I've been doing a little too much reading there these past three months, and needed a change of air. For the last few days I've been trotting around like a country postman, and am beginning to sleep again.

I still intend to come and see you at the end of this month. If, that is, you don't plan to come to Paris at all this winter.

Mille tendresses profondes de votre vieux

Gve Flaubert

qui vous chérit.

Nohant, 8 January [18]73

Yes, yes, mon vieux, you must come and see me. I don't expect to go to Paris before the end of the winter, and we don't really see each other properly there. Bring me *Saint Antoine*; I want to hear it and live it with you. And I want to welcome you with all my soul, and so does Maurice. Lina is fond of you too, and our little ones haven't forgotten you. I long for you to see how sweet and interesting my Aurore has grown. There's nothing new to tell you about me. I live so little in myself. That will be a good reason for you to talk to me about what interests me more, namely you. Let me know when you're coming so that I can spare you the awful coach journey from Châteauroux to Nohant. If you can bring Turgenev with you we'll be very glad and you'll have the most delightful travelling companion. Have you read *Fathers and Sons*?[1] Isn't it marvellous!

Come now, I really hope to see you this time. And I think our air will do you good. We're having beautiful weather!

Ton vieux camarade qui t'aime.

G. Sand

Six kisses to wish you a happy New Year.

[1] This novel, published in Russian in 1860, had been translated into French by Turgenev himself and published in that language in 1863.

342 FLAUBERT TO SAND

[Paris] 15 [January 1873]
Wednesday evening

Chère maître,

When I've recovered from my grippe I'll come to see you. But at the moment I'm too ill, and repulsive with my cough and my handkerchiefs.

I passed your invitation on to Turgenev. He would love to come with me. But is he possibly afraid of a relapse?

I'm still not very merry. The nonsense spawned by Badinguet's death is inconceivable.[1] In the past it would have made me laugh. Now such silliness makes me indignant. Have I become too moral? I've lost my sense of comedy – and perhaps of Truth!

Mille tendresses de votre vieux

Gve Flaubert

qui vous embrasse.

[1] The ex-emperor Napoleon III had died in Chislehurst, England, on 9 January 1873, following a bladder operation.

343 SAND TO FLAUBERT

Nohant, 18 January [1873]

You're not to be ill and you're not to be grumpy, mon vieux chéri troubadour. You're to cough, blow your nose, get better and say that France may be mad, mankind may be stupid, and we may be animals not properly finished, but just the same we have to love one another, ourselves, our species, and especially our friends. There are times when I feel very sad. But I look at my flowers, at the two little girls who are always smiling, at their charming mother, and at my good hard-working son whom the crack of doom would find hunting and cataloguing specimens and performing his allotted task every day, and being merry as a cricket in his rare moments of leisure.

This morning he said to me: "Tell Flaubert to come and I'll knock off work straight away. I'll do some puppet plays for him and force him to laugh."

Living with others keeps one from brooding. You're too much alone. Come here and be loved among us as fast as you can.

G. Sand

344 FLAUBERT TO SAND

[Paris,] 3 February [1873]
Monday evening

Chère maître,

Does it seem that I've forgotten you, and don't want to make the trip to Nohant? Nothing of the kind! But for the past month, whenever I've gone out I've had a return of the grippe, each time more severe. I have a horrible cough and soil one handkerchief after another. When will it end?

I've decided not to leave the house until I'm completely cured. And I'm still waiting for some word from the Bouilhet fountain committee! For what will soon be two months it's been impossible to get six inhabitants of Rouen to meet together in Rouen! That's friendship for you.

Life is one great difficulty! The slightest thing calls for enormous effort. However, something pleasant happened recently. I've had proof that I've made considerable trouble for His Excellency Michel Lévy. That scoundrel is so naive in his immorality that he doesn't even suspect the harm he's done me. I'll tell you all this in detail. Thinking me a poor insignificant fellow, he did what he pleased. Well, I'm taking revenge on behalf of all poor insignificant fellows. I'm taking a high hand with the gentlemen in the publishing business. I'm letting them keep climbing my stairs, and don't give them a definite answer, as I'm determined not to sign with any of them.[1] Because I'm fed up: and it will be many a long year before I burden the presses again.

At the moment I'm reading chemistry (without understanding a word) and medicine (Raspail); not to mention Gressent's *Le Potager moderne* and Gasparin's *L'Agriculture*.[2] In this connection it would be kind of Maurice to put together some of his experiences in husbandry for me. I'd like to know the *mistakes* he made, and the *reasoning* that underlay such mistakes.

What information *don't* I need for this book! I came to Paris this winter to collect some of it. But if my frightful cold persists, my stay here will have been fruitless. Am I going to become like the canon of Poitiers, mentioned by Montaigne, who didn't leave his room for 30 years, "being oppressed by melancholy," and who was nevertheless in excellent health "except for a cold that settled in his stomach"?[3] This by way of telling you that I see almost no one. Besides, who *is* there to see? The War thinned the ranks.

Only our good Turgenev gives me unalloyed pleasure. What a man! Such conversation! Such taste! I read *Saint Antoine* to him: he seemed to like it, and made a couple of very judicious comments.

I haven't been able to get your article on Badinguet: I count ón reading it chez vous.[4]

Speaking of reading, I have just swallowed *all* of the odious Joseph de Maistre. The way that gentleman and his works have been dinned into our ears! And the modern Socialists, who have praised him to the skies! Beginning with the Saint-Simonians and ending with A. Comte![5] France is intoxicated with authority, whatever people say. Here is a lovely idea I found in Raspail: "*Physicians should be magistrates*, in order to be able to force. . . . etc."[6]

Your Romantic and Liberal old fogey vous embrasse tendrement.

Gve Flaubert

A thousand kisses to the little ones. And tell Mme Maurice again how sorry I was not to be able to travel to Nohant with her.[7]

Everybody is tearing *La Femme de Claude* (which I haven't seen) to pieces, whereas *Les Erinnyes* will earn a mere 1,200 francs or so for Leconte de Lisle. What is one to think?[8]

---

[1] In addition to Charpentier (see p. 284), two other publishers, Lemerre and Lachaud, had come to offer Flaubert their services. But he continued to hold back, not only out of disgust with publishing, but also because he had not yet succeeded in buying back Bouilhet's rights.

[2] Preliminary reading for *Bouvard et Pécuchet*, chapters II (agriculture and gardening) and III (chemistry, medicine, etc.).

[3] *On the Affection of Fathers for their Children*: ". . . I saw some years ago a Dean of Saint-Hilaire, at Poitiers, given up to such solitude by the discomfort of his melancholy that, when I entered his chamber, it was twenty-two years that he had not stepped outside the door; and yet his faculties were all unimpaired, save for a rheum that had attacked his stomach." (Translated by George B. Ives.)

[4] An article in *Le Temps*, 30 January 1873, entitled *Dans les bois*. (Reprinted in Sand's *Dernières Pages*, pp. 3–20.)

[5] Auguste Comte greatly admired J. de Maistre's *Du Pape* (1819), which had inspired him to write his *Cours de philosophie positive* (published 1830–42). Certain elements from the doctrine of the Catholic de Maistre can be found in the writings of Claude-Henri de Saint-Simon (1760–1825), the founder of French Socialism, whose secretary Comte had been from 1817 to 1824.

[6] "The source of this quotation has not been found," Alphonse Jacobs states in a footnote here.

[7] Flaubert had been unable to accompany Lina Sand to Nohant (she had been in Paris on business) because of an impending meeting of the committee for the Bouilhet monument.

[8] *La Femme de Claude*, by the younger Dumas, had opened at the Théâtre du Gymnase on January 16th. It was a dramatization of Dumas' thesis mentioned in Letter 329, Note 3. *Les Erinnyes*, a drama in two parts after the ancient Greek, had opened at the Odéon on 6 January.

Dumas' play, though flayed by critics, was a commercial success, whereas the other, though highly praised, was thinly attended.

345 SAND TO FLAUBERT

Nohant, 5 February [18]73

I wrote to you yesterday in Croisset; Lina thought you'd gone back there. I was asking you to do me a favour that you've done me before, namely to ask your brother to use his influence to help my friend Despruneaux with his lawsuit, which is now going to the court of appeal. That letter will probably be sent on from Paris and reach you as soon as this one. It's only a matter of dropping your brother a line, if it's not a bother.[1]

What's all this about persistent bronchitis? There's only one cure, and that's a very small dose – half a centigramme – of acetate of morphine every evening when your dinner has been digested, and keep this up for at least a week. That's how I treat myself – and my family – and it always does the trick. It's so easy and quick! You feel an improvement after two or three days. I do hope you'll be better soon, chiefly for your sake, but also for my own, because then you'll come, and I'm really longing to see you.

Maurice doesn't quite know how to answer your question. He hasn't made any mistakes in his own farming activities, but although he does know about the errors other people do or may make, he says not only are they innumerable but each one is specific to the situation and conditions involved. When you're here and he can find out exactly what you're after, he can tell you anything you want to know about central France and, if you need to generalize, about world geology. His own approach has always been not to go in for wholesale innovation, but to take the method hallowed by experience and try to develop that. Experience is always a trustworthy guide; it may not tell you everything, but it never lies.

Upon which I take my leave of you, summon you, expect you, hope for you, and yet don't want to badger you. But we certainly do love you, and we want to inject you with a bit of our Berry patience, against the things of this world which we well know to be no joke! But why were we put in this world if not to be patient?

Your obstinate troubadour qui t'aime.

G. Sand

[1] Sand's list of "letters sent" mentions one written to Flaubert on 4 February. Flaubert probably forwarded it to his brother, who did not preserve it.

346 FLAUBERT TO SAND

[Paris] 12 [March 1873]
Wednesday

Chère maître,

If I'm not with you, you must blame the great Turgenev. I was preparing to leave for Nohant when he said, "Wait, and I'll go with you at the beginning of April." That was two weeks ago. I'll be seeing him tomorrow at Mme Viardot's and will ask him to advance the date, because I'm growing impatient. I feel *the need* to embrace you and talk with you. I mean it.

I'm beginning to feel myself again. What has been wrong with me these last four months? What was it that troubled me so deeply? I have no idea. What's certain is that I have been quite ill, in some undefined way. But now I'm better, and even beginning to think less often about Michel Lévy. That hatred was becoming a veritable mania, most disturbing to me. I'm not entirely over it, but the thought of the wretched creature no longer brings palpitations, spasms of anger and outrage. That's something. On the other hand I've definitely decided not to go into print with anything else, in order to steer clear of the book Merchants. Since the first of January, I own all the rights to *Madame Bovary* and *Salammbô*, and could sell both books if I wished. But I'm taking no action, preferring to go without the money and spare my nerves. That's your old troubadour for you.

I'm reading all kinds of books, and making notes for my own big one that's going to take me five or six years. And I'm meditating two or three others.[1] Enough to keep me dreaming a long time: that's the main thing. Art continues to be "in the doldrums," as M. Prud'homme puts it, and the world nowadays is no place for people of taste. One must withdraw into solitude like the rhinoceros, and wait to give up the ghost.

Best greetings to all your family, et à vous, ch; agere bon maître, mille tendresses de
    Votre

                                        Gve Flaubert

[1] Since 1871-2, Flaubert had been meditating several subjects, which he noted in his "Carnet 20", a notebook now in the Bibliothèque historique de la Ville de Paris. Three "scenarios", more or less related – *Sous Napoléon III*, *Monsieur le Préfet*, and *Un Ménage parisien* – probably have to do with the "modern Parisian novel", or "novel about the Second Empire", that he sometimes mentioned to friends. A fourth theme, of a different character, is entitled *Les Bourgeois au XIXe siècle*. For yet another project, *Harel-Bey*, see Letter 408, Note 2.

347 SAND TO FLAUBERT

                            Nohant, 15 March [18]73

At last, mon vieux troubadour, we can hope to see you soon. I was worried about you. I always am, to tell the truth – I'm not happy about your rages and prejudices. They've been going on too long; and as you say yourself, the whole thing is almost morbid. Can't you just *forget*? You live too much inside yourself, and that makes you relate everything to yourself. If you were a vain and selfish person I'd just tell myself it was normal; but in you, who are so kind and generous, it's an anomaly, a malady that has to be fought against. Of course, life is unsatisfactory, painful and irritating for everybody. But don't overlook the enormous compensations – it's ungrateful to forget them. If you get into a temper about someone or other, it's of no consequence so long as it makes you feel better; but when you stay angry and indignant for weeks or months or even years – that's very hard and unfair on those who love you and would like to spare you all trouble and disappointment. You see, I'm scolding you. But when I welcome you here I shall be thinking only of the hope and joy of seeing you well and flourishing again. We can't wait to have you with us, and we're really counting on seeing Turgenev, whom we adore as well.

I've been troubled lately with a series of painful inflammations; but that hasn't stopped me enjoying writing stories and playing with my babes. They're so sweet, and my grown-up children are so good to me I believe I shall die smiling at them. What does it matter if one has a hundred thousand enemies if one is loved by two or three good people? And don't you love me too, and wouldn't you say I was wrong to dismiss that as nothing? When I lost Rollinat, didn't you write and tell me to concentrate on those who were left to me and love *them* more? Come and let me overwhelm you with reproaches for not practising what you preached.

We're waiting for you, and preparing a fantastic *mi-carême*;[1] do try to be here for it. Laughter is a great doctor. We'll provide you with a costume for the fancy-dress. I hear you were a great success as a pastry-cook at Pauline's![2] If you're feeling better you may be sure it's because you've taken yourself in hand and allowed yourself some distraction. Paris is good for you; you're too much alone out there in that pretty house of yours.

Come and work here. You could easily send a boxful of books!

Let us know when you're coming so that we can have a carriage waiting for you at Châteauroux.

[unsigned]

[1] The third Sunday in Lent – "Mid-Lent".
[2] Since February, 1872, Flaubert had been attending Mme Viardot's Thursday soirées, but there is no mention in his correspondence of the evening to which Mme Sand refers here: perhaps it was, rather, a Carnival celebration, early in March.

348 FLAUBERT TO SAND

[Paris,] 20 [March 1873]
Thursday

Chère maître,

The gigantic Turgenev has just left my flat. We took a solemn oath: on April 12th, Easter Eve, we will dine chez vous.

It's been no small matter, reaching this decision. It's so difficult to arrange anything at all. For my part, I could easily have set out tomorrow. But I have the impression that our friend isn't very free to come and go. And I myself have things to do the first week in April.

Tonight I'm going to two fancy-dress balls!!! Now try to tell me I'm not young!

Mille tendresses de votre vieux

Troubadour
qui vous embrasse

For an example of modern fetidity, read the article on *Marion Delorme* in the last number of *La Vie Parisienne*.[1] It's worth framing. If something fetid can be framed! But we aren't all that particular these days.

[1] *La Vie Parisienne* for 15 March 1873 contains an article, signed "Ouf", entitled "Pour *La Femme de Claude* et contre *Marion Delorme*". "Ouf" attacks Victor Hugo for belittling Louis XIII and Cardinal Richelieu. "It is a disgrace that less than two years after the loss of Alsace and the abominations of the Commune, the event of the month, of the year, should be a revival of a play insulting the king and the minister who gave Alsace to France." The article says that Hugo's language resembles "*un dialecte des Sioux*", and praises Dumas *fils* for his "sincerity" despite his poor style.

349   SAND TO FLAUBERT

[Nohant] 23 March [18]73

No, the giant can't do just as he likes; I've noticed. But he's one of those people who like being ruled, and I can understand him. So long as one's in good hands – and he is.

And so we still hope to see him, but you're the only one I'm counting on for certain. I couldn't be more pleased to hear you're making an effort, going out and enjoying yourself. It's absolutely necessary in these chaotic times. If the day ever comes when we don't need to be a little drunk in order to survive, it'll mean that the world is functioning properly. But we're not there yet.

That faecal article doesn't deserve to be read. I didn't finish it: one averts one's eyes and nose from that sort of thing. But I don't think the person to whom such incense was offered up can have been very pleased.

So come with the swallows and bring *Saint Antoine* with you. Maurice will be so interested! He's more learned than me – I'm ignorant of so many things I'll be able to appreciate only the grand, poetic aspect. But I'm sure, in fact I know, that he can understand it all.

Go on bestirring yourself – it's essential – and above all go on loving us as we love you.

George Sand
ton vieux troubadour

350 SAND TO FLAUBERT

Nohant, 7 April [1873]

I've written and asked my friend General Ferri-Pisani, whom you know and who is based at Châteauroux,[1] to hire a carriage which will be waiting for you[2] at the station on the 12th, at 3.20. You should leave Paris by the 9.10 train – it's a fast train, and if you don't take that one the journey is slow and tedious. I hope the general will come here with you. If there's any change in your plans as promised, send him a telegram at Châteauroux so that he doesn't go and wait for you. He usually comes here on horseback.

We're looking forward *impatiently* to seeing you.

Ton vieux troubadour

G. Sand

[1] General Ferri-Pisani was commander-in-chief of the sub-division "Indre" of the 9th national *"région militaire"* (Tours). [J. B.]

[2] Sand uses the plural *"vous"* for "you" throughout this letter, showing that she retains a lingering hope that Turgenev will accompany Flaubert.

351 FLAUBERT TO SAND

[Paris, 9 April 1873]
Wednesday

I shall arrive at Nohant on Saturday, chère maître. But our mighty Muscovite won't be there until Monday, because: Mme Viardot's brother is coming to spend three days in Paris. That reason baffles me! However. . . .

So, it's settled, unless the heavens fall, that in 72 hours your old troubadour,

Gve Flaubert
will embrace you.

I rely on Ferri-Pisani to drive me to Nohant.

*

And so, at last, Flaubert reached Nohant for the long-desired and much-postponed visit. However, reading George Sand's entries in her diary, one is aware of disappointment. For the first time, perhaps, she realized the extent of the gulf between the two "troubadours".

FROM GEORGE SAND'S DIARY, 1873

Saturday, 12 April

. . . Flaubert arrived during dinner. He has lost rather than put on weight, and is no fatter than Plauchut, who regards himself as thin. We played dominoes; Flaubert played well, but was soon short of breath. He was happier with heated discussion. Plauchut acted the armchair democrat and withstood the broadsides. Maurice supported both alternately. I listened.

Sunday, 13 April (Easter Day)

The sun came back at last and it was fine. At the lunch table Lina saluted the season with flowers and spring chicken. We went out and looked at the garden, the farm, the cowsheds, Gustave[1] and all the other animals. Flaubert looked through the bookshelves and didn't find anything he didn't know. René[2] and the doctor[3] came to dinner; there was dancing afterwards. Flaubert put on a skirt and had a shot at the fandango. He was very funny, but gasping for breath after about five minutes. He shows his age much more than I do. But I think he looks less overweight and tired than he did. He still lives too much by the brain at the expense of the body. We deafened him with our noise. Plauchut was like a mad thing. Maurice and Aurore went out on the heath and found a *mardelle*[4] at last! She was intoxicated with delight and the fresh air. She danced in the evening. Played dominoes with the young folk. At about midnight Maurice impressed Flaubert with his butterflies.

Monday, 14 April

Lovely day; too hot at midday. Garden, Lolo's lesson – she's got a head cold and had a slight touch of fever after dinner. Flaubert read us his *Saint Antoine* from three to six and from nine till midnight. It was splendid. René and the doctor came to dinner. Ferri arrived right in the middle of the reading, listened to a couple of chapters with great pleasure, then went on to dine with Angèle;[5] he'll be back in the morning. René was enchanted, the doctor very interested, I completely captivated and gratified. Plauchut astonished, almost pole-axed. Maurice was so gripped he got a bad headache.

Tuesday, 15 April

Beautiful weather. Spent the day out of doors, chatting in the garden among the flowers, everything just right, not too much of anything in heaven or on earth. Ferri came to lunch. He's always charming; he left at two. I stayed talking with Flaubert till four o'clock, then gave Lolo her lesson. In the evening, talk and laughter.

Wednesday, 16 April

Dull, very hot day, but very pleasant. We all went out on the heath at midday to see the *mardelle* Maurice and Lolo found the other day. It's a big hollow with a peaty stream running into it; the ground is covered with tall dry ferns, but underneath there's fresh grass growing, *viola canina*,[6] fleabane, primroses and little saplings. We went round the edge of a pretty pine wood, walking through the broom. The orchises are starting to flower; a lovely pink colour. Lolo trotted along valiantly and Titite didn't do badly either. Back home in time to dress for dinner. Turgenev finally arrived. He's well, and looking younger and spry. We chatted till midnight.

Thursday, 17 April

Bad weather. I didn't go out; nor did the children. Gave Aurore her lesson. Talked to Turgenev and Flaubert. Turgenev read us a very lively comic piece. The young men came to dinner. We had turkey with truffles, *le pari de Plauchut*.[7] Afterwards we jumped about, danced, sang, shouted and generally bored Flaubert stiff – he never wants to do anything but talk about literature. It was all too much for him. Turgenev likes noise and cheerfulness; he's as much of a child as we are. He danced and waltzed. What a good and convivial genius! Maurice read us *The Ballad of the Night*:[8] he made an excellent job of it and was a great success. He impresses Flaubert with everything he does.

Friday, 18 April

Nice weather. But we've had a lot of rain, and the water in the ditch has risen a step higher. Everything is in flower, including the lilacs and the *crataegi*;[9] the St Lucy trees[10] are losing their petals already. Everyone out in the garden. Gave Lolo her lesson. Flaubert talked and was very lively and funny, but he monopolized the conversation, and Turgenev, who's much more interesting, could hardly get a word in. This evening the onslaught lasted until one o'clock. At last we parted. They leave in the morning. Plauchut is staying on to wait for me.

Saturday, 19 April

Everyday life depends more on a person's character than on his intelligence or greatness. My dear Flaubert has left me absolutely exhausted . . . I love him dearly, and he's an excellent man, but his personality is too excitable. He wears us out. It poured with rain from midday on. I gave Lolo her lesson; wrote letters; didn't go out. This evening we danced, made noise, played at dominoes, enjoyed playing the fool. We missed Turgenev. We don't know him so well and aren't so fond of him, but he has the gift of true simplicity and the charm of bonhomie.

[1] The ram. (See Letter 178.)
[2] René Simonnet, George Sand's great-nephew.
[3] Probably Dr Edouard Pissavy, the lover of Sand's daughter, Solange Clésinger.
[4] *Mardelle* or *margelle*, name given in Berry to certain subterranean passages caused by

the action of water passing through rock formations. Formerly thought to be man-made. *(Larousse du XXᵉ siècle)*

⁵ Mme Angèle Périgois, née Néraud, a friend of G. Sand living in La Châtre.

⁶ Dog-tooth violet.

⁷ See Letters 357 and 358.

⁸ A humorous poem, never published, written by George Sand, Maurice and several friends. The manuscript is in the Lovenjoul collection at Chantilly.

⁹ Hawthorne.

¹⁰ A kind of cherry (*prunus Mahaleb*) native to central Europe.

*

Both Flaubert and George Sand had aged considerably since the war. The sorrows and disillusionments of *l'année terrible* had affected them profoundly. Sand had acquired an even deeper realization of what was ultimately important to her. Turgenev's genial *savoir-vivre* naturally delighted her: he had been nurtured in a sociable atmosphere, and experienced much less difficulty than Flaubert in accommodating himself to the requirements of others.

As for Flaubert, the events of 1870–1 had heightened his sensitivity and intensified his misanthropy. Art was more than ever his consolation; and more than ever he detested noise, stupidity, childishness. (On the other hand, his insistent loquacity at Nohant, his monopolizing of conversation, was doubtless a reaction, also, from his prolonged seclusion – in which he had no one with whom he could converse.) The visit to Nohant may possibly have disappointed him also: such sensations are often intuitively mutual. Nevertheless, the letter he sent to his hostess is filled with tender, wistful gratitude.

352 FLAUBERT TO SAND

[Paris, 24 April 1873]
Thursday morning

Chère maître,

It's only 5 days since we parted, and I miss you as might some dumb animal. I miss Aurore, and the entire household, including Fadet. Yes, I do indeed. It was delightful to be with you. You are all so good, and so clever.

Why can't we live together, why is life always so badly arranged? Maurice seems to me a model of human happiness. Is there *anything* he lacks? Certainly no one envies him more than I do.

Your friends Turgenev and Cruchard[1] philosophized about all this between Nohant and Châteauroux, as they bowled comfortably along in your carriage behind two good fast horses. Long live the coachmen of La Châtre! But the rest of the journey was very unpleasant, because of our fellow-passengers on the train. I sought consolation in strong drink: the charming Muscovite had a flask of excellent brandy with him. We were both rather sad at heart, and neither spoke nor slept.

Here we found the Barodetian nonsense in full spate.[2] And, following on the heels of that production, for the past three days we've had Stoffel,[3] another bitter pill. Oh! God! God! What a trial to live in such times! You can't imagine the floods of madness engulfing us here! How right you are to live far from Paris!

I've got back to my reading, and in a week I'll begin my excursions to the countryside nearby, to choose a setting for my two characters. Following which, towards the 12th or 15th, I'll be back at my house on the river. I'd very much like to go to Saint-Gervais[4] this summer – at last – to bleach my nose and patch up my nerves. It's something I've been putting off on one pretext or another for ten years. But it's about time for a beauty treatment. Not that I aspire to be pleasing and seductive on account of my physical graces, but I really do hate the sight of myself when I look in the mirror. One has to take more care of one's looks as one gets older.

This evening I'm to see Mme Viardot. I'll go early, and we'll talk of you.

When shall we meet again? How far Nohant is from Croisset!

Take Aurore on your lap and give her lots of big kisses from me. And do the same with Mlle Titi [sic]. With Maurice, that wouldn't be very comfortable for you, perhaps, if it went on for long. As for Mme Maurice, tell her straight out that I'm very fond of her. A little pat on the head for Fadet; and to you, chère bon maître, toutes mes tendresses.

Gve Flaubert

Otherwise known as Rev. Fr. Cruchard of the Barnabites, spiritual director of the Ladies of Disillusion.

---

[1] Here and in the postscript are the first appearances of "Cruchard" in the correspondence. He is most fully identified in an article by Maurice Haloche in the *Bulletin des Amis de Flaubert*, No. 12 (1958), referring to an auction in Paris, in 1931, of items that had belonged to Mme Franklin-Grout (Flaubert's niece Caroline):

"... That same day a collector acquired, for 2,400 francs, a manuscript of six quarto pages, on blue paper, dedicated to 'Mme la baronne D. Dev., née A. D.', who is none other than George Sand.... This manuscript, entitled *Life of the Reverend Father Cruchard, by the Reverend Father Cerpet*, is a burlesque, truculent biography. Cruchard is described as having been born in the cider press of a farm at Mariquerville, near Bayeux. A pious youth, he is sent to a seminary, but is a rebellious student until a pilgrimage works a radical change. Becoming active and hard-working, he is borne by his many successes to the cathedral of Bayeux, where he becomes a celebrated preacher. His attainments, which Flaubert lists in astonishing number, attract the attention of a high official, who introduces him to the Court. There our Rev. Father gorges himself so copiously whenever the occasion presents itself that one gentleman describes him as 'the leading theologian and the leading trencherman of the realm'. Henceforth such is his reputation that all the great ladies and all the nuns clamour for him as their confessor. In that office he is indulgent and kind. But obesity increasingly bloats his body, and he begins to fall into a dotage. Nevertheless he continues light-hearted to the end, exclaiming, in what he recognizes as his last moments, '*Crack!* Hear that? The jug's had it!' (*Je sens que la cruche va tout à fait se casser.*)" *Cruche*, which means "pitcher" or "jar", is also a slang term for "blockhead", analogous to the English "old crock". M. Jacobs reminds us that Flaubert had invented the Rabelaisian Cruchard several years before, in letters to Caroline, and revived him now for the entertainment of Mme Sand. Flaubert would later tell Sand, ironically, that Cruchard was his "ideal". (Postscript to Letter 375.)

[2] In a stormy campaign, Désiré Barodet, mayor of Lyons, was running as Radical candidate for election as Deputy. His chief competitor was the government's candidate, Charles de Rémusat. Barodet's victory, on 28 April, heralded the downfall, on 24 May, of Thiers and his ministry.

[3] Baron Eugène Stoffel had been French military attaché in Berlin in 1870. In 1871 he published confidential reports of Prussian military strength which he had sent as a warning to the Thiers ministry and which he claimed had gone unheeded. For this he was reproved by the War Ministry and pensioned off. Now his nomination as Deputy from Lyons by the Bonapartists and legitimists was causing a scandal. He obtained only 27,000 votes, as against Barodet's 180,000 and Rémusat's 135,000.

[4] Saint-Gervais-les-Bains was a health resort in the Haute-Savoie. Its waters were considered beneficial for skin and intestinal ailments. (*Larousse du XXe siècle*.)

*

That same day, the 24th, George Sand arrived in Paris, "on personal, *not literary*, business", as she wrote on the 26th to Charles-Edmond. (She needed a new dental plate.) Her letter to Flaubert announcing this visit has not been found: we know of its existence from Flaubert's reply.

353 FLAUBERT TO SAND

[Paris, 27 April 1873]
Sunday morning, 10 o'clock

Chère maître,

What a pleasant surprise! You *must* come to dinner tomorrow chez Cruchard with Renan and Baudry (already invited).

As for the rest of the week, I'm free on Tuesday, Thursday and Saturday. At what time of day can I find you, apart from 6 p.m. at Magny's?

Will you dine with me here this evening, just the two of us? *But I count on you for tomorrow.* You haven't yet put your elbows on my dining table, please note,[1] and that must be rectified.

I suppose you'll be going to Mme Viardot's on Thursday. If it would be more convenient for you to come here that day, come then. We could go on to the rue de Douai after dinner.

In any case, you must give me a day. But above all don't tire yourself. Bar your door firmly against intruders.

A bientôt donc.

Votre vieux

G.

[1] That is, since he had moved to rue Murillo.

354 SAND TO FLAUBERT

[Paris, 27 April 1873]
Sunday

I'll come and dine with you tomorrow, your reverence. I'll be at home every day at 5 o'clock, but you might meet faces you don't like. It would be better if you came to Magny's, where you'd find me on my own or with Plauchut, or with others who are your friends as well as mine.

Je t'embrasse. The letter you sent to Nohant reached me here today.

G. Sand

*

The four friends dined together the next evening. The atmosphere was doubtless tense: all professed moderate republican sympathies, and Barodet was being elected. "There is nothing to detain me in Paris," Sand wrote to her children that same evening. "Wherever I've gone in the city there's been a pall of deathly gloom. Probably other neighbourhoods are triumphant; but bourgeois, scholarly and artistic Paris is appalled. I dined tonight at Flaubert's with Baudry and Renan: the latter takes it all as an unhappy chapter of history, and calmly says we must expect anything."

Fortunately there were to be other opportunities to meet: a concert by Pablo de Sarasate and Camille Saint-Saëns at Mme Viardot's on May 1, and two days later a dinner at the restaurant Véfour – Flaubert, George Sand, Turgenev and Edmond de Goncourt.

But Flaubert's mercurial behaviour was beginning to exasperate George Sand. A letter to Maurice, posted to Nohant that night of the 28th, gives a lively and picturesque account of what took place, but shows Sand irritated and displeased.

GEORGE SAND TO MAURICE SAND

[Paris, 28 April 1873]

... I've just dined with Flaubert, whose conduct was odder than ever. He'd invited Turgenev and de Goncourt as well as me, and we'd arranged to meet at Magny's at half-past 6. I arrived at the agreed time, and Turgenev came soon after. We waited a quarter of an hour, and then de Goncourt rushed up all aghast, saying, "We're not having dinner here – Flaubert's waiting for you at the Frères Provençaux." "But why?" "He says he can't breathe properly here; the rooms are too small; he's been up all night and he's tired." "But I'm tired, too," said I. "Scold him – he's an ill-mannered wretch – but do come!" "No, I'm not going to move – I'm starving. Let's all stay and have dinner here." Everyone laughed, but de Goncourt said Flaubert would go crazy, so off we bundled in a cab. We then had to go up three hundred steps to the Véfour, only to find Flaubert asleep on a sofa. I called him a beast, he went on his knees and begged forgiveness, the others split their sides laughing. The dinner was very poor – I hate that kind of food – and the room much smaller than those at Magny's. Flaubert said he was exhausted, at the end of his tether, he'd been reading a play to Carvalho from 2 till 5 o'clock in the morning, the play had been accepted with rapture, he was going back to Croisset to take *six months* rewriting it, and would come back and spend *the whole winter* in Paris having it put on; all this bored him to death, but he was doing it in memory of Bouilhet. He's becoming as obsessed about the memory of Bouilhet as Marchal's mother was about the medal.[1] Nevertheless, he was hooting with joy, delighted, the play was the only thing in the world. He couldn't talk about anything else, and wouldn't let Turgenev get a word in, much less de Goncourt. I made my escape at ten o'clock. I'll be seeing him tomorrow, but shall say I'm leaving on Monday. I've had enough of my young friend. I'm very fond of him, but he gives me a splitting headache. He doesn't like noise, but he doesn't mind the din he makes himself . . .[2]

[1] This reference to the mother of the painter Charles Marchal is unexplained.

[2] Goncourt gives a quite different description of this dinner in his *Journal*. For one thing, George Sand contradicts herself, mentioning two restaurants, Véfour and Les Frères Provençaux (which were a few doors apart): Goncourt says the dinner took place in the former. Furthermore, Goncourt makes no mention of the details given by Sand, and devotes most of his entry to an admiring account of Turgenev's conversation, especially his eloquent reminiscences of his youth in Russia.

Possibly Mme Sand is being a bit fanciful, to amuse her children – evoking some of the traits they had seen Flaubert display during his recent visit to Nohant. The two versions can scarcely be reconciled. However, George Sand's letter has the ring of reality, and Goncourt may have mistaken the occasion.

*

It is not known whether Mme Sand saw Flaubert the next day: her diary does not mention him, nor do her letters to Maurice and Lina. She left for Nohant on May 8th. Flaubert, too, soon left the city. After a brief, pleasantly nostalgic visit to his old friend Mme Roger des Genettes, at Villeneuve near Nogent-sur-Seine, he returned to Croisset on the 17th.

A few days later Sand sent him her newly published volume, *Impressions et Souvenirs*, inscribed "*A mon cher Gustave Flaubert, son vieux troubadour*".

355 FLAUBERT TO SAND

[Croisset, 31 May 1873]
Saturday

Chère maître,

Cruchard should have thanked you sooner for sending him your new book. But His Reverence is working like 18 thousand blacks. That's his excuse.

Not that that has kept him from reading *Impressions et Souvenirs*. I was already familiar with parts of it, from reading them in the past, in *Le Temps*. A pun![1]

Here is what was new to me and what struck me. (1) The first chapter. (2) The second, containing a charming and very apt passage about the Empress. How right you are in what you say about the Proletariat![2] Let's hope there'll be an end to its reign, as well as to that of the Bourgeois! and for the same reasons – as punishment for the same stupidity and the same selfishness.

"*Réponse à un ami*" I know, since it was addressed to me.[3]

The dialogue with Delacroix is enlightening. Curious, the two pages on what he thought of old Ingres.

I don't fully share your views about punctuation: that is, mine exhibits the very excesses you disapprove of.[4] And needless to say I can adduce good reasons for defending them.

"*J'allume le fagot*, etc.": I found this long passage charming.[5]

In *Thoughts of a Schoolmaster* I admire your pedagogic spirit, chère maître. And there are some things admirably suited to readers of primers.[6]

Thank you for what you say about my poor Bouilhet.[7]

I *adore* your Pierre Bonnin.[8] I've known people like him; and since those pages are dedicated to Turgenev it gives me an opportunity to ask whether you have read *L'Abandonnée*?[9] I find it simply sublime. That Scythian is a tremendous fellow.

At the moment, I'm not dealing with literature of so high an order. Far from it! I'm working, and working overtime, on *Le Sexe faible*. In a week I've rewritten the first act. It's true that I'm putting in long days: once, last week, I worked for 18 hours at a stretch! And your Cruchard is as fresh as a young girl. Not tired, no headaches. I think I may be finished with this task in three weeks. After that, God's will be done! It would be amusing if Carvalho's strange behaviour were to be "crowned with success"!

I'm afraid that Maurice may have lost his turkey with truffles. Because I want to substitute, in place of the three theologal virtues, Christ's countenance appearing in the sun. What do you think?[10] Once that change is made, and when I'll have strengthened the massacre at Alexandria and clarified the symbolism of the fantastic animals, *Saint Antoine* will *be irrevocably* finished. And I'll go back to my two characters, whom I put aside to do the play.

What a wretched way one is obliged to write for the stage! Ellipses, pauses, questions and repetitions have to be piled on if you want the thing to move. All of which is, in itself, very ugly.

I may be deceiving myself, but I think I'm doing something now that does move along very fast and will be easy to perform. We'll see.

Adieu, cher bon maître. Kiss all your family for me, especially Lolo, who'll then do the same to you: coming from her it will be sweeter.

Your idiotic old

Cruchard

friend of *Chalumeau*. (Note that name.) It's a tremendous story, but one would have to take a firm stand and tell it *right*.[11]

[1] Flaubert's pun: "in *Le Temps*"(the newspaper); and "*dans le temps*" (in the past).

[2] *Impressions et Souvenirs* is a collection of twenty-two articles by George Sand that had appeared in *Le Temps* in 1871 and 1872. Flaubert alludes here to Chapter II, in which Sand speaks with gentle irony of the mania of bourgeois ladies for imitating the Empress, and that of "the people" for adopting the bad habits of the bourgeoisie.

[3] See Letters 285 and 286. "*Réponse à un ami*" forms Chapter IV in the volume.

[4] Chapter VI in the volume. Sand prefers the simplest punctuation possible. Starting from the principle that "Punctuation is style well understood," she says it must be flexible: "there is no absolute rule." Publisher and printer must respect the author's punctuation, just as they respect other aspects of his style.

[5] "*I light the fire*": these are the opening words of Chapter VIII, dated "1871, 28 October, Nohant." Sand describes a night passed at the fireside, and evokes memories of her youth, her reading, the development of her religious concepts.

[6] See Letter 298.

[7] See Letter 315, Note 2. Sand devotes four pages to Bouilhet, composed largely of quotations.

[8] "Pierre Bonnin", Chapter XIX, written after Sand had read Turgenev's *Mémoires d'un seigneur russe*, evokes the simple life, and the loyalty, of the carpenter at Nohant.

[9] *L'Abandonnée* is one of the tales in the volume *Histoires étranges*, then recently published in Paris. Of this story Flaubert wrote that same day to Turgenev: "I don't know that you have ever shown yourself to be a greater poet and psychologist. It's a marvel, a masterpiece. And such art! What ingenuities of execution underlie that apparent simplicity!"

The French and the English titles of Turgenev's tales, and of the volumes in which they are collected, seldom correspond, making identification elusive.

[10] The penultimate sentence in *La Tentation de Saint Antoine* is: "*Tout au milieu, et dans le disque même du soleil, rayonne la tête de Jésus-Christ.*" ("In the very centre of the sky, and in the disc of the sun itself, shines the countenance of Jesus Christ.") The "three theologal virtues" are Faith, Hope, and Charity – "Charity" being "Love" in modern parlance.

[11] Chalumeau, the Roman Catholic curate of Canteleu, had been surprised while "frolicking" (M. Jacobs' term) with two girls in the Protestant cemetery. As a common noun, *chalumeau* (a pipe, or reed) can lend itself to phallic connotations.

*

Throughout June, Flaubert, at Croisset, worked steadily at *Le Sexe faible*, which he was to read to Carvalho on the 28th. On the 20th, despite his recent resolution not to burden any printing press for a long time to come, he signed a contract with Charpentier for new editions of *Madame Bovary* and *Salammbô*.

During this same time George Sand was incapacitated by a recurrence of anaemia.

Once again, letters from Croisset and Nohant crossed in the post.

356 FLAUBERT TO SAND

[Croisset, 3 July 1873]
Thursday

Why do you leave me so long without news, chère bon maître? I miss you: I do indeed.

I've finished with the Dramatic arts. Carvalho came here last Saturday to hear me read *Le Sexe faible*, and seemed pleased with it. He thinks it will be a success. But I have so little faith in the expertise of those sharpers that I have my doubts.

I'm exhausted. I sleep 10 hours a night plus two during the day, resting my poor brain.

Now I'll resume my reading for my book: it will be at least a year before I begin to write.

Where is the mighty Turgenev at the moment, do you know?

Mille tendresses à tous et à vous les meilleures,

Votre vieux

Cruchard

357 SAND TO FLAUBERT

[Nohant] 4 July [1873]

I don't know where you are at the moment, Cruchard de mon coeur, so I'm addressing this to you in Paris, whence I imagine it will be forwarded. I've been ill, your reverence – no pain, just a stupid attack of anaemia, leaving me without legs or appetite, with sweat constantly on my brow and my heart all over the place like that of a woman with child. I don't call that fair when one's getting on for seventy. Tomorrow I enter upon my 70th spring, cured after ten or so dips in the river. I've so enjoyed resting, however, that I haven't done a stroke of work since I got back from Paris, and I only open my inkwell today to write to you.

This morning we were re-reading the letter in which you say Maurice has lost his bet. He claims he won because you've taken out the theologal virtues. Wager or no, I want you to keep the new version, which fits in perfectly with the rest, whereas the theologal virtues don't.

Have you any news of Turgenev? I'm worried about him. Mme Viardot wrote a few days ago and said he'd had a fall and hurt his leg.[1] Yes, I have read *L'Abandonnée* – it's very fine, like everything he writes. I do hope his injury isn't serious! But it's always serious when the person concerned suffers from gout.

Are you still working away furiously? How unlucky you are, not to know the ineffable pleasure of doing nothing! And how lovely work will seem to me afterwards! But I shall put it off as long as possible. I'm coming more and more to believe there's nothing worth saying!

But don't *you* go thinking that. Write some good things and love your old troubadour who loves you always.

G. Sand

Love from all Nohant.

¹ Turgenev had left France for Russia early in June. The results of a fall caused him to take to his bed in Vienna, but the injuries did not prove serious. He returned to France at the end of July.

358 FLAUBERT TO SAND

[Croisset, 20 July 1873]
Sunday

I am not like Mr de Vigny: I do *not* love "the sound of the horn in the depths of the wood".¹ For the past two hours some imbecile on the island opposite has been driving me mad with his instrument! The wretch is spoiling the sunshine for me, and preventing me from enjoying the summer. The weather is splendid just now. But I'm simmering with rage. Nevertheless I want to chat with you a bit, chère maître.

First of all, greetings on your Seventieth, which seems to me to find you more robust than does the Twentieth of many another. What a Herculean constitution you have! Bathing in an icy stream indicates a degree of strength that I find astonishing and a sign of good health that's very reassuring to your friends. Live long! Take care of yourself for the sake of your darling granddaughters, for the excellent Maurice, for me, for everyone. And I would add "for Literature" were I not afraid of your lofty disdain.

There goes that horn again! This is maddening! I'm tempted to go and find the constable!

No, I do not share the kinds of disdain you profess. And, as you say, I am absolutely unacquainted with "the pleasure of doing nothing". The moment I'm not holding a book in my hands, or not thinking about writing one, I'm so bored I could scream. Life seems bearable only when it's being conjured away. Otherwise one would have to give oneself over to dissipation – and even if one did that . . . !

So: *Le Sexe faible* is finished, as far as I'm concerned, and it will be put on – so at least Carvalho promises – in January, if Sardou's *L'Oncle Sam* is released by the Censor.² Otherwise in November.

During the past six weeks I've got into the habit of looking at things from a theatrical point of view and thinking in dialogue; so, lo and behold, I've gone and written an outline for another play! It will be called *Le Candidat*. My outline fills 20 pages. But I have no one to show it to, alas! So I'll leave it in a drawer and get back to my book. I'm reading Daremberg's *Histoire de la médecine* – highly entertaining. And I've finished le sieur Garnier's *Essai sur les facultés de l'entendement*, which I find utterly idiotic.³ Such are my occupations.

He seems to have quieted down. What a relief!

A certain character named Maurice Sand seems to me to be something of a swindler. It was he, I think, who bet I wouldn't change anything in *Saint Antoine*, and he claims to have won his wager! Isn't he taking unfair advantage of young Plauchut's candour?

Not the slightest sign of life from the Muscovite! I wrote to him, a while ago, at his address in the rue de Douai. Why this silence? Has Mme Viardot eaten him?

For my summer holiday I'll go to Paris in August to do some necessary research. Then I may spend a week in Dieppe before returning here, and here I'll remain until summoned to the Vaudeville.

I don't know whether there's as much talk about the Shah in Nohant as there is in these parts. Enthusiasm has run pretty high: a little more and he'd have been proclaimed emperor! His stay in Paris spawned monarchical ideas among businessmen, shopkeepers and workers to a degree you cannot conceive. And the gentlemen of the clergy are doing very well. Very *very* well.[4]

And beyond the horizon the horrors taking place in Spain[5] maintain mankind's reputation for affability.

Kiss everybody for me, chère maître, especially Lolo.

Votre vieux Cruchard qui vous aime fort.

[unsigned]

[1] *J'aime le son du Cor, le soir, au fond des bois* is the first line of Alfred de Vigny's poem *Le Cor*.

[2] *L'Oncle Sam*, a comedy in four acts by Sardou, had been held up by the Censor for two years. According to Goncourt, the reason was economic: "When the manager of the Vaudeville begged Thiers to be allowed to put on Sardou's play, Thiers sent word that it was impossible: at the moment, Americans were the only people spending money in Paris, and it wouldn't do to hurt their feelings." (*Journal*, Vol. X, p. 124). The play opened at last on 6 November 1873.

[3] It is not clear whether Flaubert was reading Dr Charles Daremberg's *Histoire des sciences médicales* (2 vols., 1870) or his *La Médecine, histoire et doctrines* (1865). The correct title of the work by Adolphe Garnier is *Traité des facultés de l'âme* (3 vols., 1852; new edition 1872).

[4] Nassr-ed-Din, shah of Persia, had visited Paris July 6–19. He had been given a magnificent reception: display of the Versailles fountains, grand gala at the Opéra, illuminations in public parks, military review at Longchamp, official dinners, etc. There was considerable public interest: *Le Temps* printed a special daily feature. In some circles this was taken to indicate an upsurge of royalist feeling.

[5] An allusion to the "Carlist Wars", waged by the younger against the elder branch of the Spanish royal house. The French press was publishing horrifying details: massacres, bloody attacks on defenceless villages, and other inhumanities.

*

In August, Flaubert did spend some time with his niece at Dieppe, and he visited Princesse Mathilde at Saint-Gratien. For most of the month, however, he was in Paris, doing research for *Bouvard et Pécuchet*, negotiating with Carvalho about *Le Sexe faible*, and correcting proofs of a fresh printing of *Madame Bovary* for his new publisher. He returned to Croisset on September 4th, after an "epic day" spent seeking a proper setting for his two "*bonshommes*".[1] A letter from Sand awaited him.

[1] "Wednesday was an epic day," he wrote to Caroline on 5 September. "I went from Paris to Rambouillet by train, from Rambouillet to Houdan by carriage, on by train then from Houdan to Mantes in a cabriolet, to Rouen. I reached Croisset at midnight in drenching rain. Expenses: 83 francs; it's costly to be conscientious about literature!"

359 SAND TO FLAUBERT

Nohant, 30 August 1873

Where can we meet these days? where are you roosting? I'm just back from the Auvergne with all my *smala*,[1] Plauchut included. It's very fine, the Auvergne – pretty, rather. The flora is still abundant and interesting, walks are hard going, accommodation a problem. But I stood it all very well, except for the two thousand metres above sea-level at the Puy de Sancy, where the combination of cold wind and hot sun landed me with four days of fever. After that I got back into the swim, and here I mean to go on with my dips in the river until the frosts set in.

There was no more question of any kind of work, or any thought of literature, than if none of us had ever learned to read. The local "poats" pursued me with books and bouquets, but I can deal with that now by sending each of them any old work of my own in exchange. Oh, but I did see some wonderful places, and some strange volcanic landscapes where one would have liked to hear your *Saint Antoine* in a setting worthy of the subject! What purpose do such visual pleasures serve, though, and to what extent do our impressions take on permanent form? One can't tell in advance, and with the passage of time and life's procrastinations, everything tends to get jumbled together in an undistinguishable mass.

What news of your play? Have you started on your book? Or chosen vantage point? Tell me what he's up to, le Cruchard de mon coeur. Write, even if it's only a word, to say you still love us as I and as all of us here love you.

G. Sand

[1] As in Letter 93: "household".

360 FLAUBERT TO SAND

Croisset, 5 September [1873]
Friday

Arriving here yesterday, I found your letter, chère bon maître. All goes well chez vous: God be thanked for that.

I spent the entire month of May [sic, for August] wandering about: I was in Dieppe, in Paris, in Saint-Gratien, in Brie and in Beauce, looking for the kind of place I had in mind, and which I think I may finally have found, near Houdan. However, before beginning my terrifying book I'll take one last look along the road from La Loupe to L'Aigle. And that will be that.[1]

Things look promising at the Vaudeville. So far, Carvalho has been charming. So enthusiastic, in fact, that I'm a bit uneasy: one mustn't forget all those Frenchmen shouting "*A Berlin!*" and getting such a thrashing.

Not only is said Carvalho pleased with *Le Sexe faible*, but he wants me to write another play immediately. I showed him my scenario, and he'd like to put the thing on next winter.[2] However, it hasn't yet taken sufficient shape in my mind for me to begin writing dialogue. On the other hand, I'd like to get it out of the way before starting on the story of my two *bonshommes*. Meanwhile, I'm continuing to read and make notes.

You probably don't know that the Censor's office has formally banned Coët-logon's play, "because it criticizes the Empire."[3] Since in *Le Sexe faible* I have a rather ridiculous old general, I'm a bit apprehensive about what those imbeciles might do. What a splendid institution it is, Censorship! Axiom: All governments loathe Literature: one Power does not love another.

When *Mademoiselle La Quintinie* was banned, you were too stoical, chère maître, or too indifferent. We must *always* protest against injustice and Stupidity – shout, foam with rage, fight to the death. When we can. Had I your prestige and authority, I'd have made a pretty scene. Old Hugo is wrong, too, I think, to keep quiet about *Le Roi s'amuse*.[4] He often makes his presence felt on less justifiable occasions.[5]

Speaking of great men, I was told at Dieppe that our friend [the younger] Dumas is becoming extremely religious. He asked the nuns at Neuville if he might be allowed to present the awards on Prize Day, and volunteered to provide the books himself. His offers were refused! The Headmistress even made fun of him to the local ladies. People suspect he has the Chamber of Deputies in mind (noble ambition!), and I think they may be right. What a strange fellow! That's what comes of not having read the classics in one's youth. If he'd studied the masters before he started shaving, he wouldn't think Dupanloup a great man.[6] I tell you all this under the most sacred seal of secrecy. Because I'd be very sorry to offend this decent chap in any way.

In Rouen, too, processions were organized,[7] but they failed completely in their effect, with deplorable results for Fusion. What a shame! Among the stupidities of our time, Fusion perhaps stands supreme.[8] I wouldn't be surprised if we were to see little old Thiers again, would you? On the other hand, fear of clerical reaction has made many of the Reds go over to Bonapartism. One would need to have a big bump of naiveté to retain faith in any of the political parties.

Have you read *L'Antéchrist?*[9] An excellent book, I think, except for some lapses of taste – modern expressions applied to things from antiquity. Renan seems to me to be improving. I spent an evening with him recently and found him delightful.

Next week I expect our great and good Turgenev.

Well, what about you? Are you never again to enter my humble abode?

I'll be going to Paris for Sardou's opening about October 20th. And again at the beginning of December, for my rehearsals.

Greetings to the family, kisses to the children, and to you, chère maître, toutes mes tendresses.

Gve Flaubert

---

[1] Flaubert eventually settled his two copyists in Calvados, between Caen and Falaise. (See Letter 383.)

² *Le Candidat.*

³ *Les Petites Gens*, a five-act play by M. Nescio (pseudonym of the comte de Coëtlogon), seems never to have been performed or published.

⁴ Hugo's drama, *Le Roi s'amuse*, had been closed by the Censor after its first Parisian performance on 22 November 1832. Now again, in July 1873, its scheduled autumn opening at the Théâtre Saint-Martin had been cancelled: the Censor's office was still displeased by Hugo's depiction of François I as brutal and debauched. The play had its definitive Paris production only in 1882 – half a century after it was written. On the other hand, Verdi's opera *Rigoletto*, its libretto by Francesco Maria Piave derived from *Le Roi s'amuse*, but its setting moved from Paris to Mantua for related reasons, had been sung at the Opéra-Comique as early as 1857.

⁵ An allusion to Hugo's intervention in favour of members of the Commune.

⁶ Mgr Dupanloup, bishop of Orléans, a Deputy since 1871, was one of the most influential leaders of the Catholic faction in the Assembly. For Flaubert at this time the name Dupanloup – he sometimes uses it in an almost abstract sense – embodies the political activity of clerical Catholicism.

⁷ The *Conseil général des pèlerinages* (General Council of Pilgrimages), founded in 1872, had been organizing "pilgrimages" and processions in favour of the temporal power of the Pope. More recently, its aims had been "broadened" to include the restoration of the French monarchy.

⁸ The first defeat of the "fusion" between the two branches of the royal family (see Letter 278, Note 2) had not discouraged the royalists. After the fall of Thiers on 24 May 1873, and the installation of the conservative government of the duc de Broglie under the presidency of Macmahon, there no longer seemed to be serious opposition to the restoration of the monarchy. In early August the royalists, after choosing the comte de Chambord as their candidate, demanded that the Assembly be re-convened from its mid-summer recess to discuss the matter. There was alarm throughout France; the Republicans rallied and campaigned vigorously against a "return to the abuses of the Ancien Régime"; and Mac-Mahon refused the royalists' demand. [Résumé by M. Jacobs "after Lavisse and Chastenet".]

⁹ Ernest Renan's *L'Antéchrist*, the fourth book of his *Histoire des origines du christianisme*, had been published by Lévy on 9 June.

*

Flaubert continued busy with his reading for *Bouvard et Pécuchet* and the writing of *Le Candidat*: he finished the first act of the latter on 21 September.

At Nohant, the Viardots and Turgenev were again Mme Sand's guests – from 16 to 29 September, the latter arriving on the 23rd. About this time, Flaubert must have sent Sand the text of his *Vie et Travaux du R. P. Cruchard*. No accompanying letter has been found.

361 SAND TO FLAUBERT

Nohant, 3 October [18]73

The life of Cruchard is a splendid creation, and so convincing I can't tell if it's a biography you've invented or a copy of some genuine article. I needed a bit of a laugh after the departure of all the Viardots (except Viardot himself) and the great Muscovite, who was charming though extremely unwell sometimes. But when he left he was very well and cheerful, though sorry he hadn't been to see you.[1] The truth is he was ill when he was supposed to have come. Like me, he's had an upset stomach for some time. I cure myself by sobriety, whereas he – he certainly doesn't! But I forgive him: these attacks leave you very hungry, and if that's in proportion to the space you have to fill, he must be famished. What an amiable, excellent and worthy man he is! and how modest, for all his talent! Everyone here adores him, and I set the example. Everyone adores you too, Cruchard de mon coeur. But you love your work better than your friends, and in that you are inferior to the real Cruchard, who at least adored our sacred religion.

Speaking of which, I believe we shall have a Henri V. People tell me I'm looking on the black side. I don't know about that, but I do smell a whiff of sacristy triumphant. However, as long as it didn't last too long, I wouldn't mind seeing our worthy clerical bourgeois being looked down on by those whose estates they've bought and whose titles they've taken over. It would serve them right.

We're having such marvellous weather in the country! I still go every day for a cold brew in my little river; and I'm getting better. Tomorrow I hope to get back to work: I've done absolutely nothing for six months.[2] I usually take much shorter holidays, but always it's the pink of the autumn crocuses in the meadows that tells me I must buckle to. And now the time has come, back to the grindstone!

Love me as I love you. My Aurore – I haven't neglected her and she's working well – sends you a big kiss, and Lina and Maurice their love.

G. Sand

[1] Turgenev, after twice postponing a promised visit to Croisset, at last arrived there the day before Sand wrote this letter.

[2] Before her holiday she had already started on the novel *Ma Soeur Jeanne*, which was published in *La Revue des Deux Mondes* beginning on 1 January 1874.

362 FLAUBERT TO SAND

Croisset, Thursday
[30 October 1873]

Whatever happens, Catholicism will receive a terrible blow.[1] And if I were devout I'd spend my time in front of a crucifix, praying "Preserve the Republic for us, O my God!" But people *fear* the monarchy, because of what it is and because of the reaction that would ensue. Public opinion is absolutely against it. The Prefects' reports are disquieting, the army is divided between Bonapartists and republicans, and big business in Paris has come out against Henri V. Such is the information I bring from Paris, where I've just spent ten days.[2] In short, chère maître, I now think "they" will be sunk. Amen![3]

I advise you to read Cathelineau's pamphlet and the one by Ségur. Very curious. It's easy to see what's at the bottom of it all. Those people think they're living in the XIIth century.[4]

As for Cruchard . . . Carvalho asked him to make changes, and he refused. (As you know, Cruchard isn't always easy.) The said Carvalho finally realized that it was impossible to change anything in *Le Sexe faible* without distorting the essential idea of the play. But he asked if he could put on *Le Candidat* first – a play that's as yet incomplete and that he of course is enthusiastic about. Once it's finished, read over and revised, he'll probably no longer want it. In short, after *L'Oncle Sam*, if *Le Candidat* is finished, he'll run it. If not, it will be *Le Sexe faible*. Actually, I don't much care one way or the other, I'm so eager to get back to the novel that's going to take me several years. Besides, the dramatic *style* is beginning to get on my nerves. Those short little sentences, the constant sparkle – it all irritates me: it's like Seltzer water, pleasing at first but soon turning stale. So from now till January I'm going to keep "dialoguing" as best I can, but after that I'll return to serious matters.

I saw our dear Muscovite, who has the stone, and stomach pains. I worry about him. He's not robust, our friend – and I fear he's no stoic.

I called on Prince Napoléon, but he had gone out. And I heard a lot of political talk – an immense amount of it. Oh, how vast, how infinite, is human Stupidity!

I'm glad to have amused you a bit with the Cruchard biography. But I think it's something of a hybrid, and Cruchard's character isn't really consistent, don't you agree? A man so astute at managing things wouldn't have such a taste for literature. And his archaeology is out of place: it goes with a different type of ecclesiastic. Perhaps it's a transition that's lacking? Such is my humble criticism.

I read in a theatrical journal that you were in Paris. That false news filled me with false joy, chère bon maître que j'adore et que j'embrasse.

Votre vieux

Gve Flaubert

Greetings to all, and kisses to the little charmers.

---

[1] The possibility of a Restoration had by now become unlikely; and the announcement by the comte de Chambord in the newspaper *L'Union* on October 30th (the day of the present letter) that his party would not necessarily preserve the tricolour as the national flag dealt the movement a further blow.

[2] From 20 to 30 October.

[3] It has often been said that Flaubert lacked any sense of politics. However that may be, in this question of "Fusion" he displayed perspicacity. He never believed in the restoration of the monarchy – as his correspondence throughout this period abundantly testifies – for reasons at once practical, historical, and psychological. When he wrote the present letter, he had not yet learned of Chambord's announcement in *L'Union*.

[4] General Henri de Cathelineau and Mgr L. G. de Ségur, canon-bishop of the Chapter of Saint-Denis, were prominent royalists. Their pamphlets were entitled, respectively, *L'Heure à Dieu* and *Vive le Roi*.

363   SAND TO FLAUBERT

[Nohant, 10 November 1873]
Monday

Your poor old troubadour, after a severe attack of rheumatism during which he couldn't lie down or eat or even dress himself on his own, is at last on his feet again. He also had something wrong with his liver, plus jaundice, urticaria and fever – in short he was only fit for the boneyard.

But now he's on his feet – very weak, but able to write a few lines and join you in saying "Amen" to the quenching of Catholic dictatorships. But one shouldn't even call those people Catholics. They're merely clericals.

I see today from the "prints" that *L'Oncle Sam* has opened. They say it's no good, but it could still be a success.[1] So I can see you being put off; Carvalho strikes me as no less slippery and capricious than other theatre managers.

Everyone at Nohant sends you their love, and I send you most of all, but I can't write any more.

G. Sand

Working well? When shall I be able to get back to it? I'm a wet rag.

[1] Released by the Censor (cf. Letter 358, Note 2), Sardou's *L'Oncle Sam* had opened on 6 November. It ran almost continuously until early March 1874, and then again for several weeks following the failure of *Le Candidat*.

364   FLAUBERT TO SAND

[Croisset] 15 November [1873]
Saturday evening

I don't like hearing you aren't well, at the onset of what threatens to be a severe winter. Please accept a bit of advice. Go somewhere warm. Whatever the expense. Let everything else go: your health comes first.

Mightn't your bathing in the brook have brought on those rheumatic pains? My brother has just been cured of his by a month's stay at Aix in Savoie.

If it's your liver that's most seriously affected, go to Vichy. Treatments there continue through the winter. Not too much philosophy, chère maître! Think of yourself, or rather of us.

I have just finished my 4th act. And in two weeks I'll have completed the whole thing. But I can't sleep. "Macbeth does murder sleep."[1]

Votre vieux

Troubadour
vous embrasse.

Let Maurice write to me if it tires you.

[1] Flaubert writes: "*Macbeth a tué le sommeil.*" He read Shakespeare in both English and French.

Le Candidat was now finished, and Flaubert went to Paris to see to its production.

365 FLAUBERT TO SAND

Paris, 8 [December 1873]
Monday

Chère maître,
I learned yesterday from the American, Harrisse,

("*L'Américain farouche est un monstre sauvage,*
    Qui mord en frémissant le frein de l'esclavage"
M. de Voltaire – *Alzire*)[1]

that you are "completely well".
    So, might you be coming to Paris for the rehearsals of *Villemer*?
    As for me, next Thursday I read *Le Candidat* to the actors at the Vaudeville,
and rehearsals will begin immediately.

Cruchard,
qui vous embrasse, is going to be very excited! A change from the silence of
the sacristy!
    Write to me if you have time.
    A big kiss to your darlings.

[1] "The wild American is a savage monster, seething as he champs at the bit of slavery."
[2] *Le Marquis de Villemer* would be revived at the Odéon from 12 December 1873 to 23
February 1874.

*

Under the date of 9 December 1873, Sand's record of "Letters sent" notes a
reply to Flaubert's of the 8th (Letter 365). Unfortunately, all that is known of
her reply is an extract printed in a bookseller's catalogue:[1]

[1] Libreria Antiquaria Pregliasco, Turin. Catalogue No. 21, 1967.

366 SAND TO FLAUBERT

Nohant, 9 December [1873]

[. . .] So you're launched into the emotions and continual disappointments
of the theatre. Ah well, that's good, but you're in for a lot of vexation and, if I
know you, some furious rages [. . .]. I love you, mon Cruchard, all of us here
love you; please keep in touch. Ton vieux troubadour.

G. Sand

367 FLAUBERT TO SAND

[Paris, 31 December 1873]
Wednesday

I'll take advantage of a quiet moment to chat with you a little, chère bon maître.

First, give my love to all your family; and accept, every one of you, my best wishes for the New Year.

And now, here's what's been happening with your Père Cruchard:

Cruchard is very busy, but serene (or *serin?*).[1] And very cool, which surprises everyone. Yes, I assure you! No indignation! No explosions! Rehearsals for *Le Candidat* have begun, and the play will open early in February. Carvalho seems very pleased with it, but he insisted that I compress two acts into one – as a result of which the first act is inordinately long. In accomplishing that task in two days Cruchard outdid himself: he slept a total of 7 hours between Thursday morning (Christmas day) and Saturday. And feels the better for it.

Do you know what I'm about to do to make my ecclesiastical role complete? I'm going to be a godfather. Little Mme Charpentier,[2] in her enthusiasm for *Saint Antoine*, has asked me to let her give the name Antoine to the child she's about to bring into the world. I've refused to allow this young Christian to be afflicted with the name of so frenetic a man. But I've had to accept the honour being paid to me – even though it costs, or will cost me dear: imagine my old mug up there beside the baptismal font, along with babe, nurse and parents! O Civilization! Thou showest no mercy! Fine Manners! – such are thy demands!

On Sunday I attended the civil funeral of François-Victor Hugo.[3] Such a crowd! And not a sound, not the slightest disorder! Days like that are bad for Catholicism.[4] Poor old Hugo (whom I couldn't resist embracing) was very broken up, but Stoical. What did you think of the *Figaro*, scolding him for wearing a "soft hat" at his son's funeral! . . .[5]

As for politics, dead calm. The Bazaine trial is ancient history. Nothing better portrays our present state of demoralization than the pardoning of that scoundrel.[6] Besides – the power to pardon (outside the realm of theology) is the negation of justice. What right has one man to prevent the fulfilment of the law? The Bonapartists should have washed their hands of him; but not at all – they were loud in his defence, out of hatred for the 4th of September. Why do all Parties support the very rascals who exploit them? Answer: because all Parties are execrable, stupid, unjust, obtuse! Example: the story of le sieur Azor. (What a name!) He robbed the clergy. No matter! The clergy saw his trial as an attack on themselves.[7]

Talking of the Church, I have just read (straight through – I'd never done so before) Lamennais' *Essai sur l'indifférence*.[8] Now I'm thoroughly acquainted with the ghastly jokesters who have had such a disastrous influence on the 19th century. To state that the criterion of certainty lies in common sense – in other words, in fashion and custom – doesn't this open the way to Universal Suffrage? Which is, in my opinion, a disgrace to humanity.

I have also just read *La Chrétienne*, by the abbé Bautain. A book of great interest for a novelist. It's an evocation of its period, of modern Paris. Then, to purify my brain, I devoured a volume by Garcin de Tassy on *La Littérature hindoustanie*. Reading that, you can at least breathe freely.[9]

As you see, your Cruchard hasn't had his wits entirely destroyed by the theatre. Besides, I can't complain about the Vaudeville. Everyone is polite and punctual. How different from the Odéon!

Our friend Chennevières is now our superior, having been put in charge of all theatres! The artistic world is delighted by his appointment.[10]

I see the Muscovite every Sunday. He is very well, and I love him more and more.

Saint Antoine will be in proof by the end of January.[11]

Adieu, chère maître. When shall we meet again? Nohant is very far away, and I'm going to be very busy all this winter! May 1874 be good to you!

Votre vieux

G

who loves you.

[1] *Serin* – canary (colloquially, "bird-brain").

[2] The Charpentiers' first son (Georges Charpentier was now Flaubert's publisher) would be born in mid-January 1874 and christened Marcel-Gustave. He died in infancy, on 16 April 1875.

[3] Victor Hugo's second and only surviving son, who had died on 26 December, at the age of forty-five.

[4] The government of May 24th had acted to discourage civil burial by openly approving the decree of the Prefect of the Rhône which prohibited any burial after seven o'clock in the morning without the participation of a clergyman from one of the legally recognized denominations. Therefore, the number of civil burials greatly increased, often assuming the character of anti-clerical demonstrations.

[5] The account of the funeral in the *Figaro* for 30 December was particularly disagreeable. Flaubert's allusion is to the following passage:

"Immediately behind the coffin walked Victor Hugo, an overcoat hung over his shoulders and fastened around his neck by the sleeves; in his left hand he held a broad-brimmed *soft hat*. We repeat: a *soft hat*, the classic soft hat, the soft hat of Belleville, the soft hat of *La Sociale*. It was distressing, that hat, and we heard many a sad comment on this obvious concession to the populace – one that should not have been made on this occasion."

[6] Accused of surrendering the city of Metz to the enemy without having exhausted all means of defence (see Letter 265, Note 1), Maréchal Achille Bazaine had been summoned to appear before the Conseil de Guerre at Versailles, Général Duc d'Aumale presiding. The trial lasted from 6 October 1873 to 10 December, and resulted in a death sentence. The President of the Republic, Macmahon, Bazaine's former comrade-in-arms, commuted the sentence to twenty years' imprisonment.

[7] Antoine Azur (not Azor) was a bank director and founder of a Catholic publishing firm that issued news-sheets carrying religious propaganda. With the cooperation of certain bishops he organized economical excursions from Paris to Rome, and a subscription in favour of the Pope. When various of his enterprises began to fail, he made improper use of his banking customers' deposits.

⁸ The *Essai sur l'indifférence en matière de religion* had been published in two volumes in 1817 and 1823. In it, Lamennais portrays the Church as the repository of all truth.

⁹ *La Chrétienne de nos jours, lettres spirituelles*, by the abbé L. E. M. Bautain (3 vols., Paris, 1859–61). And (probably) J. H. Garcin de Tassy's *La Langue et la Littérature hindoustanie* (2 vols., 1839 and 1847).

¹⁰ Philippe de Chennevières, once one of the group who used to dine together at Magny's, had been in charge of the Musée du Luxembourg. His new title, after 23 December, was Directeur des Beaux-Arts. He was thought to be the father of Louis Bouilhet.

¹¹ On 13 December Flaubert had finally given his *Saint Antoine* to Charpentier. Publication was postponed until March, in order not to interfere with a translation to be published in a Russian magazine. The delay would also avoid possible competition with Victor Hugo's novel *Quatrevingt-Treize*, which was to appear in February.

CHAPTER X

1874

368   SAND TO FLAUBERT

[Nohant, 3 January 1874]

I've got the grippe and a headache, but, though I'm completely fuddled I want to send my love and to thank you for writing for the New Year. All Nohant loves you and *te bige*, as they say in these parts.

We wish you a magnificent success, and are glad you won't have had to pay for it with a lot of vexation. Though that wouldn't arise, in my experience, from the actors; at the Vaudeville, too, I've only come across good people. Have you got a part for my friend Parade? or for Saint-Germain – you thought him a fool one day when he may have lunched too well, but if he's a chump he's a worthy one, with an excellent heart and mind. And genuine talent!

I myself don't read all the trash you feed on – apparently the better to appreciate the good bits you intersperse them with. I've finished laughing at human stupidity. I avoid it and try to forget it. But I'm always ready to admire. That's the best recipe for good health. So I'm delighted to know I shall soon be reading *Saint Antoine* again.

Let me know how the play comes along, and don't be ill in this nasty winter. Ton vieux troubadour qui t'aime.

G. Sand

369   FLAUBERT TO SAND

[Paris] 7 February [1874]
Saturday evening

At last I have a moment to myself, chère maître, so let's chat a little.

I learned from Turgenev that you are now very well: that's the important thing. And now for news of the worthy Père Cruchard:

Yesterday I signed the final proofs of *Saint Antoine*. But the book itself won't appear before April 1st (will it be a case of April Fool?)[1] because of translations. So that's settled, and I've put it out of mind: as far as I'm concerned, *Saint Antoine* now exists only in the realm of memory. However, I won't pretend that I didn't feel very downhearted for a while, as I looked at the first proof. It's painful to bid farewell to an old friend!

As for *Le Candidat*, I think it will be on from the 20th to the 25th of this month. It's something that has cost me little effort and to which I attach small importance, so I'm not particularly concerned over the outcome.

Carvalho's departure was annoying, and worried me for a few days. But his successor, Cormon, is most assiduous.[2] So far I have only good things to say of him, as indeed of everyone else. The people at the Vaudeville are charming. Your old troubadour, whom you think of as excitable and in a perpetual rage, is being gentle as a lamb, and even meek. At first I made all the changes "they" requested. Those changes "they" then saw to be foolish, and "they" restored the original text. But I myself deleted parts that seemed to me to drag. And everything is going well, very well. Delannoy and Saint-Germain look their parts and act like angels.[3] I think we'll pull it off.

One thing is annoying. The Censor's office has spoiled the part of the little Legitimate fop,[4] and now I'm afraid that the play, which was strictly impartial in conception, may seem to flatter the reactionaries. This distresses me, because I don't want to appear to favour *any* political passions – having, as you know, a fundamental hatred of all dogmatism, of every party.

So our good friend Alexandre [Dumas] has taken the plunge! Behold him, in the Academy![5] Very modest of him, in my opinion. One has to be modest to think oneself honoured by Honours.

Have you read his preface to *Faust*?[6] Sad! Sad! To say that Goethe "is not a great man" seems to me to be going rather far! I keep looking for the reason – for what lies behind such a statement, the motive that drove him to utter such an inept piece of impudence. I can't make it out. Is there perhaps a touch of Dupanloup there somewhere?

Speaking of religion, you are probably unaware that next month will see me at the foot of the altar. Little Mme Charpentier has asked me to stand godfather to her latest. One has to accept, or risk being thought a rotter.

Adieu, chère maître. Embrace all the family for me, great and small. Et à vous, du fond du coeur

Votre vieux

Gve Fl.

[1] March 31, as it was to turn out.

[2] Carvalho had left the Vaudeville rather suddenly on 19 January 1874, to become stage director at the Opéra. He was replaced by Eugène Cormon, a playwright and producer.

[3] Delannoy and Saint-Germain played the most important roles, those of Rousselin (the candidate) and Gruchet (his opponent).

[4] The character Onésime de Bouvigny in the play. The Censor had struck out a few details pertaining to his Catholicism.

[5] The younger Dumas had been elected to the Academy on 29 January 1874.

[6] A new translation of *Faust*, by H. Bacharach, had appeared in September, 1873, with a preface by Dumas. Flaubert alludes to the following passage in that preface:

"Posterity will inscribe it on tablets of bronze: 'GOETHE, born at Frankfurt, 1749; died at Weimar, 1832: great writer, great poet, great artist.' And when the fanatics of form-for-form's-sake and art-for-art's-sake ... call on Posterity to add '*great man*', Posterity will answer 'No!'"

Flaubert apparently wanted to use this fragment ironically in the second part of *Bouvard et Pécuchet*: a newspaper clipping containing Dumas' words is among the Flaubert papers in the Municipal Library at Rouen.

370   SAND TO FLAUBERT

Noh[ant], 13 February [18]74

Everything's going well and you're pleased, mon troubadour. So we're happy here because of your happiness, and we make wishes for your success. And are waiting eagerly for *Saint Antoine* and the chance to read it again.

Maurice has had a grippe that recurs every other day. Lina and I are well, The little girls are even better. Aurore learns everything with wonderful ease and willingness. She's my life and my ideal, that child. Her progress is the only thing that gives me pleasure now. All the ast, everything I've been able to learn or create, is only of value to me insofar as it may be of use to her. If I've had some share of intelligence or goodness, it's only in order that she might have a larger one.

You haven't got children. Be a writer then, an artist, a master. It's only natural – it's your compensation, your happiness and your strength. So be sure to tell us you're pressing forward. That's clearly of vital importance to your life.

And keep well. I think these rehearsals are good for you, because they make you move about.

Nous t'embrassons tous bien tendrement.

G. Sand

371   FLAUBERT TO SAND

[Paris, 28 February 1874]
Saturday evening

Chère maître,

The opening of *Le Candidat* is set for next Friday, or possibly Saturday. Or perhaps Monday the 9th? The delay is due to Delannoy's illness. And to *L'Oncle Sam*. Because we have to wait until said *Sam* falls below 1,500 francs a night!

I think my play will be very well performed – that's all I can say. As for the rest, I have no idea. I'm quite calm as to the outcome – a state of detachment that surprises me.

If I weren't being harassed by people asking for tickets I'd forget entirely that I'm about to appear on the boards and expose myself, despite my advanced age, to the jeers of the populace. Is this stoicism – or fatigue?

I've been having (and still have) the grippe – with the result that your Cruchard is prey to general lassitude, accompanied by violent (or, rather, deep) melancholy. Hawking and coughing beside my fire, I mull over my youth. I think of all "my" dead: I wallow in black thoughts. Whether this is the result of over-activity during the past eight months, or whether it's due to the total absence of the feminine element in my life, I have never felt more abandoned, more empty, more battered. What you wrote in your last letter about your beloved granddaughters moved me profoundly. Why do I have none of that? And yet I was born with every capacity for affection. But one doesn't choose one's destiny. One submits to it. I was a coward in my youth. *I was afraid* of Life. Ultimately, all accounts are rendered.

But let's revert to something more cheerful.

His Majesty the Emperor of all the Russias has no love for the Muses. The Censor's office of that "autocrat of the North" has categorically forbidden the translation of *Saint Antoine*: the proofs came back from St Petersburg last Sunday. The French edition will be banned there as well. It's a rather serious financial loss for me.[1] The French Censor came very close to banning my play. If our friend Chennevières hadn't spoken in my favour I wouldn't be produced. The temporal powers have no love for Cruchard. How droll it is, this naive hatred of Art by Authority, by every government of whatever sort!

Have you read old Hugo's *Quatrevingt-Treize*? I like it better than his last two books.[2] There are many fine things in the first volume. But all the characters talk like Hugo – he has no gift for creating real people.

At the moment I'm reading books on hygiene. How comical they are! The complacency of the medical men who write them! Such arrogance! Such asses, most of them! I have just finished *La Gaule poétique*, by the great Marchangy (Béranger's enemy!).[3] It sent me into fits of laughter. And then, to soak myself in something great, I re-read the immense, the sacrosanct, the incomparable Aristophanes. There's a man for you! What a world it must have been, where such things were written!

Next Tuesday I'm invited to sign Mlle Viardot's marriage contract. Turgenev seems very happy about the match.

I saw Prince Napoléon, who looked to me thinner, and of a darker complexion, than formerly. He asked after you. We spoke very little about politics, thank God.

Je vous baise sur les deux joues, tendrement.

Votre vieux

　　　　　　　　　　　Gve Flaubert

[1] In a letter to his niece of 23 February, Flaubert had given the sum: ". . . so I lose the 2,000 francs I'd have been paid by the *Revue de Saint-Petersbourg* and perhaps 2 or 3,000 more that I'd have had from the sale of the Russian edition in book form and from Russian sales of the French edition." It was Turgenev who had suggested *Saint Antoine* to the Russian magazine.

[2] *L'Homme qui rit* (1869) and *L'Année terrible* (1872).

[3] *La Gaule poétique, ou l'histoire de France considérée dans ses rapports avec la poésie, l'éloquence et les beaux arts*, by L. A. F. de Marchangy (8 vols., Paris, 1815–17), had enjoyed a great success.

372   SAND TO FLAUBERT

[Nohant, 10 March 1874]

Our two little girls have had horrid grippes and taken up all my time, but I've been following the fortunes of your play in the papers. I'd come and applaud you, mon Cruchard chéri, if I could leave the beloved invalids. So it's Wednesday that they pronounce their verdict on you. The jury may be good or it may be stupid – you never can tell!

I got back to work too once I'd recuperated from the long novel[1] that the *Revue* has been publishing with some success. I'll send it to you when it comes out as a book.

And *you* must let me know what happens as soon as possible on Thursday. I needn't tell you that success and failure prove nothing – the whole thing is a lottery. It's pleasant to succeed; but for a philosophic mind it oughtn't to be very upsetting to fail. I don't know anything about the play, but I believe it will be an immediate success. As for lasting success, one can never tell how that will turn out from one day to the next.

Nous t'embrassons tous bien tendrement.

G. Sand

[1] The "long novel" is *Ma Soeur Jeanne*, running in the *Revue des Deux Mondes* from 1 January to 15 March 1874 and to be published in book form in June. The new work on which George Sand was engaged was a play, *Salcède*, which she soon abandoned.

*

Le Candidat opened on 11 March. It was an utter failure, a fiasco.

Edmond de Goncourt noted in his *Journal* that the exasperated audience "mocked and jeered at the actors"; and that when he went backstage after the final curtain he found Flaubert "railing against the intolerable manners of first-nighters." Flaubert sent a report to Sand the next day:

373   FLAUBERT TO SAND

[Paris, 12 March 1874]
Thursday, 1 o'clock

Chère maître,

If ever there was a Flop! People wanting to flatter me insist that the play will catch on with the general public, but I don't believe it for a second.

I know the defects of my play better than anyone. If Carvalho hadn't driven me crazy for a month making one foolish "correction" after another (all of which I rejected), I'd have done some retouching, or rather made some changes myself that might have altered the final result. But, as it was, I grew so disgusted with the whole business that I wouldn't have changed a line for a million francs. In a word, I'm sunk.

Besides, it has to be said that the audience was detestable, all fops and stockbrokers who had no understanding of what words *mean*. Anything poetic they took as a joke. A poet says: "I'm a man of the 1830s, you know. I learned to read from *Hernani* and would have liked to be Lara."[1] That brought a roar of ironic laughter. And more of the same.

And then the public was misled by the title. They were expecting another *Rabagas*.[2] The Conservatives were annoyed because I didn't attack the Republicans, and the Communards would have liked me to throw a few insults at the Legitimists.

My actors played superbly, Saint-Germain among the rest. Delannoy, who carries the entire play, is much distressed, and I don't know how to console him.

As for Cruchard, he is calm, very calm! He dined very well before the performance, and after it supped even better. Menu: two dozen Ostend oysters, a bottle of iced champagne, three slices of roatsbeaf [sic], truffle salad, coffee, liqueur.

Cruchard is sustained by his Religion and his Stomach.

I confess I'd have liked to make some money. But since my fiasco has nothing to do with art or feeling, I really don't give a damn. I tell myself, "At last it's over," and feel much relieved.

The worst of all was the scandal about tickets. Note that I was given 12 seats in the stalls and one box (the *Figaro* had 18 stalls and 3 boxes). I never even *saw* the chef de claque.[3] It's almost as though the management of the Vaudeville set things up for a failure. Their dream came true.

I didn't have a quarter of the seats I'd have liked to dispose of. And I bought a number – for people who then proceeded to knife me during the intervals. The "bravos" of a few faithful supporters were quickly drowned in a sea of "Shhhs." At the mention of my name after the final curtain there was some applause (for the man, not the play), together with two rounds of boos from the top gallery. And that's the truth.

This morning's newspapers – the minor press – are polite. I can't ask more of them than that.

Adieu, chère bon maitre. Don't feel sorry for me. Because I don't feel pitiable. I've been having a frightful grippe, like your little girls. But I'm better.

Et je vous embrasse trétous.[4]

Votre vieux

                                        Gve Flaubert

My man said something nice as he handed me your letter this morning. Recognizing your handwriting, he sighed, and said: "Ah, the best one wasn't there last night."

My sentiments precisely.

[1] The unworldly Flaubert is surprised that a boulevard (corresponding to "West End" or "Broadway") theatre audience should laugh at references to Romantic poetry in the midst of a satirical comedy. (*Hernani*, drama in verse by Victor Hugo, 1830; *Lara, a Tale*, poem by Byron, 1814.)

² In *Rabagas* (see Letter 329, Note 4), Sardou depicts a man of advanced opinions who sacrifices his ideals to personal interest. The play had pleased Conservatives and scandalized Republicans.

³ The *claque* was a set of applauders hired by the theatre. The author of the play was expected to reward them via their leader.

⁴ *trétous*: a Flaubertian verbal invention, combining *très* ("very") and *tous* ("all of you").

374 SAND TO FLAUBERT

[Nohant, 14 March 1874]
Saturday

I've had the same experience a couple of dozen times myself, and the worst is the disgust you speak of. One never sees or hears one's own play; it's become unrecognizable, and one's ceased to have any feelings about it. Hence the philosophy with which writers who happen to be artists accept the verdict, whatever it may be.

I'd already heard something about the opening. The audience wasn't well-disposed. The subject was too near the bone. People don't like seeing themselves as they are. There's no room in the theatre now for anything but either idealism or smut. There's an audience only for the two extremes. Any study of morals upsets those whose ways are immoral, and, as these may well be the only ways left, people dismiss as boring what they in fact find uncomfortable. Anyhow, you're not taking it to heart, and that's the right attitude to adopt until you can get your own back.

I don't know anything about the play except that it was a work of enormous talent (as Saint-Germain wrote to me recently, though he did say he didn't expect it would be to the taste of present-day audiences). Do send it to me when it's published, and then I'll tell you whether it's Cruchard or the public who got it wrong. See how the next two performances go. See if the reactions of different sections of the public say anything useful.

As for the habit of doling out tickets to everyone except the author, that's how it's always been for me too. We're too easy-going. And as for friends stabbing one in the back, it happens to everybody.

Je t'embrasse et je t'aime. Get your revenge soon; I have no worries about the future.

Love from all of us. Tell your man he's right and that he's a good fellow. The little ones are better. I'm working.

[unsigned]

375 FLAUBERT TO SAND

[Paris, 15 March 1874]
Sunday

Since there would have had to be a fight, and since Cruchard detests the idea of a struggle, I have withdrawn my play, even though there was 5 thousand francs' worth of advance sales.[1] Too bad, but I won't have my actors hissed and booed. The second night, when I saw Delannoy coming off the stage with tears in his eyes, I felt like a criminal and decided that was enough. (I'm touched by the distress of three people – Delannoy, Turgenev, and my manservant.) So it's over. I'm having the play printed; you'll receive it by the end of the week.

I'm being flayed by all parties – the *Figaro* and the *Rappel*.[2] It's unanimous. People for whom I bought tickets or did other favours are calling me a cretin – for example Monselet, who *asked* his paper to let him write an article against me.[3] All of which leaves me untouched. Never have I been less upset. I'm astonished by my own stoicism (or pride). And when I seek the reason for this I wonder whether you, chère maître, aren't partly responsible.

I remember the first night of *Villemer*, which was a triumph, and the first night of *Les Don Juan du Village*, which was a defeat. You don't know how much I admired you on those two occasions. The nobility of your character (a thing rarer even than genius) was truly edifying! And I said a prayer: "O, that I might be like her under such circumstances!" Who knows? Was I perhaps sustained by your example? Forgive the comparison.

Well, I don't give a damn, and that's the truth.

But I do confess I regret the several thousand francs I might have earned. My little money-box is empty. I had wanted to buy some new furniture for Croisset. Nothing doing!

My dress rehearsal was deadly. The entire Parisian press! They took everything as a joke. In your copy I'll underline the passages they pounced on.[4]

Yesterday and the day before, those passages no longer bothered anybody. Anyway, too late now. Perhaps Cruchard's pride carried him away.

And they wrote articles about my house, my slippers, and my dog.[5] They described my apartment, where they saw "pictures and bronzes on the walls". In fact there is nothing at all on my walls. I know that one critic was indignant with me for not paying him a call: this morning an intermediary came to tell me that, and asked, "What answer shall I give him?" – "*Merde.*" – "But Dumas and Sardou and even Victor Hugo aren't like you." – "Oh, I'm quite aware of that." – "Well, then, don't be surprised if . . ." Etc.

Adieu, chère bon maître. Amitiés aux vôtres, baisers aux chères petites et à vous toutes mes tendresses.

Gve Flaubert

P. S. Could you give me a copy or the original of the biography of *Cruchard*? I have no draft of it, and would like to re-read it, to steep myself again in "my ideal".[6]

---

[1] Two items in the newspaper *L'Evénement* seem to be correct reports of Flaubert's hesitations:

15 March: "M. Flaubert is said to have wished to cancel further performances of *Le Candidat* at the Vaudeville because of the negative though courteous verdicts of the Parisian critics. We learn, however, that he has acceded to the pressure of his friends and the management of the Vaudeville not to do so."

16 March: "At the Vaudeville, revival of *L'Oncle Sam* . . . , M. Flaubert having decided yesterday to withdraw *Le Candidat* despite box-office receipts of five thousand francs, even at this early date, for future performances."

In the opinion of some professionals, *Le Candidat* might have succeeded had Flaubert not impulsively withdrawn it. But, as mentioned above, there were apparently those at the Vaudeville itself who were against the play, and whom Flaubert would have had to "fight".

² A. Vitu, in the *Figaro* for 14 March, reproached Flaubert particularly for having included no sympathetic characters in his play – a criticism recurrently levelled against certain works by Flaubert. The review in *Le Rappel* of the same day spoke of the "*ennui glacial*" caused by the play's "puerility, naiveté, and total lack of interest".

³ Charles Monselet, dramatic critic on *L'Evénement*, wrote that "Six lines of *Madame Bovary*, chosen at random, are worth more than all of *Le Candidat*." He spoke warmly of Flaubert's human and literary qualities.

⁴ However, the *Figaro*, in its report of the dress rehearsal, had predicted a great success.

⁵ One of the reporters wrote of "the hermitage at Croisset", where Flaubert worked "shut away for weeks on end, writing at night, and sleeping on a rug during the day, with his great dog Salambô [sic], for company".

⁶ Mme Sand returned the original. It was among Flaubert's papers inherited by his niece and sold after her death. (See Letter 352, Note 1.)

*

Le Candidat was published on 28 March and *La Tentation de Saint Antoine* on the 31st. Flaubert immediately sent copies of both to Nohant.

376 SAND TO FLAUBERT

[Nohant] 3 April [18]74

We've read *Le Candidat* and we're going to re-read *Antoine*. I have no difficulty about the latter: it's a masterpiece. I'm not so happy with *Le Candidat*. It's not something that can be seen by "you", the spectator, watching events unfold and trying to take an interest in them. The subject itself is off-putting; too real for the stage, and treated too realistically. From the point of view of the theatre a real rose tree is ineffective – you need a *painted* rose tree. And there's no advantage in having one painted by a master, either. What's needed is just a rough likeness, a kind of cheat. And this applies to the play. It isn't amusing to read. On the contrary, it's depressing. It's so true to life it doesn't make one laugh, and since one can't take an interest in any of the characters one isn't interested in the action. That's not to say you can't or shouldn't write for the theatre. On the contrary, I believe you will, and do it very well. But writing to be acted is difficult, much more difficult, a hundred times more difficult than writing to be *read*. Unless one is Molière and has a well-defined society to depict, eighteen out of every twenty attempts are bound to fail. But that doesn't matter. As you've seen for yourself, one is philosophical, one soon gets used to this hand-to-hand battle, and just carries on until one hits the enemy, the public, the blockheads. If it was easy, if we were sure to succeed every time, there'd be no merit in engaging in this diabolical struggle of one against all.

You see, mon chéri – I say what I think. So you can be sure of my sincerity when I back you up unreservedly. I haven't read what the newspapers say about you. I care as little for what they think about you as for what they think about me. Individual judgments are neither here nor there. Theatre makes its impact collectively, and I've tried to read your play as a member of the public *as a whole*. Even if you'd had a success, I'd have been pleased with the success, but not with the play. Certainly, from the point of view of the writing, it shows talent: it couldn't do otherwise. But it's a case of good construction being used to build a house on an unsuitable piece of land. The architect has picked the wrong site. The subject lends itself to caricature, as in *M. Prud'homme*,[1] or to tragedy, as in *Richard d'Arlington*.[2] But you treat it *exactly*, which means that the art of the theatre disappears: for exactness belongs to photography.[3] Very few people can produce a perfectly accurate photograph; but even then it isn't art. And you are an artist par excellence! Have another go and do better! as the peasants say.

I'm writing a play at the moment[4] and I think it's very good. But as soon as it's exposed to the scrutiny of rehearsal I'll find it quite dreadful. And in reality it's just as likely to be excellent as worthless. One never knows oneself what one's doing and what one's worth, and one's best friends don't know either. They can be enchanted by a play of ours when they read it, and disenchanted when they see it on the stage. That doesn't mean they've betrayed us. They've merely been affected differently. They want to applaud, but their hands fall back in their laps. The electricity has gone. The author was mistaken, and so were they. But what does it matter? When the author's an artist, and an artist like you, he wants to try again, the wiser for the experience. I'd rather see you trying again straight away than buried in your *deux bonshommes*. I fear, from what you've told me about the subject, that it may be another case of something too true, too well observed and too accurately rendered. You have the talents for that; but you have other, greatly superior capacities as well – intuition, largeness of vision and genuine power. I notice that in the past you've employed sometimes the one set of talents and sometimes the other, amazing everyone with the extraordinary contrast. Why not combine the realistic and the poetic, the true and the fictional? Isn't the most comprehensive art an amalgam of both? You have two publics – one for *Madame Bovary* and another for *Salammbô*. Put them together in one auditorium and force them to get on with one another.

Bonsoir mon troubadour, je t'aime et je t'embrasse, nous t'embrassons tous.

G. Sand

---

[1] See Letter 47, Note 3.

[2] *Richard d'Arlington*, drama in 3 acts, in prose, by the elder Dumas in collaboration with J.-F. Beudin and P.-P. Goubaux, had opened at the Théâtre de la Porte-Saint-Martin on 10 December 1831.

³ Half a century later, Marcel Proust would discuss, in his great novel, the limitations of photographic accuracy, invoking Flaubert as an example of transcendent artistic power.

⁴ Sand read her play *Salcède* to the management of the Odéon the following 31 May. It was accepted, but "with alterations to be made by the author". It was never produced.

377   FLAUBERT TO SAND

[Paris] 8 [April 1874]
Wednesday

Chère maître,

Thank you for your long letter about *Le Candidat*. Now let me add a few critical remarks of my own.

1 The curtain should have come down after the electoral meeting, and the second half of the 3rd act should have constituted the opening of the 4th.

2 Omit the anonymous letter – it's superfluous, since Arabella tells Rousselin that his wife has a lover.

3 Reverse the order of the scenes in the 4th act: that is, begin with the announcement of Mme R[ousselin]'s rendezvous with Julien, and make Rousselin a bit more jealous. He would like to catch his wife committing adultery, but is too busy with the elections.

The exploiters aren't sufficiently developed. There should have been 10 instead of 3! Then he sacrifices his daughter. That's the end of everything. And just as he becomes aware of his own rottenness, he's elected. His dream comes true. But it brings him no happiness.

That way there would have been dramatic development, and a moral.

Whatever you may say, I think the *subject* a good one.

But I bungled it. Not one of the critics pointed out how. But I know. And that consoles me.

What do you say to La Rounat's begging me, in his article, "in the name of our old friendship", not to have the play published, because he finds it so "stupid and badly written"? And he goes on to draw a parallel between me and Gondinet.¹

One of the most comic aspects of our time is the arcana of the theatre. Anyone would think that the art of the stage was a realm inaccessible to mere human intelligence, a secret known only to those who write like cab-drivers. The element of "instant success" takes precedence over all else. It's a veritable school for demoralization! If my play had been given proper support by the management, it could have made money like any other. But would it have been any better? You know I wasn't given *a single ticket*, I never even saw the chef de claque, and I was booed by one of the managers of the theatre.²

Your friend Saint-Germain so disparaged me before, during, and after my 4 performances that I didn't send him the printed text. He found that shocking. I wonder why he should have, since he thought the audience was right to go for me about lines I consider excellent. Charpentier came close to showing him

the door, so violent were his diatribes against yours truly.[3] Please believe me
– I don't give a damn about all this. But one mustn't be a simpleton: one must
know whom one is dealing with.[4]

Since we're having a gossip, let me tell you that the clerk at our friend Lévy's
is assuring customers that "Mme Sand thinks *La Tentation de Saint Antoine*
detestable." But there are some customers who won't have that, and contradict
him – Turgenev, for example: in fact it was to Turgenev that the clerk made
his remark.

La Tentation seems to be doing well anyway. The first printing of 2 thousand
copies is sold out. Tomorrow the second will be in the shops. I've been torn
to pieces in the minor newspapers, and praised to the skies by two or three
people. Nothing of consequence has appeared as yet, and I suspect nothing
may ever appear. Renan no longer writes in the *Débats*, he tells me, and Taine
is busy with his new house at Annecy.

I've been denounced by Villemessant and Buloz,[5] both of whom can be
counted on to do everything possible to make things disagreeable for me.
Villemessant blames me for "not getting myself killed by the Prussians"! It's
all enough to make you vomit.

And you want me to overlook human Stupidity! And to forego the pleasure
of portraying it! But the Comic is Virtue's sole consolation. And besides, there's
a lofty way of taking it. That's what I'm going to try to do in my *Deux bonshommes*.
Have no fear that this book will be too realistic! On the contrary: I'm afraid it
may seem impossible, so excessively will it be concerned with ideas. This little
task that I'll be beginning in six weeks will take me four or five years: it will
have *that* virtue, at least!

Adieu, chère bon maître. Amitiés aux vôtres, et à vous toutes les tendresses
de

Cruchard

[1] Edmond Gondinet's *Le Chef de division*, a satirical comedy about bureaucracy, had
opened a few months before.

[2] Flaubert wrote to Alphonse Daudet on 17 March: "Heugel, one of the managers at
the Vaudeville, booed me! So I was told by Peragallo [a theatrical agent]." As to Flaubert's
"not being given a single ticket", his meaning is not clear. (See Letter 373.)

[3] Cf. this passage with Letters 369, 373 and 374. Perhaps the name Saint-Germain is
a lapsus here?

[4] Since this is almost the last reference to *Le Candidat* in Flaubert's letters to George
Sand, it might be appropriate to mention the later career of the play.

Two revivals are listed in the *Enciclopedia dello Spettacolo*: by Antoine, for a single night,
20 April 1910, at the Odéon in Paris; and a German "adaptation" in 1914. The latter was
by Karl Sternheim, who, according to the same modern encyclopaedia, after writing a farce
called *J. P. Morgan*, produced in 1931 the "first, pallid satire of nazism", *Aut Caesar aut nihil*,
and soon thereafter was lucky enough to leave his country alive.

Later, in 1980, 106 years after its Paris première, *Le Candidat*, revived in translation as
Candidato al Parlamento, was produced in Italy by the actor-director Tino Buazzelli. See *The
Letters of Gustave Flaubert*, II, 210.

⁵ The reason for Buloz' hostility – if it really existed – is not known. Villemessant, editor of *Le Figaro*, appears to have been hostile to Flaubert because of the latter's republican sympathies.

378 SAND TO FLAUBERT

[Nohant] 10 April [1874]

Anyone who says I don't think *Saint Antoine* is a fine and excellent work is lying, as I need hardly say. And I don't know how I'm supposed to have confided in Lévy's clerk, whom I've never even met! I do remember telling Lévy himself last summer¹ that I found the book superb and of the highest distinction.

I'd have written you an article if I hadn't refused to do one for Meurice in the last few days on V. H[ugo]'s *Quatrevingt-Treize*. I told him I was ill. The fact is, I don't know how to write articles, and I've done so many for Hugo already I've exhausted the subject. I wonder why he's never written one for me: I'm no more a journalist than he is, and I could do with his support more than he with mine.

Anyway, articles serve no more purpose nowadays than having friends in the theatre. As I said, it's a battle of all against one, and the secret, if there is one, is how to produce an electric current. The subject is therefore very important in the theatre. With a novel you have time to draw the reader to you. A completely different matter! I don't agree that there's nothing mysterious about the theatre. In one way it's *very* mysterious: you can't judge your effects in advance, and even the cleverest playwrights are wrong more often than not. You say yourself that you made mistakes. I'm working on a play now, and it's impossible for me to tell if I'm going the right way about it. And when *shall* I know? The day after the first performance, if I have it put on, which isn't certain. The only thing that's amusing is work that hasn't yet been read to anyone. All the rest is a chore and part of the "job". Horrible!

Just laugh at all the gossip. The most blameworthy people are those who relay it. I find it very strange that they say all those things against you to your friends. No one ever says anything to me; they know I wouldn't stand for it.

Be brave and glad because *Saint Antoine* is doing and selling well. What does it matter if they slate you in some paper or other? Once upon a time it did matter. But not now. The public is no longer what it was, and journalism hasn't the slightest influence on literature any more. Everyone is a critic and forms his own opinion. No one ever writes me any articles for my novels. I don't even notice.

Je t'embrasse et nous t'aimons.

Ton vieux

troubadour

¹ Michel Lévy had been a guest at Nohant from 9 to 12 July 1873.

379 FLAUBERT TO SAND

[Paris] 1 May [1874]
Friday evening

Chère maître,

"All goes well!" The insults are piling up! It's a concerto, a symphony, with all the instruments playing at full blast. I've been torn to pieces by everything from the *Figaro* to the *Revue des Deux Mondes*. Including the *Gazette de France* and the *Constitutionnel*. And it's not over yet. Barbey d'Aurevilly insulted me personally,[1] and the generous René Saint-Taillandier [sic], saying I'm "unreadable", ascribes to me ridiculous expressions I have never used.[2] So much for what's in print. What's being said is more of the same. Saint-Victor tore into me at the Brébant dinner[3] (out of servility to Michel Lévy, perhaps?), as did that excellent Charles-Edmond, etc., etc. On the other hand, I'm admired by the professors of the faculty of theology at Strasbourg, by Renan, by Père Didon the Dominican, and by the cashier at my butcher's. Not to mention a few others.[4] That's the truth.

What comes as a surprise is the hatred underlying much of this criticism – hatred for me, for my person; wilful denigration; and I keep looking for the reason. I don't feel hurt. But this avalanche of abuse does depress me. One would rather inspire good feelings than bad. However, I no longer think about *Saint Antoine* – it's over and done with.

This summer I'm going to set to work on another book of the same stamp,[5] after which I'll go back to novels pure and simple. I have two or three in my head that I'd very much like to write before I die.[6] Just now I'm spending my days in the Bibliothèque, making quantities of notes. In a fortnight I'll return to my house in the country. In July I'm going to decongest myself on a Swiss mountaintop, following the advice of Dr Hardy, who calls me "a hysterical woman", an observation I regard as profound.

Turgenev leaves next week for Russia. The trip will interrupt his picture-buying mania: our friend now spends all his time in the auction rooms. He is a man of passions! so much the better for him. And another passionate one is young Plauchut. *His* passion is Terpsichore! What a dancer! What a drawing-room gentleman! As he dances the quadrille his smile and his arms are ... exquisite! ineffable!

I greatly missed you at Mme Viardot's a fortnight ago. She sang arias from *Iphigénie en Aulide*. I can't tell you how beautiful it was – soul-stirring, utterly sublime. What an artist that woman is! What an artist! Such emotions console one for existing.

So: and you, chère bon maître: the play there's talk of – is it finished? You'll be back with Duquesnel! I pity you! Now that he's put dogs on stage at the Odéon, perhaps he'll ask you for horses! That's what we've come to. Didn't you admire the indescribable style of *La Jeunesse de Louis XIV*?[7] *Some* people get away with anything! Admit it!

And your household, from Maurice to Fadet – how goes it? Kiss the dear children for me – and let them embrace you, in return, on my behalf.

Votre vieux

Cruchard

[1] Barbey d'Aurevilly, in *Le Constitutionnel* (20 April), found *La Tentation* incomprehensible. He emphasized the difference between the book's hero and its author: "between the ardent, pious character of a very great saint ... and the most frigid, materialistic, unmoral of contemporary authors".

[2] Saint-René-Taillandier: "The last book Flaubert published, [*L'Éducation sentimentale*] was a deadly bore: this one is unreadable."

[3] The Magny dinners had not survived the war, but a few of the old habitués and some newcomers now met at the restaurant de Brébant (run by Magny's brother-in-law).

[4] In a letter written the same day to his friend Mme Roger des Genettes, Flaubert mentions favourable comments by Hugo, the Parnassians and others, including two English reviewers.

[5] *Saint Antoine* and *Bouvard et Pécuchet* are books "of the same stamp" in that each of them is predominantly a vehicle for the exposition of ideas by its characters – chiefly religious in the one, chiefly scientific in the other, and, in both, social and philosophical. Those two books thus differ fundamentally from the "straight" novels, *Madame Bovary* and *L'Éducation sentimentale*.

[6] See Letter 346, Note 1.

[7] Comedy in five acts, in prose, by the elder Dumas, first performed in Brussels, 20 January 1854. With revisions by the younger Dumas, it had been revived at the Odéon on 14 March 1874.

380 SAND TO FLAUBERT

[Nohant] 4 May [1874]

Let them say what they like, *Saint Antoine* is a masterpiece, a magnificent book. Laugh the critics to scorn. Stupid lot. The present age doesn't like lyricism, but just let's wait for the reaction: it will come for you, and it will be splendid. Rejoice in the insults: they bode well for the future.

I'm still working at my play. I'm not at all sure it's any good, but I don't let that worry me. They'll tell me the answer when it's finished, and if it doesn't seem to interest anyone I'll put it away again. It will have kept me amused for six weeks. That's the main thing for people like us.

So Plauchut is become a drawing-room favourite? Lucky old boy! He's always pleased with himself and with others, and it makes him behave like an angel. I forgive him all his airs and graces.

You were fortunate to hear the *Diva Paulita*; we had her and *Iphigénie* for a fortnight in Nohant last autumn. Yes indeed, really beautiful and great.

Try to come and see us before you go to Croisset. You would make us so happy. Nous t'aimons, et tout mon cher monde t'embrasse d'un grand bon coeur.

Ton vieux toujours troubadour

G. Sand

381   FLAUBERT TO SAND

Croisset, 26 May [1874]
Tuesday

Chère bon maître,

Here I am, back in my solitude! But I shan't stay here long, because in just under a month I'm going to spend three weeks in Rigi, to breathe a bit, clear my brain, and "de-neuroticize" myself. It's too long since I've had some good fresh air. I'm tired, and feel the need of a little rest.

After which I'll set to work on my big book, which will take me at least four years: it will have *that* virtue!

Le Sexe faible, which I sent to Carvalho at the Vaudeville, was returned to me by said Vaudeville, and likewise returned by Perrin,[1] who finds it scabrous and shocking. "A cradle and a nurse on stage at the Français! Imagine!" So I took it to Duquesnel – from whom, so far (naturally), no reply.

How pervasive it is, the Demoralization engendered by the theatre! The Rouen bourgeois, including my brother, lower their voices and look ill at ease when they speak to me about the failure of *Le Candidat* – as though I had been taken to court on a forgery charge. *Not to succeed is a crime*; and success is the measure of every Good. I find this supremely grotesque.

Explain to me why certain failures are palliated, whereas it is decreed that others merit a bed of thorns. Ah! The world is a strange place, and to try to conform to its precepts strikes me as chimerical.

Talking of the theatre, where are you with your play? And what has been decided about it?

Le bon Turgenev must be in St Petersburg? From Berlin he sent me a favourable article about *Saint Antoine*.[2] My pleasure came less from the article itself than from his having sent it. I saw a good deal of him last winter, and am increasingly fond of him.

I have also been seeing le père Hugo, who (when he isn't speaking publicly about politics) is a charming fellow.

Weren't you pleased by the fall of the De Broglie ministry? I was, extremely. But the sequel?[3] I'm still young enough to hope that the next Chamber will bring us a change for the better. However . . . ? People are so stupid! So Stupid!

Ah! *saprelotte*, how I long to see you and have a long chat. Things are badly arranged in this world. Why don't we live with those we love? The abbey of Thélème[4] is a beautiful dream! But only a dream.

Embrassez bien fort pour moi les chères petites,

et tout à vous

Cruchard*

Is there an inexpensive edition of Maurice's book on butterflies?[5]

*More Cruchard than ever. I feel imbecilic, nasty, sheikish, deliquescent – and, withal, cool and calm: i.e. in the final stage of decadence.

[1] Manager of the Théâtre-Français.

[2] *Gazette nationale de Berlin*, 13 May 1874.

[3] A temporary, non-party administration organized by President Macmahon following the fall of the exclusively rightist De Broglie coalition.

[4] A "Liberty Hall" described in Rabelais' *Gargantua*.

[4] The only known edition of Maurice Sand's *Le Monde des Papillons* is the de luxe one published by Rothschild in 1867.

*

Flaubert and Sand missed one another in Paris. She arrived there on 30 May, and the next day read *Salcède* to Duquesnel at the Odéon. He seemed pleased with it at first; but his enthusiasm cooled, and two days later he asked for changes, and especially for more "love interest". Mme Sand was reluctant to tinker with it. "Since there's no hurry," she wrote to Maurice on 2 June, "I think I'll do my novel first, to avoid going stale with the play." She returned to Nohant on 10 June, after sending Flaubert a copy of her most recently published novel, *Ma Soeur Jeanne*.

382 FLAUBERT TO SAND

Croisset, [3 June 1874]
Wednesday, 5 o'clock

Chère maître,

I have just swallowed, in one gulp, like a glass of wine, *Ma Soeur Jeanne*. I'm enchanted by it. It's amusing, and moving. Really dashing! How it carries one along!

The beginning is a model of narration: then comes the psychology; and the drama (very well prepared from the start) unfolds naturally.

Your hero is a *real* man. And yet one likes him.

Still, I think he's a bit quick in dropping Manuella – who excites me prodigiously! And Sir Richard – isn't he rather too reasonable? Those are my only cavils; and they are inappropriate, because I judge from a stance different from that of the author – something *one hasn't the right to do*.

How true it is, the love of your young man for a woman he hasn't yet seen! And his breathless race to try to see her.

While writing this I'm re-reading pages 111 and 112 – marvellous.

Manuella's story is exquisite. And the doctor's jealousy, his brutality, his carping – so right. His occasional moral reflections on his own character are quite profound beneath their seeming simplicity.

At the bottom of page 211, it seemed to Père Cruchard that he himself was being embraced: he *felt* it, like a shock! What fire! *Oh, ma chère maître!* The five or six pages that follow are among the most beautiful you have ever done. I read them over and over, to savour them.

One slight objection, however: I wonder whether page 217 is quite right, given the situation and the kind of love the señora inspires. I don't understand why you need to make them chaste, since Sir Richard arrives at the critical moment.

As for the way her nerves are differently affected by two men, one exciting her, the other soothing her – the contrast is a marvel.

Similarly Chapter XVI, the story of poor Fanny's amours.

And the dance! The bolero! I was forgetting that! What a splendid description!

One shudders with terror at the question (p. 320): "*Where is the child?*" In a play, what a wonderful ending to an act that scene would be!

And I adore the conclusion: Viane, the man of reason, yielding to spontaneity. This is very comical and very effective. Perhaps I see comedy there, where you meant none? No matter. The parallelism[1] is clear.

Whereupon, my adored and ever-young maître, ever valiant and brilliant, je vous embrasse tendrement.

Votre

Gve Flaubert

You are right to call yourself a troubadour. *Ma Soeur Jeanne* is proof of it. The entire problem lies in this: to be a troubadour without being stupid; to · create Beauty while remaining True: and you have solved it once again.

---

[1] Flaubert seems to be referring to various theories of "parallelism", concerning relations between mind and matter, that were popular at the time.

*

Travelling from 18 to 23 June with his friend Edmond Laporte in Lower Normandy, the part of the province south of the Seine, Flaubert at last found the setting he needed for *Bouvard et Pécuchet*. Then he left for Paris; and from Paris went on to Rigi, arriving on the 30th.

383 FLAUBERT TO SAND

Kaltbad Rigi (Switzerland)
Friday, 3 July [18]74

Is it true, chère maître, that you came to Paris last week? I was passing through on my way to Switzerland, and I read in a "rag" that you'd been to see *Les Deux Orphelines*,[1] taken a walk in the Bois de Boulogne, dined at Magny's, etc. – which proves that, thanks to the freedom of the Press, one's no longer master of one's own actions.[2] From which it also results that Père Cruchard holds it against you that you didn't let him know of your presence in the "New Athens". It seemed to me that people there were more stupid and dull than usual. Politics has reached the drooling-point. Incessant talk about the return of the Empire.[3] I don't believe it. Still . . . ? In which case one would have to go into exile. But where, and how?

Was it for a play that you came? I pity you, having to deal with Duquesnel. He had the manuscript of *Le Sexe faible* returned to me by the Direction des Théâtres, without a word of explanation! And in the ministerial envelope there was a letter from an underling that is really something! I'll show it to you. It's a masterpiece of impertinence. One wouldn't write that way to a chap from Carpentras submitting a vaudeville sketch to the Théâtre Beaumarchais. It was Chennevières who set that tone. So much for help from friends!

This is the same play, *Le Sexe faible*, that Carvalho was enthusiastic about last year! Now nobody wants anything to do with it. Perrin thinks it would be improper to put "a nurse and a cradle" on the stage of the Théâtre-Français. Not knowing what to do with it, I've taken it to the Théâtre de Cluny. Ah! my poor Bouilhet was right to die! But I think the Odéon might show more respect for his posthumous works.

Without suspecting any Holbachian plot,[4] I too feel my toes have been stepped on rather too often, lately. And what indulgence is shown to certain others! If I had written, for example, the preface, or letter, with which Dumas has embellished *Le Retour de Jésus*, [sic][5] imagine the laughter! The jeers! After being a legislator and a moralist, he's now becoming a theologian! And a critic! He informs us that Goethe was not a poet (preface to *Werther*).[6] His friend (and yours), Dr Favre, once spoke to me of "that fool Goethe", apropos of *Faust*! Bravo!

It's like the American, Harrisse, maintaining to me that Saint-Simon wrote badly. I exploded at that. After what I said he won't belch his stupidity in my presence again. It was at table, chez la Princesse. My violence cast a pall.

As you see, your Cruchard continues to be intolerant of any flippancy about *la Religion*.[7] He's not calming down. Quite the contrary! And more and more does he execrate the infamous Michel Lévy. The very thought of that filthy beast gives me palpitations. (God's truth.)

Let's turn to pleasanter things. Have you read a book that I consider very powerful, *La Conquête de Plassans*, by Zola?[8] It's going unnoticed. Why?

I have just read Haeckel's *La Création naturelle*.[9] Nice, very nice book. It seems to me a better exposition of Darwinism than Darwin's own works.

Le bon Turgenev has sent me news of himself from the depths of Scythia. He has found the information he needed for a book he has in mind. The tone of his letter is very lively, whence I gather he's well. He'll be back in Paris in a month.

A fortnight ago I made a little trip in Lower Normandy, where I finally discovered a good setting for my two *bonshommes*. It will be between the valley of the Orne and that of the Auge. I'll have to go back there several times.[10] So, in September I'll begin the mighty task. It frightens me; I feel overwhelmed by it in advance.

Since you're familiar with Switzerland,[11] I don't have to tell you anything about it. And you'd be too scornful were I to say how deadly dull I'm finding it. I came in obedience to doctor's orders, to un-redden my face and calm my nerves. I doubt that the remedy will have much effect: certainly the boredom will have been mortal.

I'm no man of Nature. And I'm baffled by countries that have no history. I'd give all the glaciers of Switzerland for the Vatican Museum. *That* is the place to dream in. In any case, in 3 weeks I'll be back, glued to my table with its green table-cloth – in a humble retreat that you seem never to wish to re-visit.

It's a long time since I've had a letter from you, chère maître. Send me a long one.

Je vous embrasse tendrement.

Votre vieux

Gve Flaubert

¹ A play by Adolphe Dennery and Cormon, which had opened at the Théâtre de la Porte-Saint-Martin, 29 January 1874.

² P. Véron, in the Parisian weekly *Le Monde illustré*, had compressed a number of George Sand's activities during her recent stay in Paris into the space of a fictitious single day, and ended with "What do you say to that, for a septuagenarian?"

³ Encouraged by the defeat of the royalists, the Bonapartists had become more active. Some street-violence resulted, and on 13 June the government suspended the imperialist newspaper, *Le Pays*.

⁴ See Letter 207, Note 1.

⁵ *Le Retour du Christ, Appel aux femmes*, published anonymously in 1874, with a letter-preface by the younger Dumas.

⁶ *Werther*: mistake for *Faust*. See Letter 369, Note 6.

⁷ "*la Religion*" = *l'Art*.

⁸ This, the fourth volume of *Les Rougon-Macquart*, had been published on 27 May.

⁹ *Histoire de la création des êtres organisés d'après les lois naturelles, conférences scientifiques sur la doctrine de l'évolution en général et celle de Darwin, Goethe et Lamarck en particulier.* (Translated by Ch. Letourneau. Paris, 1874.)

¹⁰ See also Letter 360.

¹¹ Sand had spent the month of September 1836 in Switzerland.

384   SAND TO FLAUBERT

[Nohant] 6 July [18]74
Seventy years old yesterday

I was in Paris from May 30th to June 10th. You weren't there. Since I got back here I've been ill with the grippe and rheumatics, and often quite unable to use my right arm. But I don't feel like staying in bed. I spend the evening with my children and forget my little woes. They'll pass; everything does.

So that's why I haven't written, even to thank you for your kind letter about my novel. In Paris I got a bit overtired. I'm getting old, and beginning to feel it. I don't get ill more often, but when I do it takes more out of me. Never mind. I've no right to complain: I'm well loved and well looked after in my nest. I press Maurice to pursue his travels without me, as I haven't the strength to go with him. He leaves tomorrow for the Cantal, with a servant, a tent, a lamp and a whole lot of tools, to examine the *micros* of his entomological constituency. When I tell him you're bored on the Rigi he can't make it out.

[7 July]

I resume the letter I started yesterday. I still find it hard to use a pen. And I've still got a pain in my side. I can't manage it. Until tomorrow.

8 July

Perhaps I'll be able to do it today. I can't bear to think you might be accusing me of forgetfulness, when what stops me from writing is a purely physical weakness that has nothing to do with my feelings.

You say they've been "stepping on your toes" too much. The only paper I read is *Le Temps*, and it's an effort for me to open even one of them and see the sort of thing it deals in. You ought to be like me, and *ignore* the critics when what they say isn't of any consequence, and even when it is. I've never really understood what use it is to the author concerned. Criticism is always based on an individual point of view which the artist doesn't recognize as valid. It's because of this kind of intellectual usurpation that people challenge the sun and the moon – which doesn't prevent those luminaries from shining tranquilly down on us.

You don't want to be a man of nature. That's your loss. It means you attach too much importance to the details of human affairs, and don't reflect that even in yourself there's a *natural* force that defies the ifs and buts of human chitchat. We are of nature, in nature, through nature and for nature. Talent, will and genius are just as much natural phenomena as lakes, volcanoes, mountains, winds, stars and clouds. What man fabricates is nice or nasty, clever or stupid; what he receives from nature is good or bad – but *is*. It exists and goes on existing. And it doesn't have to consult that fabrication of opinion called "criticism" about what it has done or what it means to do. Criticism doesn't know anything about it. The business of criticism is to babble. Nature alone can speak to the intelligence, in an imperishable language that's always the same because it never departs from eternal truth and absolute beauty. The difficulty when one travels is to *find* nature, because everywhere man has altered it, and almost everywhere he has spoiled it. That's probably why it bores you: wherever you look you see it disguised or distorted. But I presume the glaciers are still intact.

But I can't write any more. So I must tell you quickly que je t'aime et que je t'embrasse tendrement. Write and tell me how you are. I hope I'll be all right again in a few days' time. Maurice is waiting for me to be well before he leaves. I'm being as quick as I can. My little ones send their love. They're in splendid form. Aurore is fascinated by mythology (George Cox, trans. by Baudry).[1] Do you know it? It's marvellous for children and parents.

Enough – that's all I can manage. Je t'aime, don't have black thoughts, and resign yourself to being bored if the air there is good.

[unsigned]

¹ George Cox, *Les Dieux et les Héros, contes mythologiques*, translated from the English by F. Baudry and E. Delerot (Paris, 1867).

385 FLAUBERT TO SAND

Kaltbad Rigi Switzerland
Tuesday, 14 July [1874]

What's this? Ill? Pauvre chère maître! If it's rheumatism, do what my brother did: being a doctor, he doesn't believe in medicine. Last year he went to Aix-en-Savoie for the waters, and in a fortnight was cured of the pains he'd been having for six years. But for you that would mean a change – leaving Nohant and the little girls: so you'll stay where you are; and you'll be *wrong*. One must look after oneself – for the sake of those who love you.

And – by the way – you said something naughty in your last letter. What? – I suspect you of forgetting Cruchard! Come, now: for one thing I have too much vanity – and then, too much faith in you.

You don't tell me what has happened about your play at the Odéon.

Speaking of plays, I'll soon be exposing myself to the jeers of the populace and the hacks. The manager of the Théâtre de Cluny, to whom I took *Le Sexe faible*, has written me an admiring letter and is ready to put this play on in October. He's counting on "a big financial success". Amen to that!

But I remember Carvalho's enthusiasm, followed by utter cooling-off. It all makes me more scornful than ever of the self-styled experts who claim to "know". Because here's a play called "perfect" by the heads of the Vaudeville and the Cluny, "unperformable" by the head of the Français, and "in need of complete re-writing" at the Odéon. Make what you can of that! And just try to follow their advice! No matter! Since those four gentlemen are the masters of our fate because they have money, and because they are cleverer than we (never having written a line), we must believe what they say, and submit.

It's strange how much pleasure idiots take in messing about with someone else's work – paring it down, "correcting" it, playing the schoolmaster! Did I tell you that because of that sort of thing I was on very cool terms with a certain Charles-Edmond? For publication in *Le Temps*, he wanted to revise a novel I had recommended to him: one that isn't particularly splendid, but a single sentence of which he himself would be incapable of writing. I didn't hide my opinion of his procedure: *inde irae*. Still, it's impossible for me to be modest enough to regard that worthy Polack as a better judge than I of French prose!

And you want me to stay calm! Chère maître! I haven't your temperament! I'm not like you, ever soaring above the woes of this world. Your Cruchard is as sensitive as a man who has been flayed alive. And Stupidity, self-approval, injustice, exasperate him more and more. Here, the ugliness of the Germans around me completely effaces the view of the Rigi! *Nom d'un nom!!* What mugs!

Thank God, "I purge all their realm of my abhorrent sight"[1] next Tuesday. I'll be in Paris from the 24th to the 26th. And at Croisset by the beginning of August.

Embrassez pour moi tous les vôtres. And write and tell me that you're better. Votre vieux qui vous chérit,

Gve Flaubert

[1] Flaubert's adaptation of Racine's *Phèdre*, Act IV, Scene 2: "*De ton horrible aspect purge tous mes Etats.*"

*

Leaving Kaltbad on 19 July – not the 21st, as he had planned – Flaubert spent a few days in Geneva and returned to Paris on the 24th. Then, after visiting his niece in Dieppe, he returned to Croisset on the 31st. There he began his novel. But he was called to Paris on various matters on 25 August, and remained there until 17 September.

George Sand, somewhat weakened by illness, stayed quietly at Nohant. Flaubert began to worry about her. "Have you news of Mme Sand?" he asked Turgenev. "She's stopped writing to me." It was he who broke the silence.

386 FLAUBERT TO SAND

[Croisset] 26 September [1874]
Saturday

So we don't love each other any more! We don't write any more. We forget Cruchard. We neglect our old troubadour. That's bad.

What is happening with you, chère maître? With you and all of yours. Health, work, etc. For heaven's sake – or rather mine – quick, a letter, a good long one. That would be a great kindness.

As for me, after being bored as a donkey at Rigi I came home at the beginning of August and set to work on my book. The opening wasn't easy. In fact it was *excruciating*, and I thought I'd die of despair. But now it's coming along: I'm into it. Let come what may! Certainly one has to be absolutely *mad* to undertake such a book. I fear it may be fundamentally impossible – in its very conception. We'll see. Ah! If I can pull it off.... What a dream!

You doubtless know that once again I'm about to brave the storms of the footlights (splendid metaphor). "Confronting the attention of the theatre-going public," I'll appear on the boards of the Cluny probably towards the end of December. The manager of that establishment is enchanted with *Le Sexe faible*. But so was Carvalho, which didn't prevent ... You know the rest.

It goes without saying that everybody is scolding me for having the play done in such a flea-pit. But since nobody else wants it, and since I'm determined it should be performed, to earn a few sous for Bouilhet's heir, I have to go along with it. I'll keep two or three little anecdotes on this subject for our next meeting. Why is it that the theatre seems generally to turn people crazy? Once you enter that world the ordinary conditions of life no longer hold. If you have the (minor) misfortune not to succeed, your friends turn away from you. You've become disreputable. People no longer greet you! I give you my word of honour that this happened to me with *Le Candidat*. I don't believe in *conjurations holbachiques*. Nevertheless, the entire way I've been treated ever since March astonishes me. Actually I don't give a single damn, and the fate of *Le Sexe faible* worries me less than the shortest sentence of my novel.

The level of public intelligence seems to me to be sinking lower and lower! To what depths of stupidity are we descending? Belot's[1] last book sold 8 thousand copies in a fortnight. Zola's *La Conquête de Plassans*, 17 hundred in six months. And he hasn't had a single review! All those idiotic Monday critics have just been swooning over M. Scribe's *Une chaîne!*[2] . . . France is sick, very sick, whatever one may say. And my thoughts take on an ever more ebony hue.

Still, there are a few comic touches. 1st Bazaine's escape, with the episode of the sentry[3]; 2nd *L'Histoire d'un diamant*, by le sieur Paul de Musset (see *La Revue des Deux Mondes* of 1 September); 3rd the entrance to Nadar's former establishment, *near Old-England*,[4] where one can contemplate a life-size photograph of Alex Dumas, a visiting-card (with photograph) of Alex Dumas, and a terra-cotta bust of Alex Dumas. "That fool Goethe" (Dr Favre's words to me) was more modest. It's true that he "wasn't a poet" (assertion by the same Alexandre: see his preface to *Werther*).

I'm sure you're finding me a great grouser, and that you're going to reply: "What difference does it all make?"

But everything makes a difference. And we're perishing from Bunkum, from ignorance, from bumptiousness, from contempt for everything great, from love of the banal, and from imbecilic chatter. "The Europe that hates you looks at you and laughs," says Ruy Blas.[5] God! It certainly has reason to.

And

Saint Polycarpe

vous embrasse sur les deux joues.

[1] Probably Adolphe Belot's *Hélène et Mathilde*.
[2] A five-act comedy, first performed in 1841 at the Comédie-Française. Revived in the same theatre 8 September 1874.
[3] After his trial (see Letter 367, Note 6), Bazaine had been confined in the fort on the Ile Sainte-Marguérite, off Cannes. He escaped from there during the night of 9–10 August, in rather mysterious circumstances. From 14 to 17 September, several guards, accused of complicity or criminal negligence, were taken to court at Grasse. During their trial one of them declared that while he was on sentry duty facing the wing occupied by the ex-maréchal, he had been "visited on three different occasions by one of the prison guards who made indecent advances to him."
[4] "Nadar" (the pseudonym of Félix Tournachon, 1820–1910) was a celebrated photographer.
Flaubert writes "near Old England" in English. Old England, founded in 1861, was, and still is, a clothing shop on the Boulevard des Capucines, specializing in British goods. The younger Dumas was perhaps being "featured" because of his recent entry into the Académie Française.
[5] "*L'Europe qui vous hait vous regarde en riant.*" Act III, Scene 2.

387 SAND TO FLAUBERT

Nohant, 28 September [18]74

No indeed, of course we're not forgetting our Cruchard adoré, but I'm getting so tedious I don't like to write to you any more. I'm insignificant, like all people who are happy at home and used to their work. Every day is the same, and solid relationships don't change. But for almost a year my daughter has been living nearby; she bought a property that used to belong to my brother,[1] and has installed herself there in a bizarre manner. I was rather against it: I knew she'd soon tire of us, and that's what has happened. She's been steering clear of us for a couple of months now, which is all to the good, since although she has wit and charm she also has the most capricious and difficult character imaginable. I myself am very patient, but the others are not so longsuffering, and breathe a sigh of relief whenever she goes away. She's always talking about how much she loves her family and this part of the world, but that claim is perpetually contradicted by her actions and her constant running down of everything and everybody – very comical when she claims to love and admire them all. Her nature is an essentially "literary" one, in the bad sense of the word. That is, all her feelings are transposed into words and are no more than skin-deep. Nevertheless, she's happy because she thinks she's perfectly all right. I've given up worrying about her.

My health hasn't been too good this year, and I haven't been away from home. I wanted the children to leave me here alone while they took the little girls on holiday. But my kind Lina wouldn't have that, and my granddaughters have continued to flourish. Aurore is as tall and strong as if she were twelve. She's an angel of uprightness and sincerity. I'm still her teacher, and her intelligence amazes me.

I've buckled down to my annual chore and am writing my novel.[2] Facility increases with age, so I don't let myself spend more than two or three months a year on it, otherwise I might just churn it out and what I produced might not be conscientious enough. I don't even write for more than two or three hours a day; the inner work gets done while I'm painting my watercolours.

So much for me. As for Maurice, he's been on two excursions, one to Le Sancy and the other to Le Plomb in the Cantal. The local name for it is *Le pélon*, which means "lawn". It's a desolate place, but interesting, and he brought back some specimens that will be very useful for his erudite researches.

We're going to be quite lonely now. Of my three great-nephews, one is in Montpellier, the other in Lyons, in finance, and the eldest, our "big René", has been appointed deputy public prosecutor in Châteauroux, where his mother has joined him. It's not far away, but the change greatly affects our everyday life. Antoine Ludre is studying law in Paris so as to take over his father's practice. They all come here in the vacations, but in a few days from now every one of our little pigeons will have flown away.

So you're soon doomed to go and endure rehearsals. You'll get used to it some day, but there are so many pills to swallow that at first they feel like boulders. You've never told me, and so I've never known, why, after being so enthusiastic about *Le Sexe faible*, Carvalho broke his word to you.[3] He probably did so just because he'd given it. Managers are made that way, *all* of them. Why, we'll never know. Duquesnel is just the same, but as I never believe a word he tells me I'm not "caught", any more than Arnal's birds.[4] I don't blame you for going to the Cluny. It's as good a theatre as any other, and I set the example. Tell me when you go to Paris, and I'll try to be in town at the same time, though I don't expect to have any serious business to take me there.

I'm not preaching you any sermons on your misanthropy this time. I'd just be saying the same thing over and over, because it *is* the same thing over and over, and if it weren't, the world would come to an end. Ever since time began the world has seemed stupid to those who aren't stupid themselves. It was to avoid that annoyance that I became stupid myself, as fast as ever I could. Sheer egoism, no doubt.

Je t'aime et je t'embrasse. Les miens t'embrassent et t'aiment. Write to us more often, don't work too hard, and love your vieux Berrichons du bon Dieu who never stop talking about you.

Ton troubadour

[1] The château de Montgivray, near Nohant. Solange had bought it in 1873 from her cousin Léontine Simonnet, daughter of Hippolyte Chatiron.

[2] *Flamarande*, which was printed in the *Revue des Deux Mondes*, 1 February – 1 May 1875. It was later divided into two parts and published in two separately entitled volumes: *Flamarande* and *Les Deux Frères*.

[3] It was not Carvalho who had "broken his word" to Flaubert, but his successor, Cormon. Carvalho had merely wanted to stage *Le Candidat* before *Le Sexe faible*.

[4] In his note here, identifying Etienne Arnal as a well known comic actor, M. Jacobs confesses – understandably enough – that he "lacked the courage" to seek the comedian's "birds" in the welter of his innumerable skits.

388   FLAUBERT TO SAND

Paris 4 [November 1874]
Wednesday

Chère bon maître,

Your old Cruchard hasn't been very lively for the last six weeks. Stomach and intestinal pains, nervous distress, ultra-black mood – that's about the size of it. I think these may all be mere symptoms of anxiety: the frightful book I'm beginning weighs on me so heavily that it's crushing me in advance. In short, I've been in a pitiable state. Just the last two days things have been somewhat better. The change of air has revived me.

I came here for Zola's opening, which was a success.[1] Despite everything. Tomorrow I return to Croisset, and shall be back in Paris in a fortnight: the reading of *Le Sexe faible* is set for the 19th of this month.

And you? When shall I see you, after so long? How much I have to tell you! And how happy I'll be to embrace you.

Our poor Muscovite is ill in bed.

Friendly greetings to all; and to you, chère maître, les tendresses de

Gve

[1] *Les Héritiers Rabourdin*, Zola's three-act comedy, inspired by Ben Jonson's *Volpone*, had opened at the Théâtre de Cluny the previous night. Zola later wrote that hostile critics had killed the play, which had been heartily applauded by the first-night audience and, especially, by the "popular" audience the following Saturday night.

389 SAND TO FLAUBERT

Nohant, 5 November [1874]

What, mon Cruchard – you've been ill? This is what I've been afraid of. I'm always having internal trouble myself, yet I do scarcely any work; so I worry about your way of life, which combines too much intellectual effort with too much confinement. Despite the charm of Croisset, which I've seen and delighted in, the solitude that goes with it makes me anxious: there isn't anyone left to remind you to eat, drink and sleep – and above all walk. Your rainy climate turns you all into stay-at-homes. Here, where it doesn't rain enough, at least we're lured out of doors by the beautiful hot sun. That Phoebus bucks us up, whereas Phoebus Apollo does us in.

But I always talk like a philosophical Cruchard who's come to terms with his own personality, addressing a Cruchard who's a fanatical devotee of literature with a mania for production. When will you be able to say, It's time to rest? To enjoy the innocent pleasure of living for the sake of living, of marvelling as one watches other people bustling about, of giving them only the surplus of oneself? It's pleasant to mull over the things one has picked up from life, sometimes unwittingly and without comprehending them.

Old friendships are a help, but then all at once they can deal us a blow. I've just lost my poor blind Duvernet,[1] whom you met here; he passed on quietly, without knowing he was dying and without pain. Another enormous void. And my nephew, the lawyer, has been appointed to Châteauroux. His mother has gone too. So we're the only members of the family left. Fortunately we're so fond of one another that we can manage, but we can't help missing our absent friends. Plauchut left us yesterday, but he'll be back for Christmas. Maurice is already at work to give us a marvellous puppet show.

And you? If you're in Paris, won't you come and spend Christmas with us? You'll have finished with your rehearsals, you'll have had a success – perhaps you'll be in the mood to return to the material things of life and eat some truffles?

Write, get better, aime toujours ton vieux troubadour et les siens qui t'aiment aussi.

G. Sand

¹ Charles Duvernet, one of George Sand's oldest friends, died 17 October 1874. When she wrote the present letter she had just written his obituary, published in *L'Echo de l'Indre* of 6 November and reprinted in *Dernières Pages*, pp. 255–8.

*

Called to Paris for rehearsals of *Le Sexe faible*, Flaubert set out on 16 November 1874. But a few days later, furious at finding that Weinschenk, the manager of the Théâtre de Cluny, could not keep his promises, he withdrew the play and sent it to the Théâtre du Gymnase.

390   FLAUBERT TO SAND

[Paris] 2 December [1874]
Wednesday

I'm filled with remorse. To leave a letter like your last so long unanswered is a crime. I was waiting to write to you until I had something definite to tell you about *Le Sexe faible*. What is definite is that I took it away from the Cluny a week ago. The cast Weinschenk proposed to me was an odiously stupid one. And he didn't keep his promises to me. Thank God I was able to back out in time. At the moment my play is on offer at the Gymnase. No news as yet from le sieur Montigny.

I'm struggling like five hundred devils with my book, and sometimes I ask myself whether I'm not crazy to have undertaken it. But like Thomas Diafoirus I "steel myself against the difficulties,"¹ and keep going – at a snail's pace, it's true. Beside the difficulties of the writing, which are frightful, I have to learn many things of which I'm ignorant. In a month I hope to be finished with agriculture and gardening. And I'll have done only two thirds of my first chapter!

Speaking of books, read *Fromont et Risler*, by my friend Daudet, and *Les Diaboliques* by my enemy Barbey d'Aurevilly.² The latter is side-splitting. Perhaps it's due to the perversity of my nature, which makes me like pernicious things, but this work seemed to me extremely funny. Impossible to go further in the realm of the inadvertently grotesque.

Otherwise, dead calm. France is sinking slowly, like a rotten hulk. Any hope of salvage seems chimerical, even to her most solid citizens. One has to be here, in Paris, to have an idea of the universal degradation, the stupidity, the senility, in which we're floundering.

The thought of these death-throes haunts me: I'm mortally depressed. When I'm not fretting about my work I moan about myself. Really. In my leisure hours I think only of the dead. And I'm going to say something very pretentious: nobody understands me! I belong to another world. The men in my profession are so little of my profession!

There's scarcely anyone other than Victor Hugo with whom I can talk about what interests me. Two days ago he quoted to me by heart from Boileau and

Tacitus. I felt as though I had received a gift, the thing is so rare. On days when there are no politicians with him he's an adorable man.

As for the Muscovite, most of the time he's prostrate on his sofa, poor fellow! He's often in pain: no longer is he full of jokes, the way he used to be.

There's one man whom I envy above all others: your son. Why didn't I arrange my life like his? Ah! If I had two darling little girls: what a refreshment for the spirit! But one isn't master of one's fate. Gradually, without your realizing, events push you in a certain direction; and then, suddenly, one day you find yourself in a hole, alone. While awaiting the ultimate hole.

It seems to me I must be boring you with my eternal jeremiads: am I? Here's an end to them, en vous embrassant tendrement.

Votre vieux

Cruchard

I shan't be able to come to Nohant for Christmas. And you? Weren't you to come to Paris this winter?

[1] Molière: *Le Malade imaginaire*, Act II, Scene 5.
[2] *Fromont jeune et Risler aîné, moeurs parisiennes* had been published on 26 June 1874; *Les Diaboliques* on 28 November.

391   SAND TO FLAUBERT

Nohant, 8 December [18]74

Pauvre cher ami,

The sadder you grow the more I love you. How you fret, and how sensitive you are to life! For what you complain about *is* life. Yet it's never been any better, for anyone, ever. We feel it to a greater or lesser degree, we understand it more or less, and the more we're in advance of our own time the more we suffer. We move like shadows beneath a layer of clouds through which the sun shines but faintly and fitfully, and we keep appealing to the sun, which is helpless. It's up to us to clear away our own clouds.

You love literature too much. It will kill you, and you won't kill human stupidity. That poor dear stupidity which *I* don't hate – I look at it through motherly eyes. For it's a kind of infancy, and all infancy is sacred. Yet what hatred you've vowed against it, and how you make war on it! You've got too much knowledge and intelligence, mon Cruchard. You forget there's something higher than art – wisdom. And art, at its greatest, is nothing but the expression of wisdom. Wisdom comprehends everything: beauty, truth, good – and enthusiasm. It teaches us to see something outside ourselves that is higher than what is within us, and gradually, through contemplation and admiration, to come to resemble it.

But I shan't be able to change you. I shan't even be able to make you understand how I see and understand happiness; by which I mean the acceptance of life as it is! There *is* one person who could change you, though, and save you; and that's old Hugo, for in part he's a great philosopher as well as being the great artist that you need and that I am not. You should see a lot of him. I think he'll be a calming influence. I'm not stormy enough now for you to be able to understand me. But I think he's retained all his thunder, while at the same time acquiring the gentleness and mercy of age.

See him – see him often, and tell him your troubles. I can see they are big ones and tend to turn into spleen. You think too much of the dead. You're too ready to suppose they're at rest. They are not. They're like us. They're still searching. Trying to search.

All my people are well and send their love. As for me, I'm not getting better, but I hope, better or not, to carry on still, so as to bring up my granddaughters, and to love you, so long as there's breath in my body.

G. Sand

*

To try to change Flaubert, to console him, was – truly – effort wasted. His melancholy, his hypochondria, his rages, were all deeply rooted. And for some time a new worry had been looming–although he still scarcely admitted it. It arose from financial anxieties, and from a suspicion that, in that quarter, "things weren't going well." The year 1875 augured ill.

CHAPTER XI

1875

Flaubert spent the winter in Paris, seeing his friends and working, with difficulty, on *Bouvard et Pécuchet*.

Sand, continually unwell, remained at Nohant.

[Paris] 13 [January 1875]
Wednesday

Will you forgive my long delay, chère maître? But I think I must weary you with my eternal jeremiads, no? I keep repeating myself, like a sheik! I'm becoming too stupid! I bore everybody! In short, your Cruchard has turned into an intolerable old geezer – the result of his own intolerance. And since I can do nothing whatever about that, I should at least be considerate and spare others my outbursts.

For the past six months, especially, I don't know what's been the matter with me. But I feel profoundly ill, without being able to put my finger on it. And I know many people in the same state. Why? Perhaps we're all suffering from *le mal de la France*. Here in Paris, at the country's heart, one is more aware of it than at the extremities – in the provinces.

I assure you that at this moment everyone senses some strange, incomprehensible disturbance in the atmosphere. Our friend Renan is one of those who feel it most desperately. And Prince Napoléon. But there's a difference: both those men have strong nerves, whereas I'm a clear case of hypochondria. One ought to be able to resign oneself. But I can't.

I'm working as hard as possible, to avoid thinking about myself. But the book I've undertaken to write is absurdly difficult, and my feeling of impotence makes me all the more desperate.

The only thing that's kept me going during these recent weeks is my anger against Halanzier and the whole boring business of the Opéra. Note that I've never set eyes on said gentleman. No matter! What exasperates me is the importance accorded him: for a month he has been *the* great personage in Europe. Besides, the inauguration of the Opéra had its sinister side. Reyer told me it was like watching the second entry of the Prussians into Paris.[1] Splendid, isn't it?

Our dear Muscovite is still not well. And Mme Plessy complains that you never come to Paris. I do the same.

Don't tell me again that "Stupidity is sacred, like all things infantine." Because: Stupidity has no generative power. And let me continue to believe that the Dead no longer "seek" anything, and that they rest in peace. We're tormented enough on earth: let us be allowed to lie undisturbed once we're below ground.

Ah! How I envy you! How I long to have your serenity! Not to mention the rest. And your two dear little ones: I send them my love, and to you too.

Your old imbecile,

St Polycarp

¹ The new Paris Opéra, designed by the architect Charles Garnier, had been inaugurated on 5 January 1875 with much publicity and a gala programme that included the first act of *Guillaume Tell*, the first and second acts of *La Juive*, the blessing of the daggers from *Les Huguenots*, a ballet, and other spectacles. In all this, the manager, Olivier Halanzier Dufrenoy, was well to the fore. It is not clear why Flaubert should have thought the inauguration "sinister", nor what the composer and critic Ernest Reyer (1823–1909) meant by his remark about the Prussians – unless, perhaps, the occasion attracted many musical Germans to the city of Paris, so recently invaded by their military compatriots?

393   SAND TO FLAUBERT

Nohant, 16 [January 18]75

And *I* send *my* love to *you*, cher Cruchard, for the New Year, which I hope will be tolerable for you, since you don't want to hear any more about the myth of happiness. You admire my serenity. It doesn't come from my character, but from my need, now, to think only of others. It's about time. Old age is creeping on, and death has got me by the shoulders. But I'm still, if not necessary, at least very useful to my family, and as long as I have breath I shall go on thinking, speaking and working for them. Duty is the master par excellence. It's the Zeus of modern times, the son of Time who has become Time's master. It lives and acts regardless of all the world's agitation. It neither questions nor argues. It examines coolly and goes forward without looking back. Stupid Kronos swallowed stones. Zeus breaks them with a thunderbolt, and that thunderbolt is will. I'm not a philosopher, but a servant of Zeus, who deprives slaves of half of their souls but leaves the souls of the valiant intact. I haven't time to think of myself any more, to ruminate about disagreeables, to despair of the human race, to contemplate my past joys and sorrows, or to call for death. My goodness, if one were selfish one would rejoice to see it coming! So easy, to sleep in the void, or to wake into a better life! For death opens up those hypotheses, or rather that antithesis.

But someone who has to go on working mustn't call for death until exhaustion opens the gates of liberty. You've missed having children. That's the punishment of those who want to be too independent; but the pain is another

glory for those who dedicate themselves to Apollo. So don't complain about
having to work: describe your martyrdom for us. There's a good book to be
written on that subject.

You say Renan is in despair. I don't believe it. I think he's suffering, like all
who take a long and lofty view, but he must have strength in proportion to his
vision. And you tell me Napoléon V[1] thinks as he does. He'd do well to share
all his ideas. He has written me a very wise and kind letter. He now sees that
a well-run republic would be a relatively good solution; I think it's still a
possibility. It will be very bourgeois and not very ideal, but one has to start at
the beginning. We artists have no patience. We want the abbaye de Thélème[2]
straight away. But before arriving at "Do what thou wilt" we have to pass
through "Do what thou canst."

Je t'aime et je t'embrasse de tout mon coeur, mon cher Polycarpe. My
children large and small do the same. Come now, we mustn't weaken! We all
have to set an example to our friends, our relations, our fellow-citizens. And I
– don't you think I need help and support in my long but not yet finished task?
Don't you love anyone any more, not even your old troubadour, who sings
all the time but weeps often, though she conceals it like a cat hiding away
to die?

[unsigned]

---

[1] In a footnote here, Alphonse Jacobs expresses uncertainty as to whether this mark is
really a V (Roman numeral 5). If so, it is perhaps a reference to the position of Prince
Napoléon, the friend of Mme Sand and Flaubert, in the sequence of imperial successors.
"Napoléon IV" was the "Prince Impérial", son of the deposed Emperor, the young man
fated to die in 1879, at the age of 23. (See Letter 276, Note 12.) Prince Napoléon, in his
"very wise letter" (3 January 1875), had written to Mme Sand that he had come to consider
a republic the only possible form of government for modern France.

[2] See Letter 381, Note 4.

*

During the following months Flaubert, increasingly misanthropic, neglected
his friends. A persistent grippe, intestinal troubles and rheumatism all intensified his depression and spoiled his Parisian stay.

On 15 February, Sand, worried at having no news, sent him a letter now
lost. Flaubert's reply, referring to the illness that caused his silence, is also lost.
Then Sand wrote again.

394 SAND TO FLAUBERT

[Nohant] 20 February [1875]

So you're not at all well, cher vieux? But I'm not worried because it's only
a matter of nerves and rheumatism, and I've lived 70 years with all that physical
botheration and am still active. But I'm sad to hear you're anxious and ailing

and gloomy, as one's bound to be when ill. I knew the time would come when you'd be advised to walk. All your trouble comes from lack of exercise. A man of your strength and constitution ought always to have kept physically active. So don't jib at the very wise advice that sentences you to one hour's walk a day. You imagine the work of the mind takes place only in the brain; but you're much mistaken. It takes place in the legs as well. Write and tell me that a fortnight of this régime has cured you. I'm sure that's what will happen.

Je t'aime et je t'embrasse, together with my brood.

Ton vieux

Troubadour

*

It was now Flaubert's turn to be anxious. Hearing on 25 March that Mme Sand was "gravely ill", he at once sent a telegram to Maurice; and, receiving no immediate reply, wrote to Lina.

Mme Sand had, in fact, been ill – a grippe with complications – but there was no cause for immediate alarm; and it was she who answered Flaubert's telegram.

395 SAND TO FLAUBERT

[Nohant] 25 March [18]75

Don't be worried about me, mon Polycarpe. There's nothing serious the matter. Just a touch of grippe, and my right arm almost out of commission, but electricity will get the better of that. It's just a strain, they think. *I*'m much more anxious about *you*: you're ten times stronger than me, but your morale is low, whereas mine accommodates itself to everything – cravenly if you like, but maybe it's a kind of philosophy to choose to be cowardly rather than cross. Write to me and tell me you're going out and walking and are better.

I've finished checking the proofs of *Flamarande*.[1] That's the most tedious part of the whole thing. I'll send you the novel in book form. I know you don't like reading snippets.

I'm rather tired, but feel like starting again on something else. When it's not warm enough to go out I get bored if I haven't got work to do.[2] All goes well in the nest, apart from a few colds. The spring's so churlish this year! But that pale sun will soon become beloved bright-haired Phoebus Apollo again, and all will be well.

Aurore is getting so tall it's quite astonishing to hear her laugh and play like a child. As gentle and affectionate as ever. The other one's still a funny little imp.

Tell us about yourself, and love us always as we love you.

Ton vieux

troubadour

¹ Proofs for *La Revue des Deux Mondes*. For publication in book form, see Letter 387, Note 2.
² She was soon to begin her novel *Marianne*.

396 FLAUBERT TO SAND

[Paris] 27 [March 1875]
Saturday evening

Chère maître,

Once again I curse the mania for dramatization, and the pleasure certain people take in announcing "important" news! I was told that you were "very ill". Your sweet handwriting came yesterday morning to reassure me. And this morning I had Maurice's letter. So, God be praised.

What to tell you about myself? I'm not up to much: I have. . . . I don't know what. Potassium bromide has relaxed me, and given me eczema on my forehead. All kinds of abnormal things are happening to me. My depression presumably arises from some hidden cause. I feel old, worn out, disgusted with everything. And I find others as boring as I find myself.

Nevertheless, I'm working – but without enthusiasm, as one performs a task. Might it be my work that's making me ill? – because this book I've begun is a mad one.

You advised me, in one of your recent letters, to see as much as I could of old Hugo. But I must tell you that he *shattered* me the last time I saw him. The foolishness of what he said about Goethe is not to be imagined: he thought, for example, that Goethe wrote *Wallenstein*, and he attributed the *Elective Affinities* to Ancillon! He had never heard of *Prometheus*, and considered *Faust* a feeble work. The visit literally made me ill.

If the Great are thus, what can the rest be like? What occasion for exaltation is left to us?

That is why I continually lose myself in childhood memories, like an old man. I expect nothing more from life than sheet after sheet of paper to blacken with my scribbling. I feel I'm crossing an endless solitude, bound for I don't know where, and that it's I who am at once the desert, the traveller, and the camel!

Today I spent my afternoon at Amédée Achard's funeral.¹ A Protestant service – as stupid as if it had been Catholic. *Tout Paris!* And a swarm of reporters.

Your friend Paul Meurice called on me a week ago to suggest that I "cover the Salon" for *Le Rappel*. I declined the honour, because to my mind no one should presume to be critic of an art of whose technique he is ignorant. Besides – what's the use of so much criticism?

I'm being sensible. I go out every day, I take exercise. And I come home tired and more out of sorts than before. So much for the good it does me. All in all, your troubadour (not very troubadour-esque!) has become a sad piece of goods. It's to avoid boring you with my complaints that I write to you so seldom these days. Because nobody is more aware than I of my unbearableness.

Send me *Flamarande*: it will be a breath of fresh air.

Je vous embrasse tous, et vous surtout, chère maître, si grand, si fort et si doux.

Votre

Cruchard – more and more cracked[2]

"Cracked" is the right word: I can feel the contents leaking out.

---

[1] Amédée Achard (1814–75), a popular novelist.

[2] Here, implied, is the word *cruche* ("pitcher" or "jar"), from which Flaubert had derived "Cruchard". (See Letter 352, Note 1.)

397   SAND TO FLAUBERT

Nohant, 7 May [18]75

So you leave me without news of you? You say you'd rather be forgotten than keep complaining. But since that won't work and you *won't* be forgotten, complain away, but go on telling us that you exist and still love us.

Since the more you grumble the better you are, I know you won't rejoice at poor Michel's death.[1] For me it's a great loss in every way: he was absolutely devoted to me, and proved it all the time by countless attentions and services.

Everyone's well here. I feel fine now it's warmer, and am working hard. I'm also doing a lot of water-colour,[2] and reading the *Iliad* with Aurore. She won't use any other translation but Leconte de Lisle's; for her, Homer is ruined by vagueness. She's a singular mixture of precocity and childishness. She's only nine, but so tall that people take her for twelve. She's still passionately keen on dolls, but as "literary" as you or I, though she's still only learning the language.

Are you still in Paris in this fine weather? Nohant is *streaming* with flowers, from the tops of the trees to the lawns. Croisset must be even prettier, because it's cool, while our fields are struggling against drought, which is now chronic in the Berry. But if you *are* still in Paris you look out over the lovely Parc Monceau, where I hope you go for walks. You must. It's the price one has to pay to live. So walk!

And won't you come to see us? We love you just the same here whether you're sad or gay, and we'd like affection to mean something to you. But we will, and do, give it to you unconditionally.

I'm thinking of going to Paris next month. Will you be there?

G. Sand

---

[1] Michel Lévy had died on 4 May. Sand wrote an obituary article that appeared in *L'Univers illustré*, 15 May (reprinted in *Dernières Pages*, pp. 269–76).

[2] Sic: singular in Sand's text.

Flaubert returned to Croisset on 9 May.

398 FLAUBERT TO SAND

Croisset, near Rouen
10 May [1875]

Twinges of gout here and there, pains throughout my body, *invincible* depression, a sense of the futility of all things, grave doubts about the book I'm writing – that's what's the matter with me, dear and valiant maître. Add to all that, worries about money, and an ever-present longing for death, together with broodings about the past: there you have my state of mind. And I assure you that I struggle to change it. But my will is eroded. I'm incapable of decisive action. Ah! I ate my cake before my bread and butter, and old age holds out no promise of being gay. Since beginning hydrotherapy I feel somewhat less apathetic, though, and tonight I'm going to resume work, without looking back.

I have left my flat in the rue Murillo and taken a larger one adjoining the quarters just rented by my niece on the boulevard de la reine Hortense.[1] I'll be less alone next winter. For I can no longer tolerate solitude – a sign that my head is empty.

Turgenev seemed very pleased with the first two chapters of my frightful book. But perhaps Turgenev is too fond of me to be an impartial judge?

I won't budge for a long time, because I want to get ahead with my work, which bears down on me like a 500-ton weight. My niece is coming here for the whole of June. When she leaves I'll make a little archaeological and geological excursion in Calvados,[2] and that will be that.

No! I did not rejoice in Michel Lévy's death, and I even envy a death so easy. In my opinion he didn't merit it. Say what you will, that man did me much harm. He wounded me deeply. I often re-live my break with him, and the memory remains painful. It's true that I'm absurdly sensitive. What scratches others tears me to pieces. Why can't I have the capacity for enjoyment that I have for its opposite?

I love what you say about Aurore reading Homer. Oh, to have a granddaughter like her! What I'm missing in life! But one doesn't design one's fate. One accepts it. I have always lived from day to day, without plans for the future, pursuing my goal – my only goal – literature – looking neither to left nor right! Everything that existed around me has disappeared, and I find myself in a desert. To put it briefly, my life completely lacks the element of *distraction*.

To write well, one must possess a certain zest. Once gone, how retrieve it? How does one stop thinking about one's wretched self? What most ails me is my disposition. If it weren't for that, all would be well. As you see, chère bon maître, I do well to spare you my letters. Nothing is more tiresome than a grumbler.

Whereupon, je vous embrasse plus tendrement que jamais, vous et les chères petites.

Cruchard

¹ The Commanvilles had rented an apartment on the fifth floor of 240, rue du Faubourg-Saint-Honoré, on the corner of the boulevard de la Reine-Hortense (today avenue Hoche). It needed refitting, and they did not move in until October.

² For *Bouvard et Pécuchet* (end of Chapter II and first part of Chapter III). But Flaubert put his novel aside in July, and did not make this trip until September 1877.

*

Financial difficulties that had threatened the Commanvilles for some time now suddenly became acute.¹ Flaubert, suffering also on his niece's account, and involved for the first time in his life in matters of "business", found it impossible to work on his novel. On 30 June he wrote to Turgenev, who had been planning to visit Croisset:

¹ "Ernest Commanville's business consisted of buying lumber from Scandinavia, Russia, Central Europe, etc. and reselling it after having it sided in his sawmill at Dieppe. He had apparently been selling before paying. . . . In 1875 lumber prices fell disastrously, and he was caught. The extent of his obligations is not known exactly: Flaubert speaks of 1,500,000 francs." [Jacobs, quoting Jacques Suffel, *Gustave Flaubert* (1979).]

FLAUBERT TO TURGENEV

30 July 1875

My last letter was "lugubrious", you say, my dear friend. But I have cause to be lugubrious, for I must tell you the truth: my nephew Commanville *is absolutely ruined*! And I myself am going to be severely affected as a result.

What makes me desperate is the situation of my poor niece. My (paternal) heart suffers for her. Sad days are beginning: lack of money, humiliation, lives convulsed. Everything has gone wrong, and my brain no longer functions. I feel that from now on I'll be incapable of anything whatever. I shan't recover from this, my dear friend. I'm stricken to the core.

Such days as we're passing through! I don't want you to share in them, so we must postpone the visit you suggest in your letter of yesterday. We cannot have you here just now. And yet God knows that an embrace from my old Turgenev would lighten my heart! . . .

For a very long time now I haven't written to Mme Sand. Tell her I think of her more than ever. But I haven't the strength to write her.

We'll have to gather our wreckage together. It will be a long business. What shall we be left with? Not much. That's what is clearest of all. Nevertheless I hope to be able to keep Croisset. But the good days are gone, and my only prospect is a lamentable old age. The best thing that could happen to me would be to die. . . .

*

On receiving that, Turgenev enclosed it in a letter to George Sand:

Bougival, near Paris, Friday, August 13 [18]75

Dear Madame Sand,

All goes well here, but there is another friend who finds himself just now in a cruel situation – Flaubert, whose letter I enclose. I blame myself all the more for not having written to you for so long when you see that he never stops thinking of you . . . A letter from you would be a great boon to him. And when I think that I have kept his letter for ten days, ah! truly, I am furious at my own indolence and selfishness. I well know that in everything Flaubert says there is the involuntary exaggeration of an impressionable and nervous man, accustomed to an easy, unfettered life; still, I feel that he has indeed been stricken, perhaps even more deeply than he realizes. He has tenacity without energy, just as he has self-esteem without vanity. Misfortune enters into his soul as into so much butter. I have twice asked him to let me visit him at Croisset, and he has refused. In a more recent letter to me he speaks [again] of the mortal wound he has suffered.

399 SAND TO FLAUBERT

Nohant, 15 August [1875]

Mon pauvre cher vieux,

I heard only today, in a letter from our dear lazy Turgenev, of your niece's misfortune. Is it really irreparable? Her husband is young and intelligent – can't he start again, or get some employment that will mend matters? They haven't any children, and they're both young and healthy, so they don't need a fortune to live. Turgenev says your own resources are damaged by the débâcle. If it's only a question of damage, it's a serious setback, but you'll bear it philosophically. You have no vices or ambitions to cater for, and I'm sure you can adjust your life to your means. The worst trial will be the suffering of the young woman who is like a daughter to you, but you will give her courage and consolation. Now is the time to rise above your own troubles in order to lessen other people's. I'm sure that even as I write you have already calmed her mind and touched her heart. And perhaps the disaster isn't as great as it seemed to begin with. Things may lighten a little, and a new way of dealing with them emerge. That's how it usually works out, and people's worth is reflected in their energy and their hopes, always an indication of strength and intelligence. Many a man has overcome adversity by his own efforts. Be sure that better days will come, and keep telling them so, for it's true. You mustn't let your own moral and physical health be harmed by this reversal. Think about curing the people you love and forget yourself. *We'll* be thinking of you instead, and suffering for you. I am truly distressed that in the midst of your spleen you should have yet another cause for sadness.

So come, cher excellent vieux, brighten up, write us a good successful novel, and think of those who love you and whose hearts bleed when you are depressed. Love them, love us, and your energy and verve will come back to you.

Nous t'embrassons tous bien tendrement. Don't write if you don't feel like it, just send a word saying I'm better and I love you all.

G. Sand

400   FLAUBERT TO SAND

[Croisset] 18 August [1875]

Wednesday

Chère bon maître,

I haven't written to you because my news was too sad. Throughout the past year I continually sensed the approach of some great misfortune. My spleen had no other cause. Now it has come to pass. My poor niece is completely ruined, and I three quarters so. At the very best we shall have barely enough to live on, and poorly at that.

Ever since I was young I have sacrificed everything to my peace of mind. Now that's gone forever. You know that I'm not a *poseur*. Well, I long to die as soon as possible, because I am *finished*, emptied out, and older than if I were a hundred. To carry on I would have to be fired by an idea, by a subject for a book. But I no longer have *Faith*. And work of any kind has become impossible for me.

So, not only am I worried about my material future: my literary future seems to me blasted.

The logical thing would be to seek employment immediately, to find some lucrative occupation. But what could I do? Remember: I'm 54 years old, and at that age one doesn't change one's habits; one doesn't start a new life!

I've braced myself against misfortune. I've tried to be stoical. Every day I make an immense effort to work. Impossible! Impossible. My poor brain is pulverized.

Since I need to get away (it's now four months that I've been agonizing here with my poor niece), it's possible that in a fortnight's time I'll go to Concarneau, where I'll stay as long as possible. I'll be with Georges Pouchet,[1] who is continuing Coste's experiments with fish-breeding there. Perhaps the sea air will do me good and I'll come back stronger.

I fear I may have to leave Croisset. That would be the coup de grâce.

Embrassez pour moi les chères petites, et à vous toutes mes tendresses.

Votre troubadour bien embêté

Gve Flaubert

[1] Georges Pouchet, director of the Laboratory of Marine Biology at Concarneau, a branch of the Museum of Natural History in Paris. (Mme Sand had met his father in Rouen in 1866. See pp. 32 and 52.) Georges Pouchet had succeeded to the post of Victor Coste, the naturalist and expert in pisciculture (the artificial breeding of fish), who had died in 1873.

*

"Sad letter from Flaubert, depressed," Sand wrote in her diary for 20 August. She longed to help her friend, but how? The best thing she could think of for him was a post of some kind – something that would provide him with the necessary funds and at the same time prevent him from withdrawing into his grief. That same day she wrote the following letter.

SAND TO AGENOR BARDOUX [?][1]

Nohant, 20 August [18]75
Indre La Châtre

Monsieur et cher maître,

I am very alarmed by our friend Flaubert's state of depression and despair. Perhaps you know that his niece Mme Commanville has met with great financial reverses, and as some of their interests were related, Flaubert's own situation is seriously compromised, damaged and threatened. He has probably written to you about this himself, but the letter I received from him today impels me to ask you if there isn't some way of rescuing him. I am not at all practical and haven't the least idea what he means by lucrative employment. But perhaps you have some idea of how such a post might be found. Despite the despondent way he expresses this wish I believe that if a position were found he would think it his duty to accept it. I also think salvation lies for him in being obliged to work, in having a duty to fulfil: his life hitherto has suffered from the lack of such an obligation and its advantages.

Cher monsieur, if there is anything whatsoever I myself can do for him, please let me know. I am grieved by his sadness and fearful for the future. When a man of his stature loses heart one can't help fearing there's something very seriously wrong. Forgive me for writing in this way, but he is so fond of you that I naturally turn to you in great confidence and hope.

Croyez à mes sentiments bien profonds de dévouement.

George Sand

[1] Agénor Bardoux (1829–91), an old friend of Flaubert's, was at this time Under-secretary of State in the Ministry of Justice. This letter does not bear Bardoux's name, but M. Jacobs, in his notes, adduces evidence making it seem likely that he was the recipient.

401 SAND TO FLAUBERT

Nohant, 7 September [18]75

You're upset and depressed, and you make me upset too. Never mind – I'd rather have you complain than keep silent, cher ami, and I don't want you to stop writing to me.

I have great sorrows too, and often. My old friends are dying before me. One of the dearest, who brought Maurice up and on whom I was counting to help me bring up my granddaughters, has just died quite suddenly.[1] It's a great grief to me. Life is a series of blows. But there's no getting away from duty: we must just go on and do what we have to do without saddening those who suffer when we do.

I beg you to exercise your will, and not to forget we share in your distress. Tell us that things are more peaceful and that the outlook is brighter.

We love you, sad or cheerful. Write and tell us how things go.

G. Sand

[1] Jules Boucoiran, Maurice Sand's former tutor, who had died at Nîmes, 18 August 1875.

402   FLAUBERT TO SAND

[Croisset] 12 [September 1875]
Sunday

I cannot write to you at length, as I should: I haven't the physical strength.

I leave tomorrow for Deauville, where I'm going to sell my last remaining bit of land in order to save my nephew from bankruptcy.[1] From there I go to Concarneau, where I'll try to resuscitate myself. I doubt that I'll succeed.

As soon as I'm more myself I'll send you my news.

You too have been going through very sad times. My sympathy for you is the more acute because of my own heavy load.

Ah! What a relief it would be if I could leave this world!

Je vous embrasse – with what strength I have left.

Your

Gve Fl

[1] From his mother, Flaubert had inherited a farm at Deauville, called "La Cour Bénouville" – land forming part of the present race-course – which brought him an annual rent of between five and six thousand francs. Now he decided to sell it to spare his niece the humiliation of her husband's bankruptcy. Of this sacrifice, Jacques Suffel has written (*Gustave Flaubert*, p. 100): "The gesture was generous, but absurd, because he ruined himself. Nothing forced him to do this, and his sacrifice did not put Commanville in the clear. The 200,000 francs brought in by the farm covered only part of the liabilities." In other words, it would have been more practical of Flaubert to let Commanville go bankrupt, and to help Caroline out of his own income. But, for Flaubert, it was a question of "honour".

*

At Concarneau, where he arrived on 16 September, Flaubert began to relax. He had sworn that while there he would "do nothing"; but within a week he was planning a story based on the legend of Saint Julian the Hospitaller, "to see whether I am still capable of writing a sentence".

On October 1st, by arrangement with the creditors, Commanville's bankruptcy was averted. The future looked dark, however: the principal of Caroline's dowry could not be touched, but she arranged to set aside a portion of her annual income to liquidate the debt. Guarantors had to be found, and Flaubert underwent the humiliation of asking friends to serve in this capacity.

403 FLAUBERT TO SAND

Concarneau (Finistère)
Hôtel Sergent
Sunday, 30 October [1875]

Chère maître,

I still hesitate to write to you these days, because I'm afraid of wearying you with my laments – a man shedding tears about his money doesn't merit much attention. But what can I tell you? I'm neither a Stoic nor a Christian. And I feel utterly prostrated. I'll never recover from this blow. Adversity is good for nothing, however much hypocrites may assert its virtue.

My nephew has devoured half my small capital. To prevent his going bankrupt I have compromised all the rest. And now I don't know how I am to live. Nothing more can be asked of me.

To put on a good front, after all that, and console myself with words like "devotion", "duty", "sacrifice" – No! No! I have been accustomed to great independence of mind, to being completely unconcerned with the material side of existence. At my age one can't start a new life. One can't change one's habits. My heart is broken and my imagination destroyed. That's how things stand with me.

I'm seeking a subject for a novel, and not finding one to my taste. Because I've abandoned my two *bonshommes*. Shall I ever take them up again? I doubt it. I've grown very timid, very lazy, a sterile coward, a brute beast. Nevertheless, to keep myself occupied I'm going to try to "put into writing" the legend of St Julian the Hospitaller. It will be very short – perhaps thirty pages.

I go to bed at 10, get up at 9, stuff myself with lobster, and walk along the shore, mulling over my memories and my griefs, deploring my wasted life – and the next day it all begins again. I watch my companion, G. Pouchet, as he dissects molluscs and explains things in which I attempt to interest myself. I eat at the table d'hôte and hear the local bourgeois talk about hunting and sardines. Every day these gentlemen spend six hours in the café. I envy them, because they seem happy. I read *Le Siècle* and *Le Temps* regularly! Great stuff! But none of this does me good.

I've read somewhere that one of your plays is to be revived at the Français.[1] Is it true? In that case will you be coming to Paris this winter? When would it be? I shan't be there before mid-November. I have no reason to be there: quite the contrary. I dread next winter, which will be no fun for my niece and me. Perhaps she will have to sell Croisset? And I may have to look for a "job" – yes, a job, in order to live. We must await the result of the liquidation. But here

I go, talking about accursed *business*. Forgive my bad manners. And continue to love

votre vieux troubadour
bien démoli

Gve Flaubert

Embrassez bien fort pour moi les chères petites. Ah! If I had one of my own to hug! Maurice has the right idea! He arranged his life well. Why didn't I do the same?

[1] *Le Marquis de Villemer*, at the Comédie-Française, with a cast to include Mme Arnould-Plessy and Sarah Bernhardt.

404   SAND TO FLAUBERT

Nohant, 8 October [18]75

There now! Your health's improving in spite of you, if you're sleeping so long at night. The sea air forces you to live, and you've made progress – you've abandoned a subject that wouldn't have been a success. Write something more down to earth that suits everybody.

Tell me what would be for sale at Croisset if it had to be sold. Is it just a house and garden, or is there a farm and land? If it wasn't beyond my means I'd buy it and you could live there for the rest of your life. I haven't any cash, but I could try to transfer some capital. Please give me a serious answer. If I can do it, it shall be done.

I've been ill all summer – that's to say, I've been constantly unwell, but I've worked all the harder to distract myself.[1] Yes, they are going to revive *Villemer* and *Victorine* at the Théâtre-Français. But there are no definite details yet, and I don't know at what point in the autumn or winter I shall have to be in Paris.[2] When I do come I shall find you in good form and hopeful, shan't I? I believe that if out of kindness and devotion you've made a great sacrifice for your niece, who is to all intents and purposes your daughter, you will and so I think you'll be able to put all that behind you and start life again like a young man. One isn't old unless one wants to be old. Stay by the sea as long as you can. The main thing is to furbish up the physical mechanism.

It's as hot here as in high summer. I hope you'll go on having sunshine where you are. Learn about life from the molluscs! They're cleverer creatures than they're given credit for, and I personally would love to go on an excursion with Georges Pouchet! Natural history is an inexhaustible source of pleasant occupation even for those who seek only amusement, and if you got interested it would be the saving of you. But you'll save yourself anyway: you're a person of consequence, and couldn't go to pieces like some ruined grocer.

Nous t'embrassons tous du meilleur de nos coeurs.

G. Sand

¹ George Sand's right arm still gave her trouble, and intestinal disorders often kept her from eating. But she continued to work steadily: new tales, additions to her *Contes d'une grand'mère*, were appearing in *Le Temps* and in *La Revue des Deux Mondes*; she corrected proofs for the publication, in book form, of *Flamarande* and *Les Deux Frères*. She was now writing *La Tour de Percemont*, which *La Revue des Deux Mondes* started to publish 1 December 1875.

² *Le Mariage de Victorine*, a comedy in three acts, first performed in 1851, was revived at the Théâtre-Français on 7 March 1876, and *Le Marquis de Villemer* on 4 June 1877.

405   FLAUBERT TO SAND

[Concarneau, 11 October 1875] Monday

Ah, chère maître! What a great heart you have! Your letter moved me to tears. You are adorable, simply adorable. How can I thank you? What I long to do is give you a great hug.

Well, this is how things stand. My nephew has devoured half my fortune, and with the remainder I indemnified one of his creditors who wanted to put him into receivership. Once the liquidation is completed, I hope to recover approximately the amount I have risked. From now until then, we can keep going.

Croisset belongs to my niece. We have definitely decided not to sell it except in the last extremity. It is worth a hundred thousand francs (the equivalent of an annual yield of five thousand), but it brings in no income, as the upkeep is expensive. Anything that might come in from the stables, gardens, etc. is counterbalanced by the gardener's wages and the maintenance of the buildings.

My niece was married under the *régime dotal*,¹ and therefore she cannot sell a piece of land unless she immediately re-invests the proceeds in real estate or securities. So, as things stand, she cannot give Croisset to me. To help her husband, she has pledged her entire income – the only resource she had.

As you see, the situation is complicated. To live, I need 6 or 7 thousand francs a year (at least) *and* Croisset.

I may perhaps recoup the six or seven thousand francs at the end of the winter.² As for Croisset, we'll decide about it later. That is the present state of affairs. It will be a great grief to me if I have to leave this old house, so full of tender memories. For all your goodwill, I fear there is nothing you can do. Since there is no urgency at the moment, I prefer not to think about it. Like a coward, I dismiss, or rather would like to dismiss, from my mind all thoughts of the future and of "business". Am I fed up with it! And have been for five months – good God!

I continue to work a little, and take walks. But now it's growing cold and rainy. Even so, I shan't return to Paris before the 8th or 10th of November.

You approve of my abandoning my bitch of a novel. It was too much for me, I realize. And that discovery is another blow. Despite all my efforts to harden myself against fate, I feel very feeble.

Merci encore une fois, chère bon maître, je vous aime bien, vous le savez. Votre vieux

Cruchard
more than ever a stupid old wreck

¹ A legal financial clause limiting her use of her dowry.

² As usual, Flaubert is vague when writing about finances. He probably means that he may recover some income-producing capital if the liquidation of Commanville's assets, the sawmill and the adjoining land, brings in sufficient funds.

*

Flaubert changed his plans and left Concarneau on November 1st. He went straight to Paris without going to Croisset, and settled into his Paris apartment.

406 FLAUBERT TO SAND

[Paris] 240 rue du Faubourg-Saint-Honoré
Sunday [14 November 1875]

Chère maître,

I read in a newspaper yesterday that the Français is rehearsing, or will be rehearsing, *Victorine*.

So you'll be coming to Paris? How I long to give you a hug!

I've been here a week or so, and have resumed work. I'm none the merrier for that. Still, the days go by less painfully. But the old fellow's about done in, I fear.

Send me a note to tell me when we'll meet.

Votre vieux

Cruchard

407 SAND TO FLAUBERT

Nohant, 15 November [18]75

So you're in Paris, and you've left your place in the rue Murillo? And you're working? Be of good cheer – "mine truly" will come through.

I know they're rehearsing *Victorine* at the Français, but I don't know if I shall go and see the revival. I've been so ill all summer, and am still having such trouble with my innards, that I don't know if, when the time comes, I'll be up to travelling in the winter. We shall see. The hope of seeing you will spur me on, you may be sure. But I've been very shaky since I entered my seventies, and I don't know yet if I shall get myself to rights again. I did so love stumping about, but now I can't walk any more without the risk of horrible pains. But I put up patiently with such woes. I work all the more, and paint water-colours in my leisure hours. Aurore consoles and delights me. I'd have liked to live long enough to see her married. But God disposes, and we have to accept life and death as he sees fit.

This is really to say I'll come to Paris to see you if it's not *absolutely* imposs-ible. And you'll read me what you've done so far. Meanwhile, write and tell me how things go, because I certainly shan't move until the last rehearsals. I know my people, and I'm sure they'll do the best they can, and anyhow Perrin will keep an eye on them.

A tender kiss from all of us[1] – we love you, Cruchard or not.

George Sand

---

[1] "Nous te *bigeons* tous bien tendrement."

408 FLAUBERT TO SAND

[Paris] 240, rue du Faubourg-Saint-Honoré
Thursday, 16 December [1875]

Things are going a little better, so let me send you a line, chère bon maître adorable.

Let's have some order in our chat. (1) "Business"[1] (loathsome "business") is proceeding not too badly. Commanville's receiver is going to stop the liquidation and propose an arrangement to his creditors which they will probably accept. If he is allowed to keep his factory and his land, which are very valuable, he can resume work. But for that he'll need capital. He intends to form a limited company. The great difficulty is to find a Chairman [for the Board of Directors]: the rest will follow of itself. To do this can either be easy, or very difficult. One simply needs to know someone in high finance. The matter could be settled and all arrangements made in 24 hours. But we know no one in that world. Do you?

So, the future remains very uncertain. I don't want to think about it. Otherwise I'd go mad: I almost did, last summer. I say that in all seriousness.

My poor niece, who had been the most courageous of all of us, is now exhausted. I'm worried by her anaemic condition. I do my best to shake off black thoughts, and keep working despite everything.

You know that I've put aside my big novel to write a little mediaeval trifle, which won't take up more than 30 pages. It transports me into a setting more seemly than the modern world, and does me good. I'm also looking for a contemporary novel, and am pondering several ideas, all of them embryonic.[2] I'd like to do something terse and violent. But I still lack the *string* for the necklace (which is the main thing, needless to say).

Outwardly, my existence has scarcely changed. I see the same people, have the same visitors. My Sunday regulars are, first, the great Turgenev, who is nicer than ever, Zola, Alphonse Daudet, and Goncourt. You have never spoken to me about Zola and Daudet. What do you think of their books?

I read nothing at all, except Shakespeare, whom I'm going through again from start to finish. How he reinvigorates one, puts air into the lungs as if one were on a mountain top! Everything appears mediocre beside such a prodigy.

Since I go out very little, I haven't yet seen le père Hugo. But this evening I'll resign myself to pulling on my boots and going to pay him my respects.

My admiration for him is infinite; but, the Courtiers around him! ... God help us!

There is much talk about Taine's book, which is just out and which I've not yet seen.[3] The senatorial elections are providing entertainment for the public – including me. Unimaginable, the baseness, the grotesqueness, of the conversations that must be taking place in the corridors of the Assembly![4] The XIXth century is destined to see the collapse of all religions. Amen! I weep for none of them.

No news of your *Victorine*? One hears the most contradictory things about *L'Etrangère*. According to Delaunay,[5] the reaction to its reading was not enthusiastic, despite the newspapers. Augier has quarrelled with the Comédie-Française.[6] At the Odéon, a live bear is to appear on stage.[7] That's all I know on the subject of literature.

When shall we see each other? I cannot come to Nohant. And you – have you abandoned Paris forever?

Amitiés à tous les vôtres. Embrassez bien pour moi vos chères petites, et à vous votre vieux troubadour

qui vous aime

Gve Flaubert

[1] There is no further enumeration.

[2] See Letter 346, Note 1. He was also making notes for an "oriental" novel, *Harel-Bey*, about "a civilized man who barbarizes himself and a barbarian who becomes civilized. He wanted to develop the contrast between two worlds that were merging." (M.-J. Durry, op. cit., pp. 104–8.)

[3] Probably *Les Origines de la France contemporaine*, Vol. 1, *L'Ancien Régime*, published on 9 December.

[4] The Senate had recently been reconstituted. Of its 300 members 225 were to be elected by restricted "popular" vote and 75 appointed for life by the Assembly (the Chamber of Deputies). Party machinations and intrigues concerning these appointments were causing scandal.

[5] The actor Louis-Arsène Delaunay (1826–1903) had withdrawn from the tentative cast of Dumas' play, which was running into trouble at the Comédie-Française. This Delaunay is not to be confused with E. L. E. Delannoy (1817–88), also an actor and also mentioned in the letters.

[6] Not permanently. The Comédie had indeed refused Emile Augier's *Madame Caverlet*, which treats of divorce, but the play later entered the repertory.

[7] In the comedy *Les Danicheff*, by the Russian writer Pierre Newsky, adapted by the younger Dumas. It would open 8 January 1876.

409   SAND TO FLAUBERT

[Nohant] 18 and 19 December [18]75

At last I rediscover my old troubadour, after he's caused me so much sorrow and anxiety. So you're on your feet again, hopeful that external events will follow their natural courses, and, however they turn out, once more finding within yourself the power to exorcize them by work.

What do you mean by someone in "high finance"? I don't know anything about it myself, but Victor Borie is a friend of mine.[1] He'll do me a favour if it suits him. Should I write to him?

So you're going to get back to the grindstone? So am I, because I've done nothing since *Flamarande* but hang around waiting for my time to be up. I was so ill all the summer. But my peculiar yet excellent friend Favre has worked a miracle cure, and I've taken on a new lease of life.

So what shall we be doing? You'll go in for *desolation*, I'll wager, while I go in for *consolation*. I don't know what our destinies stem from. You watch them go by, analyze them, but abstain, literarily, from judging them. You confine yourself to describing them, carefully and systematically concealing your own feelings. And yet those feelings can be seen through what you write, with the result that you make your readers sadder than they were before. I'd like to make them less unhappy. I can't forget that my own conquest of despair was due to my will, and to a new way of seeing things that is completely opposite to the view I once had.

I know you disapprove of personal attitudes entering into literature. But are you right? Isn't your stand due to lack of conviction rather than aesthetic principle? One can't have a philosophy in one's soul without its showing through. But it's not for me to give you literary advice, or to offer opinions about the writer friends you mention. I've told the Goncourts myself what I think about them. As for the others, I firmly believe they have more technique and talent than I. But I think they, and above all you, lack a broad and definite view of life. Art isn't merely painting or description. Besides, real painting is full of the soul that wields the brush. Nor is art only criticism and satire. Criticism and satire depict but one aspect of truth. I want to see man as he is. Not good or bad, but good *and* bad. But there's something else about him too: nuance, subtlety, shade. And for me, that is the very goal of art. Man, being good and bad, has an inner force that leads him to be either very bad and not very good, or very good and not very bad.

It seems to me that your school of writers fails to concern itself with the depths, and tends too much to stay on the surface. By dint of striving after form it underrates content. It addresses itself to a literary audience. But that audience doesn't really exist, as such. We are human beings before we are anything else. And we want to find man at the heart of all stories and all facts. That's what was wrong with *L'Éducation sentimentale*, which I've thought about a lot, wondering why a book so weighty and well written should have aroused so much rancour. The fault lay in the fact that the characters do not *act* upon themselves. They are influenced by facts, but never grapple with them. Well, I think the main interest of a story consists precisely in what you didn't care to do. If I were you I'd try the opposite tack. You are feeding yourself up on Shakespeare again, and you're right. He makes men do battle with facts; and please note that his men always topple the facts, for better or worse, crushing them or being crushed with them.

Politics are a comedy now. We've already had tragedy – shall we end up with opera or operetta? I read my paper conscientiously every morning, but apart from that I simply can't think or be concerned about it. The reason is that it's all absolutely devoid of any ideal, and I can't take an interest in any of the people involved in the sorry business. They're all enslaved by facts, because they were born enslaved to themselves.

My dear little girls are well. Aurore is marvellous, an upright soul in a strong body. The other one is all grace and sweetness. I'm still a patient and diligent tutor, but I don't have much time for my own writing, because I can't stay up after midnight and I like to spend all the evening with the family. But the shortage of time acts as a stimulus, and makes me really enjoy working. It's like eating forbidden fruit in secret.

All my dear people send their love and are glad to hear you're better. Did I send you *Flamarande* and the photographs of the little girls? If not, drop me a line and I'll send the lot.

Ton vieux troubadour qui t'aime,

G. Sand

Please give my love to your charming niece. She wrote me such a kind and delightful letter! Tell her I beg her to take care of herself and resolve to get well soon.

What! Littré a senator! It's scarcely credible when one knows what the Senate is like. But the Chamber [of Deputies][2] deserves congratulations for this attempt at self-respect.

[1] Victor Borie, agronomist and banker, director of the Comptoir d'Escompte, had been George Sand's lover in 1847–8.
[2] See Letter 408, Note 4.

*

Now, as the association between Sand and Flaubert approaches its close, we see them again engaged in passionate debate about art and life – and still no nearer to agreement on these great themes than they had been ten years before.

410 FLAUBERT TO SAND

[Paris, about 31 December 1875]

Chère maître,

I've given a great deal of thought to your good letter of the 18th, so affectionate and maternal. I have read it at least ten times, and confess I'm not sure that I understand it. Just what do you think I should do? Be more specific.

I constantly do all I can to broaden my mind, and I write according to the dictates of my heart. The rest is beyond my control.

I don't "go in for desolation" wantonly: please believe me! But I can't change my eyes! As for my "lack of conviction", alas! I'm only too full of convictions. I'm constantly bursting with suppressed anger and indignation. But my ideal of Art demands that the artist reveal none of this, and that he appear in his work no more than God in nature. The man is nothing, the work is everything! This discipline, which may be based on a false premise, is not easy to observe. And for me, at least, it's a kind of perpetual sacrifice that I make to good taste. It would be very agreeable for me to say what I think, and relieve M. Gustave Flaubert's feelings by means of such utterances; but of what importance is the aforesaid gentleman?

I think as you do, mon maître, that Art is not merely criticism and satire. That is why I have never deliberately tried to write either the one or the other. I have always endeavoured to penetrate the soul of things and to emphasize universal truths; and have purposely avoided the fortuitous and the dramatic. No monsters, no heroes!

You say, "It's not for me to give you literary advice, or to offer opinions on your writer friends, etc." But why not? I *want* your advice. I long to hear your opinions. Who should give advice and express opinions if not you?

Speaking of my friends, you call them my "school". But I wreck my health trying not to have a school. *A priori*, I reject all schools. Those writers whom I often see, and whom you mention, admire everything that I despise, and scarcely concern themselves about the things that torment me. Technical detail, factual data, historical truth, and accuracy of portrayal I regard as distinctly secondary. I aim at *Beauty* above all else, whereas my companions give themselves little trouble over it. Where I am devastated by admiration or horror, they are unmoved; sentences that make me swoon seem very ordinary to them. Goncourt, for example, is very happy when he has picked up in the street some word that he can stick into a book; I am very satisfied when I have written a page without assonances or repetitions. I would willingly exchange all Gavarni's captions for a few such marvels as Victor Hugo's "*l'ombre était nuptiale, auguste et solennelle*," or Montesquieu's "*Les vices d'Alexandre étaient extrêmes comme ses vertus. Il était terrible dans sa colère. Elle le rendait cruel.*"[1]

In short, I try to think well *in order* to write well. But my aim is to write well – I don't conceal that.

I lack "a broad and definite view of life". You're a thousand times right! But I ask you: how can it be otherwise? You won't illuminate my darkness – mine or anyone else's – with metaphysics. The words Religion or Catholicism on the one hand, Progress, Fraternity, Democracy on the other, no longer satisfy the spiritual demands of our time. The brand-new dogma of Equality, preached by Radicalism, is demonstrated to be untrue by Physiology and History. I don't see how it is possible today to establish a new Principle any more than to respect the old ones. Hence I keep seeking – without ever finding – that Idea from which all the rest must proceed.

Meanwhile I repeat to myself what Littré once said to me: "Ah, my friend, man is an unstable compound, and the earth a most inferior planet."

Nothing comforts me more than the hope of leaving it soon and not being transported to another, which might be worse. "I should prefer not to die," Marat said. Ah, no! Enough of toil and trouble!

What I'm writing now is a little something of no consequence, which mothers can safely recommend to their daughters. The whole thing will run to only thirty pages. It will take me another two months. Such is my verve! I'll send it to you as soon as it appears – (not the verve, the little story).

I have two photographs of your darling little ones. But I do not have *Flamarande*.

So! May 1876 be kind to all of you.

Je vous embrasse tendrement, chère bon maître adorable.

Votre

Cruchard
de plus en plus rébarb*ara*tif [sic]

---

[1] "The darkness was nuptial, august and solemn" (from *Booz endormi*); and "Alexander's vices were as extreme as his virtues. His anger was terrible. It made him cruel" (from *Lysimaque*).

Marcel Proust was struck by Flaubert's admiration of Montesquieu's sentence. ". . . I imagine that what Flaubert particularly admired," Proust wrote to Léon Daudet in March, 1920, "was its wonderful, steady *continuity*. Even so, it is certainly lighter, more spontaneous, than Flaubert's own prose."

CHAPTER XII

1876

On 2 January – as we know from her list of letters written – Mme Sand sent New Year's greetings to Flaubert. And ten days later she replied at length to his credo of 31 December.

411   SAND TO FLAUBERT

Nohant, 12 January 1876

Mon chéri Cruchard,

I've been meaning to write to you every day but have had absolutely no time. At last there's a space, though; we're buried in snow. I adore this kind of weather: the whiteness is like a universal purification, and indoor amusements are even more cosy and pleasant. How can anyone hate winter in the country? Snow is one of the most beautiful sights in the whole year!

It seems my sermons aren't very clear. I have that in common with the orthodox, but I'm not one of them: I have no fixed plan about either equality or authority. You seem to think I want to convert you to some doctrine or other. Not at all – I wouldn't dream of it. Everyone sees things from his own point of view, which I acknowledge should be chosen freely. I can summarize my own point of view in a few words: not to stand in front of a misted window which shows one nothing but the reflection of one's own nose. And to see as much as possible – good, evil, near, far, around, about; and to perceive how everything, tangible or intangible, constantly gravitates towards the necessity of goodness, kindness, truth and beauty.

I don't say humanity's on the way to the heights. I happen to think it is, in spite of everything, but I don't argue about it – there's no point, because everyone judges according to what he sees, and at the moment the general prospect is meagre and ugly. In any case, I don't need to be sure that the world will be saved in order to believe in the necessity of goodness and beauty. If the world departs from this law it will perish; if its citizens reject it they will be destroyed. Other planets and other souls will trample them underfoot – no matter! But for my part, I want to tend upwards till my last gasp, not because I either expect or need to find a "haven" for myself elsewhere, but because my only pleasure is to stay with the people I love on the path that leads upward.

In other words, I shun the sewer and seek what is dry and clean, in the conviction that this is the law of my existence. Being human doesn't amount to much; we're still very close to the apes from whom we're said to descend. So be it. All the more reason to distinguish ourselves from them, and at least be worthy of the relative truth which our species has been permitted to understand: a very poor, limited, humble truth, at that! But still let us grasp it as well as we can, and not suffer it to be taken away from us.

I think you and I really agree; but I practise this simple religion and you do not, since you let yourself be got down; your heart is not convinced of it, since you curse life and wish for death like some Catholic looking for recompense, if not for eternal rest. You can't be sure, any more than anyone else, of that recompense. Life may be eternal, in which case toil is eternal too. If that's the case, let us run our course bravely. If it's otherwise and the self perishes completely, let's earn the honour of having performed our task, our duty – for we have no clear duties but towards ourselves and our fellow-creatures. What we destroy in ourselves we destroy in them. Our abasement degrades them, our falls drag them down; we owe it to them to remain upright so that they may not be laid low. The wish for a speedy death, like the desire for long life, is a weakness, and I don't want you to go on thinking of it as a right. I once thought I had that right too, though I believed then what I believe now. But I lacked strength and said, like you, "I can't help it." I was lying to myself. One can do anything. One discovers unsuspected strength when one really wants to "climb upward", to go a rung higher every day, to say to oneself, "The Flaubert of tomorrow has got to be better than the Flaubert of today, and the Flaubert of the day after tomorrow must be stronger and more lucid still." Once you feel you're on the ladder you'll soon start to mount it. Before long you will gradually be entering upon the happiest and most propitious part of life: old age. It's then that art reveals itself in all its sweetness; in our youth it manifests itself in anguish. You prefer a well-written sentence to the whole of metaphysics. I too like to see that which elsewhere fills volumes reduced to a few words; but a writer has to have understood the true content of those volumes, whether he accepts or rejects it, before he can produce the sublime summary that is the pinnacle of literary art. So we shouldn't despise the efforts the human mind has made in order to arrive at the truth.

I say this because you are extremely prejudiced as far as mere *words* are concerned. In reality, however, you read and ponder and work at things much harder than I and many another. You have acquired a degree of learning which I shall never attain. So you are a hundred times richer than any of us – and yet you howl as if you were poor. Give alms to a beggar whose mattress is stuffed with gold, but who will eat nothing but well-written sentences and carefully chosen words? Foolish fellow, dig into your mattress and eat your gold. Feed on the ideas and feelings you've amassed in your head and heart; the words and phrases, the *form* you attach such importance to, will emerge of themselves. You regard form as an end when it is only an effect. The best visible effects emerge only from emotion, and emotion comes only from conviction. No one is ever moved by something he doesn't ardently believe in.

I don't say you don't believe. On the contrary: one aspect of your life is all affection, protection of others, graceful and simple kindness, which shows that you're a more convinced believer than anyone. But as soon as you're dealing with literature you insist for some reason or other on being a different person, one who has to disappear or even annihilate himself – one who doesn't exist! What a strange obsession! What misguided "good taste"! Our work can never be better than we are ourselves.

Who's saying anything about putting your *self* on the stage? Of course that's no good, unless one's actually writing a first-person story or recording a personal experience. But to withdraw one's *soul* from what one writes – what kind of morbid fancy is that? If a writer conceals his opinion of his characters, and so leaves the reader uncertain what *he's* to make of them, then that writer is asking to be misunderstood, and the reader is bound to abandon him. For if your reader is to want to understand the story you're telling him, he must be shown clearly which of the characters are supposed to be strong and which are supposed to be weak.

L'Éducation sentimentale was misunderstood.[1] I kept telling you, but you wouldn't listen. It needed either a short preface, or some expression of disapproval, if only a significant word here or there, to condemn evil, call weakness by its right name, and draw attention to endeavour. All the characters in the book are weak and come to nothing except those whose instincts are evil: that's the criticism people make, because they haven't understood that your intention was precisely to depict a deplorable society which encourages bad instincts and ruins noble efforts. But when we are misunderstood it is always our own fault. What the reader wants most of all is to be able to grasp what we think; but you loftily refuse to comply. I understood you because I knew you. If someone had given me the book to read without any name attached, I'd have found it fine but strange, and wondered whether you were immoral, a sceptic, indifferent or in despair. You say that's how it ought to be, and that M. Flaubert would be breaking the rules of good taste if he showed what he thought and revealed his literary intentions. Wrong, absolutely wrong. Provided M. Flaubert writes seriously and well, the reader will grow fond of his personality and be ready to sink or swim with him. But when an author leaves him in doubt the reader loses interest, fails to understand the book, and puts it aside unfinished.

I've done battle before against your favourite heresy – that one writes for twenty intelligent people and lets the rest go hang. But it's not really genuine because lack of success bothers and irks you. Anyhow, the book in question, well written and important as it is, didn't meet with twenty favourable critics. So one should no more write for twenty people than for three, or for a hundred thousand. One should write for all who love reading and can benefit from a good book. Therefore one should draw upon the highest morality within one, and not make a mystery about the ethical, useful aspect of what one writes. *Madame Bovary* proved it. Although a section of the public made an outcry, the larger and saner part of it saw in the book a severe and striking judgment on a woman faithless and without conscience; a rebuke to vanity, ambition and folly. They pitied the woman, as art saw to it that they should, but the lesson was plain. And it would have been even plainer – plain to *all* – if you'd deigned to show what you thought, and what should be thought, about the woman, her husband and her lovers.

This desire to depict things as they are, and the events of life as they appear, seems to me to be based on unsound arguments. It's all one to me whether someone represents non-living things realistically or poetically, but it's a different matter when it comes to the impulses of the human heart. The writer can't abstract himself from his contemplation of these, for the writer is a man and his readers are humanity. You[2] can't prevent your story being a conversation between your reader and yourself. If you show him evil coldly, without ever showing him good, he gets angry. He wonders who is bad – he or you. You are trying to move him, to engage his feelings, but you won't succeed if you are unmoved yourself, or if you conceal your feelings so well that he thinks you indifferent. And he is right: supreme impartiality is anti-human, and a novel ought above all to be human. If it isn't, it gets no credit for being well written, well constructed and well observed. It lacks the essential quality: interest.

The reader also loses interest in a book whose characters are merely good, without any weakness or light and shade: he can see that this isn't human either. I believe that the art, the special art, of the novel resides in the conflict between the characters. But in that struggle I want to see good triumph. Let a good man be crushed by facts if necessary, but let him not be sullied or degraded by them. Let him go to the stake feeling he is more fortunate than his persecutors.

15 January 1876

I wrote the above three days ago, and every day I've been on the point of throwing it on the fire; it's long and diffuse and probably useless. When people's natures contrast on certain points it's difficult for them to comprehend each other, and I fear you will understand me no better now than before. But I send you my scribble anyway, so that you can see I'm concerned about you almost as much as about myself.

You could do with a success, after some bad luck which affected you deeply. I'm just telling you how to make success a certainty. Hold on to your worship of form; but pay more attention to content. Don't regard genuine virtue as a platitude in literature. Let it have its representative, let there be some decent and strong men among the madmen and idiots you like making fun of. Show the sound elements that exist inside even those intellectual abortions. In short, abandon the conventions of the realists and return to true reality, which is made up of a mixture of good and evil, bright and dull; but in which the desire for good nevertheless has a place and a use.

Je t'embrasse pour nous tous.

G. Sand

[1] What are considered the obscurities – whether of intention or text – of *L'Éducation sentimentale* have remained a theme of discussion. In his exchange of letters on this subject with Léon Daudet, Marcel Proust gave his view (shortly after 7 March 1920): "Flaubert had a certain concept, perhaps a bit gross [*lourde*] of beauty. To that concept he sacrificed correctness of language, and many other things. From your point of view, the first mistake in French in *L'Éducation sentimentale* is the title itself. This is certainly obscure, since you interpret it as meaning 'The education of the feelings' (*L'Éducation du sentiment*). Whereas I interpret it quite differently: '*L'Éducation purement sentimentale*' – an education in which the young man's teachers address themselves only to his feelings. If I'm right, the novel of Flaubert's to which the title *L'Éducation sentimentale* would be most appropriate is *Madame Bovary*. That heroine is certainly a victim of just such an *éducation sentimentale*."

And in an earlier letter, of September 1919, to Louis de Robert, Proust had stated: "I infinitely admire Flaubert (at least, *L'Éducation sentimentale*. That title, incidentally, is incorrect French) but I don't have to agree with an author's conclusions to admire his dialectic." The exchange with Daudet had arisen from Proust's essay *A propos du Style de Flaubert* in the *Nouvelle Revue Française* for 1 January 1920.

[2] Here Sand addresses all "Realist" writers.

*

At the same time, Sand sent Flaubert copies of *Flamarande* and *Les Deux Frères*. Flaubert found them poor: "Most upsetting" was his only comment in a letter of 5 February to Turgenev. It was not, in any case, a moment when his literary judgment of George Sand's work was likely to be indulgent. His disappointment is evident in his reply to Sand's long letter.

412 FLAUBERT TO SAND

[Paris, 6 February 1876]
Sunday evening

What a beast you must think me, chère maître! Because I haven't answered your last letter and haven't said a word about your two volumes – not to mention that a third has come from you this very morning.[1]

But for the past fortnight I've been completely engrossed in my little story, which will soon be finished. I've been obliged to do various errands, and some reading, and certain things more serious. My niece's health worries me extremely; and that sometimes so muddles my thinking that I don't know what I'm up to. As you see, I'm having a lot to bear. My niece is extremely anaemic. She is wasting away. She has been obliged to abandon painting, her only distraction. None of the usual tonics helps her in the slightest. For the last few days, on the orders of a doctor who seems to me more knowledgeable than the rest, she has been trying hydrotherapy. Will that cure her indigestion and insomnia? And strengthen her entire system? Your poor Cruchard takes less and less pleasure in existence. He's had more than enough of it – much more. But let's talk about your books! Better so.

I enjoyed them both, *Flamarande* and *Les Deux Frères*, and the proof is that I devoured them one after the other.

What a charming woman Mme Flamarande is! And M. de Salcède is such a good fellow. The account of the kidnapping of the child, the flight in the carriage, and the story of Zamora[2] are all perfect. Interest is sustained throughout – indeed it steadily mounts. In general, what impresses me in these two novels (as, in fact, in everything you write) is the natural sequence of ideas – the talent, or rather the genius, for narration. What an abominable old thing your Flamarande is! As for the servant who tells the tale and is clearly in love with Madame – I wonder why you didn't feature his jealousy more strongly.

Except for the Count, all the people in this story are virtuous – extraordinarily so. But do you think they are true to life? Are there many people like them? Of course while we're reading we accept them, because they're so skilfully presented. But afterwards?

And now, chère maître – and this is in reply to your last letter – here, I think, is the essential difference between us. You, always, in whatever you do, begin with a great leap towards heaven, and then you return to earth. You start from the *a priori*, from theory, from the ideal. Hence your forbearing attitude towards life, your serenity, your – to use the only word for it – your greatness. I, poor wretch, remain glued to the earth, as though the soles of my shoes were made of lead: everything disturbs me, everything lacerates and ravages me, though I make every effort to soar. If I tried to assume your way of looking at the world I'd become a mere laughing-stock. For no matter what you preach to me, I can have no temperament other than my own. Nor any aesthetic other than the one that proceeds from it. You accuse me of "not letting myself go" naturally. What about discipline – the virtue of discipline? What would become of that? I admire Monsieur de Buffon for putting on lace cuffs before sitting down to write. That touch of elegance is a symbol.[3] I try, naively, to have the widest possible sympathies. What more can be asked of anyone?

As for revealing my own opinion of the people I bring on stage, no, no! a thousand times no! I don't recognize my *right* to do so. If the reader doesn't draw from a book the moral it implies, either the reader is an imbecile or the book a sham, in that it lacks authenticity. For if a thing is True, it is good. Even obscene books are not immoral unless they lack truth. But that's not how it is in life.

And please note that I loathe what is commonly called "realism", even though I'm regarded as one of its high priests. Make what you can of all that.

As for the public, its taste astounds me more and more. Yesterday, for example, I went to the opening of *Le Prix Martin*,[4] a bit of buffoonery I found very witty. Yet not a word in the play brought a laugh, and the dénouement, which seemed to me particularly good, went unnoticed. To try to please readers therefore seems to me utterly chimerical. I defy anyone to tell me how one "pleases." Success is a result; it must not be a goal. I have never sought it (though I desire it), and I seek it less and less.

After my little story I'll do another:[5] I feel too unsettled to take on anything larger. I had first thought I might publish *Saint Julien* in a newspaper. But I abandoned the idea. What would be the use? I find all those shops (i.e. the newspapers) so nauseating that I prefer to keep my distance.[6]

When I call on le père Hugo I study the democrats I see there. He continues to be charming to me. But what an entourage – God help us!

Well, adieu – that's enough bile for today. I was touched by the length of your last letter. You do love me!

Et je vous le rends, en vous embrassant fortement.

Votre vieux

Gve Flaubert

[1] *La Tour de Percemont – Marianne*, two short novels in a single volume, published at the end of January.

[2] The name of a horse, in *Flamarande*.

[3] So thought Machiavelli also, in his great letter of 10 December 1513, in which he recounts, from rustic exile, his writing of *The Prince*. Seneca, too – in a letter of which Machiavelli's is possibly a conscious echo – expressed the view that decency of aspect touches on self-respect. (Seneca: *Epistolae Morales*, XCII.)

[4] A comedy by Emile Augier and Eugène Labiche, which opened at the Théâtre du Palais-Royal on 5 February 1876. A failure, quickly withdrawn.

[5] This was to be *Un Coeur simple*.

[6] Flaubert had been invited to publish *Saint Julien* in the Sunday supplement of *Le Figaro*, but had declined. However, a year later he overcame his reluctance to publish in a newspaper, and *Saint Julien* appeared in *Le Bien public*, 17–19 April 1877. The two following stories, *Un Coeur simple* and *Hérodias*, were printed at the same time in *Le Moniteur universel*, 12 to 27 April.

*

Saint Julien was finished on 17 February 1876.

413 FLAUBERT TO SAND

[Paris, 18 February 1876]
Friday evening

Ah! Thank you from the bottom of my heart, chère maître. You have given me an exquisite day: only today have I read *La Tour de Percemont – Marianne*. Having several things to finish, among them my *Saint Julien*, I had put the said volume in a drawer lest I succumb to temptation. My little novella was finished last night, and this morning I immediately took up your book and devoured it at one sitting.

I think it's perfect: two gems! *Marianne* moved me deeply, and brought tears to my eyes several times. I recognized myself in the character of Pierre.[1] Certain pages were like fragments of what my own memoirs would be, had I the talent to write as you do. How charming it all is, and poetic, and *true*! I greatly enjoyed *La Tour de Percemont*, but *Marianne* literally enchanted me. The English agree with me, because in the last number of *The Athenaeum* there's a very fine article about you.[2] Did you know that? So: this time I admire you to the full, without the slightest reservation. *Voilà*: this makes me very happy.

You have never done me anything but good, and I love you tenderly.

Everything seems to conspire to vex and torment your old Cruchard. For ten years I have had a servant who has suited me perfectly, and to whom (if I may say so without self-praise) I have been very generous. This morning he announced that he no longer wished to work for me, because "I wasn't nice to him any more." The real reason is that my new apartment is less chic than the old. Also, though I have raised his wages every year, he knows that I am poor now, and despises me for it. That sort are just as bourgeois as the rest! Don't put your faith in the People! The blind hatred they feel for us, whatever we may do for them, makes my head spin. I beg your pardon for bothering you with this domestic tittle-tattle. But my feelings are a bit hurt, and I'm sorry for myself. *C'est fini.*[3]

Now that I've finished my story I'm going to write another. The pair can make up into a little volume that I'll publish this autumn. As for publishing them in a newspaper first, no! I can't help it – I can't bear the thought of associating myself with those rags: they all disgust me.

And then, the less money I have, the less I want to earn. As soon as something seems likely to benefit me financially, it revolts me, as if it were something base. Is this pride? I expect so, don't you?

Turgenev keeps at me to get back to the big book about my two Woodlice. He's crazy about it. But the difficulties terrify me. And yet I shouldn't like to die before completing it. Because, after all, it's my testament. I may return to it four or five months from now.[4] At present I have so little self-confidence!

Nobody talks of anything except *L'Étrangère*.[5] I haven't seen the play, and can't tell you anything about it. The extracts I've seen don't strike me as exactly dazzling from the stylistic point of view. Who bothers about thee, O Beauty? How thou art despised, O Passion!

Could anything be more paltry than the business of the elections? Truly sad. Dawn is a long time coming.

Adieu, chère bon maître. Baisez bien pour moi les chères petites.

Votre vieux qui vous chérit.

Gve Flaubert

[1] Pierre André, the hero of *Marianne*, is a man of forty who has done nothing with his gifts, due to paralyzing timidity together with lack of self-confidence and ambition. For this he sometimes despises himself. In love he aims too high, then gives up, not daring to declare himself.

[2] *The Athenaeum*, 12 February 1876: ". . . *La Tour de Percemont* is a very pretty story, as good, perhaps, as anything that George Sand ever wrote. *Marianne*, too, is full of character, and it is only the greatest of writers who can develop character in stories not a hundred pages long." (unsigned.)

[3] Emile Colange, who was twenty-six when he began to work for Flaubert in 1870, did, after all, remain with him to the end.

[4] Flaubert did not return to *Bouvard et Pécuchet*, his "two woodlice", until June 1877, after the publication of *Trois Contes*. At his sudden death on 8 May 1880 it was left unfinished.

The text, never completely revised, was printed in a volume of 400 pages the next year, and has been repeatedly re-issued, usually accompanied by Flaubert's notes for the remaining pages of the book. One section of the latter, an anthology of clichés, has sometimes been printed separately. An English translation by Jacques Barzun, *The Dictionary of Accepted Ideas*, with an excellent introduction, was printed by New Directions, New York, in 1954 (revised edition 1963), and in London by The Bodley Head that same year.

 5 See Letter 408, Note 5.

414 SAND TO FLAUBERT

Nohant, 6 March [1876]

I write to you in haste this morning because M. Perrin has just notified me of the first performance of the revival of my *Mariage de Victorine*, at the Théâtre-Français.

I myself have neither the time nor the wish to go at such short notice, but I'd have liked to send a few friends. And he hasn't offered me a single ticket. I'm writing to him – and he'll get the letter tomorrow – to ask him to send you at least one ticket for the stalls. If you don't receive it, be sure it's not my fault. I have to write the same thing to five or six other people, so I'll end now, with love, so as not to miss the post.

Let me know how your niece is and give her my love.

G. Sand

*

On 7 March 1876, Flaubert was present at the opening of *Victorine*, preceded by its eighteenth-century model, *Le Philosophe sans le savoir* (by Michel Jean Sedaine, 1765).

415 FLAUBERT TO SAND

[Paris, 8 March 1876]
Wednesday, 1 o'clock

Complete success, chère maître. The actors were called back after every act, to great applause. Everybody was pleased. Exclamations from the audience. All your friends responded to your call and were sorry you weren't there.

The rôles of Antoine and Victorine were extremely well played. Little Baretta is a real jewel.

How in the world were you able to pattern *Victorine* so closely on *Le Philosophe sans le savoir* and make it *good*? That's what I can't imagine. Your play enchanted me and made me cry my eyes out, whereas the other bored me absolutely to death. I couldn't wait for it to end. Such language! The wonderment on the faces of our good Turgenev and Mme Viardot was comical to see.

In your play, what produced the greatest effect was the scene in the last act between Antoine and his daughter. Maubant is too majestic, and the actor who plays Fulgence isn't up to the part. But everything went very well. This revival will have a long run.[1]

The egregious Harrisse told me that he was going to write to you at once. So his letter will reach you before mine. I was to have set out this morning for Pont-l'Evêque and Honfleur to see a bit of the countryside that I've forgotten, but the floods have made that impossible.

My niece is better since beginning to take shower-baths.

Do read Zola's new novel, *Son Excellence Rougon*.[2] I'm very curious to know what you think of it.

A big hug from
Your old

Cruchard

[1] Was Flaubert sincere in speaking thus about *Victorine*? A few days later, on March 15th, he wrote to Mme Roger des Genettes: "Last week I was at the Français to see *Le Philosophe sans le savoir* and *Le Mariage de Victorine*. So false! So banal! So trivial!" Do those adjectives apply only to Sedaine's play?

[2] This, the sixth volume of *Les Rougon-Macquart*, had been published by Charpentier on 25 February.

416 SAND TO FLAUBERT

Nohant, 9 March 1876

So you scorn Sedaine, impious wretch! That shows how blinded you are by your theory of form. Sedaine isn't a real writer, it's true, though he doesn't fall far short. But he's a man, and he has a heart and feelings, a genuine sense of morality and a just view of human emotions. I don't care a hoot about a few outmoded ideas or some baldness of style! He says what he has to say aptly and movingly.

Dear old Sedaine! He's one of my beloved papas, and in my opinion *Le Philosophe sans le savoir* is much better than *Victorine*. The action is so affecting and well-managed! But you look only for the well-turned phrase. That's something, but only something – it isn't the whole of art, or even the half of it. A quarter at most, and when the other three quarters are good one can do without the one that isn't.

I hope you won't go to the country until the weather's better. We *had* been let off lightly, but for the last three days it's poured with rain. A deluge. It makes me ill. I couldn't have gone to Paris.

So your niece is better. Thank God!

Je t'aime et je t'embrasse de tout mon âme.

G. Sand

Please tell M. Zola to send me his book. I shall certainly read it with interest.

[Paris, 10 March 1876]
Friday evening

No! I don't "scorn" Sedaine. Because I don't scorn what I utterly fail to understand. I feel about him as I do about Pindar and Milton, both of whom are absolutely closed books to me; but I do know our Sedaine is far from being in the same class as either of them.

Tuesday's audience shared my boredom. And *Victorine*, quite apart from its intrinsic merit, gained by the contrast. Mme Viardot, whose taste is instinctively refined, said to me, "However did she" – meaning you – "manage to create *this* out of *that*?" I feel the same.

You make me a little sad, chère maître, when you ascribe to me aesthetic opinions that are not mine. I think the rounding-out of a sentence is nothing. But that *to write well* is everything. Because: "Good writing implies good feeling, good thinking, and good expression." (Buffon.)[1]

The last term of this argument is thus dependent on the two others, since it is necessary to feel strongly in order to think, and to think in order to express. Every bourgeois can have heart and delicacy, be full of the best feelings and the greatest virtues, without for that reason becoming an artist. And finally, I believe Form and Content to be two abstractions, two entities, interdependent.

The concern for external Beauty you deplore in me is for me a *method*. When I come upon a disagreeable assonance or a repetition in one of my sentences, I'm sure I'm floundering in the False. By dint of searching, I find the proper expression, which was always the *only* one, and which is, at the same time, harmonious. The word is never lacking when one possesses the idea.

Note (to return to Sedaine) that I share all his opinions and approve his predilections. From the archaeological point of view it's all very interesting, and from the humanitarian point of view very laudable. I grant you that. But for us, today, what is it? Is it eternal Art? I ask you.

Other writers of his time also formulated useful *principles*; but they did so in imperishable style, in a manner at once more specific and more universal.

In short, that the Comédie-Française should persist in offering that play as a "masterpiece" so exasperated me that when I got home, to rid myself of the taste of such pap, I took up Euripides' *Medea* before going to bed, having no other classic to hand. And lo! Aurora stole on Cruchard unawares!

I have written to Zola to send you his book. I'll also tell Daudet to send you his *Jack*.[2] I'm most curious to have your opinion of these two books, which are quite different in style and attitude, but both very remarkable.

The alarm of the Bourgeois at the elections has been fun to watch.

How I regret never seeing you! Je vous embrasse.

Votre vieux

Gve Fl

¹ Flaubert quotes from his memory of Buffon's *Discours à l'Académie* (also known as *Discours sur le style*). The correct text is: "Bien écrire, c'est tout à la fois bien penser, bien sentir et bien rendre; c'est avoir en même temps de l'esprit, de l'âme et du goût."

² *Jack, moeurs contemporaines* had been published on 9 February.

418 SAND TO FLAUBERT

Nohant, 25 March [18]76

I could say a good deal about M. Zola's novels, but it will be better to say it in an article rather than a letter, because it involves a general question that needs to be worked out at leisure.¹ I'd also like to read M. Daudet's book first – the one you mentioned, though I've forgotten the title. So do ask the publisher to send me a copy – I'll pay for it if he doesn't feel like making me a present of it. The thing's very simple, really. Briefly, while criticizing *Rougon* from the philosophical point of view, I won't retract my opinion that it's a very distinguished book, a *strong* book, as you would say, and one worthy to be placed in the front rank. But this doesn't affect my opinion that art ought to seek the truth, and that truth is not the depicting of evil. It should be the depicting of good *and* evil. A painter who sees only the one is as misleading as a painter who sees only the other. Life is not filled exclusively with monsters; society is not made up only of wretches and scoundrels. Decent folk are not in the minority, since society survives in a more or less orderly manner, without too many crimes going unpunished. Fools are in positions of power, I agree, but public conscience obliges them to respect the law. Denouncing and castigating rogues is acceptable – it's even moral; but let us be shown the other side of the coin, otherwise the unsophisticated reader – that is, the reader in general – recoils, is saddened and frightened, and denies you in order not to despair.

And how are you? Turgenev wrote that your last piece of work was very remarkable – so you're not down and out as you claim? And your niece is still making progress? I'm better too, after stomach cramps that were enough to make one go blue in the face, and were horribly persistent too. But physical pain is a salutary lesson so long as it leaves your mind free. You learn to bear and even to overcome it. You have a few bad moments when you just flop on the bed, but I always think of what my old village priest used to say when he had gout: "Either it will pass or I shall." And he used to laugh, he was so pleased with his witticism.²

My Aurore is starting to study history, and she's not very pleased with all those killers they call heroes and demi-gods. *She* calls them nasty fellows.

We're having an extraordinary spring. The ground is strewn with flowers and snow at the same time, and you get frozen fingers picking violets and anemones.

I read *L'Étrangère* in manuscript, and it's not such an example of "decadence" as you say. Some diamonds shine brightly in all that motley. Besides, decadence is a kind of metamorphosis. Mountains in travail roar and yell, but they also sing beautiful songs.

Je t'embrasse et je t'aime. Bring your legend out soon so that we can read it.

Ton vieux troubadour

G. Sand

[1] But Mme Sand did not, in the brief time left to her, write an article about Zola.
[2] See Letter 60, Note 1.

419 SAND TO FLAUBERT

[Nohant] 30 March 1876

Cher Cruchard,

I'm enthusiastic about *Jack* – please thank M. Daudet for me. Yes indeed! he has both talent and heart! And how well it's all written and observed!

I'm sending you a volume of old things that have just been put together.[1]

Je t'embrasse et je t'aime.

Ton vieux troubadour

G. Sand

[1] Probably the volume entitled *La Coupe, Lupo Liverani, Le Toast, Garnier, Le Contre-bandier*, which had been published on 18 March.

420 FLAUBERT TO SAND

[Paris, 3 April 1876]
Monday evening

Chère maître,

I received your volume this morning. I have two or three other books here lent me by various people some time ago. I'll make haste to finish them, and shall read yours at the end of the week, during a little two-day trip I have to make to Pont l'Evêque and Honfleur for my *Histoire d'un coeur simple* – a trifle at present "in the works", as M. Prud'homme would say.

I'm glad you liked *Jack*. It's a charming book, isn't it? If you knew the author you'd like him even more than his book. I've told him to send you *Risler* and *Tartarin*. You'll thank me after reading them, I'm sure.

One could write a nice article comparing *Jack* and *Rougon*. In my opinion the latter is infinitely the stronger. Don't you find that Daudet sacrifices a little to effect, to easy entertainment, to chic? He makes things easy for himself by avoiding the deeper aspects of things, he discourses interminably, gives unnecessary descriptions, and is generally prolix and too indulgent to the reader. He exploits women's sensibilities. His protagonist is a Victim rather than a Character. The episode about Cécile is bungled, and the word at the end, *délivré*, seems to me in vulgar taste. But all the things I reproach him for are the source of his success. If he corrected his faults his sales would suffer. I'll not speak of his strengths, which are excellent and many.

Rougon is much more seriously conceived and executed. And to my mind far stronger. There isn't a superfluous word. It's solid: no tricks. Nevertheless I share neither Turgenev's severity concerning *Jack* nor the "immensity" of his admiration for *Rougon*. One has charm and the other strength. But neither is concerned *above all* with what is for me the goal of Art, namely Beauty! I remember how my heart throbbed, and what violent pleasure I experienced, when I was looking at one of the walls of the Acropolis, a wall that is completely bare (the one to the left as you climb the Propylaea). Well, I wonder whether a book, quite apart from what it says, cannot produce the same effect. In the precise fitting-together of its parts, the rarity of its elements, the polish of its surface, the harmony of the whole, is there not an intrinsic Virtue, a kind of divine force, something eternal, like a principle? (I speak as a Platonist.) If this were not so, why should there be a relation between the right word and the musical word? Or why should great compression of thought always result in a line of poetry? Does it follow that the law of Numbers governs feelings and images, and that what seems to be exterior form is actually essence? If I were to keep going very long on this track I'd get myself in a fine old mess. Because on the other hand Art must be human; or rather, Art is only what we can make it. We are not free. Each of us follows his own path, willy-nilly. In short, your Cruchard no longer has a sound idea in his noddle.

But how hard it is to understand one another! Here are two men whom I greatly like and whom I consider true artists, Turgenev and Zola. For all that, they don't admire Chateaubriand's prose at all, still less Gautier's. Sentences that enrapture me seem to them hollow. Who is in error? And how to please the public, when those closest to you are thus remote? All this makes me very sad. Don't laugh.

Let's go down a few levels and talk about less important things. Victor Borie,[1] at the Société Financière: isn't he the same Borie who was, or is still, your friend? If so, could you give me a very warm letter to him? – to predispose him to consider a bit of business which, if it were to succeed, might completely re-float, financially,

votre vieux

Troubadour

Depending on how you answer, I'll explain the matter to you.

I didn't tell you that *L'Étrangère* seemed to me an example of "decadence", for the simple reason that I haven't yet seen that play.

---

[1] See Letter 409, Note 1.

421 SAND TO FLAUBERT

Nohant, 5 April [18]76

Victor Borie's in Italy. What should I write and say to him? Are you able to go and see him and explain the business in question? He's somewhere in the neighbourhood of Civitavecchia, but he moves about a lot and may not be easy to reach. I'm sure he'll welcome you with open arms, because although he's a financier to his fingertips he's remained a good friend to us and a good fellow. He hasn't told us if he's on his alum mountain[1] for long. Lina's writing to him and will know the answer to that soon. Should we say you're ready to go and see him, or that you'll wait for him to come back to Paris? Anyhow, letters addressed to him at the Albergo d'Italia in Florence will reach him until May 20th. But we have to watch out for him, as he writes only very occasionally.

No time to say more about it today. Company is arriving. I've read *Fromont et Risler*; please tell M. Daudet I stayed awake all night reading it, and I don't know which I like better, *Jack* or *Risler*. The latter's very appealing; it's practically impossible to put it down.

Je t'embrasse et je t'aime. But when are you going to let me read some Flaubert?

G. Sand

[1] Borie was at Allumiere (18 kilometres from Civitavecchia), where the French company he headed had recently leased aluminium mines from the Italian government. The mines had been expropriated in 1870 from the papacy, which had controlled them almost from the time of their opening in the sixteenth century. They have long since been abandoned.

422 FLAUBERT TO SAND

[Paris, 8 April 1876]
Saturday evening

For the moment, chère maître, don't worry about Borie. The bit of business I mentioned isn't yet ripe. But it will be in a few days. Then I'll explain it to you and probably ask you for a letter of recommendation to him. It concerns a matter that will be proposed to the Société Financière, of which he is a member. But nothing is to be done for the moment. Only it's important not to lose sight of him, in case we have to find him.

I have just seen Prince Napoléon, who asked after you. "Won't she be coming to Paris this May, as usual?" A question that I, too, ask you.

Despite my shingles, I've decided to leave the day after tomorrow for Pont-L'Evêque and Honfleur. My work is impeded by my need for certain documents: it's lamentable, how slowly it progresses. Happy are those not afflicted with the mania of Perfection! I'm aware of the futility of this, but can't

cure myself. Beautiful things are accomplished more naturally. It's not my fault!
My nerve-ends are raw when it's a question of style.

Embrassez bien les chères petites pour moi.

Votre vieux

Cruchard

qui vous aime

*

Flaubert, still in Paris, worked slowly at *Un Coeur simple* (at that time he was
still provisionally calling it *Histoire d'un coeur simple*), meanwhile outlining a
third tale, the story of St John the Baptist, which would become *Hérodias*.

George Sand, increasingly weakened by the cancer that would soon end her
life, was frequently in severe pain. Nevertheless she too continued to work: she
began a new novel, *Albine*, and gave lessons to Aurore as usual.

During more than six weeks there are no letters. But Sand must have written
to Victor Borie, who had returned from Italy, telling him to expect a visit from
Flaubert. Probably because she was too ill, she asked Lina to tell Flaubert of
the financier's favourable reply.

423   FLAUBERT TO SAND

[Paris, 29 May 1876]

Monday evening

Chère maître,

Thanks to Madame Lina's kind letter I called yesterday on V. Borie, who was
courtesy itself. My nephew took his documents to him today. Borie promised to
investigate the matter: will he?

I think he may be able to do me, indirectly, the greatest service possible. If
my poor nephew were to find the capital he needs for his work, I could recoup
part of what I have lost and live in peace to the end of my days.

I introduced myself to Borie as coming from you, and it is to you that I owe
the cordiality of his reception. I don't thank you for that (needless to say),[1] but
you can tell him that I was touched by his kind welcome (and stimulate his zeal
if you think that would be useful).

I have been hard at work lately. How I'd love to see you and read you my
mediaeval trifle! I've begun another tale, called *Histoire d'un coeur simple*. But I
have interrupted it to do some research on the period of John the Baptist: I
want to write about Herodias' feast.

Our good Turgenev leaves tonight for St Petersburg. He asks me whether
I have thanked you for your latest book. Would I be capable of such forgetfulness?

You will see from my *Histoire d'un coeur simple* (in which you will recognize
your own direct influence) that I am not as obstinate as you think. I believe you
will like the moral tendency, or rather the underlying humanity, of this little
work.[2]

Adieu, chère bon maître. My greetings to all.
Je vous embrasse bien tendrement.
Votre vieux

Gve Flaubert

[1] i.e. "thanks are unnecessary between us."

[2] *Un Coeur simple*, inspired in part by the example of Flaubert's – and his parents' – servant, Julie (who was still living), is set in parts of Normandy that he had known as a child. This tale of the servant Félicité, her laborious life, and her parrot, is probably Flaubert's best-known work after *Madame Bovary*. In our day, a fine English novel, Julian Barnes' *Flaubert's Parrot*, pays it charming tribute.

Lucien Andrieu, in *Bulletin des Amis de Flaubert*, No. 44, May 1974, "Les Domestiques de la famille Flaubert", proves that "Julie" (1804–82) was named Béatrix Caroline Hébert (always called Caroline by her family); and he supposes that "Julie" was substituted because both Mme and Mlle Flaubert were named Caroline. "Béatrix" was apparently considered unsuitable. (J. B.)

*

The day that letter reached Nohant, Mme Sand took to her bed. Doctors were powerless: intestinal blockage had reached a stage at which, in those days, it was inoperable. Nothing could relieve her. She knew she was dying.

Flaubert's Paris season was ending when he read the alarming news in the press. A telegram to Nohant brought a reassuring reply from Lina, but he soon learned that there was no hope. George Sand died on 8 June 1876, at nine in the morning, after more than a week of intense suffering.

Flaubert was among the friends who made the journey from Paris, taking the night train on the 9th, with Prince Napoléon. He wrote of the funeral to his friend Mademoiselle Leroyer de Chantepie:

> You want to know the truth about Mme Sand's last moments. It is this: she did not have any priest attend her. But as soon as she was dead, her daughter, Mme Clésinger, asked the bishop of Bourges to authorize a Catholic burial, and no one in the house (except perhaps her daughter-in-law, Mme Maurice) stood up for our poor friend's ideas. Maurice was so prostrated that he had no energy left, and then there were outside influences, miserable considerations inspired by certain bourgeois. I know no more than that. The ceremony was immensely moving: everyone was in tears, I along with the rest.

In the village church Maurice read a message from Victor Hugo: "*Je pleure une morte et je salue une immortelle*;"[1] and under a gentle rain George Sand was buried in the Nohant cemetery. "It seemed to me that I was burying my mother a second time," Flaubert later wrote to Maurice.

That same evening he took the train to Paris, and two days later was at Croisset.

On June 25 he wrote to Turgenev in Russia:

... The death of our poor poor Mme Sand grieved me immensely. I wept like a calf at her funeral, twice: the first time, when I kissed her granddaughter Aurore (whose eyes, that day, were so like hers as to be a kind of resurrection); and the second, when I saw her coffin carried past me.

There were some fine goings-on. In order not to offend "public opinion" – the everlasting and execrable "they" – her body was taken to the church. I will give you the details of this disgraceful business when I see you. I felt a tightening around my heart, I can tell you. . . .

You are right to mourn our friend, for she loved you dearly, and never spoke of you without calling you "le bon Turgenev". But why pity her? She had everything life had to offer, and will remain a very great figure.

The good country people wept copiously around the grave. We were up to our ankles in mud in the little village cemetery, and a gentle rain was falling. Her funeral was like a chapter in one of her books.

At Croisset, Flaubert finished the story in which he had told Mme Sand she would recognize her influence. "I began *Un Coeur simple* exclusively for her, solely to please her," he wrote in another letter to Maurice. "She died when I was in the middle of my work. Thus it is with all our dreams." *Un Coeur simple* was at once Flaubert's tribute and his farewell to George Sand. "One had to know her as I did," he wrote in his letter to Mlle de Chantepie, "to realize how much femininity there was in that great man, and the vast tenderness in that genius. Her name will live in unique glory as one of the great figures of France."

[1] "I mourn a woman who has died, and salute one who is deathless."

TRANSLATOR'S AFTERWORD

The volume *Trois Contes* (*Three Tales*), containing *Un Coeur simple, La Légende de Saint Julien l'Hospitalier*, and *Hérodias*, was published by Charpentier on 24 April 1877. It pleased most of the critics, and its commercial success eased Flaubert's financial stringency, though during the few years remaining to him the Commanvilles, for whom he had sacrificed so much, kept a sharp eye on his spending.

Flaubert never finished *Bouvard et Pécuchet*. After his death in May 1880, the portion he had completed – constituting, to his mind, almost all of the projected first volume – was serialized in *La Nouvelle Revue*, and published by Charpentier.

F. S.

BIBLIOGRAPHY

I. MANUSCRIPTS

A. For the FLAUBERT correspondence the essential source is the Franklin-Grout Archive, bequeathed by the author's niece to the Institut de France and housed at the Bibliothèque Spoelberch de Lovenjoul at Chantilly. The autograph letters to George Sand comprise Volume IV of series A (cote H 1358), making up almost the whole of what has survived (214 items).

One note found its way into the documents of the Aurore Lauth-Sand Archive, in the Bibliothèque historique de la Ville de Paris (dossier G).

For one of the letters still lacking an autograph we have resorted to the copy previously made by René Descharmes (René Descharmes Archive, Bibliothèque nationale; cf. especially N.a.fr. 23825).

B. As for Flaubert, the Bibliothèque Spoelberch de Lovenjoul is the principal source for the GEORGE SAND correspondence, but most of her letters to Flaubert have passed into the hands of collectors. Only a few have found their way into public libraries:

Bibliothèque Spoelberch de Lovenjoul, Franklin-Grout Archive
    (series B, Volume VI, cote H 1366): 5 letters.
Ibid., Documents George Sand, Lettres à divers (dossier E 913): 1 letter.
Bibliothèque historique de la Ville de Paris, Aurore Lauth-Sand Archive
    (dossier G): 4 letters.
Bibliothèque nationale: 1 letter.

The remaining letters the text of which could be checked against the autograph were at the time in the following collections:

Coll. Alfred Dupont (Paris), 89 letters.
Coll. Mme Vandendriessche (Roubaix), 49 letters.
Coll. Marc Loliée (Paris), 23 letters.
Coll. Jean Depruneaux (La Châtre), 5 letters.
Coll. Mme Simone André-Maurois (Paris), 2 letters.
Coll. Bernard Le Dosseur, 1 letter.
Coll. Pierre Descazeaux, 1 letter.

Most of these letters have since been dispersed at auctions, especially those in the Alfred Dupont collection (1956–9).

C. Among the documents that have supplied us with valuable information we must mention in particular:

in the Bibliothèque nationale, Aurore Lauth-Sand Archive: the George Sand *Diaries*, 1852–76 (N.a.fr. 24813 to 24838) and some of her *Carnets* (N.a.fr. 13657, 13662 and 13664);

in the Bibliothèque historique de la Ville de Paris, George Sand's letters to Maurice and Lina (Aurore Lauth-Sand Archive, dossier G, nos. 1643 to 2536);

in the Bibliothèque municipale de Rouen, the dossiers concerning *Bouvard et Pécuchet*, "Recueils de documents" (g 226 I to VIII).

2. PUBLISHED LETTERS

Lettres de George Sand à Gustave Flaubert (Nouvelle Revue, Vols. 20 and 21, 15 February, 1 and 15 March 1883).

Lettres de Gustave Flaubert à George Sand (Nouvelle Revue, Vols. 25 and 26, 15 December 1883, 1 and 15 January 1884).

George Sand, *Correspondance, 1812–76* (Paris, Calmann-Lévy, 1882–4, 6 vols. 18°) [letters to Flaubert in Vols. IV, V and VI].

Lettres de Gustave Flaubert à George Sand, introduced by a study by Guy de Maupassant (Paris, Charpentier, 1884, 12°) [this study had previously been excerpted in *La Revue bleue*, 19 and 26 January 1884].

Gustave Flaubert, *Correspondance* (Paris, Charpentier, 1887–93, 4 vols. 12° [letters to George Sand in Vols. III and IV].

Correspondance entre George Sand et Gustave Flaubert, preface by Henri Amic (Paris, Calmann-Lévy [1904], 12°) [the latest edition of this work, dated 1916, departs considerably from the earlier ones, notably in including two unpublished letters].

Oeuvres complètes de Gustave Flaubert. Correspondance (Paris, Conard, 1910, 5 vols. 18°) [letters to Sand in Vols. III and IV].

Oeuvres complètes illustrées de Gustave Flaubert. Correspondance. Text revised and edited by René Descharmes. Edition du Centenaire (Paris, Librairie de France, 1922–5, 4 vols. 8°) [letters to Sand in Vols. II and III; facsimiles of two letters from Sand to Flaubert].

Oeuvres complètes de Gustave Flaubert. Théâtre (Paris, Conard, 1927, 8°) [two letters from Sand to Flaubert].

M. Roya, *Flaubert auteur dramatique. Trois lettres inédites de George Sand (Les Nouvelles littéraires*, 19 April 1930).

Oeuvres complètes de Gustave Flaubert. Correspondance. New augmented. ed. (Paris, Conard, 1926–33, 9 vols. 8°) [letters to Sand in Vols. V, VI and VII].

Chr. Ryelandt, *Malgrétout. Histoire d'un roman. George Sand et les Ardennes (La Grive*, no. 77, April 1953) [three letters from Sand to Flaubert].

Oeuvres complètes de Gustave Flaubert. Correspondance. Supplément, collected, edited and annotated by R. Dumesnil, J. Pommier and Cl. Digeon (Paris, Conard, 1954, 4 vols. 8°) [letters to Sand in Vols. II and III].

A. F. J. Jacobs, *Flaubert et George Sand (Unpublished documents) (Revue d'Histoire littéraire de la France*, 1957, pp. 19ff.) [two letters to Flaubert].

Gustave Flaubert, *Oeuvres complètes*. Preface and notes by M. Nadeau (Lausanne, Editions Rencontre, 1964–5, 18 vols. 16°) [letters to Sand from Vol. IX].

Georges Lubin, *Un billet inédit de George Sand à Flaubert (Bulletin des Amis de Flaubert*, no. 38, May 1971).

Gustave Flaubert, *Oeuvres complètes*. New edition, based on Flaubert's unpublished mss [edited and with notes by M. Bardèche] (Paris, Club de l'Honnête Homme, 1971–5, 16 vols.) [the correspondence, in 5 vols., forms Vols. 12 to 16; letters to Sand in Vols. III (= 14) and IV (= 15)].

Dialogue des deux troubadours. Correspondence between George Sand and Gustave Flaubert, 1863–76. Preface and selection by Georges Lubin (Paris, Les Cent-Une [1978]).

Note: A new edition of the general correspondence, established in accordance with the most rigorous of modern scientific principles, is in the course of publication, in respect of both Sand and Flaubert. The *Correspondance* of George Sand, whose publication is being overseen by Georges Lubin, has gone as far as 1858; 14 volumes have so far appeared since 1964 in Classiques Garnier. No letters to Flaubert therefore appear in it as yet, for the two writers began to correspond only in 1863. The same applies to the *Correspondance* of Flaubert, published by Jean Bruneau in the Bibliothèque de la Pléiade; the first volume, for the years 1830 to 1851, came out in 1973.

3. GENERAL WORKS

Every general work concerning the two writers necessarily includes a description of the relations between Sand and Flaubert. We mention only those we have found particularly useful.

Wladimir Karénine (pen-name of Mme Varvara Komarov), *George Sand, sa vie et ses oeuvres* (Paris, Plon-Nourrit, 1899–1926, 4 vols. 8°) [especially Vol. IV, pp. 240–8, 503–9, 551–7 and *passim*].

René Dumesnil, *Gustave Flaubert, l'homme et l'oeuvre* (Paris, Desclée de Brouwer, 1932) [3rd ed. 1947; pp. 211–14 and *passim*].

Hélène Frejlich, *Flaubert d'après sa correspondance* (Paris, S.F.E.L.T., 1933).

Alfred Colling, *Gustave Flaubert* (Paris, Fayard, 1941).

André Maurois, *Lélia ou la vie de George Sand* (Paris, Hachette, 1952) [pp. 481–8, 497–9, 513–19 and *passim*].

Pierre Salomon, *George Sand* (Coll. "Connaissance des Lettres", Paris, Hatier-Boivin, 1953) [*passim*].

Jacques Suffel, *Gustave Flaubert* (Coll. "Classiques du XIXᵉ siècle", Paris, Editions universitaires, 1958) [new edition: Paris, Nizet, 1979].

Claude Digeon, Flaubert (Coll. "Connaissance des Lettres", Hatier, 1970).

4. PRINCIPAL DOCUMENTARY WORKS AND ARTICLES

Juliette Adam, *Mes souvenirs* (Paris, A. Lemerre, 1902–10) [*passim*, but especially Vol. III, *Mes sentiments et nos idées avant 1870*, pp. 162–7, 413–16; Vol. VI, *Nos amitiés politiques avant l'abandon de la revanche*, pp. 374–5].

Antoine Albalat, *Gustave Flaubert et ses amis* (Paris, Plon, 1927) [chap. XIII, pp. 257–81].

Lucien Andrieu, *Les Dédicaces des livres envoyés à Flaubert et conservés à l'Hôtel de ville de Canteleu (Bulletin des Amis de Flaubert*, no. 24, May 1964).

Casimir Carrère, *George Sand amoureuse. Ses amants, ses amitiés tendres* (Ed. La Palatine, 1967) [pp. 434–46].

Marie Cordroc'h, *Répertoire des lettres publiées de George Sand* (Paris, A. Colin [1962]) [first published in *Revue d'Histoire littéraire de la France*, 1959, Vol. 2 to 1961, Vol. 4].

E. and J. de Goncourt, *Journal. Mémoires de la vie littéraire* (Ed. de l'Imprimerie nationale de Monaco, 22 vols. 1956–8) [*passim* in almost every volume, but especially in Vols. VII, VIII and X].

A. F. J. Jacobs, *Flaubert et George Sand. Reclassement de leur correspondance (Bulletin du Bibliophile*, 1956, no. 6, pp. 269–304).

A. F. J. Jacobs, *George Sand à Croisset et Flaubert à Nohant (Bulletin des Amis de Flaubert*, no. 8, 1956).

René Joly, *Les Livres offerts par George Sand à Flaubert (Le Livre et l'Estampe*, no. 38, 1964).

Halpérine-Kaminsky, *Yvan Tourgueneff d'après sa correspondance avec ses amis français* (Paris, Fasquelle, 1901).

Georges Lubin, *Quelques billets inédits de Flaubert à la famille Sand (Bulletins des Amis de Flaubert*, no. 23, December 1963).

Georges Lubin, *Flaubert et le monument de George Sand (Bulletin des Amis de Flaubert*, no. 37, December 1970).

Claude Tricotel, *Comme deux troubadours. Histoire de l'amitié Flaubert-Sand* (Paris, Société d'édition d'enseignement supérieur, 1978).

Jules Troubat, *La Salle à manger de Sainte-Beuve* (3rd ed., Paris, Mercure de France, 1910) [ch. VI, p. 152ff.].

For historical and political events our chief sources, apart from the leading journals of the period, are the following works:

Jacques Chastenet, *Histoire de la Troisième République*, Vol. I: *L'Enfance de la Troisième, 1870–79* (Paris, Hachette, 1952).

Georges Dubosq, *La Guerre de 1870–71 en Normandie*, episodes and details, from the latest documents . . . (Rouen, press of the *Journal de Rouen*, 1905, Lg 8°.

Ernest Lavisse, *Histoire de France contemporaine*, Vols. VI, VII and VIII, by Ch. Seignobos (Paris, Hachette, 1921) [Vol. VI: *La Révolution de 1848 – Le second Empire*; Vol. VII: *Le Déclin de l'Empire et l'établissement de la IIIe République*; Vol. VIII: *L'Evolution de la IIIe République*].

Yvan Lecler, *Crimes écrits. La Littérature en procès au 19e siècle* (Paris, Plon, 1991).

5. ARTICLES ARISING OUT OF THE PUBLICATION OF THE LETTERS IN *NOUVELLE REVUE* AND IN THE MAUPASSANT EDITION

Anon., *George Sand und Gustave Flaubert (Nuova Antologia,* 1883, p. 137).

Anon., *George Sand and Gustave Flaubert (The Nation,* Vol. 29, 1884, pp. 337ff.).

Anon., *Realism and Decadence in French Fiction* . . . , *G. Flaubert: Lettres à George Sand and Other Works (The Quarterly Review,* Vol. 171, July–October 1890, pp. 57–91) [major article concerned not only with Flaubert and Sand but also with Balzac, Stendhal, Zola, Daudet, Bourget, Taine, Loti, Brunetière and E. Tissot].

Anon., *The French Decadence: G. Flaubert, Lettres à George Sand (The Quarterly Review,* Vol. 174, January–April 1892, pp. 479–504) [deceptive title: the article is exclusively concerned with Maupassant].

Paul Bourget, *Les Lettres de Flaubert à George Sand (Débats,* 10 Feb. 1884) [article reprinted in *Essais de psychologie contemporaine,* Paris, Plon, 1901, pp. 185–96].

Ferd. Brunetière, *La Correspondance de Flaubert avec George Sand (Revue des Deux Mondes,* 1 Feb. 1884, pp. 695–705) [article reprinted in *Histoire et Littérature,* Vol. II, Paris, Calmann-Lévy, 1885, pp. 127–48].

A. Caccianiga, *Tra Croisset e Nohant. Flaubert e la Sand (L'Illustrazione Italiana,* no. 53, 18 Dec. 1887, pp. 430–54).

M. Gaucher, *Causerie littéraire: Lettres de Gustave Flaubert à George Sand (Revue bleue,* 9 Feb. 1884).

N. H. Kennard, *Gustave Flaubert and George Sand (The Nineteenth Century,* Vol. XX, July–December 1886, pp. 693–708).

H. Klein, *Gustave Flaubert in seinen Briefen an George Sand (Unsere Zeit, Deutsche Revue der Gegenwart,* 1884, Vol. II, pp. 753–62).

H. Michel, *Lettres de George Sand à Gustave Flaubert (Le Temps,* 14 April 1883).

6. ARTICLES ARISING OUT OF THE PUBLICATION OF THE AMIC EDITION

Lucien Descaves, *L'Epistolière (Le Journal,* 19 June 1904) [concerning the George Sand centenary; includes a few words about her relationship with Flaubert and their correspondence].

René Doumic, *George Sand* . . . *Le génie de l'écrivain. La Correspondance avec Flaubert (Revue hebdomadaire,* 10 April 1909) [lecture to the Société des Conférences, 31 March 1909].

Emile Faguet, *Revue dramatique: George Sand critique* [about her, about Flaubert, Dumas fils, the question of realism, etc.] *(Suppl. du Journal des Débats,* 28 July 1904).

H. Gillot, *Correspondance entre George Sand et Gustave Flaubert (Zeitschrift für neufranzösische Sprache und Literatur,* 1907, pp. 175–90).

Heinrich Mann, *Eine Freundschaft: Gustave Flaubert und George Sand* (München-Schwabing, E. W. Bonsels, 1905, 8°).

7. SUNDRY ARTICLES

J. B.[= Jules Bertaut], *Flaubert et George Sand* (*Le Temps*, 1 Dec. 1921).

Ch. Clerc, *George Sand: Epitaphe pour la tombe d'Emma Bovary* [pastiche] (*Revue hebdomadaire*, 16 Oct. 1920, Vol. X, pp. 321–2).

G. P. Gooch, *The Second Empire, XII. George Sand and Flaubert* (*Contemporary Review*, Dec. 1958) [slightly deceptive title: in this chapter the two writers are treated separately].

Georges Lubin, *Flaubert et George Sand* (*Bulletin des Amis de Flaubert*, no. 31, Dec. 1967).

J. Merlant, *Un entretien inconnu de Flaubert et de George Sand sur Rousseau* (Montpellier, Poulet, 1912).

Maurice Nadeau, Introduction to Vol. 12 of his *Oeuvres complètes de Flaubert* (pp. 11–22).

P. Souday, *Flaubert et George Sand* (*Le Temps*, 12 Dec. 1921).

8. TRANSLATIONS

Translations exist in several languages of Flaubert's "selected correspondence", including certain letters he addressed to his friends. Only one translation has, to our knowledge, been devoted to George Sand's letters:

Gustave Flaubert, *Briefe an George Sand* [tr. by E. von Hollander], *mit einem Essay von Heinrich Mann* ["*Flaubert und die Kritik*"], Potsdam, Gustav Kiepenheuer, 1919 (Der Liebhaberbibliothek 22nd vol.), 253 pp.

For the two writers' dialogue:

The George Sand – Gustave Flaubert Letters, translated by Aimée McKenzie (New York, Boni and Liveright, 1921), with introduction by Stuart P. Sherman.

INDEX

[Page numbers in roman type indicate references by Flaubert and Sand in letters and diary entries. Page numbers in italics indicate references by the Editors in the Introduction, linking passages and footnotes.]

Calamatta, Luigi – *cont'd.*
of his life, until he was appointed to teach
the subject in Milan. He had met Sand
about 1835 and engraved or executed
several portraits of her. In 1862 his only
daughter, Lina, became the wife of Maurice
Sand.) 136, *137*, 138, 139
Calamatta, Mme (Lina's mother), 140
Calvados, *321*, 367
Candidat, Le (Flaubert), 318, 320, *321*, *322*,
324,*325*,326,*326*,327,332,333,*335*,335–8,
338–9,339–40,341,*342*,346,354,*356*
Cannes, 57, 60, 62, 63, 89, 92, 93, 97, *98*
Canteleu, *12*, 18, 32, 86, 106, 315, *316*
Carnac, *3*, 22, 24
Caro, Elme-Marie (1826–87, philosopher),
197
Caroline (Flaubert's niece) *see* Commanville
Carré, Michel (1819–72, dramatist), *La Petite
Fadette*, 156, *157*
Carvalho (Léon Carvaille, 1825–97, Director
of the Vaudeville theatre), 283, *283*, 314,
315, 316, 317,*319*, 320, 324, 325, 327, 332,
332, 335, 346, 349, 352, 353, 356,*356*
Cathelineau, General Henri de, 323–4,*324*;
L'Heure à Dieu, *324*
Cauterets, 278
Cavalier, Georges (1841–78. Nicknamed
Pipe-en-Bois, graduate of the Ecole
Polytechnique, he was Bohemian
rabble-rouser in the theatre.) 247, *248*
Cayeux, 84
Cécile, character in *Jack*, 395
Cervantes, Miguel de, *Don Quixote*, 130, 138
César, nickname of Napoleon III, 362, *363*
Césarine Dietrich (Sand), x, *204*, *210*
Céséna, A. de (1810–89, critic), 167
Chaillot, 77, *78*
Chalumeau (curate of Canteleu), 315,*316*
Chamber of Deputies, 92, 206, 321, 346, 378,
378, 380
Chambord, comte de (1820–83, Henry V in
the event of a restoration), 233, *233*,*322*,
323,*324*
Champagne, *85*, 86, 99, 100, 101, 204
Champfleury, Jules Husson, known as
(1821–89, journalist, novelist, leader of the
realist school), *Les Amoureux de
Sainte-Périne*, 59,*59*
Changarnier, N. A. T. (1793–1877, general
and statesman), 75, *76*
Charles VI (King of France from 1380 to
1422), 69, *69*
Charles-Edmond, Charles-Edmond Choïecki,
known as (1822–99. Born in Poland, he had
to leave his country in 1844 on account of
his opposition to the Russian occupiers. He

wrote novels and plays and became literary
editor of *Le Temps*, then Senate Librarian.)
256, *258*, 260, 267–8, 280, 292, *293*,*312*,
344, 352
Charles-Edmond and Foussier, Edouard, *La
Baronne*, 252, *252*, 256
Charpentier, Georges (1846–1905, Flaubert's
publisher after the writer's quarrel with
Lévy), *284*,*302*, 316,*328*,*329*, 341,*392*
Charpentier, Marcel-Gustave (son), *328*
Charpentier, Marguerite (wife), 327, 332
Château des coeurs, Le (Flaubert), 20, 20, 22,
23, 31,*33*, 36, 75, *76*, 165, 166, *166*, 168,
168, 169, 172, 174, 175, *175*, 177, 184–5
Château de Meudon, 213
Chateaubriand, F. R. de (1768–1848,
statesman and writer), 130, 248, 396
Châteauroux, 89, 173, 176, *176*, 187, 305,
307, 310, 355,*357*
Chatiron, Emilie (1793–1870, wife of
Hippolyte), *187*
Chatiron, Hippolyte (1799–1848. Son of
George Sand's father by a servant girl at
Nohant; he was Sand's childhood playmate.
After a brief military career he settled at
Montgivray, between Nohant and La
Châtre, where he lived as a small-scale
landed gentleman.) 28, *29*,*356*
Chatrian, Alexandre (1826–90, novelist), *295*
Chaussée, Coralie de la (daughter of Mme
Vasse de Saint-Ouen), 18
Chennevières, Philippe de (1820–99, Director
of the Beaux-Arts), 328,*329*, 334, 349
Chevalier, Ernest (1820–87. Flaubert's first
childhood friend and schoolmate at the
Rouen lycée, then at law school in Paris.
Later the two practically lost touch.) 3
Chilly, Charles de (1807–72, Director of the
Odéon), 20, *20*, 36, *49*, 75, *76*, 115, 144,
156, 158, 159, *161*, 161–2, 163, *164*, 178,
199, 236, *236*, 238, 239, 245, 247,*253*, 275
Chopin, Frédéric (1810–49, Sand's lover,
1838–47), *vii*, *54*
Cicero, 152
Clairon, Mlle (1723–1803, tragic actress), *126*
Clairville, L. F. (1811–79, wrote plays about
sprites), 256
Clamart, *231*
Claye, Jules (1806–86, printer), 276
Clésinger, Solange (1828–99. Daughter of
Sand possibly by Stephane Ajasson de
Grandsagne. In 1847 she married the
sculptor Auguste Clésinger but left him a
few years later. The couple had produced
two children, who both died young. After
the separation Solange led a hectic life. Her
difficult character led to frequent rows with

Nérac, with his maidservant/mistress Jeanny
Dalias.) 80, *80*
Dudevant, Maurice *see* Sand, Maurice
Dudevant, Solange *see* Clésinger, Solange
Duguéret, Elisa (1841–91, actress at the
Odéon who took the role of Daphne in
Douilhet's *Faustine* in 1864), 39
Dumaine, L. F. (1831–93. Director of La
Gaîté Theatre), 20–1, 22
Dumas *fils*, Alexandre (1824–95. Bastard son
recognized by his father, he became one of
the most celebrated men of his era, thanks
to his novel, his plays and his controversial
opinions. After discovering, in the course of
a visit to Poland in 1851, the letters George
Sand had addressed to Chopin, he returned
them to the lady; this good-hearted act
underlay an enduring and affectionate
friendship. His relationship with Flaubert,
whom he met around 1864–5, was less
solid, because Flaubert had a low opinion of
his gifts and style.) *10*, 16, *16*, 39, 53, *54*,
66, 113, 145, 150, 196, 213, *213–14*, *223*,
224, *236*, 246, 256, 294, 321, 332, *332*,
333, 338, *345*, 354, *354*, *378*; *La Dame aux
camélias*, 101, 294, *295*; *L'Etrangère*, 378,
378, 390, 394, 396; *La Femme de Claude*,
302, *302*, *306*; *L'Homme-Femme*, 283, *283*;
Les Idées de Madame Aubray, *65*, 66, 193,
193; *La Lettre de Junius*, *233*; preface to
Faust, 332, *332*, 349, *350*; preface to *Retour
de Jésus*, 349, *350*; preface to *Théâtre complet*,
151; preface to *Werther*, 354
Dumas *père*, Alexandre (1803–70), 293; *Le
Chevalier de la Maison-rouge*, 166, *166*; *La
Jeunesse de Louis XIV*, 344, *345*; *Richard
d'Arlington*, 340, *340*
Dumesnil, René, x
Dumont, character in *Nanon*, 290
Dumouriez, General C. F. (1739–1823), *230*
Dupanloup, Mgr F. A. D. (1802–78, Bishop
of Orléans), 321, *322*, 332
Dupin de Francueil, Aurore, Baronne
Dudevant (1748–1821, daughter of the
Maréchal de Saxe, and George Sand's
grandmother), *213*
Duplan, Jules (1822–70. A businessman who
had to sell off his house in 1862 as a result
of financial difficulties. He became secretary
to Cernuschi, an Italian politician who had
fled to France, and accompanied him on a
long voyage in the Orient. He was a very
close friend of Flaubert from 1851; Flaubert
entrusted him with a great deal of research
for his books and all manner of errands in
Paris. Duplan also had the habit of combing
the papers for articles and reviews to send

his friend for his interest.) *4*, *76*, 146, *169*,
185, *185*, 186–7, *188*
Duquesnel, Félix (1832–1915, ran the Odéon
with Chilly), 20, *20*, 35, 36, *49*, *133*, 156,
162, 163, 177, 178, 185, 238, 247, 275, 277,
278–9, 282–3, *283*, 294, 344, 346, *347*,
349, 356
Duranty, L. E. E. (1833–80, journalist and
novelist), 167
Durry, M. J., *266*, *378*
Dussardier, character in *L'Éducation
sentimentale*, *111*
Duvernet, Charles (1807–74, journalist,
childhood friend of Sand, living at the
château du Coudray, near Nohant), 175,
216, 357, *358*
Duvernet, Mme, 175
Duveyrier, Charles (1803–66. Lawyer,
follower of Saint-Simon, founder of *Crédit –
*in which Sand had planned in 1850 to
publish extracts from her *Histoire de ma vie*.
Under the Second Empire his concern was
industry and business. As a playwright he
put on revues, plays, operas with his brother
Anne – known as Mélesville – Scribe and
others.) 33–4, 35, 203; *Michel Perrin*, 34

Echo de l'Indre, L', *358*
Eclaireur de l'Indre, L', *xv*
Éducation sentimentale, L' (Flaubert), 1843–4
version, *3*; 1869 version, *16*, 32, *33*, *37*, *63*,
79, *88*, *91*, *105*, *108*, *109*, *111*, *119*, *134*,
141, *141*, *145*, *146*, 147, 150, *159*, 166, *166*,
167–8, *169*, 169–72, 178, 179, *185*, 196,
237, *238*, 276, *345*, 379, 385, *386–7*;
Sand's article on, 169–72
Elle et Lui (Sand), *265*
Emilien, character in *Nanon*, 290
Enfant prodigue, L' (Flaubert), 175
England, The English, *219*, 389
Enghien, *111*, 259
Epictetus, 287
Epiphanius, Saint, 183, *183*
Erckmann, Emile (1822–99, novelist), *295*
Erckmann-Chatrian, *L'Illustre Docteur Mathéus*,
295, *295*
Erdeven, 22
Espinasse, Mme (Widow of General Espinasse
killed at Magenta; since 1862 she was a
lady-in-waiting to Princesse Mathilde.) 160,
160
Etretat, 84, 87
Eugène Louis, Prince Imperial (1856–79),
213, *214*, *223*, *230*
Eugénie, Empress (1826–1920), 189, 190,
190–1, 191, 205, *213*, 315, *316*

s'amuse, 321, *321*, *322*; *Ruy Blas*, 253, *253*,
256, 262, *263*, 264, *283*, 354
Hyacinthe, Charles Loyson, Le Père
(1827–1912. A Dominican friar who
became a Carmelite. He was an eloquent
preacher who tried to reconcile Catholicism
with modern ideas. He was excommunicated
in 1869, left his order, married and pursued
his calling in Geneva.) 114, 117

Idées d'un Maître d'école, Les ("Thoughts of a
Schoolmaster": Sand), *258*
Ideville, Henri d' (1830–87, historian and
political thinker), *283*
Impressions et Souvenirs (Sand), *238*, *243*, *283*,
314, 314–15
Indépendance belge, L', 248
Ingres, J. A. D. (1780–1867, painter), 315
Isidore, nickname for Napoleon III, 94, *96*,
132, 152, 211, 232, 233
Italy and Italians, 88, 229, 397

Janvier de la Motte, Eugène (1823–84. Prefect
of the Eure, later member of Chamber of
Deputies, friend of the Flauberts.) 265–6,
266
Jonson, Ben, *Volpone*, *357*
Joséphine, Empress, *59*
Journal officiel, Le, *169*, *281*
Journal d'un voyageur pendant la guerre (Sand),
222, *223*
Jouvencel, H. F. P. de (1817–97, politician),
150, *151*
Julien Duprat, character in *Le Candidat*,
341
Julio, Flaubert's greyhound, *284*
Jumièges, 85, 86, 87

Kaltbad-Rigi *see* Rigi
Kant, Emmanuel (1724–1804, German
philosopher), 269; *The Critique of Pure
Reason*, 262, 266
Kératry, Emile, comte de (1832–1905,
politician), *207*, 208
Kervéguen, vicomte de (1811–68, politician),
99, *99*

Labiche, Eugène (1815–88, dramatist), 143;
Le Prix Martin, *389*
La Bouille, 18
La Châtre, *vii*, *34*, 81, 111, 178, 216, *216*,
310, *310*
Lachaud, publisher, *302*

Lacordaire, J. B. H. (1802–61, famous
Dominican preacher and religious writer),
246, *248*
Lacretelle, P. H. de (1815–99, writer and
politician), *241*
Ladmirault, General L. R. P. de (1808–98,
Governor of Paris, 1871–8), 293, *293*, 294
La Fargue, editor of *Le Figaro*, 235, *236*
La Fontaine, Jean de (1621–95), "The Oak
and the Reed", *59*; "Ode to the King", *61*
Lagier, Suzanne (1833–93, actress and singer,
friend of Flaubert and the Goncourts), 229,
230
La Harpe, J. F. de (1739–1803, poet), 134
Lamartine, A. de (1790–1869, poet), *17*, 139,
139; "La Marseillaise de la paix", 209
Lamber, Juliette *see* Adam
Lambert, Esther (wife of Eugène), 102, *102*,
105, 107, 108, 158
Lambert, Eugène (1825–1900. Painter and
friend of Maurice Sand in Delacroix's
studio. He came to Nohant in 1844 and
stayed there twelve years. His marriage left
him well-to-do. He settled in Paris and
specialized in painting cats and dogs.) *102*,
158, 222
Lambrou, doctor at Luchon, 278
La Messine, Alice, nicknamed Toto (Juliette
Adam's daughter), *113*
Lammenais, Félicité-Robert de (1782–1854),
Essai sur l'indifférence, 327, *329*
Langrune, 84
Lansberg, Mathieu, 97
Lanterne, La, 115, *115*, 229, *291*
Laporte, Edmond (1832–1906. Friend of Jules
Duplan, he lived at Grand-Couronne,
across the Seine, and from 1868 became a
close friend of Flaubert. Just as Duplan had
done before 1870, he combed numerous
works, particularly for the second volume of
Bouvard et Pécuchet. Flaubert rewarded him
with an autograph manuscript of *Trois Contes*
adorned with a splendid dedication.
Commanville's financial difficulties led to
the two friends' quarrelling in 1879.) *284*,
348
La Rounat, Léon (1823–86, theatre director
and critic), 148, 161, *162*, 341
Latouche, Henri de (1785–1851, poet,
novelist, journalist, and George Sand's early
mentor), *252*
Latour-Saint-Ybars, Isidore (1807–91, lawyer,
journalist and playwright), 162–3;
L'Affranchi de Pompée, 161, *161*, 163, *164*,
177, 178, 179, 181, 182, *182*
Laur, Francis (1844–1934, "Cascaret".
Engineer, inventor and journalist who went